DEMENTIA

Person-centered care for persons with dementia has been developed and expanded over the last few decades. Speech-language pathologists are uniquely positioned to understand the striking impact that communication challenges have on persons with dementia and their caregivers, and can lead the charge to improve access to communication and participation. This volume serves as a starting point and reference manual for those who want to provide person-centered and life-enhancing services to persons with dementia, and to inspire the continued generation of quality research to demonstrate the value of cognitive-communication, behavioral, and caregiver interventions. It serves as a call to action for an interprofessional team of healthcare providers across healthcare settings to promote meaningful life engagement in persons with dementia using evidence-based assessment and intervention approaches.

This volume provides background on the evolution of caring for persons with dementia, as well as a description of the diagnostic process for dementia syndromes and the cognitive and communication characteristics of dementias with an emphasis on Alzheimer's dementia. Its chapters cover the person-centered assessment process for persons with cognitive and communicative disorders of dementias; intervention approaches for the wide variety of cognitive, communicative, eating/swallowing, and behavioral symptoms and consequences of dementia syndromes; reimbursement and documentation issues for various settings in which persons with dementia are seen; and issues and challenges of quality of life and end-of-life care.

Ellen M. Hickey, Ph.D., CCC–SLP, is an Associate Professor of speech-language pathology at Dalhousie University. Her teaching, practice, and research specialize in quality of life and treatment for persons with neurogenic communication disorders, including the cognitive-communicative disorders caused by dementia syndromes.

Michelle S. Bourgeois, Ph.D., CCC–SLP, ASHA Fellow, is a Professor of speech-language pathology at the University of South Florida. She specializes in interventions for persons with dementia and their caregivers. She has published numerous research articles, training manuals and CDs, and books on dementia interventions.

DEMENTIA

Person-Centered Assessment and Intervention

Second Edition

Edited by Ellen M. Hickey and Michelle S. Bourgeois

Routledge
Taylor & Francis Group

NEW YORK AND LONDON

Second edition published 2018
by Routledge
711 Third Avenue, New York, NY 10017

and by Routledge
2 Park Square, Milton Park, Abingdon, Oxon, OX14 4RN

Routledge is an imprint of the Taylor & Francis Group, an informa business

© 2018 Taylor & Francis

First edition published by Psychology Press 2009

Library of Congress Cataloging in Publication Data
Names: Hickey, Ellen M. (Ellen Mary) editor. | Bourgeois, Michelle S., editor.
Title: Dementia: person-centered assessment and intervention/edited by
Ellen M. Hickey and Michelle S. Bourgeois.
Description: 2nd edition. | New York: Routledge, 2018. | Revised edition
of: Dementia: from diagnosis to management: a functional approach/
Michelle S. Bourgeois and Ellen M. Hickey, 2009. | Includes
bibliographical references and index.
Identifiers: LCCN 2017020918| ISBN 9781138859906 (hbk: alk. paper) | ISBN
9781138859913 (pbk: alk. paper) | ISBN 9781315103891 (ebk)
Subjects: LCSH: Dementia.
Classification: LCC RC521.B68 2018 | DDC 616.8/31–dc23
LC record available at https://lccn.loc.gov/2017020918

ISBN: 978-1-138-85990-6 (hbk)
ISBN: 978-1-138-85991-3 (pbk)
ISBN: 978-1-315-10389-1 (ebk)

Typeset in Bembo
by Wearset Ltd, Boldon, Tyne and Wear

This book is dedicated to all of the individuals with dementia and their families who are striving to maintain a good quality of life. You are everyday heroes.

CONTENTS

ABOUT THE COVER

"A House for My Wife" by John L.

John is a person with dementia who lives in a nursing home. He enjoys expressing himself through painting. He has a unique style of painting, starting with 3 or 4 horizontal lines, and then adding on top of the lines. His paintings often reflect his love for his family.

Immersed in this painting, John took htis time in choosing colors. In one session, he completed the blue, brown, green, and yellow areas, as well as the diamond shape. He didn't feel it was finished so he returned to it again at another session. It was then he decided to add the stars to the sky and the orange house with the red roof. "A house for my wife," he said and put down his brush, satisfied his picture was complete.

ACKNOWLEDGMENTS

As we noted in the first edition, this book represents the accumulation of knowledge and experiences we have gleaned from the many persons with dementia and their caregivers with whom we have worked for nearly three decades. We have been motivated by your strength and courage to put forth our best efforts. Again, we thank you for your patience and for understanding that we did not always have the answers to your questions or solutions to your challenges. Thank you for teaching us and allowing us to share your world. Thanks in particular to John L. and his family, who graciously provided the cover art for the book.

Everyone who supported us in this endeavor cannot possibly be acknowledged here, but special thanks are extended to the Goldstein, Bourgeois, and Hickey families for their unfaltering love and support. Special thanks also to Stephen Sakalauskus, John Michael and Emma Jean Hadley, and Evelin Viera for their friendship, kindness, and good humor. Thanks also to the rest of our family, friends, colleagues, and students who supported us throughout this process. In particular, Rebecca Allen and Pamela Coulter, deserve a heartfelt thank you for their hard work and contributions.

Completion of this book would not have been possible without the enthusiasm and encouragement provided by our colleagues, Natalie Douglas and Becky Khayum. You went above and beyond what you were originally asked to do, and did so with gusto! We would also like to thank our other outstanding co-authors, Tammy Hopper, Nidhi Mahendra, Stuart Clearly, Jennifer Brush, and Renee Kinder, for your excellent contributions. Your ideas and expertise have enhanced each chapter. Your dedication to improving the lives of people with dementia and their caregivers is extraordinary. We are fortunate to have such amazing collaborators. We owe you all a debt of gratitude!

This book would not have been possible without the support of many agencies and collaborators who made both the research and clinical endeavors possible over the years. We would also like to acknowledge the many researchers worldwide who have developed and investigated the ideas discussed throughout the book, and the clinicians who work tirelessly to improve the quality of lives of people with dementia and their families.

Last but not least, we extend much gratitude to Georgette Enriquez and Brian Eschrich for their guidance in the process of writing this book. Your patience, consideration, and encouragement is much appreciated. Thank you!

This book is dedicated to all of the individuals with dementia and their families who are striving to maintain a good quality of life. You are everyday heroes.

CONTRIBUTORS

Jennifer Brush, Brush Development Company, Chardon, OH, USA.

Stuart Cleary, University of Alberta, Canada.

Pamela Coulter, Dalhousie University, Canada.

Natalie F. Douglas, Central Michigan University, USA.

Tammy Hopper, University of Alberta, Canada.

Becky Khayum, MemoryCare Corporation, Aurora, IL, USA.

Renee Kinder, Encore Rehabilitation Services, Louisville, KY, USA.

Nidhi Mahendra, San Jose State University, USA.

1

INTRODUCTION

History and Philosophy of Treatment in Dementia

Michelle S. Bourgeois and Ellen M. Hickey

Clinicians from many disciplines have ventured to provide appropriate and effective interventions for the diverse behavioral symptoms that define the neurologically degenerative condition known as dementia. Problems with memory in older adults have been described for thousands of years, with the medical community describing changes in cognitive, psychiatric, and intellectual functioning that were not common features of aging. In addition to dementia, other terms for similar behavioral symptoms included *amentia, dotage, imbecility, insanity, idiocy, organic brain syndrome*, and *senility* (Boller & Forbes, 1998; Torack, 1983). The first edition of the *Diagnostic and Statistical Manual of Mental Disorders* (*DSM*; American Psychiatric Association [APA], 1952) described dementia as an organic brain syndrome (OBS) that was differentiated from an acute brain syndrome due to its chronic and irreversible nature (Boller & Forbes, 1998). Subsequent editions of the *DSM* reflected the evolution of terminology from OBS to *senile and presenile dementia* to the current *major neurocognitive disorder (NCD)*, which is defined as "a decline from previous level of performance in one or more cognitive domains (memory impairment, abstract thinking, personality, judgment, language, praxis, constructional abilities, or visual recognition) that interferes with independence in work, social activities, and relationships with others" (5th ed.; *DSM-5*; APA, 2013).

As early as the 15th and 16th centuries, the cause of "insanity" was attributed to syphilis, and was referred to as *general paresis of the insane or neurosyphilis*. The late 19th and early 20th centuries brought a more precise and analytic approach to the differentiation of clinical symptoms. As clinicians observed and documented the specific characteristics of individuals, new diagnostic classifications emerged. In 1892, Arnold Pick described one of the pathologies that causes frontotemporal lobar degeneration. Alois Alzheimer published the first account of Alzheimer's disease in 1906. Kraepelin differentiated "senile" and "presenile" forms of dementia in 1910 (Amaducci, Rocca, & Schoenberg, 1986). "Cortical" and "subcortical" dementias were first proposed by Von Stockert in the 1930s to describe lesions appearing in the brain stem and deep gray matter (Whitrow, 1990). Primary degenerative dementias became the popular nosology in 1980, with the third edition of the *DSM* (APA, 1980) (3rd ed.; *DSM-III*; APA, 1980). Advances in neuroimaging and neuropathology, as well as in the clinical fields of neuropsychology and speech-language pathology (SLP), have resulted in considerable evolution of our understanding of the heterogeneity of diseases that cause dementia syndromes. Dementia with Lewy bodies, corticobasal degeneration, subcortical gliosis, frontotemporal dementia, primary progressive aphasia, and HIV-associated dementia are some of the most recently identified diseases that cause dementia syndromes (5th ed.; *DSM-5*; APA, 2013).

The recognition of a disease was soon followed by the identification of treatments for the undesirable symptoms. The earliest accounts of intervention for dementia symptoms were the use of a rotating chair, which was suggested for mental conditions related to congested blood in the brain, and the hyperbaric oxygen chamber, thought to re-oxygenate brain tissues causing dementia (Cohen, 1983). Julius Wagner von Jauregg, the first psychiatrist to win the Nobel Prize, discovered in 1917 that malaria inoculations improved six of nine patients with neurosyphillis (Whitrow, 1990). Recently, pharmacologic therapies have provided small benefits for improving cognition, including cholinesterase inhibitors (e.g., donepezil) for persons with mild-moderate Alzheimer's dementia, and a N-methyl-D-aspartate receptor antagonist (memantine) for persons with mild to severe Alzheimer's dementia (Farrimond, Roberts, & McShane, 2012; Tan et al., 2014), but it is unclear if these treatments are effective for persons with atypical dementias (Li, Hai, Zhou, & Dong, 2015). When behavioral disturbances including depression, agitation, aggression, and hallucinations require treatment, clinicians sometimes try a variety of neuroleptic, antidepressant, anxiolytic, and anticonvulsant medications, but not without risk of serious side effects (Corbett, Burns, & Ballard, 2014; Reus et al., 2016).

Research and policy development have encouraged a person-centered care approach (Kitwood, 1997), which resembles the kind of care and quality of life that most people would choose if given the opportunity. Person-centered care is anchored in values and beliefs that return the locus of control to older adults and their caregivers to support their quality of life (QoL). The main tenets of person-centered care call on care providers to promote choice, dignity, respect, self-determination, and purposeful living. The growing emphasis on person-centered (Kitwood, 1997; Ryan, Byrne, Spykerman, & Orange, 2005) resulted in a culture change in models of long-term care, and governments began to legislate more holistic care. The United States Congress passed the Omnibus Budget and Reconciliation Act of 1987 (OBRA; American Health Care Association, 1990) that mandates physical, cognitive, and communicative evaluations of residents, the development of a care plan upon admission to a nursing home, and periodic reassessments. When deficits in cognitive and communicative functioning are identified, the plan of care should include referral to the speech-language pathologist (SLP) for further assessment of treatment needs.

The past few decades have seen an explosion of interest in holistic and nonpharmacological approaches to intervention, which is ideally provided by an interprofessional team of healthcare professionals, with the person with dementia and family at the center of the team. Speech-language pathologists have only begun to develop assessment and treatment approaches for the cognitive and communication deficits that accompany dementia in the past 30 years (Bayles et al., 2005). Bayles, Kaszniak, and Tomoeda (1987) first documented the cognitive-linguistic deficits and skills of persons with dementia across the stages of brain degeneration, providing the resources that clinicians needed to assist in the differential diagnosis of people presenting with dementia symptoms. At that time, when a person was diagnosed with a degenerative neurological condition, the role of the SLP was to direct the family to supportive services in the community, including nursing homes.

From the mid-1980s, when behavioral treatments for the language and cognitive deficits of persons with dementia began to appear, thoughts about therapeutic intervention began to shift from futile to possible (Hopper, 2003). Evidence began to document the presence of spared abilities that could be used to design effective cognitive-communicative interventions that support or modify the client's behaviors directly (e.g., Camp, Foss, O'Hanlon, & Stevens, 1996; Hopper, Bayles, & Kim, 2001) or to assist caregivers to change their own coping strategies and behaviors (e.g., Bourgeois, Schulz, Burgio, & Beach, 2002). Effective nonpharmacological interventions to reduce responsive behaviors and to compensate for cognitive deficits include: direct interventions (person-centered care, communication skills training, redirection techniques, social and activity stimulation); environmental modifications; and caregiver education (e.g., Cohen-Mansfield, Thein, Marx, Dakheel-Ali, & Freedman, 2012; Hopper et al., 2013; Livingston et al., 2014). Psychological treatments can help to decrease depression and anxiety in persons with dementia (Orgeta, Qazi, Spector, & Orrell, 2014). Finally, exercise by people with dementia may improve performance of activities of daily living (ADLs) (Forbes, Forbes, Blake, Thiessen, & Forbes, 2015).

As noted above, caring for persons with dementia saw a major shift with the development of social models of health and disability. The World Health Organization developed the *International Classification of Impairment, Disability, and Handicap* (ICIDH; WHO, 1980), which evolved into the *International Classification of Functioning, Disability, and Health* (ICF; WHO, 2001). The ICF guides clinicians in understanding the effects of a medical condition on an individual, while examining how the person's context influences level of disability and functioning. The ICF can be used with individuals or populations to facilitate holistic approaches for assessment and intervention for people with chronic conditions. Figure 1.1 depicts the ICF components as (a) impairments of body structures and functions, (b) activity limitations related to the execution of a task or action, and (c) participation restrictions that limit involvement in life situations. These components are influenced by a variety of environmental and personal factors that act as supports or barriers to meaningful participation.

Within the field of speech-language pathology, the ICF (WHO, 2001) has inspired development of frameworks for communication disability and participation (e.g., Baylor, Burns, Eadie, Britton, & Yorkston, 2011; Threats, 2006, 2007). The Living with Aphasia: Framework for Outcome Measurement (A-FROM; Kagan et al., 2008) is an integrated, social model that was empirically derived from focus groups and visually depicts the relationship among impairment, participation, personal factors, and the environment. Personal values, identity, and feelings are given equal weight when compared to the impairment itself (see Figure 1.2). Although designed for people with aphasia, the domains of the model can easily be applied to life participation of individuals with dementia as well. Indeed, the goal of treatment for persons with dementia is improvement of the lived experience, as noted in the center most section of Figure 1.2. One of the many useful components of this model is that it urges clinicians to consider conversation as an

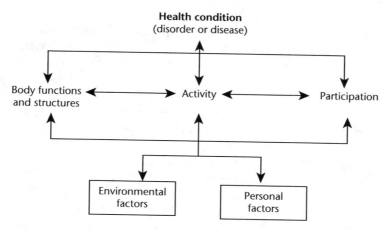

FIGURE 1.1   The *International Classification of Functioning, Disability, and Health*
Source: ICF; WHO, 2001.

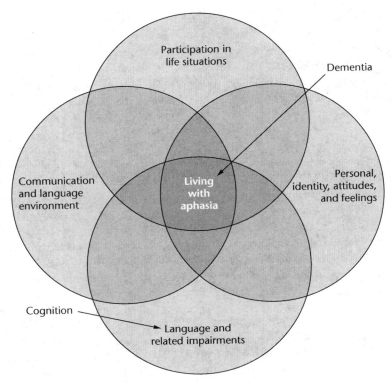

FIGURE 1.2 Living with Aphasia: Framework for Outcome Measurement (A-FROM) Adapted for Use as a Life Participation for Persons with Dementia Model

Source: Adapted with permission from the Aphasia Institute, Toronto, Canada. Kagan, A., Simmons-Mackie, N., Rowland, A., Huijbregts, M., Shumway, E., McEwen, W., Threats, T., & Sharp, S. (2007). Counting what counts: A framework for capturing real-life outcomes of aphasia intervention. *Aphasiology, 22*(3), 258–280.

ADL, and to recognize that context is key in working on communication. These elements can be applied to our work with persons with dementia in the form of a life participation approach for dementia.

Other social models have been developed to explain responsive behaviors of persons with dementia, and to promote development of person-centered care that maximizes functioning and quality of life. Some models aim to explain responsive behaviors as reflecting the theory of "unmet needs" (e.g., Algase et al., 1996; Kunik et al., 2003). These models encourage us to identify interventions for unmet needs of the person with dementia by examining the person, the caregivers, and the environment to improve quality of life for people with dementia and their caregivers (see Chapter 3 for details), and applied in the assessment and intervention chapters (see Chapters 6–8). The evolution in philosophy of care and policies regarding care has sparked a new attitude toward working with persons with dementia, with an increased focus on maximizing independent functioning and participation for as long as possible and on enhancing the quality of life of persons with dementia as well as their caregivers (Bourgeois, Brush, Elliot, & Kelly, 2015). These models have contributed to our guiding principles for intervention for persons with dementia, which will be explained in Chapter 4 and applied throughout the intervention chapters.

Assessment instruments have been designed to identify not only the degree of impairment and the resulting activity limitations and participation restrictions, but also to determine the preserved strengths of an individual that can be used to develop interventions to address person-centered, meaningful goals (see Chapter 5 for more details). Interventions can target any aspect of the ICF. Impairment-based interventions for persons with dementia are primarily pharmacological interventions, and some behavioral interventions. Other interventions aim to improve participation and engagement in meaningful activities. The development of two innovative approaches has shaped the way that the interprofessional team provides care for persons with dementia: the strength-based needs approach (e.g., Eisner, 2013) and Montessori-based approaches (e.g., Bourgeois et al., 2015; Camp & Skrajner, 2004; Elliot, 2011). These approaches encourage care providers to view persons with dementia as still having preserved competencies that can be capitalized upon to promote a satisfying life. Thus, the focus of most behavioral interventions is to find stimuli or strategies that compensate for the impairments, supporting the persons with dementia to maximize participation in daily life at a level that is meaningful and satisfying to them, their families, and others in their social environment. Interventions have been developed to promote functional behaviors related to memory, communication, ADLs, and eating and swallowing, and will be discussed in Chapters 6 through 8. Other interventions are targeted toward caregivers, and these will be discussed in Chapters 9 and 10.

As SLPs in the United States began to deliver more assessments and interventions for persons with dementia, they experienced some frustration with Medicare reimbursement claims denials. Claims reviewers had the misconception that the assessment and treatment of cognitive functioning were the responsibilities of psychologists and occupational therapists, not SLPs (Bayles et al., 2005). Various task forces of the American Speech-Language-Hearing Association (ASHA) developed documents designed to educate claims reviewers and legislators about the cognitive and communicative needs of persons with dementia and the role of the SLP with persons with dementia. The first of these documents was a technical report in which the relationship between cognition and language was defined, the role of the SLP in evaluating and treating persons with dementia was described, and the responsibilities of the SLP on an interdisciplinary cognitive intervention team were outlined (ASHA, 1987). A position paper on the roles of SLPs and audiologists in working with older persons specifically stated that speech and hearing professionals were required to provide services in the areas of needs identification, evaluation, treatment, resource referrals, counseling, discharge planning, services documentation, research, quality assurance, and advocacy (ASHA, 1988). The third document comprised SLP guidelines for serving persons with language, socio-communicative, and/or cognitive-communicative impairments (ASHA, 1991). In addition to the SLP roles outlined for serving these persons (identification, assessment, intervention, collaboration, case management, education, advocacy), specific competencies required to perform each role were described.

In a document outlining the preferred practice patterns of SLPs and audiologists (ASHA, 1993), several additional areas of responsibility were outlined for persons providing services to individuals with dementia, including screening for potential language problems. In addition, assessment of cognitive strengths and deficits was recommended, as well as follow-up services to monitor cognitive-communicative status and the maintenance of intervention effects. A second document on preferred practice patterns added additional definitions for assessment, diagnosis, and treatment of persons with cognitive-communication disorders (ASHA, 1997). Specific procedures for assessing impairments, strengths, deficits, contributing factors, and functional communication were included, as well as advocating for the selection of treatment goals to improve oral and written language and cognitive-communicative behavior.

As the evidence accumulates to justify the involvement of SLPs in the identification, diagnosis, and treatment of persons with cognitive-communication disorders, the above cited documents have been updated in the areas of the knowledge and skills needed by SLPs (ASHA, 2005a, 2005b)

TABLE 1.1 American Speech-Language-Hearing Association (ASHA) Position Statement on the Roles of Speech-Language Pathologists Working With Individuals With Dementia-Based Communication Disorders

Identification	Identifying persons at risk for dementia, taking into account the incidence and prevalence of dementia in different culturally and linguistically diverse populations.
	Screening individuals who present with language and communication difficulties, including hearing screening.
	Providing prevention information to individuals and groups known to be at risk for dementia, as well as to individuals working with those at risk.
Assessment	Selecting and administering clinically, culturally, and linguistically appropriate approaches to diagnosis and assess cognitive-communication functioning and swallowing across the course of the underlying disease complex.
	Determining the need for further assessment and/or referral for other services from other professionals, such as an audiologist for hearing and balance problems.
Intervention	Selecting and administering clinically, culturally, and linguistically appropriate evidence-based practice techniques for intervention of cognitive-communication and swallowing disorders with persons with dementia and their caregivers.
	Recommending environmental modifications that support communication.
Counseling	Providing culturally and linguistically appropriate counseling for individuals with dementia and their significant others and caregivers about the nature of their dementia and its course.
Collaboration	Consulting and collaborating with individuals with dementia, family members, and other personal and professional caregivers to develop intervention plans to maximize cognitive-communication and functional abilities at the highest level throughout the underlying disease course.
Case management	Serving as a case manager, coordinator, or team leader to ensure appropriate and timely delivery of a comprehensive management plan.
Education	Developing curricula and training programs.
	Educating, supervising, and mentoring future SLPs in research, assessment, diagnosis, and treatment of cognitive-communication problems associated with dementia.
	Educating families, caregivers, other professionals, third-party payers, legislators, and the public regarding the communication needs of individuals with dementia and the role of SLPs in diagnosing and managing cognitive communication and swallowing disorders associated with dementia.
Advocacy	Advocating for services for individuals with dementia at the local, state, and national levels.
	Serving as an expert witness.
Research	Remaining informed of research in the area of dementia.
	Helping advance the knowledge base of cognitive-communication problems in the dementias and of treatment efficacy through research.

Source: American Speech-Language-Hearing Association (2007).

and their roles in addressing the needs of this population (ASHA, 2007; see Table 1.1). In addition, leaders in the field have spearheaded efforts to review systematically the published treatment research to develop evidence-based practice guidelines for clinicians to manage the cognitive-communication disorders of persons with neurological disorders, including dementia (e.g., Golper et al., 2001; Hopper et al., 2013).

The Executive Board of the Academy of Neurological Communication Disorders and Sciences (ANCDS) developed and published guidelines based on research evidence to support clinical decision-making in the management of persons with neurological conditions. The ANCDS Ad hoc Practice Guidelines Coordinating Committee directed the individual writing committees to focus on developing practice guidelines instead of practice standards, which require a high degree of certainty based on Class I empirical evidence. Instead, practice guidelines are recommendations for management procedures that have a moderate degree of clinical certainty based on Class II evidence or a strong consensus from Class III evidence (Miller et al., 1999). Class I evidence requires one or more well-designed, randomized, controlled clinical trials; Class II evidence requires one or more well-designed, observational clinical studies with concurrent controls such as single-case or cohort controls; and Class III evidence is provided by expert opinion, case series, case reports, or historical controls (Golper et al., 2001). A lack of published Class I studies limits development of practice standards currently; alternatively, some practice guidelines have been developed and hold the most promise for guiding clinicians and researchers in the development of treatment approaches. There is a continued need to systematically generate data with more clients with dementia and with more diverse characteristics that will eventually lead to well-designed Class I studies. Throughout the book, we discuss the degree and quality of available evidence for interventions discussed.

In conclusion, the field of dementia care is no longer in its infancy. Thirty years of attention to diagnostic description and classification, as well as intervention alternatives, have generated scientific evidence from which clinicians and researchers can base clinical decisions. Speech-language pathologists are uniquely positioned to understand the striking impact that communication challenges have on persons with dementia and their caregivers. Communication is a basic human right (www.internationalcommunicationproject.com), and SLPs can lead the charge to improve access to communication and participation for persons with dementia. We are prepared to guide our clients and their caregivers through the challenges of dementia with the ultimate objective of experiencing the best quality of life possible. This volume aims to serve as a reference manual and the starting point for those who want to provide person-centered and life-enhancing services to persons with dementia, and to inspire the continued generation of quality research to demonstrate the value of cognitive-communication intervention. This book also serves as a call to action for healthcare providers in general, and SLPs in particular, to promote meaningful life engagement in persons with dementia through the use of evidence-based assessment and intervention approaches.

References

Algase, D. L., Beck, C., Kolanowski, A., Whall, A., Berent, S., Richards, K., & Beattie, E. (1996). Need-driven dementia-compromised behavior: An alternative view of disruptive behavior. *American Journal of Alzheimer's Disease, 11*(6), 10–19. doi:10.1177/153331759601100603.

Amaducci, L. A., Rocca, W. A., & Schoenberg, B. S. (1986). Origin of the distinction between Alzheimer's disease and senile dementia: How history can clarify nosology. *Neurology, 36*, 1497–1499. http://dx.doi.org/10.1212/WNL.36.11.1497.

American Health Care Association. (1990). *Long term care survey: Regulations, forms, procedures, guidelines.* Washington, DC: Author.

American Psychiatric Association (APA). (1952). *Diagnostic and statistical manual of mental disorders (DSM)*. Washington, DC: Author.

American Psychiatric Association (APA). (1980). *Diagnostic and statistical manual of mental disorders (DSM-III;* 3rd ed.). Washington, DC: Author.

American Psychiatric Association (APA). (2013). *Diagnostic and statistical manual of mental disorders (DSM-5;* 5th ed.). Washington, DC: Author.

American Speech-Language-Hearing Association (ASHA). (1987). Role of speech-language pathologists in the habilitation and rehabilitation of cognitively impaired individuals. *ASHA, 29*(6), 53–55.

American Speech-Language-Hearing Association (ASHA). (1988). The roles of speech-language pathologists and audiologists in working with older persons. *ASHA, 30*(3), 80–84.

American Speech-Language-Hearing Association (ASHA). (1991). Guidelines for speech-language pathologists serving persons with language, socio-communicative, and/or cognitive-communicative impairments. *ASHA, 33*(Suppl. 5), 21–28.

American Speech-Language-Hearing Association (ASHA). (1993). Preferred practice patterns for the professions of speech-language pathology and audiology. *ASHA, 35*(Suppl. 11), i–iii, 1–102.

American Speech-Language-Hearing Association (ASHA). (1997). *Preferred practice patterns for the professions of speech-language pathology and audiology*. Rockville, MD: Author.

American Speech-Language-Hearing Association (ASHA). (2005a). Knowledge and skills needed by speech-language pathologists providing services to individuals with cognitive-communication disorders. *ASHA* (Suppl. 25), 2–9.

American Speech-Language-Hearing Association (ASHA). (2005b). Roles of speech-language pathologists in the identification, diagnosis, and treatment of individuals with cognitive-communication disorders: Position statement. *ASHA* (Suppl. 25), 1–2.

American Speech-Language-Hearing Association (ASHA). (2007). *Scope of practice in speech-language pathology* [scope of practice]. doi:10.1044/policy.SP2007-00283.

Bayles, K. A., Kaszniak, A. W., & Tomoeda, C. K. (1987). *Communication and cognition in normal aging and dementia*. Austin, TX: Pro-Ed.

Bayles, K. A., Kim, E. S., Azuma, T., Chapman, S. B., Cleary, S., Hopper, T., … Zientz, J. (2005). Developing evidence-based practice guidelines for speech-language pathologists serving individuals with Alzheimer's dementia. *Journal of Medical Speech-Language Pathology, 13*(4), xiii–xxv.

Baylor, C., Burns, M., Eadie, T., Britton, D., & Yorkston, K. (2011). A qualitative study of interference with communicative participation across communication disorders in adults. *American Journal of Speech-Language Pathology, 20*, 269–287. doi: 10.1044/1058-0360(2011/10-0084).

Boller, F., & Forbes, M. M. (1998). History of dementia and dementia in history: An overview. *Journal of Neurological Sciences, 158*, 125–133. http://dx.doi.org/10.1016/S0022-510X(98)00128-2.

Bourgeois, M. S., Brush, J., Elliot, G., & Kelly, A. (2015). Join the revolution: How Montessori for aging and dementia can change long-term care culture. *Seminars in Speech and Language, 36*, 209–214. http://dx.doi.org/10.1055/s-0035-1554802.

Bourgeois, M. S., Schulz, R., Burgio, L. D., & Beach, S. (2002). Skills training for spouses of patients with Alzheimer's disease: Outcomes of an intervention study. *Journal of Clinical Geropsychology, 8*, 53–73. doi:10.1023/A:1013098124765.

Camp, C. J., Foss, J. W., O'Hanlon, A. M., & Stevens, A. B. (1996). Memory interventions for persons with dementia. *Applied Cognitive Psychology, 10*, 193–210.

Camp, C. J., & Skrajner, M. J. (2004). Resident-assisted Montessori programming (RAMP): Training persons with dementia to serve as group activity leaders. *The Gerontologist, 44*, 426–431. doi:10.1093/geront/44.3.426.

Cohen, G. D. (1983). Historical views and evolution of concepts. In B. Reisberg (Ed.), *Alzheimer's disease: The standard reference* (pp. 29–33). New York: Free Press.

Cohen-Mansfield, J., Thein, K., Marx, M., Dakheel-Ali, M., & Freedman, L. (2012). Efficacy of nonpharmacologic interventions for agitation in advanced dementia: A randomized, placebo-controlled trial. *Journal of Clinical Psychiatry, 73*, 1255–1261.

Corbett, A., Burns, A., & Ballard, C. (2014). Don't use antipsychotics routinely to treat agitation and aggression in people with dementia. *BMJ, 349*: g6420. doi:10.1136/bmj.g6420.

Eisner, E. (2013). *Engaging and communicating with people who have dementia: Finding and using their strengths.* Baltimore: Health Professions Press.

Elliot, G. (2011). *Montessori Methods for Dementia™: Focusing on the person and the prepared environment.* Oakville, Canada: Dementiability Enterprises.

Farrimond, L. E., Roberts, E., & McShane, R. (2012). Memantine and cholinesterase inhibitor combination therapy for Alzheimer's disease: A systematic review. *BMJ Open, 2*(3).

Forbes, D., Forbes, S. C., Blake, C. M., Thiessen, E. J., & Forbes, S. (2015). Exercise programs for people with dementia. *Cochrane Database of Systematic Reviews, Issue 4.* Art. No.: CD006489. DOI: 10.1002/14651858.CD006489.pub4.

Golper, L. C., Wertz, R. T., Frattali, C. M., Yorkston, K. M., Myers, P., Katz, R., … Wambaugh, J. (2001). *Evidence-based practice guidelines for the management of communication disorders in neurologically impaired individuals: Project introduction.* Retrieved January 2, 2016 from www.ancds.org/assets/docs/EBP/practice guidelines.pdf.

Hopper, T. L. (2003). "They're just going to get worse anyway": Perspectives on rehabilitation for nursing home residents with dementia. *Journal of Communication Disorders, 36,* 345–359. http://dx.doi.org/10.1016/S0021-9924(03)00050-9.

Hopper, T., Bayles, K. A., & Kim, E. S. (2001). Retained neuropsychological abilities of individuals with Alzheimer's disease. *Seminars in Speech and Language, 22,* 261–273.

Hopper, T., Bourgeois, M., Pimental, J., Qualls, C., Hickey, E., Frymark, T., & Schooling, T. (2013). An evidence-based systematic review on cognitive training for individuals with dementia. *American Journal of Speech-Language Pathology, 22,* 126–145.

Kagan, A., Simmons-Mackie, N., Rowland, A., Huijbregts, M., Shumway, E., McEwen, S., … Sharp, S. (2008). Counting what counts: A framework for capturing real-life outcomes of aphasia intervention. *Aphasiology, 22,* 258–280. http://dx.doi.org/10.1080/02687030701282595.

Kitwood, T. (1997) *Dementia reconsidered: The person comes first.* Buckingham, UK: Open University Press.

Kunik, M., Martinez, M., Snow, A., Beck, C., Cody, M., Rapp, C. et al. (2003). Determinants of behavioral symptoms in dementia patients. *Clinical Gerontologist, 26*(3–4), 83–89.

Li, Y., Hai, S., Zhou, Y., & Dong, B. R. (2015). Cholinesterase inhibitors for rarer dementias associated with neurological conditions. *Cochrane Database of Systematic Reviews, Issue 3.* Art. No.: CD009444. doi: 10.1002/14651858.CD009444.pub3.

Livingston, G., Kelly, L., Lewis-Holmes, E., Baio, G., Morris, S., Patel, N., Omar, R., Katona, C., & Cooper, C. (2014). Non-pharmacological interventions for agitation in dementia: Systematic review of randomized controlled trials. *British Journal of Psychiatry, 205,* 436–442.

Miller, R. G., Rosenberg, J. A., Gelinas, D. F., Misumoto, H., Newman, D., Sufit, R., … Oppenheimer, E. A. (1999). Practice parameter: The care of the patient with amyotrophic lateral sclerosis (an evidence-based review). *Neurology, 52,* 1311–1325. doi: http://dx.doi.org/10.1212/WNL.52.7.1311.

Orgeta, V., Qazi, A., Spector, A. E., & Orrell, M. (2014). Psychological treatments for depression and anxiety in dementia and mild cognitive impairment. *Cochrane Database of Systematic Reviews, Issue 1.* Art. No.: CD009125. doi: 10.1002/14651858.CD009125.pub2.

Reus, V., Fochtmann, L. J., Eyler, A. E., Hilty, D. M., Horvitz-Lennon, M., Jibson, M. D., … & Yager, J. (2016). The American Psychiatric Association practice guideline on the use of antipsychotics to treat agitation or psychosis in patients with dementia. *Am J Psychiatry 173*(5), 543–546.

Ryan, E. B., Byrne, K., Spykerman, H., & Orange, J. B. (2005). Evidencing Kitwood's personhood strategies: Conversation as care in dementia. In: B. H. Davis (Ed.), *Alzheimer talk, text and context: Enhancing communication.* New York: Palgrave Macmillan.

Tan, C. C., Yu, J. T., Wang, H. F., Tan, M. S., Meng, X. F., Wang, C. et al. (2014). Efficacy and safety of donepezil, galantamine, rivastigmine, and memantine for the treatment of Alzheimer's disease: A systematic review and meta-analysis. *Journal of Alzheimer's Disease, 41*(2), 615–631.

Threats, T. (2006). Towards an international framework for communication disorders: Use of the ICF. *Journal of Communication Disorders, 39*(4), 251–265. doi.org/10.1016/j.jcomdis.2006.02.002.

Threats, T. (2007). Access for persons with neurogenic communication disorders: Influences of personal and environmental factors of the ICF. *Aphasiology, 21*(1), 67–80. doi.org/10.1080/02687030600798303.

Torack, R. M. (1983). The early history of senile dementia. In B. Reisberg (Ed.), *Alzheimer's disease: The standard reference* (pp. 23–28). New York: Free Press.

Whitrow, M. (1990). Wagner-Jauregg and fever therapy. *Medical History, 34*, 294–310. doi:10.1017/S0025727300052431. https://doi.org/10.1017/S0025727300052431.

World Health Organization (1980). *International classification of impairments, disabilities, and handicaps: A manual of classification relating to the consequences of disease.* Geneva: World Health Organization. Retrieved February 21, 2006 from http://apps.who.int/iris/bitstream/10665/41003/1/9241541261_eng.pdf.

World Health Organization. (2001). *International classification of functioning, disability, and health.* Retrieved February 21, 2006 from www3.who.int/icf/icftemplate.cfm.

2

CLINICAL AND PATHOPHYSIOLOGICAL PROFILES OF VARIOUS DEMENTIA ETIOLOGIES

Tammy Hopper, Ellen M. Hickey, and Michelle S. Bourgeois

Dementia is a syndrome, or collection of cognitive and behavioral symptoms, caused by an underlying disease. Although the dementia syndrome is characterized by a core set of diagnostic criteria, expression of the syndrome will vary depending on the underlying neuropathology, as well as across individuals with a particular disease. The most common diseases that cause dementia are age-related; thus, with the growing aging population comes an increase in the incidence and prevalence of dementia. More people are seeking information about dementia from their medical providers and other sources, including the Internet, which often leads to referrals for testing. More individuals being tested leads to several benefits: a larger database of clinical cases to analyze, improved methods for more specific and reliable diagnoses, and enhanced treatment options. Advances in determining the underlying causes of the spectrum of dementia diagnoses are accelerating; the need for accurate and reliable methods for differentiating among dementia syndromes remains a priority for clinicians who are faced with clients and their presenting symptoms. This chapter outlines the range of different diseases and disorders that can cause dementia, their pathophysiological markers, and their associated cognitive and behavioral symptoms.

The term dementia[1] is referred to as Major Neurocognitive Disorder (NCD) in the fifth edition of the *Diagnostic and Statistical Manual of Mental Disorders* (5th ed.; *DSM-5*; American Psychiatric Association [APA], 2013). The criteria for a diagnosis of Major NCD (see Box 2.1) include: (A) Evidence of significant cognitive decline from a previous level of performance in one or more cognitive domains (complex attention, executive function, learning and memory, language, perceptual–motor, or social cognition) based on: (1) concern of the individual or knowledgeable informant or the clinician that there has been a significant cognitive decline, and, (2) a substantial impairment in cognitive performance, preferably documented by standardized neuropsychological testing; (B) The cognitive deficits interfere with independence in everyday activities; (C) The cognitive deficits do not occur exclusively in the context of a delirium (an acute confusional state); (D) The cognitive deficits are not better explained by another mental disorder (e.g., major depression, schizophrenia).

The *DSM-5* includes a two-step procedure for diagnosis in which people are first classified as having Major NCD and then the underlying etiology of the clinical syndrome is coded (Petersen

---

1. The term dementia is "retained as an alternative" to the term Major NCD in the *DSM-5* (APA, 2013, p. 607), and will be used throughout this chapter.

Box 2.1 *DSM-5* Diagnostic Criteria for Major Neurocognitive Disorder (NCD) (also known as dementia) (APA, 2013)

A. Evidence of significant cognitive decline from a previous level of performance in one or more cognitive domains:

- complex attention
- executive function
- learning and memory
- language
- perceptual-motor
- social cognition

Based on:

1. Concern of the individual or knowledgeable informant or the clinician that there has been a significant cognitive decline.
2. A substantial impairment in cognitive performance, preferably documented by standardized neuropsychological testing.
B. The cognitive deficits interfere with independence in everyday activities (i.e., minimally, requiring assistance with complex instrumental activities of daily living such as paying bills).
C. The cognitive deficits do not occur exclusively in the context of a delirium (an acute confusional state).
D. The cognitive deficits are not better explained by another mental disorder (e.g., major depression, schizophrenia).

---

et al., 2014). Dementia is most commonly caused by Alzheimer's disease (AD), an irreversible, progressive neurological disorder that ultimately results in death (Alzheimer's Association, 2016). Other conditions that cause dementia include neurodegenerative diseases (e.g., Parkinson's disease, Huntington's disease, frontotemporal lobar degeneration, Lewy Body disease), vascular diseases (e.g., stroke), infections (e.g., Creutzfeldt-Jacob disease), traumatic brain injury, and certain substances (e.g., alcohol) and medications. Given the multiple potential causes of dementia, and the fact that some causes are more treatable than others (Clarfield, 2003), a comprehensive, multi-disciplinary clinical assessment of cognitive and noncognitive symptoms is crucial for accurate diagnosis.

Additionally, it is important to note that one neuropathology can cause a variety of clinical dementia syndromes (e.g., Alzheimer's disease can cause Alzheimer dementia, primary progressive aphasia, or posterior cortical atrophy; frontotemporal lobar degeneration can cause behavioral variant–frontal temporal dementia, primary progressive aphasia). Likewise, some clinical dementia syndromes can be caused by a variety of neuropathologies (e.g., primary progressive aphasia can be caused by Alzheimer's disease or frontotemporal lobar degeneration). Further, the clinical diagnostic process is not always clear cut, and diseases can be misdiagnosed based on cognitive and physical examination; however, the use of expensive neuroimaging tests must be balanced against the benefit of the information to be gained (Thomas et al., 2017). Thus, families and persons with dementia can become confused about the diagnostic process and conclusions. Speech-language pathologists and other health professionals, therefore, should understand the difference between the underlying neuropathologies and the clinical dementia syndromes so that they may educate and counsel persons with dementia and their families (Khayum, 2016). See Figure 2.1 for a flowchart (Khayum, personal communication) developed from the Northwestern Care Pathway Model (Morhardt et al., 2015) that can be used to explain the diagnostic process to persons with dementia and their families.

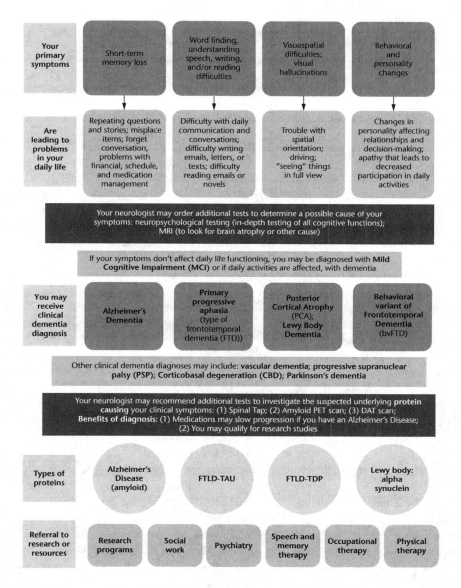

FIGURE 2.1 Northwestern Care Pathway Model to Dementia Care (Morhardt et al., 2015)

Source: Used with permission from Becky Khayum and colleagues.

Box 2.2 Common Diseases and Conditions that Cause Dementia Syndromes

- Alzheimer's disease
- Parkinson's disease
- Frontotemporal lobar degeneration
- Lewy Body disease
- Vascular diseases
- Huntington's disease
- Infections
- Traumatic brain injury
- Substances/medications

Screening and Diagnosis of Dementia

The realization that one's memory and cognitive functioning might be changing is frightening. Most people in this situation monitor their periodic memory lapses and wait until they reach their anxiety threshold to schedule an appointment with their doctor. Others seek out a referral at the earliest sign of a problem. Fears may lead to denial or minimization of symptoms, and hiding symptoms from family and friends. Family members and friends may show similar patterns of reluctance or eagerness to investigate increasing cognitive issues. For example, a family member who does not drive may believe that it will be safe for the person with cognitive changes to continue driving as long as a passenger is present in the vehicle. At the other end of the continuum, some family members who notice cognitive changes become fearful for the safety of that person and attempt to limit the person's responsibilities, restrict or prohibit driving, and begin to search for alternative living situations before a diagnosis has been made or those limitations become necessary. A thorough medical examination is needed to begin the process of confirming or explaining the underlying causes of the symptoms. Community memory screenings offer a quick and no cost way to start the process.

Community Memory Screenings

Free Memory Screenings are frequently offered in the community as a public service by hospitals, geriatric assessment centers, university-affiliated memory disorder clinics, other medical establishments, social service resource centers (e.g., Alzheimer Resource Centers), state-funded agencies (e.g., an Area Agency on Aging or a Department of Elder Affairs), and national organizations (e.g., the Alzheimer's Association or the Alzheimer's Foundation of America). As of 2015, the Alzheimer's Foundation of America has launched the National Memory Screening Program, an ongoing initiative conducted in collaboration with community organizations to promote early detection of memory problems and encourage appropriate intervention. Memory-screening events may also be part of a larger community health fair where citizens can obtain free health information and participate in a variety of health screenings (e.g., for blood pressure, cholesterol, bone density, and falls risk). These memory screenings are typically advertised in local newspapers and in public service announcements on the radio and television.

The memory screening is designed to provide a quick assessment of cognitive abilities using screening instruments, such as the *Mini Mental State Exam* (MMSE; Folstein, Folstein, & McHugh,

1975; MMSE-2; Folstein & Folstein, 2010) or the *Montreal Cognitive Assessment* (MoCA; Nasreddine et al., 2005). Review of the person's medications for potential drug interactions or memory-impairing drugs (i.e., Benadryl used as a sleep aid), screening for depression and other medical and mental health concerns, and the identification of any recent traumatic life events (e.g., the death of a family member or a divorce) are also included in a memory-screening protocol, which usually takes approximately 30 minutes. A compilation of the information gathered in this quick session can be helpful in determining if there appear to be reasonable explanations for the memory symptoms or if more extensive testing is warranted. The person is then counseled to follow up with his or her medical provider. Informational brochures about normal aging and memory, memory-enhancing strategies, and memory loss prevention are available from a variety of sources listed at the end of this chapter.

Medical Assessment

The medical examination begins with a careful documentation of the presenting complaint and history of symptoms to identify areas of change in medical condition (e.g., pain, weight, sleep, and activity), cognitive functioning (e.g., language, orientation, initiation and execution of activities, visuospatial difficulties), and noncognitive functioning (e.g., change in personality, behavioral disturbance, motor functioning, and psychiatric symptoms). Family members or significant others often provide helpful information, particularly if they live with the person. The physician will pay particular attention to the report of symptom onset, rate of progression, and severity of symptoms. A sudden onset will signal the potential for cardiovascular etiology (e.g., stroke), whereas a gradual insidious onset is expected for a diagnosis of Alzheimer's disease. Although there is some controversy about the extent to which the symptoms of dementia might be reversible (Jack et al., 2011), the importance of accurate differential diagnosis of conditions that might respond to medical treatment is irrefutable. The symptom list will guide the physician in conducting the physical examination and selecting other areas of investigation. Box 2.3 summarizes the diagnostic process that the physician and team undergoes with the client and family to determine if there is a dementia syndrome and which disease is present.

The Physical Examination. The physical examination begins with a review of medical conditions. Existing medical conditions may explain impaired cognitive symptoms; for example, cardiovascular disease, diabetes, hypothyroidism, anoxic or hypoxic conditions, liver and renal disease, and other metabolic conditions can all contribute to impaired attention, concentration, and memory. Appropriate treatment of these medical conditions may improve cognition. The physical exam may reveal evidence of cardiovascular-respiratory impairments, as indicated by measuring pulse and blood pressure and listening to the heart, lungs, and abdomen. The person's current medications for these medical conditions are reviewed and evaluated against self- and family-reports of their effectiveness for managing the symptoms of that condition. Sometimes, the addition of a medication or changes in medication dosing can exacerbate cognitive symptoms; reevaluation after a period of adjustment to medications is usually indicated.

Blood Chemistry: Metabolic and Nutritional Factors. When the person presents with previously undiagnosed symptoms and an explanatory medical condition is not obvious, blood screening is usually ordered. Current recommended routine laboratory analyses remain the same as those proposed by Knopman et al. (2001) and include a complete blood count, serum electrolytes, glucose, blood urea nitrogen and creatinine, folate, thyroid-stimulating hormone, and vitamin B_{12}. Testing for Lyme disease, syphilis, and HIV is also advisable when risk factors for those conditions are present. Chronic alcoholism is often revealed when nutritional deficiencies are documented from blood chemistries; untreated long-term alcohol abuse is thought to contribute to the dementia symptoms seen in Wernicke-Korsakoff syndrome (Thompson, Guerrini, & Marshall, 2012), discussed in a later section of this chapter.

Neurological Examination. A focused neurological examination is needed to determine if there are specific neurological conditions that could explain the cognitive concerns. The neurologist will complete a cranial and spinal nerve examination to look for signs of facial weakness; abnormal eye movements; visual field defects; posture, gait, and movement disorders; grasp, sucking, and snout reflexes; vibratory and proprioceptive sensation deficits that would signal specific neurological conditions. Extrapyramidal signs suggest Lewy body disease, Parkinson's disease, or Huntington's disease, although they are often present in AD as well (Karantzoulis & Galvin, 2014). Ataxia and proprioceptive changes are associated with vitamin B_{12} deficiency. Increased lower-limb tone, brisk reflexes, and apraxic gait are seen in frontal pathologies, such as those from normal-pressure hydrocephalus (Patterson & Clarfield, 2003).

Furthermore, mental status, language functioning, and mood may provide signs that are used to differentiate among focal impairments secondary to vascular lesions, psychotic symptoms related to psychiatric illness (such as major depression), or the gradual deterioration of cognitive functioning in dementia. Neurologists often administer quick cognitive screening measures, such as the MoCA (Nasreddine et al., 2005), and the MMSE (Folstein et al., 1975) to determine global mental status. Age-, culture-, and education-related norms (Crum, Anthony, Bassett, & Folstein, 1993; Grigoletto, Zappalà, Anderson, & Lebowitz, 1999) are available for more accurate interpretation of MMSE results. Additionally, the MMSE-2 (Folstein & Folstein, 2010) is more sensitive to subcortical cognitive deficits than the original MMSE and is also available in eight languages, and three dialects of Spanish. Language and mood are typically assessed informally throughout the evaluation process from responses to direct questioning about the client's symptoms and history. Older persons with depression tend to score lower on the MMSE (Folstein, Folstein, & Folstein, 2011).

Family and Psychosocial History. The person's psychosocial history is needed for an accurate interpretation of medical and neurological information. Information is gathered, usually by a social worker, to document presence of relatives with dementia or other high-risk medical conditions, education level and occupation, social supports and resources, hobbies/activities, and living arrangements. When there is evidence that first-degree relatives experienced dementia symptoms, or had medical conditions with known cognitive symptoms, the person is more likely at increased risk for dementia (Alzheimer's Association, 2016). The extent and composition of the person's social network should be ascertained, including family, friends, care providers, and the resources and support they provide to them. Maintaining social relationships and friendships and participating in social activities (e.g., church, cards and board games, and book clubs) might delay cognitive decline (DiMarco et al., 2014). Some researchers advocate activities that require clients to learn new information (e.g., a second language and a musical instrument) to foster the potential development of new neuronal pathways and increase cognitive reserve (Antoniou, Gunasekera, & Wong, 2013).

The relationship between educational attainment and dementia risk has received much scrutiny in recent years. Since the publication of Snowdon's (2001) investigation of the cognitive and educational histories of a community of nuns, the potential neuroprotective effects of education have been studied. In a recent systematic review, Meng and D'Arcy (2012) report the findings of several studies in which there is evidence to support the protective effects of increased education levels against several types of dementia. They interpret these findings in the context of the cognitive reserve hypothesis, which posits that individuals with higher levels of education develop a buffer or reserve through enhanced neuronal connections that helps them compensate for the early brain changes associated with several neurodegenerative diseases.

However, some scientists believe that the increased risk of dementia among those with lower educational attainment may be explained by other factors common to people in lower socio-economic groups (McDowell, Xi, Lindsay, & Tierney, 2007), such as increased risk for disease in general and less access to medical care and adequate nutrition. Information about diet, exercise, and alcohol consumption is valuable also for evaluating psychosocial functioning. Aerobic exercise may also have a protective benefit. Higher midlife fitness levels seem to be associated with lower hazards of developing dementia later in life (Defina et al., 2013). On the other hand, late life depression is associated with a higher risk of dementia, particularly vascular dementia and Alzheimer's dementia (Diniz, Butters, Albert, Dew, & Reynolds, 2013).

Accurately determining the needs of a person who lives alone is often difficult, especially if there are few visitors to monitor the physical status of the home and the daily living habits. The presence of a spouse or adult children ensures more accurate and detailed information, although psychological issues, such as grief, anger, and fear, can temper its veracity. An overburdened caregiver puts him or herself and the care recipient at risk for negative physical and emotional outcomes. This interview process is critical for determining the entire range of resources the client and caregiver will need following the medical diagnosis.

Pharmacological Assessment. Medication review is a vital component of the comprehensive dementia evaluation because of the cognition-impairing effects of some common medications and the prevalence of polypharmacy (the use of multiple medications and/or unnecessary medications; Maher, Hanlon, & Hajjar, 2014) among older adults. Confusion and apathy may be seen in an older person taking over-the-counter sedatives (e.g., Benadryl). Multiple medications for a range of health conditions can impact cognitive function and alter drug pharmacokinetics, including prescription and over-the-counter drugs as well as herbal remedies. For example, the prescription drug Coumadin and the over-the-counter medications aspirin and gingko biloba are all anticoagulants, which if taken together could thin the blood more than the prescribing physician intended. Many types of medicines have known memory-impairing properties, including analgesics, antipsychotics, anticholinergics, anxiolytics, barbiturates, sedatives, hypnotics, antidepressants, antihistamines, and some urinary agents (Massey & Ghazvini, 2005). Nonprescription drug use should also be reported to the clinician for its potential contribution to impaired cognitive functioning. In addition, noncompliance with medication regimens often exacerbates known medical conditions and can be the result of forgetting or refusing to take the drugs as prescribed. Finally, the neurotoxic effects of drug and alcohol abuse, often overlooked in the elderly, can be ameliorated if detected and treated appropriately.

Neuropsychological Assessment. Another critical component of the diagnosis of dementia is the neuropsychological examination. Neuropsychology is the study of brain, cognitive, affective, and behavioral functioning based on performance in a variety of assessments. The primary function of neuropsychological testing is to determine whether the person's performance is pathological or normal given age, gender, education, and cultural background (Taylor & Monsch, 2004). Different patterns of performance on tests of cognition (e.g., attention, memory), language, praxis, visuospatial ability, and executive function also help to diagnose the different types of dementia. Neuropsychological assessments repeated over time are useful for documenting disease progression and the effects of treatment. These assessments will be described in Chapter 5.

Prior to conducting a neuropsychological assessment, age-related changes in vision and hearing must be considered. Visual impairment is common among older adults and may be due to refractive error (and corrected with lenses/glasses) or nonrefractive error related to macular degeneration or diabetic retinopathy (Chou et al., 2013). Macular degeneration, glaucoma, and cataracts are other disorders of the eye that the clinician should look for in a chart review or interview prior to neuropsychological assessment. Simple tests of reading may be used to screen for visual ability;

however, clinicians should refer to appropriate healthcare professionals (e.g., optometrists, occupational therapists) for more in-depth evaluations as indicated.

Hearing loss is common among older adults and may be even more prevalent among older adults with cognitive impairment. Over the past several years, researchers have found an association between hearing loss and cognitive impairment (Kiely, Gopinath, Mitchell, Luszcz, & Anstey, 2012) as well as hearing loss and higher incident dementia (Lin et al., 2011). In a recent study, Nirmalasari, Mamo, Nieman, and Simpson (2017) reported that among 133 individuals over the age of 50 who visited a memory clinic, almost two-thirds exhibited hearing loss (using the World Health Organization's definition of hearing loss as a pure-tone average (PTA) of 0.5–4 kHz tones in the better ear of >25 dB). The mechanisms underlying the association between cognitive and hearing impairment remain unknown; however, researchers have posited that the relationship may result from a common neuropathology underlying both hearing loss and cognitive decline, deleterious effects of social isolation caused by both hearing and cognitive loss, or increased cognitive load caused by hearing loss (Albers et al., 2015; Lin & Albert, 2014). Regardless of the cause, the relationship between cognitive impairment and hearing loss means that clinicians must be aware of hearing health prior to neuropsychological assessment to ensure appropriate differential diagnoses, and refer to audiologists where necessary. If a client with a hearing loss has hearing aids, then the clinician should ensure that the aids are worn during the neuropsychological assessment, and that they have working batteries in place.

Neuroimaging Assessment. Although not necessary for a clinical diagnosis of dementia, the use of neuroimaging techniques may increase the physician's certainty of a dementia diagnosis (McKhann et al., 2011) and the results may assist in identification of the various etiologies of dementia (APA, 2013). Therefore, physicians commonly use structural neuroimaging with either computed tomography (CT) or magnetic resonance imaging (MRI) scans in routine initial assessment for dementia. CT provides an X-ray image of intracranial structures to detect brain tumors, subdural hematomas, hydrocephalus, cerebral lesions, cortical atrophy, and ventricular and white matter changes. CT may be useful for recognizing focal lesions when there are few focal neurological signs. The most widely used neuroimaging technique to investigate anatomical changes and neurodegeneration is structural MRI (Risacher & Saykin, 2013). Structural MRI is often preferred over CT scans, as MRI uses electromagnetic forces to create a spatial representation of brain tissue and produces improved resolution and superior soft tissue contrast of the images.

A variety of other neuroimaging techniques are also used for investigation of dementia, usually in a research context (Risacher & Saykin, 2013). These include molecular-imaging approaches to complement the structural-imaging techniques by depicting cerebral blood flow, the distribution of radioactive-labeled drugs, and biochemical reactions to specific enzymes in the brain. For example, functional MRI (fMRI) detects the modulation of hemoglobin during a task as blood flows through the brain. Magnetic resonance spectroscopy (MRS) examines biochemical changes by measuring radio frequencies (Risacher & Saykin, 2013). Single photon emission computed tomography (SPECT) uses gamma ray-emitting substances to generate images that reflect the biochemical status of cells, including blood flow, synaptic density, and tumor metabolism (Bhogal et al., 2013).

Positron emission tomography (PET) measures cerebral glucose metabolism by injecting radio-labeled ligands, among them fluorodeoxyglucose (FDG) that measures glucose metabolism, tracers that assess beta-amyloid deposits (e.g., Pittsburgh Compound B; PiB), and tracers that assess neurotransmitter systems (Risacher & Saykin, 2013). PET studies allow for assessment of functional changes in brain metabolism and neurotransmitter and other protein levels, which can provide important information about degenerative changes in different types of dementia (Risacher & Saykin, 2013). Positive PET amyloid imaging and decreased FDG uptake on PET, along with

---

Box 2.3 Diagnostic Process for Dementia

Two-step procedure for diagnosis:

1. classified as having Major NCD.
2. underlying etiology of the clinical syndrome is coded (Petersen et al., 2014).

Based on the following components of the medical assessment:

- Physical examination, e.g., status of current medical conditions – heart, renal, liver functions.
- Blood chemistry: metabolic and nutritional factors, e.g., vitamin deficiencies, electrolyte balance.
- Neurological examination, e.g., visual field defects, movement and gait disorders.
- Family and psychosocial history, e.g., family history of Alzheimer's disease, social network.
- Pharmacological assessment, e.g., polypharmacy or noncompliance issues.
- Neuropsychological assessment, e.g., memory, language, praxis tests.
- Neuroimaging assessment, e.g., MRI or CT.
- Biomarkers, e.g., cerebrospinal fluid measures of tau protein.

---

disproportionate atrophy on structural MRI in temporal and parietal cortices are cited as biomarkers of AD (McKhann et al., 2011). Other biomarkers will be discussed in the section that follows.

Neuropathology, Biomarkers, and Genetics

Much research is under way in the areas of biomarkers and genetics with neuropathologically confirmed dementia, with the goal of developing accurate and reliable laboratory tests as well as treatments for disorders that cause dementia. Biomarkers are biological markers or factors that can be measured to indicate the presence or absence of a disease (Alzheimer's Association, 2016). Biomarkers in diseases that cause dementia can be categorized into imaging modalities (as described above), and cerebrospinal fluid (CSF) measures; currently, no blood-based or urine-based biomarkers are available for routine clinical use (Ahmed et al., 2014). Fluid biomarkers that have been included in the diagnostic criteria for the pathophysiological Alzheimer's disease are CSF measures of brain amyloid beta protein deposition, as well as elevated CSF tau (McKhann et al., 2011). The *DSM-5* approach to diagnosis of dementia involves the characterization of the syndrome, with a subsequent task of determining its etiology, such as AD, frontotemporal lobar degeneration, Lewy body disease, or vascular cognitive impairment (Petersen et al., 2014). In the future, biomarkers are likely to be incorporated into the decision process, but most are not validated at present for use in routine clinical practice; these remain areas of major research interest (Jack et al., 2011; Petersen et al., 2014).

The genetics of different types of dementia are also being studied. For example, mutations in the presenilin-1 (on chromosome 14) and presenilin-2 (on chromosome 1) genes are linked to autosomal dominant familial AD (Albert et al., 2011; Alzheimer's Association, 2016). In addition, there are genetic risk factors for progression to late-onset/sporadic Alzheimer's dementia, including the presence of one or two alleles in the apolipoprotein E (APOE) gene. Individuals with two ε4 alleles have an increased risk; the ApoE2 allele may serve a protective role (Bertram, Lill, & Tanzi, 2010). Genetic testing can be carried out on a symptomatic or predictive basis (Loy, Schofield, Turner, & Kwok, 2014). Symptomatic genetic testing in dementia does not change clinical management; however, it can help confirm the diagnosis in cases of uncertainty (Loy et al., 2014).

Progression from Normal Aging to Dementia

The most common clinical dementia syndromes are associated with advanced age; however, dementia is not a part of normal aging. In fact, healthy aging is associated with only subtle declines in cognition (Harada, Love, & Triebel, 2013). When dementia does develop, in most cases it is insidious. Scientists now recognize a long period of time prior to a diagnosis of dementia during which older adults experience cognitive decline that may signal the presence of neuropathology and eventual dementia. Subjective Cognitive Decline is the term used to describe a stage in which older adults report a perceived decline in their cognitive abilities but are asymptomatic upon evaluation with objective measures (Jessen et al., 2014). Because the onset of the neuropathology of Alzheimer's disease is thought to occur decades before overt cognitive decline in Alzheimer's dementia, researchers are focused on examining the earliest stages at which intervention can be initiated to delay dementia onset. The presence of Subjective Cognitive Decline is associated with increased risk of future cognitive decline and progression to Mild Cognitive Impairment (MCI) and dementia (Jessen et al., 2014).

MCI was introduced as a clinical entity in the 1980s (Petersen et al., 2014), and is often a transitional phase from cognitive changes of normal aging and, perhaps Subjective Cognitive Decline, to those of dementia. The diagnosis of MCI includes the following core clinical criteria: Concern regarding a change in cognition, impairment in one or more cognitive domains, preservation of independence in functional activities, and no significant impairment in social and occupational functioning (Albert et al., 2011). The *DSM-5* (APA, 2013) criteria for Mild NCD are essentially the same as those developed by Albert and colleagues (2011) for MCI. Also, in the *DSM-5*, mild NCD precedes Major NCD/dementia (Petersen et al., 2014).

MCI, like dementia, can be caused by a variety of etiologies. Therefore, in recent years, researchers have attempted to discriminate among different subtypes of MCI, according to the underlying disorder. People with MCI, based on the core clinical criteria outlined above, could be classified into one of two categories: amnestic MCI (a-MCI) in cases of prominent cognitive impairments in episodic memory, or non-amnestic MCI (na-MCI) in cases of prominent cognitive impairments in domains other than memory (Petersen et al., 2014). Importantly, not all individuals who experience MCI will progress to dementia. Progression rates vary, depending on sampling methods used; for example, progression rate to dementia is 10–15% per year in specialized referral clinics versus approximately 5–10% in the general population (Petersen et al., 2014). Therefore, a thorough medical examination and follow up are necessary to identify early changes and to provide people with information about the likelihood of progression. One robust marker for predicting the progression from MCI to AD is hippocampal atrophy (Jack et al., 2008).

Clinical Dementia Syndromes and their Underlying Neuropathologies

As mentioned previously, dementia is not a disease, it is a clinical syndrome caused by an underlying disease. Dementia syndromes are primarily subtyped according to presumed etiology (APA, 2013) and based on the comprehensive medical and neuropsychological examination. Frequently,

Box 2.4 *DSM-5* Diagnostic Criteria for Mild NCD (also known as MCI) (APA, 2013)

A. Evidence of modest cognitive decline from a previous level of performance in one or more cognitive domains:

- complex attention
- executive function
- learning and memory
- language
- perceptual-motor
- social cognition

Based on:

1. concern of the individual or knowledgeable informant or the clinician that there has been a mild cognitive decline; and,
2. a modest impairment in cognitive performance, preferably documented by standardized neuropsychological testing.
B. The cognitive deficits do not interfere with capacity for independence in everyday activities.
C. The cognitive deficits do not occur exclusively in the context of a delirium.
D. The cognitive deficits are not better explained by another mental disorder.

different etiologies occur together (e.g., Alzheimer's disease and vascular disease) and it may be difficult to attribute symptoms to one disease state. As new knowledge is gained on clinico-pathological correlations between syndromes and diseases, new and more specific diagnostic categories emerge. The following descriptions of clinical dementia syndromes and their underlying etiologies, therefore, reflect current evidence generated for that classification and the frequency of the diagnosis, and are not an endorsement of any particular classification schema that is subject to change with additional research. Table 2.1 presents common characteristics of the most frequently occurring dementia subtypes.

Alzheimer's Dementia. Alzheimer's disease and "senile dementia" were first described by Dr. Alois Alzheimer in 1907. The most common form of Alzheimer's disease develops over a long period of time before the presentation of clinical symptoms. When clinical symptoms become significant enough to interfere with social and occupational functioning, the syndrome is referred to as Alzheimer's dementia. Alzheimer's dementia is the most common form of dementia (60–80% of cases), with half of the cases caused solely by Alzheimer's disease and half caused by Alzheimer's disease plus another disorder (Alzheimer's Association, 2016). In the United States, Alzheimer's dementia afflicts approximately 11% of all individuals over the age of 65 and up to one-third of those over the age of 85 (Hebert, Weuve, Scherr, & Evans, 2013). Currently more than 5 million people in the United States have a diagnosis of Alzheimer's dementia or a related dementia (Hebert et al., 2013), over 500,000 in Canada (Alzheimer Society of Canada, 2010), and more than 35 million worldwide (World Health Organization, 2012).

Whereas a small percentage of cases of Alzheimer's dementia are a result of genetic mutation and have an early onset before age 65 (Schreiber, Bird, & Tsuang, 2014), the vast majority of

TABLE 2.1 Characteristics of Common Dementia Syndromes

	Alzheimer's Dementia	Vascular Dementia	Bv-Frontotemporal Dementia	Dementia with Lewy Bodies	Parkinson's Disease Dementia
Prevalence	60–70% of cases	20–30% of cases	5–10%	15–20% of cases	18–30% of people with PD
Onset	Slow, gradual progression	Abrupt, stepwise progression	Slow, gradual	Slow, gradual	Slow, gradual, and fluctuating
Cognitive Abilities	Episodic memory deficits; word finding deficits (early) Working memory (mid) Remote memory (later) Executive dysfunction (early)	Focal symptoms (some early; others late) Attention, executive functions impaired early	Executive dysfunction; relative sparing of memory (early)	Gradually fluctuating Similar to Alzheimer's dementia Attention (early) Executive dysfunction (early)	Similar to Dementia with Lewy Bodies Fluctuating cognition Executive dysfunction (early)
Motor Abilities	Variable	Co-occurs with extrapyramidal symptoms, gait problems, paresis, facial weakness	Variable; extrapyramidal symptoms sometimes occur; features of motor neuron disease may be present	Extrapyramidal symptoms often occur	Extrapyramidal symptoms; resting tremor, bradykinesia, and cogwheel rigidity; dysarthria
Language Abilities	Mild word finding (early) Semantics, pragmatics and reading comprehension impaired later	Focal language deficits variable	Relatively spared early on; later mutism may occur	Verbal fluency deficits (early) Otherwise intact (early) Similar to AD	Less language impairment than Alzheimer's dementia Early pragmatic deficits
Visuospatial Abilities	Progressive decline	Visual field deficits	Intact (early)	Deficits (early)	Intact (early)
Behavior	Delusions, hallucinations, agitation, repetitive behaviors (mid) Ambulation, eating, and swallowing (late)	Depression, agitation, anxiety, and apathy (early)	Profound early changes in mood, personality, and social conduct; apathy or disinhibition	Visual hallucinations, delusions, and depression (early)	Depression, mood changes Medication-related delusions and hallucinations

Alzheimer's dementia cases (~95%) have a late onset, occurring at or after age 65. The risk factors for late-onset Alzheimer's dementia include age and gender (male–female proportion = 1.2 : 1.5 respectively); women have higher incidence in Europe, but not reliably in the United States (Prince et al., 2013). Other risks may include family history of Alzheimer's dementia; lower educational, social, and economic status; MCI; history of moderate to severe traumatic brain injury; and cerebrovascular risk factors (smoking, hypertension, diabetes, hyperlipidemia; Reitz & Mayeux, 2014), as well as depression, physical inactivity (midlife), obesity, and smoking (Deckers et al., 2015). Studies of potential environmental and neurotoxic factors, such as aluminum, lead, and pesticide exposure, remain inconclusive. Certain genetic risk factors have been linked to Alzheimer's dementia, most notably the Apolipoprotein E (Apo E) gene on chromosome 19. Of the three Apo E alleles (e2, e3, e4), the e4/e4 genotype is associated with 8–12 times the risk of Alzheimer's dementia (Loy et al., 2014).

The neuropathology in Alzheimer's disease consists of amyloid plaques and neurofibrillary tangles (Jack et al., 2013). Amyloid plaques are extracellular aggregations of the amyloid-Beta peptide that are found throughout the brain, and neurofibrillary tangles are found within neurons, resulting from hyperphosphorylation of the microtubule-associated protein tau (Risacher & Saykin, 2013). Amyloid accumulation is thought to precede the formation of tangles during the long preclinical period of the disease (Jack et al., 2013). The result is widespread cell death. Structural MRI of cerebral volume loss shows a pattern that begins in the entorhinal cortex, involves the medial temporal lobe and hippocampus, as well as medial parietal cortex (Bhogal et al., 2013), with relative sparing of occipital and primary sensory-motor cortices until later in the disease course. It is important to note that new research provides evidence that Alzheimer's disease is not a unitary disease; rather, it has distinct subtypes including the ones that cause primary progressive aphasia as well as the progressive visuospatial impairments of posterior cortical atrophy (Mesulam et al., 2014). What differentiates these subtypes is the pattern or distribution of the Alzheimer's neuropathology. This pattern defines the clinical presentation of the syndrome. In Alzheimer's dementia, consistent with the distribution of the neuropathology, memory impairment is often the earliest symptom.

Not all aspects of memory are impaired to the same extent. Episodic memory is typically prominently impaired and semantic memory deficits, noted as word-finding problems, are common (Weintraub, Wickland, & Salmon, 2012). Remote, autobiographical memory gradually deteriorates over time as compared to healthy aging, however, remote memory is relatively better preserved than more recent episodic memories (Morris & Mograbi, 2013). Although span memory remains relatively intact in early Alzheimer's dementia, the central executive function of working memory is impaired (Stopford, Thompson, Neary, Richardson, & Snowden, 2012).

By definition, multiple cognitive domains are affected in Alzheimer's dementia. In the early stages, lapses in attention and concentration may be present, often with awareness of these occurrences. Executive functioning, or the ability to plan, organize, and initiate an action or event, also may be impaired early, along with complex attention deficits (Weintraub et al., 2012). Visuospatial abilities have been reported to decline in a progressive fashion over time (Johnson, Storandt, Morris, & Galvin, 2009). Together, these cognitive changes contribute to the deficits observed in everyday functioning and begin to affect communication behaviors.

Although language is less affected than memory, language changes can be detected long before an Alzheimer's dementia diagnosis is confirmed (Mesulam et al., 2008). Language impairment worsens as semantic memory and other cognitive processes that support language are impacted. Eventually, pragmatic language abilities decline as the person has more difficulty with appropriate use of language in social situations. Phonology and syntax are relatively preserved compared to semantics and pragmatics (Croot, Hodges, Xuereb, & Patterson, 2000). Reading comprehension and oral reading remain relatively preserved until later in the course of Alzheimer's dementia (Bourgeois, 2013). In the late stages, verbal language becomes severely impaired in expression and comprehension. In the late stages, persons with Alzheimer's dementia often display incoherent mumbling and eventual mutism. Affective responses (e.g., smiling and pleasant vocalizations) to familiar sensory stimuli, cues, and music may be difficult to distinguish from reflexive behavior (Bayles, Kaszniak, & Tomoeda, 1987; Lubinski, 1995). (Language symptoms across stages will be described in more detail in Chapter 3.)

Behavioral and neuropsychiatric symptoms occur in approximately 80% of individuals with dementia seen in specialty clinics (APA, 2013). Lyketsos et al. (2011) reviewed behavioral and neuropsychiatric symptoms associated with Alzheimer's dementia. Among the most prevalent are sleep disorders, mood disorders (apathy, depression), delusions (e.g., theft, persecution, house is not home, infidelity, abandonment, and phantom boarder); hallucinations (visual, auditory, gustatory, olfactory, and haptic); agitation and combativeness. Restlessness; pacing; wandering; and repetitive behaviors are also commonly reported (van der Linde et al., 2016).

Vascular Dementia (VaD). Vascular disease encompasses a group of cerebrovascular pathologies that can cause cognitive impairment. When the cognitive impairment is severe enough to meet criteria for a diagnosis of dementia, the condition is referred to as vascular dementia, which accounts for at least 20% of cases of dementia, and thus is the second most common cause of dementia in older adults (Gorelick et al., 2011). Defining neuropathological changes associated with VaD is challenging because of heterogeneous lesion locations and types (Khan, Kalaria, Corbett, & Ballard, 2016). Factors contributing to impairment and the VaD phenotype include origin and type of vascular occlusion, presence of hemorrhage, distribution of arterial territories, and the size of vessels involved (Khan et al., 2016). Vascular dementia is most commonly seen with extensive confluent white matter lesions (leukoaraiosis), multiple lacunes and bilateral small thalamic infarcts (Bhogal et al., 2013; Iadecola, 2013; Jellinger, 2013). When extensive ischemic injury to the subcortical white matter occurs, usually due to chronic untreated hypertension, it is labeled Binswanger disease; when multiple infarcts occur due to large artery lesions, it is referred to as multi-infarct dementia (Khan et al., 2016). Pure VaD appears to be rare (Perneczky et al., 2016), as the neuropathologies of VaD tend to coexist with other types of neurodegeneration, including Alzheimer's disease.

Recent studies have highlighted the role of cerebrovascular disease, not only as a primary cause of cognitive impairment (as in VaD), but also as a factor that exacerbates the expression of dementia caused by other diseases/disorders (Gorelick et al., 2011; Toledo et al., 2013). The major risk factors for VaD are the same as those for cardiovascular disease and include hypertension, diabetes, hyperlipidemia, and smoking (Gorelick et al., 2011). Another key risk factor is the hereditary condition of cerebral autosomal dominant arteriopathy with subcortical infarcts and leukoencephalopathy (CADASIL) (APA, 2013).

The onset and progression of VaD may vary from acute onset with stepwise decline (fluctuations and plateaus of varying durations), to a slowly progressive course that is similar to that seen in Alzheimer's dementia (APA, 2013). A characteristic of subcortical white matter infarctions is gait impairment, often seen in VaD, and marked by hesitation and diminished stride length and step height (Werring & Camicioli, 2016). Focal lesions can result in pyramidal symptoms (e.g., hemiparesis, hypertonia, and abnormal reflexes), pseudobulbar affect (e.g., exaggerated emotional responses, dysarthria, dysphagia, and gag reflex), and visual field defects (Khan et al., 2016).

The cognitive impairments in VaD are likewise quite variable depending on the nature and distribution of the underlying pathology. People with VaD do not consistently have a profound episodic memory deficit and the recent guidelines for the diagnosis of vascular cognitive disorders and dementia reflect this fact, with an emphasis on deficits in speed of information processing, complex attention, and frontal executive functioning (Sachdev et al., 2014). Language changes may be focal in nature and coexist with hemiparesis, facial weakness, visual field defects, and extrapyramidal signs (Erkinjuntti, 2000). Neuropsychiatric symptoms are common as well. In a study of almost 500 people with VaD, 92% of the sample reported behavioural and psychological symptoms; apathy, depression, agitation/aggression, aberrant motor behavior, and hallucinations were common and varied depending on the type of VaD (Staekenborg et al., 2010).

Frontemporal Lobar Degenerations (FTLD). FTLD are a group of neurodegenerative diseases that are characterized by distinct molecular types and several clinical phenotypes (Mesulam et al., 2014), among them behavioral variant frontotemporal dementia (bv-FTD), primary progressive aphasia, and motor neuron dysfunction (Knopman & Roberts, 2011; McKhann et al., 2001). It is noteworthy that there is a significant clinical, pathological, and genetic overlap between FTLD and the atypical Parkinsonian syndromes, progressive supranuclear palsy, and corticobasal degeneration (Seltman & Matthews, 2012), which will be discussed in later sections of this chapter. In some classifications, supranuclear palsy and corticobasal degeneration are considered to be types of FTLD (Alzheimer's Association, 2016). Common to all types of FTLD is marked atrophy in frontal and anterior temporal lobes, without senile plaques, neurofibrillary tangles, or Lewy bodies (Josephs et al., 2012).

The prevalence and onset of FTLD is challenging to determine because of insensitive diagnostic criteria and inadequate recognition of the condition (Knopman & Roberts, 2011; Onyike & Diehl-Schmid, 2013), though diagnostic criteria have improved for bv-FTD (Gorno-Tempini et al., 2011; Rascovsky et al., 2011). Current prevalence estimates show that FTLD accounts for approximately 5–10% of all cases of pathologically confirmed dementia (Alzheimer's Association, 2016; Brunnström, Gustafson, Passant, & Englund, 2009; Seltman & Matthews, 2012). Onset of FTLD tends to occur earlier in life, with most cases diagnosed between the ages of 45–64 years of age, with a mean age of onset of 53 (Ratnavalli, Brayne, Dawson, & Hodges, 2002). Persons with FTLD may be symptomatic as early as 35 years of age (Franczak, Kerwin, & Antuono, 2004), and FTD is the most common type of dementia in people younger than 65 years. Survival with FTLD varies across studies from 3 to 14 years, with variability across phenotypes, with people who have motor neuron dysfunction having the shortest survival (Onyike & Diehl-Schmid, 2013). Median survival was 9.9 years in a study of 354 people with FTLD, with family history associated with shorter survival (Chiu et al., 2010).

Behavioral-variant FTD (bv-FTD) is most commonly associated with pathological non-Alzheimer tau accumulation, as in Pick's disease, and sometimes with accumulation of another protein called TDP-43 (Whitwell et al., 2011). Brain imaging is necessary to increase diagnostic certainty (Piguet, Hornberger, Mioshi, & Hodges, 2011). Upon neuroimaging and at autopsy, there is widespread atrophy in the frontal lobes, anterior cingulate, anterior insula, and thalamus (Risacher & Saykin, 2013). Behavioral-variant FTD must begin with evidence, by history or direct observation, of progressive deterioration of behavior and/or cognitive function (Rascovsky et al., 2011; Seltman & Matthews, 2012). There is a strong family history of bv-FTD; approximately 40% of cases have a family history and an estimated 10–20% of cases have autosomal dominant inheritance pattern (APA, 2013).

Diagnostic criteria for possible bv-FTD include recurrence or persistence of at least three of the following behavioral/cognitive symptoms: early behavioral disinhibition (e.g., loss of manners); early apathy or inertia; early loss of sympathy or empathy; early perseverative, stereotyped, or compulsive/ritualistic behavior (e.g., complex, compulsive, or ritualistic behaviors, or stereotypy of speech); hyperorality and dietary changes (e.g., binge eating, increased cigarette consumption, or oral exploration or consumption of inedible objects); and executive function deficits with relative sparing of memory and visuospatial functions (Rascovsky et al., 2011). Probable bv-FTD is based on meeting criteria for possible bv-FTD, as well as exhibiting significant functional decline and imaging results consistent with bv-FTD, though there is marked variability in symptom profiles in the initial presentation (Karantzoulis & Galvin, 2011).

The presence of greater executive function deficits than memory deficits helps to differentiate bv-FTD from Alzheimer's dementia, as does the presence of social disinhibition, euphoria, stereotypical and aberrant motor behavior, and changes in eating preference (Piguet et al., 2011). Language changes are mostly in the expressive domain initially, with reduced output, increasing reliance on stereotypical remarks, perseverative and then echolalic responses, and eventual mutism. Comprehension, naming, reading, and written output are usually well preserved, as are visual perception and spatial and motor skills (Franczak et al., 2004). Thus, these clients are sometimes diagnosed with psychiatric disorders prior to the correct diagnosis of bv-FTD.

Primary Progressive Aphasia (PPA). Primary Progressive Aphasia is commonly caused by FTLD, but it might also be caused by Alzheimer's disease, corticobasal degeneration, progressive supranuclear palsy, or other neurodegenerative diseases. The Alzheimer's disease that causes PPA is distinct from the typical late-onset Alzheimer's disease that causes the Alzheimer's dementia syndrome (Mesulam et al., 2014). There is a two-step diagnostic process for PPA. First, the person must demonstrate a primary language disorder based on Mesulam's (2001) criteria; then, the variant of PPA should be identified (Gorno-Tempini et al., 2011). A diagnosis of PPA, according to Mesulam (2001), requires three criteria: (1) prominent clinical feature is difficulty with language, (2) impairments in activities of daily living related to language use (e.g., using the telephone), and (3) aphasia is the most prominent deficit for at least two years at the onset of the disorder. The diagnosis of PPA is ruled out if the pattern of deficits can be better accounted for by another neurodegenerative or psychiatric diagnosis, if the prominent deficits are in cognitive domains other than language, and if there are prominent behavioral disturbances at the outset. Once PPA is identified, then the deficits are further classified into one of three PPA variants, and may be based on clinical, imaging supported, or definite pathologic diagnosis (Gorno-Tempini et al., 2011).

The PPA variants include: progressive nonfluent aphasia (nv-PPA), or a semantic variant progressive aphasia (sv-PPA), and logopenic variant (Gorno-Tempini et al., 2011), although not all patients with PPA can be classified into one subtype and may simultaneously fit two subtypes (Mesulam et al., 2014). Nonfluent aphasia variant-PPA presents initially with a slowly progressive deterioration of language abilities, with at least one core feature of agrammatism or effortful speech (often apraxia of speech). There must also be two out of three other features: impaired complex syntax comprehension, spared word comprehension, and spared object knowledge. People with nv-PPA often have early word-finding difficulties, phonemic paraphasias, and agrammatic errors, but visuospatial and memory skills remain relatively intact and personality and behavioral symptoms are rare (Kertesz & Harciarek, 2014; Mesulam, 2001). Eventually, the person with PPA may develop ideomotor apraxia, progress from nonfluent aphasia to mutism, and display some behavioral symptoms. Other cognitive deficits may present late in the disease process. People with nv-PPA may eventually display other motor disturbances that are consistent with CBD or PSP, but most often the underlying neuropathology is FTLD (Gorno-Tempini et al., 2011). Structural imaging analyses demonstrate that people with nv-PPA show atrophy primarily in the anterior perisylvian regions, including Broca's area, insular cortex, premotor cortex, with involvement of the caudate and thalamus later in the disease (Risacher & Saykin, 2013).

On the other hand, semantic variant-PPA is marked by a progressively deteriorating fluent aphasia that is well-articulated, effortless, syntactically correct, but anomic and empty of content (Gorno-Tempini et al., 2011). This variant is also sometimes referred to as semantic dementia or PPA-semantic, though there is not consensus on whether semantic dementia is distinct from sv-PPA. Persons with sv-PPA must display the two core features of impaired confrontation naming and impaired single-word comprehension; the anomia is severe, particularly when compared with other language domains. Three of four other diagnostic features must also be displayed, including: impaired object knowledge object identity, surface dyslexia or dysgraphia, spared repetition, and spared speech production (linguistically and motorically). Additionally, autobiographical and episodic memory, single-word repetition, reading aloud, and writing are well preserved (Gorno-Tempini et al., 2011). People with sv-PPA have asymmetrical cortical atrophy (more pronounced in the left hemisphere) affecting ventral and lateral regions of the anterior temporal lobes along with the anterior hippocampus and amygdala (Risacher & Saykin, 2013). The most common neuropathology in sv-PPA is FTLD (Gorno-Tempini et al., 2011).

The third type of PPA, the logopenic variant PPA (lv-PPA; also known as logopenic PPA), was the most recently described variant (Gorno-Tempini et al., 2011). Diagnosis is based on presence of two core features: impaired single-word retrieval and impaired sentence repetition of sentences; three out of four other characteristics must also be present: phonologic errors, spared single-word comprehension and object knowledge, spared motor speech, and absence of frank agrammatism (Gorno-Tempini et al., 2011). Rate of language production is slowed by word retrieval difficulties rather than agrammatism or motor speech difficulties, though naming impairments are not as severe as in sv-PPA and naming errors are more likely phonological paraphasias. Neuroimaging reveals atrophy in the left posterior perisylvian or parietal areas or hypoperfusion in these areas on SPECT or PET. Logopenic PPA is sometimes considered to be an FTD variant, although this condition may also be caused by Alzheimer's disease and is not specific to FTLD (Harris et al., 2013; Mesulam et al., 2014).

Dementia with Lewy Bodies (DLB). Lewy Body disease is caused by abnormal depositions of the Lewy Body, a neuronal inclusion comprised of aggregated α-synuclein in the frontal and temporal lobes and basal ganglia (Mayo & Bordelon, 2014). Lewy bodies are found in brainstem nuclei in both Parkinson disease (PD) as well as in DLB, although in DLB there is a concomitant presence of Lewy bodies in the cortex and subcortical white matter (Mayo & Bordelon, 2014). When dementia occurs in the presence of Lewy bodies, it is called Dementia with Lewy Bodies (DLB; McKeith, Taylor, Thomas, Donaghy, & Kane, 2016). DLB is ranked as the second or third most commonly occurring cause of dementia, accounting for 15–20% of cases, although prevalence estimates vary (Vann Jones & O'Brien, 2014). More males than females are affected by DLB (Boot et al., 2013). Risk factors of DLB include advanced age, hypertension, hyperlipidemia, and carriers of one or more APOE ε4 alleles (Mayo & Bordelon, 2014).

The core features of the consensus clinical diagnostic criteria for DLB are: fluctuating cognition with pronounced variations in attention and alertness, recurrent visual hallucinations that are typically well formed and detailed, and spontaneous motor features of parkinsonism (McKeith et al., 2005, 2016). The motor features of parkinsonism include tremor, rigidity, bradykinesia, gait abnormality, and postural change, as well as procedural memory deficits (Kaur et al., 2013). Neuropsychiatric symptoms are salient features of DLB, and in addition to hallucinations include the presence of depression, apathy, anxiety, agitation, delusions, or paranoia (Ballard, Aarsland, Francis, & Corbett, 2013; Ballard et al., 1999, 2004). Rapid eye movement (REM) sleep behavior disorder is also a common early symptom of DLB and is a parasomnia characterized by dream enactment behaviors in the setting of excessive motor activity during REM sleep (Ma et al., 2016). Persons with DLB tend to have better verbal episodic memory, but more trouble with visual-perceptual tasks, than those with DAT.

Parkinson's Disease Dementia (PDD). Parkinson's disease is a neurodegenerative extra-pyramidal disorder that affects 1.5–2.5% of persons over the age of 70, and is more common in males than females (Pringsheim, Jette, Frolkis, & Steeves, 2014). The disease is associated with neuronal loss in the substantia nigra, which produces dopamine, an inhibitory neurotransmitter (Weintraub & Stern, 2005). The hallmark symptoms of this disease include resting tremor, brady-kinesia, rigidity, and postural instability (Weintraub & Stern, 2005). These symptoms are responsive to medications (e.g., levodopa and carbidopa), particularly early in the disease process.

Dementia develops in 18–30% of people with Parkinson's disease. Histological evidence – including neuritic plaques, neurofibrillary tangles, loss of pigmented neurons in the substantia nigra, and Lewy body inclusions – suggests multiple pathologies (Irwin et al., 2012; Kehagia, Barker, & Robbins, 2010). The pattern of symptoms in PDD resembles that of DLB more so than AD (Kehagia et al., 2010). Dementia DLB and PDD are characterized by the combination of dementia and parkinsonism and are frequently accompanied by other symptoms, such as visual hallucinations, fluctuating cognition, and REM sleep behavioral disturbance, as well as auto-nomous dysfunction and excessive daytime sleepiness (Aarsland, Ballard, Rongve, Broadstock, & Svenningsson, 2012). Cognitive problems such as aphasia, apraxia, and agnosia are relatively absent in people with PDD compared with those with AD (Klingelhoefer & Reichmann, 2014). In the later stages of PDD and DLB, the diseases may be indistinguishable, clinically as well as pathologi-cally; currently, the separation between PDD and DLB is done on an arbitrary basis considering the temporal course of the onset of dementia and the parkinsonian motor symptoms (Klingel-hoefer & Reichmann, 2014). The similarity between DLB and PDD can make differential dia-gnosis difficult, but the consensus is that if cognitive deficits occur first or within one year, then it is DLB; if cognitive deficits occur more than one year after the motor deficits, then the diagnosis is PDD (McKeith et al., 2005). The common neuropsychiatric symptoms that accompany PD are similar to those that occur in DLB (mood fluctuations, hallucinations, depression, anxiety, agita-tion, and irritability; APA, 2013). Anti-parkinsonian drugs also affect circadian rhythms and sleep-wake regulating systems (French & Muthusamy, 2016).

Dementia Due to Progressive Supranuclear Palsy (PSP) and Corticobasal Degen-eration (CBD). Progressive supranuclear palsy is a rare degenerative neurological disease that is sometimes confused with PD because of the overlap in symptoms of rigidity, dysarthria, and dementia; however, PSP is distinguished by the feature of vertical eye gaze paralysis, with falls as another prominent feature (Litvan et al., 1996). Onset of PSP is usually after 60 years old, with no cases reported of onset before 40 years (Donker Kaat, Boon, Kamphorst, Duivenvoorden, & van Swieten, 2007). Median survival was eight years in a study of 197 people with PSP (Chiu et al., 2010). Tau proteins are found in the basal ganglia and brainstem, and functions of the subthalamic nucleus, substantia nigra, and globus pallidus most severely affected (Dickson, Ahmed, Algom, Tsuboi, & Josephs, 2010; Donker Kaat, Chiu, Boon, & van Swieten, 2011); frontal regions may be affected by atrophy and neurofibrillary tangles (Donker Kaat et al., 2007). There have been reports of familial aggregation (see Im, Kim, & Kim, 2015 for a review).

Similar to PD, executive function impairments are the primary cognitive symptom in people with dementia due to PSP, with evidence of impaired new learning, reduced verbal fluency, and preserved recognition memory (Gerstenecker, Mast, Duff, Ferman, & Litvan, 2012). The neuropsychiatric symptoms of PSP have more characteristics of frontal lobe dysfunction, including high degrees of apathy and disinhibition (Kobylecki et al., 2015; Madhusoodanan et al., 2014). There are variable findings with respect to impacts on language functioning (Kim & McCann, 2015). Dysarthria is one of the most common and prominent features of PSP, with a mix of hypokinetic, spastic, and ataxic dysarthrias, and sometimes progressing to anar-thria (see Kim & McCann, 2015, for a more complete review of communication in people with PSP).

Corticobasal degeneration is another syndrome that may resemble PD and PSP due to symp-toms of rigidity and cognitive impairment (Bruns & Josephs, 2013). The distinguishing features of

CBD are the asymmetric nature of the rigidity and the presence of dystonia, focal reflex myoclonus, and at least one cortical sign (limb apraxia, cortical sensory loss, or alien limb phenomenon (Bruns & Josephs, 2013). Speech and language disorders are often the first signs of CBD, with dysarthria (mixed with spastic and/or hypokinetic features are most common, but ataxic or hyperkinetic components are possible), apraxia of speech, or progressive aphasia (nonfluent) present in 30–40% of cases (Blake, Duffy, Boeve, Ahlskog, & Maraganore, 2003; Boeve, 2000; Josephs & Duffy, 2008). Aphasic language syndromes and dementia have been identified in persons with CBD, with prominent executive function, verbal fluency, and visuospatial deficits (Frattali, Grafman, Patronas, Makhlouf, & Litvan, 2000). Severe depression and apathy are the two most common neuropsychiatric symptoms in CBD (Armstrong, 2014). Primary progressive apraxia of speech may be the first presenting symptom in persons with PSP or CBD (Duffy et al., 2015; Josephs et al., 2012).

Dementia Due to Huntington's Disease (HD). Huntington's disease is a hereditary and progressive neurodegenerative disorder of the basal ganglia, noted for motor, cognitive, and neuropsychiatric impairments (Ross & Tabrizi, 2011). Neuronal loss occurs in the caudate nucleus, putamen, and globus pallidus, with reduction of neurotransmitters, and frontal lobe atrophy (Ross & Tabrizi, 2011). HD symptoms tend to arise in persons between 35 and 42 years old, and disease duration is approximately 15–17 years; however, there may also be an early or a late onset of the disease.

The earliest signs of HD include neuropsychiatric symptoms, such as apathy, depression, and symptoms of obsessive compulsive disorder, as well as personality changes such as irritability and impulsivity (APA, 2013; Thompson et al., 2012; van Duijn et al., 2014). Cognitive deficits in early HD include a selective pattern of attention, executive function, and immediate memory deficits, with relative preservation of semantic memory and delayed recall (Papoutsi, Labuschagne, Tabrizi, & Stout, 2014). The neuropsychiatric symptoms may predate motor symptoms by up to a decade and seem to be unrelated to the cognitive and motor symptoms (Thompson et al., 2012).

The motor symptoms of HD, such as involuntary movement abnormalities, chorea, akinesia, dyskinesia, gait problems, bradykinesia, and saccadic eye movements, appear later in the disease process (Thompson et al., 2012). Beginning with a generalized cognitive slowing, communication is affected by decreased conversational initiation, diminished topic maintenance, and comprehension of abstract concepts. Over time, deficits in problem-solving abilities, memory skills, executive functioning, and the ability to perceive and interpret emotion in facial expressions interfere with communicative interactions (Labuschagne et al., 2013). When the motor symptoms surface, speech production is affected with hyperkinetic dysarthria, characterized by dysprosody, harsh vocal quality, and difficulty timing respiratory support with phonation and articulation. Increased evidence of dysarthria leads to severe reductions in speech intelligibility and the need for alternative modes of communication (Klasner & Yorkston, 2000).

Dementia Due to Human Immunodeficiency Virus (HIV). Up to 40% of people living with HIV have mild cognitive impairment (Harding & Robertson, 2015) known as HIV-associated neurocognitive disorder (HAND). When HAND progresses to having a significant impact on daily life activities, it meets the criteria for a diagnosis of HIV-associated dementia (HAD), or Major NCD due to HIV Infection (APA, 2013). The availability of combination antiretroviral therapy (cART) since 1996 has successfully controlled HIV viremia, improved immune function, and led to significant improvements in morbidity, life expectancy, and neurological outcomes for people who are HIV-infected (Heaton et al., 2011). As a result, there has been a significant drop in the prevalence of dementia (HAD) to less than 5% of individuals who have access to cART (Brew & Chan, 2014; Chan & Brew, 2014; Clifford & Ances, 2013). In a retroactive study of people admitted to an infectious disease unit, researchers compared the prevalence of neurological disorders related to HIV in the pre-highly active anti-retroviral therapy (HAART) versus HAART eras (Matinella et al., 2015). They found that HAD was more likely in people with co-morbidities, particularly hepatitis C and drug abuse. Furthermore, those who developed neurological complications were more likely to have higher viral loads and were more likely to be either untreated or unaware of their HIV status prior to hospitalization. This points to the need for early detection and treatment. Additionally, people with HIV are living longer due to improved immunological status in the HAART era, and are therefore at risk of other age-related diseases that cause dementia.

In those individuals with mild NCD and major NCD from HIV infection, structural imaging shows cerebral atrophy particularly in anterior cingulate, lateral temporal cortex, primary motor and sensory cortices, frontal and parietal lobes, as well as focal white matter lesions typically in subcortical regions (Risacher & Saykin, 2013). Unlike other neurodegenerative disorders, the mild NCD associated with HIV is not invariably progressive; rather, an NCD due to HIV infection can resolve, improve, worsen, or have a fluctuating course (APA, 2013). Cognitive impairments reflect the neurological damage that occurs in the disease. Episodic memory is impaired early, with attention and executive function deficits common with frontal lesions (Woods, Moore, Weber, & Grant, 2009). With subcortical deficits, early effects on speech are extrapyramidal and occur with gait disturbances with psychomotor slowing (Woods et al., 2009).

Dementia Due to Prion Disease. Prion diseases, also known as transmissible spongiform encephalopathies (TSEs), are a group of neurodegenerative conditions that are transmissible, progressive, and uniformly fatal (Song & Zhang, 2015). Creutzfeldt-Jakob Disease (CJD) is a form of human TSE, and causes a rare form of progressive dementia. Approximately 15% of cases of CJD are inherited (familial CJD; Song & Zhang, 2015) due to mutations in the prion protein gene on chromosome 20; approximately 85% of human prion disease are transmissible or sporadic CJD (Puoti et al., 2012). It predominantly affects those of middle to old age, with a mean age of death in the late 60s. The cause of the sporadic CJD disease remains unknown. People classically present with memory impairment and cognitive decline accompanied by neurological features such as ataxia, extrapyramidal and pyramidal signs, and myoclonus (Puoti et al., 2012). The clinical course is usually rapidly progressive and the person typically becomes bedbound, akinetic, and mute within weeks to months (Holman et al., 2010).

The neuropathological features of CJD include spongiform degeneration, fibrous astrocytes, and microvacuolation of the neocortex with some prion protein-positive plaques (Prusiner, 2001). Structural imaging studies show widespread cortical atrophy (Risacher & Saykin, 2013). Cognitive and neuropsychiatric symptoms include progressive memory loss, aphasia, depression, anxiety, delusions, and bizarre or uncharacteristic behavior (Cummings, 2003). The rapid progression and early onset differentiate it from other forms of dementia.

Dementia Due to Traumatic Brain Injury. Traumatic brain injury (TBI) is defined as impact to the head or other mechanism of rapid movement/displacement of the brain within the skull with one or more of the following: loss of consciousness, posttraumatic amnesia, disorientation or confusion, neurological signs (e.g., seizure, visual field cuts; APA, 2013). Traumatic brain injury is most commonly caused by falls and motor vehicle accidents and has its highest prevalence in very young children, older adolescents, and seniors (APA, 2013). Mechanisms of TBI include focal lesions, such as contusions, as well as diffuse axonal injury (DAI). In DAI, neuronal axons are damaged through mechanical loading of the brain during rapid head accelerations with or without impact (Johnson, Stewart, & Smith, 2013). The frontal and temporal lobes and their related circuitry (e.g., subcortical white matter, basal ganglia, and thalamus) are particularly vulnerable to the effects of DAI (Rabinowitz & Levin, 2014).

The neurocognitive profile of individuals post-TBI is variable owing to the severity and type of injuries sustained. In acute stages of moderate to severe TBI, impaired consciousness and posttraumatic amnesia (PTA) are neurobehavioral hallmarks (Rabinowitz & Levin, 2014). Post-traumatic amnesia is the transitory period of confusion and amnesia following TBI which leaves a gap in memory (Rabinowitz & Levin, 2014). According to consensus definitions and reflected in the DSM-5 (APA, 2013), moderate and severe TBI are characterized by loss of consciousness for longer than 30 minutes and/or PTA persisting for at least 24 hours. The cognitive domains that are most often affected by TBI include memory, attention, processing speed, and executive functioning, with more severe TBI resulting in additional deficits in communication, visuospatial processing, intellectual ability, and awareness of deficit (Rabinowitz & Levin, 2014). Behavioral and psychological symptoms are common sequalae and include disturbances in emotional function and regulation (e.g., irritability, disinhibition, apathy; Rao, Koliatsos, Ahmed, Lyketsos, & Kortte, 2015). The key factors differentiating a major NCD/dementia post-TBI from other types of dementia is that onset is sudden and is a direct result of the TBI, and course of recovery is variable, not necessarily worsening in a progressive fashion as in degenerative cases such as Alzheimer's disease.

Although a single mild TBI will not result in a Major NCD/dementia, there is growing evidence that repetitive mild TBI can trigger the development of chronic traumatic encephalopathy (CTE), a progressive neurodegeneration characterized by the widespread deposition of hyperphosphorylated tau (p-tau) as neurofibrillary tangles (McKee et al., 2009). Chronic traumatic encephalopathy is associated with memory disturbances, behavioral and personality changes, parkinsonism, and speech and gait abnormalities (McKee et al., 2013), and its neuropathological expression is marked by atrophy of the cerebral hemispheres, medial temporal lobe, thalamus, mammillary bodies, and brainstem (McKee et al., 2013). In addition to the association between repetitive brain injury and later cognitive impairment, several studies have identified a history of just a single moderate to severe TBI as an epigenetic risk factor for the later development of clinical syndromes neurodegenerative dementia, such as AD (Johnson et al., 2009).

Substance-Induced Dementia. Substance-induced NCDs are characterized by impairments in cognition that persist beyond the duration of intoxication and acute withdrawal following substance use (APA, 2013). The actual prevalence of dementia following substance abuse is unknown, and is considered rare; however, minor NCD is common and may be persistent (APA, 2013). Neuropathologically, imaging studies show that prolonged, excessive alcohol use is associated with permanent changes to the brain, including markedly decreased neuron density, volume shrinkage, altered glucose metabolism, and perfusion of the frontal lobes (Ridley, Draper, & Withall, 2013). Cognitive deficits associated with mild or major NCD with alcohol etiology include impairments in executive functions, visuospatial function, and memory and learning abilities (APA, 2013; Ridley et al., 2013).

The relative contributions of the direct toxic effect of alcohol and the impact of thiamine deficiency to lasting neurological damage remains speculative (Ridley et al., 2013). Individuals with alcohol use disorders are at high risk of thiamine deficiency, which can lead to Wernicke's encephalopathy (WE), an acute neurological disorder characterized by nystagmus and ataxia (APA, 2013; Lough, 2012). Long-term outcomes of WE can include development of Korsakoff syndrome (KS), the features of which include a profound amnesia and tendency to confabulate (APA, 2013; Ridley et al., 2013).

Box 2.5 Case Example

Rebecca Smith, a real estate professional from upstate New York, visits her mother in Florida for a long weekend. When she arrives, her mother is happy to see her and spends the next several hours chatting about family members and the recent events in the neighborhood. Rebecca soon notices that her mother has repeated the same stories about the man across the street watching her from his window and the kids who run through her yard, knocking over the garbage cans, and has asked about her grandson's recent recital several times. She notices piles of mail and magazines on the countertops and newspapers stacked up in the corner of the living room. When Rebecca offers to fix a snack before bedtime, she finds expired and rotting food in the refrigerator. In the bathroom she notices many pill containers on the counter, some empty and others with pills of various sorts mixed together. Rebecca realizes her mother is more impaired than she thought from her daily telephone conversations. In the morning, she checks in with a neighbor, who expresses relief that she is visiting and confirms her worst fears. She schedules an emergency visit with her mother's physician, whose nurse reviews the contents of the brown bag she has brought with them: 14 medications, and a variety of vitamins and nutritional supplements. To her surprise, her mother readily admits to the nurse that she is having trouble sleeping, does not have much of an appetite or much interest in her usual hobbies and activities, and is afraid to drive her car to the store. When the doctor questions her, she comments that her brain is fuzzy now that she is retired and doesn't have to keep track of daily appointments.

This is a common story and one that will have a relatively positive outcome. The physician will order a variety of diagnostic tests, blood work, and a CT scan, and refer her for neuropsychological testing. Rebecca will take her mother to visit local assisted living residences and help her to choose an acceptable home. She will arrange to have an agency provide daily meals, an occasional companion, and weekly housekeeping services. In the next month, she will visit more frequently to help her pack and move to her new home. When the dementia diagnosis is eventually made, Rebecca's mother will have made a satisfactory transition to a safe environment.

Not all situations turn out this well … much education is still needed.

Conclusion

The diagnosis of clinical dementia syndromes is a complex process requiring the expertise of many professionals and the observations of those close to the person. From initial questions about everyday memory lapses, to the medical investigation of metabolic systems and the radiological assessment of brain structure and function, to the neuropsychological evaluations of cognitive processes, the investigation of all symptoms necessitates the cooperation and communication of a diverse group of practitioners. The diagnostic process will be a lengthy and often frustrating experience for clients and caregivers who would prefer quick and definitive answers to their concerns. Unfortunately, the degenerative nature of many of the dementia etiologies will result in changing symptoms and diagnoses over the course of the person's illness. Furthermore, many etiologies co-exist such that dementia symptoms present a "mixed" profile (e.g., VaD + AD; Substance-induced dementia + TBI). To the extent that professionals work in an interdisciplinary fashion, using information gathered from multiple sources to inform their decisions, improved diagnostic outcomes will result. With much research effort toward development of

---

Box 2.6 Resources and Websites for Information about Dementia

- Alzheimer's Association: www.alz.org/
- Alzheimer's Foundation of America: www.alzfdn.org/
- Alzheimer Society of Canada: www.alzheimer.ca/en
- Dementia Society of America: www.dementiasociety.org/
- *What is Vascular Dementia?*, Alzheimer's Society: www.alzheimers.org.uk/site/scripts/documents_info.php?documentID=161
- *Cognitive Changes*, National Multiple Sclerosis Society: www.nationalmssociety.org/Symptoms-Diagnosis/MS-Symptoms/Cognitive-Changes
- *Cognition and MS*, Multiple Sclerosis Society of Canada: https://mssociety.ca/library/document/LrvdiAzUK01SbsCcafFt938eQhNP2IJ7/original.pdf
- *Cognitive Issues in Parkinson's Disease*, American Parkinson Disease Association: www.apdaparkinson.org/cognitive-issues-in-parkinsons-disease/
- *Diffuse Lewy Body Disease*, Parkinson Canada: www.parkinson.ca/site/c.kgLNIWODKpF/b.8647145/k.6D4A/Diffuse_Lewy_Body_Disease.htm
- *Dementia*, American Speech-Language-Hearing Association: www.asha.org/public/speech/disorders/dementia/
- Mayo Clinic: www.mayoclinic.org/diseases-conditions/dementia/basics/tests-diagnosis/con-20034399?_ga=1.225368858.1436415849.1423143192
- Medline Plus: https://medlineplus.gov/alzheimersdisease.html
- https://medlineplus.gov/alzheimerscaregivers.html
- National Memory Screening: http://nationalmemoryscreening.org/screening-sites-info.php

---

disease-modifying pharmacological treatments, it may become more and more important for the correct neuropathology to be identified in a person presenting with a dementia syndrome. This may lead to a better selection of treatment choices and improved quality of life for clients and their families. The following chapters will address in more detail the assessment of cognitive, language, and behavioral symptoms of dementia, and the range of interventions available. See Box 2.6 for additional resources on information about dementia.

References

Aarsland, D., Ballard, C., Rongve, A., Broadstock, M., & Svenningsson, P. (2012). Clinical trials of dementia with Lewy bodies and Parkinson's disease dementia. *Current Neurology and Neuroscience Reports, 12,* 492–501. doi: 10.1007/s11910-012-0290-7.

Ahmed, R. M., Paterson, R. W., Warren, J. D., Zetterberg, H., O'Brien, J. T., Fox, N. C., ... Schott, J. M. (2014). Biomarkers in dementia: Clinical utility and new directions. *Journal of Neurology, Neurosurgery, & Psychiatry, 85,* 1426–1434. doi:10.1136/jnnp-2014-307662.

Albers, M. W., Gilmore, G. C., Kaye, J., Murphy, C., Wingfield, A., Bennett, D. A., ... Zhang, L. I. (2015). At the interface of sensory and motor dysfunctions and Alzheimer's disease. *Alzheimer's & Dementia, 11,* 70–98. http://dx.doi.org/10.1016/j.jalz.2014.04.514.

Albert, M. S., DeKosky, S. T., Dickson, D., Dubois, B., Feldman, H. H., Fox, N. C., ... Phelps, C. H. (2011). The diagnosis of mild cognitive impairment due to Alzheimer's disease: Recommendations from the National Institute on Aging–Alzheimer's Association workgroups on diagnostic guidelines for Alzheimer's disease. *Alzheimer's & Dementia, 7,* 270–279. http://dx.doi.org/10.1016/j.jalz.2011.03.008.

Alzheimer's Association. (2016). *2016 Alzheimer's disease facts and figures.* Alzheimer's Association: Author. Retrieved from www.alz.org/documents_custom/2016-facts-and-figures.pdf.

Alzheimer Society of Canada. (2010). *Rising tide: The impact of dementia on Canadian society.* Retrieved from www.alzheimer.ca/~/media/Files/national/Advocacy/ASC_Rising_Tide_Full_Report_e.pdf.

American Psychiatric Association. (2013). *Diagnostic and statistical manual of mental disorders* (5th ed.). Washington, DC: Author.

Antoniou, M., Gunasekera, G. M., & Wong, P. C. (2013). Foreign language training as cognitive therapy for age-related cognitive decline: A hypothesis for future research. *Neuroscience & Biobehavioral Reviews, 37*, 2689–2698. http://dx.doi.org/10.1016/j.neubiorev.2013.09.004.

Armstrong, M. J. (2014). Diagnosis and treatment of corticobasal degeneration. *Current Treatment Options in Neurology, 16*(3), 1–12. doi:10.1007/s11940-013-0282-1.

Ballard, C., Aarsland, D., Francis, P., & Corbett, A. (2013). Neuropsychiatric symptoms in patients with dementias associated with cortical Lewy bodies: Pathophysiology, clinical features, and pharmacological management. *Drugs & Aging, 30*, 603–611. doi:10.1007/s40266-013-0092-x.

Ballard, C., Holmes, C., McKeith, I., Neill, D., O'Brien, J., Cairns, N., … Perry, R. (1999). Psychiatric morbidity in dementia with Lewy bodies: A prospective clinical and neuropathological comparative study with Alzheimer's disease. *American Journal of Psychiatry, 156*, 1039–1045. doi:10.1176/ajp.156.7.1039.

Ballard, C. G., Jacoby, R., Del Ser, T., Khan, M. N., Munoz, D. G., Holmes, C., … McKeith, I. G. (2004). Neuropathological substrates of psychiatric symptoms in prospectively studied patients with autopsy-confirmed dementia with Lewy bodies. *American Journal of Psychiatry, 161*, 843–849. http://dx.doi.org/10.1176/appi.ajp.161.5.843.

Bayles, K. A., Kaszniak, A. W., & Tomoeda, C. K. (1987). *Communication and cognition in normal aging and dementia.* Boston: Little, Brown & Company.

Bertram, L., Lill, C. M., & Tanzi, R. E. (2010). The genetics of Alzheimer disease: Back to the future. *Neuron, 68*, 270–281. http://dx.doi.org/10.1016/j.neuron.2010.10.013.

Bhogal, P., Mahoney, C., Graeme-Baker, S., Roy, A., Shah, S., Fraioli, F., … Jäger, H. R. (2013). The common dementias: A pictorial review. *European Radiology, 23*, 3405–3417. doi:10.1007/s00330-013-3005-9.

Blake, M. L., Duffy, J. R., Boeve, B. F., Ahlskog, E. J., & Maraganore, D. M. (2003). Speech and language disorders associated with corticobasal degeneration. *Journal of Medical Speech-Language Pathology, 11*(3), 131–146. Retrieved from www.pluralpublishing.com/journals_JMSLP.htm.

Boeve, B. F. (2000). Corticobasal degeneration. In C. H. Adler & J. E. Ahlskog (Eds.), *Parkinson's disease and movement disorders: Diagnosis and treatment guidelines for the practicing physician* (pp. 253–262). Totowa, NJ: Humana Press.

Boot, B. P., Orr, C. F., Ahlskog, J. E., Ferman, T. J., Roberts, R., Pankratz, V. S., … Boeve, B. F. (2013). Risk factors for dementia with Lewy bodies: A case-control study. *Neurology, 81*(9), 833–840. doi:10.1212/WNL.0b013e3182a2cbd1. Epub 2013 Jul 26.

Bourgeois, M. S. (2013). *Memory and communication aids for people with dementia.* Baltimore: Health Professions Press.

Brew, B. J., & Chan, P. (2014). Update on HIV dementia and HIV-associated neurocognitive disorders. *Curr Neurol Neurosci Rep, 14*(8), 468. doi:10.1007/s11910-014-0468-2.

Brunnström, H., Gustafson, L., Passant, U., & Englund, E. (2009). Prevalence of dementia subtypes: A 30-year retrospective survey of neuropathological reports. *Archives of Gerontology and Geriatrics, 49*, 146–149. http://dx.doi.org/10.1016/j.archger.2008.06.005.

Bruns, M. B., & Josephs, K. A. (2013). Neuropsychiatry of corticobasal degeneration and progressive supranuclear palsy. *International Review of Psychiatry, 25*, 197–209. http://dx.doi.org/10.3109/09540261.2013.766154.

Chan, P., & Brew, B. J. (2014). HIV associated neurocognitive disorders in the modern antiviral treatment era: Prevalence, characteristics, biomarkers, and effects of treatment. *Current HIV/AIDS Reports, 11*, 317. doi:10.1007/s11904-014-0221-0.

Chiu, W. Z., Donker Kaat, L., Seelaar, H., Rosso, S. M., Boon, A. J., Kamphorst, W., & Van Sweiten, J. C. (2010). Survival in progressive supranuclear palsy and frontotemporal dementia. *Journal of Neurology, Neurosurgery, & Psychiatry, 81*(4), 441–445.

Chou, C. F., Cotch, M. F., Vitale, S., Zhang, X., Klein, R., Friedman, D. S., Klein, B. E., & Saaddine, J. B. (2013). Age-related eye diseases and visual impairment among U.S. adults. *American Journal of Preventative Medicine, 45*(1), 29–35. doi:10.1016/j.amepre.2013.02.018.

Clarfield, A. M. (2003). The decreasing prevalence of reversible dementias: An updated meta-analysis. *Archives of Internal Medicine, 163*, 2219–2229. doi:10.1001/archinte. 163.18.2219.

Clifford, D. B., & Ances, B. M. (2013). HIV-associated neurocognitive disorder. *The Lancet Infectious Diseases, 13*, 976–986. http://dx.doi.org/10.1016/S1473-3099(13)70269-X.

Croot, K., Hodges, J. R., Xuereb, J., and Patterson, K. (2000). Phonological and articulatory impairment in Alzheimer's disease: A case series. *Brain & Language, 75*, 277–309. doi:10.1006/brln.2000.2357.

Crum, R. M., Anthony, J. C., Bassett, S. S., & Folstein, M. F. (1993). Population-based norms for the Mini-Mental State Examination by age and educational level. *Journal of the American Medical Association, 269*, 2420–2421. doi:10.1001/jama.1993. 03500180078038.

Cummings, J. L. (2003). *The neuropsychiatry of Alzheimer's disease and related dementias.* London, England: Martin Dunitz.

Deckers, K., van Boxtel, M. P. J., Schiepers, O. J. G., de Vugt, M., Sanchez, J. L. M., Anstey, K. J., … Köhler, S. (2015). Target risk factors for dementia prevention: A systematic review and Delphi consensus study on the evidence from observational studies. *International Journal of Geriatric Psychiatry, 30*, 234–246. doi:10.1002/gps.4245.

DeFina, L. F., Willis, B. L., Radford, N. B., Gao, A., Leonard, D., Haskell, W. L., … Berry, J. D. (2013). The association between midlife cardiorespiratory fitness levels and later-life dementia: A cohort study. *Annals of Internal Medicine, 158*, 162–168. doi:10.7326/0003-4819-158-3-201302050-00005.

Di Marco, L. Y., Marzo, A., Muñoz-Ruiz, M., Ikram, M. A., Kivipelto, M., Ruefenacht, D., … Frangi, A. F. (2014). Modifiable lifestyle factors in dementia: A systematic review of longitudinal observational cohort studies. *Journal of Alzheimer's Disease, 42*, 119–135. doi:10.3233/JAD-132225.

Dickson, D. W., Ahmed, Z., Algom, A. A., Tsuboi, Y., & Josephs, K. A. (2010). Neuropathology of variants of progressive supranuclear palsy. *Current Opinion in Neurology, 23*, 394–400.

Diniz, B. S., Butters, M. A., Albert, S. M., Dew, M. A., & Reynolds, C. F. (2013). Late-life depression and risk of vascular dementia and Alzheimer's disease: Systematic review and meta-analysis of community-based cohort studies. *The British Journal of Psychiatry, 202*(5), 329–335. doi:10.1192/bjp.bp. 112.118307.

Donker Kaat, L., Boon, A. J. W., Kamphorst, W., Duivenvoorden, H. J., & van Swieten, J. C. (2007). Frontal presentation in progressive supranuclear palsy. *Neurology, 69*(8), 723–729. doi:10.1212/01. wnl.0000267643.24870.26.

Donker Kaat, L., Chiu, W., Boon, A., & van Swieten, J. (2011). Recent advances in Progressive Supranuclear Palsy: A review. *Current Alzheimer Research, 8*(3), 295–302.

Duffy, J., Strand, E. A. Clark, H., Machulda, M., Whitwell, J. L., & Josephs, K. A. (2015). Primary progressive apraxia of speech: Clinical features and acoustic and neurologic correlates. *American Journal of Speech-Language Pathology, 24*, 88–100.

Erkinjuntti, T. (2000). Vascular dementia: An overview. In J. O'Brien, D. Ames, & A. Burns (Eds.), *Dementia* (2nd ed.) (pp. 623–634). London, England: Arnold.

Folstein, M. F., & Folstein, S. E. (2010). *Mini-Mental State Examination®* (2nd ed.). Lutz, FL: Psychological Assessment Resources.

Folstein, M., Folstein, S., & Folstein, J. (2011). The Mini-Mental State Examination®: A brief cognitive assessment. In M. T. Abou-Saleh, C. L. E. Katona, & A. Kumar (Eds.), *Principles and practice of geriatric psychiatry* (3rd ed.) (pp. 145–146). Chichester, UK: John Wiley & Sons.

Folstein, M. F., Folstein, S. E., & McHugh, P. R. (1975). "Mini-mental state": A practical method for grading the cognitive state of patients for the clinician. *Journal of Psychiatric Research, 12*(3), 189–198.

Franczak, M., Kerwin, D., & Antuono, P. (2004). Frontotemporal lobe dementia. In R. W. Richter, & B. Z. Richter (Eds.), *Alzheimer's disease: A physician's guide to practical management* (pp. 137–141). New York: Humana Press, Inc.

Frattali, C. M., Grafman, J., Patronas, N., Makhlouf, F., & Litvan, I. (2000). Language disturbances in corticobasal degeneration. *Neurology, 54*, 990–992. http://dx.doi.org/10.1212/WNL.54.4.990.

French, I. T., & Muthusamy, K. A. (2016). A review of sleep and its disorders in patients with Parkinson's disease in relation to various brain structures. *Frontiers in Aging Neuroscience, 8*, 1–17. doi:10.3389/fnagi.2016.00114.

Gerstenecker, A., Mast, B., Duff, K., Ferman, T. J., & Litvan, I. (2012). Executive dysfunction is the primary cognitive impairment in progressive supranuclear palsy. *Archives of Clinical Neuropsychology, 28*, 104–113. https://doi.org/10.1093/arclin/acs098.

Gorelick, P. B., Scuteri, A., Black, S. E., DeCarli, C., Greenberg, S. M., Iadecola, C., … Seshadri, S. (2011). Vascular contributions to cognitive impairment and dementia: A statement for healthcare professionals from the American Heart Association/American Stroke Association. *Stroke, 42*, 2672–2713. https://doi.org/10.1161/STR. 0b013e3182299496.

Gorno-Tempini, M. L., Hillis, A. E., Weintraub, S., Kertesz, A., Mendez, M., Cappa, S. F., … & Grossman, M. (2011). Classification of primary progressive aphasia and its variants. *Neurology, 76*, 1006–1014. http://dx.doi.org/10.1212/WNL.0b013e31821103e6.

Grigoletto, F., Zappalà, G., Anderson, D. W., & Lebowitz, B. D. (1999). Norms for the Mini-Mental State Examination in a healthy population. *Neurology, 53*, 315–320. http://dx.doi.org/10.1212/WNL.53.2.315.

Harada, C. N., Love, M. C. N., & Triebel, K. L. (2013). Normal cognitive aging. *Clinics in Geriatric Medicine, 29*, 737–752. http://dx.doi.org/10.1016/j.cger.2013.07.002.

Harding, K. E., & Robertson, N. P. (2015). HIV-associated neurocognitive disorders. *Journal of Neurology, 262*, 1596–1598. Doi:10.1007/s00415-015-7783-7.

Harris, J. M., Gall, C., Thompson, J. C., Richardson, A. M., Neary, D., du Plessis, D., … Jones, M. (2013). Sensitivity and specificity of FTDC criteria for behavioral variant frontotemporal dementia. *Neurology, 80*, 1881–1887. http://dx.doi.org/10.1212/WNL.0b013e318292a342.

Heaton, R. K., Franklin, D. R., Ellis, R. J., McCutchan, A. M., Letendre, S. L., LeBlanc, S., … Taylor, M. J. (2011). HIV-associated neurocognitive disorders before and during the era of combination anti-retroviral therapy: Differences in rates, nature, and predictors. *Journal of NeuroVirology, 17*, 3–16. doi:10. 1007/s13365-010-0006-1.

Hebert, L. E., Weuve, J., Scherr, P. A., & Evans, D. A. (2013). Alzheimer disease in the United States (2010–2050) estimated using the 2010 census. *Neurology, 80*, 1778–1783. http://dx.doi.org/10.1212/WNL.0b013e31828726f5.

Holman, R. C., Belay, E. D., Christensen, K. Y., Maddox, R. A., Minino, A. M., Folkema, A., … Schonberger, L. B. (2010). Human prion diseases in the United States. *PLOS One, 5*(1), e8521. doi:10.1371/journal.pone.0008521.

Iadecola, C. (2013). The pathobiology of vascular dementia. *Neuron, 80*, 844–866. http://dx.doi.org/10.1016/j.neuron.2013.10.008.

Im, S. Y., Kim, Y. E., & Kim, Y. J. (2015). Genetics of progressive supranuclear palsy. *Journal of Movement Disorders, 8*(3), 122–129. doi:10.14802/jmd.15033.

Irwin, D. J., White, M. T., Toledo, J. B., Xie, S. X., Robinson, J. L., Van Deerlin, V., … Trojanowski, J. Q. (2012). Neuropathologic substrates of Parkinson disease dementia. *Annals of Neurology, 72*, 587–598. doi:10.1002/ana.23659.

Jack, C. R., Jr., Weigand, S. D., Shiung, M. M., Przybelski, S. A., O'Brien, P. C., Gunter, J. L., … Petersen, R. C. (2008). Atrophy rates accelerate in amnestic mild cognitive impairment. *Neurology, 70*, 1740–1752. http://dx.doi.org/10.1212/01.wnl.0000281688.77598.35.

Jack, C. R., Albert, M. S., Knopman, D. S., McKhann, G. M., Sperling, R. A., Carrillo, M. C., … Phelps, C. H. (2011). Introduction to the recommendations from the National Institute on Aging–Alzheimer's Association workgroups on diagnostic guidelines for Alzheimer's disease. *Alzheimer's & Dementia, 7*, 257–262. http://dx.doi.org/10.1016/j.jalz.2011.03.004.

Jack, C. R., Jr., Knopman, D. S., Jagust, W. J., Petersen, R. C., Weiner, M. W., Aisen, P. S., … Trojanowski, J. Q. (2013). Update on hypothetical model of Alzheimer's disease biomarkers. *Lancet Neurology, 12*, 207–216. doi:10.1016/S1474-4422(12)70291-0.

Jellinger, K. A. (2013). Pathology and pathogenesis of vascular cognitive impairment: A critical update. *Frontiers in Aging Neuroscience, 5*, 1–19. https://doi.org/10.3389/fnagi.2013.00017.

Jessen, F., Amariglio, R. E., Van Boxtel, M., Breteler, M., Ceccaldi, M., Chételat, G., … Wagner, M. (2014). A conceptual framework for research on subjective cognitive decline in preclinical Alzheimer's disease. *Alzheimer's & Dementia, 10*, 844–852. http://dx.doi.org/10.1016/j.jalz.2014.01.001.

Johnson, D. K., Storandt, M., Morris, J. C., & Galvin, J. E. (2009). Longitudinal study of the transition from healthy aging to Alzheimer disease. *Archives of Neurology, 66*(10), 1254–1259. doi:10.1001/archneurol.2009.158.

Johnson, V. E., Stewart, W., & Smith, D. H. (2013). Axonal pathology in traumatic brain injury. *Experimental Neurology, 246*, 35–43. http://dx.doi.org/10.1016/j.expneurol. 2012.01.013.

Josephs, K. A., & Duffy, J. R. (2008). Apraxia of speech and nonfluent aphasia: A new clinical marker for corticobasal degeneration and progressive supranuclear palsy. *Current Opinion in Neurology, 21*, 688–692. doi:10.1097/WCO.0b013e3283168ddd.

Josephs, K. A., Duffy, J. R., Strand, E. A., Machulda, M. M., Senjem, M. L., Master, A. V., … Whitwell, J. L. (2012). Characterizing a degenerative syndrome: Primary progressive apraxia of speech. *Brain, 135*, 1522–1536. doi:10.1093/brain/aws032.

Karantzoulis, S., & Galvin, J. E. (2014). Distinguishing Alzheimer's disease from other major forms of dementia. *Expert Review of Neurotherapeutics, 11*, 1579–1591. http://dx.doi.org/10.1586/ern.11.155.

Kaur, B., Harvey, D. J., DeCarli, C. S., Zhang, L., Sabbagh, M. N., & Olichney, J. M. (2013). Extrapyramidal signs by dementia severity in Alzheimer's disease and dementia with Lewy bodies. *Alzheimer Disease and Associated Disorders, 27*, 226. doi:10.1097/WAD.0b013e31826f040d.

Kehagia, A. A., Barker, R. A., & Robbins, T. W. (2010). Neuropsychological and clinical heterogeneity of cognitive impairment and dementia in patients with Parkinson's disease. *The Lancet Neurology, 9*(12), 1200–1213.

Kertesz, A., & Harciarek, M. (2014). Primary progressive aphasia. *Scandinavian Journal of Psychology, 55*(3), 191–201. doi:10.1111/sjop.12105.

Khan, A., Kalaria, R. N., Corbett, A., & Ballard, C. (2016). Update on vascular dementia. *Journal of Geriatric Psychiatry and Neurology, 29*, 281–301. doi:10.1177/0891988716654987.

Khayum, B. (2016, November). *Toss the workbooks: Person-centered, evidence-based interventions for people with dementia.* Paper presented at the Annual Convention of the American Speech-Language-Hearing Association, Philadelphia.

Kiely, K. M., Gopinath, B., Mitchell, P., Luszcz, M., & Anstey, K. J. (2012). Cognitive, health, and sociodemographic predictors of longitudinal decline in hearing acuity among older adults. *The Journals of Gerontology: Series A, Biological Sciences and Medical Sciences, 67*, 997–1003. doi:10.1093/gerona/gls066.

Kim, J.-H., & McCann, C. M. (2015). Communication impairments in people with progressive supranuclear palsy: A tutorial. *Journal of Communication Disorders, 56*, 76–87.

Klasner, E. R., & Yorkston, K. M. (2000). AAC for Huntington disease and Parkinson's disease: Planning for change. In D. R. Beukelman, K. M. Yorkston, & J. R. Reichle (Eds.), *Augmentative and alternative communication for adults with acquired neurologic disorders.* Baltimore: Paul H. Brookes.

Klingelhoefer, L., & Reichmann, H. (2014). Dementia: The real problem for patients with Parkinson's disease. *Basal Ganglia, 4*, 9–13. http://dx.doi.org/10.1016/j.baga.2014.03.003.

Knopman, D. S., DeKosky, S. T., Cummings, J. L., Chui, H., Corey-Bloom, J. … & Stevens, J. C. (2001). Practice parameter: Diagnosis of dementia (an evidence-based review). *Neurology, 56*, 1143–1153.

Knopman, D. S., & Roberts, R. O. (2011). Estimating the number of persons with frontotemporal lobar degeneration in the US population. *Journal of Molecular Neuroscience, 45*, 330–335. doi:10.1007/s12031-011-9538-y.

Kobylecki, C., Jones, M., Thompson, J. C., Richardson, A. M., Neary, D., Mann, D. M. A., … Gerhard, A. (2015). Cognitive–behavioural features of progressive supranuclear palsy syndrome overlap with frontotemporal dementia. *Journal of Neurology, 262*, 916–922. doi:10.1007/s00415-015-7657-z.

Labuschagne, I., Jones, R., Callaghan, J., Whitehead, D., Dumas, E. M., Say, M. J., … Stout, J. C. (2013). Emotional face recognition deficits and medication effects in pre-manifest through stage-II Huntington's disease. *Psychiatry Research, 207*, 118–126. http://dx.doi.org/10.1016/j.psychres.2012.09.022.

Lin, F. R., & Albert, M. (2014). Hearing loss and dementia: Who's listening? *Aging and Mental Health, 18*, 671–673. http://dx.doi.org/10.1080/13607863.2014.915924.

Lin, F. R., Metter, E. J., O'Brien, R. J., Resnick, S. M., Zonderman, A. B., & Ferrucci, L. (2011). Hearing loss and incident dementia. *Archives of Neurology, 68*, 214–220. doi:10.1001/archneurol.2010.362.

Litvan, I., Agid, Y., Calne, D., Campbell, G., Dubois, B., Duvoisin, R. C., … Zee, D. S. (1996). Clinical research criteria for the diagnosis of progressive supranuclear palsy (Steele-Richardson-Olszewski syndrome): Report of the NINDS-SPSP International Workshop. *Neurology, 47*, 1–9. doi:http://dx.doi.org/10.1212/WNL.47.1.1.

Lough, M. E. (2012). Wernicke's encephalopathy: Expanding the diagnostic toolbox. *Neuropsychology Review, 22*(2), 181–194. doi:10.1007/s11065-012-9200-7.

Loy, C. T., Schofield, P. R., Turner, A. M., & Kwok, J. B. J. (2014). Genetics of dementia. *The Lancet, 383*, 828–840. http://dx.doi.org/10.1016/S0140-6736(13)60630-3.

Lubinski, R. (1995). *Dementia and communication*. San Diego, CA: Singular Publishing Group.

Lyketsos, C. G., Carrillo, M. C., Ryan, J. M., Khachaturian, A. S., Trzepacz, P., Amatniek, J., … Miller, D. S. (2011). Neuropsychiatric symptoms in Alzheimer's disease. *Alzheimer's & Dementia, 7*, 532–539. http://dx.doi.org/10.1016/j.jalz.2011.05.2410.

Ma, J.-F., Hou, M.-M., Tang, H.-D., Gao, X., Liang, L., Zhu, L.-F., … Chen, S.-D. (2016). REM sleep behavior disorder was associated with Parkinson's disease: A community-based study. *BMC Neurology, 16*, 123. doi:10.1186/s12883-016-0640-1.

Madhusoodanan, S., Wilkes, V., Preston Campbell, R., Serper, M., Kojo Essuman, E., & Brenner, R. (2014) Psychiatric symptoms of progressive supranuclear palsy: A case report and brief review. *Neuropsychiatry, 4*, 27–32. Retrieved from www.openaccessjournals.com/journals/neuropsychiatry.html.

Maher, R. L., Hanlon, J., & Hajjar, E. R. (2014). Clinical consequences of polypharmacy in elderly. *Expert Opinion on Drug Safety, 13*, 57–65. http://dx.doi.org/10.1517/14740338.2013.827660.

Massey, A., & Ghazvini, P. (2005). Involvement of neuropsychiatric pharmacists in a memory disorder clinic. *The Consultant Pharmacist, 20*, 514–518. https://doi.org/10.4140/TCP.n.2005.514.

Matinella, A., Lanzafame, M., Bonometti, M. A., Gajofatto, A., Concia, E., Vento, S., Monaco, S., & Ferrari, S. (2015). Neurological complications of HIV infection in pre-HAART and HAART era: A retrospective study. *Journal of Neurology, 262*, 1317–1327. doi:10.1007/s00415-015-7713-8.

Mayo, M. C., & Bordelon, Y. (2014). Dementia with Lewy bodies. *Seminars in Neurology, 34*, 182–188. doi:10.1055/s-0034-1381741.

McDowell, I., Xi, G., Lindsay, J., & Tierney, M. (2007). Mapping the connections between education and dementia. *Journal of Clinical and Experimental Neuropsychology, 29*, 127–141. http://dx.doi.org/10.1080/13803390600582420.

McKee, A. C., Cantu, R. C., Nowinski, C. J., Hedley-Whyte, E. T., Gavett, B. E., Budson, A. E., … Stern, R. A. (2009). Chronic traumatic encephalopathy in athletes: Progressive tauopathy after repetitive head injury. *Journal of Neuropathology & Experimental Neurology, 68*, 709–735. http://dx.doi.org/10.1097/NEN.0b013e3181a9d503.

McKee, A. C., Stein, T. D., Nowinski, C. J., Stern, R. A., Daneshvar, D. H., Alvarez, V. E., … Cantu, R. C. (2013). The spectrum of disease in chronic traumatic encephalopathy. *Brain, 136*, 43–64. https://doi.org/10.1093/brain/aws307.

McKeith, I. G., Dickson, D. W., Lowe, J., Emre, M., O'Brien, J. T., Feldman, H, … Yamada, M. (2005). Diagnosis and management of dementia with Lewy bodies: Third report of the DLB consortium. *Neurology, 65*, 1863–1872. doi:10.1212/01.wnl.0000187889.17253.b1.

McKeith, I., Taylor, J. P., Thomas, A., Donaghy, P., & Kane, J. (2016). Revisiting DLB diagnosis: A consideration of Prodromal DLB and of the diagnostic overlap with Alzheimer disease. *Journal of Geriatric Psychiatry & Neurology, 29*(5), 249–253.

McKhann, G. M., Albert, M. S., Grossman, M., Miller, B., Dickson, D., & Trojanowski, J. Q. (2001). Clinical and pathological diagnosis of frontotemporal dementia. *Archives of Neurology, 58*, 1803–1809. doi:10.1001/archneur.58.11.1803.

McKhann, G. M., Knopman, D. S., Chertkow, H., Hyman, B. T., Jack, C. R. Jr., Kawas, C. H., … Phelps, C. H. (2011). The diagnosis of dementia due to Alzheimer's disease: Recommendations from the National Institute on Aging–Alzheimer's Association workgroups on diagnostic guidelines for Alzheimer's disease. *Alzheimer's & Dementia, 7*, 263–269. http://dx.doi.org/10.1016/j.jalz.2011.03.005.

Meng, X., & D'Arcy, C. (2012). Education and dementia in the context of the cognitive reserve hypothesis: A systematic review with meta-analyses and qualitative analyses. *PLoS One, 7*(6), e38268. http://dx.doi.org/10.1371/journal.pone.0038268.

Mesulam, M. (2001). Primary progressive aphasia: Differentiation from Alzheimer's disease. *Annals of Neurology, 49*, 425–432. doi:10.1002/ana.410220414.

Mesulam, M.-M., Weintraub, S., Rogalski, E. J., Wieneke, C., Geula, C., & Bigio, E. H. (2014). Asymmetry and heterogeneity of Alzheimer's and frontotemporal pathology in primary progressive aphasia. *Brain, 137*, 1176–1192. doi:10.1093/brain/awu024.

Mesulam, M., Wicklund, A., Johnson, N., Rogalski, E., Léger, G. C., Rademaker, A., et al. (2008). Alzheimer and frontotemporal pathology in subsets of primary progressive aphasia. *Ann. Neurol. 63*, 709–719. doi:10.1002/ana.21388.

Morhardt, D., Weintraub, S., Khayum, B., Robinson, J., Medina, J., ... Rogalski, E. J. (2015). The CARE Pathway Model for dementia: Psychosocial and rehabilitative strategies for care in young-onset dementias. *Psychiatric Clinics of North America, 38*(2), 333–352.

Morris, R. G., & Mograbi, D. C. (2013). Anosognosia, autobiographical memory and self-knowledge in Alzheimer's disease. *Cortex, 49*, 1553–1565. http://dx.doi.org/10.1016/j.cortex.2012.09.006.

Nasreddine, Z. S., Phillips, N. A., Bédirian, V., Charbonneau, S., Whitehead, V., Collin, I., ... Chertkow, H. (2005). The Montreal Cognitive Assessment, MoCA: A brief screening tool for mild cognitive impairment. *Journal of the American Geriatrics Society, 53*, 695–699. doi:10.1111/j.1532-5415.2005.53221.x.

Nirmalasari, O., Mamo, S. K., Nieman, C. L., & Simpson, A. (2017). Age-related hearing loss in older adults. *International Psychogeriatrics, 29*(1), 115–121. doi:https://doi.org/10.1017/S1041610216001459.

Onyike, C. U., & Diehl-Schmid, J. (2013). The epidemiology of frontotemporal dementia. *Int Rev Psychiatry, 25*(2), 130–137.

Papoutsi, M., Labuschagne, I., Tabrizi, S. J., & Stout, J. C. (2014). The cognitive burden in Huntington's disease: Pathology, phenotype, and mechanisms of compensation. *Movement Disorders, 29*, 673–683. doi:10.1002/mds.25864.

Patterson, C. J., & Clarfield, A. M. (2003). Diagnostic procedures for dementia. In V. O. Emery & T. Oxman (Eds.), *Dementia: Presentations, differential diagnosis, and nosology* (pp. 61–88). Baltimore: Johns Hopkins University Press.

Perneczky, R., Tene, O., Attems, J., Giannakopoulos, P., Ikram, M. A., Federico, A., Sarazin, M., & Middleton, L. T. (2016). Is the time ripe for new diagnostic criteria of cognitive impairment due to cerebrovascular disease? Consensus report of the International Congress on vascular dementia working group. *BMC Med., 14*(1), 162. doi:10.1186/s12916-016-0719-y.

Petersen, R. C., Caracciolo, B., Brayne, C., Gauthier, S., Jelic, V., & Fratiglioni, L. (2014). Mild cognitive impairment: A concept in evolution. *Journal of Internal Medicine, 275*, 214–228. doi:10.1111/joim.12190.

Piguet, O., Hornberger, M., Mioshi, E., & Hodges, J. R. (2011). Behavioral-variant frontotemporal dementia: Diagnosis, clinical staging, and management. *Lancet Neurology, 10*(2), 162–172. doi:10.1016/S1474-4422(10)70299-4.

Prince, M., Bryce, R., Albanese, E., Wimo, A., Ribeiro, W., & Ferri, C. P. (2013). The global prevalence of dementia: A systematic review and metaanalysis. *Alzheimer's & Dementia, 9*, 63–75. http://dx.doi.org/10.1016/j.jalz.2012.11.007.

Pringsheim, T., Jette, N., Frolkis, A., & Steeves, T. D. L. (2014). The prevalence of Parkinson's disease: A systematic review and meta-analysis. *Movement Disorders, 29*, 1583–1590. doi:10.1002/mds.25945.

Prusiner, S. (2001). Shattuck lecture: Neurodegenerative diseases and prions. *New England Journal of Medicine, 344*, 1516–1526. doi:10.1056/NEJM200105173442006.

Puoti, G., Bizzi, A., Forloni, G., Safar, J. G., Tagliavini, F., & Gambetti, P. (2012). Sporadic human prion diseases: Molecular insights and diagnosis. *The Lancet Neurology, 11*(7), 618–628.

Rabinowitz, A. R., & Levin, H. S. (2014). Cognitive sequelae of traumatic brain injury. *Psychiatric Clinics of North America, 37*, 1–11. http://dx.doi.org/10.1016/j.psc.2013.11.004.

Rao, V., Koliatsos, V., Ahmed, F., Lyketsos, C., & Kortte, K. (2015). Neuropsychiatric disturbances associated with traumatic brain injury: A practical approach to evaluation and management. *Seminars in Neurology, 35*, 64–82. doi:10.1055/s-0035-1544241.

Rascovsky, K., Hodges, J. R., Knopman, D., Mendez, M. F., Kramer, J. H., Neuhaus, J., ... Miller, B. L. (2011). Sensitivity of revised diagnostic criteria for the behavioral variant of frontotemporal dementia. *Brain, 134*, 2456–2477. https://doi.org/10.1093/brain/awr179.

Ratnavalli, E., Brayne, C., Dawson, K., & Hodges, J. R. (2002). The prevalence of frontotemporal dementia. *Neurology, 58*, 1615–1621. http://dx.doi.org/10.1212/WNL.58.11.1615.

Reitz, C., & Mayeux, R. (2014). Alzheimer disease: Epidemiology, diagnostic criteria, risk factors and biomarkers. *Biochemical Pharmacology, 88*, 640–651. http://dx.doi.org/10.1016/j.bcp.2013.12.024.

Ridley, N. J., Draper, B., & Withall, A. (2013). Alcohol-related dementia: An update of the evidence. *Alzheimer's Research & Therapy, 5*(3). doi:10.1186/alzrt157.

Risacher, S. L., & Saykin, A. J. (2013). Neuroimaging biomarkers of neurodegenerative diseases and dementia. *Seminars in Neurology, 33*, 386–416. doi:10.1055/s-0033-1359312.

Ross, C. A., & Tabrizi, S. J. (2011). Huntington's disease: From molecular pathogenesis to clinical treatment. *The Lancet Neurology, 10*, 83–98. http://dx.doi.org/10.1016/S1474-4422(10)70245-3.

Sachdev, P., Kalaria, R., O'Brien, J., Skoog, I., Alladi, S., Black, S. E., … Scheltens, P. (2014). Diagnostic criteria for vascular cognitive disorders: A VASCOG statement. *Alzheimer Disease and Associated Disorders, 28*, 206–218. doi:10.1097/WAD.0000000000000034.

Schreiber, M., Bird, T. D., & Tsuang, D. W. (2014). Alzheimer's disease genetics. *Current Behavioral Neuroscience Reports, 1*, 191–196. doi:10.1007/s40473-014-0026-x.

Seltman, R. E., & Matthews, B. R. (2012). Frontotemporal lobar degeneration. *CNS Drugs, 26*, 841–870. doi:10.2165/11640070-000000000-00000.

Snowdon, D. (2001). *Aging with grace*. New York: Bantam.

Song, W., & Zhang, R. (2015). Creutzfeldt-Jakob disease. In L. Hongjun (Ed.), *Radiology of infectious diseases: Volume 1* (pp. 53–63). The Netherlands: Springer.

Staekenborg, S. S., Su, T., van Straaten, E. C. W., Lane, R., Scheltens, P., Barkhof, F., & van der Flier, W. M. (2010). Behavioural and psychological symptoms in vascular dementia; differences between small- and large-vessel disease. *Journal of Neurology, Neurosurgery & Psychiatry, 81*, 547–551. doi:10.1136/jnnp. 2009.187500.

Stopford, C. L., Thompson, J. C., Neary, D., Richardson, A. M. T., & Snowden, J. S. (2012). Working memory, attention, and executive function in Alzheimer's disease and frontotemporal dementia. *Cortex, 48*, 429–446. http://dx.doi.org/10.1016/j.cortex. 2010.12.002.

Taylor, K., & Monsch, A. (2004). The neuropsychology of Alzheimer's disease. In R. Richter & B. Richter (Eds.), *Alzheimer's disease: A physician's guide to practical management* (pp. 109–120). Totowa, NJ: Humana Press.

Thomas, A., Attems, J., Colloby, S. J., O'Brien, J. T., McKeith, I., Walker, R., … Walker, Z. (2017). Autopsy validation of 123I-FP-CIT dopaminergic neuroimaging for the diagnosis of DLB. *Neurology, 88*(3), 276–283.

Thompson, J. C., Harris, J., Sollom, A. C., Stopford, C. L., Howard, E., Snowden, J. S., & Craufurd, D. (2012). Longitudinal evaluation of neuropsychiatric symptoms in Huntington's disease. *The Journal of Neuropsychiatry and Clinical Neurosciences, 24*(1), 53–60. http://dx.doi.org/10.1176/appi.neuropsych. 11030057.

Thomson, A. D., Guerrini, I., & Marshall, E. J. (2012). The evolution and treatment of Korsakoff's syndrome: Out of sight, out of mind? *Neuropsychology Review, 22*:81–92. doi:10.1007/s11065-012-9196-z.

Toledo, J. B., Arnold, S. E., Raible, K., Brettschneider, J., Xie, S. X., Grossman, M., … & Trojanowski, J. Q. (2013). Contribution of cerebrovascular disease in autopsy confirmed neurodegenerative disease cases in the National Alzheimer's Coordinating Centre. *Brain, 136*, 2697–2706. https://doi.org/10.1093/brain/awt188.

van der Linde, R. M., Dening, T., Stephan, B. C., Prina, A. M., Evans, E., & Brayne, C. (2016). Longitudinal course of behavioral and psychological symptoms of dementia: A systematic review. *British Journal of Psychiatry, 209*(5), 366–377. doi:10.1192/bjp.bp. 114.148403.

van Duijn, E., Craufurd, D., Hubers, A. A. M., Giltay, E. J., Bonelli, R., Rickards, H., … Landwehrmeyer, G. B. (2014). Neuropsychiatric symptoms in a European Huntington's disease cohort (REGISTRY). *Journal of Neurology, Neurosurgery & Psychiatry, 85*, 1411–1418. doi:10.1136/jnnp-2013-307343.

Vann Jones, S. A., & O'Brien, J. T. (2014). The prevalence and incidence of dementia with Lewy bodies: A systematic review of population and clinical studies. *Psychological Medicine, 44*, 673–683. https://doi.org/10.1017/S0033291713000494.

Weintraub, D., & Stern, M. B. (2005). Psychiatric complications in Parkinson Disease. *American Journal of Geriatric Psychiatry, 13*, 844–851. http://dx.doi.org/10.1097/00019442-200510000-00003.

Weintraub, S., Wicklund, A. H., & Salmon, D. P. (2012). The neuropsychological profile of Alzheimer disease. *Cold Spring Harbor Perspectives in Medicine, 2*(4), a006171. doi:10.1101/cshperspect.a006171.

Werring, D. J., & Camicioli, R. M. (2016). Vascular gait disorders: What's the matter with the white and gray matter? *Neurology, 86*, 1177–1178. doi:10.1212/WNL.0000000000002529: 1526-632X.

Whitwell, J. L., Jack, C. R., Jr., Parisi, J. E., Knopman, D. S., Boeve, B. F., Petersen, R. C., … Josephs, K. A. (2011). Imaging signatures of molecular pathology in behavioral variant frontotemporal dementia. *Journal of Molecular Neuroscience, 45*(3), 372–378. doi:10.1007/s12031-011-9533-3.

Woods, S. P., Moore, D. J., Weber, E., & Grant, I. (2009). Cognitive neuropsychology of HIV-associated neurocognitive disorders. *Neuropsychology Review, 19*, 152–168. doi:10.1007/s11065-009-9102-5.

World Health Organization (2012). *Dementia: A public health priority*. Geneva: Author.

3

COGNITIVE-COMMUNICATIVE CHARACTERISTICS

Profiling Types of Dementia

Nidhi Mahendra, Ellen M. Hickey, and Michelle S. Bourgeois

Dementia is a progressive, neurodegenerative syndrome that is characterized by declines in a person's cognition, language, functional communication, and behavior. There are many causes of dementia, each accompanied by characteristic cellular-molecular pathology, associated neuropathology, structural protein abnormalities, clinical symptoms, and cognitive-communicative characteristics. Alzheimer's dementia (AD) is the leading type of dementia, followed by vascular dementia (VaD) and dementia with Lewy bodies (DLB) (Alzheimer's Association, 2016; Plassman et al., 2007). Frontotemporal lobar degeneration (FTLD) is a newer diagnosis that is less common than AD and VaD, and recent advances in neuroimaging and longitudinal study have revealed several variants of FTLD. This chapter focuses on describing the clinical profile of AD, and includes some information on other types of dementias. Both strengths and deficits in cognition (i.e., memory, attention, perception, executive function, and visuospatial and constructional skills) and communication (i.e., auditory comprehension, spoken language production, reading, writing, and pragmatic skills) are described. Before proceeding, we must recognize the important caveat that mixed dementia is much more common than previously known. Some estimates suggest that half the persons diagnosed with dementia show pathological evidence of simultaneously having more than one cause of dementia (Schneider, Arvanitakis, Bang, & Bennett, 2007).

This chapter begins with a review of cognitive processing, particularly focusing on human memory systems, given that memory impairments appear early as a notable clinical feature of the most common dementias, such as AD, VaD, and DLB. The chapter then focuses on the cognitive-communicative changes accompanying AD and other common dementia types. Throughout this book, language is regarded as an integral aspect of cognition that cannot be separated from cognition. Understanding and producing language is essential to performing many cognitive operations, which is why cognitive deficits frequently manifest as disordered language and functional communication. Breakdowns in communication often manifest as responsive behaviors, such as disruptive vocalizations and repetitive questions. Finally, the relationship among cognition, communication, and behavior is discussed.

Cognitive Skills and Deficits in AD and other Dementias

Memory

Human memory is conceptualized as a multidimensional construct with distinct processing components. British psychologist Alan Baddeley (1995) emphasized three interdependent components for processing information – encoding, consolidation, and retrieval. Information enters our system through our five senses and is held very briefly in sensory memory. Then it is held temporarily in working memory while being actively manipulated. Working memory (which replaced the less precise concept of short-term memory) is a dynamic, limited-capacity buffer that was first described by Baddeley and Hitch (1974). Long-term memory (LTM) allows us to store information permanently and results from more lasting neurochemical changes in the brain. Long-term memory is comprised of two systems of stored knowledge – the declarative or explicit ("knows that" system) and the nondeclarative or implicit ("knows how") system. Declarative memory consists of semantic and episodic memory, whereas non-declarative memory consists of priming, procedural memory, habits, and conditioned responses. Figure 3.1 illustrates how different types of memory are involved in information processing. Box 3.1 lists these components of the human memory system with examples of each type of memory.

Sensory Memory. Sensory memory is a very brief, modality-specific store of information that comes in directly from our senses (i.e., hearing, vision, touch, taste, and smell). Vestibular and somatosensory stimuli (i.e., pain, temperature, and proprioception) also enter sensory memory (Gardner, Martin, & Jessell, 2000; Zu Eulenburg, Muller-Forell, & Dieterich, 2013). Information in sensory memory may become associated with other behaviors and stimuli, and then transferred to working memory and even to LTM, for later retrieval (Emery, 2000). Some researchers are

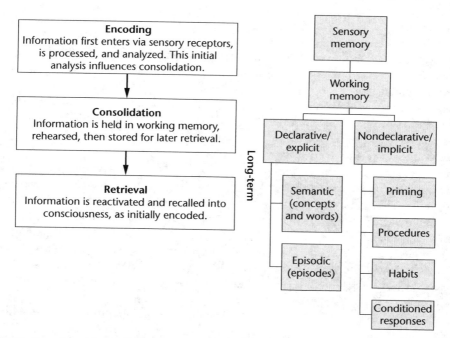

FIGURE 3.1   Interdependent Information Processing Elements on the Left Side; Memory Model on the Right Side

Source: Adapted from: Bayles & Tomoeda, 2013; Mahendra & Hopper, 2017; Squire & Schacter, 2002.

Box 3.1 Types of Memory and Examples

- Sensory memory: The information you see, hear, touch, taste, smell – held for 1–2 seconds.
- Working memory: Saying a phone number to yourself repeatedly as you prepare to dial it.
- Long-term memory.

  - Declarative or Explicit memory

    - Semantic memory: The Eiffel tower is in Paris, France; lemons are yellow and sour.
    - Episodic memory: I saw the Eiffel tower on my trip to Paris in 2002; I enjoyed fresh lemonade after lunch this afternoon.

  - Nondeclarative or Implicit memory

    - Priming: You are told 10 words related to 'sleep' (e.g., drowsy, tired, bed). When asked to recall these words, you recall "sleep" even though it was not on the original list because it is conceptually related to the words you heard.
    - Procedural memory: Learning to play a sport or a musical instrument; learning a strategy for solving puzzles, such as Sudoku.
    - Habits: Going to brew a pot of coffee first thing every morning without conscious thought; biting on your pen when concentrating hard on something.
    - Conditioned responses: When your mood improves as soon as you hear a specific song; when you are sick and feel better after having specific comfort foods.

---

interested in how sensory memory develops, is maintained over a person's lifetime, and shapes behavior. For instance, in a study of the human auditory system, the effects of early exposure to rich sensory stimulation (e.g., childhood musical training) seem to be cumulative and contribute to more robust sensory processing later in life, possibly allowing a person to better cope with downstream declines in sensory function (Skoe & Kraus, 2014). Similar to cognitive reserve, this finding supports the concept of a sensory reserve that, in conjunction with LTM, may contribute to the automatic nature of many behavioral responses.

When specific sensory stimuli do not result in expected behaviors, one possibility is that the sensory receptors are impaired (e.g., from age-related changes in vision and hearing) and sensory stimuli are not being perceived. If sensory supports (e.g., glasses, hearing aids) fail to enhance perception and recognition, the person might have agnosia (e.g., auditory or visual agnosia, prosopagnosia for impaired face recognition), or there could be an impairment of encoding and association of the stimulus to relevant information in LTM. These failures in encoding stimuli and associating them to appropriate responses could manifest as perseverative behaviors, such as repeatedly touching objects or staring too long at a person, indicating difficulty recognizing routine stimuli in the environment.

In AD, there is evidence for relatively spared sensory processing in early and middle stages, as compared to later stages. This is attributed to the later neuropathological involvement of the primary motor, sensory, and visual isocortical areas (Serrano-Ponzo, Frosch, Masliah, & Hyman, 2011) that form the neurobiological substrates for sensory memory. However, the performance of persons with AD deteriorates on more complex visual tasks involving backward masking (Miller,

1996), visual memory for faces (Damasio, 1999; Seelye, Howieson, Wild, Moore, & Kaye, 2009), visual association (Lindeboom, Schmand, Tulner, Walstra, & Jonker, 2002) and retention (Massman, Butters, & Delis, 1994). Further, multiple investigators have demonstrated that poor visual memory (as quantified by errors on *Benton's Visual Retention Test*; Benton, 1974), is associated with an increased risk of AD (Kawas et al., 2003), and that low scores on visual association tasks predicted episodic memory impairment (Meyer et al., 2016) and the onset of dementia prior to diagnosis (Lindeboom et al., 2002).

Similarly, anosmia and early impairments in olfactory memory, odor recognition, and odor identification are well documented in AD (Kovacs, 2004; Peters et al., 2003; Schofield, Ebrahimi, Jones, Bateman, & Murray, 2012), worsen with progression of AD (Devanand, 2016; Devanand et al., 2000; Nordin & Murphy, 1998; Schofield et al., 2012), and have been documented in persons with Parkinson's disease (PD) (Pearce, Hawkes, & Daniel, 1995). Further, odor identification deficits also predict conversion from MCI to AD (Tkalčić, Spasić, Ivanković, Pokrajac-Bulian, & Bosanac, 2011). Researchers have also found evidence of vestibular dysfunction (Chong, Horak, Frank, & Kaye, 1999; Previck, 2012), impaired mobility, and altered standing balance in AD when compared to age- and gender-matched controls (Suttanon et al., 2012). Additionally, persons with AD have more difficulty visually suppressing incongruent stimuli during balance tasks than healthy controls and persons with PD (Chong et al., 1999). This greater difficulty suppressing distractors is related to the adverse effect of AD on inhibitory processes (Amieva, Phillips, Della Salla, & Henry, 2004). These impairments in vestibular function, mobility, balance, and suppressing distraction explain why persons with AD are at increased risk for falls, despite lack of any overt impairment of gross motor skills.

Working Memory. After sensory memory, incoming information moves to working memory, a dynamic, short-duration, limited capacity buffer that allows us to hold on to information briefly while we process it and actively manipulate it. Working memory is unique in that it holds information exactly as it comes in via sensory memory, but also manipulates it and activates related information from LTM, as needed. Baddeley (1986) first described the structure of working memory as consisting of a supervisory central executive, a phonological loop for manipulating auditory information, and a visuospatial sketchpad for manipulating visual and spatial information. The central executive controls the other working memory components, makes decisions about resource allocation for particular tasks, and directly relates information to LTM. Subsequently, Baddeley (2000) proposed an additional component of working memory, namely, the episodic buffer that closely interfaces with LTM. This episodic buffer integrates information across domains (e.g., verbal and visual) and serves to chronologically order information (Baddeley, 1992, 2000).

Working memory is disrupted early in AD (Baddeley, Baddeley, Bucks, & Wilcock, 2001; Stopford, Thompson, Neary, Richardson, & Snowden, 2012) resulting in impaired word repetition (Stopford et al., 2012), reduced memory span capacity (Gagnon & Belleville, 2011), and rapid forgetting (Au, Chan, & Chiu, 2003; Gagnon & Belleville, 2011). Further, the central executive is involved early in AD (Baddeley, 1992; Lafleche & Albert, 1995; Stopford et al., 2012) and directly contributes to difficulty on divided attention tasks that require the concurrent completion of two tasks (Belleville, Chertkow, & Gauthier, 2007). These working memory impairments are related to the adverse effect of AD on speed of processing (van Deursen, Vuurman, Smits, Verhey, & Reidel, 2009), divided attention (Morris, 1996), and executive function (Baudic et al., 2006; Collette, Delrue, Van Der Linden, & Salmon, 2001). Beyond impaired performance on working memory tasks used in standardized assessment (e.g., digit span, paired associate learning), caregivers consistently report rapid forgetting of recent information (e.g., the answer to a question), difficulty holding on to information (e.g., the topic of an ongoing conversation), and difficulty integrating new information with older information from LTM.

Declarative or Explicit Memory: Semantic and Episodic Memory. Long-term memory consists of two major systems – declarative memory and nondeclarative memory. Declarative memory is knowledge that can be consciously retrieved and declared, and includes semantic memory and episodic memory. Semantic memory is a rich network of concepts and their associations that form our world knowledge, not tied to a specific memory. Difficulty accessing semantic memory manifests as anomia, one of the earliest language symptoms in dementia. Semantic memory impairments underlying anomia have also been documented in healthy older adults (Barresi, Nicholas, Connor, Obler, & Albert, 2000; Connor, Spiro, Obler, & Albert, 2004), who may be unable to retrieve a word occasionally and talk around the target or substitute a plausible alternative to convey intended meanings.

Semantic memory is often spared early on in AD and is regarded as being better spared than originally thought (Bayles & Kim, 2003), given that concepts and facts in semantic memory are typically overlearned, stored, and accessed repeatedly over time. As AD progresses, access to semantic memory is increasingly compromised (Bayles, Tomoeda, Kazniak, & Trosset, 1991). Anomia is a common feature in the language profile of persons with AD (March, Wales, & Pattison, 2003; Perry & Hodges, 2000; Van der Hurk & Hodges, 1995), some types of FTLD (Khan, Wakefield, Blackburn, & Venneri, 2013), DLB (Lambon Ralph et al., 2001; Schneider et al., 2012), and Huntington's disease (Salmon & Filoteo, 2007). The semantic variant of PPA (sv-PPA) is a fluent language variant of frontotemporal lobar degeneration. Unlike AD, sv-PPA is characterized by much more severe, progressive, and multimodal dissolution of semantic knowledge (Landin-Romero, Tan, Hodges, & Kumfor, 2016). These semantic memory deficits in sv-PPA extend across a variety of word retrieval tasks (Adlam et al., 2006). Language deterioration will be described more later.

The other component of declarative memory is episodic memory, which is our capacity for consciously recollecting knowledge of episodes, specific incidents, and events from our lives, with their associated temporospatial contexts. This type of memory system allows you to remember a short story, and to recall events and autobiographical information. Episodic memory is the last to mature (Tulving, 1983), and is instrumental in supporting rapid learning of new information (Squire & Dede, 2015). Episodic memory depends on the integrity of the entorhinal cortex and the hippocampus in the medial temporal lobe, these being the regions where neuropathological changes associated with AD are first observed.

Episodic memory is highly vulnerable to the effects of aging and AD, and is affected early and severely in persons with AD (Baddeley et al., 2001; Bayles & Tomoeda, 2013; Budson, 2009; Craik, 2000; Salmon & Bondi, 2009). Episodic memory deficits are often among the first symptoms reported by family caregivers of persons with AD (Bayles, 1991). When episodic memory fails, there is significant impact on everyday activities. People with dementia frequently forget appointments, to take medications, or that they have already eaten a meal. Episodic memory impairments also pose safety risks when persons with dementia forget to turn off a stove, lock a door, or forget their wallet while out on an errand. Persons with AD have great difficulty recalling recent events, including autobiographical memories. Whereas episodic recollection of autobiographical memories is impaired in preclinical stages and in early AD, semantic knowledge pertaining to autobiographical memories was spared until moderate stages of AD (Seidl, Lueken, Thomann, Geider, & Schröder, 2011). Persons with advanced AD are notably impaired on measures of autobiographical memory, such as *Autobiographical Memory Enquiry* (AME; Borrini, Dall'Ora, Della Sala, Marinelli, & Spinnler, 1989), autobiographical fluency for names, recent public events, and famous faces; yet their remote memory for public events was relatively preserved (Sartori, Snitz, Sorcinelli, & Daum, 2004). Prospective memory, i.e., memory for planned tasks and future events is significantly impaired in both AD and VaD (Livner, Laukka, Karlsson, & Bäckman, 2009).

Compared to persons with AD, episodic memory impairments are not as dramatic on imme-diate and delayed measures of verbal recall in VaD (Golden et al., 2005; Levinoff, 2007). Persons with DLB too may not present with significant memory impairment at first (McKeith, Taylor, Thomas, Donaghy, & Kane, 2016). Persons with the behavioral variant of frontotemporal demen-tia (bv-FTD) and the language variants or the primary progressive aphasias (PPA), have relatively spared episodic memory (Gorno-Tempini et al., 2011). A striking characteristic of persons with sv-PPA is the spared ability to remember day-to-day events (e.g., keeping appointments, inde-pendent travel, and shopping) alongside severe word comprehension and word retrieval deficits (Moss, Kopelman, Cappelletti, de Mornay Davies, & Jaldow, 2003). Persons with sv-PPA show relatively preserved recollection of recent autobiographical memories with somewhat poorer remote autobiographical memories (Graham & Hodges, 1997; Landin-Romero et al., 2016).

Finally, in discussing retrieval from declarative memory, there are clinically relevant differences between free and cued recall, recall versus recognition, and immediate versus delayed retrieval. Prominent deficits in free recall are seen in AD (Hopper, 2003; Salmon, 2000; Van Liew et al., 2016). Episodic recall is also consistently impaired in other dementias, such as VaD (Cerciello, Isella, Proserpi, & Papagn, 2016; Mahendra & Engineer, 2009), PD, HD (Paulsen, 2011; Van Liew et al., 2016), Multiple Sclerosis (MS), and PSP (Caine et al., 1986; Knoke, Taylor, & Saint-Cyr, 1998; Pillon et al., 1994). Across dementia types, free recall (without cues) is much more impaired than cued recall (e.g., providing a semantic cue for a pictured object, showing a family photo with a written cue) or recognition memory.

In comparing recall and recognition performance in AD, Bayles and Tomoeda (1993) noted significantly impaired free recall on a word-learning task, but improved cued recall and recogni-tion memory. Mahendra (2001) also reported that persons with AD performed very poorly on delayed free recall of a short story, yet were able to correctly answer most questions about this story in a multiple-choice recognition task. Similarly, when comparing persons with AD, VaD and FTLD on a 24-item word-learning task, persons with VaD and FTLD demonstrated better free recall and stronger sensitivity to semantic cues than those with AD (Cerciello et al., 2016). Further, persons with VaD had a higher rate of forgetting across conditions while those with FTLD had better performance on free recall, cued recall, and recognition. This initial sparing of episodic recall in FTLD occurs because the neuropathology in FTLD does not characteristically involve the medial temporal lobes (Glosser, Gallo, Clark, & Grossman, 2002), responsible for episodic memory. In summary, performance of persons with dementia is influenced by the material being recalled (e.g., word list or a story), recall index (free recall, cued recall, or recognition), the type of dementia, and dementia severity. See Box 3.2 for examples of free recall, cued recall, and recognition.

Nondeclarative (or Implicit) Memory: Priming, Procedures, Habits, and Condition-ing. Nondeclarative memory is the learning-by-doing system, where skills and action patterns are learned by repeated practice, providing varied unconscious, implicit mechanisms for learning information is expressed via performance rather than recollection (Budson, 2009; Schacter, 1987; Squire & Dede, 2015). Nondeclarative memory encompasses priming, motor procedures and skills, habits and conditioned responses (Bayles & Tomoeda, 2013; Seger & Spiering, 2011). Priming is an implicit, unconscious form of memory that refers to an enhanced ability to detect, identify, or respond to a stimulus after recent exposure to it, or to a related stimulus. Thus, when a stimulus or a desired response is primed by previous exposure, we can access it rapidly and without conscious processing. Persons with AD perform comparably to age-matched controls on picture priming tasks (Ballastceros, Reales, & Mayas, 2007), visual perceptual priming tasks (Salmon & Fennema-Notestine, 1996), and repetition priming tasks (Fleischman et al., 1995; Ober & Shenaut, 2014). These find-ings relate to a larger literature on relatively spared implicit memory in AD.

Box 3.2 Examples of Free Recall, Cued Recall, and Recognition

1. Free recall

   a. Examiner (after telling the client a short story): Now, I'd like you to tell me that story. Client: *"Let's see … I think it was about a young person. That's all I have."*

   b. Examiner: "What is the name of this place?" Client: "Mountain View home."

2. Cued recall

   a. Examiner (following initial response above): "What was the item that got lost in this story?" Client: *"I think it was a wallet."*

   b. Examiner (following no response to initial question): "It starts with Mou–." Client: "Mountain View home."

3. Recognition

   a. Examiner: (following response above): "Is the person in this story a man or a woman?" Client: *"A woman."*

   b. Examiner (same sequence of cues as above, no response): "Are we at Southwood or Mountain View home?" Client: "Mountain View home."

Another component of nondeclarative memory is procedural memory, which allows us to learn motor tasks and procedures (e.g., to play a sport or to use a tool), and to develop cognitive skills (e.g., word and number games) by repeatedly performing them. Schacter and Tulving (1994) described procedural memory as "knowing how" to perform a task, in contrast with fact-based, declarative memory. Procedural memory is impaired in dementia due to HD (Heindel, Butters, & Salmon, 1988) yet is relatively spared in AD, likely because motor procedures are typically learned via repeated practice over time, thus becoming automatic and independent of conscious recall. Other examples of procedural memory include completing basic and instrumental ADLs.

A third aspect of implicit memory is habit memory. Habits are well-rehearsed, behavioral routines that we use in our daily lives without conscious thought. The basal ganglia play a crucial role in acquiring habits, which are described as unconscious, automatic, inflexible, and learned slowly and incrementally (Seger & Spiering, 2011). For instance, we implicitly know our early morning routines and do specific tasks as soon as we wake up, usually performing them without a thought. Habits are not merely restricted to things we do but also include our thoughts and beliefs. Finally, conditioned responses are learned or reflexive responses produced automatically in response to specific stimuli. Such conditioned responses are learned in direct association with specific stimuli, and include behaviors such as greetings. In other instances, a stimulus gets conditioned over time to evoke a specific response based on either positive or negative consequences. For example, being presented a bouquet of flowers may either delight a person or cause immediate concern due to allergies. Likewise, music and foods can elicit either positive or negative affect based on their associations. This understanding of conditioned responses has implications for using stimuli that directly evoke positive communicative responses, as this type of implicit memory is preserved in most dementias. For example, even persons with moderate-to-severe AD verbally acknowledged and thanked the examiner when presented with a gift (Bayles, Tomeda, Cruz, & Mahendra, 2000).

Evidence for relatively spared implicit memory functioning in early to middle stages of dementia comes from priming studies in AD (Fleischman & Gabrieli, 1998). Morris and Kopelman

TABLE 3.1 Cognitive Profiles Across Major Dementia Types

	Alzheimer's Disease (AD)	Va Vascular Dementia (VaD)	Dementia with Lewy Bodies (DLB)	Parkinson's Disease (PD)	Huntington's Disease (HD)	Progressive Supranuclear Palsy (PSP)	Multiple Sclerosis (MS)
Attention							
Sustained	Less impaired	Less impaired	Fluctuating	Good	Impaired	More impaired	Impaired
Divided	More impaired	More impaired	More impaired	Impaired	More impaired	More impaired	Impaired
Memory							
Working	Impaired	More impaired	More impaired	More impaired	More impaired	More impaired	Impaired
Episodic	More impaired	Impaired	Impaired	Less impaired	More impaired	Impaired	Impaired
Semantic	Less impaired	Impaired	Limited research	Less impaired	Less impaired	Impaired	Impaired
Procedural	Less impaired	Impaired	Less impaired	More impaired	More impaired	More impaired	Unimpaired
Executive Function	Impaired	Impaired	Impaired	Impaired	Impaired	Impaired	Impaired
Visuospatial Function	Impaired	More impaired	Very impaired, with hallucinations	Impaired	Impaired	Very impaired	Impaired

(1986) first documented normal priming effects in AD, asking participants to name pictures and later demonstrating increased naming speed when repeatedly exposed to the same pictures. Similar sparing of implicit memory for nonverbal tasks was demonstrated when persons with AD improved their speed and accuracy on a pursuit rotor task with repeated practice (Heindel, Salmon, Shults, Walicke, & Butters, 1989). Procedural memory is also relatively preserved in the semantic variant of PPA, or sv-PPA (Bier et al., 2015), while being more impaired in VaD (Libon et al., 1998), in PD (Koenig, Thomas-Antérion, & Laurent, 1999; Roy, Park, Roy, & Almeida, 2015; Zgaljardic, Borod, Foldi, & Mattis, 2003), and in HD (Heindel et al., 1989). In HD, implicit memory is more compromised than episodic memory (Paulsen, 2011). See Table 3.1 for an at-a-glance comparison of cognitive profiles across major dementia types.

As described here, typical encoding, consolidation, and storage of information for later retrieval is disrupted in dementia, which disrupts the retention and learning of new information. Importantly, however, persons with AD can learn new information when encoding, consolidation, and retrieval processes are supported and strengthened (e.g., Camp, 2001; Rusted & Sheppard, 2002; van Halteren-van Tilborg, Scherder, & Hulstijn, 2007). The relative sparing of nondeclarative memory in AD has great potential when designing functional interventions using spaced retrieval training (Camp & McKitrick, 1992; Hopper et al., 2013; Mahendra, 2011; Materne, Luszcz, & Bond, 2014), graphic cues (Bourgeois, 2014), or augmentative alternative communication systems (Fried-Oken, Beukelman, & Hux, 2011; Fried-Oken et al., 2012) to help compensate for explicit memory deficits in everyday activities. These cognitive-communicative interventions will be described in Chapter 6.

Attention

Attention is the process of focusing on a stimulus of choice for a length of time (sustained attention), to a specific stimulus while suppressing or ignoring a competing stimulus (selective attention), attending to multiple stimuli or tasks at the same time (divided attention), or switching back and forth from one task or stimulus to another (attention switching) (Biel & Hula, 2016; Norman & Shallice, 1986). Examples of simple tasks used to examine attention include having the person visually scan for a certain letter in a display of random letters, or to listen for a certain letter in a recording of random letters being stated. In divided attention tasks, for example, the person is asked to attend to two different letters or symbols at the same time. Common attention-switching tasks include asking a person to switch between: scanning for two different letters when given a signal; naming fruits and then vegetables; making a trail alternating between letters and numbers, or sorting cards by color then by shape. The impact of attention impairments on daily activities depends on dementia severity and the type of attention process involved. Persons with milder impairments, or difficulty only with complex attention, are typically unable to drive or manage finances. With more severe impairments, affecting basic sustained and selective attention tasks, there can be difficulty paying attention long enough to complete a basic ADL task such as brushing hair.

Performance on complex tasks of attention requires the integrity of sensory functions, speed of processing, and executive control processes, such as decision-making and inhibition (Baddeley et al., 2001; Foldi, Lobosco, & Schaefer, 2002). Differentiating between attention and executive function deficits can be difficult when analyzing performance on tasks requiring divided attention and attention switching. In general, when a task is familiar, has been practiced, or has functional and personal relevance, healthy adults and persons with dementia require less cognitive effort and perform better. This is important for clinicians, as we can enhance client performance by attending to how information is presented (e.g., reduce the number of choices, present stimuli sequentially not simultaneously) (Foldi et al., 2002).

In early stages of dementia, performance is not impaired on simple tasks that require sustained attention (Assal & Cummings, 2003). Persons with mild dementia may have spared performance on sustained attention tasks such as listening for the presence or absence of a pure tone, or for a change in pattern amid a series of tones (Lines et al., 1991; Perry, Watson, & Hodges, 2000). Certain components of selective attention are relatively intact in early stages (e.g., simply selecting a target stimulus), yet as task complexity increases due to similarity between a target and a distractor, persons with dementia consistently experience more confusion, increased errors, and longer response times (Baddeley et al., 2001; Foldi, Jutagir, Davidoff, & Gould, 1992; Foldi et al., 2005; McGuiness, Barrett, Craig, Lawson & Passmore, 2010). Compared to AD, VaD is usually characterized by more notable deficits in attention (Levy & Cheline, 2007; McGuiness et al., 2010). Persons with DLB demonstrate significant fluctuations in attention and vigilance (Ballard et al., 2001; McKeith et al., 2016), with periods of time in which alertness and concentration are impaired, and the person has limited awareness of their immediate environment (Ballard, Aarsland, Francis, & Corbett, 2013; McKeith et al., 2016; Walker et al., 2000).

A quick look at Table 3.1 shows that all dementias adversely impact divided attention. In AD, divided attention deficits appear relatively early (Collette, Delrue, Van Der Linden, & Salmon, 2001; McGuiness et al., 2010). For instance, persons with AD have difficulty listening for a target word while simultaneously entering digits on a keyboard (Perry & Hodges, 1999) and persons with PD demonstrated more difficulty than healthy older controls while buttoning a shirt and simultaneously generating possible first names of women (Teixeira & Alouche, 2007). Similarly, performance on complex tasks of divided attention, such as driving (Fitten et al., 1995) and computer-administered visual attention measures (Whelihan, DiCarlo, & Paul, 2005) also confirms early-appearing deficits in dementia.

Executive Functions. Executive functions include varied processes, such as initiation, response inhibition of inappropriate or irrelevant responses, task persistence, organization and sequencing, generative thinking for problem-solving, and self-monitoring of performance (Assal & Cummings, 2003; Lezak, Howieson, Bigler, & Tranel, 2012; Sohlberg & Mateer, 2001). Together, executive functions ensure a person's success, independence, and flexibility for social and occupational functioning. Executive function is at the heart of many basic and instrumental activities of daily living (IADLs), such as shopping, preparing meals, managing finances, taking medications, completing chores, using the telephone or computer, and taking public transit. All dementia types adversely influence executive function and IADLs.

Another important component of executive function is the concept of Theory of Mind (TOM), which refers to the ability to attribute mental states, thoughts (cognitive component), and feelings (affective component) to others (Cuerva et al., 2001; Heitz et al., 2016). For example, in a conversation, adults make judgments about what is shared knowledge and what needs to be explained, and make decisions about whether to tell a listener certain information based on how they think that listener will respond (e.g., not telling someone about a party that they were not invited to, in order to avoid hurting their feelings). Another example is making decisions about how and when to deliver bad news based on what we perceive of the other person's mental state at a given time. Theory of Mind has been studied in children with and without cognitive or communication disorders, and is beginning to receive attention in dementia research (Youmans & Bourgeois, 2010).

Across dementia types, executive dysfunction appears early and progressively declines as dementia severity increases. These executive function impairments are easily observed on traditional or functional assessment measures. Persons with early AD (Perry & Hodges, 1999) and those with FTLD (Johnson, Head, Kim, Starr, & Cotman, 1999) demonstrated executive dysfunction on traditional measures such as Trail Making Part B (Reitan & Wolfson, 1985). On executive function measures that specifically test planning, (e.g., *Tower of London*; Shallice, 1982), set shifting and response inhibition (*Wisconsin Card Sorting Test*; Heaton, Chelune, Talley, Kay, & Curtiss, 1993), performance in early stages of dementia is better in AD than in PSP (Grafman, Litvan, Gomez, & Chase, 1990), FTLD (Rosen et al., 2002), DLB (Downes et al., 1999), or in MS (Rao, Leo, Bernardin, & Unverzagt, 1991).

By the middle stages of AD, individuals demonstrate prominent planning deficits on the *Tower of London* task, because of forgetting task rules and using strategies that violate task rules (Rainville et al., 2002). This illustrates the juxtaposition of how episodic memory deficits and the inability to inhibit inappropriate responses combine to impact task performance. In PD, the earliest signs of executive dysfunction present as difficulties with task initiation and planning (Zgaljardic et al., 2003), whereas in DLB, affected individuals demonstrate perseveration and cognitive inflexibility during decision-making (Slachevsky et al., 2004). The behavioral variant of frontotemporal dementia (bv-FTD) is characterized by prominent changes in executive functions, personality, and behavior (Gorno-Tempini et al., 2011). The complexity of executive functions tasks is demonstrated in findings that even in healthy older adults, a significant relationship was observed between performance on the *Everyday Problems Test for Cognitively Challenged Elderly* (EPCCE; Willis, 1993) and scores on the *Mini-Mental State Exam* (Willis et al., 1998).

Whereas TOM was first studied in autism and schizophrenia, there has been growing interest in studying TOM in neurodegenerative diseases. TOM deficits have been reported earliest in FTD (Gregory et al., 2002) and in DLB (Heitz et al., 2016), and also occur in sv-PPA (Duval et al., 2012), HD (Allain et al., 2011), in amyotrophic lateral sclerosis or ALS (Meier, Charleston, & Tippett, 2010), PSP (Ghosh et al., 2012), in corticobasal degeneration (Kluger & Heilman, 2007), and in PD (Roca et al., 2010). In comparison to these dementias, there is some evidence that TOM knowledge might be spared in AD based on studies (Heitz et al., 2016) in which persons with AD performed similar to healthy controls on specific measures, such as the *Faux Pas Recognition* test and a *Facial Emotion Recognition Test* (Ekman & Friesen, 1975). Observational studies of nonverbal communicative behaviors of persons with AD using an ethnographic approach found that persons with AD communicated effectively using nonverbal behaviors and could interpret others' nonverbal behaviors and respond accordingly (Hubbard, Cook, Tester, & Downs, 2002). Other studies reveal TOM deficits in mild AD, proportional to the degree of cognitive impairment (Cuerva et al., 2001). These discrepant findings likely stem from differing task demands and methodology used to study TOM, and the influence of existing executive, episodic, and working memory deficits on performance. Youmans and Bourgeois (2010) provided visual supports to persons with AD to control for the effects of variable memory deficits, and confirmed TOM impairments.

Perceptual and Visuospatial Function. There are distinct aspects of visual perception that are relevant for understanding visuoperceptual and visuospatial function in persons with dementia. Visual perception is the ability to interpret visual information and requires visual acuity, visual orientation, and visual search functions. Many persons with dementia experience declines in visual acuity and/or age-related conditions of the eye (e.g., cataracts, glaucoma, diabetic retinopathy, macular degeneration) that impact the ability to process visual information. Separate from this, persons with dementia also have genuine difficulty interpreting visual stimuli with visuospatial and constructional deficits appearing early on, including in preclinical stages (Weintraub, Wickland, & Salmon, 2012). Visuoperceptual skills include discriminating between objects, perceiving physical features (e.g. size, color, contour), part-to-whole processing, perceiving color contrasts, and the ability to distinguish foreground from background. Visuoperceptual skills also are critical in everyday activities for identifying simple objects (e.g., a razor versus a toothbrush), recognizing familiar faces, constructional tasks like drawing or copying a figure, participating in hobbies (e.g., crafts), completing occupational tasks (e.g., using a cash register or a computer), or driving.

Considering the earlier described changes in visual memory, it is not surprising that persons with dementia demonstrate changes in visual perception and visuospatial functioning. Common perceptual problems in dementia include auditory agnosias (Hodges, 2001), visual perception deficits (Caselli, 2000), achromatopsia (color perception), prosopagnosia or facial recognition (Seelye et al., 2009), and in later stages, propopagnosia (i.e., recognizing oneself) also has been documented (Simard, van Reekum, & Myran, 2003). Impairments of visual perception may also influence reading comprehension performance in dementia. For example, Silveri and Leggio (1996) found that in persons with AD, visual perception deficits explained reading comprehension performance, investigated using word-to-picture matching tasks with foils that shared lexical-semantic, phonological, or visual-perceptual features. Similarly, Glosser and colleagues (2002) also documented reading impairments associated with visual-processing deficits in AD. Clinically, it is important to differentiate between deficits of visual acuity and visuospatial cognition. For example, Rizzo, Anderson, Dawson, and Nawrot (2000) demonstrated no difference between healthy controls and persons with AD on measures of visual acuity, stereoacuity, and on discriminating the direction of motion. Yet, persons with AD performed significantly worse than controls on measures of visual attention, visuospatial construction, and visual memory.

Thus, visuoperceptual deficits can easily compromise functional behaviors, socially acceptable responses, and even the safety of a person with dementia. For example, a client with dementia may perceive a carpet with bold, black dots as actual holes in a damaged floor and be afraid to walk across the room; may become easily alarmed, mistaking their spouse for a stranger; or misperceive the signals that a stovetop is still hot. (See Chapter 5 for information about assessment of perception.) The impact of these perceptual difficulties on functional tasks, like driving, is particularly important for clinicians designing interventions. For example, in an experimental driving task to compare the ability of healthy older adults and those with mild dementia to detect landmarks and identify traffic signs, poor performance of drivers with dementia was predicted by performance on measures of visual perception, attention, memory, and executive function (Uc, Rizzo, Anderson, Shi, & Dawson, 2005). Further, driving safety worsened as the cognitive load and task complexity increased.

Different patterns of perceptual deficits have been documented across dementia syndromes. Visuospatial impairments are commonly reported in AD and in PD with dementia (PDD) (Assal & Cummings, 2003; Stern, Richards, Sano, & Mayeux, 1993), with deficits in PDD worse than those in AD on *Block Design* and *Ravens Progressive Matrices* (Huber, Shuttleworth, & Freidenberg, 1989). Visuospatial impairments are worse in AD compared to VaD (Fitten et al., 1995). However, related deficits in visual memory have been observed in persons with AD, VaD, and PD when drawing the complex *Rey-Osterrieth* figure from memory (Freeman et al., 2000). Visuospatial dysfunction is a hallmark of DLB and among the earliest symptoms of DLB, including complex visual hallucinations (Ferman & Boeve, 2007; McKeith et al., 2016). The prominent visuospatial deficits seen in persons with DLB can be assessed using tests of object size discrimination, form discrimination, overlapping figure identification, and visual counting tasks (Mori et al., 2000; Shimamura et al., 1998). These researchers additionally observed that persons with AD outperform persons with DLB on tests of picture arrangement, block design, and object assembly. Similarly, on visual memory tests, Noe and colleagues (2004) found that persons with DLB performed worse than those with AD, and performed similar to those with PD. Finally, visuospatial impairments also are documented in MS (Rao et al., 1991). Visual hallucinations are common in persons with DLB (Ballard et al., 2013).

One clinical consideration is that poor performance on visual and visuospatial tasks may result from failure to understand or to retain task instructions. Further, more complex visuospatial tasks require the integration of multiple cognitive domains (e.g., attention and memory), thereby, making it difficult to attribute poor performance to any one cognitive component. For example, the popularly used *Clock Drawing Task* requires attention, memory, executive function, and visuospatial skills. Similarly, difficulties on complex visuospatial tasks do not reliably predict the performance of a person with dementia on more functional tasks of reading. Despite prominent deficits on abstract tasks, persons in the late stages of dementia are able to read simple words and sentences, respond to greetings and compliments and correct misinformation (Bayles et al., 2000), while retaining the ability to respond to familiar pictures and written materials in memory books (Bourgeois & Mason, 1996; Hoerster, Hickey, & Bourgeois, 2001).

Language Skills and Deficits in AD and Other Dementias

The effects of dementia on linguistic communication are best understood by appreciating the inextricable link between memory and language. The signature memory impairments in AD disrupt the comprehension and production of language, directly contributing to communicative impairments (Bayles, 2001; Ferris & Farlow, 2013). Spoken language production is uniquely complex and involves precisely sequencing phonemes to form words, selecting appropriate vocabulary, using syntax to form grammatical sentences, and sequencing and organizing sentences to convey meaning. These phonemes, words, and grammatical forms are learned, stored in memory, and retrieved in real time when a speaker conveys a message to a listener. Thus, we typically use semantic and episodic memory stores during communication while our rule-governed knowledge of phonology, morphology, and syntax is supported by the procedural or implicit memory system (Ullman, 2013). Similarly, when comprehending and producing written language, we apply rules to combine graphemes to spell written words, and to combine written words into sentences.

Together, impairments of attention, working memory, episodic memory, executive function, and visuospatial ability interfere with language production and comprehension, varying by type and severity of dementia. In AD, working and episodic memory deficits explain diminished performance on language comprehension and production tasks. Bayles (2003) suggested that reduced working memory span, difficulty focusing attention, and impaired activation of information in LTM do not reveal a loss of linguistic knowledge, particularly when tasks involved short instructions presented at a comfortable rate of speech, using short commands, supported by contextual and written supports. Table 3.2 summarizes the cognitive-communicative changes seen in AD in early, middle, and late stages.

Spoken Language Production

Phonology and Motor Speech Production. Persons with AD retain their ability to select and sequence phonemes for speech production over the course of the disease. Persons with AD rarely make noticeable phonological errors or have motor speech disorders (Appell, Kertesz, & Fisman, 1982). Recently, Meilan and colleagues (Meilan et al., 2014) used spectrographic analyses to study temporal and acoustic characteristics in the speech of healthy older adults and persons with Alzheimer's disease. They found that select measures such as the number of voice breaks, shimmer (i.e., extent of variation in expiratory airflow), and the noise-to-harmonics-ratio (i.e., amplitude of noise compared to tonal components of speech) reliably differentiated persons with AD from healthy older controls.

When more pronounced changes in articulatory patterns or motor speech production are observed early on, a diagnosis other than AD is likely indicated or it is possible that the person presents with a mixed dementia resulting from the combined effects of AD and another dementia type. For instance, apraxia of speech, a disorder of motor planning and programming resulting

TABLE 3.2 Cognitive-Communicative Profiles by Stage of Alzheimer's Disease (AD)

Stages of Alzheimer's Disease	Impaired Cognitive-Communicative Abilities	Relatively Spared Cognitive-Communicative Abilities
Early Stage		
Expressive Language	Difficulty with word retrieval	Spared phonology, syntax, and pragmatics
Receptive Language	Ability to comprehend abstract language and complex conversation	Well-preserved oral reading and simple writing tasks
Attention	Prominent selective and divided attention deficits	Spared comprehension of concrete language and short, yes-no questions; spared reading comprehension
Memory	Deficits in episodic and working memory	Spared alertness and sustained attention
Executive Function	Pervasive difficulty completing IADLs (e.g., shopping, paying bills)	Spared sensory and nondeclarative memory (e.g., procedures, skills, priming, conditioned responses)
Visuospatial Function	Mild deficits on more complex tasks	Somewhat spared metacognition, seen as awareness of memory deficits or of anomia
Middle Stage		
Expressive Language	Increasing difficulty with empty speech, anomia, and discourse breakdowns	Retained speech fluency, phonology and syntax; spared oral reading of familiar words and short text; relatively preserved pragmatics
Receptive Language	Difficulty comprehending multi-step commands; impaired reading comprehension	Reading comprehension of familiar and meaningful words and phrase; ability to follow short conversations on personally relevant topics (e.g., hobbies, opinions)
Attention	Pervasive impairment	
Memory	Profound deficits in episodic and working memory	
Executive Function	Difficulty planning, switching response sets, and inhibiting inappropriate responses	
Visuospatial Function	Increasing visuospatial deficits	
Late Stage		
Expressive Language	Inability to express needs and wants; repetitive, disruptive vocalizations; near-mutism in end-stage	Occasional responses to tangible, culturally familiar and meaningful sensory stimuli (e.g., smiles, music)
Receptive Language	Severely limited spoken and written language comprehension	May recognize and respond to familiar tactile, visual, and affective cues (e.g., hand-holding)
Attention	Severely affected attention, fluctuating alertness	May respond to personal attention and presence of a companion
Memory	Severely affected including recognition of familiar persons	
Executive Function	Severely affected	
Visuospatial Function	Severely affected	

from cortical lesions, may occur in corticobasal degeneration (CBD; Blake, Duffy, Boeve, Ahlskog, & Maraganore, 2003; Josephs & Duffy, 2008) or primary progressive apraxia of speech (PPAOS; Duffy et al., 2015; Josephs et al., 2012).

Some dementia types may be characterized by one of the seven types of dysarthria, a group of neuromuscular execution disorders affecting speech due to deficits in strength, speed, coordination, tone, and/or range of motion of the speech musculature (Duffy, 2012). Dysarthrias occur commonly in PD, HD, PSP, CBD, and ALS; the type of dysarthria depends on the neuropathology of the disease (Assal & Cummings, 2003; Campbell-Taylor, 1995; Duffy, 2012). Sometimes a motor speech disorder is an early sign of a neurodegenerative disease (Duffy, 2012). For example, in PD, motor speech changes, such as abnormal phonation and respiration with impaired pitch and loudness control, are often early signs of the disease (Campbell-Taylor, 1995). Up to 89% of people with PD exhibit hypokinetic dysarthria (Liotti et al., 2003), characterized by reduced vocal intensity, short rushes of speech, and impaired articulation and speech intelligibility (Duffy, 2012; Pinto et al., 2004). Many of the diseases that cause motor speech disorders may also cause dementia; see Duffy (2012) for a comprehensive description of motor speech disorders in degenerative diseases.

Syntax. Grammatical knowledge is considered largely spared in AD, likely due to reliance on nondeclarative memory for the rules of syntax in a particular language. Early studies revealed that persons with mild to moderate AD did not present with frank agrammatism (Kempler, 1995) and were able to produce language of similar grammatical complexity as persons without dementia (Hier, Hagenlocker, & Shindler, 1985; Kempler, Curtiss, & Jackson, 1987). Syntactic ability appears intact across tasks, e.g., spontaneous utterance production (Kempler et al., 1987), sentence comprehension (Schwartz, Marin, & Saffran, 1979), and writing to dictation (Kempler et al., 1987). The pervasive cognitive decline in AD results in reduced syntactic complexity (de Lira, Ortiz, Campanha, Bertolucci, & Minett, 2011), characterized by reduced sentence length, more frequent use of formulaic language and fixed expressions (Bridges & Van Lancker Sidtis, 2013), and diminished propositional content as analyzed from interview transcripts of persons with mild dementia compared to persons without dementia (Lyons et al., 1994).

Semantics. Language tasks affected earliest in AD stem from episodic and semantic memory deficits and include difficulty with retrieving words or anomia (Bayles & Tomoeda, 2013; Obler, Dronkers, Koss, Delis, & Friedland, 1986), describing objects and concepts (Mardh, Nägga, & Samuelsson, 2013; Reilly, Peelle, Antonucci, & Grossman, 2011), and maintaining discourse coherence and cohesion (Bayles & Tomoeda, 2013; Dijkstra, Bourgeois, Allen & Burgio, 2004). In AD, confrontation naming and generative naming abilities are significantly impaired when compared to age-matched healthy older controls (Arkin & Mahendra, 2001; Bayles & Tomoeda, 1983, 2013; Clark et al., 2009; Sailor, Antoine, Diaz, Kuslansky, & Kluger, 2004). When compared to healthy older adults, Sailor et al. (2004) reported that persons with AD had slower memory search processes and were less likely to name atypical exemplars of a category. Unlike healthy older adults, persons with early dementia are not easily able to retrieve a target word or spontaneously use a compensatory strategy.

Subtle differences on naming and verbal fluency tasks have been reported by etiology. Bayles and Tomoeda (1983) reported that persons with HD did not exhibit difficulty on the *Boston Naming Test* until later in the disease. Similarly, persons with PD usually have milder naming deficits and do not demonstrate paraphasias throughout the disease course (Huber, Shuttleworth, & Freidenberg, 1989). Compared to performance patterns seen in AD, verbal fluency is worse overall in PSP, PD, HD, and VaD (Huber et al., 1989; Lafosse et al., 1997; Mahendra & Engineer, 2009; Pillon, Dubois, Ploska, & Agid, 1991). Category fluency is worse in AD, whereas letter fluency is better in PSP and HD than in AD (Rosser & Hodges, 1994), and better in AD than VaD (Duff Canning, Leach, Stuss, Ngo, & Black, 2004; Mahendra & Engineer, 2009).

Recent evidence suggests that the nature of the naming deficit in AD changes with disease progression (Silagi, Bertolucci, & Ortiz, 2015). In the early stages, persons with AD have difficulty with quickly accessing semantic memory, thus demonstrating semantic paraphasias and some instances of no-responses (Chenery, Murdoch, & Ingram, 1996; Silagi et al., 2015). In moderate stages of AD, semantic stores begin to degrade, impacting naming performance by resulting in more frequent semantic paraphasias, greater number of no-responses (an indicator of pure anomia), more errors arising from visual perception deficits (Huber et al., 1989; Shuttleworth & Huber, 1988; Silagi et al., 2015), and overall greater variability in performance (Chenery et al., 1996; Silagi et al., 2015). Together, these studies show that there are quantitative (i.e., more errors) in naming performance as AD progresses, and qualitative changes (i.e., distinct types of errors). However, information that is personally relevant may be relatively preserved, as people with AD show consistently better naming of personally relevant people, places, and objects than those not personally relevant (Snowden, Griffiths, & Neary, 1994).

Similar to the aforementioned explanations for the nature of naming difficulty in AD, Kempler (1995) suggested that impaired lexical access more likely explains semantic retrieval difficulties than a deterioration of underlying lexical representations for multiple reasons. First, persons with AD use circumlocution in confrontation–naming tasks and often produce the intended word after saying something similar or describing the object (Bayles & Tomoeda, 1983). Second, comprehension is better than production of the same words, and persons with AD spontaneously use gestures indicating the use of an object that they have not been able to name (Kempler, 1988). Finally, phonemic cues aid retrieval (Neils, Brennan, Cole, Boller, & Gerdeman, 1988) suggesting that underlying semantic representations were accessible via phonemic cues. Other investigators have suggested that naming deficits are related to attention and concentration problems (Cannatà, Alberoni, Franceschi, & Mariani, 2002; Selnes, Carson, Rovner, & Gordon, 1988). Still other researchers attribute impaired confrontation naming in persons with AD, HD, and PD to a semantic features deficit theory (Frank, McDade, & Scott, 1996), which suggests that failure to activate important semantic features of an object results in decreased ability to name the object.

Discourse and Pragmatics. Pragmatics is the social use of language and is typically assessed through discourse production, by eliciting and analyzing a sample of connected language using one or more discourse genres. Discourse is a series of connected utterances, organized around a topic and can be generated by describing a picture, answering open-ended questions, having a monologue, and engaging in topic-specific or naturalistic conversation. Discourse can be evaluated in terms of its coherence and cohesion. Coherence is about how a conversation makes logical sense to a listener based on the salience and relevance of the ideas and concepts expressed by the speaker (Ulatowska & Chapman, 1995). Cohesion concerns the grammatical and lexical relationship of words in a sentence, and sentences in a paragraph. Impaired coherence has been documented in persons with AD, based on evidence of irrelevant, incorrect, or missing information in topic-directed discourse (Ripich & Terrell, 1988; Ulatowska et al., 1988). Examples of measures of cohesion in discourse are use of reference, connectors, and verb tense (Ulatowska & Chapman, 1995). For instance, referential errors, greater use of pronouns, and vague terms (e.g., "thing," "stuff") reveal cohesion impairments in discourse (Dijkstra, Bourgeois, Petrie, Burgio, & Allen-Burge, 2002; Hier et al., 1985; Ripich & Terrell, 1988).

Early discourse deficits in AD have been attributed to deficits in encoding (Kempler, 1995) and in word-finding (Nicholas, Obler, Albert, & Helms-Estabrooks, 1985). Across discourse tasks, persons with AD typically produce less relevant content, more tangential responses, and shorter fragmented sentences (Bucks, Singh, Cuerden, & Wilcock, 2000; Ehrlich, Obler, & Clark, 1997; Nicholas et al., 1985; Ripich & Terrell, 1988; Tomoeda & Bayles, 1993). In picture description tasks, persons with probable AD and MCI were significantly impaired on measures of gist production and picture details than age-matched controls (Chapman et al., 2002), and subtle declines were noted in lexico-semantic processing characterized by anomia, semantic paraphasias, fewer error repairs, and fewer themes identified from the picture (Forbes, Venneri, & Shanks, 2002). Yet, in other picture description research, individuals with mild AD produced meaningful, on-topic, descriptive, and figurative statements (Hopper, Bayles, & Kim, 2001). Of note, the complexity of instructions and stimuli used to elicit discourse can influence client performance, as can dementia severity and concomitant sensory deficits. For example, persons with AD performed better with pictures that contained less information than with more complex pictures (Ehrlich et al., 1997).

During conversation, persons with dementia sometimes make irrelevant or vague comments, and repeat already stated ideas. However, in response to appropriate supports and cues, persons with AD are able to participate in casual conversation (Bourgeois, 1993; Egan, Berube, Racine, Leonard, & Rochon, 2010; Hopper et al., 2001) and provide on-topic opinions in response to questions (Arkin & Mahendra, 2001; Mahendra & Arkin, 2003). By the middle stages of AD, discourse breakdowns and pragmatic impairments are more pronounced. Persons with AD have difficulty maintaining the topic of a conversation and acknowledging their communication partner's perspective (Kempler, 1995; Nicholas et al., 1985; Ripich & Terrell, 1988). Utterances become increasingly inaccurate, repetitive, or lacking in information. However, some social conventions such as turn-taking and eye contact, remain mostly intact. People in the late stages of AD may still attempt to respond to their name or to social greetings, and may express pleasure even when expressive output is rather limited (Bayles et al., 2000).

Oral Reading. The ability to read aloud remains relatively intact until the later stages of AD. For example, single-word reading ability was evident on the Functional Linguistic Communication Inventory (Bayles & Tomoeda, 1994), even in individuals with late-stage AD. Reading is likely to be most impaired in persons with sv-PPA given the inexorable loss of semantic knowledge, and because surface dyslexia is one of its identifying features (Gorno-Tempini et al., 2011). Further, reading involves the interaction of orthographic, phonologic, and semantic systems (Patterson et al., 1994). Patterson et al. (1994) found intact oral reading ability for high-frequency words and words with regular phoneme-grapheme correspondence in persons with sv-PPA, and difficulties with irregularly spelled words and pseudowords. Noble, Glosser, and Grossman (2000) did not find this same pattern of oral reading in persons with AD, FTD, and PPA.

Written Language Production

In general, written language has not been extensively studied in dementia. In general, performance on writing tasks correlates with dementia severity and spoken language performance. Persons with AD demonstrate spared mechanics of writing and well-preserved syntax in writing samples yet reduced language complexity, shorter sentences with fewer words and units of information, spelling errors, and greater use of empty and indefinite phrases (Aarsland, Høien, & Larsen, 1995; Forbes-McKay, Shanks, & Venneri, 2014; Groves-Wright, Neils-Strunjas, Burnett, & O'Neill, 2004; Horner, Heyman, Dawson, & Rogers, 1988; Kemper et al., 1993; Rapcsak, Arthur, Bliklen, & Rubens, 1989). Spelling of irregular words is frequently impaired (Rapcsak et al., 1989) while spelling and writing of single, regular words and nonwords is preserved, as is the ability to spell high-frequency words compared to low-frequency words (Hughes, Graham, Patterson, & Hodges, 1997).

On sentence-level writing, information content, sentence length, number of clauses, and use of verb forms and conjunctions decline as dementia severity increases (Kemper et al., 1993). Syntax is accurate, though simpler, in persons with moderate dementia. On more complex, narrative–writing tasks, persons with dementia have difficulty retrieving information from LTM (Henderson, Buckwalter, Sobel, Freed, & Diz, 1992; LaBarge, Smith, Dick, & Storandt, 1992). By the middle stages of AD, a marked reduction in the ability to write is evident, and perseveration of words and letters is common. Persons with late stage AD are usually unable to respond to writing tasks.

Snowdon and colleagues had a unique opportunity to evaluate writing samples (autobiographies) of 93 women entering the convent when they were in their early 20s and then correlate linguistic features of the writing samples with their cognitive functioning in their later years (ages 75–95). They found that two measures of linguistic ability in early life, idea density and grammatical complexity, were associated with low cognitive test scores in late life, with idea density having stronger and more consistent associations with poor cognitive function. In addition, Alzheimer's disease was confirmed upon autopsy of 14 of the women who had low idea density in early life and died during the study period. The authors concluded that low linguistic ability in early life was a strong predictor of cognitive function and Alzheimer's disease in late life (Snowdon et al., 1996).

Auditory Comprehension

Auditory comprehension in persons with dementia is adversely affected as a result of the pervasive effects on attention and working memory (Kempler, Almor, Tyler, Andersen, & MacDonald, 1998). Social withdrawal and isolation may be a presenting sign of auditory comprehension difficulties. Auditory comprehension appears intact for simple and concrete language, but is impaired for abstract language even in the early stages (Kempler, Van Lancker, & Read, 1988). On a picture–sentence matching task, in which the syntactic complexity of sentences ranged from simple active to center-embedded object relative sentences, persons with MCI demonstrated slight difficulties in syntactic processing compared to healthy controls (Bickel, Pantel, Eysenbach, & Schröder, 2000). Similarly, Waters and Caplan (2002) documented preserved syntactic comprehension in persons with early AD, despite working memory deficits. Further, until the middle stages of the disease, persons with AD can comprehend two- and three-step commands and respond accurately to concrete questions (Bayles & Tomoeda, 1994; Hopper et al., 2001).

In a study of discourse comprehension, persons with early- and middle-stage AD demonstrated poorer comprehension of narratives than healthy controls; yet, participants in both groups better understood main ideas than details, and better understood literal than inferential information (Welland, Lubinski, & Higginbotham, 2002). As AD progresses, comprehension is facilitated when instructions conveyed are short, syntactically simple, and personally relevant. In severe AD, comprehension performance declines for one-step commands, multiple-choice and yes–no questions (Bayles & Tomoeda, 1993), and for sentence–picture matching tasks (Bickel et al., 2000). Comprehension of nonverbal language, such as tone of voice and facial expression, remains relatively spared throughout AD, which is useful information for caregivers when interacting with affected individuals.

Reading Comprehension

In AD, the ability to comprehend written information frequently mirrors auditory comprehension abilities, with gradual decline in the ability to understand text, compared to reading performance pre-diagnosis. Reading comprehension deficits may be attributed to breakdowns in visuoperceptual function, oculomotor function, sustained attention, episodic and working memory (Fernández et al., 2016; Kempler, 1988), or in executive control mechanisms. This makes reading rather effortful for persons with dementia and results in needing to frequently re-read material and difficulty with understanding the gist and processing details. These challenges with reading often cause persons with dementia to lose interest in reading, and to gradually withdraw from reading for leisure.

Persons with dementia are impaired in their ability to draw inferences from discourse-level written material and to answer questions based on content (Creamer & Schmitter-Edgecombe, 2010; Small, Kemper, & Lyons, 1997). In studying single-word reading, several investigators have demonstrated retained ability to read aloud single words without comprehension in moderate and even severe stages of AD (Bayles & Tomoeda, 1994; Raymer & Berndt, 1996). Related to this, findings from some researchers reveal that reading comprehension of single words (Strain, Patterson, Graham, & Hodges, 1998), particularly personally relevant single words, remains spared into moderate stages of AD (Bourgeois, 1992). Grober and Bang (1995) studied sentence comprehension in AD using written sentences that were either paired with pictures simultaneously or removed from view prior to picture presentation. They evaluated the effects of semantic versus syntactic cues on sentence comprehension, finding that sentence comprehension improved when semantic cues were available and demands on working memory were minimized. There is evidence for the utility of such written cues to reshape responsive behaviors (e.g., Bourgeois, Burgio, Schulz, Beach, & Palmer, 1997; Bourgeois et al., 2003) and to improve conversation regarding personally relevant topics (e.g., Benigas & Bourgeois, 2012; Bourgeois, 1992, 1993; Bourgeois & Mason, 1996; Hoerster et al., 2001). See Chapter 6 for a description of use of personalized written cues for persons with dementia.

Vascular Dementia

Vascular dementia is characterized by early-appearing impairments of executive function, attention, and visuospatial function (Levy & Chelune, 2007; Randolph, 1997) with these typically being worse in severity than in AD. However, persons with VaD perform better than those with AD on measures of immediate and delayed verbal memory (Golden et al., 2005), on category fluency tasks, and others tasks that tap into semantic memory. Additionally, persons with VaD perform worse on letter fluency tasks than on category fluency tasks (Mahendra & Engineer, 2009; Poore, Rapport, Fuerst, & Keenan, 2006). On the Arizona Battery for Communication Disorders of Dementia (ABCD; Bayles & Tomoeda, 1993), Mahendra and Engineer (2009) noted that persons with VaD had impaired performance on category naming, object description, and concept definition tasks. Researchers also have documented discourse breakdowns in VaD including empty speech, repetitious statements, tangential responses, and sentence fragments (Mahendra & Engineer, 2009; Vuorinen, Laine, & Rinne, 2000). Figure 3.2 illustrates some differences in performance in VaD versus AD on figure copying, clock drawing, and sentence writing tasks.

Primary Progressive Aphasias

The syndromes associated with FTLD warrant special mention in the description of language characteristics. There are three categories of variants of FTLD – a behavioral variant (bv-FTD), three language variants (called the primary progressive aphasias, or PPAs), and motor variants. Persons with bv-FTD do not initially present with language or memory deficits per se, rather with executive function impairments and significant behavioral changes. Frequently, pragmatics are particularly affected due to disinhibition, stereotypical and repetitive behaviors, apathy, and reduced interest in social interactions. Persons with FTD may perseverate unduly on the same topic, violate turn-taking, and abruptly change conversational topics or leave utterances incomplete. The PPA types are a fluent or semantic variant (sv-PPA), nonfluent and agrammatic variant

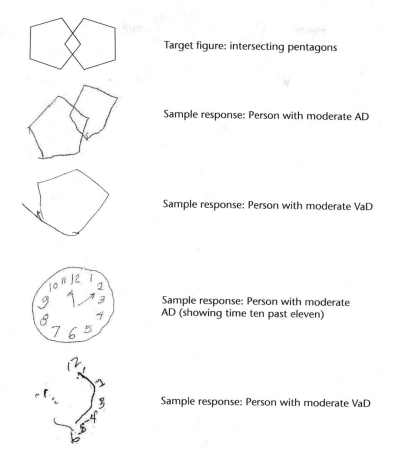

Target figure: intersecting pentagons

Sample response: Person with moderate AD

Sample response: Person with moderate VaD

Sample response: Person with moderate
AD (showing time ten past eleven)

Sample response: Person with moderate VaD

FIGURE 3.2 Comparison of Figure Copying, Clock Drawing, and Written Sentence Generation in Persons with Alzheimer Dementia Versus Vascular Dementia

(nfv-PPA), and a more recently detailed logopenic variant (lv-PPA). These PPAs are characterized by progressive difficulties with producing and comprehending language. Language impairments must be documented for a diagnosis of any of the three identified PPA types (Gorno–Tempini et al., 2011).

When PPA is accompanied by speech that is nonfluent and agrammatic and characterized by anomia and paraphasias, the term *nonfluent or agrammatic PPA (nfv-PPA)* is used. This variant has characteristics similar to Broca's aphasia with spared semantic memory yet significant reduction in expressive speech, impaired repetition, and impaired syntactic processing (e.g., difficulty conjugating verbs). These nonfluent symptoms in nfv-PPA gradually will progress to mutism (Nestor & Hodges, 2000).

When PPA is characterized by speech that is fluent with no syntactic errors and poor auditory comprehension, with severe anomia, surface dyslexia, and an accompanying loss of semantic or conceptual knowledge, the term *semantic variant* or sv-PPA is used. Early in sv-PPA, affected persons present with circumlocutions, semantic paraphasias, and marked impairment on confrontation naming and category fluency tasks (Sapolsky et al., 2011). Over time, as semantic knowledge disintegrates, the severity of anomia increases, as do conversational breakdowns and difficulty comprehending language. Table 3.3 presents the cognitive-communicative characteristics of these four major FTD subtypes.

TABLE 3.3 Cognitive–Communicative Characteristics across FTLD Subtypes

	Behavioral Variant (bv-FTD)	Semantic Dementia (sv-PPA)	Nonfluent PPA (nfv-PPA)	Logopenic PPA (lv-PPA)
Attention				
Sustained	Good	Good	Unimpaired	Good
Divided	Impaired early	Impaired	Impaired	Impaired
Memory				
Sensory	Good	Less impaired	Good	Good
Working	Less impaired	Less impaired	Impaired	Impaired
Episodic	Less impaired	Impaired	Impaired	Impaired
Semantic	Less impaired	Very impaired	Less impaired	Less impaired
Procedural	Less impaired	Less impaired	Less impaired	Good
Executive Function	Impaired	Impaired	Less impaired	Impaired
Visuospatial Function	Impaired	Less impaired	Less impaired	Somewhat spared
Speech	Fluent	Fluent, no syntactic errors	Nonfluent, agrammatic	Reduced rate, paucity of speech
Language	No paraphasias or anomia	Frank anomia; surface dyslexia; loss of conceptual knowledge	Paraphasias present; anomia with spared concept knowledge	Few paraphasias; anomia; impaired single-word comprehension

The logopenic variant of PPA (lv-PPA), which has been identified most recently (Gorno-Tempini et al., 2011; Mahendra, 2012), is characterized by a unique profile of speech and language characteristics that differ from post-stroke aphasia as well as from sv-PPA and nfv-PPA. Persons with logopenic PPA present with overall reduced verbal output (Kertesz et al., 2003), reduced speech rate, use of grammatically simpler but correct sentence structure, and routine word-finding difficulty (Gorno-Tempini et al., 2004, 2011). Further, persons with lv-PPA have impaired auditory comprehension (Henry & Gorno-Tempini, 2010), repetition ability (Gorno-Tempini et al., 2004, 2008), reading (Brambati, Ogar, Neuhaus, Miller, & Gorno-Tempini, 2009), and spelling (Sepelyak et al., 2011).

Behavioral Characteristics

Responsive Behaviors in Persons with Dementia

Behavioral changes in persons with dementia are a direct result of declines in attention, memory, executive function, visuospatial function, and linguistic communication. These deficits can be observed in persons with dementia as disorientation, forgetfulness, delayed responses, reduced mental flexibility, and difficulty self-monitoring. Responsive behaviors that occur in people with dementia due to these challenges commonly include being forgetful and confused, engaging in repetitive vocalizations and other disruptive communication attempts (e.g., shouting), and sometimes becoming agitated and aggressive, or apathetic. The frequency, intensity, and antecedents to these responsive behaviors vary across individuals, the type and severity of dementia, and a variety of environmental factors. In early stages, people with dementia experience challenges in daily functions and activities; they may get lost or disoriented while driving, forget to schedule appointments, forget the location of important items, repeat questions and entire conversations, and experience personality changes and irritable affect. Typically, these responsive behaviors are noticed by family members and may cause conflict, as well as prompt a consult with a physician.

As dementia progresses, responsive behaviors become more varied, frequent, and difficult to manage. Cohen-Mansfield (2000) developed a taxonomy to describe dementia-related behaviors along two dimensions (physical versus verbal, and aggressive versus nonaggressive); see Figure 3.3 for examples of the behaviors in each of the four resulting quadrants. In the middle stages, disruptive and repetitive vocalizations can be especially frustrating for family members, who may attempt to reason and respond to the person with dementia only to find themselves repeating the exact information just a few minutes later. These situations reveal the severity and irreversibility of memory impairments in AD. If not noticed earlier, the functional decline becomes obvious to caregivers. Further, other behaviors such as inappropriately close interactions with strangers, reckless behavior (e.g., with finances), hoarding, hallucinations, delusions, and angry outbursts often become the reason why caregivers begin to feel burnt out. This stage requires careful attention to triggers leading to responsive behaviors and use of positive strategies to prevent the behaviors (e.g., written cues, predictable routines, a supportive environment).

In the later stages, as the more agitated behaviors subside, the person's responsive behaviors slow down and become very repetitive as apathy and lethargy set in. The person is no longer able to engage with the environment and requires assistance for all ADLs. Caregivers report that, counter-intuitively, this period requiring more physical care of the person with dementia is comparatively less stressful because the person's behaviors have mellowed out and are more predictable.

The different dementia syndromes share some behavioral characteristics and have some unique symptoms. In early AD, memory impairments are the dominant clinical signature, causing

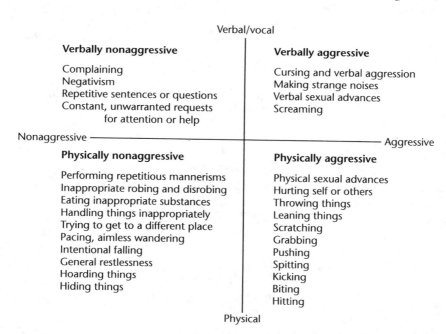

FIGURE 3.3 Behaviors in the CMAI Organized by Dimensions

Source: Reprinted with permission from J. Cohen-Mansfield.

progressive changes in mood, anxiety, agitation, and aggression (Han et al., 2014). In later AD, behaviors are characterized by hallucinations, delusions, and apathy, with changes in sexual behavior, hoarding, and altered night-time routines. Persons with DLB experience complex, fully-formed visual hallucinations, delusions, mood changes, gait changes, and sleep disorders (Cummings, 2003). Parkinson's disease dementia commonly results in mood changes, hallucinations, anxiety, apathy, depression, and irritability (Aarsland, Litvan, & Larsen, 2001; Cummings, 1995). In VaD, depression, agitation, and anxiety are more common and more severe than in AD (Aharon-Peretz, Kliot, & Tomer, 2000); delusions, personality changes, disinhibition, unexpected incontinence, and symptoms associated with specific areas of focal damage (e.g., anosognosia from right parietal lesion or aphasia from left hemisphere lesions) also may be seen (Cummings, 2003). The behavioral variant of FTLD results in prominent behavioral symptoms early in the disease process, most notably disordered personal conduct, dramatically altered personality, and disinhibition (Cummings, 2003). Additionally, FTLD is accompanied by distractibility, indifference, and apathy, as well as by obsessive-compulsive tendencies and stereotypic behaviors. The lack of depressive symptoms and later onset of memory impairments distinguishes FTLD from AD (Levy et al., 1998). Based on an analysis of the *Clinical Dementia Rating Scale* (Morris, 1993), after matching for age and MMSE score, bv-FTD caused more severe impairments than AD or sv-PPA in judgment, problem solving, community affairs, home and hobbies, and personal care (Rosen et al., 2004). In late stages of dementia, access to vocabulary is severely limited and only limited functional communication is possible.

Responsive behaviors can be explained using a biopsychosocial model and a theory of unmet needs – the *Need-Driven Compromised Behavior Model* (Algase et al., 1996, Beck et al., 1998), seen in Figure 3.4. Persons with dementia have varied biological, physical, cognitive social, emotional, and spiritual needs that they are often unable to communicate due to cognitive-communicative deficits. Often, these behavioral expressions of needs are misinterpreted as maladaptive behaviors that require a restrictive intervention (i.e., physical or chemical restraint). Physical and chemical restraints do not build esteem and violate the dignity of persons with dementia, often leading to worse responsive behaviors. Perhaps the best case against such restraints is that they do not address the need of the person with dementia that led to the responsive behavior in the first place.

Relationships Among Cognitive-Communicative Characteristics and Behaviors in Dementias

Responsive behaviors can be explained by deficits in memory and communication that make it difficult for the person to communicate needs. Teasing apart the specific deficit that is causing a behavior can be difficult, as there can be more than one explanation for a behavior. Sensory memory deficits might prevent the recognition of common objects, people, or locations, resulting in confusion and, possibly, agitation. Working memory deficits might result in failure to hold on to information while it is being manipulated, impacting ability to follow verbal instructions, keep track of a conversation, or process the answer to a question. Inability to access degraded information from LTM leads to errors in selecting communicative responses appropriate for the situation, or sequencing the steps of a procedure for a hobby or ADL, leading to loss of interest in long-term hobbies and avoidance of communicative situations. For instance, a person with dementia likely does not respond to the prompt, "It's time to get ready," with the behaviors of getting up, and putting on a coat and shoes. Such lack of expected responses to common, previously familiar, sensory stimuli can make a person with dementia appear uncooperative, unresponsive, hesitant, or confused, while simultaneously causing frustration for caregivers. The solution is for the caregiver or clinician to examine the cause of this failure to respond. Perhaps the statement was not encoded

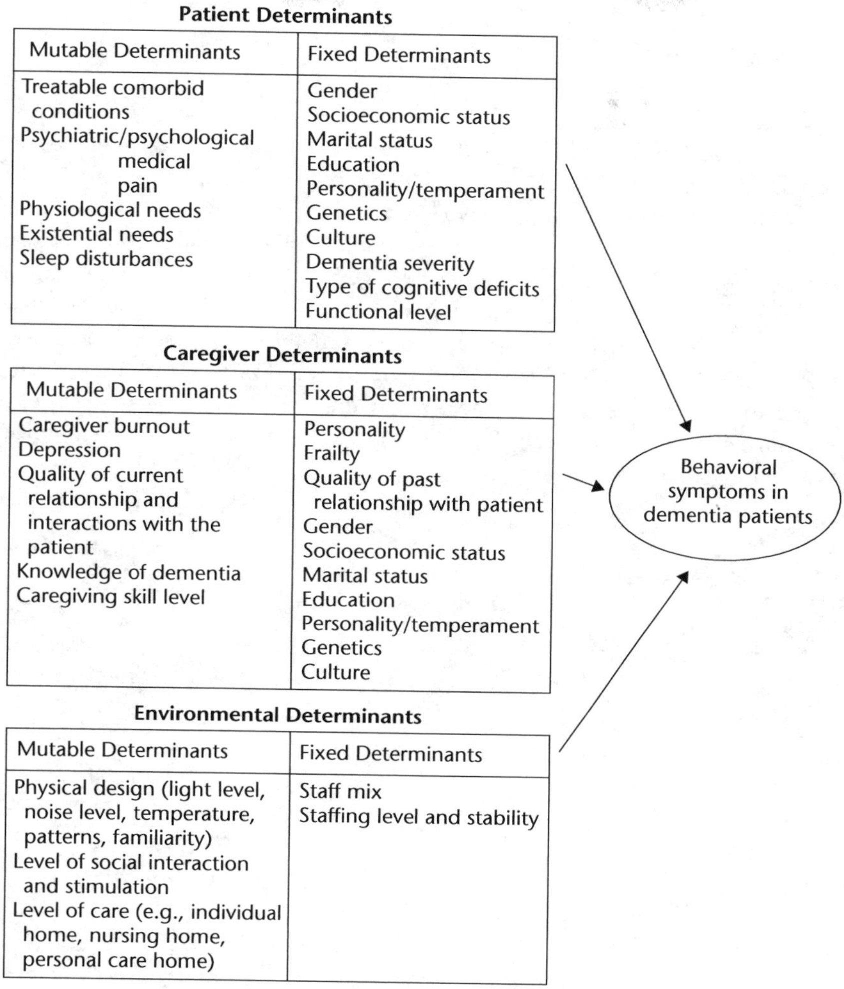

Patient Determinants

Mutable Determinants	Fixed Determinants
Treatable comorbid conditions Psychiatric/psychological 　　medical 　　pain Physiological needs Existential needs Sleep disturbances	Gender Socioeconomic status Marital status Education Personality/temperament Genetics Culture Dementia severity Type of cognitive deficits Functional level

Caregiver Determinants

Mutable Determinants	Fixed Determinants
Caregiver burnout Depression Quality of current 　relationship and 　interactions with the 　patient Knowledge of dementia Caregiving skill level	Personality Frailty Quality of past 　relationship with patient Gender Socioeconomic status Marital status Education Personality/temperament Genetics Culture

Environmental Determinants

Mutable Determinants	Fixed Determinants
Physical design (light level, 　noise level, temperature, 　patterns, familiarity) Level of social interaction 　and stimulation Level of care (e.g., individual 　home, nursing home, 　personal care home)	Staff mix Staffing level and stability

Behavioral symptoms in dementia patients

FIGURE 3.4 Determinants of Behavioral Symptoms in Persons with Dementia

Source: Kunik et al., 2003. Reprinted with permission.

auditorily, leading to no response or a delayed response; or working memory deficits prevent holding onto the sentence to allow comprehension; or semantic stores are degraded and prevent comprehension. Further, specific responsive behaviors, such as wandering, pacing, sundowning, and repetitive questions can be explained as problems with encoding, consolidation, and retrieval, as illustrated in Box 3.3.

Any behavior represents an interaction between a person and their environment. (See Table 3.4 for types of memory deficits and related difficulties and responsive behaviors.) Caregivers should reframe responsive behaviors (e.g., disruptive vocalizations or striking out) as unsuccessful communicative attempts, and enact strategies to respond to the needs of the person with dementia. From this vantage point, a speech-language pathologist (SLP) has a key role in helping build communication bridges by providing supports to both persons with dementia and their caregivers, in accordance with the life participation approach (see Chapters 1 and 4 for descriptions of relevant social models). The SLP (often in collaboration with other health professionals) can facilitate the

---

Box 3.3 Case Study

Mr. Araujo asks his wife to get a broom from the kitchen closet so that he can sweep the leaves off the front porch. She does not return after a short amount of time. He goes in to look for her, and finds her holding the fridge door open and looking inside. He might think she was deliberately disregarding his request. More likely, however, she fully intended to get the broom and return to the task of sweeping leaves, but became distracted being in the kitchen, opened the fridge, and lost track of her intended plan. When asked to recall the original request, she may not remember the request, nor be able to respond what she was looking for in the fridge, or if she was planning to eat or drink something. The cause of this change of plans may be that the original request to get the broom was understood but not held suffi-ciently long in working memory to enable completing the task. Thus, when a distractor appeared while completing the original task, it triggered a new behavior, preventing comple-tion of the original request.

TABLE 3.4 Classifying Language Deficits and Responsive Behaviors by Memory Subsystem

Sensory Memory	Working Memory	Long-Term Memory
Problems with registration, recognition, and identification	Problems with encoding and decoding	Problems with retrieval
Visual agnosia: does not recognize common objects; puts objects in wrong places	Repetitive questions; failure to encode answer	Word-finding problems: specific words, facts, and names of familiar persons, places, and events; uses wrong name
Sundowning: does not recognize own home	Follows caregiver; forgets caregiver is temporarily in the other room	States erroneous information: lying and accusations
Repetitive tactile manipulation; does not recognize object	Uncooperative, may not follow directions: failure to encode or decode verbal stimuli	Disruptive vocalization: inability to access words to express wants and needs
Delusions; misidentifies people, objects, places		Forgets how to dress, bathe, feed, and toilet self
Hallucinations: sees people and objects that are not there	Agitation, pacing: failure to encode responses to anxiety-induced behavior	Forgets how to use telephone and other familiar implements
Distracted by other sensory stimuli; sensory overload		Does not complete tasks
		Apathy: forgets what to do
		Wandering: forgets where to go

---

assessment of the behavior and unmet needs, and then develop an intervention plan, and consult with nursing personnel on a functional maintenance plan. Intervention usually involves encourag-ing both the caregivers and person with dementia to use alternate modes of verbal and nonverbal expression to communicate with each other about needs and care, and to engage the person in meaningful interactions and activities, while preserving their dignity and autonomy.

Clinicians can develop interventions to modify responsive behaviors using visual and auditory cues or low-tech AAC boards, especially when behaviors are expressed verbally (e.g., repeated requests or questions). If physically nonaggressive behaviors, such as wandering or restlessness, are interpreted as memory impairments (i.e., forgets destination, or forgets what to do), SLPs may attempt interventions to increase awareness and orientation of place and to facilitate engagement in meaningful activities. Verbally and physically aggressive behaviors also can be identified as viable targets for cognitive-communicative intervention. It is important to consider that these difficult behaviors are in fact, attempts to communicate an unmet need and, when ignored or misinterpreted, result in increasing frustration and escalating intensity of the behavior in question. Physically aggressive behaviors directed at others (i.e., hitting, kicking) might be expressions of extreme displeasure, discomfort, or resentment. Alternatively, these aggressive behaviors may simply be inappropriate attempts to gain attention or seek interaction. In such cases, it may be essential to first respond to a client's need for social conversation and companionship.

Efforts to identify the triggers of responsive behaviors will involve soliciting information from the person and others in the environment, and even observing the person and the situation. Sometimes, there are external stimuli such as a loud overhead speaker, a cold room, or physical pain that distress a client; other times, the person is lonely and bored, and becomes anxious sitting in a room alone. A knowledgeable caregiver's perspective may be needed to understand the responsive behavior. An SLP may observe potential causes that have gone unnoticed by the typical caregivers by reading chart notes, talking to the nursing and/or dietary staff, and carefully studying the environment to consider modifications.

Finally, clinicians need to take ownership of their role in contributing to person-centered care by scanning the physical, cognitive, social, and attitudinal environment in which our clients live, to determine what causes or reinforces a client's responsive behaviors, and what supports meaningful engagement. The challenge is to find ways to enhance positive, pleasant, and meaningful communicative interactions and engagement in activities. In Chapter 5, the role of the SLP in assessing cognitive-communicative abilities and deficits, responsive behaviors, and the impact on participation and quality of life is further described. Chapters 6 through 8 describe the role of the SLP in designing and delivering interventions to address meaningful engagement in activities and improved quality of life despite the cognitive-communicative impairments of dementia. Chapters 9 and 10 provide discussion of family and staff caregiver interventions using the framework of the impact of cognitive-communicative skills and deficits on adaptive behaviors and caregiving interactions.

Conclusion

This chapter provided a detailed description of the effects of AD and select dementias on multiple domains of cognition and communication. Studying the dementia syndromes and their cognitive-communicative profiles reveals both shared and distinctive characteristics across dementia types. Perhaps, even more importantly, these profiles reveal that there are residual strengths in each dementia syndrome just as there are hallmark areas of significant impairment. Another perspective introduced in this chapter is how these cognitive-communicative changes are reflected in responsive behaviors seen in persons with dementia. This understanding directly informs our approach to comprehensive assessment, and sets the stage for clinicians to conduct person-centered assessments that reveal both strengths and limitations so that this data may strongly support evidence-based treatment planning for all persons with dementia. Finally, as our understanding of distinct dementia syndromes improves, much more research is needed to better understand profiles of cognitive-communicative function in order to drive the development of innovative clinical interventions.

Acknowledgments

Preparation of this chapter was partly supported by a grant to the first author from The California Wellness Foundation *(Grant # 2012–048: 2012–2017).*

References

Aarsland, D., Høien, T., & Larsen, J. (1995). Alexia and agraphia in dementia of the Alzheimer type. In M. Bergener & S. Finkel (Eds.), *Treating Alzheimer's and other dementias* (pp. 298–308). New York: Springer.

Aarsland, D., Litvan, I., & Larsen, J. P. (2001). Neuropsychiatric symptoms of patients with progressive supranuclear palsy and Parkinson's disease. *Journal of Neuropsychiatry and Clinical Neurosciences, 13*(1), 43–49.

Adlam, A-L., Patterson, K., Rogers, T., Nestor, P., Salmond, C., Acosta-Cabronero, J., & Hodges, J. (2006). Semantic dementia and fluent primary progressive aphasia: Two sides of the same coin? *Brain, 129*(11): 3066–80. doi:10.1093/brain/awl285.

Aharon-Peretz, J., Kliot, D., & Tomer, R. (2000). Behavioral differences between white matter lacunar dementia and Alzheimer's disease: A comparison on the neuropsychiatric inventory. *Dementia and Geriatric Cognitive Disorders, 11*(5), 294–298.

Algase, D. L., Beck, C., Kolanowski, A., Whall, A., Berent, S., Richards, K., & Beattie, E. (1996). Need-driven dementia-compromised behavior: An alternative view of disruptive behavior. *American Journal of Alzheimer's Disease and Other Dementias, 11*(6), 10–19.

Allain, P., Havet-Thomassin, V., Verny, C., Gohier, B., Lancelot, C., Besnard, J., Fasotti, L., & Le Gall, D. (2011). Evidence for deficits on different components of theory of mind in Huntington's disease. *Neuropsychology, 25*, 741–751.

Alzheimer's Association (2016). 2016 Alzheimer's disease facts and figures. *Alzheimer's and Dementia, 12*(4), 1–80.

Amieva, H., Phillips, L. H., Della Sala, S., & Henry, J. D. (2004). Inhibitory functioning in Alzheimer's disease. *Brain, 127*, 949–964.

Appell, I., Kertesz, A., & Fisman, M. (1982). A study of language functioning in Alzheimer patients. *Brain and Language, 17*(1), 73–91.

Arkin, S., & Mahendra, N. (2001). Discourse analysis of Alzheimer's patients before and after intervention: Methodology and outcomes. *Aphasiology, 15*(6), 533–569.

Assal, F., & Cummings, J. L. (2003). Cortical and frontosubcortical dementias: Differential diagnosis. In V. O. Emery & T. E. Oxman (Eds.), *Dementia: Presentations, differential diagnosis, and nosology* (pp. 239–262). Baltimore: Johns Hopkins University Press.

Au, A., Chan, A. S., & Chiu, H. (2003). Verbal learning in Alzheimer's dementia. *Journal of the International Neuropsychological Society, 9*(3), 363–375.

Baddeley, A. D. (1986). *Working memory.* Oxford, UK: Oxford University Press.

Baddeley, A. (1992). Working memory. *Science, 255*(5044), 556–569.

Baddeley, A. (1995). The psychology of memory. In A. D. Baddeley, B. A. Wilson, & F. N. Watts (Eds.), *Handbook of memory disorders* (pp. 3–26). New York: John Wiley.

Baddeley, A. D. (2000). The episodic buffer: A new component of working memory? *Trends in Cognitive Science, 4*, 417–423.

Baddeley, A. D., Baddeley, H. A., Bucks, R. S., & Wilcock, G. K. (2001). Attentional control in Alzheimer's disease. *Brain, 124*(8), 1492–1508.

Baddeley, A. D., & Hitch, G. (1974). Working Memory. In G. H. Bower (Ed.), *The psychology of learning and motivation: Advances in research and theory* (Vol. 8, pp. 47–89). New York: Academic Press.

Ballard, C., Aarsland, D., Francis, P., & Corbett, A. (2013). Neuropsychiatric symptoms in patients with dementias associated with cortical Lewy bodies: Pathophysiology, clinical features, and pharmacological management. *Drugs & Aging, 30*, 603–611. doi:10.1007/s40266-013-0092-x.

Ballard, C., O'Brien, J., Gray, A., Cormack, F., Ayre, G., Rowan, E., … Tovee, M. (2001). Attention and fluctuating attention in patients with dementia with Lewy bodies and Alzheimer disease. *Archives of Neurology, 58*(6), 977–982.

Ballasteros, S., Reales, J. M., & Mayas, J. (2007). Picture priming in normal aging and Alzheimer's disease. *Psicothema, 19*(2), 239–244.

Barresi, B. A., Nicholas, M., Connor, L. T., Obler, L. K., & Albert, M. L. (2000). Semantic degradation and lexical access in age-related naming failures. *Aging, Neuropsychology, and Cognition, 7*(3), 1–10.

Baudic, S., Dalla Barba, G., Thibaudet, M. C., Smagghe, A., Remy, P., & Trakov, L. (2006). Executive function deficits in early Alzheimer's disease and their relations with episodic memory. *Archives of Clinical Neuropsychology, 21*(1), 15–21.

Bayles, K. A. (1991). Age at onset of Alzheimer's disease: Relation to language dysfunction. *Archives of Neurology, 48*(2), 155–159.

Bayles, K. A. (2001). Understanding the neuropsychological syndrome of dementia. *Seminars in Speech and Language, 22*(4), 251–260.

Bayles, K. A. (2003). Effects of working memory deficits on the communicative functioning of Alzheimer's dementia patients. *Journal of Communication Disorders, 36*(3), 209–219.

Bayles, K. A., & Kim, E. S. (2003). Improving the functioning of individuals with Alzheimer's disease: Emergence of behavioral interventions. *Journal of Communication Disorders, 36*(5), 327–343.

Bayles, K. A., & Tomoeda, C. K. (1983). Confrontation naming impairment in dementia. *Brain and Language, 19*(1), 98–114.

Bayles, K. A., & Tomoeda, C. K. (1993). *The Arizona battery of communication disorders of dementia.* Austin, TX: Pro-Ed.

Bayles, K. A., & Tomoeda, C. K. (1994). *Functional linguistic communication inventory.* Austin, TX: Pro-Ed.

Bayles, K. A., & Tomoeda, C. K. (2013). *Cognitive-communication disorders of dementia: Definition, diagnosis and treatment* (2nd ed.). San Diego, CA: Plural Publishing, Inc.

Bayles, K. A., Tomoeda, C. K., Cruz, R. F., & Mahendra, M. (2000). Communication abilities of individuals with late-state Alzheimer disease. *Alzheimer Disease and Associated Disorders, 14*(3), 176–181.

Bayles, K. A., Tomoeda, C. K., Kaszniak, A. W., & Trosset, M. W. (1991). Alzheimer's disease effects on semantic memory: Loss of structure or impaired processing? *Journal of Cognitive Neuroscience, 3*(2), 166–182.

Beck, C., Frank, L., Chumbler, N. R., O'Sullivan, P, Vogelpohl, T. S., Rasin, J., … Baldwin, B. (1998). Correlates of disruptive behavior in severely cognitively impaired nursing home residents. *The Gerontologist, 38*(2), 189–198.

Belleville, S., Chertkow, H., & Gauthier, S. (2007). Working memory and control of attention in persons with Alzheimer's disease and mild cognitive impairment. *Neuropsychology, 21*(4), 458–469.

Benigas, J. E., & Bourgeois, M. S. (2012). Evaluating oral reading and reading comprehension in patients with dementia: A comparison of generic and personally relevant stimuli. *Non-Pharmacological Therapies in Dementia, 2*(1), 41–54.

Benton, A. L. (1974). *Revised visual retention test: Clinical and experimental application* (4th ed.). New York: Psychological Corporation.

Bickel, C., Pantel, J., Eysenbach, K., & Schröder, J. (2000). Syntactic comprehension deficits in Alzheimer's disease. *Brain and Language, 71*(3), 432–448.

Biel, M., & Hula, W. (2016). Attention. In M. Kimbaro (Ed.). *Cognitive-communication disorders* (2nd ed.). San Diego, CA: Plural Publishing.

Bier, N., Brambati, S., Macoir, J., Paquette, G., Schmitz, X., Belleville, S., Faucher, C., & Joubert, S. (2015). Relying on procedural memory to enhance independence in daily living activities: Smartphone use in a case of semantic dementia. *Neuropsychological Rehabilitation, 25*(6), 913–935. doi:10.1080/09602011.2014.997745.

Blake, M. L., Duffy, J. R., Boeve, B. F., Ahlskog, J. E., & Maraganore, D. M. (2003). Speech and language disorders associated with corticobasal degeneration. *Journal of Medical Speech-Language Pathology, 11*(3), 131–146.

Borrini, G., Dall'Ora, P., Della Sala, S., Marinelli, L., & Spinnler, H. (1989). Autobiographical memory: Sensitivity to age and education of a standardized enquiry. *Psychological Medicine, 19*(1), 215–224.

Bourgeois, M. S. (1992). Evaluating memory wallets in conversations with patients with dementia. *Journal of Speech and Hearing Research, 35*(6), 1344–1357.

Bourgeois, M. S. (1993). Effects of memory aids on the dyadic conversations of individuals with dementia. *Journal of Applied Behavior Analysis, 26*(1), 77–87.

Bourgeois, M. (2014). *Memory & communication aids for people with dementia*. Baltimore: Health Professions Press.

Bourgeois, M. S., Burgio, L. D., Schulz, R., Beach, S., & Palmer, B. (1997). Modifying repetitive verbalization of community dwelling patients with AD. *The Gerontologist, 37*(1), 30–39.

Bourgeois, M. S., Camp, C., Rose, M., White, B., Malone, M., Carr, J., & Rovine, M. (2003). A comparison of training strategies to enhance use of external aids by persons with dementia. *Journal of Communication Disorders, 36*(5), 361–378.

Bourgeois, M. S., & Mason, L. A. (1996). Memory wallet intervention in an adult day care setting. *Behavioral Interventions, 11*(1), 3–18.

Brambati, S. M., Ogar, J., Neuhaus, J., Miller, B. L., & Gorno-Tempini, M. L. (2009). Reading disorders in primary progressive aphasia: A behavioral and neuroimaging study. *Neuropsychologia, 47*(8–9), 1893–1900.

Bridges, K. A., & Van Lancker Sidtis, D. (2013) Formulaic language in Alzheimer's disease. *Aphasiology, 27*(7), 799–810. doi:10.1080/02687038.2012.757760.

Bucks, R. S., Singh, S., Cuerden, J. M., & Wilcock, G. K. (2000). Analysis of spontaneous, conversational speech in dementia of Alzheimer type: Evaluation of an objective technique for analysing lexical performance. *Aphasiology, 4*(1), 71–91.

Budson, A. E. (2009). Understanding memory dysfunction. *The Neurologist, 15*: 71–79.

Caine, E. D., Bamford, K. A., Schiffer, R. B., Shoulson, I., & Levy, S. (1986). A controlled neuropsychological comparison of Huntington's disease and multiple sclerosis. *Archives of Neurology, 43*(3), 249–254.

Camp, C. J. (2001). From efficacy to effectiveness to diffusion: Making the transitions in dementia intervention research. *Neuropsychological Rehabilitation, 11*(3–4), 495–517.

Camp, C. J., & McKitrick, L. A. (1992). Memory interventions in Alzheimer's-type dementia populations: Methodological and theoretical issues. In R. L. West & J. D. Sinnott (Eds.), *Everyday memory and aging: Current research and methodology* (pp. 155–172). New York: Springer-Verlag.

Campbell-Taylor, I. (1995). Motor speech changes. In R. Lubinski (Ed.), *Dementia and communication* (pp. 70–82). San Diego, CA: Singular Publishing.

Cannatà, A., Alberoni, M., Franceschi, M., & Mariani, C. (2002). Frontal impairment in subcortical ischemic vascular dementia in comparison to Alzheimer's disease. *Dementia and Geriatric Cognitive Disorders, 13*(2), 101–111.

Caselli, R. (2000). Visual syndromes as the presenting feature of degenerative brain disease. *Seminars in Neurology, 20*(1), 139–144.

Cerciello, M., Isella, V., Proserpi, A., & Papagno, C. (2016). Assessment of free and cued recall in Alzheimer's disease and vascular and frontotemporal dementia with the 24-item Grober and Buschke test. *Neurological Sciences*, doi:10.1007/s10072-016-2722-7.

Chapman, S. B., Zientz, J., Weiner, M., Rosenberg, R., Frawley, W., & Burns, M. H. (2002). Discourse changes in early Alzheimer's disease, mild cognitive impairment, and normal aging. *Alzheimer Disease and Associated Disorders, 16*(3), 177–186.

Chenery, H. J., Murdoch, B. E., & Ingram, J. C. L. (1996). An investigation of confrontation naming performance in Alzheimer's dementia as a function of disease severity. *Aphasiology, 10*(5), 423–441.

Chong, R. K. Y., Horak, F. B., Frank, J., & Kaye, J. (1999). Sensory organization for balance: Specific deficits in Alzheimer's but not in Parkinson's disease. *Journal of Gerontology, 54*(3), M122–M128.

Clark, L. J., Gatz, M., Zheng, L., Chen, Y. L., McCleary, C., & Mack W. J. (2009). Longitudinal verbal fluency in normal aging, preclinical, and prevalent Alzheimer's disease. *American Journal of Alzheimer's Disease and Other Dementias, 24*, 461–468.

Cohen-Mansfield, J. (2000). Approaches to the management of disruptive behavior. In M. P. Lawton & R. Rubenstein (Eds.), *Interventions in dementia care: Toward improving quality of life* (pp. 39–65). New York: Springer.

Collette, F., Delrue, G., Van Der Linden, M., & Salmon, E. (2001). The relationships between executive dysfunction and frontal hypometabolism in Alzheimer's disease. *Brain and Cognition, 47*, 272–275.

Connor, L. T., Spiro, A., III, Obler, L. K., & Albert, M. L. (2004). Change in object naming ability during adulthood. *Journal of Gerontology Series B: Psychological Sciences and Social Sciences, 59*(5), 203–209.

Craik, F. I. M. (2000). Age-related changes in human memory. In D. C. Park & N. Schwarz (Eds.) *Cognitive aging: A primer* (pp. 75–92). Philadelphia: Taylor and Francis.

Creamer, S., & Schmitter-Edgecombe, M. (2010). Narrative comprehension in Alzheimer's disease: Assessing inferences and memory operations with a think-aloud procedure. *Neuropsychology, 24*(3), 279–290.

Cuerva, A. G., Sabe, L., Kuzis, G., Tiberti, C., Dorrego, F., & Starkstein, S. (2001). Theory of mind and pragmatic abilities in dementia. *Neuropsychiatry, Neuropsychology and Behavioral Neurology, 14*(3), 153–158.

Cummings, J. L. (1995). Behavioral and psychiatric symptoms associated with Huntington's disease. *Advances in Neurology, 65*, 179–186.

Cummings, J. L. (2003). *The neuropsychiatry of Alzheimer's disease and related dementias*. London, UK: Martin Dunitz.

Damasio, A. R. (1999). *The feeling of what happens: Body and emotion in the making of consciousness*. New York: Harcourt, Brace.

de Lira, J. O., Ortiz, K. Z., Campanha, A. C., Bertolucci, P. H. F., & Minett, T. S. C. (2011). Microlinguistic aspects of the oral narrative in patients with Alzheimer's disease. *International Psychogeriatrics, 23*(3), 404–412.

Devanand, D. P. (2016). Olfactory identification deficits, cognitive decline, and dementia in older adults. *American Journal of Geriatric Psychiatry, 24*(12), 1151–1157. doi:10.1016/j.jagp. 2016.08.010.

Devanand, D. P., Michaels-Marston, K. S., Liu, X., Pelton, G. H., Padilla, M., Marder, K., … Mayeux, R. (2000). Olfactory deficits in patients with mild cognitive impairment predict Alzheimer's disease at follow-up. *American Journal of Psychiatry, 157*(9), 1399–1405.

Dijkstra, K., Bourgeois, M. S., Allen, R. S., & Burgio, L. D. (2004). Conversational coherence: Discourse analysis of older adults with and without dementia. *Journal of Neurolinguistics, 17*, 263–283.

Dijkstra, K., Bourgeois, M., Petrie, G., Burgio, L., & Allen-Burge, R. (2002). My recaller is on vacation: Discourse analysis of nursing home residents with dementia. *Discourse Processes, 33*(1), 53–76.

Downes, J. J., Priestly, N. M., Doran, M., Ferran, J., Ghadiiali, E., & Cooper, P. (1999). Intellectual, mnemonic, and frontal functions in dementia with Lewy bodies: A comparison with early and advanced Parkinson's disease. *Behavioral Neurology, 11*(3), 173–183.

Duff Canning, S. J., Leach, L., Stuss, D., Ngo, L., & Black, S. E. (2004). Diagnostic utility of abbreviated fluency measures in Alzheimer disease and vascular dementia. *Neurology, 62*(4), 556–562.

Duffy, J. (2012). *Motor speech disorders: Substrates, differential diagnosis, and management* (3rd ed.). St. Louis, MO: Elsevier Mosby.

Duffy, J., Strand, E. A. Clark, H., Machulda, M., Whitwell, J. L., & Josephs, K. A. (2015). Primary progressive apraxia of speech: Clinical features and acoustic and neurologic correlates. *American Journal of Speech-Language Pathology, 24*, 88–100.

Duval, C., Bejanin, A., Piolino, P., Laisney, M., de La Sayette, V., Belliard, S., Eustache, F., & Desgranges, B. (2012). Theory of mind impairments in patients with semantic dementia. *Brain, 135*, 228–241.

Egan, M., Berube, D., Racine, G., Leonard, C., & Rochon, E. (2010). Methods to enhance verbal communication between individuals with Alzheimer's disease and their formal and informal caregivers: A systematic review. *International Journal of Alzheimer's Disease, 2010*, 1–12. doi:10.4061/2010/906818.

Ehrlich, J. S., Obler, L. K., & Clark, L. (1997). Ideational and semantic contributions to narrative production in adults with dementia of the Alzheimer type. *Journal of Communication Disorders, 30*(2), 79–99.

Ekman, P., & Friesen, W. (1975). *Pictures of facial affect*. Palo Alto, CA: Consulting Psychologists Press.

Emery, V. O. B. (2000). Language impairment in dementia of the Alzheimer type: A hierarchical decline? *International Journal of Psychiatry in Medicine, 30*(2), 145–164.

Ferman, T. J., & Boeve, B. F. (2007). Dementia with Lewy Bodies. *Neurology Clinics, 25*(3), 741–761.

Fernández, G., Manes, F., Politi, L. E., Orozco, D., Schumacher, M., Castro, L., Agamennoni, O., & Rotstein, N. P. (2016). Patients with mild Alzheimer's Disease fail when using their working memory: Evidence from the eye tracking technique. *Journal of Alzheimers Disease, 50*(3), 827–838. doi:10.3233/JAD-150265.

Ferris, S. H., & Farlow, M. (2013). Language impairment in Alzheimer's disease and benefits of acetylcholinesterase inhibitors. *Clinical Interventions in Aging, 8*, 1007–1014.

Fitten, L. J., Perryman, K. M., Wilkinson, C. J., Little, R. J., Burns, M. M., Pachana, N., … Ganzell, S. (1995). Alzheimer and vascular dementias and driving. *Journal of the American Medical Association, 273*(17), 1360–1365.

Fleischman, D. A., & Gabrieli, J. D. E. (1998). Repetition priming in normal aging and Alzheimer's disease: A review of findings and new theories. *Psychology and Aging, 13,* 88–119.

Fleischman, D. A., Gabrieli, J. D. E., Reminger, S., Rinaldi, J., Morrell, F., & Wilson, R. (1995). Conceptual priming in perceptual identification for patients with Alzheimer's disease and a patient with right occipital lobectomy. *Neuropsychology, 9*(2), 187–197.

Foldi, N. S., Jutagir, R., Davidoff, D., & Gould, T. (1992). Selective attention skills in Alzheimer's disease: Performance on graded cancellation tests varying in density and complexity. *Journal of Gerontology, 47*(3), 146–153.

Foldi, N. S., Lobosco, J. J., & Schaefer, L. A. (2002). The effect of attentional dysfunction in Alzheimer's disease: Theoretical and practical implications. *Seminars in Speech and Language, 23*(2), 139–150.

Foldi, N. S., Schaefer, L. A., White, R., Johnson, R. E. C., Berger, J. T., Carney, M. T., & Macina, L. O. (2005). Effects of graded levels of physical similarity and density on visual selective attention in patients with Alzheimer's disease. *Neuropsychology, 19*(1), 5–17.

Forbes, K. E., Venneri, A., & Shanks, M. F. (2002). Distinct patterns of spontaneous speech deterioration: An early predictor of Alzheimer's disease. *Brain & Cognition, 48*(2–3), 356–361.

Forbes-McKay, K. E., Shanks, M. F., & Venneri, A. (2014). Charting the decline in spontaneous writing in Alzheimer's disease: A longitudinal study. *Acta Neuropsychiatrica, 26*(4), 246–252.

Frank, E. M., McDade, H. L., & Scott, W. K. (1996). Naming in dementia secondary to Parkinson's, Huntington's, and Alzheimer's diseases. *Journal of Communication Disorders, 29*(3), 183–197.

Freeman, R. Q., Giovannetti, T., Lamar, M., Cloud, B. S., Stern, R. A., Kaplan, E., & Libon, D. J. (2000). Visuocontructional problems in dementia: Contributions of executive systems functions. *Neuropsychology, 14*(3), 415–426.

Fried-Oken, M., Beukelman, D. R., & Hux, K. (2011). Current and future AAC research considerations for adults with acquired cognitive and communicative impairments. *Assistive Technology, 24*(1), 56–66.

Fried-Oken, M., Rowland, C., Daniels, D., Dixon, M., Fuller, B., … Oken, B. (2012). AAC to support conversation in persons with moderate Alzheimer's disease. *Augmentative and Alternative Communication, 28*(4), 219–231.

Gagnon, L. G., & Belleville, S. (2011). Working memory in mild cognitive impairment and Alzheimer's disease: Contribution of forgetting and predictive value of complex span tasks. *Neuropsychology, 25*(2), 226–236. doi:10.1037/a0020919.

Gardner, E. P., Martin, J. H., & Jessell, T. M. (2000). The bodily senses. In E. Kandel, J. Schwartz, & T. Jessell (Eds.), *Principles of neural science* (pp. 430–450). New York: McGraw-Hill.

Ghosh, B. C., Calder, A. J., Peers, P. V., Lawrence, A. D., Acosta-Cabronero, J., & Pereira, J. M., Hodges, J. R., & Rowe, J. B. (2012). Social cognitive deficits and their neural correlates in progressive supranuclear palsy. *Brain, 135,* 2089–2102.

Glosser, G., Baker, K. M., de Vries, J. J., Alavi, A., Grossman, M., & Clark, C. M. (2002). Disturbed visual processing contributes to impaired reading in Alzheimer's disease. *Neuropsychologia, 40*(7), 902–909.

Glosser, G., Gallo, J. L., Clark, C. M., & Grossman, M. (2002). Memory encoding and retrieval in frontotemporal dementia and Alzheimer's disease. *Neuropsychology, 16*(2), 190–196.

Golden, Z., Bouvier, M., Selden, J., Mattis, K., Todd, M., & Golden, C. (2005). Differential performance of Alzheimer's and vascular dementia patients on a brief battery of neuropsychological tests. *International Journal of Neuroscience, 115,* 1569–1577.

Gorno-Tempini, M. L., Brambati, S. M., Ginex, V. et al. (2008). The logopenic or phonological variant of primary progressive aphasia. *Neurology, 71*(16), 1227–1234.

Gorno-Tempini, M. L., Dronker, N. F., Rankin, K. P. et al. (2004). Cognition and anatomy in three variants of primary progressive aphasia. *Annals of Neurology, 55*(3), 335–346.

Gorno-Tempini, M. L., Hillis, A. E., Weintraub, S., Kertesz, A., Mendez, M., … Grossman, M. (2011). Classification of primary progressive aphasia and its variants. *Neurology, 76*(11), 1006–1014.

Grafman, J., Litvan, I., Gomez, C., & Chase, T. N. (1990). Frontal lobe function in progressive supranuclear palsy. *Archives of Neurology, 47*(5), 553–558.

Graham, K. S., & Hodges, J. R. (1997). Differentiating the roles of the hippocampal complex and the neocortex in long-term memory storage: Evidence from the study of semantic dementia and Alzheimer's disease. *Neuropsychology, 11*(1), 77–89.

Gregory, C., Lough, S., Stone, V., Erzinclioglu, S., Martin, L., Baron-Cohen, S., & Hodges, J. R. (2002). Theory of mind in patients with frontal variant frontotemporal dementia and Alzheimer's disease: Theoretical and practical implications. *Brain, 125*(4), 752–764.

Grober, E., & Bang, S. (1995). Sentence comprehension in Alzheimer's disease. *Developmental Neuropsychology, 11*(1), 95–107.

Groves-Wright, K., Neils-Strunjas, J., Burnett, R., & O'Neill, M. J. (2004). A comparison of verbal and written language in Alzheimer's disease. *Journal of Communication Disorders, 37*(2), 109–130.

Han, K. H., Zaytseva, Y., Bao, Y., Pöppel, E., Chung, S. Y., Kim, J. W., & Kim, H. T. (2014). Impairment of vocal expression of negative emotions in patients with Alzheimer's disease. *Frontiers in Aging Neuroscience, 26*(6), 101. doi:10.3389/fnagi.2014.00101.

Heaton, R. K., Chelune, G. J., Talley, J. L., Kay, G. G., & Curtiss, G. (1993). *Wisconsin Card Sorting Test (WCST), Revised and expanded*. Lutz, FL: Psychological Assessment Resources.

Heindel, W. C., Butters, N., & Salmon, D. P. (1988). Impaired learning of a motor skill in patients with Huntington's disease. *Behavioral Neuroscience, 102*(1), 141–147.

Heindel, W. C., Salmon, D. P., Shults, C. W., Walicke, P. A., & Butters, N. (1989). Neuropsychological evidence for multiple implicit memory systems: A comparison of Alzheimer's, Huntington's, and Parkinson's-disease patients. *Journal of Neuroscience, 9*(2), 582–587.

Heitz, C., Noblet, V., Phillipps, C., Cretin, B., Vogt, Phillippi, N., … Blanc, F. (2016). Cognitive and affective theory of mind in dementia with Lewy bodies and Alzheimer's disease. *Alzheimer's Research and Therapy, 8*(10). doi:10.1186/s13195-016-0179-9.

Henderson, V. W., Buckwalter, J. G., Sobel, E., Freed, D. M., & Diz, M. M. (1992). The agraphia of Alzheimer's disease. *Neurology, 42*(4), 777–784.

Henry, M. L., & Gorno-Tempini, M. L. (2010). The logopenic variant of primary progressive aphasia. *Current Opinion in Neurology, 23*(6), 633–637.

Hier, D., Hagenlocker, K., & Shindler, A. (1985). Language disintegration in dementia on a picture description task. *Brain and Language, 25*, 117–133.

Hodges, J. R. (2001). Frontotemporal dementia (Pick's disease): Clinical features and assessment. *Neurology, 56* (Suppl. 4), S6–S10.

Hoerster, L., Hickey, E. M., & Bourgeois, M. S. (2001). Effects of memory aids on conversations between nursing home residents with dementia and nursing assistants. *Neuropsychological Rehabilitation, 11*(3–4), 399–427.

Hopper, T. L. (2003). "They're just going to get worse anyway": Perspectives on rehabilitation for nursing home residents with dementia. *Journal of Communication Disorders, 36*(5), 345–359.

Hopper, T., Bayles, K. A., & Kim, E. S. (2001). Retained neuropsychological abilities of individuals with Alzheimer's disease. *Seminars in Speech and Language, 22*(4), 261–273.

Hopper, T., Bourgeois, M., Pimentel, J., Qualls, C. D., Hickey, E., Frymark, T., & Schooling, T. (2013). An evidence-based systematic review on cognitive interventions for individuals with dementia. *American Journal of Speech-Language Pathology, 22*(1), 126–145.

Horner, J., Heyman, A., Dawson, D., & Rogers (1988). The relationship of agraphia to the severity of dementia in Alzheimer's disease. *Archives of Neurology, 45*(7), 760–763.

Hubbard, G., Cook, A., Tester, S., & Downs, M. (2002). Beyond words: Older people with dementia using and interpreting nonverbal behavior. *Journal of Aging Studies, 16*(2), 155–167.

Huber, S. J., Shuttleworth, E. C., & Freidenberg, D. L. (1989). Neuropsychological differences between the dementias of Alzheimer's and Parkinson's disease. *Archives of Neurology, 46*(12), 1287–1291.

Hughes, J. C., Graham, N., Patterson, K., & Hodges, J. R. (1997). Dysgraphia in mild dementia of Alzheimer's type. *Neuropsychologia, 35*(4), 533–545.

Johnson, J. K., Head, E., Kim, R., Starr, A., & Cotman, C. W. (1999). Clinical and pathological evidence for a frontal variant of Alzheimer's disease. *Archives of Neurology, 56*(10), 1233–1239.

Josephs, K. A., & Duffy, J. R. (2008). Apraxia of speech and nonfluent aphasia: A new clinical marker for corticobasal degeneration and progressive supranuclear palsy. *Current Opinion in Neurology, 21*, 688–692. doi:10.1097/WCO.0b013e3283168ddd.

Josephs, K. A., Duffy, J. R., Strand, E. A., Machulda, M. M., Senjem, M. L., Master, A. V., … Whitwell, J. L. (2012). Characterizing a degenerative syndrome: Primary progressive apraxia of speech. *Brain, 135*, 1522–1536. doi:10.1093/brain/aws032.

Kawas, C. H., Corrada, M. M., Brookmeyer, R., Morrison, A., Resnick, S. M., Zonderman, A. B., & Arenberg, D. (2003). Visual memory predicts Alzheimer's disease more than a decade before diagnosis. *Neurology, 60*(7), 1089–1093.

Kemper, S., LaBarge, E., Farraro, F. R., Cheung, H., Cheung, H., & Storandt, M. (1993). On the preservation of syntax in Alzheimer's disease: Evidence from written sentences. *Archives of Neurology, 50*(1), 81–86.

Kempler, D. (1988). Lexical and pantomime abilities in Alzheimer's disease. *Aphasiology, 2*(2), 147–159.

Kempler, D. (1995). Language changes in dementia of the Alzheimer type. In R. Lubinski (Ed.), *Dementia and communication* (pp. 98–114). Philadelphia: Decker.

Kempler, D., Almor, A., Tyler, L. K., Andersen, E. S., & MacDonald, M. E. (1998). Sentence comprehension deficits in Alzheimer's disease: A comparison of off-line vs. on-line sentence processing. *Brain and Language, 64*, 297–316.

Kempler, D., Curtiss, S., & Jackson, C. (1987). Syntactic preservation in Alzheimer's disease. *Journal of Speech, Language, and Hearing Research, 30*(3), 343–350.

Kempler, D., Van Lancker, D., & Read, S. (1988). Proverb and idiom interpretation in Alzheimer disease. *Alzheimer Disease and Associated Disorders, 2*(1), 38–49.

Kertesz, A., Davidson, W., McCabe, P. et al. (2003). Primary progressive aphasia: Diagnosis, varieties, evolution. *Journal of the International Neuropsychological Society, 9*(5), 710–719.

Khan, K., Wakefield, S., Blackburn, D., & Venneri, A. (2013). Faster forgetting: Distinguishing Alzheimer's disease and frontotemporal dementia with delayed recall measures. *Alzheimer's and Dementia, 9*(4), Suppl. P 526. doi:http://dx.doi.org/10.1016/j.jalz.2013.04.259.

Kluger, B. M. & Heilman, K. M. (2007). Dysfunctional facial emotional expression and comprehension in a patient with corticobasal degeneration. *Neurocase, 13*, 165–168.

Knoke, D., Taylor, A. E., & Saint-Cyr, J. A. (1998). The differential effects of cueing on recall in Parkinson's disease and normal subjects. *Brain and Cognition, 38*(2), 261–274.

Koenig, O., Thomas-Antérion, C., & Laurent, B. (1999). Procedural learning in Parkinson's disease: Intact and impaired components. *Neuropsychologia, 37*(10), 1103–1109.

Kovacs, T. (2004). Mechanisms of olfactory dysfunction in aging and neurodegenerative disorders. *Ageing Research Review, 3*, 215–232.

Kunik, M. E., Martinez, M., Snow, A. L., Beck, C. K., Cody, M., Rapp, C. G., … Hamilton, J. D. (2003) Determinants of behavioral symptoms in dementia patients. *Clinical Gerontologist, 26*(3–4), 83–89.

LaBarge, E., Smith, D. S., Dick, L., & Storandt, M. (1992). Agraphia in dementia of the Alzheimer type. *Archives of Neurology, 49*(11), 1151–1156.

Lafleche, G., & Albert, M. S. (1995). Executive function deficits in mild Alzheimer's disease. *Neuropsychology, 9*, 313–320.

Lafosse, J. M., Reed, B. R., Mungas, D., Sterling, S. B., Wahbeh, H., & Jagust, W. J. (1997). Fluency and memory differences between ischemic vascular dementia and Alzheimer's disease. *Neuropsychology, 11*(4), 514–522.

Lambon Ralph, M. A., Powell, J., Howard, D., Whitworth, A. B., Garrard, P., & Hodges, J. R. (2001). Semantic memory is impaired in both dementia with Lewy bodies and dementia of Alzheimer's type: A comparative neuropsychological study and literature review. *Journal of Neurology, Neurosurgery, and Psychiatry, 70*(2), 149–156.

Landin-Romero, R., Tan, R., Hodges, J. R., & Kumfor, F. (2016). An update on semantic dementia: Genetics, imaging and pathology. *Alzheimer's Research and Therapy, 8*(1), 52. doi:http://doi.org/10.1186/s13195-016-0219-5.

Levinoff, E. J. (2007). Vascular dementia and Alzheimer's disease: Diagnosis and risk factors. *Geriatrics and Aging, 10*(1), 36–41.

Levy, J. A., & Chelune, G. J. (2007). Cognitive behavioral profiles of neurodegenerative dementias: Beyond Alzheimer's disease. *Journal of Geriatric Psychiatry and Neurology, 20*, 227–238.

Levy, M. L., Cummings, J. L., Fairbanks, L. A., Masterman, D., Miller, B. L., Craig, A. H., … Litvan, I. (1998). Apathy is not depression. *Journal of Neuropsychiatry and Clinical Neurosciences, 10*(3), 314–319.

Lezak, M. D., Howieson, D. B., Bigler, E. D., & Tranel, D. (2012). *Neuropsychological assessment* (5th ed.) New York: Oxford University Press.

Libon, D. J., Bogdanoff, B., Cloud, B. S., Skalina, S., Giovannetti, T., Gitlin, H. L., & Bonavita, J. (1998). Declarative and procedural learning, quantitative measures of the hippocampus, and subcortical white alterations in Alzheimer's disease and ischemia vascular dementia. *Journal of Clinical and Experimental Neuropsychology, 20*(1), 30–41.

Lindeboom, J., Schmand, B., Tulner, L., Walstra, G., & Jonker, C. (2002). Visual association test to detect early dementia of the Alzheimer type. *Journal of Neurology, Neurosurgery and Psychiatry, 73*, 126–133.

Lines, C. R., Dawson, C., Preston, G. C., Reich, S., Foster, C., & Traub, M. (1991). Memory and attention in patients with senile dementia of the Alzheimer type and in normal elderly subjects. *Journal of Clinical and Experimental Neuropsychology, 13*(5), 691–702.

Liotti, M., Ramig, L. O., Vogel, D., Cook, C. I., Ingham, R. J., Ingham, J. C., … Fox, P. T. (2003). Hypophonia in Parkinson disease: Neural correlates of voice treatment revealed by PET. *Neurology, 60*(3), 432–440.

Livner, A., Laukka, E. J., Karlsson, S., & Bäckman, L. (2009). Prospective and retrospective memory in Alzheimer's disease and vascular dementia: Similar patterns of impairment. *Journal of Neurological Sciences, 283*(1–2), 235–259. doi:10.1016/j.jns.2009.02.377.

Lyons, K., Kemper, S., LaBarge, E., Ferraro, F. R., Balota, D., & Storandt, M. (1994). Oral language and Alzheimer's disease: A reduction in syntactic complexity. *Aging, Neuropsychology, and Cognition, 1*(4), 271–281.

Mahendra, N. (2001). Interventions for improving the performance of individuals with Alzheimer's disease. *Seminars in Speech & Language, 22*(4), 289–302.

Mahendra, N. (2011). Computer-assisted spaced retrieval training of faces and names for persons with dementia. *Non-Pharmacological Therapies in Dementia, 1*(3), 217–237.

Mahendra, N. (2012). The logopenic variant of primary progressive aphasia: Effects on linguistic communication. *SIG 15 Perspectives on Gerontology, 17*, 50–59. doi:10.1044/gero17.2.50.

Mahendra, N., & Arkin, S. M. (2003). Effect of four years of exercise, language, and social interventions on Alzheimer discourse. *Journal of Communication Disorders, 36*(5), 395–422.

Mahendra, N., & Engineer, N. (2009). Effects of vascular dementia on cognition and linguistic communication: A case study. *Perspectives on Neurophysiology and Neurogenic Speech and Language Disorders, 19*(4), 106–115.

Mahendra, N., & Hopper, T. (2017). Dementia and related neurocognitive disorders. In I. Papathanasiou, P. Coppens, & C. Potagas (Eds.). *Aphasia and related neurogenic communication disorders* (2nd ed., pp. 455–494). Boston: Jones and Bartlett Publishers.

March, E., Wales, R., & Pattison, P. (2003). Language use in normal ageing and dementia of the Alzheimer type. *Clinical Psychologist, 7*(1), 44–49.

Mardh, S., Nägga, K., & Samuelsson, S. (2013). A longitudinal study of semantic memory impairment in patients with Alzheimer's disease. *Cortex, 49*(2), 528–533.

Massman, P. J., Butters, N. M., & Delis, D. C. (1994). Some comparisons of verbal deficits in Alzheimer dementia, Huntington disease, and depression. In V. O. B. Emery & T. E. Oxman (Eds.), *Dementia: Presentations, differential diagnosis, and nosology* (pp. 232–248). Baltimore: Johns Hopkins University Press.

Materne, C. J., Luszcz, M. A., & Bond, M. J. (2014). Once-weekly spaced retrieval training is effective in supporting everyday memory activities in community dwelling older people with dementia. *Clinical Gerontologist, 37*(5), 475–492.

McGuiness, B., Barrett, S. L., Craig, D., Lawson, J., & Passmore, A. P. (2010). Attention deficits in Alzheimer's disease and vascular dementia. *Journal of Neurology, Neurosurgery, and Psychiatry, 81*(2), 157–159.

McKeith, I., Taylor, J. P., Thomas, A., Donaghy, P., & Kane, J. (2016). Revisiting DLB diagnosis: A consideration of Prodromal DLB and of the diagnostic overlap with Alzheimer disease. *Journal of Geriatric Psychiatry & Neurology, 29*(5), 249–253.

Meier, S. L., Charleston, A. J., & Tippett, L. J. (2010). Cognitive and behavioral deficits associated with the orbitomedial prefrontal cortex in amyotrophic lateral sclerosis. *Brain, 133*, 3444–3457.

Meilan, J. J. G., Martinez-Sanchez, F., Carro, J., Lopez, D. E., Millian-Morell, L., & Arana, J. M. (2014). Speech in Alzheimer's disease: Can temporal and acoustic parameters discriminate dementia? *Dementia and Geriatric Cognitive Disorders, 37*, 327–334.

Meyer, S. R., Spaan, P. E., Boelaarts, L., Ponds, R. W., Schmand, B., & de Jonghe, J. F. (2016). Visual associations cued recall: A paradigm for measuring episodic memory decline in Alzheimer's disease. *Neuropsychology, Development and Cognition. Section B. Aging, neuropsychology and cognition, 23*(5), 566–577.

Miller, E. (1996). The assessment of dementia. In R. Morris (Ed.), *The cognitive neuropsychology of Alzheimer-type dementia* (pp. 291–309). New York: Oxford University Press.

Mori, E., Shimomura, T., Fujimori, M., Hirono, N., Imamura, T., Hashimoto, M., ... Hanihara, T. (2000). Visuoperceptual impairment in dementia with Lewy bodies. *Archives of Neurology, 57*(4), 489–493.

Morris, J. C. (1993). The Clinical Dementia Rating (CDR) Scale: Current version and scoring rules. *Neurology, 43*(11), 2412–2414.

Morris, R. G. (1996). Attentional and executive dysfunction. In R. Morris (Ed.), *The cognitive neuropsychology of Alzheimer-type dementia* (pp. 49–70). New York: Oxford University Press.

Morris, R. G., & Kopelman, M. D. (1986). The memory deficits in Alzheimer-type dementia: A review. *Quarterly Journal of Experimental Psychology, 38*(4), 575–602.

Moss, H. E., Kopelman, M. D., Cappelletti, M., de Mornay Davies, P., & Jaldow, E. (2003). Lost for words or loss of memories? Autobiographical memory in semantic dementia. *Cognitive Neuropsychology, 20*(8), 703–732.

Neils, J., Brennan, M. M., Cole, M., Boller, F., & Gerdeman, B. (1988). The use of phonemic cueing with Alzheimer's disease patients. *Neuropsychologia, 26*(2), 351–354.

Nestor, P., & Hodges, J. (2000). Non-Alzheimer dementias. *Seminars in Neurology, 20*(4), 439–446.

Nicholas, M., Obler, L. K., Albert, M. L., & Helms-Estabrooks, N. (1985). Empty speech in Alzheimer's disease and fluent aphasia. *Journal of Speech and Hearing Research, 28*(3), 405–410.

Noble, K., Glosser, G., & Grossman, M. (2000). Oral reading in dementia. *Brain and Language, 74*(1), 48–69.

Noe, E., Marder, K., Bell, K. L., Jacobs, D. M., Manly, J. J., & Stern, Y. (2004). Comparison of dementia with Lewy bodies to Alzheimer's disease and Parkinson's disease with dementia. *Movement Disorders, 19*(1), 60–67.

Nordin, S., & Murphy, C. (1998). Odor memory in normal aging and Alzheimer's disease. *Annals of the New York Academy of Sciences, 855*(1), 686–693.

Norman, D. A., and Shallice, T. (1986). Attention to action: Willed and automatic control of behavior. In R. J. Davidson, G. E. Schwartz, & D. Shapiro (Eds.), *Consciousness and self-regulation* (Vol. 4, pp. 1–18). New York: Plenum.

Ober, B. A., & Shenaut, G. K. (2014). Repetition priming of words and nonwords in Alzheimer's disease and normal aging. *Neuropsychology, 28*(6), 973–983.

Obler, B. A., Dronkers, N. F., Koss, E., Delis, D. C., & Friedland, R. P. (1986). Retrieval from semantic memory in Alzheimer-type dementia. *Journal of Clinical and Experimental Neuropsychology, 8*(1), 75–92.

Patterson, K. E., Graham, N., & Hodges, J. R. (1994). Reading in dementia of the Alzheimer type: A preserved ability? *Neuropsychology, 8*(3), 395–407.

Paulsen, J. S. (2011). Cognitive impairment in Huntington disease: Diagnosis and treatment. *Current Neurology and Neuroscience Reports, 11*(5), 474–483. doi:10.1007/s11910-011-0215-x.

Pearce, R. K. B., Hawkes, C. H., & Daniel, S. E. (1995). The anterior olfactory nucleus in Parkinson's disease. *Movement Disorders, 10*, 283–287.

Perry, R. J., & Hodges, J. R. (1999). Attention and executive deficits in Alzheimer's disease: A critical review. *Brain, 122*(3), 383–404.

Perry, R. J., & Hodges, J. R. (2000). Differentiating frontal and temporal variant frontotemporal dementia from Alzheimer's disease. *Neurology, 54*(12), 2277–2284.

Perry, R. J., Watson, P., & Hodges, J. R. (2000). The nature and staging of attention dysfunction in early (minimal and mild) Alzheimer's disease: Relationship to episodic and semantic memory impairment. *Neuropsychologia, 38*(3), 252–271.

Peters, J. M., Hummel, T., Kratzsch, T., Lotsch, J., Skarke, C., & Frolich, L. (2003). Olfactory function in mild cognitive impairment and Alzheimer's disease: An investigation using psychophysical and electrophysiological techniques. *American Journal of Psychiatry, 160*(11), 1995–2002.

Pillon, B., Deweer, B., Michon, A., Malapani, C., Agid, Y., & DuBois, B. (1994). Are explicit memory disorders of progressive supranuclear palsy related to damage to striatofrontal circuits? Comparison with Alzheimer's, Parkinson's, and Huntington's diseases. *Neurology, 44*(7), 1264–1270.

Pillon, B., Dubois, B., Ploska, A., & Agid, Y. (1991). Severity and specificity of cognitive impairment in Alzheimer's, Huntington's, and Parkinson's, and progressive supranuclear palsy. *Neurology, 41*(5), 634–643.

Pinto, S., Thobois, S., Costes, N., Le Bars, D., Benabid, A.-L., Broussolle, E., … Gentil, M. (2004). Subthalamic nucleus stimulation and dysarthria in Parkinson disease: A PET study. *Brain, 127*(3), 602–625.

Plassman, B. L., Langa, K. M., Fisher, G. G., Heeringa, S. G., Weir, D. R., Ofstedal, M. B. et al. (2007). Prevalence of dementia in the United States: The Aging, Demographics, and Memory Study (ADAMS). *Neuroepidemiology, 29*, 125–132.

Poore, Q. E., Rapport, L. J., Fuerst, D. R., & Keenan, P. (2006). Word list generation performance in Alzheimer's disease and vascular dementia. *Aging Neuropsychology & Cognition, 13*, 86–94.

Previc, F. H. (2013). Vestibular loss as a contributor to Alzheimer's disease. *Medical Hypotheses, 80*(4). doi:10.1016/j.mehy.2012.12.023.

Rainville, C., Amieva, H., Lafont, S., Dartigues, J.-F., Orgogozo, J.-M., & Fabrigoule, C. (2002). Executive function deficits in patients with dementia of the Alzheimer type: A study with a Tower of London task. *Archives of Clinical Neuropsychology, 17*(6), 513–530.

Randolph, C. (1997). Differentiating vascular dementia from Alzheimer's disease: The role of neuropsychological testing. *Clinical Geriatrics, 5*(8), 77–84.

Rao, S. M., Leo, G. J., Bernardin, L., & Unverzagt, F. (1991). Cognitive dysfunction in multiple sclerosis. I. Frequency, patterns, and prediction. *Neurology, 41*(5), 685–691.

Rapcsak, S. Z., Arthur, S. A., Bliklen, D. A., & Rubens, A. B. (1989). Lexical agraphia in Alzheimer's disease. *Archives of Neurology, 46*(1), 65–68.

Raymer, A. M., & Berndt, R. S. (1996). Reading lexically without semantics: Evidence from patients with probable Alzheimer's disease. *Journal of the International Neuropsychological Society, 2*(4), 340–349.

Reilly, J., Peelle, J. E., Antonucci, S. M., & Grossman, M. (2011). Anomia as a marker of distinct semantic memory impairments in Alzheimer's disease and semantic dementia. *Neuropsychology, 25*(4), 413–426.

Reitan, R. M., & Wolfson, D. (1985). *The Halstead-Reitan Neuropsychological Test Battery: Theory and clinical interpretation*. Phoenix, AZ: Neuropsychology Press.

Ripich, D. N., & Terrell, B. Y. (1988). Patterns of discourse cohesion and coherence in Alzheimer's disease. *Journal of Speech and Hearing Disorders, 53*(1), 8–14.

Rizzo, M., Anderson, S. W., Dawson, J., & Nawrot, M. (2000). Vision and cognition in Alzheimer's disease. *Neuropsychologia, 38*(8), 1157–1169.

Roca, M., Torralva, T., Gleichgerrcht, E., Chade, A., Arevalo, G. G., Gershanik, O., & Manes, F. (2010). Impairments in social cognition in early medicated and unmedicated Parkinson disease. *Cognitive and Behavioral Neurology, 23*, 152–158.

Rosen, H. J., Hartikainen, K. M., Jagust, W., Kramer, J. H., Reed, B. R., Cummings, J. L., … Miller, B. L. (2002). Utility of clinical criteria in differentiating frontotemporal lobar degeneration (FTLD) from AD. *Neurology, 58*(11), 1608–1615.

Rosen, H. J., Pace-Savitsky, K., Perry, R. J., Kramer, J. H., Miller, B. L., & Levenson, R. W. (2004). Recognition of emotion in the frontal and temporal variants of frontotemporal dementia. *Dementia and Geriatric Cognitive Disorders, 17*(4), 277–281.

Rosser, A., & Hodges, J. R. (1994). Initial letter and semantic category fluency in Alzheimer's disease, Huntington's disease, and progressive supranuclear palsy. *Journal of Neurology, Neurosurgery, and Psychiatry, 57*(11), 1389–1394.

Roy, S., Park, N. W., Roy, E. A., & Almeida, Q. J. (2015). Interaction of memory systems during acquisition of tool knowledge and skills in Parkinson's disease. *Neuropsychologia, 66*, 55–66. doi:10.1016/j.neuropsychologia.2014.11.005.

Rusted, J., & Sheppard, L. (2002). Action-based memory in Alzheimer's disease: A longitudinal look at tea making. *Neurocase, 8*(1–2), 111–126.

Sailor, K., Antoine, M., Diaz, M., Kuslansky, G., & Kluger, A. (2004). The effects of Alzheimer's disease on item output in verbal fluency tasks. *Neuropsychology, 18*(2), 306–314.

Salmon, D. P. (2000). Disorders of memory in Alzheimer's disease. In L. S. Cermak (Ed.), *Handbook of neuropsychology (Vol. 2): Memory and its disorders* (2nd ed., pp. 155–195). Amsterdam: Elsevier.

Salmon, D. P., & Bondi, M. W. (2009). Neuropsychological assessment of dementia. *Annual Review of Psychology, 60*, 257–282.

Salmon, D. P., & Fennema-Notestine, C. (1996). Implicit memory. In R. G. Morris (Ed.), *The cognitive neuropsychology of Alzheimer-type dementia* (pp. 105–127). New York: Oxford University Press.

Salmon, D. P., & Filoteo, J. V. (2007). Neuropsychology of cortical versus subcortical dementia syndromes. *Seminars in Neurology, 27*(1), 7–21.

Sapolsky, D., Domoto-Reilly, K., Negreira, A., Brickhouse, M., McGinnis, S., & Dickerson, B. C. (2011). Monitoring progression of primary progressive aphasia: Current approaches and future directions. *Neurodegenerative Disease Management, 1*, 43–55.

Sartori, G., Snitz, B. E., Sorcinelli, L., & Daum, I. (2004). Remote memory in advanced Alzheimer's disease. *Archives of Clinical Neuropsychology, 19*(6), 779–789.

Schacter, D. L. (1987). Implicit memory: History and current status. *Journal of Experimental Psychology: Learning, Memory, and Cognition, 13*(3), 501–518.

Schacter, D. L. & Tulving, E. (1994). *Memory systems 1994.* Cambridge, MA: MIT Press.

Schneider, J. A., Arvanitakis, Z., Bang, W., & Bennett, D. A. (2007). Mixed brain pathologies account for most dementia cases in community-dwelling older persons. *Neurology, 69*, 2197–2204.

Schneider, J. A., Arvanitakis, Z., Yu, L., Boyle, P. A., Leurgans, S. E., & Bennett, D. A. (2012). Cognitive impairment, decline and fluctuations in older community-dwelling subjects with Lewy bodies. *Brain, 135*(10), 3005–3014. doi:10.1093/brain/aws234.

Schofield, P. W., Ebrahimi, H., Jones, A. L., Bateman, G. A., & Murray, S. R. (2012). An olfactory stress test may predict preclinical Alzheimer's disease. *BMC Neurology, 2*, 12–24. doi:10.1186/1471-23 77-12-24.

Schwartz, M. F., Marin, O. S. M., & Saffran, E. M. (1979). Dissociations of language function in dementia: A case study. *Brain and Language, 7*(3), 277–306.

Seelye, A. M., Howieson, D. B., Wild, K. V., Moore, M. M., & Kaye, J. A. (2009). Wechsler Memory Scale–III Faces test performance in patients with mild cognitive impairment and mild Alzheimer's disease. *Journal of Clinical and Experimental Neuropsychology, 31*(6), 682–688.

Seger, C. A., & Spiering, B. J. (2011). A critical review of habit learning and the basal ganglia. *Frontiers in Systems Neuroscience, 5*, 1–9.

Seidl, U., Lueken, U., Thomann, P. A., Geider, J., & Schröder, J. (2011). Autobiographical memory deficits in Alzheimer's disease. *Journal of Alzheimer's Disease, 27*(3), 567–574.

Selnes, O. A., Carson, K., Rovner, B., & Gordon, B. (1988). Language dysfunction in early- and late-onset possible Alzheimer's disease. *Neurology, 38*(7), 1053–1056.

Sepelyak, K., Crinion, J., Molitoris, J., Epstein-Peterson, Z., Bann, M., Davis, C., Newhart, M., Heidler-Gary, J., Tsapkini, K., & Hillis, A. E. (2011). Patterns of breakdown in spelling in primary progressive aphasia. *Cortex, 47*(3), 342–352.

Serrano-Ponzo, A., Frosch, M. P., Masliah, E., & Hyman, B. T. (2011). Neuropathological alterations in Alzheimer disease. *Cold Spring Harbor Perspectives in Medicine, 1*(1)a006189. doi:10.1101/cshperspect.a006189.

Shallice, T. (1982). Specific impairments of planning. *Philosophical Transactions of the Royal Society B: Biological Sciences, 298*(1089), 199–209.

Shimamura, T., Mori, E., Yamashita, H., Imamura, T., Hirono, N., Hashimoto, M., … Hanihara, T. (1998). Cognitive loss in dementia with Lewy bodies and Alzheimer disease. *Archives of Neurology, 55*(12), 1547–1552.

Shuttleworth, E. C., & Huber, S. J. (1988). The naming disorder of dementia of Alzheimer type. *Brain and Language, 34*(2), 222–234.

Silagi, M. L., Bertolucci, P. H. F., & Ortiz, K. Z. (2015). Naming ability in patients with mild to moderate Alzheimer's disease: What changes occur with the evolution of the disease. *Clinics, 70*(6), 423-428. doi:10.6061/clinics/2015(06)07.

Silveri, M. C., & Leggio, M. G. (1996). Influence of disorders of visual perception in word-to-picture matching tasks in patients with Alzheimer's disease. *Brain and Language, 54*(2), 326–334.

Simard, M., van Reekum, R., & Myran, D. (2003). Visuospatial impairment in dementia with Lewy bodies and Alzheimer's disease: A process analysis. *International Journal of Geriatric Psychiatry, 18*(5), 387–391.

Skoe, E., & Kraus, N. (2014). Auditory reserve and the legacy of auditory experience. *Brain Sciences, 4*(4): 575–593. doi:10.3390/brainsci4040575.

Slachevsky, A., Villalpando, J. M., Sarazin, M., Hahn-Barma, V., Pillon, B., & Dubois, B. (2004). Frontal assessment battery and differential diagnosis of frontotemporal dementia and Alzheimer disease. *Archives of Neurology, 61*(7), 1104–1107.

Small, J. A., Kemper, S., & Lyons, K. (1997). Sentence comprehension in Alzheimer's disease: Effects of grammatical complexity, speech rate, and repetition. *Psychology and Aging, 12*(1), 3–11.

Snowden, J., Griffiths, H., & Neary, D. (1994). Semantic dementia: Autobiographical contribution to preservation of meaning. *Cognitive Neuropsychology, 11*(3), 265–288.

Snowdon, D., Kemper, S., Mortimer, J., et al. (1996). Linguistic ability in early life and cognitive function and Alzheimer's Disease in late life. *JAMA, 275*(7), 528–532.

Sohlberg, M. M., & Mateer, C. A. (2001). *Introduction to cognitive rehabilitation: Theory and practice.* New York: Guilford Press.

Squire, L. R., & Dede, A. J. O. (2015). Conscious and unconscious memory systems. *Cold Spring Harbor Perspectives in Biology, 7,* a021667. doi:10.1101/cshperspect.a021667.

Squire, L. R., & Schacter, D. L. (2002). *Neuropsychology of memory* (3rd ed.). New York: Guilford Press.

Stern, Y., Richards, M., Sano, M., & Mayeux, R. (1993). Comparison of cognitive changes in patients with Alzheimer's and Parkinson's disease. *Archives of Neurology, 50*(10), 1040–1045.

Stopford, C. L., Thompson, J. C., Neary, D., Richardson, A. M., & Snowden, J. S. (2012). Working memory, attention and executive function in Alzheimer's disease and frontotemporal dementia. *Cortex, 48*(4), 429–446.

Strain, E., Patterson, K., Graham, N., & Hodges, J. R. (1998). Word reading in Alzheimer's disease: Cross-sectional and longitudinal analyses of response time and accuracy data. *Neuropsychologia, 36*(2), 155–171.

Suttanon, P., Hill, K. D., Said, C. M., Logiudice, D., Lautenschlager, N. T., & Dodd, K. J. (2012). Balance and mobility dysfunction and falls risk in older people with mild to moderate Alzheimer disease. *American Journal of Physical Medicine and Rehabilitation, 91*(1), 12–23. doi:10.1097/PHM.0b013e31823caeea.

Teixeira, N. B., & Alouche, S. R. (2007). Dual task performance in Parkinson's disease. *Brazilian Journal of Physical Therapy, 11*(2), 113–117.

Tkalčić, M., Spasić, N., Ivanković, M., Pokrajac-Bulian, A., & Bosanac, D. (2011). Odor identification deficit predicts clinical conversion from mild cognitive impairment to dementia due to Alzheimer's disease. *Translational Neuroscience, 2*(3), 233–240. doi:10.2478/s13380-011-0026-1.

Tomoeda, C. K., & Bayles, K. A. (1993). Longitudinal effects of AD on discourse production. *Alzheimer Disease and Associated Disorders, 7*(4), 223–236.

Tulving, E. M. (1983). *Elements of episodic memory.* New York: Oxford University Press.

Uc, E. Y., Rizzo, M., Anderson, S. W., Shi, Q., & Dawson, J. D. (2005). Driver landmark and traffic sign identification in early Alzheimer's disease. *Journal of Neurology, Neurosurgery, and Psychiatry, 76*(6), 764–768.

Ulatowska, H. K., Allard, L., Donnell, A., Bristow, J., Haynes, S. M., Flower, A., & North, A. J. (1988). Discourse performance in subjects with dementia of the Alzheimer type. In H. Whitaker (Ed.), *Neuropsychological studies in nonfocal brain damage* (pp. 108–131). New York: Springer-Verlag.

Ulatowska, H. K., & Chapman, S. B. (1995). Discourse studies. In R. Lubinski (Ed.), *Dementia and communication* (pp. 115–132). Philadelphia: Decker.

Ullman, M. T. (2013). The role of declarative and procedural memory in disorders of language. *Linguistic Variation, 13*(2), 133–154. doi:10.1075/lv.13.2.01ull.

Van Deursen, J. A., Vuurman, E. F., Smits, L. L., Verhey, F. R., & Riedel, W. J. (2009). Response speed, contingent negative variation and P300 in Alzheimer's disease and MCI. *Brain and Cognition, 69*(3), 592–599. doi:10.1016/j.bandc.2008.12.007.

Van Halteren-Van Tilborg, I. A., Scherder, E. J., & Hulstijn, W. (2007). Motor-skill learning in Alzheimer's disease: A review with an eye to the clinical practice. *Neuropsychology Review, 17*(3), 203–212.

Van der Hurk, P. R., & Hodges, J. R. (1995). Episodic and semantic memory in Alzheimer's disease and progressive supranuclear palsy: A comparative study. *Journal of Clinical and Experimental Neuropsychology, 17*(3), 459–471.

Van Liew, C., Santoro, M. S., Goldstein, J., Gluhm, S., Gilbert, P. E., & Corey-Bloom, J. (2016). Evaluating recall and recognition memory using the Montreal Cognitive Assessment: Applicability for Alzheimer's and Huntington's diseases. *American Journal of Alzheimer's Disease and Other Dementias, 31*(8), 658–663.

Vuorinen, E., Laine, M., & Rinne, J. (2000). Common patterns of language impairment in vascular dementia and in Alzheimer's disease. *Alzheimer Disease and Associated Disorders, 14*(2), 81–86.

Walker, M. P., Ayre, G. A., Cummings, J. L., Wesnes, K., McKeith, I. G., O'Brien, J. T., & Ballard, C. G. (2000). Quantifying fluctuation in dementia with Lewy bodies, Alzheimer's disease, and vascular dementia. *Neurology, 54*(8), 1616–1624.

Waters, G. S., & Caplan, D. (2002). Working memory and on-line syntactic processing in Alzheimer's disease: Studies with auditory moving windows presentation. *Journal of Gerontology: Psychological Sciences, 57B,* 298–311.

Weintraub, S., Wickland, A. H., & Salmon, D. P. (2012). The neuropsychological profile of Alzheimer disease. *Cold Spring Harbor Perspectives in Medicine, 2*(4), a006171. doi:10.1101/cshperspect.a006171.

Welland, R. J., Lubinski, R., & Higginbotham, D. J. (2002). Discourse Comprehension Test: Performance of elders with dementia of the Alzheimer type. *Journal of Speech, Language, and Hearing Research, 45*(6), 1175–1187.

Whelihan, W. M., DiCarlo, M. A., & Paul, R. H. (2005). The relationship of neuropsychological functioning to driving competence in older persons with early cognitive decline. *Archives of Clinical Neuropsychology, 20*(2), 217–228.

Willis, S. L. (1993). *Test manual for the Everyday Problems Test for Cognitively Challenged Elderly.* University Park, PA: Pennsylvania State University.

Willis, S. L., Allen-Burge, R., Dolan, M. M., Bertrand, R. M., Yesavage, J., & Taylor, J. L. (1998). Everyday problem solving among individuals with Alzheimer's disease. *The Gerontologist, 38*(5), 569–577.

Youmans, G., & Bourgeois, M. (2010). Theory of mind in individuals with Alzheimer-type dementia. *Aphasiology, 24,* 515–534.

Zgaljardic, D. J., Borod, J. C., Foldi, N. S., & Mattis, P. (2003). A review of the cognitive and behavioral sequelae of Parkinson's disease: Relationship to frontostriatal circuitry. *Cognitive and Behavioral Neurology, 16*(4), 193–210.

Zu Eulunburg, P., Muller-Forell, W., & Dieterich, M. (2013). On the recall of vestibular sensations. *Brain Structure and Function, 218*(1), 255–267.

4

SETTING THE STAGE FOR PERSON-CENTERED CARE

Intervention Principles and Practical Considerations

Ellen M. Hickey, Renee Kinder, Becky Khayum, Natalie F. Douglas, and Michelle S. Bourgeois

This chapter will set up the case for intervention with persons with dementia by discussing the following topics: guiding principles of interventions, settings in which health professionals work with persons with dementia, and reimbursement considerations. Regardless of the treatment setting, speech-language pathologists (SLPs) will encounter persons with neurodegenerative conditions with symptoms ranging from mild to severe, and must be prepared to provide skilled services that are person-centered. The overarching aims of the interventions described throughout this book are to maximize independent functioning and improve participation and quality of life. The interventions may also benefit family and professional caregivers by increasing their quality of life and/or decreasing their burden. General principles of intervention for persons with dementia are delineated, then suggestions are provided for applying those principles to support individuals with dementia across service delivery settings (e.g., home to assisted living to nursing home). The differences in functional behaviors, the environment, and communication partners will be outlined for each setting to lead clinicians toward developing logical, person-centered treatment goals. Examples of functional and reimbursable goals will be provided. The section on reimbursement considerations was developed for clinicians working in the United States; however, some of the general ideas for documentation of services could be applicable in other countries as well.

As noted in Chapter 1, social models of health and disability have impacted the evolution of care for persons with dementia. When combined with the idea that communication is a basic human right (www.internationalcommunicationproject.com), social models of care assist clinicians in addressing a wider variety of treatment targets that go beyond a focus on impairments to those that maximize functional abilities, participation, and quality of life. Useful social models for dementia care include: the *International Classification of Functioning, Disability, and Health* (ICF; WHO, 2001); the Living with Aphasia: Framework for Outcome Measurement (Kagan et al., 2008); the Unmet Needs Models (e.g., Algase et al., 1996; Kunik et al., 2003), and strength-based models (e.g., Eisner, 2013). Given the nature of degenerative diseases, treatment most often emphasizes participation in life activities.

Power, Anderson, and Togher (2011) provide an illustrative case study of a problem-solving process that uses the ICF (WHO, 2001) in the SLP management of a person with Huntington's disease. Quantitative and qualitative data are converged to develop person-centered care that addresses the individual's current needs while also planning for the future. At the time of evaluation, the client and the client's mother reported that conversation was difficult to follow, and that socializing was dependent on others. Treatment plans included maximizing engagement with the client's children and providing opportunities for authentic connection. Care was taken to plan for the progression of the disease in attempts to maximize positive communication exchanges throughout the lifespan. The client's values and specific activities, participation restrictions, and perceived barriers drove the treatment decisions, illustrating how the relationship between person-centered care and the ICF is a natural one.

Social models of disability look at people with chronic health conditions in the context of society and recognize that care should be provided in a holistic manner that supports maximizing independence and engagement, as well as enhancing quality of life of persons with dementia. These models require that holistic assessment include an examination of the environmental factors that impact functioning. This includes both the physical (e.g., building design, personal and private spaces) and social environment (e.g., caregivers, volunteers, other residents), which will be discussed in detail in Chapter 7. Effective intervention programs are often multidimensional to address the variety of factors that impact persons with dementia. For example, needs in several areas, including sensory stimulation, social interaction, and meaningful activities, were prevalent in a sample of people with dementia in a long-term care community (Cohen-Mansfield, Dakheel-Ali, Marx, Thein, & Regier, 2015). Thus, "Unmet Needs" models (e.g., Algase et al., 1996; Kunik et al., 2003) are useful tools when assessing responsive behaviors of people with dementia and formulating person-centered care plans.

This chapter will also address considerations related to reimbursement for services, issues that cause ongoing consternation amongst healthcare providers. We want to make it clear that SLP services for cognitive-communicative deficits ARE reimbursable by US Medicare and private insurance companies (Kander, 2013; Satterfield & Sampson, 2015). Further, in the context of progressive conditions, the courts have ruled that Medicare cannot deny services due to lack of progress, as maintenance of function is a reimbursable service (Kander, 2013). Of course, documentation issues and third-party payer regulations change frequently, so the guidelines described here are broad. Recommendations of websites are provided so clinicians may keep current on these important issues. As most clinicians deal with denials from third-party payers at some point in their careers, strategies for appealing claims are also provided.

Some Guiding Principles for Functional Intervention

Clinicians must keep in mind that, for the most part, the interventions discussed in the following chapters have not been shown to change brain function or the impairments resulting from dementia, nor are they designed to do so. Rather, they increase behaviors that maximize independence and support participation and engagement in everyday life. The following three principles of dementia intervention are proposed as guidelines for selecting functional treatment goals and outcomes. We propose that clinicians consider adopting these principles to guide the goals of dementia intervention: (1) to maximize independent functioning for as long as possible, (2) to maintain quality of life through supported participation and engagement in desired activities, and (3) to achieve these goals through procedures that are personally relevant to the client and are trained within functional contexts.

1 Maximize Independent Functioning as Long as Possible

Intervention should begin in the earliest stages of the degenerative condition. This way, the individual is aware of his or her own deficits and remaining skills, can communicate desired goals and personal preferences, can identify memory strategies currently used, and can participate in planning and implementing the most effective compensatory strategies now and for future functional losses. An ideal approach is to enhance areas of strength and to reduce demands on impaired systems. As dementia symptoms progress, external communication and memory aids, as well as environmental modifications, should be designed and implemented to promote maximal function. This way, the person can maximize independence across the stages of the disease. For example, Bourgeois (2014) has developed a method to design effective external graphic cueing systems that maximize conversational communication and ability to follow ADL sequences, and other skills, which will be described further in Chapter 5.

2 Maintain Quality of Life via Supported Participation and Engagement

Activities that define the individual's lifestyle, personality, and identity must be identified to match compensatory strategies and the potential need for caregiver or partner training with specific activities. A variety of life activities ranging from employment to volunteer jobs to leisure activities can be analyzed for potential compensatory supports that can be implemented by the individual or by trained caregivers or peers. Personally meaningful life activities can be identified using one of the several innovative tools that have been developed to support conversations with persons with aphasia (e.g., Life Interests and Values Cards, LIV; Haley, Womack, Helm-Estabrooks, Lovette, & Goff, 2013) or persons with dementia (e.g., VoiceMyChoice™; Bourgeois, Camp, Antenucci, & Fox, 2016). These tools are described in Chapter 11.

Once meaningful participation goals are identified, then cognitive-communicative or other interdisciplinary treatments can be applied. For example, Arkin (1996, 2001) designed a supported volunteer program in which college students were paired with adults with dementia and accompanied them to their volunteer activities (e.g., an animal shelter or a hospital) for enhanced socialization and cognitive support to complete the activities. Positive outcomes of such intergenerational programming are becoming better described and studied in the literature (Weeks, MacQuarrie, Begley, Nilson, & MacDougall, 2016; Low, Russell, McDonald, & Kaufmann, 2015). Interventions that address quality of life, and support participation and engagement are described throughout the intervention chapters (Chapters 6 through 10), from cognitive-communication treatments to swallowing treatments to interdisciplinary programs and environmental modifications to caregiver approaches.

3 Emphasize Personal Relevance and Contextual Training

The importance of selecting treatment targets and activities based on the person's lifelong interests and habits is paramount in addressing motivation and treatment adherence issues. As clinicians, we know that the client who is motivated and has participated in the selection of treatment targets and activities will be most likely to carry out the treatment plan; likewise, we usually do not have much optimism for those who must be cajoled and convinced to attempt a specific protocol or strategy. Therefore, it is ideal to be planning treatment and compensatory strategy implementation with early-stage, motivated persons; however, when that window of opportunity has closed, the next best option is to know what interests and activities are held in high regard by the client and to plan modifications and supports that will facilitate the maintenance of those activities. For example, Camp (1999), Eisner (2001, 2013), and Elliot (2011) have developed approaches for the selection of interest-appropriate materials and activities that are based on the personal strengths and interests of the individual. These treatments are described in Chapter 7.

The principle of providing treatment in the context where the desired behavior is to be used is particularly important with persons with cognitive disorders, where the expectation for generalization to other situations and contexts may be limited. To the extent possible, it is necessary

---

Box 4.1 Guiding Principles for Functional Intervention with Persons with Dementia

1. Maximize Independent Functioning as Long as Possible
2. Maintain Quality of Life via Supported Participation and Engagement
3. Emphasize Personal Relevance and Contextual Training

---

to provide training and practice in the specific environment where the behavior is to occur so that there is no need to plan (and hope) for generalization of the behavior from the training context to the desired location. Additionally, modifications to the visual support or other aspects of the situation can also be made on the spot, preventing the acquisition of incomplete or erroneous components of the target behavior. If a more traditional training venue is used (e.g., therapy room), there is increased potential for delayed training effects (at best) or failure to use the compensatory strategy; e.g., training use of the facility's neighborhood activity calendar in the SLP's office is less likely to result in use of the calendar than training that is done in the neighborhood, where the person can practice walking to look at the calendar.

Treatment Considerations and Communication Supports Across Settings

Home and Community

Most persons (75%) with dementia will experience the full course of their illness while living at home and participating in the community (Jones, Dwyer, Bercovitz, & Strahan, 2009). In the early stages, speech–language treatment is likely to be provided in an outpatient clinic, under Medicare Part B. In the later stages, or if the person with dementia has other health complications, they may be eligible to receive speech–language treatment through home health services, under Medicare Part A. It is critical that family members attend treatment sessions in an outpatient clinic along with the person with dementia, to facilitate generalization of treatment strategies and target behaviors to the home environment.

During the pre-diagnosis phase, many persons will adopt memory and communication supports (e.g., planners, calendars, written notes, shopping lists, and maps) for typical age-related changes. Individuals may seek specialized assessment because of their emerging symptoms and may receive a diagnosis of Mild Neurocognitive Disorder (NCD; formerly Mild Cognitive Impairment); if the cognitive or language changes are beginning to impact daily functioning, they may receive a diagnosis of early-stage dementia. For some individuals who have decreased insight or awareness of their impairments, family members may initiate the formal assessment process. Individuals in the early stages of the disease and their family members are often anxious and overwhelmed by the neurodegenerative diagnosis and are seeking additional disease education, support, counseling, resources, as well as strategies. Speech-language pathologists may play several important roles, including providing additional disease education and counseling, providing services to train use of cognitive-communicative strategies (e.g., Bourgeois, 2013), and referring individuals and their families to other professionals, such as social workers or elder law attorneys.

In the early stages of the disease process, overt memory and language supports need to be implemented to maintain everyday activities in the home and community; such memory and communication supports constitute augmentative and/or alternative communication (AAC) tools that aid in enhancing life participation (Bourgeois, Fried-Oken, & Rowland, 2010). For some persons in the early stages, the goal may be to provide strategies that allow the individual to maintain work status as long as possible. This may include education and training with employers and/or coworkers and family members. Persons who are already retired may benefit from strategies aimed to increase participation in desired volunteer opportunities or other activities around the community.

As the disease progresses, caregivers assume responsibility for daily activities, and a range of memory and communication supporting systems can be implemented to maintain participation, engagement, and quality of life. The extent to which these memory supports maintain satisfactory functioning in the home will largely depend on the caregiver's attitude, skills, and health. Caregivers who are willing and able to seek advice and implement suggestions for addressing difficult behaviors may be successful in keeping their loved ones at home for the duration of the illness. These caregivers need to learn strategies for maintaining functional behaviors and to modify techniques as their loved one declines.

Some families who are financially able may choose to hire a private duty caregiver to assist in the care of the diagnosed individual. Whereas some families may hire a caregiver only a few days a week for several hours to provide respite, other families may hire full-time care or a live-in caregiver to enable their loved one to stay at home in the later stages. Both family members and hired caregivers need education and training on strategies to facilitate functional recall and communication during daily activities. Memory/communication books and interest albums keep their loved ones conversing about familiar people and activities. Memo boards and reminder cards provide some independence in remembering important facts and reducing repeated questions. As well, activity modifications keep the person engaged in familiar lifelong hobbies. See Figure 4.1 for examples of these types of memory and communication aids.

Adult Day Program

When the caregiver begins to experience the stressors of providing continuous care, an adult day program can provide a welcome respite. In this setting, the person with dementia has the opportunity for social interaction and participation in stimulating activities that supplement those that are available in the home. Staff members are trained to recognize the signs of memory impairment and to respond in appropriate ways. Activities are designed to provide opportunities for engagement at the appropriate level of cognitive ability.

FIGURE 4.1 Memory Supports for Home and Community Settings

Some caregivers do not utilize an adult day program or other respite opportunities because of fears that the person will refuse to participate or will feel abandoned. Others may not be able to take advantage of these programs due to lack of financial resources or fear of costs (Alzheimer's Association, 2016). The Alzheimer's Association's (2016) *Special Report on the Personal Financial Impact of Alzheimer's Disease on Families*, based on a survey of 3,524 caregivers, found that the costs of caregiving can have devastating impacts on families, including the possibility of food insecurity and poor nutrition and health for all family members. Many families lack knowledge about government assistance programs for older people. Other researchers have found that barriers to seeking help are more prevalent in minority populations, with obstacles related to knowledge, societal, and healthcare factors (Mukadam, Cooper, & Livingston, 2013). Programs such as adult day centers may be more successful if they are culturally tailored to the participants' needs (Seabrooke & Milne, 2009).

Speech-language pathologists who are working with persons with dementia, who are attending or are considering joining a program, may help to create written memory supports that can be very useful in helping the person (and his or her caregiver) transition to this new setting. Reminder cards that state, "I am spending the day with friends. My wife will pick me up at 4:30," or a memory wallet with pages that describe the facility and activities (e.g., "I enjoy my time at Joe's Place," "I play pool with Fred and Sam," and "The meals are delicious") can help prepare people with dementia for their day at the center. Staff can prompt individuals with dementia to read their card or memory wallet when they ask questions about leaving. People should be encouraged to bring their memory book to the center to share with other individuals. Activity staff often design group discussions around common topics in memory books, such as "Let's talk about our parents," or "Where did everyone go to school?" Volunteers in adult day care centers may make memory books for persons with dementia and use them for group activities (Bourgeois & Mason, 1996).

Another useful suggestion for day care staff is to prepare a simple, large-print list of the day's activities at the center that can be copied and sent home with each person. When the caregiver asks the person about the past day, instead of the typical response, "We didn't do anything," the person can read the list of activities and comment about each one. This memory-supporting tool is particularly useful for alleviating the guilt many caregivers feel about having others care for their family member. Figure 4.2 shows examples of memory and communication supports for adult day care, including an example of a daily schedule to prompt conversation about the day's events. Speech-language pathologists working with an individual who attends an adult day program may find it helpful to provide instructions for a manager at the program to implement specific strategies to help the person with dementia more fully participate in the program's activities (e.g., memory and communication aids).

FIGURE 4.2 Memory Supports for Adult Day Care

Independent and Assisted Living Facilities

Residents of independent and assisted living facilities are usually transitioning from the totally independent living environment of their own homes to the semi-independent and semi-supervised situation of a private room or apartment in a communal living situation. Speech-language treatment is often provided by a therapy company that is present within the facility, under Medicare Part B. For those who qualify for home health services, treatment may be provided under Medicare Part A. Some companies have therapists that travel to multiple independent and assisted living facilities to provide treatment coverage. The focus of intervention in this setting is on environmental engineering to create a positive, supportive communication environment to assist the person in maintaining or increasing activities and participation and ensuring safety. Interventions should be functional and contextualized. Depending upon the person's unique dementia clinical profile (memory loss, language deficits, visuospatial deficits, behavioral changes, or a combination of these symptoms), the SLP can implement interventions that capitalize on preserved abilities to increase independence, safety, and engagement in desired activities. Caregivers should be trained to facilitate the use of external cognitive and communication aids for some individuals, while others may require environmental modifications that enhance visuospatial function or behavioral strategies that help to manage aggressive or impulsive behaviors.

Independent and assisted living communities frequently have different levels of support and services that are available for their residents. Speech-language pathologists may provide guidance for families and facility staff regarding the appropriate level of care for an individual; e.g., some individuals may reside in independent living, but require daily medication reminders or escorts to meals and activities, while others may need to transition from independent living to assisted living, where more constant supervision and support are provided.

Some people welcome the comforts, safety, and social benefits of living with other people and transition easily. Others resist the limitations imposed by a reduced living space, the periodic monitoring of their activities, and the privacy issues that accompany residential living. Personal losses can also create barriers to successful acclimation to a new living arrangement; some residents grieve for lost possessions, their deceased partners, their former home and neighborhood, and their independence. They may withdraw from socialization, avoid communal meals, and decline invitations to participate in activities. If individuals are also suffering from memory loss and cognitive decline, they may experience periods of disorientation and confusion in their new surroundings. Memory-supportive tools can ease a difficult transition. A memory album that illustrates the home that has just been left, including pictures of the different rooms with the personal objects, furniture, and memorabilia, can be a comfort (see Figure 4.3). Including some written text explaining the circumstances of the move is helpful: e.g., "My heart condition worries my family. I will be safer living close to other people," and "I was often lonely at home alone. Here I will make many

FIGURE 4.3 Memory Supports for Assisted Living

new friends." Staff can suggest that people read their memory book when they get confused or ask to be taken home. Other repetitive requests, such as wanting to drive their car, can be redirected with a memory book page that states, "I enjoyed driving my car around town, but now I don't have to worry about the gas and insurance. Whenever I need to go somewhere, my son drives me in his car."

Independent and assisted living facilities typically support residents in their daily functions with written text in various formats. A quick stroll through an assisted living facility will uncover writing in the form of identification signs on resident rooms and staff offices, newspapers and magazines, menus posted near the dining room, activity schedule boards, and staff name tags. Signs can be useful in promoting positive behaviors and activities; significant reductions in dehydration were the result of posting a sign to drink a beverage in an innovative nursing home in Australia that used the ABLE model (Roberts, Morley, Walters, Malta, & Doyle, 2015) (see Figure 4.4; see Chapter 7 for more information about the ABLE model and other innovative long-term care models). A variety of sign colors and lettering choices were evaluated by asking residents with dementia their preferences; contrary to expectations, residents consistently chose bright green, bright magenta, and bright royal blue over white backgrounds, and white lettering instead of black (Brush, Camp, Bohach, & Gertsberg, 2015). The implementation of the preferred signs significantly increased wayfinding. Clinicians working in this environment can encourage their clients to read and respond appropriately to signs and other written cues.

When the text is too small or too complex, suggestions for modifying these written supports can be made to other staff, who may have the needed supplies for making suggested changes. For example, visually enhancing the day on an activity calendar with a colorful frame can increase the likelihood that residents will be able to find the day's activities. Having a separate blackboard for

FIGURE 4.4 Example of a Sign to Encourage Hydration

Source: Used with permission from Anne Kelly.

the day's activities is even more helpful for many persons with dementia. Some clinicians have been successful in convincing the local newspaper to publish a large-print insert of news and announcements once a week for subscribers who used to enjoy reading the paper but now have visual and cognitive limitations (Lou Eaves, October 2000, personal communication); adult literacy resources are also useful (e.g., News for You at www.newreaderspress.com/news-for-you-online). Printed invitations to attend a specific facility activity may make the reluctant resident feel welcome, and a daily printed menu slipped under the resident's door may entice him or her to try a meal in the dining room. A large-print directory of important telephone numbers by the telephone in the person's room, with notes about when specific family members are at work or home, can help the person feel it is possible to contact family when needed.

Long-Term Care

Persons with dementia may transition to a long-term care facility when their medical needs or behavioral challenges are no longer able to be met in the home environment or assisted living facility. Long-term care may be provided at memory units that are within a Continuing Care Retirement Community (CCRC) or skilled nursing facility (SNF), or a stand-alone memory care community. Speech–language treatment may be provided under several different payment sources, including outpatient services under Medicare Part B, Home Health services under Medicare Part A, or skilled rehabilitation under Medicare Part A (see "Rehabilitation and Skilled Nursing" section), or under private insurance for those who are younger than 65 years.

Barriers to care in the long-term care setting often include a lack of meaningful activities for residents, and under-staffed units with frequent turnover of staff members. Sometimes staff members could benefit from more training on dealing with cognitive-communicative needs to help them to provide care for residents' daily needs. Fortunately, many states are beginning to mandate dementia training (e.g., the Alzheimer's Disease Initiative of the state of Florida; http://elderaffairs.state.fl.us/doea/alz.php). The Alzheimer's Association has developed the CARES online training and certification program (www.alz.org/care/alzheimers-dementia-online-tools.asp) to increase access to appropriate knowledge about dementia and management strategies. Speech–language pathologists are frequently asked to assess swallowing in this setting, but may not be contacted when a resident is experiencing restlessness or agitation as a result of their communication, memory, or visuospatial deficits; the Alzheimer's Association has a useful booklet for care staff to bring awareness to the continuum of responsive behaviors that might be appropriate for referral to other professionals including SLPs (www.alz.org/national/documents/brochure_DCPRphases1n2.pdf/). Staff in-services and ongoing training is critical to ensure that residents are being appropriately referred for cognitive and language services (see Chapter 10).

The transition to long-term care can be facilitated with written or picture supports like those used in the assisted living facility. The focus of intervention continues to be on environmental engineering and providing memory supports. Memory books and wallets, reminder cards, and memo boards can all include text explaining the move to the new facility (e.g., "My new home is Magnolia Manor. I am safe here"). A memory book containing personal biographical information and pictures, or an interest album about a favorite hobby, can be useful for quiet times when staff is busy and the person can review the book independently. Repeated requests for the family can be answered truthfully if the resident has a guest book in which family members write notes about their visits and when they will be back: "I see here that your son writes he will be back to visit on Tuesday; that's tomorrow." Family photos and other personal memorabilia should be labeled in large print; it is the experience of many long-term care staff that when they ask about the people in the photos, the resident either cannot remember the accurate names or makes mistakes in naming them. As noted in Chapter 7, staff can use a family video to comfort or redirect a resident who is displaying confused and agitated behaviors. Clinicians can suggest to family that they video record themselves and other family members having a conversation with their relative; or for those residents who do not have family to make a personal video, Video Respite tapes can be used (Caserta & Lund, 2002; Lund, Hill, Caserta, & Wright, 1995; https://videorespite.com/). Alternatively, family may choose to provide a device such as a tablet computer or iPad that can digitally store multiple pictures and videos. Finally, in assisted living and long-term care, the SLP may also promote socialization with other residents for persons with dementia. As noted in Chapter 6, this may alleviate some of the social isolation that is prevalent among those with cognitive or communication disorders in nursing homes. Figure 4.5 provides examples of memory supports for long-term care settings.

Rehabilitation and Skilled Nursing

Individuals in any stage of dementia, from mild to severe language and cognitive symptoms, may require sub–acute rehabilitation. A person with dementia in this setting is, by nature of the medical condition that necessitated this placement, in a temporary situation that can be disorienting and disagreeable. Coming from acute care, the effects of pain medications and the residual effects of anesthesia may still be contributing to increased cognitive dysfunction. If the medical condition (e.g., hip fracture) and the rehabilitation are painful, the person will not be in the best frame of mind to cooperate with therapy. In these situations, the person's care planning is usually conducted by a team of professionals, including the physician, social worker, SLP, OT, PT, and nursing staff. Therefore, the therapeutic intervention plan must address the person's need to understand and cooperate with demands from multiple therapists and nurses. Medicare reimbursement in this setting is provided through Medicare Part A, the Prospective Payment System, with Resource Utilization Groups (RUG) levels corresponding to the intensity of nursing and skilled therapy each individual requires (to be discussed later in this chapter).

As in acute care, SLPs have a role in this setting to provide consultation services to the other professionals in the form of advice about the cognitive, communicative, and cueing needs of the person with dementia. In rehabilitation, however, the treatment plan is likely to be more intensive, with more active involvement of all therapists. The SLP may initiate individual cognitive-communication goals related to medical, social, and emotional needs, as well as to enhance the achievement of goals in other disciplines. Although co-treatment sessions with PT/OT are typically difficult due to the minutes needing to be split for reimbursement, SLPs can provide the best care through an interdisciplinary approach that includes frequent collaboration with other disciplines. For example, if the primary focus of rehabilitation is physical recovery, the SLP can best serve the client's needs by ensuring that the PT's instructions are presented in a format that the

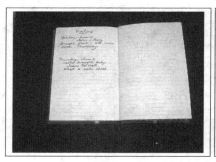

FIGURE 4.5 Memory Supports for Long–Term Care

person with dementia can understand and remember. Consultation about length of verbal commands, repetition of the same verbal command, and the use of written commands with picture supplements should be offered. Figure 4.6 illustrates examples of memory aids used for physical therapy. The objective of the consultation should be the enhancement of therapy outcomes and the most independent placement possible upon discharge.

During this skilled stay, SLPs have a unique opportunity to provide intensive treatment not only to increase cognitive and language function for the rehabilitation environment, but also to work with the individual's family members to discuss strategies for the discharge environment. If the person with dementia will be returning home, the SLP can target goals for increased independence and safety in this anticipated discharge environment. For example, the SLP might collaborate with family members to create a personalized memory and communication wallet during treatment sessions to be used in the home environment. Materials can be printed, laminated, and put together during the sessions, and family members can be trained to write the answers to repetitive questions or personally relevant words that are difficult to retrieve in dry erase marker on the laminated pages. While this memory and communication aid can be used in the rehabilitation environment (e.g., family members can write down when they visited and when they plan to return to the facility), it will be an important compensatory tool upon returning home.

Acute Care

When a person with dementia enters an acute care setting, it is often because of a medical condition that requires anesthesia, is painful, or is treated with strong medications. In these cases, the effects of impaired cognition and the consequences of the medical intervention exacerbate the person's inability to function appropriately or at premorbid levels. The change in environment, which may be confusing in and of itself, may also magnify these problems. Persons with dementia are likely to be disoriented, to have difficulty communicating basic needs, and to have needs in social closeness in the acute care setting. Nurses often provide medical instructions verbally (e.g., "The call button is right here. Use it when you feel you need to get up") with the expectation

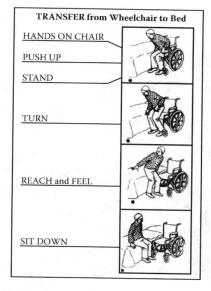
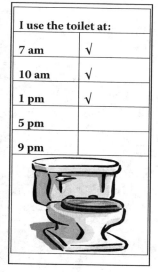

FIGURE 4.6 Memory Supports for Rehab Settings

that their patients understand and will remember later in the day. Unfortunately, most patients with impaired cognition or language prior to a medical intervention are even more impaired immediately after the intervention, and are therefore unable to respond appropriately. Family members are often called upon to monitor their loved ones around the clock, or to hire a sitter/companion.

While the role of SLPs in swallowing is imperative in acute care, SLPs also have an important role to play in ensuring that the patient in acute care can communicate his or her wants and needs effectively, including those pertaining to safe swallowing and nutrition. Therefore, SLPs need to assess the patient's functional hearing and vision to recommend to nursing staff the appropriate cues and strategies for the person in bed. Nurses in collaboration with SLPs have developed some useful no-tech AAC tools for communicating with nonspeaking patients in acute care (e.g., Garrett, Happ, Costello, & Fried-Oken, 2007). Figure 4.7 provides examples of memory supports for the acute care setting.

The SLP should be involved in staff education and training in the use of cognitive-communicative strategies that will enhance care and quality of life. SLPs must keep in mind that persons with dementia in the acute care setting may fatigue more quickly and may have high anxiety levels. Therefore, treatments need to be efficient and strategies must be easy to implement by other staff and family members. Some simple written tools can facilitate comprehension of nursing instructions and increase orientation in the acute care setting. However, these cues are often provided ineffectively, such as by writing too much or not making the cues portable. Alternatively, large-print statements, posted on the patient's bedside tray and within eye range, can help patients to remember where they are, how to call for help, and other important messages relevant to their medical condition (see Figure 4.7). Thus, staff in-services are important for teaching nurses how to make appropriate written cueing systems for the care needs of an individual and how to implement them for maximum effects. Family caregivers should also be taught strategies that will enhance communication for medical needs as well as social and emotional needs (see Chapter 9 for more on family caregivers).

Hospice Care

When a person has a life-limiting illness and further medical intervention is deemed futile, hospice care incorporating the principles of palliative care is recommended to facilitate the best possible quality of life through relief of suffering and control of symptoms, as well as death with dignity, using a multidisciplinary approach (Last Acts Palliative Care Task Force, 1998). The Last Acts Palliative Care Task Force identified the following principles of palliative care: (a) respecting an individual's goals, preferences, and choices; (b) comprehensive caring (physical, psychological, social, and spiritual support); (c) utilizing the strengths of interdisciplinary resources; (d) acknowledging and addressing caregiver concerns; and (e) building systems and mechanisms of support (www.lastacts.org/). The role of the SLP at this stage of the patient's journey is to evaluate the

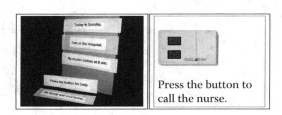

FIGURE 4.7 Memory Supports for Acute Care

person's communicative strengths and communication needs, develop communication strategies, and train caregivers and family members in the most effective ways to support communication with the dying person (Pollens, 2004). Specific examples of communication needs of dying patients (e.g., to communicate their final wishes, or to express their gratitude to someone) are detailed in Chapter 11.

Hospice care is funded by Medicare Part A, if the prognosis for life span is six months or less. A dilemma exists for providers of persons with dementia: determining at what point the six-month prognosis can be made for end of life. There are Medicare guidelines for characterizing this point, but this determination is not that clear cut (Covinsky, Eng, Lui, Sands, & Yaffe, 2003; Hurley & Volicer, 2002; Schonwetter et al., 2003). Severe declines in functional status (swallowing, mobility, communication, and continence) are associated with the beginnings of the terminal stage. Based on other literature, Allen, Kwak, Lokken, and Haley (2003) suggested that dementia may be a contributor to death far more than is recognized, and that criteria for providing hospice care be expanded. One suggestion was to determine the typical and atypical behavioral features of end-stage dementia so that family members may be educated on what to expect and so that caregivers may know when intervention is necessary. Thorough assessment is needed to determine the cause of atypical behaviors and to provide appropriate need-based and strength-based interventions. Some of the atypical behaviors may be indicators of pain requiring pain management. Hospice should be instituted more frequently and sooner with persons in the late stages of dementia (Allen et al., 2003).

Obtaining Referrals

Sometimes in medical settings, SLPs receive automatic referrals for dysphagia consultations, but may not be consulted readily for individuals who have cognitive-communication disorders. Because of high productivity expectations in long-term care facilities especially, SLPs may be required to build their own caseloads by screening residents for cognitive or communication decline, particularly in subacute rehab, independent/assisted living, and long-term care settings. As we have delineated in this book, the SLP's role is to work with persons with cognitive-communication disorders, even if those disorders result from degenerative diseases. Without intervention, many individuals with reduced communication abilities are at risk for decreased activities, participation, and quality of life. Because many other healthcare professionals are not aware of the full scope of practice of the SLP for treating this population, one of the best ways to increase appropriate referrals and build caseloads is the ongoing education and training of other healthcare professionals, including facility staff members, in addition to primary care physicians, neurologists, neuropsychologists and social workers in the community (see Box 4.2 for concrete examples).

Reimbursement and Documentation Issues

Navigating Reimbursement Guidelines

The navigation of regulatory reimbursement and documentation requirements for provision of skilled SLP services can be a significant challenge when working with individuals with dementia. Reimbursement of skilled SLP services for persons with dementia begins with having an adequate understanding of payer regulatory guidelines and best practices for billing and coding. Information is available on government websites and through the American Speech-Language-Hearing Association (ASHA) (see Box 4.13 at the end of the chapter for links to resources to keep up to date with changing guidelines). ASHA has been involved in advocacy for ensuring reimbursement of SLP services, and they provide support and useful summaries of information. The *ASHA Leader* is

---

Box 4.2 Examples of Education and Training Opportunities to Increase Appropriate Referrals

- Provide frequent and reoccurring in-services or "lunch and learns" with handouts to other healthcare professionals.
- Devise a one-page laminated handout that describes a "Trigger List" for SLP referrals, with a focus upon cognitive-communication symptoms. Post at nurses' stations and social work offices in healthcare facilities; at central home health office for referral coordinator; at referring physician and memory clinic offices.
- Establish a weekly "Rounds," an interdisciplinary team meeting where new or challenging cases are discussed by all healthcare disciplines. These discussions not only facilitate ongoing collaboration, but other healthcare professionals have an opportunity to learn about SLP interventions for individuals with dementia through case studies.

---

another good resource for tips on Medicare documentation. Luckily, most hospitals and rehabilitation companies have staff with primary responsibilities of keeping up with third-party payer regulations to support clinicians, but SLPs still need to be knowledgeable about the guidelines related to documentation and reimbursement. Because our focus is on dementia care, the emphasis of the discussion will be on Medicare A, which is the primary payer of skilled SLP services in inpatient geriatric care (e.g., skilled nursing facilities. The information in this half of the chapter is geared for SLPs working in the United States; however, some of the concepts can be useful in other countries too (e.g., documenting skilled services; creating treatment plans that are reasonable and necessary; documenting reasonable expectation for progress).

Regulatory Guidance

Current regulations that guide resident care for Medicare beneficiaries in skilled nursing facilities were implemented as part of the Omnibus Budget Reconciliation Act of 1987 (OBRA '87) which dramatically changed the way Skilled Nursing Facilities (SNFs) approached resident care thereby radically modifying nursing home regulations and the survey process. OBRA required that the federal government establish a requirement for comprehensive assessment as the foundation for planning and delivering care to nursing home residents. In addition, OBRA mandated that facilities "provide necessary care and services to help each resident attain or maintain their highest practicable physical, mental, and psychosocial wellbeing," and "ensure that the resident obtains optimal improvement or does not deteriorate within the limits of a resident's right to refuse treatment, and within the limits of recognized pathology and the normal aging process" (Code of Federal Regulations [CFR] Title 42, Part 483.25).

Medicare provides regulatory guidelines in a variety of sources, including the Medicare Benefit Policy Manual (MBPM; CMS, 2016), regionally specific local coverage determinations (LCDs), and national coverage determinations (NCDs). The information in the reimbursement section of this chapter is predominantly from the guidelines for the minimum documentation requirements that are provided in the Medicare Benefit Policy Manual Chapter 15 Section 220 (CMS, 2016; www.cms.gov/Regulations-and-Guidance/Guidance/Manuals/downloads/bp102c15.pdf). Requirements include an active evaluation and plan of care for skilled services which is certified by a physician or nonphysician practitioner (NPP), progress reports, and treatment encounter notes (aka daily notes).

Services provided to a Medicare beneficiary in the SNF setting must be skilled in nature and may include nursing services, rehabilitation services, or a combination of both. Skilled Nursing Facility Part A benefits include coverage for up to 100 days in a benefit period, which begins on the day an individual is admitted as an inpatient and ends when the person has not had any inpatient hospital care (or skilled care in a SNF) for 60 days in a row. If an individual is admitted into a hospital or a SNF after one benefit period has ended, a new benefit period begins. For a person to be eligible for SNF services under Medicare Part A, the person must have days available in the benefit period, and must have a 3-day qualifying stay in an acute hospital or be transferred to the SNF within 30 days of discharge from an acute hospital. Once a person is eligible for a SNF Medicare Part A stay, there are four criteria that must be met for Medicare to cover the SNF care (see Box 4.3).

When the criteria are met and services are provided for persons covered by skilled Medicare Part A benefits, services are reimbursed based on the amount and frequency of therapy services across all disciplines including PT, OT, and SLP, and are captured in a resource utilization group (RUG) category. Under the SNF Prospective Payment System (PPS), payment is made based on the RUG category that a patient falls into based on the amount of skilled therapy that the person needs and receives. The categories for rehabilitation services are: "Rehab Ultra High" (RU), "Rehab Very High" (RV), "Rehab High" (RH), "Rehab Medium" (RM), and "Rehab Low" (RL) (see Box 4.4).

Medicare Coverage for Speech-Language Pathology Services

Per the Medicare Benefit Policy Manual, SLP services are those services provided within the scope of practice of SLPs and necessary for the diagnosis and treatment of speech and language disorders, which result in communication disabilities and for the diagnosis and treatment of swallowing disorders (dysphagia), regardless of the presence of a communication disability. A qualified SLP meets one of the following requirements: (1) The education and experience requirements for a Certificate of Clinical Competence in SLP granted by ASHA; or (2) meets the educational requirements for certification and is in the process of accumulating the supervised experience required for certification; (3) services of SLP assistants are not currently recognized by Medicare.

Box 4.3 Four Criteria to be Eligible for Medicare Part A Coverage

1. The patient requires skilled nursing services or skilled rehabilitation services, i.e., services that must be performed by or under the supervision of professional or technical personnel (see §§30.2–30.4); are ordered by a physician and the services are rendered for a condition for which the patient received inpatient hospital services or for a condition that arose while receiving care in a SNF for a condition for which he received inpatient hospital services.
2. The patient requires these skilled services on a daily basis (see §30.6).
3. As a practical matter, considering economy and efficiency, the daily skilled services can be provided only on an inpatient basis in a SNF (see §30.7.).
4. The services delivered are reasonable and necessary for the treatment of a patient's illness or injury, i.e., are consistent with the nature and severity of the individual's illness or injury, the individual's particular medical needs, and accepted standards of medical practice. The services must also be reasonable in terms of duration and quantity.

Box 4.4 Rehab Resource Utilization Group Categories and Criteria (RUGs)

Rehab	Rehabilitation Rx 720 minutes/week minimum
Ultra High	AND at least one rehabilitation discipline five days/week
(RU)	AND A second rehabilitation discipline three days/week
Rehab	Rehabilitation Rx 500 minutes/week minimum
Very High (RV)	AND At least one rehabilitation discipline five days/week
Rehab	Rehabilitation Rx 325 minutes/week minimum
High (RH)	AND At least one rehabilitation discipline five days/week
Rehab	Rehabilitation Rx 150 minutes/week minimum
Medium (RM)	AND five days any combination of three rehabilitation disciplines
Rehab	Rehabilitation Rx 45 minutes/week minimum
Low	AND three days any combination of three rehabilitation disciplines
(RL)	AND six days of 2+ nursing rehabilitation services

Conditions for Skilled Care

Per the Medicare Benefit Policy Manual, certain conditions must be met for a person to receive skilled rehabilitation services, including the following: (1) Services must be directly and specifically related to an active written treatment plan that is based on an initial evaluation performed by a qualified therapist after admit to the SNF that is approved by the physician after any needed consultation with the qualified therapist. (2) Services must be of a level of complexity and sophistication, or the condition of the patient must be of a nature that requires the judgment, knowledge, and skills of a qualified therapist. (3) The services must be provided with the expectation, based on the assessment made by the physician of the patient's restoration potential, that the condition of the patient will improve materially in a reasonable and generally predictable period; or, the services must be necessary for the establishment of a safe and effective maintenance program; or, the services must require the skills of a qualified therapist for the performance of a safe and effective maintenance program. (4) The services must be considered under accepted standards of medical practice to be specific and effective treatment for the person's condition. (5) The services must be reasonable and necessary for the treatment of the person's condition; this includes the requirement that the amount, frequency, and duration of the services must be reasonable.

Establishing a Therapy Plan of Care (POC)

Development and certification of treatment plans requires that an SLP completes a true "hands-on" assessment which is then followed by timely certification of the plan of care. Plan of care requirements as outlined in Chapter 15 Section 220 of the Medicare Benefit Policy Manual (CMS, 2016) require that the SLP provide: a clear distinction between screening, evaluation, and re-evaluation; that the person's history and the onset or exacerbation date is clear in conjunction with current symptoms; that prior level of functioning and baseline abilities are provided; and that recommended frequency and duration of care follow acceptable standards of practice for the person's specific condition. See Box 4.5 for the standard steps for establishing a plan of care, and a

---

Box 4.5 Standard Steps for Establishing a Plan of Care (POC)

Step One: Screen
Step Two: Obtain physician order to evaluate
Step Three: Evaluate and determine if skilled intervention is necessary
Step Four: Establish a plan of care
Step Five: Write a clarification order
Step Six: Have plan of care certified
Step Seven: Re-evaluate as appropriate
Step Eight: Recertify when necessary

---

description of each step follows the box. Following the development of a comprehensive plan of care, continued documentation is required to support skilled levels of care, including weekly progress reports, daily notes, and discharge summaries.

Step One: Screening. SLPs typically initiate or receive referrals for resident needs in two ways: either they receive a direct order from a physician; or they recognize the need for evaluation during a screening process. Initial screenings or regular routine reassessments are not covered services. Screening simply helps the clinician to determine if further evaluation will be warranted. Therefore, no clinical judgments or skilled recommendations can be made from screening alone, as skilled recommendations require an established plan of care with MD certification. Skilled nursing facilities will often request that rehab clinicians screen residents upon admission to the facility, on a quarterly and annual basis, and any time there is a functional decline or improvement in status to identify potential changes in function that may necessitate the need for skilled care, and to prevent functional declines. Additionally, residents, family members, and other members of the facility interdisciplinary team may request screenings if they see a change in resident function for which SLP services may be indicated. The process of screening does not have the same requirement as an evaluation in that a "hands on" assessment is not required. Therefore, sources for obtaining information often include resident observation and interview; a thorough review of the medical record including physician progress reports, nursing daily and weekly notes, dietary records, and physical and occupational therapy documentation.

Step Two: Obtaining Physician Orders (Evaluation, Clarification, Additional, and Discharge Orders). After completion of a screen, if an SLP sees the need for further evaluation, request for an *evaluation order* should be made to the physician. After the signed order is received, the SLP can complete an evaluation specific to the person's needs, and then the SLP should request the physician's signature on the assessment document. Subsequently the physician's signature on the plan of care (POC) acts as certification/clarification of services after evaluation. Many skilled nursing facilities will also request that the SLP complete a *clarification order* outlining target area(s), anticipated frequency and duration of care, and planned skilled interventions as orders are often used as the facility's guide for any changes in a resident's care, which is transferred over onto the individualized care plan. *Additional orders* are needed after initiation of the initial SLP care plan if: there are significant updates that affect long-term goals or the addition of new interventions not included on the initial care plan (e.g., initial order for dysphagia alone, but SLP determines need for communication treatment). Recertification of a care plan will often be accompanied by clarification orders.

On occasion an SLP may receive an order for services that are not warranted, or an order for one specific area of function when another is clinically indicated. In these cases, *discharge orders* are needed, and if deemed necessary, orders for the appropriate clinical area should be requested.

For example, in some skilled nursing facilities, all people admitted under Medicare Part A PPS will have standing orders as follows: "Physical, Occupational and Speech Therapy to Eval/Treat as indicated." This form of an order is often built into the facility's Policy and Procedure or a portion of the electronic medical record (EMR). This, however, does not require that an evaluation be completed in the absence of need. Therefore, an SLP can screen the resident first and complete an order request, such as: "Please discharge ST order to Eval/Treat as not clinically indicated at this time."

Additionally, if an SLP requests orders for one target area and needs orders for an additional area or in addition to the initial area, an order request should be made. For example, if an SLP receives an order such as, "ST to evaluate and treat for dysphagia," however, needed orders for language, then a change is requested such as, "ST order to evaluate and treat for dysphagia received, however, order needed for language, therefore request evaluation and treatment orders for language alone." Likewise, if an SLP receives an order for only one needed area and needs multiple, then a change is requested, "ST received order to evaluate and treat for dysphagia alone, requesting additional evaluation and treatment order for language."

Step Three: Evaluate and Determine Need for Skilled Care. Per the Medicare Benefit Policy Manual Section 220, an *evaluation* is a "hands on" service that helps the clinician to determine the need for a skilled service. Evaluations may be warranted under three conditions: (1) for a new diagnosis; (2) following screening, when there has been an evidenced change from prior level of function (PLOF); or (3) when an individual evidences an increased desire or ability to participate in skilled intervention, whereas they were limited previously. Evaluation judgments are essential to the development of the plan of care, including goals and the selection of interventions. The need for skilled care is determined by the key elements listed in Box 4.6.

To begin, the evaluation should address the person's history in conjunction with the onset or exacerbation date of the current symptoms or conditions. The onset/exacerbation date refers to the date of the functional change that indicated the need for skilled care. For individuals with chronic conditions, the onset date may not be the date of diagnosis for the condition; instead, it may relate to the exacerbation date of the disease process. Alternatively, for new conditions, such as new onset CVA/TBI, the onset date will be the date of the new insult. Onsets should be documented in conjunction with current symptoms to justify the need for skilled services (see Box 4.7).

Based on the evaluation, the therapist will establish the POC and *determine the need for skilled services*. Skilled services per the Medicare Benefit Policy Manual, Chapter 15, Section 220.2 must adhere to the following three key criteria: (1) services must follow evidenced-based practice; (2) services must be at such a level of complexity and sophistication that only a skilled clinician can provide the care; (3) determinations cannot be made solely on diagnosis alone, and established frequency and duration of care must be individualized. The services must be specific and effective treatments for the person's condition. Per Medicare, acceptable *evidence-based practices* are found in: Medicare manuals, contractors Local Coverage Determinations (LCDs) and National Coverage Determinations (NCDs), and guidelines and literature of the professions of SLP.

Box 4.6 Key Elements of Evaluation Documentation

- Clear documentation related to onset date in conjunction with current symptoms
- Inclusion of objective and subjective measures
- Established baseline measures in comparison to prior level of function
- Realistic, functional, measureable short-term objectives and long-term goals

---

Box 4.7 Examples of Onset of Condition

- Mrs. Adams presents with a medical diagnosis of Alzheimer's dementia with recent exacerbation resulting in acute care stay and functional changes in ability to follow directions during activities of daily living.
- Mr. Lee has a significant medical diagnosis of Alzheimer's dementia with recent declines in cognitive function as evidenced by cognitive testing completed by his Primary Care Physician (PCP) during an Annual Wellness Visit.

Skilled services should be provided at a *level of complexity and sophistication* that require a qualified therapist; those services that do not require the performance or supervision of a therapist are not skilled and are not considered reasonable or necessary therapy services. Therefore, if the Medicare contractor determines the services could have been safely and effectively performed only by or under the supervision of such a qualified professional, it shall presume that such services were properly supervised. Determinations on whether skilled interventions are warranted are not made based on *medical diagnosis* or prognosis alone, though it is a valid factor. Therefore, the presence of a diagnosis of dementia should not be the primary consideration for skilled need.

Each person should have *individualized frequency and duration* of care based on the specific clinical needs. Additionally, Medicare states that there must be an expectation that the person's condition will improve significantly in a reasonable (and generally predictable) amount of time, or the services must be necessary for the establishment of a safe and effective maintenance program. The amount, frequency, and duration of the services must be reasonable under accepted standards of practice.

Step Four: Establish the Plan of Care (POC). Following evaluation, the clinician will develop the formal care plan (see Box 4.9). To begin, *prior level of function* (PLOF) should be clearly defined. This is the person's level of functional status prior to the onset of the functional decline that necessitated the need for skilled care. Additionally, the initial assessment establishes the *baseline data* necessary for evaluating expected rehabilitation potential, setting realistic goals, and measuring communication status at periodic intervals. Methods for obtaining baseline function should include

---

Box 4.8 List of Skilled SLP Services for People with Dementia

Skilled services include the following:

1. Diagnosing and assessing communication and cognitive skills
2. Designing treatment programs
3. Establishing compensatory skills
4. Analyzing and modifying behaviors to improve functional abilities
5. Conducting task analyses to establish a hierarchy of tasks and cues to direct a client toward a goal
6. Training the client and staff and family caregivers to implement a *restorative/rehabilitative-based* treatment program (i.e., skills can improve) or a *maintenance-based plan*
7. Re-evaluating the client based on a change in condition (i.e., either an increase or a decrease in status)

Box 4.9 Key Elements of the Plan of Care (POC)

- Clearly defined prior level of functioning (PLOF)
- Diagnostic and assessment testing services which ascertain the type and causal factor(s) identified during the evaluation
- Baseline abilities for all target areas
- Goals (realistic, long-term, functional goals)
- Established duration of therapy, frequency of therapy, and definition of the Type of Service
- Clarification on whether the plan is anticipated to be rehabilitative/restorative or maintenance based

---

objective or subjective baseline diagnostic testing (standardized or nonstandardized), followed by interpretation of test results and clinical findings. Goals should not be created for areas that do not have documented baseline measures. The clinician compares baselines to the PLOF to establish the basis for the interventions and to assist the clinician with determining appropriate frequency and duration of care; greater changes may require more intensive interventions. As the difference between baseline and prior level of function decreases, preparations for discharge planning should be in action and frequency should be tapered to promote carryover of newly learned skills and to promote the highest level of independence upon discharge from skilled care.

Treatment goals should be established based on clinical findings with realistic, long–term, functional targets that are established with the *reasonable expectation of measurable functional improvement* in a generally predictable period. To strengthen plans, short-term objectives should be included to clarify the steps needed to achieve long-term goals. All short-term objectives and long-term goals must be measurable, for example, by using a percentile (i.e., 50%), number of clinical trials (5/10 trials), or duration of a behavior. *"In order to" statements* need to be attached to all short-term objectives and long–term goals to clarify true functional outcomes for each target area (see examples in Box 4.10 and Box 4.11).

Box 4.10 Example of a Long-Term Goal and Short-Term Objectives for Auditory Comprehension

Long-term goal:

- Patient will demonstrate auditory comprehension of simple conversation with 100% accuracy and no cues in order to improve receptive communication skills (goal target four weeks).

Short-term objectives:

- Within two weeks, patient will follow one-step commands with 100% accuracy in order to enhance patient's ability to follow directions for activities and ADLs.
- Within two weeks, patient will understand yes/no questions with 100% accuracy in order to communicate basic wants/needs.

Box 4.11 Modifying Short-Term Objectives to Show Progress in Functional Behaviors

With progress, modify:

1. Level of complexity of the behavior:

   - Words, phrases, sentences, and conversation
   - Copy written words, write to dictation, and spontaneously write
   - Find sections in memory book, find specific information, make entries, and use book independently

2. Level and types of cueing, assistance, and prompts:

   - Minimal, moderate, or maximum
   - Tactile, verbal, or visual

3. Context:

   - In treatment sessions
   - In one-on-one conversation with another resident or staff member
   - In conversation with family caregivers
   - In group conversation or activity

4. Time intervals and immediacy of responses:

   - Recall after five-minute delay, one-hour delay, and 24-hour delay
   - Respond within 30 seconds, 15 seconds, and five seconds

5. Percentage of accuracy/frequency of occurrence (# of repetitions/# of trials)

The *frequency and duration*, or number of times per week and number of weeks, of skilled treatment must be specified in the care plan. If care is anticipated to extend beyond the 90 calendar day limit for certification of a plan, it is desirable, although not required, that the clinician also estimate the duration of the entire episode of care in this setting. Frequency and duration should be patient specific, related to level of functional decline, and appropriate based on evidence-based practice patterns. Frequency and duration alone may not be used to determine medical necessity, but they should be considered with other factors such as condition, progress, and treatment type to provide the most effective and efficient means to achieve the person's goals. For example, it may be clinically appropriate, medically necessary, most efficient and effective to provide short-term intensive treatment or longer-term and less frequent treatment depending on the individual's needs. Additionally, Medicare recommends that therapists taper the frequency of visits as the person progresses toward an independent level or reaches maximum benefit with the need for a caregiver assisted self-management program upon discharge from care.

Following updates to Chapter 15 of the Medicare Benefit Policy Manual succeeding the Jimmo versus Sibelius ruling which challenged the Medicare "improvement standard," therapists are now required to clarify from the start of care (SOC) whether services will be *restorative/rehabilitative-* or *maintenance-based* in nature. Therefore, evaluation, re-evaluation, and assessment documented in the Progress Report should describe objective measurements which, when compared, show improvements in function, decrease in severity, or rationalization for an optimistic outlook to justify continued treatment. *Rehab/restorative* therapy is defined as intervention aimed at addressing recovery or improvement in function and, when possible, restoration to a previous level of health and wellbeing (i.e., PLOF). *Maintenance-based plans* are programs established by a therapist that consist of activities and/or mechanisms that will assist people in maximizing or maintaining the progress they made during therapy, or to prevent or slow further deterioration.

Individuals with chronic conditions can benefit from either level of care. Per the Medicare Benefit Policy Manual (CMS, 2016), rehabilitative therapy may be needed, and improvement in a person's condition may occur, even when a chronic, progressive, degenerative, or terminal condition exists. For example, a terminally ill patient may begin to exhibit self-care, mobility, and/or safety dependence requiring skilled therapy services. The fact that full or partial recovery is not possible does not necessarily mean that skilled therapy is not needed to improve the person's condition or to maximize functional abilities. The deciding factors are always whether the services are considered reasonable, effective treatments for the person's condition and require the skills of a therapist, or whether they can be safely and effectively carried out by nonskilled personnel.

Step Six: Obtaining Certification for POC. The *certification* is the Physician's/Non Physician Practitioner's (NPP) approval of the POC, indicated by their signature in a timely manner, occurring within 30 days. A dated signature must be located on the POC or some other document that indicates approval for the POC. Following, when initial certification expires, a recertification must be completed within 30 days.

Step Seven: Re-evaluate as Appropriate. A re-evaluation is not a routine, recurring service but is focused on evaluation of progress toward current goals, making a professional judgment about continued care, modifying goals and/or treatment or terminating services. Re-evaluations are usually focused on the current treatment and might not be as extensive as initial evaluations. Continuous assessment of the person's progress is a component of ongoing therapy services and is not payable as a re-evaluation. Additionally, they are covered only if the documentation supports the need for further tests and measurements after the initial evaluation. Indications for a re-evaluation include new clinical findings, a significant change in condition, or failure to respond to

---

Box 4.12 Examples of Documenting Reasonable Expectation for Progress

- Understanding of conversational speech improved when shorter sentences with simple vocabulary were used, background noise was reduced (e.g., radio and television turned off), and client was alerted to attend to conversation before speaking to him. This suggests that training and instruction to the client and his caregivers will help the client to understand conversation related to his medical care and social and emotional needs.

- The client displays intact reading skills, which suggests that she could benefit from use of external aids, such as written and photo cueing systems, to increase her ability to follow directions in therapy, to use compensatory strategies for specific deficits and medical precautions, and to maintain attention for task completion.

- Given graphic cueing systems (written sentences and photos), the client was able to produce appropriate verbal language at the phrase/sentence level. This suggests that training the client to use these types of compensatory strategies would allow him to become a functional communicator for basic, social, and emotional needs.

the therapeutic interventions outlined in the plan of care. They may be appropriate prior to planned discharge for the purposes of determining whether goals have been met, or for the use of the physician or the treatment setting at which treatment will be continued.

Step Eight: Recertify When Necessary. When initial certification expires, a recertification must then be completed and certified within 30 days.

Coding for Documentation and Billing

Clinicians should also be aware of the two primary coding systems used in healthcare. For Medicare and most insurers, clinicians must use the International Classification of Diseases, 10th Revision (ICD-10; American Medical Association [AMA], 2017) Clinical Modification to code for diagnoses. (The current ICD-10-CM replaced the ICD-9-CM (9th Revision) on October 1, 2015.) The ICD-10 codes identify the condition for which we are evaluating or treating the client/patient. The SLP must identify the ICD-10 codes for the medical diagnosis and for the communication and/or swallowing diagnosis. The ICD-10 codes must be recorded on the initial evaluation and plan of treatment, discharge paperwork, and any monthly summaries and continuation plans.

The second is the Health Care Common Procedures Coding System (HCPCS), which includes Level I Current Procedural Terminology, also known as CPT codes. The CPT codes represent the procedures and services that we provide to a client/patient. The HCPCS Level II codes are used to report supplies, equipment, and devices. CPT codes are used across all healthcare providers, but there are certain categories that may be used by speech-language pathologists. The codes allow billing that is either time-based or procedure-based, and these are based on relative value units (RVUs) developed by Centers for Medicare and Medicaid Services (CMS) policy makers. Time-based codes are billed in 15-minute increments, and procedure-based codes are billed per procedure. Additional guidelines, including times for each 15-minute increment, can be found in the ASHA report on 2017 Medicare Fee Schedule for Speech-Language Pathologists (ASHA, 2017; see the report at www.asha.org/members/issues/reimbursement/medicare.) See Table 4.1 for information about specific codes that are used for SLP services and at the CMS website (www.cms.gov/Regulations-and-Guidance/Guidance/Manuals/downloads/bp102c15.pdf).

Conclusion

This chapter aimed to introduce guiding principles for working with people with dementia and their families, the variety of treatment settings, and the SLP scope of practice across these settings. Next, we provided an introduction to reimbursement issues, with a focus on developing a plan of care for people who are being seen in Medicare A funded services (e.g., skilled nursing/subacute rehabilitation). Please see Table 4.2 for a summary of setting descriptions and associated clinical procedures and reimbursement for SLP practice with people with dementia and their caregivers. The goal is to inspire SLPs to embrace their full scope of practice with people with dementia and their families. Complete descriptions of assessment procedures and intervention approaches are in the following chapters.

TABLE 4.1 Current Procedural Terminology (CPT) Codes (CPT; American Medical Association, 2017) and Medicare Reimbursement Information (CMS, 2016) for SLP Evaluation

Code	Descriptor	Interpretation Time Included	Minimum Minutes Required
92626	Evaluation of auditory rehab status – first hour	No	31–60 minutes Use 92627 for each additional 30 minutes beyond 60 minutes
96125	Standardized Cognitive Performance Testing (e.g., Ross Information Processing Assessment) per hour of a qualified health professional's time, both face-to-face time administering test to the patient and time interpreting these test results and preparing the report – per hour Includes use of norm-referenced/standardized tools and criterion referenced tools	Med B★: Yes Med A★★: Initial Evaluation – No★★; Re-evaluation – Yes (when conducted as part of treatment; see RAI Manual, Chapter 3, Section O, p. 17)	0 units = 0–30 minutes 1 unit = 31–90 minutes 2 units = 91–150 minutes and so on (below 31 minutes is not billable)
96105	Assessment of Aphasia (includes assessment of expressive and receptive speech and language function, language comprehension, speech production ability, reading, spelling, and/or writing, (e.g., by BDAE) with interpretation and report – per hour Requires use of norm-referenced/standardized test	Med B★: Yes Med A★★: Initial Evaluation – No; Re-evaluation – Yes (when conducted as part of treatment; see RAI Manual, Chapter 3, Section O, p. 17)	0 units = 0–30 minutes 1 unit = 31–90 minutes 2 units = 91–150 minutes and so on (below 31 minutes is not billable) 0 units = 0–30 minutes 1 unit = 31–90 minutes 2 units = 91–150 minutes and so on (below 31 minutes is not billable)
92607	Evaluation for prescription for speech-generating AAC device face to face with the patient – first hour		31–60 minutes Use 92608 for each additional 30 minutes beyond 60 minutes

Notes
★ 96105 and 96125 billing for Medicare Part B beneficiaries follows the definition of codes set forth per local coverage determination definitions, therefore, allowing SLP to account for interpretation time in assessment.
★★ Med A – Initial evaluation time goes under Non-MDS; re-evaluation time goes under MDS. Documentation time goes under non-MDS on 1 hr codes that have documentation and interpretation time in the definition.
(Please note: all information from the Medicare Benefit Information Policy Model; CMS, 2016 – www.cms.gov/Regulations-and-Guidance/Guidance/Manuals/downloads/bp102c15.pdf)

Box 4.13 Resources for Clinicians

General Information on Medicare Regulations and Plans
- Medicare Benefits Policy Manual – Centers for Medicare and Medicaid Services (CMS, 2016) (www.cms.gov/Regulations-and-Guidance/Guidance/Manuals/downloads/bp102 c15.pdf)
- Center for Medicare Advocacy: www.medicareadvocacy.org, or call 1–860–456–7790 or 1–800–262–4414
- Medicare: www.medicare.gov, or call 1–800–MEDICARE (1–800–633–4227)
- Medicare Rights Center: www.medicarerights.org, or call 1–888–466–9050 (HMO appeals hotline)

Information on Reimbursement Issues
- American Speech-Language-Hearing Association (ASHA): www.asha.org
- *Billing and Reimbursement*, American Speech-Language-Hearing Association: www.asha. org/practice/reimbursement/
- *2017 Medicare Fee Schedule for Speech-Language Pathologists*, American Speech-Language-Hearing Association: www.asha.org/uploadedFiles/2017-Medicare-Physician-Fee-Schedule-SLP.pdf
- Contact the *Health Care Economics & Advocacy team* at reimbursement@asha.org if you are having difficulty getting reimbursed for cognitive services
- Contact the *Speech-Language Pathology Health Care Services team* at healthservices@asha. org if you have questions about cognitive assessments
- *Medicare Funding of AAC Technology – Assessment/Application Protocol*, The Rehabilitation Engineering Research Center on Communication Enhancement (AAC-RERC): evaluation and report protocols; http://aac-rerc.psu.edu/index.php/pages/show/id/27

Information on Coding Systems
- Current Procedural Technology codes, American Medical Association: www.ama-assn. org/practice-management/cpt
- HCPCS codes: www.cms.hhs.gov/MedHCPCSGenInfo/
- ICD-10 codes: www.cdc.gov/nchs/icd/icd10cm.htm

TABLE 4.2 Summary of Settings, Referral Sources, and Procedures for SLP Services

Setting	Referral Sources	Evaluation Description	Plan of Care: Typical Frequency/Duration	Setting Description	Reimbursement	Education/Training
Home Health Services	Local hospitals; skilled nursing facilities; local memory clinics and physician offices	Brief evaluation, typically 30–45 minutes, to assess how cognitive, communication, or swallowing deficits are impacting primary medical needs and safety in home environment	Treatment typically provided for 30–45 minutes 1–3 times a week. Certification period for home health episode is 90 days, but SLP visits may be limited depending on other disciplines involved	Permanent residence; ranges from mild symptoms, potentially through severe symptoms with strong caregiver support	Medicare Part A; Private insurance (e.g., Blue Cross Blue Shield; United Health Care; Cigna)	Family members; private caregivers (paraprofessional or professional aides; informal caregivers/ friends; other rehab professionals)
Outpatient clinic	Local memory clinics; primary care physicians; neurologists	Comprehensive evaluation, typically 45–120 minutes in length and thorough investigation of all cognitive and language domains	Treatment typically provided for 30–60 minutes 1–2 times a week. Average duration ranges from 4–12 weeks	Office type setting; typically mild to moderate symptoms with strong caregiver support	Medicare Part B; Private insurance (Blue Cross Blue Shield; United Health Care; Cigna)	Family members; other communication partners identified by client and family; other rehab professionals
Adult Day Program	Local memory clinics; local hospitals; rehab programs; family self referral	Comprehensive evaluation, typically 45–120 minutes in length and thorough investigation of all cognitive and language domains	Treatment typically provided on a short-term basis to promote maximum life participation in the program; dependent upon funding sources	Respite setting, during day hours; most programs designed for individuals with late-mild to moderate symptoms	Private pay programs (no Medicare reimbursement)	Program staff; family members

Independent/ Assisted Living	Facility staff members (director of resident services; staff from nursing, recreation, dining, housekeeping; other rehab staff); local physician offices	Depending on funding source (outpatient therapy vs. home health), see descriptions above. Evaluation focuses on safety, level of assistance needed, and life participation in the facility	Depending on funding source (outpatient therapy vs. home health), see descriptions above	Permanent residence with various levels of care and services; typically designed for individuals with mild-moderate symptoms, unless full-time private duty caregiver is hired	Outpatient services: Medicare Part B; Private insurance (Blue Cross Blue Shield; United Health Care; Cigna) Home Health Services: Medicare Part A; Private insurance (Blue Cross Blue Shield; United Health Care; Cigna) Hospice care	Nurses staff; recreation staff; dining staff; housekeeping staff; other rehab professionals
Long-Term Care	Facility physicians; facility staff (director of resident services; staff from nursing, recreation, dining, housekeeping; other rehab staff; social worker)	Depending on funding source (outpatient therapy vs. SNF). Evaluation focuses on increased safety and life participation in LTC environment	Depending on funding source (outpatient therapy vs. SNF) up to five times weekly, see descriptions above	Long-term: Permanent residence for individuals with severe cognitive symptoms and/or complex medical conditions SNF: stay up to 100 days for skilled nursing and rehabilitation	Outpatient services: Medicare Part B; Skilled Nursing/Rehab Facility (SNF): Medicare Part A; Hospice care	Nurses; nursing assistants; recreation staff; dining staff; housekeeping staff; other rehab professionals

continued

TABLE 4.2 Continued

Setting	Referral Sources	Evaluation Description	Plan of Care: Typical Frequency/Duration	Setting Description	Reimbursement	Education/Training
Subacute Rehabilitation	Local hospitals; facility physicians; facility nurses; other rehab staff	Evaluation time frequently limited to 15–30 minutes since evaluation minutes do not apply to establishing RUG levels. Brief cognitive, communication or swallowing evaluations. Pair with a treatment session and perform dynamic assessment that may be billed as therapy session to add on 30–45 more minutes	Intensive treatment, often 3–5 days a week, for 30–60 minutes for up to 100 days during subacute rehabilitation stay, to prepare individual for anticipated discharge setting	Short-term stay (0–90 days), with intensive nursing care and therapy, any severity of dementia symptoms	Medicare Part A: Prospective Payment System/RUG levels	Nurses; nursing assistants; recreation staff; dining staff; housekeeping staff; other rehab professionals
Acute Care	Hospital physicians and staff members	Brief evaluation to assess ability to communicate needs, pain; may be longer assessment if needed for differential diagnosis; length based on medical status, tolerance	Treatment typically provided daily while person is hospitalized.	Short-term stay (typically less than 1 week) for acute medical needs, any severity of dementia symptoms	Medicare Part A	Nursing staff; family; other rehab professionals
Hospice	Local hospitals, home health companies, physician offices	Brief evaluation to assess basic comfort care needs, and communicating end of life wishes	Treatment typically limited to a few visits to establish recommendations for swallowing for pleasure feedings, communicating basic needs	Service provided in any setting near end of life	Medicare Part A	Hospice staff members (nurses); family; private caregivers (paraprofessional or professional aides

Appendix 4.1: Care Plan: Communication Strategies

Problem No.	Date	Problems and Strengths	Goals	Approach	Discipline	Goal Analysis
1	01/13/2017	Mrs. LeBlanc has cognitive-communication deficits that impact:				
		1. ability to communicate medical, basic, social, and emotional needs	1. Mrs. LeBlanc will indicate pain by pointing to a visual scale and answering yes–no questions with verbal and visual prompts.	1. Use visual aids, including memory and communication cards, visual scales, reminder cards, a calendar, name tags, and signs.	All	
			2. Mrs. LeBlanc will indicate basic needs during care routines by pointing to written and/or pictured choices.	2. Encourage Mrs. LeBlanc to respond to questions related to care routines and medical needs; use written cues as needed.	All	
		2. orientation to place	3. Mrs. LeBlanc will converse about personally relevant topics related to social and emotional needs.	3. Encourage Mrs. LeBlanc to discuss personally relevant information related to social and emotional needs with use of conversation/memory books.	All	
		3. recall of daily activities.	4. Mrs. LeBlanc will be oriented to place with visual aids and verbal cues.	4. Use a multiple-choice format to increase response to questions related to meals and basic needs (e.g., "Do you want juice or water?").	All	
			5. Mrs. LeBlanc will decrease repetitive questions with use of reminder cards and graphic schedules.	5. When conversing, ask open-ended questions that do not have a right or wrong answer, and make comments and positive statements related to Mrs. LeBlanc's interests.	All	
			6. Mrs. LeBlanc will increase participation in activities with cues to use activity schedule & reminder cards.	6. Provide praise and meaningful communication when Mrs. LeBlanc is engaging in appropriate behavior.	All	
				7. Speech tx for cognitive-communication deficits.	SLP	

Appendix 4.2: Care Plan: Dysphagia Strategies

Problem No.	Date	Problems and Strengths	Goals	Approach	Discipline	Goal Analysis
2	01/13/2017	Mrs. LeBlanc has dysphagia and receives a mechanically altered diet.	1. Mrs. LeBlanc will be free of signs and symptoms of aspiration with the least restrictive diet and liquids.	1. Diet as ordered.	Dietary	
			2. Mrs. LeBlanc will refer to external memory aid to implement safe swallowing techniques.	2. Dysphagia evaluation and treatment with SLP.	SLP	
			3. Mrs. LeBlanc will maintain adequate oral intake for nutrition and hydration needs.	3. Cue Mrs. LeBlanc to sit upright for all p.o. intake.	SLP, nursing	
				4. Cue Mrs. LeBlanc to alternate liquids and solids – use verbal cues and written cue cards.	SLP, nursing	
				5. Cue for oral clearance as needed – provide models and verbal cues.	SLP, nursing	
				6. Cue to clear throat and cough if Mrs. Smith has wet voice quality – provide models and verbal cues.		

References

Algase, D. L., Beck, C., Kolanowski, A., Whall, A., Berent, S., Richards, K., & Beattie, E. (1996). Need-driven dementia–compromised behavior: An alternative view of disruptive behavior. *American Journal of Alzheimer's Disease, 11*(6), 10–19. doi:10.1177/153331759601100603.

Allen, R., Kwak, J., Lokken, K., & Haley, W. (2003). End-of-life issues in the context of Alzheimer's disease. *Alzheimer's Care Quarterly, 4*(4), 312–330.

Alzheimer's Association. (2016). *2016 Alzheimer's disease facts and figures*. Retrieved from www.alz.org/documents_custom/2016-facts-and-figures.pdf.

American Medical Association. (2017). *CPT 2017 professional edition: E-book*. Retrieved from https://commerce.ama-assn.org/store/catalog/productDetail.jsp?product_id=prod2730005&sku_id=sku2750005&navAction=push#usage-tab.

American Speech-Language-Hearing Association. (2017). 2017 coding and billing for audiology and speech-language pathology. Rockville, MD: ASHA Press. Retrieved from www.asha.org/eWeb/OLSDynamicPage.aspx?webcode=olsdetails&title=2017+Coding+and+Billing+for+Audiology+and+Speech-Language+Pathology.

Arkin, S. M. (1996). Volunteers in partnership: An Alzheimer's rehabilitation program delivered by students. *The American Journal of Alzheimer's Disease & Other Dementias, 11*(6), 12–22. doi:10.1177/153331759601100103.

Arkin, S. M. (2001). Alzheimer rehabilitation by students: Interventions and outcomes. *Neuropsychological Rehabilitation, 11*, 273–317. doi:10.1080/09602010143000059.

Bourgeois, M. (2013). Therapy techniques for Mild Cognitive Impairment. *Perspectives on Neurophysiology and Neurogenic Speech and Language Disorders, 23*(1), 23–34.

Bourgeois, M. S. (2014). *Memory & communication aids for people with dementia*. Baltimore: Health Professions Press.

Bourgeois, M. S., Camp, C. J., Antenucci, V., & Fox, K. (2016). VoiceMyChoice™: Facilitating understanding of preferences of residents with dementia. *Advances in Aging Research, 5*, 131–141. http://dx.doi.org/10.4236/aar.2016.56013.

Bourgeois, M., Fried-Oken, M., & Rowland, C. (2010). AAC strategies and tools for persons with dementia. *The ASHA Leader, 15*(3), 8–11. https://doi.org/10.1044/leader.FTR1.15032010.8.

Bourgeois, M., & Mason, L. A. (1996). Memory wallet intervention in an adult day care setting. *Behavioral Interventions: Theory and Practice in Residential and Community-Based Clinical Programs, 11*, 3–18.

Brush, J., Camp, C., Bohach, S. & Gertsberg, N. (2015). Developing a signage system that supports wayfinding and independence for persons with dementia. *Canadian Nursing Home, 26*(1), 4–11.

Camp, C. J. (1999). *Montessori-based activities for persons with dementia: Volume 1*. Beachwood, OH: Menorah Park Center for Senior Living.

Caserta, M., & Lund, D. (2002). Video respite in an Alzheimer's care center: Group versus solitary viewing. *Activities, Adaptation, & Aging, 27*(1), 13–26. doi:http://dx.doi.org/10.1300/J016v27n01_02.

Centers for Medicare & Medicaid Services (CMS) (2016). *Medicare benefit policy manual*. Baltimore: Author.

Cohen-Mansfield, J., Dakheel-Ali, M., Marx, M. S., Thein, K., & Regier, N. G. (2015). Which unmet needs contribute to behavior problems in persons with advanced dementia? *Psychiatry Research, 228*(1), 59–64.

Covinsky, K. E., Eng, C., Lui, L. Y., Sands, L. P., & Yaffe, K. (2003). The last 2 years of life: Functional trajectories of frail older people. *Journal of the American Geriatrics Society, 51*, 492–498. doi:10.1046/j.1532-5415.2003.51157.x.

Eisner, E. (2001). *Can do activities for adults with Alzheimer's disease: Strength-based communication and programming*. Austin, TX: Pro-Ed Inc.

Eisner, E. (2013). *Engaging and communicating with people who have dementia: Finding and using their strengths*. Baltimore: Health Professions Press.

Elliot, G. (2011). *Montessori Methods for Dementia™: Focusing on the person and the prepared environment*. Oakville, Canada: Dementiability Enterprises.

Garrett, K. L., Happ, M. B., Costello, J. M., & Fried-Oken, M. B. (2007). AAC in the intensive care unit. In D. R. Beukelman, K. L. Garrett, & K. M. Yorkston (Eds.), *Augmentative communication strategies for adults with acute or chronic medical conditions* (pp. 17–57). Baltimore: Paul H. Brookes Publishing Co.

Haley, K. L., Womack, J., Helm-Estabrooks, N., Lovette, B., & Goff, R. (2013). Supporting autonomy for people with aphasia: Use of the life interests and value cards (LIV). *Topics in Stroke Rehabilitation, 20*, 1, 22–35. http://dx.doi.org/10.1310/tsr2001-22.

Hurley, A. C., & Volicer, L. (2002). "It's okay, mama, if you want to go, it's okay." *Journal of the American Medical Association, 288*, 2324–2331. doi:10.1001/jama.288.18.2324.

Jones, A. L., Dwyer, L. L., Bercovitz, A. R., & Strahan, G. W. (2009). The national nursing home survey: 2004 overview. *Vital Health Statistics, 13*(167), 1–155.

Kagan, A., Simmons-Mackie, N., Rowland, A., Huijbregts, M., Shumway, E., McEwen, S., ... Sharp, S. (2008). Counting what counts: A framework for capturing real-life outcomes of aphasia intervention. *Aphasiology, 22*, 258–280. http://dx.doi.org/10.1080/02687030701282595.

Kander, M. (2013, April). Policy analysis: Medicare must cover services that maintain function: A recent settlement eliminates the need for "functional progress" and allows patients with progressive conditions to receive maintenance services. *The ASHA Leader, 18*, 18–19. https://doi.org/10.1044/leader.PA2.18042013.18.

Kunik, M. E., Martinez, M., Snow, L. A., Beck, C. K., Cody, M., Rapp, C. G., ... DeVance Hamilton, J. (2003). Determinants of behavioral symptoms in dementia patients. *Clinical Gerontologist, 26*, 83–89. doi:10.1300/J018v26n03_07.

Last Acts Palliative Care Task Force. (1998). Precepts of palliative care. *Journal of Palliative Medicine, 1*, 109–112.

Low, L. F., Russell, F., McDonald, T., & Kauffman, A. (2015). Grandfriends, an intergenerational program for nursing-home residents and preschoolers: A randomized trial. *Journal of Intergenerational Relationships, 13*, 227–240.

Lund, D. A., Hill, R. D., Caserta, M. S., & Wright, S. D. (1995). Video Respite™: An innovative resource for family, professional caregivers, and persons with dementia. *The Gerontologist, 35*, 683–687. doi:10.1093/geront/35.5.683.

Mukadam, N., Cooper, C., & Livingston, G. (2013). Improving access to dementia services for people from minority ethnic groups. *Current Opinion in Psychiatry, 26*(4), 409–414.

Pollens, R. (2004). Role of the speech-language pathologist in palliative hospice care. *J Palliat Med., 7*, 694–702.

Power, E., Anderson, A., & Togher, L. (2011). Applying the WHO ICF framework to communication assessment and goal setting in Huntington's disease: A case discussion. *Journal of Communication Disorders, 44*, 261–275. http://dx.doi.org/10.1016/j.jcomdis.2010.12.004.

Roberts, G., Morley, C., Walters, W., Malta, S., & Doyle, C. (2015). Caring for people with dementia in residential aged care: Successes with a composite person-centered care model featuring Montessori-based activities. *Geriatric Nursing, 36*(2), 106–110.

Satterfield, L., & Sampson, M. (2015). Capturing cognition in skilled nursing facilities: What SLPs need to know to correctly perform – and document – cognitive evaluations for Medicare beneficiaries. *The ASHA Leader, 20*, 32–33. doi:10.1044/leader.BML.20122015.32.

Schonwetter, R. S., Han, B., Small, B. J., Martin, B., Tope, K., & Haley, W. E. (2003). Predictors of six-month survival among patients with dementia: An evaluation of hospice Medicare guidelines. *American Journal of Hospice Palliative Care, 2*, 105–113.

Seabrook, V., & Milne, A. (2009). Early intervention in dementia care in an Asian community: Lessons from a dementia collaborative project. *Quality in Ageing and Older Adults, 10*(4), 29–36. doi:10.1108/14717794200900029.

Weeks, L. E., MacQuarrie, C., Begley, L., Nilsson, T., & MacDougall, A. (2016). Planning an intergenerational shared site: Nursing-home staff perspectives. *Journal of Intergenerational Relationships, 14*, 288–300. http://dx.doi.org/10.1080/15350770.2016.1229550.

World Health Organization. (2001). *International classification of functioning, disability, and health*. Geneva: Author.

5

ASSESSMENT OF COGNITION, COMMUNICATION, AND BEHAVIOR

Ellen M. Hickey, Becky Khayum, and Michelle S. Bourgeois

Appropriate person-centered and functional intervention is dependent on assessment that allows for identification of the person's cognitive and communicative deficits associated with dementia, as well as pinpointing functional strengths. The American Speech-Language-Hearing Association (ASHA) guidelines emphasize the primary role that speech-language pathologists (SLPs) play in the assessment, diagnosis, and treatment of adults with cognitive-communicative disorders (ASHA, 2005, 2007). As noted in Chapters 1 and 4, the development and application of social models of health and disability have been influential in the evolution of care for persons with dementia. Clinical researchers have been inspired by the World Health Organization's International Classification of Functioning, Disability, and Health (ICF; WHO, 2001) to develop frameworks of communication disability and participation that can guide holistic assessment and intervention procedures (e.g., Baylor, Burns, Eadie, Britton, & Yorkston, 2011; Threats, 2006, 2007).

In particular, the Life Participation Approach for Aphasia (LPAA; Chapey et al., 2001) and later the Aphasia Framework for Outcomes Measurement (A-FROM; Kagan et al., 2008) use a person-centered philosophy of assessment and care to focus upon a person's ability to participate in meaningful life activities at desired levels. While the LPAA and A-FROM were designed specifically for persons with aphasia, their principles can be applied to clients with any communication diagnoses, including individuals with neurodegenerative conditions (see Chapter 4 for more on social models). These social models challenge clinicians to conduct assessments and to measure outcomes based on what is important to the person with dementia and their family or staff caregivers, keeping the aim of our clinical services on facilitating more robust life participation. Thus, assessments for treatment planning and for measuring outcomes should capture participation in desired life activities and perceptions of quality of life.

Based on the social models of care, Bourgeois (2013, 2015) has developed a new approach to "Flip the Rehab Model" from a traditional model that is directed by the clinician to one that is more person-centered, allowing the client's and caregivers' needs to direct the assessment and intervention processes toward functional and meaningful participation in daily life. In the more traditional assessment model, the clinician begins with standardized testing that highlights the impairments of the person with dementia, often leading to intervention that is not person-centered or functional. In contrast, the "Flip the Rehab Model" approach makes the individual's and family's concerns the focus of the assessment process and emphasizes the development of a person-centered care plan. This type of person-centered approach coincides with the movement toward reporting patient/family satisfaction and patient-reported outcomes (Black et al., 2016). This chapter will describe assessment processes and procedures, with an emphasis on how to implement a person-centered, "Flip the Rehab Model" approach, based on the principles of life participation. (See Chapter 11 for quality of life assessment.)

Factors to Consider in Planning for Assessment

Purpose of Assessment

The SLP needs to carefully consider the purpose of the assessment: Is the clinician a part of a team that is either screening individuals for potential cognitive problems or conducting diagnostic evaluations to provide a medical diagnosis for an individual with progressive cognitive or language impairments? Or is the clinician working in a setting where the purpose of assessment is ultimately to provide treatment that will increase safety, independence, and life participation? If the clinician is doing treatment, then assessment must also be planned to measure treatment outcomes. Regardless of the type and purpose of the assessment, the clinician formulates hypotheses, then tests and revises these hypotheses using formal and informal testing procedures. The purpose and nature of an assessment are guided by the type of information the referral source seeks to gain. Examples of potential referral sources include physicians, other rehabilitation professionals, family caregivers, or the client themselves. Referral sources may want to know if the client shows signs of a disease or injury, the level of care needed for discharge planning, if the client demonstrates a change in condition (increase or decrease in function), if the client has benefited from treatment, or if the client shows potential to benefit from treatment. The type of information the referral source seeks may vary with level of care being provided, such as acute care, subacute rehabilitation, long-term care, home care, adult day care, or hospice (see Chapter 4 for information on settings).

Specific assessment procedures are chosen based on the purpose and type of information sought. Comprehensive assessment batteries are used when the purpose is to contribute information to a diagnostic team. However, more functional assessment is conducted when the purpose is to develop a person-centered intervention plan. During intervention, assessment of progress should be ongoing, with the treatment plan being modified as needed if the client is not achieving goals. Regardless of the referral source and purpose, the person with dementia and family members should be placed at the center of the diagnostic and care planning processes, with a focus on their concerns regarding the diagnosis and impact on daily life participation.

Selecting and Interpreting Assessment Tools

Selection of assessment tools (ranging from observation and interview protocols to formal and informal tests) and interpretation of results will be influenced by a clinician's assumptions and understanding of the effects of normal aging versus dementia syndromes on cognition and communication. As noted in Chapter 2, dementia is not a result of normal aging, but cognitive processes do slow with age, which may impact a variety of communicative processes (e.g., word retrieval). Demographic factors, including age, education, and linguistic and cultural background, should be considered when selecting and interpreting assessment tools. In the past, there have been few tools available that included people in their 80s or 90s in the normative sample; likewise, normative samples tend to be mostly English-speaking, white, middle-class Americans. Slow progress has been made, however, in extending normative samples into upper age ranges and in making assessment tools available in a variety of languages. The MMSE-2, however, has norms up to 100 years and in eight languages plus three dialects of Spanish (Folstein & Folstein, 2010), and the Self-administered Gerocognitive Examination (SAGE) (Scharre et al., 2010) has norms up to 90 years of age and versions in five languages to date. Test norms must be used cautiously if normative data for upper age ranges are limited or nonexistent, or if the person's demographic background does not match the normative sample (e.g., cultural, linguistic, or educational background) (Sloan & Wang, 2005).

Clinicians must also consider the person's sensory and physical abilities and limitations in selecting assessment tools. At times, clinicians might modify assessment tasks if no tools are available that have appropriate sensory stimuli or tasks that are appropriate for the person's needs (e.g., if the person is blind, deaf, or has a limb or speech motor impairment). For example, older adults may need larger print size or a modified background (e.g., a yellow background with large black print) to enhance processing of written or picture stimuli; or they may require use of amplification to ensure they can hear the instructions. If the tasks are modified, then test norms may not be used, but useful information might still be gained with cautious interpretation of the results.

If the purpose of assessment is to determine service needs, practitioners should be aware of how their own biases and perceptions of an older person's treatment potential might impact their assessment process and recommendations for rehabilitation. Standardized tests alone should never be used to make person-centered intervention and placement decisions; rather, a variety of functional assessments must be used to determine the cognitive-communicative needs and strengths of the individual as pertains to daily activities and life participation. ASHA (2004) describes functional assessment of communication as measurement of the ability to communicate in daily living contexts, taking into consideration environmental modifications, adaptive equipment, the time required to communicate, and the listener's familiarity with the client.

Finally, various tools are more likely to be used by specific members of the interdisciplinary team (e.g., the physician or neurologist, neuropsychologists, nurse, and/or the SLP). Specific tools should be chosen in accordance with the purpose of the assessment and the domains of the client's functioning that are being assessed, as defined by the World Health Organization's (WHO, 2001) International Classification of Functioning, Disability, and Health (ICF) and the life participation approach. SLPs can conduct assessments that address any of the ICF domains: structures and functions, activities and participation, quality of life, and contextual factors. Regardless of the tools used, individual client characteristics and desires must be considered when interpreting assessment results and making clinical decisions.

Payer Source and Medical Setting

Healthcare resources will have an impact on the type of assessment and amount of time for assessment. Resources may vary according to the geographical context and healthcare setting where the assessment is being conducted. As well, the payer source for the evaluation and subsequent treatment also impacts the length and nature of the assessment process, particularly in the United States. For example, in the United States, an outpatient clinic may allow 60–75 minutes for an in-depth, comprehensive assessment, whereas subacute settings may have policies stipulating that assessments are limited to 15–30 minutes since the assessment minutes do not count towards the RUG levels, which determine reimbursement rates under Medicare Part A (see Chapter 4 for a detailed explanation of the Resource Utilization Group levels and policies). We do not believe that a full assessment can be accomplished in 15 minutes, however, clinicians may do diagnostic treatment trials as part of assessment for treatment planning, and these minutes can be counted toward RUG levels; additionally diagnostic treatment gives a better sense of treatment potential than a standardized test does. The plan of care, which includes the recommended frequency and duration of treatment, is also influenced by medical setting and payer source or resources. Similarly, documentation for reimbursement will vary depending upon the payer source. See Chapter 4 for more information on the types of settings where SLPs work with persons with dementia and their families, and the considerations typical of each setting.

Types of Assessment

Screenings are designed to determine if there is any problem that warrants a more detailed evaluation, which may lead to a diagnostic evaluation or to assessment for treatment planning. Diagnostic evaluations are designed to identify specific impairments in structures and functions that may contribute to a differential diagnosis, usually conducted with a team. Assessment for treatment planning is designed to identify the client's desired goals and to determine the individual and environmental factors that may act as facilitators or barriers to those goals; assessment of treatment potential is also an important part of treatment planning. Clinicians should plan to conduct assessment throughout the intervention period to determine the client's responsiveness to treatment and to measure functional outcomes. These types of assessments and relevant procedures will be described further with an emphasis on assessment for treatment planning and measuring outcomes. See Table 5.1 for a summary of the pros and cons of various types of assessment procedures used in treatment planning and for examples of commonly used measures.

Screenings. In general, a screening is used to determine if there is a problem that warrants a more detailed evaluation. The SLP may be involved in screening an individual to determine if: (1) a diagnostic assessment is warranted (e.g., sign of a new problem), or (2) there is a change in condition in any ICF domain, documented by nurses, physicians, or other therapists, that warrants further assessment and intervention (i.e., increase or decrease in impairment, activities, or participation). Screening procedures will vary depending on the type of facility and its policies. Typically in long-term care, periodic reassessments of residents are required to ensure that they are functioning at their maximum potential (e.g., American Health Care Association, 1990). In many nursing homes, screening procedures include only a chart review and possibly an interview with caregivers; hands-on assessment with the resident is not permitted unless a referral for an evaluation is received. Evidence for a new problem or a change in condition may be in the professionals' evaluations or progress notes, as well as in other standard assessment tools, such as the Resident Assessment Instrument 3.0 (RAI; CMS, 2016). The RAI includes the Minimum Data Set 3.0 (MDS 3.0), and documents all functional systems and many behaviors, with 19 systems coded, including vision, hearing (and comprehension), speech and language (section B), cognition (section C), mood, behaviors, daily activity preferences, and functional status, and swallowing, as well as all other bodily systems. There is also an international version, the interRAI, for use outside the United States. See Box 5.1 for examples of change in condition.

In community-based screenings (e.g., memory screenings at senior centers), procedures usually include an interview with the client and caregiver and a global cognitive measure (e.g., the Mini-Mental State Exam [MMSE]; Folstein, Folstein, & McHugh, 1975), or the SAGE (Scharre et al., 2010), or brief assessments of depression, discourse, orientation, and/or memory. Community-based screenings may have the benefit of earlier detection and referral for dementia diagnosis than traditional methods of referral, such as primary care physician referral (Barker et al., 2005). Regardless of the location or format of a screening, if a change in condition, disease process, or functional performance of daily activities is suspected or identified, then a referral for a full evaluation should be obtained from the physician.

Diagnostic Evaluations. The type of evaluation that follows a screening will depend on whether there has been an evaluation to determine medical diagnosis. For example, someone who had suspected deficits identified at a community memory screening should be referred for a medical

TABLE 5.1 Types of Assessment Tools, Examples, and Their Pros and Cons for Treatment Planning

Standardized global cognitive measures, e.g.
- Mini–Mental State Examination-2 (MMSE-2; Folstein & Folstein, 2010)
- Montreal Cognitive Assessment (MoCA; Nasreddine et al., 2005)
- Global Deterioration Scale (GDS; Reisberg, Ferris, deLeon, & Crook, 1982)
- Burns Brief Inventory of Communication and Cognition (Burns, 1997)
- Saint Louis University Mental Status Examination (SLUMS; Tariq et al., 2006)
- Self-Administered Gerocognitive Examination (SAGE; Scharre et al., 2010).
  - Pros: Obtain ballpark idea of functioning and severity level, ease of interprofessional communication when well-known tests are used (MMSE or MoCA)
  - Cons: Not specific enough to determine individual's strengths and weaknesses; does not diagnose dementia

Comprehensive standardized test battery for impairments, e.g.
- Arizona Battery for Communication Disorders in Dementia (ABCD; Bayles & Tomoeda, 1993)
- Standardized Touchscreen Assessment of Cognition (STAC; Coles & Carson, 2013)
- Repeatable Battery for the Assessment of Neuropsychological Status (RBANS; Garcia, Leahy, Corradi, & Forhetti, 2008; Randolph, 1998)
  - Pros: Comprehensive measures that document impairments; may identify relative strength areas; use subtests to document for reimbursement
  - Cons: Too lengthy to give in one sitting; may not help identify successful, functional treatment domains; not usually sensitive to changes due to treatment

Standardized test batteries for activities, e.g.
- Functional Linguistic Communication Inventory (FLCI; Bayles & Tomoeda, 1994)
- Assessment of Language-Related Functional Activities (ALFA; Baines, Martin, & McMartin Heeringa, 1999)
- Rivermead Behavioural Memory Test – 3rd ed. (RBMT-3; Wilson et al., 2008)
- Functional Standardized Touchscreen Assessment of Cognition (FSTAC; Coles & Carson, 2013)
- Functional Assessment of Verbal Reasoning and Executive Strategies (MacDonald & Johnson, 2005)
  - Pros: More functional tasks; may indicate types of cues and stimuli to use for treatment
  - Cons: Tasks may be too decontextualized to give indicator of everyday communication abilities; not sensitive to changes due to treatment

Functional assessment for treatment potential:
- Bourgeois Oral Reading Screen (Bourgeois, 2013; see Appendix 5.5)
- Spaced Retrieval Screen (Brush & Camp, 1998; see Appendix 5.6)
  - Pros: Determines comprehension, expectation for effectiveness of cueing and learning potential; can create personally relevant stimuli for individual clients; brief
  - Cons: Stimuli may not be personally relevant; few trials

Assessment of responsive behaviors, e.g.
- Behavioral Pathology in Alzheimer's Disease Rating Scale (BEHAVE-AD; Reisberg et al., 1987)
- Cohen-Mansfield Agitation Inventory (CMAI; Cohen-Mansfield, 1986)
- The Nursing Home Behavior Problem Scale (Ray, Taylor, Lichtenstein, & Meador, 1992)
- Caregiver interview & forms (behavior diary and behavior log; Bourgeois & Hopper, 2005, Tables 3–5)
  - Pros: Important for identifying specific behaviors to target in intervention; easy for staff to use
  - Cons: Requires input from others (family and professionals); might be more efficient to ask staff for specific behaviors seen

Observational protocols, e.g.
- Functional Goals Screening Protocol: Community Clients With Dementia (Bourgeois & Rozsa, 2006; see Appendix 5.8)
- Screening Protocol to Monitor Residents With Dementia (Rozsa & Bourgeois, 2006; see Appendix 5.7)
  - Pros: Important for identifying treatment goals, cueing strategies, and setting specifics (partners, activities, and locations)
  - Cons: Requires observation over time, different locations, and multiple informants

continued

TABLE 5.1 Continued

Interview protocols, e.g.
- Personal Wants, Needs, and Safety Assessment Form (Bourgeois, 2013; see Appendix 5.2)
- Memory Aid Information Form (community version) (Bourgeois, 2013; see Appendix 5.3)
- Memory Aid Information Form – Nursing Home Version (Bourgeois, 2013; see Appendix 5.4)
  - Pros: Necessary for personalized treatment materials and appropriate goal planning
  - Cons: Requires input from others (family and professionals)

Box 5.1 Examples of Change in Condition

1. Increase in body functions, activities, and/or participation:

    - Nurses' notes (long-term care): "Much more alert than she has been since admission; beginning to demonstrate agitated behaviors." May indicate alertness sufficient to participate in rehabilitation, and a new functional need in communication skills, requiring further assessment.

2. Decrease in body functions, activities, and/or participation:

    - Nurses' notes (long-term care): "Refusing to eat solid foods and has lost weight." May indicate a decrease in swallowing ability, requiring further assessment.
    - Nurses' notes (home health): "Increasing difficulty with medication management and remembering to go to appointments, less interaction with family." May indicate decreased memory ability that is impacting health and life participation, requiring further assessment.
    - Physician's notes (out-patient): "Daughter reports difficulty with money management and use of her cell phone that impacts participation in day to day activities." May indicate increased memory and executive function deficits impacting life participation, requiring further assessment.

---

exam, leading to a complete diagnostic evaluation, often conducted by a team that includes neurology and neuropsychology and may also include geriatrics, nursing, pharmacy, and social work (see Chapter 2 for details of the medical diagnostic process). A full complement of language and cognitive assessment batteries could be completed to: identify cognitive and language signs and symptoms that are characteristic of a certain disease process or course of a disease; pinpoint the location of the lesion (e.g., cortical versus subcortical signs); give input to determine prognosis. The cognitive battery might be completed solely by neuropsychology, in which case the SLP should be familiar with the assessment results to understand the cognitive–linguistic strengths and weaknesses that have been revealed. Alternatively, there might be an SLP on the team who will work collaboratively with neuropsychology to determine the cognitive–communication impairments and strengths.

In the diagnostic process, static assessment (or formal assessment) procedures are used, following standardized test protocols. An advantage of standardized tests is that they may simplify the process of communicating with other professionals if there is mutual familiarity with the instruments (e.g., a score from the well-known MMSE might communicate more to other team members than a lesser known SLP test). Over time, a skilled clinician will acquire vast amounts of information from administration of a familiar battery to interpret the client's performance on these tests; however, clinicians must be aware of the many biases that exist in standardized measures, particularly when the age, education, and cultural background of the person being assessed does not match the normative sample (APA, 2014; Sloan & Wang, 2005). Other potential limitations include over or under testing, lack of sensitivity, lack of specificity, lack of ecological validity, and failure to uncover reasons for difficulties or to uncover strategies or modifications that may improve performance (Turkstra et al., 2005; Ylvisaker & Feeney, 1998; Ylvisaker, Szekeres, & Feeney, 2001).

Assessment for Treatment Planning and Measuring Outcomes. Most SLPs work in settings where treatment of cognitive-communication impairments is the primary focus, and clients already have a medical diagnosis of a clinical dementia syndrome. Thus, the purpose will more often be assessment for treatment planning and measuring functional outcomes. The person with dementia, family members, and/or staff members are usually seeking interventions that will increase independence, safety, and life participation. In assessments for treatment planning and measuring functional outcomes, SLPs should apply the "Flip the Rehab model" approach (Bourgeois, 2014, 2015) to ensure a person-centered process (see details below). Assessment for treatment planning is designed to: identify the concerns and desired goals of the person with dementia and the family and staff caregivers; obtain a profile of individual strengths and weaknesses that will inform intervention procedures and strategies; and determine treatment potential. In planning for functional outcomes, the clinician will identify how to improve the client's functional behaviors by either treating the cognitive, language, and communication deficits, or by modifying the environment.

Dynamic assessment (or informal assessment) is used to tailor assessments for individual needs. Hypotheses generated by standardized instruments can be tested in more ecologically valid contexts by manipulating test procedures to determine what increases or decreases performance, such as changing length, complexity, or physical characteristics of stimuli, or providing various cues (Turkstra et al., 2005; Ylvisaker & Feeney, 1998; Ylvisaker et al., 2001). This way, clinicians determine how strengths can be used to compensate for cognitive and communicative needs (Ylvisaker & Feeney, 1998).

Additionally, carefully designed interviews, observations, and experiments in natural settings can make up for most of the concerns of formal testing. Limitations of informal assessment include potential for biased interpretations of results due to lack of norms. Inexperienced clinicians may have difficulty interpreting findings if the behaviors observed are not extreme or do not fit into an obvious pattern. Furthermore, replication of informal assessment procedures to compare performance over time or across clients can be challenging, due to a lack of standardized procedures. Despite these challenges, dynamic assessment is invaluable in identifying the starting point for a treatment plan and developing a hierarchy of difficulty for the individual, which may vary from client to client.

"Flip the Rehab Model" Assessment Procedures

The remainder of this chapter will focus upon elaborating on the "Flip the Rehab Model" approach to assessment. This approach allows a clinician to conduct an assessment methodically, with objective data, while placing the focus of the assessment on the person with dementia and family members, to create a person-centered, functional treatment plan.

First, case history is derived from chart review, interviews and observations with the client and caregivers are conducted, including assessment of responsive behaviors, followed by dynamic and static assessment procedures. Next, choices are made about the use of standardized tests for activities and participation and/or structures and functions, based on the information that is needed to flesh out the details of a treatment plan. Lengthy standardized tests are rarely useful or warranted for assessment for treatment planning or measuring outcomes; instead, tests or subtests are chosen to answer specific questions. This process culminates in the formulation of person-centered intervention goals and functional outcomes that focus on life participation. Additionally, persons with dementia and their family members will likely need disease education, support, and counseling throughout the assessment and treatment process, services which may be shared across team members, particularly a social worker. See Appendix 5.1 for a checklist that may be considered when implementing the "Flip the Rehab" model approach.

Case History and Observations

Chart Review and Interviews. Case history information is gathered at the beginning of a person-centered assessment to gather comprehensive information that will inform the direction of the remainder of the assessment. Relevant case history data are derived from a chart review of medical records and from the client and/or caregivers. Information is gathered about specific concerns, personal and medical history, sensory abilities and deficits (e.g., indications of hearing or vision deficits). The client's and caregiver's goals for assessment and their desired treatment goals and outcomes should also be obtained. Whenever possible, a variety of informants should be interviewed (e.g., clients, family, and staff caregivers). The care setting will influence the amount of case history information and the number and type of caregivers available, as well as the goals for assessment and treatment.

The person with dementia (as much as able) and caregivers should describe: the client's previous and current activities and interests; the level of current participation; expected outcomes for future activities and participation; and supports (e.g., memory strategies) and barriers (e.g., responsive behaviors) to participation. Protocols have been developed to gather information about the client's wants, needs, interests, and hobbies, as well as information about safety and content for memory aids (Bourgeois, 2013; see Appendices 5.1–5.3). The medical record should be reviewed prior to the interview, whenever possible, to see relevant information collected from the individual, family, or staff. This essential information will help to determine treatment goals and to set criteria for desired treatment outcomes. See Tables 5.2 and 5.3 for examples of forms completed by a caregiver to indicate the client's current daily schedule and routine, and future desired participation in activities. If the person with dementia has a hard time participating in an interview

TABLE 5.2 Daily Schedule and Routine Form

	Monday	Tuesday	Wednesday	Thursday	Friday	Saturday	Sunday
8 a.m.	Breakfast	Breakfast	Breakfast	Breakfast	Breakfast	Breakfast	Breakfast
9 a.m.	Dressed	Dressed	Dressed	Dressed	Dressed	Dressed	Dressed
10 a.m.	Senior Center		Senior Center		Grocery Store		Church
11 a.m.							
Noon	Lunch	Lunch	Lunch	Lunch	Lunch	Lunch	Lunch
1 p.m.							
2 p.m.							
3 p.m.							
4 p.m.							
5 p.m.	Dinner	Dinner	Dinner	Dinner		Dinner	Dinner
6 p.m.	TV News	TV News	TV News	TV News	Dinner at Son's house	TV News	TV News
7 p.m.		Choir Practice					
8 p.m.							
9 p.m.	Bed	Bed	Bed	Bed	Bed	Bed	Bed

TABLE 5.3 Desired Participation Form

Environment/Activity (Include activities that person used to engage in, but doesn't anymore)	People	Frequency of Contact	Problems	Participation Goal (to be completed with SLP)
Home	Me Wife, Mary	24–7	Lots of arguments Loss of intimacy Boredom and restlessness	Increased meaningful activities to participate in together and individually; increased use of positive communication strategies to facilitate meaningful daily conversations
Church	Minister, Friends: Bob & Jane Smith, Marie Gauthier, many others	Sunday service, Tuesday choir practice	Forgets names, sometimes gets distracted and becomes lost during prayers, songs	Increased attention during church services and choir practice with use of visual memory aids and cues from spouse/choir members
Senior Center	Men's Group	Wednesday	Forgets names, trouble following conversations	Increased recall of names with use of name badges; increased comprehension of conversations with staff's use of visual and graphic supports
Grocery store	Clerk	Friday	Gives incorrect money	Pay via debit card instead of cash
Son's home	Son, Spouse, T. (6 yrs), M. (2 yrs)	Once/week	Yells at kids	Increased meaningful activities identified to participate in with grandchildren, that will decrease agitation/outbursts
Listening to classical music at home	Alone	Never (used to do this daily)	Forgets to turn on the radio; if he remembers, can't operate the buttons on the radio	Will listen to classical music on a daily basis again with use of schedule board and visual cues on the radio buttons

about current and desired participation, visual supports can be used for choice-making, such as VoiceMyChoice and Talking Mats.

Preference Assessment. A labeled picture card category-sorting procedure is an effective procedure for eliciting valid and reliable preferences and opinions about current and desired participation directly from persons with dementia. This type of tool is based on Montessori methods (Camp, 2006; Camp & Skrajner, 2004; van der Ploegg, Eppinstall, Camp, & Runci, 2013). The structured format of a Montessori category-sorting task supports memory and communication processes in persons with dementia, even in its later stages (Orsulic-Jeras, Schneider, Camp, Nicholson, & Helbig, 2001). In addition, the reading of personally relevant, functional materials has been shown to be relatively preserved in persons with dementia (even in the later stages of dementia) and to be effective for retrieval of long-term memories (Bourgeois, 1990, 1992, 2013). One such visually formatted decision-making tool is Talking Mats® (www.talkingmats.com/); this was not originally designed for people with dementia, but it has been shown useful in decision-making situations with persons with dementia (Murphy, Gray, Achterberg, Wyke, & Cox, 2010).

A card-sorting task was combined with written cues to create a novel procedure (i.e., an enhanced visual/sorting procedure) called VoiceMyChoice™ (VMC; Bourgeois, Camp, Antenucci, & Fox, 2016), which is used to elicit opinions about preferred activities and QoL indicators from persons with dementia. This tool can be delivered by a nurse or other clinician and has the potential to improve the quality of the data generated by the residents (i.e., they will verbalize more and with less confusion). Bourgeois, Brush, Douglas, Khayum, and Rogalski (2016) randomly assigned 27 residents with moderate dementia to two conditions and compared the 10-minute preference card sorting task (VMC) condition (see Figure 5.1) to a control condition

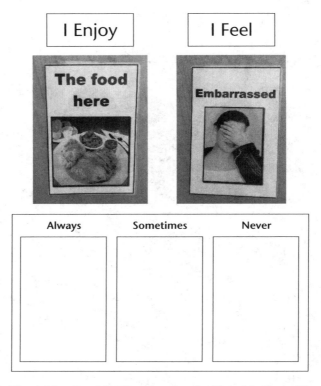

FIGURE 5.1 Sample Visual Stimuli and Sorting Template for VoiceMyChoice™

Source: VMC; Bourgeois, Camp, Antenucci, & Fox, 2016.

consisting of a 10-minute card matching activity using the materials from VMC. Results from pre- and post-administrations of the VMC Preference assessment tool administered to both residents and their nursing assistant revealed that convergence scores between members of NA-Resident dyads increased significantly after the use of VMC for both the English and non-native English dyads, but not in the control condition.

Observations and Behavior Logs. Structured observations of communication in the natural environment allow for the collection of activity and participation data, supports and barriers to participation, and the client's own or caregivers' reactions to deficits, as well as environmental data, which are all necessary for developing personally relevant and functional goals. Observation protocols can be used to determine the range of behaviors and factors that affect behaviors in the natural environment with other residents as well as with staff, family, visitors, or volunteers. For example, the Environment & Communication Assessment Toolkit (ECAT; Brush, Calkins, Bruce, & Sanford, 2011) evaluates the personal and public spaces of the person, identifying low-cost, person-centered environmental modifications, such as visual cues and signs, lighting changes, and ambient noise reduction, to improve the individual's participation in activities of daily living, leisure activities, or social communication (Bruce, Brush, Sanford, & Calkins, 2013).

Information should be gathered about how deficits impact relationships and roles in society currently, as well as projections for the future (e.g., living arrangement and health status). For example, attention and working memory deficits may limit the person's ability to comprehend conversational language, which may then restrict the person's ability to comprehend complex conversations, resulting in withdrawal from social situations. The support or barriers from frequent communication partners will impact whether this withdrawal occurs (e.g., availability, willingness, and supportiveness of communication partners, and communication demands and expectations). The client should be observed for participation, communication, and behaviors in a variety of natural contexts whenever possible (e.g., at home, in the person's own kitchen or bathroom; dining room, lounge, and activities room of an assisted living facility or long-term care unit). For outpatient clinic settings, caregivers can bring in video recordings of the individual in the home environment, if direct observation is not possible. Relevant background information (e.g., level of caregiver support) that impacts the client's participation in the home and community, or residence must be considered.

Responsive Behavior Assessment

Cognitive and communication deficits can often result in responsive behaviors (e.g., repetitive questions, disruptive vocalizations, wandering, or passivity) that affect everyday functional status. Accordingly, measurement of responsive behaviors is another important aspect of assessment for treatment planning and for measuring treatment outcomes. Kennedy (2002) recommended describing behaviors in a systematic fashion with quantitative measures of the presence or absence of a desired behavior, such as the frequency, rate, magnitude, and duration of behaviors, and the situations in which they occur. Thus, the clinician should identify, describe, and count the frequency of caregiver and client complaints, seeking answers to questions such as the following: What are the specific concerns or problems? Where do they occur, and at what time of day? How often do they occur? What are the consequences – who says and does what, and does it work? What is causing the activity limitation or participation restriction? What impact does this have on quality of life?

For in-patient or residential care settings, other caregivers can be enlisted to observe the client's behavior and record data about natural situations in addition to the SLP's observations. See Table 5.4 for an example of an informal Behavior Diary and Behavior Log. Of note, these behavior

TABLE 5.4 Behavior Diary and Behavior Log

Date	Time	Describe the Behavior	How Often?

Day	Count Problem: Cannot find room	Count Problem: Asks what time it is
Monday		
Tuesday		
Wednesday		
Thursday		
Friday		
Saturday		
Sunday		

diaries and logs can have a treatment effect with both the client and the caregiver. The simple act of recording the data can break the cycle of the antecedent-behavior-consequence by providing a different consequence. See Box 5.2 for an example of how data collection breaks the antecedent-behavior-consequence cycle. Furthermore, some caregivers have reported that their own perceptions have changed about the frequency or intensity of a behavior based on keeping these data. For instance, a problem that *seems* to happen 10 times a day may *actually* happen only once a day, which may not seem as troublesome when the objective data are reviewed, if the behavior is not dangerous.

In addition to these simple data tracking sheets, several more formal protocols have been developed to identify responsive behaviors and care needs from the perspective of caregivers. Examples of the more well-known rating scales are listed here. Behavioral Pathology in Alzheimer's Disease Rating Scale (BEHAVE-AD; Reisberg et al., 1987) assesses seven areas of behaviors:

Box 5.2 Breaking the Antecedent-Behavior-Consequence Cycle Through Data Collection

A nurse typically tries to reason with a person about a repetitive question, such as "when can I get my hair done?" The nurse responds to the question each time, sometimes telling the person not to worry about it, sometimes giving a specific answer. The nurse becomes annoyed at constantly being disrupted by these repetitive questions, which shows in her tone, making the person more anxious. The nurse is instructed to take data about the context of the behavior, recording the antecedent-behavior-consequence cycle. Each occurrence, she leaves the situation to record the behavior and the antecedent in the diary. This eliminates reinforcement or attention for the responsive behavior, which eliminates the behavior itself.

paranoid and delusional ideations, anxieties and phobias, activity disturbances, hallucinations, aggressiveness, diurnal rhythm disturbances, and affective disturbance. The Cohen–Mansfield Agitation Inventory (CMAI; Cohen-Mansfield, 1986) assesses 29 agitated behaviors, based on four factors: aggressive, physically nonaggressive, verbally agitated, and hiding and hoarding behaviors; nursing assistants provide information for nurses to score this assessment in long-term care settings. The Nursing Home Behavior Problem Scale (NHBPS; Ray, Taylor, Lichtenstein, & Meador, 1992) is a 29-item rating of severe problem behaviors that have occurred in the past 3 days.

The Multidimensional Observation Scale for Elderly Subjects (MOSES; Helmes, Csapo, & Short, 1987) includes measurement of five areas of cognitive and psychosocial functioning (self-care, disoriented behavior, depressed and anxious mood, irritable behavior, and withdrawn behavior) with 40 items in a forced-choice format. The ADAS Non-Cognitive Functions Test (ADAS-noncog; Rosen, Mohs, & Davis, 1984) has 10 items: tearfulness, depression, concentration, uncooperativeness, delusions, hallucinations, pacing, motor activity, tremors, and appetite. Versions of the ADAS are also available in French, German, Spanish, Italian, Korean, Finnish, Danish, Greek, Hebrew, and Japanese. Regardless of the tool used to document responsive behaviors, the clinician should be aware that these types of subjective reporting measures are subject to bias by the staff member completing it, and that clinicians should also conduct their own observations (Vance et al., 2003), and gather information from a variety of sources.

Assessment for treatment planning should be designed not only to identify and describe responsive behaviors but also to determine the cause of responsive behaviors and to plan strategies to reduce response behaviors by capitalizing on the client's strengths. Clinicians should keep in mind that responsive behaviors represent some attempt to interact in the environment or to communicate an unmet need, as discussed in Chapters 1 and 3 (e.g., Algase et al., 1996; Kunik et al., 2003; see Box 5.3). Clinicians should describe the contextual variables that impact a client's

---

Box 5.3 Responsive Behaviors: Assessment Process and Examples

1. Identify type and frequency of responsive behaviors

   - Most frequent: repetitive questions.
   - Most problematic: wandering and leaving the house at night.

2. Identify intervention strategies

   - Strategies for leaving the house at night should be addressed first, as this behavior presents a danger to the client – e.g., changing types of door locks, putting an alarm on the doors.
   - Strategies for addressing repetitive questions can then be reviewed and personalized.

3. Develop outcome measures specific to the responsive behaviors being targeted

   - Frequency, magnitude of target behaviors – e.g., number of attempts to leave the house at night, number of attempts that are successful.
   - See Table 5.4 for examples of behavior diaries and logs on which to record responsive behaviors. Pre-post data can be collected using these forms.
   - Note: Standardized measures would not be valid as outcome measures, as they do not reflect the specific functional behavior targeted.

behaviors and functioning, categorized by client, caregiver, and environmental variables, with each category identified by both fixed (i.e., not changeable) and mutable (i.e., changeable) variables (Kunik et al., 2003). This description of contextual variables should help the care team to plan environmental changes and personalized strategies to resolve responsive behaviors and improve participation.

Sensory Screening

Regardless of the purpose for assessment, screenings of sensory functioning (i.e., hearing and vision) should always be conducted to ensure that the client can perceive assessment stimuli and potential cues for functional and compensatory treatment strategies. The MDS 3.0 (CMS, 2016) includes general, functional items regarding hearing and vision (see Box 5.4). In addition to the MDS 3.0, hearing screening involves a pure-tone audiometric screening and word recognition testing, and checks hearing aids. Vision screening includes checking the condition of the client's glasses and functional visual recognition. Simply washing the client's glasses and making sure that they are worn properly may influence a client's performance. Vision recognition may be impacted by font size and figure–ground contrasts. This is screened using tasks such as sign recognition, or reading one's name or simple sentences in a variety of print sizes and contrasts. There are some tools that have been developed for font size assessment (Brush et al., 2011; Elliott, 2011), with the use of five to eight sentences in different font sizes (from large to small) that the person is asked to read aloud (see Figure 5.2). The ECAT (Brush et al., 2011) also includes a font size assessment with five sentences in different sizes for oral reading, as well as a gray scale contrast tool to determine whether the signs available in the environment have sufficient contrast for persons with dementia to be able to read them. Alternatively, clinicians can easily make their own font size

---

Box 5.4 Hearing, Vision, Speech, Language, and Mental Status Screening Questions from the Minimum Data Set (MDS)

Hearing (with device, if used): scored from 0 (normal hearing) to 3 (highly impaired); check for presence of hearing aid.

Vision (with device, if used) – Ability to see in adequate light: scored from 0 (adequate, sees fine detail) to 4 (severely impaired, no vision or sees only light; does not follow objects); check for glasses, contacts, or magnifying glass.

Speech Clarity: scored from 0 (normal, distinct) to 2 (no speech).

Makes Self Understood (verbal and nonverbal expression): scored from 0 (understood) to 3 (rarely/never understood).

Ability to Understand Others (with hearing aid, if used): scored from 0 (understands) to 3 (rarely/never understands).

Brief Interview for Mental Status (BIMS): total score of 0 to 15, includes immediate and delayed three-word recall, temporal orientation.

Staff Assessment for Mental Status (if unable to complete the BIMS):

- Short- and long-term memory: each scored 0 (OK) to 1 (problem)
- Memory/recall ability: check for temporal and place orientation, staff names and faces
- Cognitive skills for daily decision-making: scored from 0 (independent; consistent/reasonable) to 3 (severely impaired; never/rarely makes decisions).

I am fine.

How are you?

What a nice day.

Tried and true.

Live, laugh and learn.

Smile and the world smiles with you.

FIGURE 5.2 Example of a Reading Screen

Source: Elliott, 2011; www.dementiability.com.

assessment or test different backgrounds (e.g., yellow paper with black text) to determine optimal visual presentation for the client's best performance. Lastly, observations are made regarding the client's scanning abilities and attention to right and left visual fields.

Assessment of Activities and Participation

After completion of the person-centered interview and observation process, procedures should be targeted toward the structured evaluation of the client's everyday activities and participation. A variety of functional behaviors related to communication, ADLs, IADLs, and responsive behaviors should be assessed (see Box 5.5 for examples of communication-related daily activities). The clinician should emphasize those ADLs or responsive behaviors that the person with dementia or caregivers described as being the most problematic for life participation. Both activity abilities and limitations should be noted, with limitations characterized in terms of nature, duration, and quality, as per the ICF (WHO, 2001). For instance, a client might be able to make requests, but the nature of the requests reflects poor pragmatic abilities or inappropriate behaviors; or a client may be able to read instructions to complete simple meal preparation, but may take an excessive amount of time to do so.

If a client's deficits are limiting the ability to perform one or more ADLs or IADLs, then the clinician needs to identify strengths that may be used in designing compensatory strategies, so that

---

Box 5.5 Examples of Communication-Related ADLs and IADLs

- Engaging in conversations with significant others should be considered an ADL
- Making requests for basic needs
- Reading prescription labels
- Writing checks and managing money
- Making grocery lists and following recipes to prepare meals
- Following a to-do list or reading instructions related to home management
- Using the telephone
- Using a calendar to keep track of appointments
- Reading and writing e-mails or letters
- Using the Internet for personal needs and interests

---

the client may continue to perform these activities. ADL and IADL measures that include communication skills (e.g., telephone use) and higher-order cognitive skills (e.g., money management) may be used in treatment planning, as well as for measuring the outcomes of speech-language pathology treatments. These ADL and IADL tools have better ecological validity than impairment-oriented assessment tools, as they address everyday needs of the client.

Assessing ADLs and IADLs

Dementia–Specific ADL/IADL Measures. There are a variety of ADL and IADL tools that were developed specifically for persons with dementia. These tools are more commonly administered by other interprofessional team members, usually occupational therapists, but it is important for SLPs to glean information from all parts of the medical record and team assessment results. Some of these tools are meant to determine the person's "stage" of disease. Clinicians should be aware, though, that the practice of determining the person's stage of dementia, which effectively "labels" the person, in assessment for treatment planning is often too prescriptive and results in use of generic intervention approaches thought to be appropriate for that stage. Without an assessment of strengths and treatment potential, the emphasis on staging may limit the treatment options available to individuals, which is the antithesis of a person-centered approach (Bourgeois, Brush, Douglas, Khayum, & Rogalski, 2016).

Two examples of ADL/IADL tools used in staging are the Functional Assessment Staging (FAST; Reisberg, 1987) and the Allen Diagnostic Module – 2nd edition (ADM-2; Earhart, 2006), which also has a screening version, the Allen Cognitive Level Screen – 5 (ACLS-5; Allen, Austin, David, Earhart, McCraith, & Riska-Williams, 2007). The FAST assesses physical and instrumental ADLs, with 16 items. The FAST was designed to provide a valid and reliable assessment of the progression of functional loss through the course of the degenerative illness (i.e., stages), and is based on caregiver interview. Clinicians should be aware that the FAST may underestimate the communicative abilities of persons with late-stage dementia (Bayles, Tomoeda, Cruz, & Mahendra, 2000). The ADM-2 and ACLS-5 were developed from the Allen Cognitive Scales (Allen, Earhart, & Blue, 1992) and include craft-based performance assessments that were developed using the cognitive disabilities model. The purpose of the ADM-2 is to assess global cognitive abilities, learning potential, and performance abilities.

The Disability Assessment in Dementia Scale (DADS; Gélinas, Gauthier, McIntyre, & Gautier, 1999) can be completed as either a questionnaire or an interview with the caregiver. The caregiver is asked to identify the client's ability to initiate and perform basic ADLs and IADLs, and consists of 46 items that can be categorized into three domains: initiation, planning and organization, and performance. The DADS was developed for use in clinical trials, and has been shown to be sensitive to change over time, with good reliability and validity (Feldman et al., 2001; Gélinas et al., 1999). Despite this, the utility of this test is questionable for typical clinical populations. Consequently, the Activities of Daily Living Questionnaire Scale (ADLQ; Johnson, Barion, Rademaker, Rehkemper, & Weintraub, 2004; Oakley, Lai, & Sunderland, 1999) was developed for use in more typical outpatient settings. The ADLQ is based on an interview with a caregiver, and measures functioning in six areas of ADLs: self-care, household care, employment and recreation, shopping and money, travel, and communication. The ADLQ has good reliability and validity and is sensitive to change over time.

General ADL/IADL Measures. Tools that were not developed specifically for persons with dementia can be useful for this population. Several of these tools assess performance in simulated everyday activities. For example, the Rivermead Behavioral Memory Test, 3rd edition (RBMT-3; Wilson et al., 2008) is a well-studied measure of everyday memory functioning, which has a variety of simulated everyday tasks (e.g., recalling faces, routes, and stories). The RBMT-3 is more ecologically valid than the impairment-based memory tests, but some of the tasks are still quite contrived (e.g., route finding). The RBMT-3 is a performance-based assessment of orientation; immediate and delayed verbal, visual, procedural, and prospective recall; and novel task learning. The novel task is new in this edition, and involves a six-piece puzzle that the client must assemble in a set order and position with three learning trials and a delayed trial. There is also a larger normative sample, extending up to 96 years, and includes people with brain injury. Two parallel forms are available to prevent practice effects (note that four forms were included in earlier versions).

Similarly, tests of attention and executive functions that are based on simulations have been developed. The Test of Everyday Attention (TEA; Robertson, Ward, Ridgeway, & Nimmo-Smith, 1994) is a performance-based test of attention that simulates functional activities, such as using the elevator or telephone, listening for lottery numbers, and searching a map. Sustained, selective, divided, and alternating attention can be measured in a variety of tasks using these everyday functional behaviors. In addition to the ecological validity provided through use of everyday behaviors, other advantages include parallel forms of the TEA so that repeated measurement does not result in learning effects, and standardization on adults with hearing impairments (Robertson et al., 1994) and those with dementia (Robertson, Ward, Ridgeway, & Nimmo-Smith, 1996).

The Behavioral Assessment of the Dysexecutive Syndrome (BADS; Wilson, Alderman, Burgess, Emslei, & Evans, 1996) has seven subtests that simulate everyday tasks to assess cognitive flexibility, problem solving, planning, and self-monitoring. The BADS has norms that extend to 87 years for healthy adults and 76 years for adults with brain injury. The BADS does not have psychometric data for test–retest reliability; otherwise, it does have adequate psychometric properties. Likewise, the Behavioral Dyscontrol Scale (BDS; Belanger et al., 2005) can be used with persons with AD. The BDS contains nine items that require motor responses in the following areas: alternating hand sequences, inhibition, learning complex motor sequences, alphanumeric sequencing, and awareness of deficit or insight. The BDS is scored using a three-point scale. Reliability and validity were demonstrated with older adults. The BDS discriminates between persons with AD and MCI, but not between those with MCI and typical older adults (Belanger et al., 2005). In addition, the BDS predicts performance in ADLs, after controlling for severity of memory deficits.

ADL and IADL Rating Scales. Other ADL and IADL rating scales were developed for rehabilitation populations in general: the Functional Independence Measure (FIM) Uniform Data

System for Medical Rehabilitation (State University of New York at Buffalo, 1993), the Functional Assessment Measure (FAM; Hall, 1997; Hall, Hamilton, Gordon, & Zasler, 1993), and the Rehabilitation Institute of Chicago Functional Assessment Scale – Version II (RIC-FAS II; Heinemann, 1989). The Functional Activities Questionnaire (FAQ; Pfeffer, Kurosaki, Harrah, Chance, & Filos, 1982) was developed with a group of people with MCI and a group with dementia in the standardization. The FAQ has been assessed for use across four ethnic groups in the United States, with no difference across groups, but there were effects of age, education, and depression (Tappen, Roselli, & Engstrom, 2010). These rating scales are used by clinicians to indicate level of assistance in functional activities, for example, dressing, bathing, grooming, money management, meal preparation, and communication. The client is given a score from 7 (independent) to 1 (dependent) for each behavior on each of the scales.

Assessing Communication Activities

Dementia-Specific Communication Measures. Speech-language pathologists most often administer tools designed to assess communication activities. A relatively quick and useful test designed for adults with dementia is the Functional Linguistic Communication Inventory (FLCI; Bayles & Tomoeda, 1994). The FLCI subtests include greeting and naming, comprehension of signs, object to picture matching, word reading and comprehension, following commands, and pantomime. While the tasks are mostly decontextualized, they tend to use more functional stimuli and some are embedded in a more conversational context. Another tool, which was developed for assessing persons with dementia in long-term care environments, is the Communication Outcome Measure of Functional Independence (COMFI; Santo Pietro & Boczko, 1997).

The COMFI scale has been used in several research studies, and would also be a useful functional assessment tool in clinical settings, as it measures psychosocial interaction, communication and conversation, mealtime independence, and cognition, based on observation during mealtimes. Psychometric properties, however, have not been tested widely. For persons with severe communication impairments who communicate only through nonverbal expressions of affect, the Observed Emotion Rating Scale (Lawton, Van Haitsma, & Klapper, 1999; Lawton, Van Haitsma, Perkinson, & Ruckdeschel, 1999) can be used. This tool is completed by a clinician based on a 10-minute observation period, during which the duration of affective states (pleasure, anger, anxiety and fear, sadness, interest, and contentment) is recorded on a five-point scale, from never occurs to occurred for more than five minutes.

General Communication Measures. The Functional Standardized Touchscreen Assessment of Cognition (FSTAC; Coles & Carson, 2013; www.cognitive-innovations.com/fstac.html) is an innovative assessment tool that is useful for high-level clients, particularly in rehabilitation or home care, that comes in the form of an iPad app. The FSTAC examines cognitive abilities and breakdowns during 14 functional tasks that range from simple to complex and are completed with the integration of real-life distractions, such as text messages, phone messages, and noise. The FSTAC app generates a report of the client's cognitive (e.g., general knowledge, auditory and visual attention and short-term memory, language comprehension, executive functions) and functional (e.g., money and medication management, grocery shopping, phone skills, recalling tasks) performance.

The Communicative Activities of Daily Living, 3rd edition (CADL-3; Holland, Fromm, & Wozniak, 2017), measures performance in a variety of simulated communication activities (e.g., visit to the doctor, telephone use, and checkbook and pill bottle comprehension). The CADL-3 was designed for use with adults with acquired neurological disorders. The standardization sample included primarily persons with right- and left-hemisphere strokes, and a smaller number of persons with traumatic brain injury and other neurological diagnoses. The participants were mostly non–Hispanic White, with a few representatives from racial and ethnic minorities. The CADL-3 has good psychometric properties, but requires further testing with persons with dementia.

The Assessment of Language-Related Functional Activities (ALFA; Baines et al., 1999) also directly targets the performance of functional activities during the assessment, such as telling time, counting money, addressing an envelope, solving daily math problems, writing a check, balancing a checkbook, understanding medicine labels, using a calendar, reading instructions, using the telephone, and writing a phone message. For each functional activity, the clinician records an objective, quantitative score, so that functional gains may be captured over time.

The Functional Assessment of Communication Skills for Adults (ASHA-FACS; Frattali, Thompson, Holland, Wohl, & Ferketic, 1995) involves observation of the client's ability to perform everyday communication activities such as using the telephone, reading television guides and newspapers, and having a conversation in four domains: social communication; communication of basic needs; reading, writing, and number concepts; and daily planning. Rating scales are completed for each item. The ASHA-FACS manual provides information on the adequacy of its psychometric properties.

The Assessment for Living with Aphasia, 2nd edition (ALA-2; Kagan et al., 2013) is a self-report measure used to obtain valuable information regarding the impact of the individual's aphasia on all domains of the Living with Aphasia: Framework for Outcome Measurement (A-FROM; Kagan et al., 2008): communication and language environment, personal identify, attitudes and feelings, life participation, and severity of impairment. The A-FROM was designed with the ICF (WHO, 2001) domains in mind (see Chapter 4 for more information on the A-FROM). The focus of the assessment is on the person's perception of their aphasia and its impact on their participation in life situations and daily activities (e.g., work performance, recreational activities, relationships with family members and friends, daily conversations, activities of daily living). While this tool was designed for people with aphasia specifically, it can be useful for persons with dementia or primary progressive aphasia.

Another communication domain that has particular relevance for the development of functional treatment goals is reading. Reading comprehension can be assessed using either formal or informal reading comprehension measures. Neuropsychologists often administer the Wechsler Test of Adult Reading (WTAR) (Holdnack, 2001) to get an estimate of the person's premorbid reading function and IQ. The WTAR consists of 50 irregularly spelled words (maximum score = 50 points); raw scores are standardized by age and demographic classification. The WTAR scores have good stability over time and predictive validity, but may underestimate premorbid IQ in patients with more severe damage and AD (McFarlane, Welch, & Rodgers, 2006), and therefore, be of limited use in treatment planning.

In the absence of dementia-specific standardized reading measures, those that have been constructed for persons with aphasia can be used. Those that include functional items, such as common traffic signs, medication labels, telephone directories, and menus, may be a better indicator of preserved reading abilities than decontextualized assessments of single word or sentence comprehension. For example, the functional reading subtest of the Reading Comprehension Battery for Aphasia, 2nd edition (RCBA-2; LaPointe & Horner, 1998) and subtests of the CADL-3 (Holland et al., 2017) are more useful for functional assessment than reading subtests of comprehensive standardized aphasia batteries. Even if the client is not able to perform the tasks on standardized instruments, informal and personalized reading assessment using the client's name, address, and other functional words and phrases provides direct evidence of reading ability that can be useful for devising strategies for functional behaviors.

Communication Rating Scales. Because many other rating scales for ADLs did not address communication abilities in detail, the Functional Communication Measures (FCM; Frattali et al.,

1995) were developed by the ASHA Task Force on Treatment Outcome and Cost Effectiveness. This tool was designed to measure change in FCM rating to demonstrate achievement of functional outcomes resulting from clinical intervention. The clinician rates the client for 13 different communication variables on a seven-point scale, before and after treatment. The FCM scales can be used with any population. Other quick tools designed for people with aphasia or other cognitive-communicative disorders could be used, such as the Communication Effectiveness Index (CETI; Lomas et al., 1989). On the CETI, a communication partner is asked to rate the client on a variety of everyday communication situations (e.g., reading the newspaper and talking in a group).

Discourse Measures. Persons with a primary progressive aphasia profile often display discourse production and comprehension deficits early in the disease process. Those persons with Alzheimer's dementia and other types of dementia syndromes also display discourse production and comprehension deficits as the disease progresses. Discourse production and comprehension can be analyzed by obtaining samples of monologue and/or dialogue tasks (Togher, 2001). Monologues are most often used in clinical settings, and may be composed of narrative (i.e., picture description) or procedural tasks (i.e., activity description). Dialogue samples may be collected through interview, conversation, or debate tasks. Discourse samples can be analyzed with quantitative and/or qualitative techniques that can result in rich detail, although these rich analyses are often too time consuming for clinicians in busy clinical settings.

Examples of quantitative microlinguistic (i.e., phonology, semantics, syntax, and morphology) measures include number of word finding errors or number of different words produced per narrative (e.g., Chapman et al., 2002; Ehrlich, Obler, & Clark, 1997; Tompkins, 1995), and of macrolinguistic measures include cohesion and coherence, or accuracy and completeness of main concepts (Nicholas & Brookshire, 1993, 1995). These structured samples may be confusing for a person with cognitive deficits and may not elicit a typical discourse sample. Additionally, clinicians must consider cultural norms for communication when assessing clients from diverse backgrounds; some tasks or analyses may not be appropriate. Also, the time-consuming nature of discourse analyses is a barrier to clinical use in many settings; an advantage, however, is that the structure allows the procedures to be easily replicated to examine change over time.

The Discourse Abilities Profile (Terrell & Ripich, 1989) assesses the presence or absence of discourse features in a variety of tasks, including narrative discourse, procedural discourse, and spontaneous conversation, and was designed specifically for use with persons with dementia. Discourse features coded range from specific narrative features, procedural features, turn taking, and types of speech acts to general discourse behaviors. The Profile of Pragmatic Impairment in Communication (PPIC; Hays, Niven, Godfrey, & Linscott, 2004) was developed using Gricean principles and assesses the client's production and comprehension of literal content as well as intended meaning, and other rules of conversation, such as social style, subject matter, and aesthetics. The PPIC demonstrated good reliability and validity, and results relate to cognitive abilities.

Dynamic and authentic assessment procedures, such as the Communicative Profiling System (Simmons-Mackie & Damico, 1996), provide thorough and useful information about a client's communication. Qualitative analyses of discourse samples offer the richest descriptions, particularly Conversation Analysis (CA; e.g., Damico, Oelschlaeger, & Simmons-Mackie, 1999; Damico & Simmons-Mackie, 2003; Perkins, Whitworth, & Lesser, 1998; Tetnowski & Franklin, 2003). The results of CA can be combined with results of cognitive-neuropsychological findings for comprehensive treatment planning (Damico & Simmons-Mackie, 2003; Tetnowski & Franklin, 2003). The benefit of using either of these qualitative analyses is the strong ecological validity of the results. A significant disadvantage is the time-consuming nature of such analyses, if done thoroughly. Thus, we recommend that an experienced clinician learn the principles of qualitative analyses to enhance observations between a client and a typical communication partner (e.g., family and/or staff caregiver). Of note, production of written narratives can be assessed in a similar fashion, with the expectation that similar micro- and macro-linguistic deficits would be seen.

Formal and informal measures of discourse comprehension may be used to document difficulties comprehending lengthy, complex, and/or abstract discourse. In persons with dementia, these deficits are due to attention, memory, reasoning, and/or language deficits. On such measures (e.g., Discourse Comprehension Test, 2nd edition, Brookshire & Nicholas, 1997) persons with dementia are expected to have greater difficulty with comprehension of abstract language and/or details than with main ideas (Welland, Lubinski, & Higginbotham, 2002). They may also have difficulty with increasing length and complexity due to processing demands. Other resources, though not dementia specific, provide reviews of comprehension measures (e.g., Lezak, Howleson, Bigler, & Tranel, 2012; Meyers, 1998; Tompkins, 1995).

Engagement Measures. Other less traditional assessment tools for SLPs include measures of engagement, including domains such as positive and negative affect, and passive and active engagement. Although SLPs have not commonly measured behaviors related to engagement, they are relevant as these behaviors do represent communicative functioning. These behaviors allow caregivers to determine whether the person's needs for engagement are being met. For example, a person might display responsive behaviors (e.g., complaining, yelling, agitation, etc.) to indicate that needs are not being met. This is an opportunity for the SLP (and other interprofessional team members, such as occupational therapy and therapeutic recreation) to identify meaningful and engaging activities for that individual, implement the activity program, measure the effects of the engagement intervention, and then share the effective program with the rest of the caregivers.

Researchers have been developing measures of engagement to document the many functional behaviors that have the potential to be affected by nonpharmacological and behavioral interventions, such as Montessori-based Dementia Programming® (Camp, 2006). The Menorah Park Engagement Scale (MPES) (Camp, 2010) measures four types of engagement (constructive, passive, non-engagement, and other engagement). Similarly, the Observational Measurement of Engagement Assessment (OME; Cohen-Mansfield, Dakheel-Ali, Jensen, Marx, & Thein, 2012) is a validated measure that measures: *Duration* of time in seconds that the participant is engaged with the stimulus; *Attention to the Stimulus*; and *Attitude to Stimulus* (positive or negative facial expression, verbal content, and physical movement).

Assessment of Body Structures and Functions

Comprehensive assessment of body structures and functions is an essential aspect of differential diagnosis (WHO, 2001). An interprofessional team will use static, impairment-based standardized tests as part of a diagnostic assessment process that leads to an individual's diagnosis of dementia. Assessment of cognitive domains includes attention, perception, memory, and executive functions (e.g., insight, inhibition, initiation, and planning). Assessment of language domains includes spoken and written language production and auditory and reading comprehension. As noted above, the cognitive assessment battery completed by neuropsychology might suffice for diagnosis, or sometimes an SLP will conduct further static, impairment-based cognitive-linguistic assessments. However, there is no need for this type of assessment during assessment for treatment planning or measuring outcomes. Clinicians should keep in mind that impairment-oriented assessment tends to encourage impairment-oriented intervention; thus, static impairment-based assessment is often *not* the most effective approach for developing a functional treatment plan for individuals with dementia or for measuring functional outcomes. However, it is recognized that there can be policies around reimbursement in the United States that require SLPs to administer a diagnostic test.

In that case, a brief assessment should be administered, and then move on to informal and functional assessment procedures.

In assessment for treatment planning, the clinician seeks information that will assist in developing compensatory strategies for impairments by capitalizing on strengths. In the "Flip the Rehab Model" approach, the use of standardized testing should occur *after* the completion of person-centered interviews, observation, and assessment of activity and life participation, rather than at the beginning of the assessment process as is done in a more traditional rehabilitation model. After determining how the person with dementia experiences activity limitations and participation restrictions, and identifying desired activities, standardized tests may be used to further assess how cognitive-linguistic processes are likely impacting the ability to participate in each specific activity. Using dynamic assessment procedures, rather than the standardized approach, usually reveals the most useful information regarding what accounts for success or failure in various tasks (see Box 5.6).

Although there can be variability across individuals with the same diagnosis, clinicians should be knowledgeable about the types of strengths and impairments that are likely to be present in people with various dementia syndromes (see Chapters 2 and 3 for detailed information on dementia syndromes). For example, dynamic assessment of body structures and functions can identify strengths in reading comprehension and oral reading abilities in persons with Alzheimer's dementia. These strengths can be used to develop written cues for conversation and memory (Bourgeois, 1992). For individuals with Primary Progressive Aphasia, impairment-based assessment may provide a more comprehensive clinical profile of language strengths and weaknesses (e.g., word-finding, fluency, and grammatical construction for oral expression; single word comprehension vs. comprehension of grammatically complex sentences; presence of alexia and agraphia), which can guide treatment planning for training of functional communication strategies, along with written and picture-based communication supports (Croot, Nickels, Laurence, & Manning, 2009; Mesulam, Weineke, Thompson, Rogalski, & Weintraub, 2012).

Specific types of impairment-based assessment procedures are described below, which may be used to supplement the person-centered assessment in the "Flip the Rehab Model" approach.

Box 5.6 Examples of Variables to Manipulate in Dynamic Assessment

- Modality of stimuli
  - Visual cues – text and/or pictures to accompany verbal commands
  - Auditory cues – reading aloud the written commands for tasks

- Modality of responses
  - Pointing to written or picture choices instead of verbal response
  - Gesture response in addition to verbal response
  - Verbal responses instead of written responses

- Complexity of stimuli
  - Reduce number of choices
  - Change array of choices from horizontal to vertical presentation
  - Decreasing the linguistic complexity or length of commands or other materials
  - Personalizing the stimuli

Global measures of cognition are generally brief and can be completed by persons with shorter attention spans, which makes them preferable for severely impaired persons, as compared to lengthy cognitive assessment batteries or multiple measures of specific cognitive processes. Furthermore, many of the tasks on specific cognitive assessments are decontextualized, making it even more difficult for persons with severe deficits to understand the tasks (Mungas, Reed, & Kramer, 2003). A thorough discussion of these tools is beyond the scope of this chapter. There are other valuable resources for comprehensive overviews of impairment-based tools, such as the book, *Neuropsychological Assessment* (5th edition) (Lezak et al., 2012), which is used widely by neuropsychologists and other health professionals.

Global Dementia Rating Scales

Mental status rating scales are used to translate cognitive impairments into global stages of disease, or severity of cognitive deficits. There are two types of mental status rating scales: interview-based and client-administered. Earlier, staging was used to classify clients and predict relative treatment outcomes (Albert, 1994); trends have shifted however, and among some skilled nursing and rehabilitation facility corporations in the United States, staging has become used widely to implement prescriptive intervention approaches. Although the skills and behaviors included in various global dementia rating scales could provide important information for assessment for treatment planning, clinicians are cautioned against this prescriptive treatment planning approach by stage, as this is contrary to person-centered care. Additionally, the evidence-based treatment approaches that can be used in intervention for persons with dementia were not developed for specific stages of dementia, but a range of cognitive impairment (Bourgeois, 2015). More importantly, the clinician must identify the particular cognitive strengths and challenges in a client, regardless of stage, so that personalized interventions and strategies can be planned. Some of the more commonly used global cognitive tools will be discussed; the reader is again referred to other resources for detailed descriptions of such tools, such as Lezak et al. (2012).

Interview-Based Rating Scales. Measures such as the Global Deterioration Scale for Age-Related Cognitive Decline and Alzheimer's Disease (GDS; Reisberg et al., 1982), the Clinical Dementia Rating Scale (CDR; Morris, 1993), and the Clinician Interview-Based Impression of Change Plus Caregiver Information (CIBIC-Plus; Schneider, Colin, Lyness, & Chui, 1997) involve subjective evaluation of a person's cognitive skills (e.g., memory, orientation, judgment, problem solving, community affairs, home and hobbies, personal care, psychiatric symptoms, and performance on psychometric tests) based on an interview with a caregiver by a skilled clinician. The caregivers provide information regarding behavioral functioning, from which the clinician subjectively evaluates clients' cognitive skills (e.g., memory, orientation, judgment, problem solving, community affairs, home and hobbies, personal care, psychiatric symptoms, and performance on psychometric tests). Isella and colleagues (2006) have reported promising evidence for the reliability and validity of informant-based scales for assessing cognitive impairment and decline in dementia.

The CDR involves interviews with both the client and the caregiver. There are seven domain scores: memory, orientation, judgment, problem solving, community activities, home and hobbies, and personal care. The CDR differentiates the types of impairment profiles seen in AD, frontotemporal dementia (FTD), and semantic dementia (SD) (Rosen et al., 2004). The GDS rates seven severity levels, or stages, of dementia: for example, 1 (normal), 3 (early confusion), 5 (middle dementia), and 7 (late dementia). Clinicians determine the GDS score using all sources of available information, which might include a structured interview regarding cognitive, behavioral, and functional abilities, including memory, orientation, judgment, problem solving, community affairs, home and hobbies, personal care, psychiatric symptoms, and performance on psychometric tests. Clinicians should be aware that the GDS might underestimate the communicative abilities of persons with severe dementia (Bayles et al., 2000). The CIBIC-Plus (Schneider et al., 1997) is an elaborate scale, with scores based on interviews with both persons with dementia and caregivers. The CIBIC-Plus evaluates four domains: general, cognitive, behavioral, and activities of daily living (ADLs). The CIBC-Plus is used often in clinical trials and can provide comprehensive evidence of treatment efficacy, and may be useful in future prevention trials (Reisberg, 2007).

Client–Administered Scales. The best-known client-administered mental status rating scale is the MMSE (Folstein et al., 1975), which has been revised as the MMSE-2 (Folstein & Folstein, 2010); the MMSE-2 is available in many languages. This tool is used widely across healthcare settings because it is quick to administer, and gives a broad idea of a client's cognitive functioning. The MMSE screens orientation to time and place, language (name two objects, repeat a sentence, follow a three-step command, read aloud and follow a written command, and write a sentence), visuospatial construction (design copy), immediate and delayed verbal memory (three-word recall), and mental control (count backward from 100 by 7). Severity levels are determined by criterion scores. Because it is used so frequently, the MMSE simplifies communication across healthcare providers who are familiar with the interpretation of its scores and cognitive severity levels.

Age-, culture-, and education-related norms are available for more accurate interpretation of MMSE results (Crum, Anthony, Bassett, & Folstein, 1993; Dufouil et al., 2000; Grigoletto, Zappala, Anderson, & Lebowitz, 1999; Jones & Gallo, 2002; Mungas, Marshall, Weldon, Haan, & Reed, 1996). Crum and colleagues (1993) suggested different cutoff scores for normal performance based on education: 29/30 for persons with 9–12 years of education; 26/30 for persons with 5–8 years of schooling, and 22/30 for persons with 0–4 years of schooling. Clinicians must also consider that the tasks are highly dependent on language abilities, so persons with focal language disturbances will likely appear to be more cognitively impaired than they are. The MMSE-2 (Folstein & Folstein, 2010) is more sensitive to subcortical cognitive deficits than the original MMSE and is also available in eight languages and three dialects of Spanish. Older persons with depression tend to score lower on the MMSE (Folstein, Folstein, & Folstein, 2011).

The Montreal Cognitive Assessment (MoCA; Nasreddine et al., 2005) is a reliable global cognitive measure that is more sensitive than the MMSE in detecting early AD and MCI. The MoCA screens a variety of cognitive and language processes: attention (trails, digit span, and serial 7s), orientation, visuoconstructional skills (cube and clock draw), delayed word recall, and language (confrontation naming, repetition, verbal fluency, and abstraction). There are 30 possible points on the MoCA, with the cutoff score for "normal" at 26.

The Self-Administered Gerocognitive Exam (SAGE, Scharre et al., 2010) (available at https://wexnermedical.osu.edu/brain-spine-neuro/memory-disorders/sage) is a brief self-administered cognitive screening instrument used to identify mild cognitive impairment (MCI). The test has a sensitivity of 79 percent and a false positive rate of 5 percent in detecting cognitive impairment from normal subjects. It is not appropriate for individuals who are not literate or visually impaired.

The Saint Louis University Mental Status Examination (SLUMS) (Tariq et al., 2006) is another brief cognitive screening tool that assesses orientation, memory, executive function, and attention. It was designed to have a greater range of scores in order to better detect impairments at the mild level as well as language impairments (Buckingham et al., 2013).

The Alzheimer's Quick Test (AQT; Wiig, 2002) is a test that is sensitive to early cognitive decline of persons with MCI or dementia. The AQT can be administered in approximately 5–10 minutes. The AQT includes five sets of timed naming tasks, with scoring for both accuracy and timing of responses, which results in criterion-referenced scores that fall in ranges of normal, less accurate or slower than normal, nonnormal, and pathological. Advantages of the AQT are good reliability for repeated administration, sensitivity to early parietal lobe dysfunction, and utility with a broad range of ages and cultural backgrounds. The AQT has been standardized on persons aged 15–72. Results can be interpreted according to various dementia profiles.

Comprehensive Cognitive Assessment Batteries

Dementia-Specific Cognitive Measures. There are a variety of comprehensive assessment batteries of cognitive and behavioral functioning that assess the client at the body structure and function levels. A brief description of some of the commonly used comprehensive batteries in dementia diagnosis follows. The Dementia Rating Scale – 2 (DRS-2; Jurica, Leitten, & Mattis, 2001) evaluates attention, initiation, construction, conceptualization, perseveration, praxis, abstraction, and verbal and nonverbal recent memory, with scores ranging from 0 to 144 (cutoff for mild impairment is 123). The DRS-2 can be used with adults ranging from 56 to 105 years old to sensitively measure and characterize degree of dementia, with performance profiles that differentiate AD from Parkinson's disease (PD) and Huntington's disease (HD) (Johnson-Greene, 2004; Mungas et al., 2003). Advantages of the DRS-2 include its usefulness with persons with lower levels of cognitive function and as a longitudinal measure. A disadvantage of the DRS-2 is that it does not provide normative data for persons who have fewer than eight years of education, or for ethnic minorities; however, it does provide age- and education-corrected normative data (Johnson-Greene, 2004).

The Consortium to Establish a Registry for Alzheimer's Disease Neuropsychological Assessment (CERAD; Welsh et al., 1994) battery includes subtests for language (e.g., verbal fluency and confrontation naming), constructional praxis, memory (free recall, and delayed recall and recognition), and the MMSE. When used with the CDR and the DRS, the CERAD battery can be used to obtain a diagnostic impression of AD alone, AD associated with other disorders, or non-AD dementia.

The Repeatable Battery for the Assessment of Neuropsychological Status (RBANS; Randolph, Tierney, Mohr, & Chase, 1998) includes 12 subtests yielding six indices, such as visuospatial, memory, attention, and language abilities. Norms for standard scores are available for persons from 20 to 89 years old. Parallel forms were designed for repeated test administration to prevent learning effects. Test administration takes up to 30 minutes. The RBANS was designed to identify abnormal cognitive decline in older adults, and can be used in differentiating dementia types, including AD, HD (Randolph et al., 1998), and PD (Beatty et al., 2003). Yet, Beatty and colleagues warned that the diagnosis of dementia should not be made using the RBANS alone. The RBANS can also be used to screen for cognitive deficits in younger adults with greater sensitivity than the MMSE and DRS (Randolph et al., 1998), as well as in older adults (Duff et al., 2005). Caution should be used in interpreting results for persons with lower education levels (Gontkovsky, Mold, & Beatty, 2002). Component analyses found significant differences between probable Alzheimer's disease and non–Alzheimer's type dementia groups on the memory component score, but not on other component scores or on RBANS index scores (Garcia, Leahy, Corradi, & Forchetti, 2008).

The Alzheimer's Disease Assessment Scale – Cognitive (ADAS-cog; Rosen et al., 1984) is a cognitive testing instrument widely used in clinical drug trials. The ADAS-cog consists of 11 items that measure memory (recognition and recall), language (comprehension and production), praxis (constructional and ideational), and orientation, and takes approximately 30 minutes to administer. There are 70 points possible, with an expected mean decline of 9 points per year in untreated persons with AD, and an increase of 3–4 points is likely to reflect clinical improvement (Mohs, 2006). Versions of the ADAS are also available in French, German, Spanish, Italian, Finnish, Korean, Danish, Greek, Hebrew, and Japanese.

The Severe Impairment Battery (SIB; Saxton, McGonigle-Gibson, Swihart, Miller, & Boller, 1990; Saxton, McGonigle, Swihart, & Boller, 1993) was developed specifically for persons with severe cognitive deficits, for whom other neuropsychological instruments are not sensitive to change or result in "floor" effects. The SIB allows these persons to participate in testing through use of gestural cues and by capitalizing on preserved skills. The SIB has norms for persons 51–91 years old, with strong psychometric properties and good reliability on repeated administration (Saxton, McGonigle-Gibson, Swihart, Miller, & Boller, 1990; Schmitt et al., 1997). Thus, the SIB is useful in drug trials for participants with severe dementia. The SIB was designed to be administered by SLPs, occupational therapists, or neuropsychologists in approximately 30 minutes. For persons with very severe deficits, this testing may not be possible, so a short form was developed (SIB-S), which takes approximately 10–15 minutes to administer (Saxton et al., 2005). The SIB-S is as sensitive to change, and assesses the same nine cognitive domains, as the original SIB: expressive language, memory (verbal and nonverbal), social interaction, color naming, praxis, reading, writing, fluency, and attention. An advantage of the SIB is that standardized translations are available in German, French, and Italian, and the SIB-S is available in English and French.

Cognitive–Linguistic Assessment Measures Often Used by SLPs. The Arizona Battery of Communication in Dementia (ABCD; Bayles & Tomoeda, 1993) is a comprehensive assessment battery that includes four screening tasks (speech discrimination, visual perception, visual field, and visual agnosia), and 14 subtests in the areas of mental status, concept definition, verbal learning and memory, linguistic comprehension and expression, and visuospatial construction, and is therefore used extensively in diagnostic settings. The benefits of the ABCD are that it is standardized with an extensive population of clients across the cognitive continuum, and that it is thorough for assessing a variety of cognitive domains. The ABCD differentiates Alzheimer's dementia from normal functioning and from aphasia. It also can be used to determine severity of cognitive deficits. A challenge in using the ABCD is that it is quite lengthy and time consuming. Thus, the full battery is rarely administered in its entirety, but clinicians may choose specific subtests to probe further specific cognitive domains that will assist them developing an effective treatment plan.

Given resource limitations, clinicians usually need to use quicker measures in assessment for treatment planning. A measure developed specifically for use by SLPs, but not specifically for dementia, is the Cognitive-Linguistic Quick Test (CLQT; Helm-Estabrooks, 2001). The CLQT can be completed in less than 30 minutes, and assesses orientation, attention, verbal and visual memory, confrontation naming, auditory comprehension, and executive functions. The CLQT includes the clock-drawing task (Freedman et al., 1994), which is sensitive to attention, memory, executive functions, and visuospatial construction deficits, and is particularly well suited to persons with lower education levels (Barrie, 2002; Royall, Cordes, & Polk, 1998). The CLQT provides subscale scores and severity levels for attention, memory, language, and executive functions, as well as a global score and severity level. The CLQT also provides a separate perseveration score, which is a sensitive indicator of brain injury (Helm-Estabrooks, 2001). Norms are provided for persons 18–89 years old, and the nonclinical standardization samples included African American, Latino, and White participants. The clinical standardization sample had fewer minorities, and included persons with right-, left-, and bilateral hemisphere strokes, closed head injury, and AD. The CLQT is also available in Spanish. Test–retest reliability is adequate for most tasks; interrater reliability and validity are adequate.

Another cognitive-linguistic battery not developed specifically for dementia but often used by SLPs is the Ross Information Processing Assessment – Geriatric (RIPA-G; Ross-Swain & Fogle,

1996). The RIPA–G assesses attention; orientation; working, recent, and remote memory; verbal organization and reasoning; and auditory and reading comprehension. The standardization sample included residents of skilled nursing facilities who were 65–98 years old and had cognitive-linguistic deficits from a variety of medical conditions (e.g., chronic obstructive pulmonary disease, Alzheimer's, and stroke), as well as healthy control subjects who were 65–94 years old. The RIPA–G is a variation of the original test, which is often used with younger clients (i.e., under 72 years): the Ross Information Processing Assessment – 2 (RIPA-2; Ross-Swain, 1996). The standardization sample of the RIPA-2 included persons with traumatic brain injury, ages 15–77 years old. There are some psychometric limitations to be aware of with the RIPA versions, but the revisions have stronger reliability and validity than the original RIPA. The internal consistency and interrater reliability of the RIPA-2 are adequate.

An innovative measure, created by an SLP and an occupational therapist, the Standardized Touchscreen Assessment of Cognition (STAC; Coles & Carson, 2013; www.cognitive-innovations.com/stac.html), comes in the form of an iPad app. The STAC is both comprehensive and efficient and might be useful for people in the early stages of dementia. Cognitive domains assessed include: attention, memory, sequencing, visual scanning and attention, executive function, processing speed, and language. The assessment can be completed by clients on their own or with the help of a rehabilitation assistant; for clients with dementia, an assistant would likely be needed. The STAC app automatically produces a score sheet. Additionally, the app has two forms of the test to reduce practice effects if the test is administered more than once within a short period of time. Normative data are provided for people up to 85 years old, and the app is constantly updating the normative data so that each time the test is initiated, the most recent data is used in scoring. The STAC was validated with neurotypical adults by Wallace and colleagues (2016), but requires further testing with those with cognitive disorders.

Domain-Specific Assessment Tools

Domain-specific assessments can be used to characterize specific deficits and document decline over time, or to further assess areas of weakness and strengths to gather information that is useful for designing a functional treatment plan. During the assessment process, the SLP should also keep in mind what is known about various dementia syndromes. In the early stages of different types of clinical dementia syndromes, a single cognitive or language domain may be impacted by neurodegenerative disease, as described in the Northwestern Care Pathway Model to dementia care (Morhardt et al., 2015). Alzheimer's dementia, the most commonly occurring dementia syndrome, is characterized by a prominent impairment in short-term episodic memory. Memory and executive function assessments are particularly useful in characterizing deficits and documenting decline in persons with mild cognitive impairment and early dementia (Mungas et al., 2003).

Many of the atypical dementias have different clinical presentations during the initial onset of symptoms, corresponding with the neuroanatomical region where the neurodegenerative disease first starts in the brain, and knowledge of these presentations can help SLPs to plan assessments and intervention. (Please see Chapters 2 and 3 for more details on various dementia syndromes.) For example, an individual diagnosed with Posterior Cortical Atrophy or Primary Progressive Aphasia may not be able to use text-based visual and graphic cueing systems as successful compensatory tools, compared to an individual with Alzheimer's dementia. As individuals with atypical dementia progress, multi-domain impairments will appear. For these individuals, the initial domain of impairment (e.g., memory, language, visuospatial skills, behavioral changes) will likely remain the most impaired domain throughout all stages of the disease process.

Many domain-specific instruments are designed specifically to be used by (neuro)psychologists; SLPs may use the results of these assessments to guide their treatment planning. Language is the one domain where SLPs might do more specific assessment than neuropsychologists. If there is a specific reason for wanting more information about language processing across modalities, impairment-oriented aphasia measures (Boston Diagnostic Aphasia Examination-3, BDAE-3; Goodglass, Kaplan, & Barresi, 2000; Western Aphasia Battery-Revised, WAB-R; Kertesz, 2006) may be administered to clients with dementia, or just the relevant subtests could be used. The Northwestern Anagram Test (NAT) (Weintraub et al., 2009) was developed to assess syntax competence when clients do not have intact speech production, particularly PPA. Similarly, the Northwestern Assessment of Verbs and Sentences (NAVS) (Cho-Reyes & Thompson, 2012; Thompson, 2012) assesses the comprehension and production of single action verbs and verbs in sentences, and canonical and noncanonical sentences.

Other psycholinguistic measures (e.g., Psycholinguistic Assessments of Language Processing in Aphasia, PALPA; Kay, Lesser, & Coltheart, 1992) could be used to examine specific language domains (i.e., semantics, syntax, and phonology, pragmatics, and discourse) if there is a particular need for this information. Comprehensive aphasia batteries sample a wide range of behaviors efficiently, but the administration of an entire aphasia battery to clients with dementia is not often possible in one sitting, and is rarely necessary. Instead, dynamic assessment with specific tasks can be conducted to determine specific linguistic characteristics that account for success or failure in communication and participation in everyday activities. Because the focus of this text is on functional management of communication and behaviors in persons with dementia, a complete review of impairment-oriented language measures will not be provided. There are many other resources available for such information (e.g., Bayles & Tomoeda, 2013; Lezak et al., 2012).

Assessment of Treatment Potential and Functional Outcomes

Treatment Potential

Assessment of treatment potential is one of the most essential parts of assessment for treatment planning, as it allows the clinician to determine the client's responsiveness to treatment techniques or compensatory strategies. This may also be an important part of the evaluation when considering reimbursement issues. Many third-party payers require that clinicians report on prognosis for improvement with treatment, and document a statement of reasonable expectation for achieving the desired treatment outcomes. Observation and informal assessment procedures can be used in trial therapy to assess treatment potential. For example, many clients with Alzheimer's dementia have preserved oral reading and reading comprehension abilities that can be capitalized on in designing compensatory strategies (Bourgeois, 1992; Bourgeois et al., 2002). Documentation of responsiveness to written cues is useful for stating reasonable expectation for progress in treatment, but impairment-oriented reading measures are not often useful for this purpose.

The Bourgeois Oral Reading Screen (Bourgeois, 2013) is an informal tool that can be used to document responsiveness to written cues (see Appendix 5.5). This tool is a five-item oral reading measure in two font sizes that is used to determine the appropriate font size for reading materials. Asking the client to read aloud and comment on each page provides valuable information about the font size that is read with ease and comprehension of written sentences. Because several of the items on this measure are written in the first person (e.g., My sister is 75 years old. I live in Swissvale.), the comments of the persons taking the test can be judged as indicative of comprehension (e.g., "My sister would never tell her age"; "I don't think I live in Swissvale") (Bourgeois et al., 2002).

Difficulty with this oral reading task does not necessarily dictate that a client cannot use written cues. Dynamic assessment should be used to determine if the client is able to respond to enlarged or enhanced cues. If the client does not read the sentences as instructed, the clinician can manipulate the physical characteristics of the stimuli (e.g., increasing font size, copying onto yellow paper, or showing one sentence and picture at a time). If the client attends to the stimuli, but appears confused by the task, then the clinician should use the client's personally relevant information to determine if the client can use written cues for conversations about personal information (e.g., "My name is Francine." "I live in Halifax."). Also, refer back to the sensory screening section of this chapter for font size assessment tools, as the display of text (font size, background) can make a big impact on performance and treatment potential (Brush et al., 2011; Elliot, 2011). The clinician should also do dynamic assessment to determine what types of pictures (e.g., black and white line drawings versus familiar photos) work best for the client.

Another particularly useful trial therapy tool is the Spaced Retrieval Screen (Brush & Camp, 1998; see Appendix 5.6), which determines learning potential and documents expectation for structured training to improve targeted behaviors. In this task, the client learns the clinician's name. If the client can recall the name at a 1-minute delay in three trials, there is expectation that spaced retrieval training will be a successful intervention procedure for training other facts and strategies. If the client does not seem motivated by the task, then a different target can be used, particularly one that the clinician knows is problematic (e.g., the client's room number).

Finally, the client's stimulability for treatment should be assessed through observation of the client in everyday routines. The client is observed in the natural environment to establish the types of cues and stimuli that evoke a response, as well as describing the types of behaviors the client produces. This information is used to design stimuli and tasks that will provide opportunities for the client to perform the target behaviors in the natural setting. Bourgeois has developed several forms to assist clinicians in documenting the types of behaviors that would be conducive to functional goal development. See Appendices 5.6 and 5.7 for the Screening Protocol to Monitor Residents with Dementia (Rozsa & Bourgeois, 2006) and the Functional Goals Screening Protocol: Community Clients with Dementia (Bourgeois & Rozsa, 2006), respectively. These forms are used to document cognitive and communication behaviors, and attention and receptivity to a variety of sensory stimuli and environmental variables. The clinician should observe the client's responsiveness to visual stimuli (e.g., pictures, colors, and signs), auditory cues (e.g., talking or music), and tactile stimuli (e.g., materials with a variety of textures). The clinician also should use the procedures described previously to provide an indication of the client's attempts and desire to interact with others or engage with the environment (e.g., frequency of initiation, and active versus passive participation). This allows the clinician to observe whether the client interacts with others, engages in activities, and actively or passively participates in the setting.

Functional Outcomes

Impairment-based measures are not recommended for measuring functional outcomes for two reasons: (1) most interventions for dementia are not designed to remedy the impairments of dementia, but rather they aim to target functional behaviors; (2) most impairment-based measures are not sensitive to change due to treatment. Instead, measures of activities and participation, such as those described above, are sometimes used to assess functional outcomes. There are limitations even with these measures, as they may not be related to the behaviors being treated. Additionally, patient-/client-reported outcomes and patient/client/family satisfaction are linked increasingly to policy development and reimbursement in governments and organizations around the world (Black et al., 2016). In the United States, this has led to the development of Quality Indicators to measure a continuum of factors. Since 2004, much effort has gone into the development, validation, and standardization of new measures that are brief and available for free to be administered in several formats (i.e., paper, iPad, and computer) (http://commonfund.nih.gov/, 2017). The patient-reported outcomes measurement system (PROMIS) is comprised of Neuro-QoL (Quality of Life in Neurological Disorders; Cella et al., 2011; Gershon et al., 2012), the NIH Toolbox™ (Neurobehavioral measures of cognition, emotion, sensation, and motor function), and others, and is available at http://HealthMeasures.net/. Also see Chapter 11 for more information on PROMIS and the Neuro-QoL.

Rather than administering a standardized test that is not designed as a treatment outcome measure and is not sensitive to change due to treatment, clinicians should measure changes in the specific behaviors that are being treated and the functional activities that are impacted (Bourgeois, 1998). For example, to examine outcomes of using memory aids (collections of picture and sentence stimuli in a book or wallet format) with persons with dementia, the SLP can measure the number of statements of fact (including novel statements) versus ambiguous utterances during pre-post conversation probes (Bourgeois, 1990, 1992, 1993; Bourgeois & Mason, 1996). Outcome measures for a written reminder card treatment (index cards, memo boards, and memory book pages) for disruptive vocalizations (i.e., repetitive questions and demands) can include pre-post measures by the caregiver of the number of times the disruptive vocalizations occur (Bourgeois, Burgio, Schulz, Beach, & Palmer, 1997). Conversational behaviors that were measured in a behavioral intervention, "Breakfast Club," included questioning, use of each other's names, eye contact, and topic maintenance (Santo Pietro & Boczko, 1998). (More information on these interventions and their outcomes will be described in Chapter 6.) Likewise, clinicians can construct their own data collection tools to measure gains made in treatment; preferably this is done in ongoing assessment to determine whether an intervention approach is benefiting the person or if changes need to be made to the treatment plan. This way, the clinician can see when a client has achieved the goal and treatment can be discontinued on that goal.

Reporting Results to Family Caregivers

During the process of assessment and following intervention SLPs need to discuss the assessment results with family caregivers. Here, we offer several tips from our own experiences regarding considerations for providing this information. First, the SLP should be aware of the client's and family's cultural background and educational levels and provide information in a way that is respectful of their knowledge and perspectives. Be cautious in providing information to family members; for example, if you are not sure of an answer, be honest about that. Be sensitive to the impact of your judgments regarding the client and the care being provided. Emphasize that you are describing what you see now and that you may be missing important information that they may provide. Start with some positive results, always highlighting strengths in addition to reporting weaknesses. Focus on what is important to know for immediate care as well as for helping the family to plan for the future. Finally, be collegial and collaborative in developing and implementing a plan of care; reinforce family efforts to follow through with treatment strategies, and gently encourage those who are less involved. Keep in mind that family caregivers often have an overwhelming amount of responsibilities; stress that the recommended strategies are meant to facilitate their communication or to make caregiving less stressful and their family member's quality of life better.

Writing Functional Goals Aligned with the "Flip the Rehab" Approach

Developing a plan of care with corresponding goals is an essential component of the evaluation process. Goal writing was discussed in Chapter 4 with respect to ensuring reimbursement, and those considerations apply here as well. To ensure that your plan of care is client-directed, rather than clinician-directed, your treatment goals should directly align with the person's and family's primary concerns. See Table 5.5 for an example.

The following components should be true for each targeted goal, following the person-centered, life participation model: (1) targets an area of concern expressed by the person with the condition, a family member, and/or a caregiver/staff member; (2) focuses on a meaningful, functional activity; (3) is realistic for the person to meet, based upon the level of visual, auditory, and tactile cueing that is being recommended. If goals are developed based upon these criteria, they will align with the "Flip the Rehab" approach, which provides client-directed, person-centered care, with a focus on increasing meaningful life participation.

TABLE 5.5 Client-Directed Goal Formation

Primary Concern	Corresponding Functional Goal
1. "I have trouble remembering people's names." – Mr. Smith	Mr. Smith will use communication boards with personal pictures and graphic cues to retrieve 9/10 names of friends and family members in response to open-ended questions, given min verbal cues, to increase ability to participate in daily conversations with spouse and friends in the community.
2. "The TV remote seems to be broken all the time … I can't find my favorite channel." – Mr. Smith	Mr. Smith will sequence 3/3 steps to operate the TV remote, with use of visual sequencing aid and graphic cues, to increase sequencing ability for operating complex devices around the home to increase participation in leisure activities.
3. "He asks me what day it is and where we are going at least 20 times a day!" – Mr. Smith's spouse	Mr. Smith will decrease frequency of perseverative questions regarding daily schedule to $<3\times$ / day $\times$ 1 week, per spouse behavior log, with reference to graphic cues in memory wallet, given minimal gestural and verbal cues, to increase functional recall for schedule management.
4. "He is constantly losing his wallet and phone … we can never get out the door because something is missing." – Mr. Smith's spouse	Mr. Smith will locate 3/3 functional objects around the home with use of organizational strategies + graphic memory aids, given min verbal cues, to increase IADL/ADL participation.

Case 5.1 Illustration of a Functional Assessment for Treatment Planning in Home Care

Mr. Fitzpatrick, an 82-year-old retired teacher, was referred to speech therapy through a home health care agency following his discharge from cardiac rehabilitation. His medical records documented a prior diagnosis of vascular dementia, with increased confusion and agitation. His wife was adamant about caring for him at home, though the medical team questioned whether this would be possible. During the SLP's first meeting with Mr. Fitzpatrick, she first completed interviews and interest inventories with Mr. Fitzpatrick and his wife, in line with the "Flip the Rehab Model" approach, which revealed that he wanted to return to his hobbies of taking care of his plants, preparing simple meals, and reading. His wife was concerned about his safety awareness and outbursts when he got frustrated, and he complained, "My wife mixes everything up whenever I try to do anything, and there's nothing interesting in the newspaper anymore." After completing the interview and observation process, the SLP screened his cognitive function (Montreal Cognitive Assessment [MoCA]), hearing and vision function, functional reading ability (Bourgeois Oral Reading Screen [BORS]), and ability to learn her name (Spaced Retrieval Screen). Assessments revealed moderate cognitive-linguistic deficits, adequate hearing for one-on-one communicative interactions, adequate vision to read 14-font print, and ability to recall new information after a one-minute delay. The SLP developed a plan of treatment using visual reminder cards for the sequences of steps in Mr. Fitzpatrick's hobbies, and worked with his wife to design memory books and boxes related to his interests instead of reading the newspaper. Treatment also included training his wife to prompt Mr. Fitzpatrick to use the written cue cards for his hobbies.

Case 5.2 Illustration of Assessment for Treatment Planning in Long-Term Care

Mrs. Seinfeld is admitted to long-term care after her husband, who was her primary caregiver at home, dies. The SLP routinely screens all new admissions. Based on a brief interview with the nursing staff and a review of Mrs. Seinfeld's medical records, the SLP requests a referral for cognitive-linguistic evaluation and treatment. Nursing staff report that they do not always understand what Mrs. Seinfeld is requesting, especially when she becomes agitated. Responsive behaviors reported by nursing staff include refusal to bathe or change her clothes, repetitive questions regarding the whereabouts of her husband, and wandering into other residents' rooms. The SLP conducts an evaluation using the MoCA to determine current level of impairment, and the Bourgeois Oral Reading Screen and Spaced Retrieval Screen to determine potential to benefit from written cues and to learn new skills and strategies. Mrs. Seinfeld has moderate cognitive deficits, with preserved reading ability and good responsiveness to the spaced retrieval technique. The SLP obtains information from the case history and the activities department interest inventory that are in the medical record. She also obtains photos and additional information from Mrs. Seinfeld's granddaughter, who lives nearby. Functional goals include the use of graphic cue cards to increase compliance with bathing and dressing, a memory wallet for increased quality and satisfaction with conversational interactions, and interest books for engagement during alone times. Nursing staff will be included in the training, so that they will learn to use effective communication techniques and cueing systems in care routines, and activities staff will be included so that they will use cueing systems to enhance social interaction and participation in facility programs.

Conclusion

Person–centered care for persons with dementia and their families has evolved with the impetus of social models of care. When considering assessment in person–centered care, clinicians must first identify the purpose of the assessment (e.g., diagnostic versus treatment planning or measuring functional outcomes). Most of the time, clients come to a speech-language pathologist with a diagnosis already made by a medical team; however, sometimes speech-language pathologists are part of that team. If the client is receiving services directed toward intervention, then the clinician should engage in an assessment process that ultimately results in a person-centered treatment plan with functional goals. We suggest the use of the "Flip the Rehab Model" approach to ensure that the focus remains on meaningful goals for the client and caregivers. This approach allows the clinician to gather useful, objective data without putting the client through unnecessary testing that does not inform a person-centered treatment plan. Assessment procedures in the "Flip the Rehab Model" approach include sensory screening, interviews, observations, preference assessment, and responsive behavior assessment. Once this information is collected, the clinician might use formal or informal assessment tools to examine activities and participation. If there is information that would be useful from measures of body structures and function, then choose tools that would give the necessary information. Treatment procedures can be selected based on assessment of treatment potential, which should show the clinician the types of cues and strategies to which the person responds well. The assessment for treatment planning process culminates with goal setting and development of a plan of care. Treatment goals should directly align with the person's and family's primary concerns, and a plan should be made for measuring functional outcomes.

Appendix 5.1: "Flip the Rehab Model" Check List

√ when completed:		
	If requested, administer screening to determine if assessment is needed (in many settings, screenings are not needed, if the physician or family members are reporting a change in functional status at the time of the referral)	
	Review of medical and psychosocial history	
		Specific dementia diagnosis (e.g., Alzheimer's dementia vs. Primary Progressive Aphasia vs. Lewy body dementia)?
		Years since onset of cognitive or language changes (earlier, most salient symptoms limited to one domain, e.g., short term memory vs. language; later, multiple domains impacted)?
		Psychosocial considerations reported (e.g., family history, current level of support, understanding of diagnosis)?
	Person-centered interview with the individual, family members, and other caregivers	
	Observation of individual in their environment	
	Sensory Screening	
	Dynamic Assessment of life participation in daily activities (includes IADLs and ADLs) using formal and informal measures	
	Static Assessment: Further investigation of areas of impairment that are directly impacting life participation, using selected standardized tests	
	Counseling, support, education, and training throughout assessment	
	Goal Formulation: person-centered; impairment-based vs. compensatory, activity/participation-based goals	

Appendix 5.2: Personal Wants, Needs, and Safety Assessment Form

Assessing the Wants, Needs, and Safety of:	(name)

Environment: Home Hospital Assisted Living Nursing Home (circle one)

Wants: The expression of personal preferences, likes, and dislikes

Likes:	Dislikes:

Needs: The satisfaction of physical comforts and emotional needs

Physical: Pain:	Emotional:

Safety: The prevention of harm to one's self or others

Medication: Falls prevention: Eating: Personal hygiene:	
Environmental constraints:	
Emergency contacts:	

Source: © Michelle S. Bourgeois.

Appendix 5.3: Memory Aid Information Form

Please complete this biographical information for:

(Name): _____

(Nickname): _____

Family Information

Mother: **Father:**

Name: _____   Name: _____

Date of Birth: _____   Date of Birth: _____

Birthplace: _____   Birthplace: _____

Date of Death: _____   Date of Death: _____

Brothers: **Sisters:**

Names: _____   Names: _____

_____   _____

Wife/Husband

Name: _____   Date of Birth: _____

Birthplace: _____   Date of Marriage: _____

Location of Marriage (city, state): _____

Date of Death (if applicable): _____

Children:

Names:

1. _____   2. _____   3. _____   4. _____

Spouse: (include married name for daughters)

1. _____   2. _____   3. _____   4. _____

Grandchildren:

1. _____   2. _____   3. _____   4. _____

1. _____   2. _____   3. _____   4. _____

1. _____   2. _____   3. _____   4. _____

What are the current occupations of these children?

1. _____   2. _____   3. _____   4. _____

Where are the children and grandchildren currently living (city, state)?

1. _____   2. _____   3. _____   4. _____

Your Family Member's Life History

Date of Birth: _____ Place of Birth: _____

Childhood home (city, state): _____

High school: _____ College: _____

Military Service:

Branch: _____ When: _____

Occupation(s): _____ When:

_____ _____

_____ _____

_____ _____

Special Honors/awards:

_____

_____

_____

Hobbies, favorite leisure activities (past and/or present):

_____

Clubs, social organizations: _____

Held office? _____

Church or temple: _____

Church- or temple-related activities or involvements (for example, deacon, choir,

etc.) _____

Places lived as an adult: ### When:

_____ _____

_____ _____

Favorite pets (past and/or present):

_____ _____

Memorable vacations:

Where: _____

When: _____

With whom: _____

Best friends: _____

_____

Any other memorable events, details: _____

_____

Responsive Behaviors: Describe any other specific concerns or issues you are having and how often they occur (example: My mother asks to go to church every 10 minutes).

_____

_____

_____

_____

Daily Schedule: Please complete a daily schedule for your family member including all routine activities.

	Usual Daily Schedule	Special Activities
7:00 a.m.		
7:30		
8:00		
9:00		
9:30		
10:00		
10:30		
11:00		
11:30		
12 Noon		
12:30 p.m.		
1:00		
1:30		
2:00		
2:30		
3:00		
3:30		
4:00		
4:30		
5:00		

5:30 _____

6:00 _____

6:30 _____

7:00 _____

7:30 _____

8:00 _____

8:30 _____

9:00 _____

9:30 _____

10:00 _____

10:30 _____

11:00 _____

11:30 _____

12 Midnight _____

Any other activities that your family member participates in during his/her spare time but which

is not part of the daily schedule? _____

_____

_____

Source: © Michelle S. Bourgeois.

Appendix 5.4: Memory Aid Information Form: Nursing Home Version

Name: _____

Room #: _____

Roommate: _____

Friends: _____

Breakfast: time: _____ favorite foods: _____

Lunch: time: _____ favorite foods: _____

Dinner: time: _____ favorite foods: _____

Location of meals: _____

Daily activities (what activity, with whom, location, who takes client to the activity, and any other information pertaining to daily schedule):

Approximate morning wake-up time: _____

Approximate bedtime: _____

Everyday: _____

_____

_____

Monday: _____

Tuesday: _____

Wednesday: _____

Thursday: _____

Friday: _____

Saturday: _____

Sunday: _____

Family who visit: _____

_____

_____

Other family: _____

_____

_____

Staff members: (name and activity): _____

_____

_____

_____

_____

Other Information: _____

_____

_____

Likes   **Dislikes**

_____   _____

_____   _____

_____   _____

_____   _____

Interests and Hobbies

_____

_____

_____

Source: © Michelle S. Bourgeois.

Appendix 5.5: Bourgeois Oral Reading Measure

Source: Bourgeois (2013).

Appendix 5.6: Spaced Retrieval Screen

1. *(NO DELAY)* "Today we are going to practice remembering my name. My name is _____ . What is my name?" Correct: "That's right. I am glad that you remembered."

2. *(SHORT DELAY)* "Good. I will give you more opportunities to practice as I am working with you today. Let's try again. What is my name?" Correct: "That's right. I am glad that you remembered."

3. *(LONG DELAY)* "You are doing well remembering my name for a longer period of time, and that's the idea. I would like you to always remember my name. I will be practicing this with you during therapy by asking you often. What is my name?" Correct: "That's right; you are remembering for a longer period of time. You did a great job remembering my name."

If the client is incorrect at any level three times in a row, this client is not appropriate for SR training; say, "Thanks for trying so hard. Let's work on something else now."

Source: Brush and Camp (1998).

dix 5.7: Screening Protocol to Monitor Residents with Dementia

Resident's Name: _____

Date of Screening: _____

Medical Diagnosis: _____

Date of Birth: _____ Age: _____ Sex: _____

PART 1: RESIDENT INTERVIEW

A. Personal Information

Family		Occupation	
Hobbies		Dislikes	

Premorbid Basic Reading Ability	Yes	No	Unable to answer
Premorbid Basic Writing Ability	Yes	No	Unable to answer
Wears Hearing Aid	Yes	No	
Wears Glasses	Yes	No	For some activities
Other Languages Spoken	Yes	No	Other: _____

B. MMSE Score: _____ Mild = 20–23; Moderate = 12–19; Severe = <12

Strengths: _____ Weaknesses: _____

C. Conversational Sample:

Tell me about your stay here at (name of facility).

Discourse Features	Present	Absent	No Opportunity
Takes turns	_____	_____	_____
Relinquishes turn	_____	_____	_____
Maintains topic	_____	_____	_____
Initiates new topic	_____	_____	_____
Transitions from topic	_____	_____	_____
Requests clarification	_____	_____	_____
Clarifies	_____	_____	_____

D. Orientation to Environment:

Show me to your room	Able	Requires assistance (Mild Mod Max)	Not able
Show me to the dining area	Able	Requires assistance (Mild Mod Max)	Not able
Show me the activities room	Able	Requires assistance (Mild Mod Max)	Not able
Show me the activities board	Able	Requires assistance (Mild Mod Max)	Not able

E. Memory Book Use: (Use clinician's memory book if resident does not have one)

If resident has book:

Does resident have memory book?	Yes	No
Is book readily available for resident's use?	Yes	No
Does resident engage in conversation about book?	Yes	No
Does resident maintain topic?	Yes	No
Does resident make novel comments?	Yes	No
Does resident make error statements (false comments)?	Yes	No
Does resident transition from page to page?	Yes	No

Observations:

F. Reading Screening (Based on memory book): Pass Fail **Level:** Full sentence Short phrase Single word

G. Spaced-Retrieval Screening: Pass Fail

Observations:

PART 2: RESIDENT OBSERVATION

A. Social Communication Observation (direct or from staff):

Resident communicates wants and needs in various settings	Able	Requires assistance	Not able
Resident makes likes/dislikes knowne	Able	Requires assistance	Not able
Resident converses with staff	Able	Requires assistance	Not able
Resident initiates conversations with others	Able	Requires assistance	Not able

B. Presence of Responsive Behaviors:

Behavior	According to	Description (including time of day)

C. Swallowing:

Presence of dysphagia Yes No If applicable: Oral Pharyngeal Esophageal

Date of most recent evaluation: _____

Alternative means for nutrition/hydration: Yes   No   If yes: _____

CURRENT DIET (Check)

Regular diet	Thin liquids	Sips from cup
Mechanical soft	Nectar thick	No straw
Puree	Honey thick	Cueing required
Clear liquids	No liquids	Other:
Full liquids	Nothing by mouth	

D. Activities of Daily Living: Assistance Requirements (Circle)

Mobility	Independent	Cane	Walker	Wheelchair
Meals/eating	Independent	Minimal assistance	Moderate assistance	Dependent
Grooming	Independent	Minimal assistance	Moderate assistance	Dependent
Dressing	Independent	Minimal assistance	Moderate assistance	Dependent
Toileting	Independent	Minimal assistance	Moderate assistance	Dependent

Source: © Angela Halter Rozsa, M.S. CCC–SLP & Michelle Bourgeois, Ph.D. CCC–SLP.

Appendix 5.8: Functional Goals Screening Protocol: Community Clients with Dementia

Name: _____ Date of Screening: _____

Medical Diagnosis: _____

Date of Birth: _____ Age: _____ Gender: _____

PART 1: CLIENT INTERVIEW

A. Personal Information

Family		Occupation	
Lives with:		Hobbies	
Friends		Activities	
Preferences		Dislikes	

Premorbid Basic Reading Ability	Yes	No	Unable to answer
Premorbid Basic Writing Ability	Yes	No	Unable to answer
Wears Hearing Aid	Yes	No	
Wears Glasses	Yes	No	For some activities
Other Languages Spoken	Yes	No	Other: _____

B. MMSE Score: _____ Mild = 20–23; Moderate = 17–19; Severe = <17

Strengths: _____ Weaknesses: _____

C. Conversational Sample:

Tell me about your family (or what you did for a living):

Discourse Features	Present	Absent	No Opportunity
Takes turns	_____	_____	_____
Relinquishes turn	_____	_____	_____
Maintains topic	_____	_____	_____
Initiates new topic	_____	_____	_____
Transitions from topic	_____	_____	_____
Requests clarification	_____	_____	_____
Clarifies	_____	_____	_____

D. Orientation to Environment:

Show me where the bathroom is?	Able	Requires assistance (Mild Mod Max)	Not able
Show me where your telephone is?	Able	Requires assistance (Mild Mod Max)	Not able
Show me where I can get a glass of water?	Able	Requires assistance (Mild Mod Max)	Not able

E. Auditory and Tactile Behaviors:

Is attentive when others are talking?	Yes	No
Holds, squeezes, manipulates objects?	Yes	No
Is bothered by noises (radio, TV)?	Yes	No
Rubs, smoothes, explores surface with hands?	Yes	No
Is attentive to or participates in music, singing?	Yes	No
Hits, bangs, slaps objects or surfaces?	Yes	No

F. Visual and Functional Reading Behaviors: (Use newspaper, magazine, other written materials in the home)

Prompt client to "Tell me something interesting from this paper (magazine, mail, etc.)"

Does client read aloud from the materials?	Yes	No
Does client make comments about the topic?	Yes	No
Does client engage others with the materials (ask questions, point)?	Yes	No
Does client turn pages to find another topic?	Yes	No
Does client notice objects in the near/far distance?	Yes	No

Observations:

G. Reading Screening (Bourgeois, 1992):

Print: Small/24 correct Large/24 correct

Observations:

H. Spaced-Retrieval Screening (Brush & Camp, 1998):

Immediate   30 sec   60 sec   Pass   Fail

Repeat after me (short statement):

Observations:

PART 2: CLIENT OBSERVATION

A. Social Communication Observation (direct or from caregiver):

Client communicates wants/needs in various settings	Able	Requires assistance	Not able
Client makes likes/dislikes known	Able	Requires assistance	Not able
Client converses with others	Able	Requires assistance	Not able
Client initiates conversations with others	Able	Requires assistance	Not able

B. Presence of Responsive Behaviors:

Behavior	According to	Description (including time of day)

C. Swallowing:

Presence of dysphagia   Yes   No   If applicable: Oral   Pharyngeal   Esophageal

Date of most recent evaluation: _____

Alternative means for nutrition/hydration: Yes   No   If yes: _____

CURRENT DIET (Check)

Regular diet	Thin liquids	Sips from cup
Mechanical soft	Nectar thick	No straw
Puree	Honey thick	Cueing required
Clear liquids	No liquids	Other:
Full liquids	Nothing by mouth	

D. Activities of Daily Living: Assistance requirements (Circle)

Mobility	Independent	Cane	Walker	Wheelchair
Meals/eating	Independent	Minimal assistance	Moderate assistance	Dependent
Grooming	Independent	Minimal assistance	Moderate assistance	Dependent
Dressing	Independent	Minimal assistance	Moderate assistance	Dependent
Toileting	Independent	Minimal assistance	Moderate assistance	Dependent

Source: © Michelle Bourgeois & Angela Halter Rozsa.

References

Albert, M. S. (1994). Brief assessments of cognitive function in the elderly. In M. P. Lawton & J. A. Teresi (Eds.), *Annual review of gerontology and geriatrics focus on assessment techniques* (Vol. 4, pp. 93–106). New York: Springer.

Algase, D. L., Beck, C., Kolanowski, A., Whall, A., Berent, S., Richards, K., & Beattie, E. (1996). Need-driven dementia-compromised behavior: An alternative view of disruptive behavior. *American Journal of Alzheimer's Disease and Other Dementias, 11*(6), 10, 12–19.

Allen, C., Austin, S. L., David, S. K., Earhart, C. A., McCraith, D. B., & Riska-Williams, L. (2007). *Manual for the Allen Cognitive Level Screen – 5 (ACLS-5) and Large Allen Cognitive Level Screen – 5 (LACLS – 5)*. Camarillo, CA: ACLS and LACLS Committee.

Allen, C., Earhart, C., & Blue, T. (1992). *Occupational therapy treatment goals for the physically and cognitively disabled*. Bethesda, MD: AOTA.

American Health Care Association. (1990). *The long term care survey: Regulations, forms, procedures, guidelines*. Washington, DC: Author.

American Psychological Association (2014). Guidelines for psychological practice with older adults. *American Psychologist, 69*(1), 34–65. doi:10.1037/a0035063.

American Speech-Language-Hearing Association (ASHA). (2004). Evaluating and treating communication and cognitive disorders: Approaches to referral and collaboration for speech-language pathology and clinical neuropsychology [Technical report]. *ASHA Supplement, 23*, 47–58.

American Speech-Language-Hearing Association (ASHA). (2005). Roles of speech-language pathologists in the identification, diagnosis, and treatment of individuals with cognitive-communication disorders: Position statement. *ASHA Supplement, 25*, 1–2.

American Speech-Language-Hearing Association (ASHA). (2007). *Scope of practice in speech-language pathology [Scope of practice]*. doi:10.1044/policy.SP2007-00283.

Baines, K. A., Martin, A. W., & McMartin Heeringa, H. (1999). *Assessment of Language-Related Functional Activities* (ALFA). Austin, TX: Pro-Ed.

Barker, W., Luis, C., Harwood, D., Loewenstein, D., Bravo, M., Ownby, R., & Duara, R. (2005). The effects of a memory screening program on the early diagnosis of Alzheimer disease. *Alzheimer Disease & Associated Disorders, 19*(1), 1–7.

Barrie, M. A. (2002). Objective screening tools to assess cognitive impairment and depression. *Topics in Geriatric Rehabilitation, 18*(2), 28–46.

Bayles, K. A., & Tomoeda, C. K. (1993). *Arizona battery for communication disorders in dementia*. Tuscon, AZ: Canyonlands Publishing.

Bayles, K. A., & Tomoeda, C. K. (1994). *Functional linguistic communication inventory test manual*. Tucson, AZ: Canyonlands.

Bayles, K. A., & Tomoeda, C. K. (2013). *Cognitive-communication disorders of dementia: Definition, diagnosis, and treatment* (2nd ed.). San Diego, CA: Plural Publishing.

Bayles, K. A., Tomoeda, C. K., Cruz, R. F., & Mahendra, N. (2000). Communication abilities of individuals with late-stage Alzheimer disease. *Alzheimer Disease & Associated Disorders, 14*(3), 176–181.

Baylor, C., Burns, M., Eadie, T., Britton, D., & Yorkston, K. (2011). A qualitative study of interference with communicative participation across communication disorders in adults. *American Journal of Speech-Language Pathology, 20,* 269–287. doi:10.1044/1058-0360(2011/10-0084).

Beatty, W., Ryder, K., Gontkovsky, S., Scott, J. G., McSwan, K., & Bharucha, K. (2003). Analyzing the subcortical dementia syndrome of Parkinson's disease using the RBANS. *Archives of Clinical Neuropsychology, 18*(5), 509–520.

Belanger, H. G., Wilder-Willis, K., Malloy, P., Salloway, S., Hamman, R. F., & Grigsby, J. (2005). Assessing motor and cognitive regulation in AD, MCI, and controls using the Behavioral Dyscontrol Scale. *Archives of Clinical Neuropsychology, 20*(2), 183–189.

Black, N., Burke, L., Forrest, C. B., Ravens Sieberer, U. H., Ahmed, S., Valderas, J. M., ... Alonso, J. (2016). Patient-reported outcomes: pathways to better health, better services, and better societies. *Qual Life Res, 25,* 1103–1112. doi:10.1007/s11136-015-1168-3.

Bourgeois, M. S. (1990). Enhancing conversation skills in Alzheimer's Disease using a prosthetic memory aid. *Journal of Applied Behavior Analysis, 23*(1), 29–42.

Bourgeois, M. S. (1992). Evaluating memory wallets in conversations with patients with dementia. *Journal of Speech, Language, and Hearing Research, 35*(6), 1344–1357.

Bourgeois, M. S. (1993). Effects of memory aids on the dyadic conversations of individuals with dementia. *Journal of Applied Behavior Analysis, 26*(1), 77–87.

Bourgeois, M. S. (1998). Functional outcomes assessment of adults with dementia. *Seminars in Speech and Language, 19*(3), 261–279.

Bourgeois, M. (2013). *Memory & communication aids for people with dementia.* Baltimore: Health Professions Press.

Bourgeois, M. (2014, March). *A functional approach to assessment in dementia: Some new ideas.* Paper presented at ASHA Healthcare Conference, Las Vegas, NV.

Bourgeois, M. (2015, November). *Innovative treatments for persons with dementia.* Paper presented at ASHA Research Symposium, Denver, CO.

Bourgeois, M., Brush, J., Douglas, N., Khayum, R., & Rogalski, E. (2016). Will you still need me when I'm 64, or 84, or 104? The importance of Speech-Language Pathologists in promoting the quality of life of aging adults in the United States into the future. *Seminars in Speech and Language, 37,* 185–200.

Bourgeois, M. S., Burgio, L. D., Schulz, R., Beach, S., & Palmer, B. (1997). Modifying repetitive verbalization of community dwelling patients with AD. *The Gerontologist, 37*(1), 30–39.

Bourgeois, M., Camp, C., Antenucci, V., & Fox, K. (2016). VoiceMyChoice™: Facilitating understanding of preferences of residents with dementia. *Advances in Aging Research, 5,* 131–141.

Bourgeois, M., & Hopper, T. (2005, February). *Evaluation and treatment planning for individuals with dementia.* Proceedings of the American Speech-Language-Hearing Association Health Care Conference, Palm Springs, CA.

Bourgeois, M., LaPointe, L., Dijkstra, K., Bays, G., Lasker, J., & Johnson, K. (2002, May). *Unexpected evidence of reading comprehension during oral reading in dementia.* Presented at the International Clinical Phonetics and Linguistics Association Conference, Hong Kong.

Bourgeois, M. S., & Mason, L. A. (1996). Memory wallet intervention in an adult day care setting. *Behavioral Interventions, 11*(1), 3–18.

Bourgeois, M., & Rozsa, A. (2006). Functional goals screening protocol: Community clients with dementia. In D. Beukelman, K. Garrett, & K. Yorkston (Eds.), *AAC interventions for adults in medical settings: Integrated assessment and treatment protocols.* Baltimore: Brookes.

Brookshire, R., & Nicholas, L. (1997). *Discourse comprehension test* (2nd ed.). Minneapolis, MN: BRK.

Bruce, C., Brush, J. A., Sanford, J. A., & Calkins, M. P. (2013). Development and evaluation of the environment and communication assessment toolkit with speech-language pathologists. *Seminars in Speech and Language, 34*(1), 42–51. doi:10.1055/s-0033-1337394.

Brush, J., Calkins, M., Bruce, C., & Sanford, J. (2011). *Environment and Communication Assessment Toolkit for Dementia Care (ECAT).* Baltimore: Health Professions Press.

Brush, J. A., & Camp, C. J. (1998). Using spaced-retrieval as an intervention during speech-language therapy. *Clinical Gerontologist, 19*(1), 51–64.

Buckingham, D., Mackor, K., Miller, R., Pullam, N., & Molloy, K. (2013). Comparing the cognitive screening tolls: MMSE and SLUMS. *Pure Insights, 2(3).* Available at http://digitalcommonswou.edu/pure/volz/1ssl/3.

Burns, M. (1997). *Burns brief inventory of communication and cognition*. San Antonio, TX: Pearson.

Camp, C. (2006). Montessori-based Dementia Programming™ in long-term care: A case study of disseminating an intervention for persons with dementia. In R. C. Intrieri, & L. Hyer (Eds.), *Clinical applied gerontological interventions in long-term care* (pp. 295–314). New York: Springer.

Camp, C. (2010). Origins of Montessori programming for dementia. *Non-Pharmacologic Therapies in Dementia, 1*(2), 163–174.

Camp, C., & Skrajner, M. (2004). Resident-assisted Montessori programming (RAMPTM): Training persons with dementia to serve as group activity leaders. *The Gerontologist, 44*, 426–431.

Cella, D., Nowinski, C., Peterman, A., Victorson, D., Miller, D., Lai, J.-S., & Moy, C. (2011). The Neurology Quality of Life measurement initiative. *Arch Phys Med Rehabil, 92*(10 Suppl), S28–S36. doi:10.1016/j. apmr.2011.01.025.

Centers for Medicare & Medicaid Services (CMS) (2016). *Long-term care facility Resident Assessment Instrument 3.0 User's Manual, Version 1.14*. Washington, DC: Department of Health & Human Services. Retrieved on February 20, 2017 from www.cms.gov/Medicare/Quality-Initiatives-Patient-Assessment-Instruments/NursinghomeQualityInits/MDS30RAIManual.html.

Chapey, R., Duchan, J. F., Elman, R. J., Garcia, L. J., Kagan, A., Lyon, J., & Simmons-Mackie, N. (2000, February). Life participation approach to aphasia: A statement of values for the future. *The ASHA Leader, 5*, 4–6.

Chapman, S. B., Zientz, J., Weiner, M., Rosenberg, R., Frawley, W., & Burns, M. H. (2002). Discourse changes in early Alzheimer disease, mild cognitive impairment, and normal aging. *Alzheimer Disease & Associate Disorders, 16*(3), 177–186.

Cho-Reyes, S., & Thompson, C. K. (2012; online). Verb and sentence production and comprehension. Northwesters Assessment of Verbs and Sentences (NAVS). *Aphasiology*. doi:10.1080/02687038.2012.693584.

Cohen-Mansfield, J. (1986). Agitated behaviors in the elderly. II. Preliminary results in the cognitively deteriorated. *Journal of the American Geriatrics Society, 34*(10), 722–727.

Cohen-Mansfield, J., Dakheel-Ali, M., Jensen, B., Marx, M., & Thein, K. (2012). An analysis of the relationships among engagement, agitated behavior, and affect in nursing home residents with dementia. *International Psychogeriatrics, 2*(5), 742–752.

Coles, H., & Carson, S. (2013). *Standardized Touchscreen Assessment of Cognition* (STAC) and *Functional Standardized Touchscreen Assessment of Cognition* (FSTAC). Fairport, NY: Cognitive Innovations LLC. Retrieved from www.cognitive-innovations.com.

Croot, K., Nickels, L., Laurence, F., & Manning, M. (2009). Impairment- and activity/participation-directed interventions in progressive language impairment: Clinical and theoretical issues. *Aphasiology, 23*(2), 125–160.

Crum, R. M., Anthony, J. C., Bassett, S. B., & Folstein, M. F. (1993). Population-based norms for the Mini-Mental State Examination by age and educational level. *Journal of the American Medical Association, 269*(18), 2386–2391.

Damico, J. S., Oelschlaeger, M., & Simmons-Mackie, N. (1999). Qualitative methods in aphasia research: Conversation analysis. *Aphasiology, 13*(9–11), 667–680.

Damico, J. S., & Simmons-Mackie, N. N. (2003). Qualitative research and speech-language pathology: A tutorial for the clinical realm. *American Journal of Speech-Language Pathology, 12*(2), 131–143.

Duff, K., Schoenberg, M. R., Patton, D., Paulsen, J. S., Bayless, J. D., Mold, J., & Adams, R. L. (2005). Regression-based formulas for predicting change in RBANS subtests with older adults. *Archives of Clinical Neuropsychology, 20*(3), 281–290.

Dufouil, C., Clayton, D., Brayne, C., Chi, L. Y., Dening, T. R., Paykel, E. S., & Huppert, F. A. (2000). Population norms for the MMSE in the very old: Estimates based on longitudinal data. *Neurology, 55*(11), 1609–1613.

Earhart, C. A. (2006). *Allen Diagnostic Module – 2nd edition: Manual and assessments* (ADM-2). Colchester, CT: S&S Worldwide.

Ehrlich, J. S., Obler, L. K., & Clark, L. (1997). Ideational and semantic contributions to narrative production in adults with dementia of the Alzheimer's type. *Journal of Communication Disorders, 30*(2), 79–99.

Elliot, G. (2011). *Montessori Methods for Dementia™: Focusing on the person and the prepared environment*. Oakville, Ontario, Canada: Dementiability Enterprises.

Feldman, H., Sauter, A., Donald, A., Gélinas, I., Gautier, S., Torfs, K., & Mehnert, A. (2001). The Disability Assessment for Dementia Scale: A 12-month study of functional ability in mild to moderate severity Alzheimer's disease. *Alzheimer Disease & Associated Disorders, 15*(2), 89–95.

Folstein, M. F., & Folstein, S. E. (2010). *Mini-Mental State Examination®* (2nd ed.). Lutz, FL: Psychological Assessment Resources.

Folstein, M., Folstein, S., & Folstein, J. (2011). The Mini-Mental State Examination®: A brief cognitive assessment. In M. T. Abou-Saleh, C. L. E. Katona, & A. Kumar (Eds.), *Principles and practice of geriatric psychiatry* (3rd ed., pp. 145–146). Chichester, UK: John Wiley & Sons.

Folstein, M. F., Folstein, S. E., & McHugh, P. R. (1975). "Mini-mental state": A practical method for grading the cognitive state of clients for the clinician. *Journal of Psychiatric Research, 12*(3), 189–198.

Frattali, C. M., Thompson, C. M., Holland, A. L., Wohl, C. B., & Ferketic, M. M. (1995). The FACS of life: ASHA FACS – a functional outcome measure for adults. *ASHA, 37*(4), 40–46.

Freedman, M., Leach, L., Kaplan, E., Winocur, G., Shulman, K. I., & Delis, D. C. (1994). *Clock drawing: A neuropsychological analysis.* New York: Oxford University Press.

Garcia, C., Leahy, B., Corradi, K., & Forhetti, C. (2008). Component structure of the Repeatable Battery for the Assessment of Neuropsychological Status in dementia. *Archives of Clinical Neuropsychiatry, 23*, 63–72.

Gélinas, I., Gauthier, L., McIntyre, M., & Gautier, S. (1999). Development of a functional measure for persons with Alzheimer's disease: The disability assessment for dementia. *American Journal of Occupational Therapy, 53*(5), 471–481.

Gershon, R. C., Lai, J. S., Bode, R., Choi, S., Moy, C., Bleck, T., Miller, D., Peterman, A., & Cella, D. (2012). Neuro-QOL: Quality of life item banks for adults with neurological disorders: Item development and calibrations based upon clinical and general population testing. *Qual Life Res, 21*(3), 475–486.

Gontkovsky, S. T., Mold, J. W., & Beatty, W. W. (2002). Age and educational influences on RBANS index scores in a nondemented geriatric sample. *The Clinical Neuropsychologist, 16*(3), 258–263.

Goodglass, H., Kaplan, E., & Barresi, B. (2000). *The Boston diagnostic aphasia examination*, 3rd ed. (BDAE-3). San Antonio, TX: Psychological Corporation.

Grigoletto, F., Zappala, G., Anderson, D. W., & Lebowitz, B. D. (1999). Norms for the Mini-Mental State Examination in a healthy population. *Neurology, 53*(2), 315–320.

Hall, K. M. (1997). The Functional Assessment Measure (FAM). *Journal of Rehabilitation Outcomes, 1*(3), 63–65.

Hall, K. M., Hamilton, B. B., Gordon, W. A., & Zasler, N. D. (1993). Characteristics and comparisons of functional assessment indices: Disability rating scale, functional independence measure and functional assessment measure. *The Journal of Head Trauma Rehabilitation, 8*(2), 60–74.

Hays, S-J., Niven, B., Godfrey, H., & Linscott, R. (2004). Clinical assessment of pragmatic language impairment: A generalizability study of older people with Alzheimer's disease. *Aphasiology, 18*(8), 693–714.

Heinemann, A. W. (1989). *Rehabilitation Institute of Chicago: Functional assessment scale – revised.* Chicago: Rehabilitation Institute of Chicago.

Helm-Estabrooks, N. (2001). *Cognitive linguistic quick test: Examiner's manual.* San Antonio, TX: Psychological Corporation.

Helmes, E., Csapo, K. G., & Short, J.-A. (1987). Standardization and validation of the Multidimensional Observation Scale for Elderly Subjects (MOSES). *The Journals of Gerontology, 42*(4), 395–405.

Holdnack, H. A. (2001). *Wechsler Test of Adult Reading: WTAR.* San Antonio, TX: The Psychological Corporation.

Holland, A. L., Fromm, D., & Wozniak, L. (2017). *Communicative activities of daily living: CADL-3* (3rd ed.). Austin, TX: Pro-Ed.

Isella, V., Villa, L., Russo, A., Regazzoni, R., Ferrarese, C., & Appollonio, I. (2006). Discriminative and predictive power of an informant report in mild cognitive impairment. *J Neurol Neurosurg Psych, 77*(2), 166–171.

Johnson, N., Barion, A., Rademaker, A., Rehkemper, G., & Weintraub, S. (2004). The Activities of Daily Living Questionnaire: A validation study in patients with dementia. *Alzheimer Disease & Associated Disorders, 18*(4), 223–230.

Johnson-Greene, D. (2004). Test review: Dementia Rating Scale-2 (DRS-2): By P. J. Jurica, C. L. Leitten, and S. Mattis: Psychological Assessment Resources, 2001. *Archives of Clinical Neuropsychology, 19*(1), 145–147.

Jones, R. N., & Gallo, J. J. (2002). Education and sex differences in the Mini-Mental State Examination: Effects of differential item functioning. *The Journals of Gerontology Series B: Psychological Sciences and Social Sciences, 57*(6), P548–P558.

Jurica, P. J., Leitten, C. L., & Mattis, S. (2001). *Dementia rating scale* (DRS-2; 2nd ed.). Lutz, FL: Psychological Assessment Resources.

Kagan, A., Simmons-Mackie, N., Rowland, A., Huijbregts, M., Shumway, E., McEwen, S., ... Sharp, S. (2008). Counting what counts: A framework for capturing real-life outcomes of aphasia intervention. *Aphasiology, 22*(3), 258–280. http://dx.doi.org/10.1080/02687030701282595.

Kagan, A., Simmons-Mackie, N., Victor, J. C., Carling-Rowland, A., Hoch, J., Huijbregts, M., et al. (2013). *Assessment for living with aphasia* (2nd ed.). (*ALA*). Toronto, ON: Aphasia Institute.

Kay, J., Lesser, R., & Coltheart, M. (1992). *PALPA: Psycholinguistic assessments of language processing in aphasia.* Hove, England: Lawrence Erlbaum Associates.

Kennedy, M. (2002). Principles of assessment. In R. Paul (Ed.), *Introduction to clinical methods in communication disorders* (1st ed.). Baltimore: Brookes.

Kertesz, A. (2006). *Western aphasia battery – revised* (WAB-R). New York: Harcourt Brace Jovanovich.

Kunik, M. E., Martinez, M., Snow, A. L., Beck, C. K., Cody, M., Rapp, C. G., & Hamilton, D. J. (2003). Determinants of behavioral symptoms in dementia patients. *Clinical Gerontologist, 26*(3–4), 83–89.

LaPointe, L. L., & Horner, J. (1998). *Reading comprehension battery for aphasia (RCBA-2).* Austin, TX: Pro-Ed.

Lawton, M. P., Van Haitsma, K., & Klapper, J. (1999). Observed Emotion Rating Scale. Retrieved February 14, 2017 from www.abramsoncenter.org/PRI (scales page).

Lawton, M. P., Van Haitsma, K., Perkinson, M., & Ruckdeschel, K. (1999). Observed affect and quality of life in dementia: Further affirmations and problems. *Journal of Mental Health and Aging, 5*(1), 69–81.

Lezak, M. D., Howleson, D. B., Bigler, E. D., & Tranel, D. (2012). *Neuropsychological assessment* (5th ed.). New York: Oxford University Press.

Lomas, J., Pickard, L., Bester, S., Elbard, H., Finlayson, A., & Zoghaib, C. (1989). The Communicative Effectiveness Index: Development and psychometric evaluation of a functional communication measure for adult aphasia. *Journal of Speech and Hearing Disorders, 54*(1), 113–124.

MacDonald, S., & Johnson, C. J. (2005). Assessment of subtle cognitive-communication deficits following acquired brain injury: A normative study of the Functional Assessment of Verbal Reasoning and Executive Strategies (FAVRES). *Brain Injury, 19(11),* 895–902.

McFarlane, J., Welch, J., & Rodgers, J. (2006). Severity of Alzheimer's disease and effect on premorbid measures of intelligence. *British Journal of Clinical Psychology, 45*(4), 453–463.

Mesulam, M. M., Weineke, C., Thompson, C., Rogalski, E., & Weintraub, S. (2012). Quantitative classification of Primary Progressive Aphasia at early and mild impairment stages. *Brain, 135,* 1537–1553.

Meyers, P. S. (1998). *Right hemisphere damage: Disorders of communication and cognition.* San Diego, CA: Singular.

Mohs, R. (2006). *ADAS-Cog: What, why and how?* Retrieved on May 13, 2006, from www.alzheimer-insights.com/insights/vol.3no1/vol.3no1.htm.

Morhardt, D., Weintraub, S., Khayum, B., Robinson, J., Medina, J., O'Hara, M., ... Rogalski, E. (2015). The CARE Pathway Model for Dementia: Psychosocial and rehabilitative strategies for care in young onset dementias. *Psychiatric Clinics of North America, 38*(2), 333–352.

Morris, J. C. (1993). The Clinical Dementia Rating (CDR): Current version and scoring rules. *Neurology, 43*(11), 2412–2414.

Mungas, D., Marshall, S. C., Weldon, M., Haan, M., & Reed, B. R. (1996). Age and education correction of Mini-Mental State Examination for English- and Spanish-speaking elderly. *Neurology, 46*(3), 700–706.

Mungas, D., Reed, B. R., & Kramer, J. H. (2003). Psychometrically matched measures of global cognition, memory, and executive function for assessment of cognitive decline in older persons. *Neuropsychology, 17*(3), 380–392.

Murphy, J., Gray, C., van Achterberg, T., Wyke, S., & Cox, S. (2010). The effectiveness of the Talking Mats framework in helping people with dementia to express their views on wellbeing. *Dementia, 9*(4), 454–472. doi:10.1177/1471301210381776.

Nasreddine, Z. S., Phillips, N. A., Bédirian, V., Charbonneau, S., Whitehead, V., Collin, I., & Chertkow, H. (2005). The Montreal Cognitive Assessment (MOCA): A brief screening tool for mild cognitive impairment. *Journal of the American Geriatrics Society, 53*(4), 695–699.

Nicholas, L. E., & Brookshire, R. H. (1993). A system for quantifying the informativeness and efficiency of the connected speech of adults with aphasia. *Journal of Speech, Language, and Hearing Research, 36*(2), 338–350.

Nicholas, L. E., & Brookshire, R. H. (1995). Presence, completeness, and accuracy of main concepts in connected speech of non-brain-damaged adults and adults with aphasia. *Journal of Speech, Language, and Hearing Research, 38*(1), 145–156.

Oakley, F., Lai, J. S., & Sunderland, T. (1999). A validation study of the Daily Activities Questionnaire: An activities of daily living assessment for people with Alzheimer's disease. *Journal of Outcome Measurement, 3*(4), 297–307.

Orsulic-Jeras, S., Schneider, N., Camp, C., Nicholson, P., & Helbig, M. (2001). Montessori-based dementia activities in long-term care: Training and implementation. *Activities, Adaptation & Aging, 25*(3–4), 107–120.

Perkins, L., Whitworth, A., & Lesser, R. (1998). Conversing in dementia: A conversation analytic approach. *Journal of Neurolinguistics, 11*(1–2), 33–53.

Pfeffer, R. I., Kurosaki, T. T., Harrah, C. H., Jr., Chance, J. M., & Filos, S. (1982). Measurement of functional activities in older adults in the community. *The Journal of Gerontology, 37*(3), 323–329.

Randolph, C. (1998). *Repeatable Battery for the Assessment of Neuropsychological Status (RBANS).* San Antonio, TX: Psychological Corporation.

Randolph, C., Tierney, M. C., Mohr, E., & Chase, T. N. (1998). The Repeatable Battery for the Assessment of Neuropsychological Status (RBANS): Preliminary clinical validity. *Journal of Clinical Experimental Neuropsychology, 20*(3), 310–319.

Ray, W. A., Taylor, J. A., Lichtenstein, M. J., & Meador, K. G. (1992). The Nursing Home Behavior Problem Scale. *The Journal of Gerontology, 47*(1), M9–M16.

Reisberg, B. (1987). Functional assessment staging (FAST). *Psychopharmacology Bulletin, 24*(4), 653–659.

Reisberg, B. (2007). Global measures: Utility in defining and measuring treatment response in dementia. *International Psychogeriatrics, 19*(3), 421–456.

Reisberg, B., Borenstein, J., Franssen, E., Salob, S., Steinberg, G. … Georgotas, A. (1987). BEHAVE-AD: A clinical rating scale for the assessment of pharmacologically remediable behavioral symptomatology in Alzheimer's disease. In A. Fisher, I. Hanin, & C. Lachman (Eds.), *Alzheimer's disease: Problems, prospects, and perspectives.* New York: Springer.

Reisberg, B., Ferris, S. H., de Leon, M. J., & Crook, T. (1982). The global deterioration scale for assessment of primary degenerative dementia. *The American Journal of Psychiatry, 139*(9), 1136–1139.

Robertson, I. H., Ward, T., Ridgeway, V., & Nimmo-Smith, I. (1994). *The Test of Everyday Attention.* Gaylord, MI: Northern Speech Services.

Robertson, I. H., Ward, T., Ridgeway, V., & Nimmo-Smith, I. (1996). The structure of normal human attention: The Test of Everyday Attention. *Journal of the International Neuropsychological Society, 2*(6), 525–534.

Rosen, H. J., Narvaez, J. M., Hallam, B., Kramer, J. H., Wyss-Coray, C., Gearhart, R., & Miller, B. L. (2004). Neuropsychological and functional measures of severity in Alzheimer disease, frontotemporal dementia, and semantic dementia. *Alzheimer Disease & Associated Disorders, 18*(4), 202–207.

Rosen, W. G., Mohs, R. C., & Davis, K. L. (1984). A new rating scale for Alzheimer's disease. *The American Journal of Psychiatry, 141*(11), 1356–1364.

Ross-Swain, D. (1996). *Ross Information Processing Assessment–2* (RIPA-2). Austin, TX: Pro-Ed.

Ross-Swain, D., & Fogle, P. (1996). *Ross Information Processing Assessment–Geriatric* (RIPA-G). Austin, TX: Pro-Ed.

Royall, D. R., Cordes, J. A., & Polk, M. (1998). CLOX: An executive clock drawing task. *Journal of Neurology, Neurosurgery, and Psychiatry, 64*(5), 588–594.

Rozsa, A., & Bourgeois, M. (2006). Screening protocol to monitor residents with dementia. In D. Beukelman, K. Garrett, & K. Yorkston (Eds.), *AAC interventions for adults in medical settings: Integrated assessment and treatment protocols.* Baltimore: Brookes.

Santo Pietro, M. J., & Boczko, R. (1997). *Communication outcome measure of functional independence (COMFI Scale).* Vero Beach, FL: The Speech Bin.

Santo Pietro, M. J., & Boczko, F. (1998). The Breakfast Club: Results of a study examining the effectiveness of a multi-modality group communication treatment. *American Journal of Alzheimer's Disease and Other Dementias, 13*(3), 146–158.

Saxton, J., Kastango, K. B., Hugonot-Diener, L., Boller, F., Verny, M., Sarles, C. E., & DeKosky, S. T. (2005). Development of a short form of the Severe Impairment Battery. *The American Journal of Geriatric Psychiatry, 13*(11), 999–1005.

Saxton, J., McGonigle, K. L., Swihart, A. A., & Boller, F. (1993). *Severe impairment battery*. Bury St. Edmunds, UK: Thames Valley.

Saxton, J., McGonigle-Gibson, K. L., Swihart, A. A., Miller, V. J., & Boller, F. (1990). Assessment of the severely demented patient: Description and validation of a new neuropsychological test battery. *Psychological Assessment: A Journal of Consulting and Clinical Psychology, 2*(3), 298–303.

Scharre, D., Chang, S., Murden, R., Lamb, J., Beversdorf, D., Kataki, M., Nagaraja, H., & Borenstein, R. (2010). Self-administered Gerocognitive Examination (SAGE): A brief cognitive assessment instrument for mild cognitive impairment (MCI) and early dementia. *Alzheimer Dis Assoc Disord, 24*(1), 64–71.

Schmitt, F. A., Ashford, W., Ernesto, C., Saxton, J., Schneider, L. S., Clark, C. M., & Thal, L. J. (1997). The severe impairment battery: Concurrent validity and the assessment of longitudinal change in Alzheimer's disease. *Alzheimer Disease & Associated Disorders, 11*, 51–56.

Schneider, L. S., Colin, J. T., Lyness, S. A., & Chui, H. C. (1997). Eligibility of Alzheimer's disease clinic patients for clinical trials. *Journal of the American Geriatrics Society, 45*(8), 923–928.

Simmons-Mackie, N., & Damico, J. (1996). Accounting for handicaps in aphasia: Communicative assessment from an authentic social perspective. *Disability & Rehabilitation, 18*(11), 540–549.

Simmons-Mackie, N., Kagan, A., Victor, J. C., Carling-Rowland, A., Mok, A., Hoch, J. S., … Streiner, D. L. (2014). The assessment for living with aphasia: Reliability and construct validity. *International Journal of Speech-Language Pathology, 16*(1), 82–94. doi:10.3109/17549507.2013.831484.

Sloan, F. A., & Wang, J. (2005). Disparities among older adults in measures of cognitive function by race or ethnicity. *The Journals of Gerontology Series B: Psychological Sciences and Social Sciences, 60*(5), P242–P250.

State University of New York at Buffalo, Research Foundation. (1993). *Guide for use of the Uniform Data Set for Medical Rehabilitation: Functional independence measure*. Buffalo, NY: Author.

Tappen, R. M., Roselli, M., & Engstrom, G. (2010). Evaluation of the Functional Activities Questionnaire (FAQ) in cognitive screening across four American ethnic groups. *Clin Neuropsychol, 24*(4), 646–661.

Tariq, S. H., Tumosa, N., Chibodl, J. T., Perry, H. M., & Morley, J. E. (2006). The Saint Louis University Mental Status (SLUMS) Examination for detecting mild cognitive impairment and dementia is more sensitive than the Mini-Mental Status examination (MMSE): A pilot study. *AM J Geriatr Psychiatry, 14*, 900–910.

Terrell, B. Y., & Ripich, D. N. (1989). Discourse competence as a variable in intervention. *Seminars in Speech Language Disorders, 10*(4), 282–297.

Tetnowski, J. A., & Franklin, T. C. (2003). Qualitative research: Implications for description and assessment. *American Journal of Speech-Language Pathology, 12*(2), 155–164.

Thompson, C. K. (2012). *Northwestern Assessment of Verbs and Sentences*. Evanston, IL: Northwestern University.

Threats, T. (2006). Towards an international framework for communication disorders: Use of the ICF. *Journal of Communication Disorders, 39*(4), 251–265. doi.org/10.1016/j.jcomdis.2006.02.002.

Threats, T. (2007). Access for persons with neurogenic communication disorders: Influences of personal and environmental factors of the ICF. *Aphasiology, 21*(1), 67–80. doi.org/10.1080/02687030600798303.

Togher, L. (2001). Discourse sampling in the 21st century. *Journal of Communication Disorders, 34*(1–2), 131–150.

Tompkins, C. A. (1995). *Right hemisphere communication disorders: Theory and management*. San Diego, CA: Singular.

Turkstra, L., Ylvisaker, M., Coelho, C., Kennedy, M., Sohlberg, M. M., Avery, J., & Yorkston, K. (2005). Practice guidelines for standardized assessment of persons with traumatic brain injury. *Journal of Medical Speech-Language Pathology, 13*(2), ix–xxviii.

van der Ploegg, E., Eppinstall, B., Camp, C. J., & Runci, S. (2013). A randomized crossover trial to study the effect of personalized, one-to-one interaction using Montessori-based activities on agitation, affect, and engagement in nursing home residents with dementia. *International Psychogeriatrics, 25*(4), 565–575.

Vance, D. E., Burgio, L. D., Roth, D. L., Stevens, A. B., Fairchild, J. K., & Yurick, A. (2003). Predictors of agitation in nursing home residents. *The Journals of Gerontology Series B: Psychological Sciences and Social Sciences, 58*(2), P129–P137.

Wallace, S., Donoso Brown, E., Fairman, A., Beardshall, L., Olexsovich, A., Taylor, A., & Schreiber, J. (2016). Validation of the standardized touchscreen assessment of cognition with neurotypical adults. *NeuroRehabilitation*, 1–10. doi:10.3233/NRE-161428.

Weintraub, S., Mesulam, M.-M., Wieneke, C., Rademaker, A., Rogalski, E., & Thompson, C. (2009). The Northwestern Anagram Test: Measuring sentence production in Primary Progressive Aphasia. *AM J Alzheimers Dis Other Demen.*, *24*(5), 408–416. doi:1177/1533317509343104.

Welland, R. J., Lubinski, R., & Higginbotham, D. J. (2002). Discourse comprehension test performance of elders with dementia of the Alzheimer type. *Journal of Speech, Language, and Hearing Research, 45*(6), 1175–1187.

Welsh, K. A., Butters, N., Mohs, R. C., Beekly, D., Edland, S., Fillenbaum, & Heyman, A. (1994). The Consortium to Establish a Registry for Alzheimer's Disease (CERAD): Part V. A normative study of the neuropsychological battery. *Neurology, 44*(4), 609–614.

Wiig, E. H. (2002). *Alzheimer's quick test: Assessment of parietal function.* San Antonio, TX: Psychological Corporation.

Wilson, B. A., Alderman, N., Burgess, P., Emslei, H., & Evans, J. J. (1996). *Behavioral assessment of the dysexecutive syndrome (BADS).* Bury St. Edmunds, UK: Thames Valley.

Wilson, B. A., Greenfield, E., Clare, L., Baddeley, A., Cockburn, J., Watson, P., … Crawford, J. (2008). *The Rivermead Behavioural Memory Test – 3rd Ed. (RBMT-3).* London, UK: Pearson Assessment.

World Health Organization. (2001). *International classification of functioning, disability, and health.* Retrieved February 21, 2006, from www3.who.int/icf/icftemplate.cfm.

Ylvisaker, M., & Feeney, T. (1998). *Collaborative brain injury intervention: Positive everyday routines.* San Diego, CA: Singular.

Ylvisaker, M., Szekeres, S., & Feeney, T. (2001). Communication disorders associated with traumatic brain injury. In R. Chapey (Ed.), *Language intervention strategies in aphasia and related neurogenic communication disorders* (4th ed., pp. 745–808).

6

COGNITIVE AND COMMUNICATIVE INTERVENTIONS

Ellen M. Hickey and Michelle S. Bourgeois

The philosophy of dementia care has evolved substantially over the past few decades. In the past, the therapeutic potential of persons with dementia was viewed with a nihilistic attitude due to the degenerative nature of dementia, and the lack of effective interventions for reversing or slowing the inevitable decline in cognitive and behavioral symptoms (Hopper, 2003, 2016). The past two decades have seen the evolution of a more holistic and humanistic approach intended to maintain function, prevent excess disability, and improve quality of life (QoL), and an explosion of dementia intervention research. As described in earlier chapters, the changes in approaches to care for people with dementia have been motivated by the broad movement to use social models of healthcare, as well as the shift toward person-centered care for persons with dementia (Kitwood, 1997; Mitchell & Agnelli, 2015) and the theory of "unmet needs" in persons with dementia (e.g., Algase et al., 1996; Kunik et al., 2003). This shift toward holistic care has also taken place in speech-language pathology, notably, with the development of the Living with Aphasia: Framework for Outcome Measurement (A-FROM; Kagan et al., 2008), which can be modified slightly and applied as a "Living with Dementia" framework. As well, intervention research continues to develop with the aim of maximizing functioning and QoL (Bourgeois, Brush, Elliot, & Kelly, 2015). (See Chapters 1 and 4 for more information on the evolution of dementia care and social models, and Chapter 3 for the theory of unmet needs.)

Nonpharmacological (environmental and behavioral) intervention approaches for persons with dementia have been the subject of much study over the past few decades, with growing evidence that they can provide benefits to persons with dementia at the level of their cognitive and communicative impairments as well as participation and QoL (e.g., Egan, Bérubé, Racine, Leonard, & Rochon, 2010; Olazarán et al., 2010; Orrell et al., 2014). Furthermore, speech-language pathologists (SLPs) are now integral members of the care team providing nonpharmacological interventions for persons with dementia and their families in the United States. The American Speech-Language-Hearing Association (ASHA, 2005) position statement on the role of the SLP statement working with persons with cognitive-communicative disorders recommends that SLPs teach functional skills and develop compensatory strategies, and work with support systems. This role is developing and expanding in other countries too, such as Canada and Ireland, although there are barriers as noted in SLP surveys. For example, in Canada, while SLPs are largely aware of interventions for this population, the most frequently reported barriers were lack of funding for SLP positions in long-term care, and patients with more acute conditions were considered more of a priority in hospital settings, particularly those with dysphagia (Hopper, Cleary, Oddson, Donnelly, & Elgar, 2007). In Ireland, speech-language therapists reported that they did not feel knowledgeable or confident about evidence-based interventions for persons with dementia, nor did they have an optimal team approach for dementia care in their work settings (Gill & McCabe, 2016).

Beginning in 2001, the Academy of Neurologic Communication Disorders and Sciences (ANCDS) with support from ASHA and the Department of Veteran's Affairs, reviewed the evidence on nonpharmacological interventions that could be used by SLPs working with persons with dementia. As a result, seven systematic review papers were published (Bayles et al., 2005, 2006; Boyle et al., 2006; Hopper et al., 2005; Mahendra, Kim et al., 2006; Mahendra, Hopper et al., 2006; Zientz et al., 2007a, 2007b). More recently, a team of researchers from ANCDS and ASHA's National Center for Evidence-Based Practice (NCEP) worked together to update the systematic review on cognitive interventions for persons with dementia (Hopper et al., 2013). Additionally, many systematic reviews on cognitive interventions for persons with dementia from other fields, as well as systematic reviews of cognitive rehabilitation in general, can guide SLPs working with persons with dementia.

As discussed in Chapter 5, we suggest that clinicians should "Flip the Rehab Model" (Bourgeois, 2014, 2015) to further promote person- and caregiver-centered care. We recommend that a functional approach to assessment be used to develop a person-centered treatment plan that reflects three general principles of intervention: (a) maximize independent functioning as long as possible; (b) maintain QoL via supported participation and engagement; and (c) emphasize personal relevance and contextual training. (See Chapter 4 for a description of these principles.) This chapter will describe evidence-based interventions for cognitive-communicative abilities of persons with dementia that adhere to these principles; we also consider the International Classification of Functioning, Disability, and Health (ICF; WHO, 2001) in the discussion.

The ICF can be used to categorize intervention approaches as targeting the person's body structures/functions or activities and participation, or changes can be made to the environment that can influence participation and QoL. Using this framework, body structures and functions are treated through either pharmacological interventions or behavioral approaches that are designed to develop new or support existing neural connections and pathways to overcome cognitive deficits, such as memory, sensory perception, and language, among others. Current practice regarding pharmacological interventions will be described briefly, but a complete description is beyond the scope of this chapter. Cognitive stimulation/training approaches that target cognitive impairments will also be described. The emphasis with cognitive rehabilitation is in the activities and participation domain. There are several specific cognitive rehabilitation procedures that SLPs can use that capitalize on preserved strengths to develop compensatory strategies for functional activities for persons with dementia (Bourgeois, 1992b; Bourgeois et al., 2015; Camp et al., 1997; Camp & Skrajner, 2004). Case examples will be used to illustrate these approaches, and available evidence will be summarized. (See Chapter 7 for more on non-pharmacological/environmental and behavioral intervention approaches.)

Pharmacological Intervention Approaches

Given the market potential of pharmacological treatments for the diseases that cause dementia, significant research resources have gone into developing medications for AD. Research efforts have searched for disease-modifying medical and pharmacological treatments to prevent or stop the course of Alzheimer's disease and other diseases that cause dementia (Sun, Nelson, & Alkon, 2015). A wide variety of pharmacological treatment approaches have been explored, such as antioxidants, hormone replacement, and anti-inflammatory therapies, that aim to reduce or manipulate brain A or tau protein, and to address insulin resistance, but there are none currently approved for use (Ehret & Chamberlin, 2015). Other types of medical and surgical disease-modifying treatments are being explored, such as stem cells, deep brain stimulation, and transcranial magnetic stimulation, with some success in experimental trials, but these treatments are not available for use outside of research (Sun et al., 2015). At the time of writing, only symptom-modifying pharmacological treatments are approved for use with persons with dementia.

Pharmacological Interventions for Cognitive Symptoms

The currently available pharmacological treatments for AD have focused on managing the symptoms of dementia by targeting the functioning of either acetylcholine and glutamate, using cholinesterase inhibitors (ChEIs) and a partial N-methyl-D-aspartate (NMDA) antagonist, respectively (Alzheimer's Disease Education and Referral Center [ADEAR], 2016; Buckley & Salpeter, 2015; Sun et al., 2015; Tan et al., 2014; Wong, 2016). There are four ChEIs available for use, including galantamine, rivastigmine, and donepezil, which aim to boost the availability of acetylcholine in the brain by reducing the amount of the enzyme that breaks down this neurotransmitter. The ChEIs are used primarily with persons with mild to moderate AD with modest benefits shown to delay or prevent cognitive symptoms from becoming worse, and they may improve ADL functioning and help to control some of the behavioral symptoms of AD for about 1 year (ADEAR, 2016). Donepezil can also be used in the severe stages of AD, and is given at a higher dose (Cummings et al., 2013), and has been shown to improve the language subscale of the Severe Impairment Battery (SIB; Saxton, McGonigle, Swihart, & Boller, 1993) (Ferris et al., 2011). Also, a rivastigmine patch is now available for use in persons with severe AD (Jeffrey, 2013). Tsoi and colleagues (2016) investigated earlier initiation of drug treatments, and found that starting the drugs six months earlier did not result in better outcomes in cognition, behavior, physical function, or clinical status than those who started later.

There is one NMDA antagonist available for use, memantine, which aims to block the NMDA type of glutamate receptors when they are excessively activated (but not during normal synaptic activity) (Esposito et al., 2013). Memantine is for people with moderate to severe AD (Reisberg et al., 2003; Wong, 2016). Memantine somewhat delays the worsening of cognitive abilities and results in a modest improvement in ADL functioning, but no impact on the behavioral symptoms in persons with AD (Esposito et al., 2013; Kavanagh et al., 2011).

Because these two types of drugs work differently, they can be used together. For example, donepezil is now being used in combination with memantine in people with moderate to severe AD, and there might be a small advantage compared to either drug alone, but there is no added benefit in those with mild to moderate AD (Farrimond, Roberts, & McShane, 2012; Schneider, Dagerman, Higgins, & McShane, 2011; Tan et al., 2014). When used in combination with donepezil, there may be additional benefit with a small improvement in quality-adjusted life years, and even delayed institutionalization of persons with AD (Lachaine, Beauchemin, Legault, & Bineau (2011).

Most of the research on symptomatic pharmacological interventions has been conducted with persons with AD. Persons with VaD and PD have demonstrated improvements with donepezil and galantamine (Aarsland, Laake, Larsen, & Janvin, 2002; Black et al., 2003). A systematic review of eight randomized controlled trials did not find a benefit to using ChEIs with persons with Huntingtons, disease (HD), CADASIL, multiple sclerosis, progressive supranuclear palsy, or frontotemporal dementia (Li, Hai, Zhou, & Dong, 2015). A review of three studies that used rivastigmine with persons with vascular dementia did not find any strong support for its use, but frequent gastrointestinal side effects (Birks, McGuinness, & Craig, 2013). A narrative review concluded that donepezil and rivastigmine can be used for the cognitive and psychiatric symptoms in persons with Parkinson's dementia (PDD) or dementia with Lewy bodies (DLB), but memantine had more variable results (Ikeda, 2017).

Despite the large amounts of resources put into both research about and clinical use of these drugs, by and large, these treatments continue to yield less than satisfactory results with small effects that are of questionable clinical significance (Buckley & Salpeter, 2015; Schneider et al., 2011; Tsoi et al., 2016). Often the results shown are scores on the ADAS-Cog, or occasionally the MMSE, or SIB, with questionable clinical significance of a one- or two-point change. Additionally, most studies follow participants for less than one year, and research questions tend to revolve around measuring cognitive and global outcomes; however, practical questions remain around use in daily practice, and research is needed on long-term treatment efficacy, timing of initiation, and duration of use and how the drugs should be discontinued (Parsons, 2016; Tija et al., 2014; Wong, 2016). People with advanced dementia are receiving medications that are of questionable benefit, costing health systems significant amounts of money (Tija et al., 2014). Additional research is needed on who responds to treatment. Some researchers have also suggested that the problem with small effects might be due to drugs that only work on one neurotransmitter, or aspect of the problem, at a time (Esposito et al., 2013; Lam, Hackett, & Takechi, 2016). Given available evidence, the medical community recommends use of ChEIs or memantine with persons with AD (ADEAR, 2016; Laver, Dyer, Whitehead, Clemson, & Crotty, 2016).

Antioxidant Use to Prevent or Slow Cognitive Decline

The search for strategies to prevent or slow the progression of cognitive symptoms led to theories about the relationships among stress, diet, inflammation, and hormones and dementia, with these theories leading to subsequent therapeutic recommendations. Attempts have been made to reverse the negative effects of oxidative stress with antioxidant compounds, such as vitamin supplements and specific foods, with contradictory findings. In their discussion of a variety of antioxidants in the brain (e.g., vitamins, melatonin, alpha–Lipoic acid, garlic, and statin and anti–inflammatory medications), Lam and colleagues (2016) reported that there is compelling evidence that antioxidants may prevent cognitive decline; however, more human research is required.

A review of four studies on vitamin E found no benefit for preventing the progression of MCI to AD, or for improving cognitive function or decreasing behavioral and psychological symptoms of dementia (BPSD) in persons with AD; there may be a moderate benefit of slowing functional decline, which was found in one study (Farina, Llewellyn, Isaac, & Tabet, 2017). Two reviews of fruit and vegetable consumption had conflicting findings (Cao et al., 2016; Jiang et al., 2017). Some food intake patterns were related to a decreased risk of dementia, including: unsaturated fatty acids, antioxidants, vitamin B, and a Mediterranean diet; whereas intake of aluminum, low vitamin D levels, and smoking were related to higher risk of dementia, and more research is needed on fish and alcohol (Cao et al., 2016). Ginkgo biloba might be as effective as donepezil for slowing cognitive decline and improving functional abilities and behavior, but without the drug side effects, for persons with vascular dementia (Zeng et al., 2015) or Alzheimer's dementia (Tan et al., 2015; Yang et al., 2014); however, the evidence for ginkgo biloba is low quality (Laver et al., 2016). Some studies on statin use have been positive, but a review of four studies found that there is no evidence to recommend statins as a treatment for Alzheimer's disease, despite evidence that it does lower cholesterol in the treatment group (McGuinness, Craig, Bullock, Malouf, & Passmore, 2014).

Pharmacological Interventions for Behavioral and Psychological Symptoms

The pharmacological treatments that target cognitive function have shown little, if any, benefit for ameliorating BPSDs, including mood disturbance, altered perception, agitation, aggression, anxiety, and sleep and appetite disturbances. Other medications, including antipsychotics, anxiolytics, sedatives, and antidepressants have been used for BPSDs, but lack efficacy (Reus et al., 2016). Many of these drugs can improve one problem while creating another. Because of safety problems, researchers have turned to other potential types of pharmacological management; e.g., medical cannabis oil containing Tetrahydrocannabinol (THC) is being studied for effectiveness and safety, and might be a potentially promising treatment option after much larger and higher quality studies are done (Assaf et al., 2016).

Efficacy data are not promising for the use of neuroleptic medications to reduce BPSDs in persons with dementia, and significant risks have been identified, such as increased mortality with use of antipsychotics and cognitive decline in those taking antipsychotics for more than 12 weeks (Ballard, Creese, Corbett, & Aarsland, 2011; Corbett, Burns, & Ballard, 2014; Reus et al., 2016; Tampi & Tampi, 2014). Therefore, clinicians are advised to use pharmacological interventions as a last resort (Reus et al., 2016). Despite the warnings, people with dementia continue to be prescribed these drugs (Ballard et al., 2011; Corbett et al., 2014). For those who have been taking antipsychotic medications, however, discontinuation of these medications must be done carefully, and with consideration of the evidence for possible relapse; most will be able to discontinue, but those who had more severe BPSDs before treatment might not tolerate the withdrawal (Declercq et al., 2013).

Another issue to be concerned with is polypharmacy, which is a common problem amongst older adults, including those living in long-term care facilities, though persons with cognitive impairment might have less polypharmacy (Jokanovic et al., 2015; Moyle et al., 2017), leading to deprescribing programs in geriatric care (e.g., Reeve, Bell, & Hilmer, 2015). Care providers are being encouraged to implement more person-centered approaches to care that capitalize on environmental modifications and behavioral interventions to maximize functional behaviors in persons with dementia (Brodaty & Arasaratnam, 2012; Livingston et al., 2014; Reus et al., 2016). If environmental and behavioral interventions are not effective and the person has the potential to cause harm or the condition has not improved within 30 days, then pharmacological approaches should be tried using the practice guidelines (Reus et al., 2016). Until scientists discover the underlying causes and effective cures for these diseases, clinicians and families should rely on behavioral, nonpharmacological interventions to address the symptoms of dementia that interfere with daily life. See Box 6.7 at the end of the chapter for websites to obtain more information about pharmacological treatments for persons with dementia.

Nonpharmacological Intervention Approaches

Prior to the mid-1980s, the behavioral treatment literature consisted of single studies on diverse approaches representing the continuum of disciplines that were struggling to figure out how best to care for persons with dementia. Bourgeois' (1991) review of the treatment literature revealed four categories of approaches: environmental, stimulus control, reinforcement, and group therapy. The effects of these interventions were mostly noted in the areas of engagement, social interaction, and cooperation, with some anecdotal effects on specific communication behaviors. These effects, however, were not compelling to professionals or families who wanted treatment to result in the return to previous behavior patterns. Without evidence that robust changes in responsive behaviors could result from direct treatment, many professionals advocated an indirect approach, focusing on providing support and coping mechanisms to the caregiver (e.g., Clark, 1995).

Bourgeois (1991) challenged clinicians to develop specific interventions for persons with dementia that are designed to: address functional skills important in daily life and likely to recruit naturally occurring reinforcement; choose intervention procedures that are built on preserved skills and abilities; and select goals to match the constraints and opportunities of the environment. Since then, professionals in a wide variety of disciplines have continued to produce a plethora of therapeutic strategies and approaches with varying degrees of empirical support. Many of the non-pharmacological interventions are ultimately designed to improve the QoL of these individuals and their families by enhancing communication, improving performance of activities of daily living, maintaining functional behavior, and reducing responsive behaviors and psychotic symptoms (Cohen-Mansfield, 2005). Evidence is growing to show that nonpharmacological (environmental and behavioral) intervention approaches for persons with dementia are at least as effective as pharmacological approaches for improving cognitive abilities for specific tasks, modifying behaviors and communication, and improving QoL or mood (e.g., Egan et al., 2010; Olazarán et al., 2010; Orrell et al., 2014). Other evidence shows that pharmacological interventions do not add any benefit on top of nonpharamacological approaches (Yesavage et al., 2008). Some evidence has also been documented that multicomponent interventions can delay institutionalization of persons with dementia with modest resource utilization (Olazarán et al., 2010).

Classification of and Evidence for Cognitive Interventions

Researchers have classified three types of cognitive interventions: cognitive stimulation, cognitive training, and cognitive rehabilitation (e.g., Bahar-Fuchs, Clare, & Woods, 2013; Hopper et al., 2013; Huntley et al., 2015). *Cognitive stimulation* is the least specific intervention approach, often conducted in groups, and entails engaging the individual in stimulating activities and discussions that involve multiple cognitive domains (e.g., reminiscence therapy, reality orientation, and social activity, and sensorimotor activities). *Cognitive training* uses structured intervention with specific exercises or tasks that aim to restore one specific cognitive function (e.g., attention, executive functions, episodic memory), with gradual increases in task difficulty. This type of treatment is usually delivered individually, and may be computerized or noncomputerized. *Cognitive rehabilitation* is the most person-centered and ecologically valid of the three types of cognitive interventions. In general, cognitive rehabilitation interventions are designed to support our clients in achieving desired functional behaviors using individualized strategies that capitalize on preserved strengths, not to "fix" the impairments in persons with dementia (Hopper et al., 2013). Unfortunately, this classification of interventions is not used consistently, which makes it more difficult to evaluate their evidence overall and consumers of the research must use caution in interpreting results. A summary of overall evidence for each type of intervention is provided before describing examples of specific cognitive interventions.

Cognitive Stimulation. Individual studies and systematic reviews on cognitive stimulation and/or training are accruing. Most of the studies have included participants with mild to moderate dementia. A Cochrane review of 15 studies found that cognitive stimulation provides a consistent cognitive benefit, as well as self-reported improvements in QoL and wellbeing and staff reported ratings of communication and social interaction, but not mood, ADLs, or responsive behaviors (Woods, Aguirre, Spector, & Orrell, 2012). Two systematic reviews with strict inclusion criteria, analyzing only high-quality randomized controlled trials (RCTs), provided evidence for the benefits of cognitive stimulation for persons with dementia (Aguirre, Woods, Spector, & Orrell, 2013; Alves et al., 2013). Aguirre et al. (2013) found improvements in global cognitive functioning, with some evidence for improvements on measures of communication, social interaction, and wellbeing. Alves et al. (2013) also found that these benefits can be attained in a cost-effective manner.

If participants are also taking cholinesterase inhibitors (e.g., donepezil), the benefits of cognitive stimulation are in addition to any that might be seen with the medication (Aguirre et al., 2013; Woods et al., 2012). Qualitative research on cognitive stimulation also found that there were cognitive benefits, including changes in everyday life, as well as satisfaction with the treatment (Spector, Gardner, & Orrell, 2011).

Cognitive Training. Conversely, studies of cognitive training for persons with dementia have poor to modest evidence (e.g., Bahar-Fuchs et al., 2013; Hopper et al., 2013; Huntley et al., 2015; Kallio, Öhman, Kautiainen, Hietanen, & Pitkälä, 2017). Many studies that purport to investigate cognitive training or cognitive rehabilitation are actually reality orientation or cognitive stimulation interventions, which complicates interpretation of results across studies (Bahar-Fuchs et al., 2013). Thus, consumers of this research must read the details of the method to determine what type of cognitive intervention approach was provided. A meta-analysis of 11 cognitive training studies found no significant differences overall between intervention and control groups (Bahar-Fuchs et al., 2013). When individual studies do show benefits, participants tend to improve only on the actual tasks trained or tests with similar tasks. Improvements in overall cognitive functioning or generalization to other treatment settings or tasks should not be expected from cognitive training tasks that are focused on specific tasks or information (Hopper et al., 2013). Kallio et al. (2017) warned that common limitations in the studies (e.g., inaccurate definitions of cognitive training, inadequate sample sizes and randomization procedures) may have created inflated results. A general conclusion across systematic reviews is that more and better studies are needed to determine the efficacy of cognitive stimulation and cognitive training, and that studies need to include measures to determine generalization to daily life activities and wellbeing.

Cognitive Rehabilitation. The purpose of cognitive rehabilitation is to maximize independence and meaningful engagement in daily life at levels that are satisfying to clients, their families, and others in their social environments. Chapter 5 explains the "Flip the Rehab Model" that allows us to perform assessments that lead to person-centered goals that can be addressed using cognitive rehabilitation procedures. Treatment strategies used in cognitive rehabilitation for the memory deficits of persons with dementia have been described as either internal (to the individual) or external in focus (Bourgeois, 1991, 2014) (see Table 6.1). Internal strategies involve some mental manipulation of the information to be remembered, and include: method of loci, categorization, visual imagery, association, face-name/name-learning, rehearsal, attention and number or story mnemonics (Sohlberg & Turkstra, 2011). Internal strategies require recognition of their purpose, conscious rehearsal, and the ability to apply them at the relevant time. External strategies, or external cueing systems and aids, compensate for memory and communication deficits by capitalizing on preserved strengths, particularly oral reading and reading comprehension (Bourgeois, 2014; Hopper et al., 2013). External aids come in a wide variety of forms and are personalized to match the person's desired goals/needs and profile of deficits and strengths, as described later.

The cognitive rehabilitation procedures used to train use of external strategies has an impact on their successful implementation, and there is evidence that spaced retrieval training is effective for

TABLE 6.1 Examples of Internal and External Memory Strategies and Demands

Internal Strategies Require:	*External Strategies Require:*
Effortful, conscious processing	Automatic processing
Active memory search to recall information	Recognition of information based on experience and practice
Internal monitoring of information	External monitoring of information
Mental representation inside the brain	Physical, permanent products in the environment

persons with mild to moderate dementia (Hopper et al., 2013). Evidence for cognitive rehabilitation for persons with dementia has largely come from single-case experimental designs with persons with mild to moderate dementia. Studies have shown that persons with mild to moderate dementia can learn or relearn information or skills, with transfer to everyday contexts, and they can use external memory aids to compensate for their deficits (Anderson, Arens, Arens, & Coppens, 2001; Camp, Bird, & Cherry, 2000; Clare et al., 2000, 2001, 2002). Internal memory strategies and external memory and communication strategies and training procedures will be described in detail later in the chapter.

Given the need for larger studies and higher-quality evidence, a multicenter randomized trial, the ETNA3 study, was conducted at 40 sites in France (Amieva et al., 2016). This was a unique study in that it included 655 persons with mild to moderate dementia and their family caregivers, different types of cognitive intervention approaches to look at cognitive stimulation, training, and rehabilitation. Treatment took place in 1.5 hour weekly sessions for 6 weeks followed by maintenance sessions every 6 weeks for 21 months. Participants were randomly assigned to reminiscence therapy (stimulation) groups focused personal themes with personal stimulus materials brought from home, cognitive training groups with two levels of structured cognitive tasks related to ADLs (e.g., calculations for money management), or individualized cognitive rehabilitation that addressed personal goals identified by the participant and caregiver using errorless learning. Caregivers of persons in the cognitive stimulation and training groups attended their own education and support groups. Caregivers of those in the cognitive rehabilitation intervention received support via weekly telephone sessions. The control group received usual care at the memory clinics and day programs where the study took place. None of these intervention approaches delayed the dementia progression over the 24 months of the study, and support was not found for reminiscence therapy or for cognitive training in terms of outcome measures of cognitive, functional abilities, behaviors, depression, QoL, or caregiver burden. However, modest evidence was found to support individualized cognitive rehabilitation, with less functional decline at 24 months post, and some clinically significant improvements in terms of behavior and caregiver burden. An important finding is that cognitive rehabilitation decreased resource utilization by delaying institutionalization of persons with mild to moderate dementia.

Examples of Cognitive Interventions

Reality Orientation. Reality orientation was the first cognitive stimulation intervention specifically designed to address the confusion and disorientation of persons with dementia, which was meant to be a "hopeful, therapeutic process" but became rigid over time (Folsom, 1968; Woods et al., 2012). The purpose of RO is to maintain previously acquired skills by providing prompts and cues, rather than to teach new skills. Prompts and cues are usually in the form of a standard set of orientation facts, such as the date, location, next anticipated holiday, outside weather conditions, the day's activities and menu that are often posted in a common area on a white board or poster. Applications of RO may involve a daily group treatment program, 1 : 1 reality-based conversation with staff throughout the day, or a combined group therapy and 1 : 1 program.

The benefits of RO have been examined in a range of studies, including some randomized controlled trials and systematic reviews (e.g., Spector, Davies, Woods, & Orrell, 2000; Woods et al., 2012). Benefits have been recorded in cognitive and behavioral domains when compared to no treatment or an alternative treatment, but there is minimal evidence for maintenance of gains, which has not been measured in all studies. Suggestions have been made for 24-hour RO rather than classroom-based, and using visual cues for functional orientation information. In a more recent study of 14 persons with mild to moderate dementia who were receiving donepezil, those in the treatment group received weekly RO sessions for six months (Camargo, Justus, & Retzlaff, 2015). For those in the treatment group, their scores on several neuropsychological tests were statistically significantly improved, but generalization to functional use was not shown. The researchers concluded that RO should be offered on a long-term basis to persons with dementia. In fact, RO is a standard practice in most nursing homes. Whether persons with dementia are living in a long-term care facility or at home, caregiver assistance is likely necessary to attend to and understand the posted information (Box 6.1 lists tips for maximizing the benefits of RO).

Validation Therapy. Naomi Feil developed validation therapy in response to RO, which she found to be overly confrontational, thereby contributing to social withdrawal and hostility on the part of the person with dementia (Feil, 1992; Feil & de Klerk-Rubin, 1992). Validation therapy involves recognizing, acknowledging, and empathizing with the person's expression of feelings and their reality and nonverbal ways. Feil has suggested the use of specific techniques for particular situations, with an emphasis on nonverbal communication (e.g., touch, eye contact, and tone of voice). Feil proposed four stages of resolution for persons with dementia, but experimental valida- tion of these stages and a person's progression through them is lacking. Likewise, evidence for this approach is sparse, and most of the evidence is anecdotal. A systematic review revealed only three studies that met the criteria, and none showed statistically significant results between validation therapy and the control condition (Neal & Barton Wright, 2003). There is a need for better designed studies to determine whether this technique is beneficial.

Reminiscence Therapy. Reminiscence therapy is another verbal therapeutic approach that has existed since the 1960s, and is often conducted in discussion groups with persons with demen- tia (Dempsey et al., 2014). Each discussion has a theme that taps into preserved remote memories for positive experiences and events (e.g., life events such as getting married, a first job, holidays and travel). The discussion is supported with props, such as photographs, objects, music, and videos that highlight the theme. Tangible objects, or props, can be very useful in supporting memory and communication of persons with dementia in reminiscence (Pimentel, 2009) (see Box 6.2 for a case example).

A modern adaptation of reminiscence therapy is the use of information and communication technologies to provide multimedia stimuli in reminiscence sessions (Astell et al., 2010; Lazar, Thompson, & Demiris, 2014). For example, Computer Interactive Reminiscence Conversation

---

Box 6.1 Tips for Maximizing the Potential of Reality Orientation (RO) Cues

- Ensure the information on the RO board is meaningful and useful to the residents.
- Schedule of daily activities, name of facility.
- Provide opportunities to practice using the information in meaningful ways.
- "Today is Tuesday – Bingo day!"
- "Today is Saturday – my daughter comes on Saturdays."
- Make portable and personalized cues so that the information is with the person with dementia when needed, rather than posted on a wall down the hall.
- A cue card (described below) that the person can carry to have important information available when needed (e.g., "My room is 421." "I stay at Isleview Manor.")
- Enhance RO stimuli with training, or with routine and repetitive exposure.

(Also see Bourgeois, 2013)

Box 6.2 Case Examples: Reminiscence with Props

Two clients, Mrs. Baldwin and Mr. Tremblay, were referred for SLP services to improve their communication with staff, reduce responsive behaviors, and increase participation and engagement. The SLP conducted person-centered assessments using the process outlined in Chapter 5, including discourse samples. Both clients readily engaged in conversation, but Mrs. Baldwin's conversational skills were marked by repetitive statements and questions ("I used to drive a Ford. We went to New York City a lot. When is my daughter coming?"), while Mrs. Tremblay's conversational skills were marked by unintelligible comments and neologisms. Both clients showed good social skills, such as appropriate eye contact, use of tone, and turn-taking.

For treatment, the SLP engaged the clients in reminiscence using family photos (unlabeled). Their language was again marked by the same deficits. With Mrs. Baldwin, the SLP encouraged reminiscence and at the same time, asked her to help roll a skein of yarn into a ball. While Mrs. Baldwin rolled the yarn, she began to tell the student about the boarding house that she used to run, the meals that she prepared, the chores that she did, and the knitting and sewing that she would do for her family and her tenants. There were few statements repeated and much new information was gained that was helpful to the whole care team.

With Mrs. Tremblay, the SLP encouraged reminiscence while asking her if she would like to hold a cat (a toy cat that made noises and movements), as she had learned from her son that the client was a big animal lover and they had many cats in their home. Mrs. Tremblay patted the cat and spoke intelligibly to the cat, and in a nurturing way. She began to the tell the SLP about her love for cats and that she also had a rabbit when she was a girl. The SLP then showed the client her engagement ring and asked if she had any advice about marriage. The client began to talk at length about the best age to get married, not to wait on her husband too much, and how many children to have. The team was then able to incorporate more of the clients' histories into their conversations with them and learned to facilitate their engagement with concrete objects and actions.

Aid (CIRCA) is technology for reminiscence that was developed in Scotland and is comprised of software with a touch screen display that allows users to interact with multimedia information (Astell et al., 2010). Users choose from seven possible themes, and then choose the photos (with captions), music, or video clips from that category. The content in the CIRCA software is specific to the region where it was developed, and needs to be adapted for use in other regions, as was done in British Columbia with the development of CIRCA-BC (Purves, Phinney, Hulko, Puurveen, & Astell, 2014). Purves and colleagues found that the technology provides a focus for joint attention for the persons discussing the reminiscence materials. They also highlighted the growing diversity of many communities and the need to consider the shared versus distinct social histories of members of the community (e.g., Indigenous peoples, immigrants). A systematic review found that interactive technology supports older adults with dementia in engaging in reminiscence (Lazar et al., 2014). Use of multimedia tablet technology might also benefit family and staff caregivers by offering a less time-consuming way to enhance their interactions with people with dementia than gathering pictures, documents, music, and objects from a variety of sources, though Lazar et al. (2014) point out that the technology is still too complicated for many family members to use independently. As this technology continues to evolve, this type of intervention holds promise for use in interactions with volunteers as well.

Evidence for reminiscence therapy is mixed, though several systematic reviews have reported its benefits; limitations in study methodology continue to limit the strength of the evidence, as per several (e.g., Cotelli, Manenti, & Zanetti, 2012; Elias, Neville, & Scott, 2015; Kim et al., 2006; Lazar et al., 2014). These systematic reviews reported that outcome measures from group reminiscence therapy have documented benefits in terms of improved cognition, communication, and reduced depression, as well as other benefits sometimes reported, including reduced loneliness, social isolation, and increased wellbeing and self-esteem, but questions remain about generalization of the effects to other times or locations and maintenance of treatment effects. Newer studies aim to improve the strength of evidence. For example, Chiang and colleagues (2010) used a waitlist control group design with three waves of intervention, and found decreased depression and loneliness and increased psychological wellbeing in men with dementia. On the other hand, the large, multicentre randomized trials by Amieva et al. (2016) and Woods et al. (2016) found no difference between the reminiscence group and the control group. Furthermore, the REMCARE trial (Woods et al., 2016) examined whether joint reminiscence sessions with caregivers was effective. Though there were no differences between the intervention and control groups, secondary analyses revealed that those who attended more sessions had more improvements on outcome measures of autobiographical memory, QoL, and relationship quality. Notably, though, the results were negative for caregivers, and those who attended more sessions had more anxiety and caregiving stress. These results do not support the use of joint group reminiscence therapy with caregivers, which is not clinically effective or cost effective.

Breakfast Club. The Breakfast Club (Boczko, 1994; Santo Pietro & Boczko, 1997, 1998) is a communication stimulation approach consisting of a group treatment protocol delivered by an SLP to a small group of residents. Multisensory cues are provided to facilitate communication during the preparation, serving, and eating of a breakfast meal. The purposes of the treatment are to maintain conversational, pragmatic, organizational, and decision-making skills through the stimulation of all senses (auditory, visual, olfactory, gustatory, and tactile) and procedural memories (including linguistic, motor, and reading) to prevent isolation, learned helplessness, and the deterioration of communication skills. Many therapeutic principles specifically designed to facilitate communicative interactions are incorporated, such as the use of a structured routine or format for the session; a variety of stimuli to trigger associations with previously learned verbal, social, and motor behaviors; and individualized verbal cueing strategies to optimize the participation of each group member. A variety of language facilitation procedures are used: a continuum of question formats from open-ended to paired-choice to yes–no; the use of a cueing hierarchy (visual, semantic); the use of carrier phrases; and direct modeling of responses. Table 6.2 shows the 10-step protocol for a one-hour session.

Evaluation of the Breakfast Club protocol delivered over a 12-week period to 20 persons with mid-stage dementia revealed improvements in psychosocial interaction, communication, conversation, mealtime independence, and cognitive function. When compared to control subjects who participated in small conversation groups, the Breakfast Club participants demonstrated significant increases in psychosocial interaction and communication (Santo Pietro & Boczko, 1998). In addition, anecdotal reports of increased attention, use of other participants' names during the session, decreased distractibility, fewer off-topic comments and interruptions, increased humorous remarks, reduced agitation and anxiety, and increased social interaction in other areas of the facility were indicative of the potential usefulness of this protocol in maintaining skills necessary for QoL. Originally designed to be delivered by SLPs, a more practical approach in most settings would be for SLPs (and perhaps occupational therapists) to evaluate residents and make recommendations for involving people in a program run by nursing assistants.

TABLE 6.2 Breakfast Club Procedures

1. Group assembly, greeting, and nametag distribution

2. Facilitated discussion of juice
   "Can you read the name of this juice?" (visual cue)
   "This one has lots of vitamin C." (semantic cue)
   "You want a cold glass of _____." (carrier phrase)

3. Facilitated discussion of coffee
   Facilitator shows coffee pot and ground coffee (visual cue)
   Facilitator passes coffee around for members to smell (olfactory cue)
   "What's something hot to drink in the morning?" (semantic cue)
   "Do you want your coffee black or with milk?" (paired choice)

4. Facilitated discussion and selection of breakfast choice for the day

5. Facilitated discussion of food preparation

6. Facilitated execution and sequencing of food production

7. Facilitated distribution of prepared food

8. Facilitated discussion of another beverage option

9. Facilitated conversation on a variety of general-interest topics during meal

10. Group termination protocol, including cleanup, nametag return, and goodbyes

Source: Adapted from Santo Pietro and Boczko (1997).

Elder Rehab. Arkin (2001, 2007, 2011) addressed the issue of maintenance of cognitive intervention gains in her program of research, which saw community-residing persons with AD participating in cognitive interventions with undergraduate student volunteers. Two different learning strategies (quiz format versus repetition) on fact recall were examined. Participants who listened to audiotapes of a narrative with quiz questions learned more and retained the information longer than participants who listened to audiotapes narrating the information twice. This study is limited in generalizability, however, due to the small number of subjects. The intervention was expanded twice, first into the Volunteers in Partnership (VIP) program and then into the Elder Rehab program (Arkin, 1996, 1999, 2001). In these programs, university student volunteers participated in community activities (e.g., museum visits, bicycling, shopping, or volunteer work) and structured language stimulation (e.g., verbal fluency and conversation) with persons with AD (Arkin, 1996). In Elder Rehab, the students deliver a variety of memory and language stimulation activities (Arkin, 2005), as well as participate in physical exercise and a weekly one-hour volunteer service task (e.g., animal shelters, nursing homes, child daycare centers).

Arkin demonstrated maintenance or improvements in discourse and memory abilities of Elder Rehab participants (Arkin, 1997, 1999, 2001, 2007). At the end of the academic semester, seven of 12 participants improved on post-test discourse, picture description, and proverb interpretation tasks. A follow-up study (Mahendra & Arkin, 2003) evaluated the potential contribution of attention and physical activity by comparing two groups. Both received the same amount of physical exercise, memory training, and supervised volunteer work; the experimental group also received structured language stimulation while the control group engaged in unstructured conversation. Both groups performed similarly on post-intervention language testing. After four years of participation, four participants maintained or improved performance on all discourse measures compared to pre-treatment testing. Additional research with a larger population of subjects is needed

---

Box 6.3 Videos on YouTube depicting Arkin's Elder Rehab Program Implemented by Volunteers

- A memory quiz completed with support from a student volunteer – www.youtube.com/watch?v=Bf2xMe5BC_U
- Use of video feedback regarding performance on an autobiographical quiz – www.youtube.com/watch?v=GeoOt_LE4RM
- Olderadultsandstudentsvolunteeringtogether–www.youtube.com/watch?v=F3CvRU8kwqU–
- Exercise + language stimulation – www.youtube.com/watch?v=XnIPmLHMfMY

---

to understand the relative contributions of the different intervention components. Although Arkin's programs have utilized university student volunteers, Mahendra and Arkin suggested that staff, family caregivers, or other volunteers could also fill this role.

Computerized Cognitive Training. An increasingly popular approach to cognitive training is the use of computer programs and computer brain games, designed to target specific cognitive skills, such as memory, attention, and processing speed in order to reduce the effects of cognitive aging and to prevent the onset of dementia (Rogalski & Quintana, 2013). Systematic reviews of computerized cognitive training studies reveal small benefits overall, with better outcomes for computerized than pencil–and–paper conditions (Kueider, Parisi, Gross, & Rebok, 2012; Lampit, Hallock, & Valenzuela, 2014). Evidence showed that training multiple domains had more of an impact than single–domain training, and that while there were working memory and speed of processing gains, there were no benefits for executive functions or verbal memory in single–domain training, and these areas might require new technologies or combined interventions (Kueider et al., 2012; Lampit et al., 2014; Owen et al., 2010). In terms of treatment delivery, this type of training can be done in groups and sessions should be 30–60 minutes long, and not more than three times per week; home–based training was not effective; additionally, factors such as age, cognitive level, and noncognitive factors appear to influence outcomes (Lampit et al., 2014).

An RCT comparing the use of the Brain Fitness Program (Posit Science, 2013) with a control condition consisting of educational videos, with the same dosage of five hours per week for eight weeks, found significant improvements in processing speed and generalized effects to untrained measures of memory and attention (Smith et al., 2009). Eight studies that looked at video games, such as *Big Brain Academy: Wii Degree* (Nintendo, 2007) and *Rise of Nations* (Microsoft Game Studios, 2003), found some evidence for improved speed of processing and reaction time effects but limited transfer of training to other cognitive skills (Kueider et al., 2012). A study with 11,430 participants of a variety of ages found that training on computerized brain games for several hours per week for six weeks resulted in practice effects in trained cognitive tasks, but no transfer to closely related untrained tasks (Owen et al., 2010).

In spite of the less than stellar results of computer-based cognitive training programs for normally aging adults, there has been an equally strong interest in trying out this approach with persons with MCI and early AD. A review of 10 studies found that computer-based cognitive training was feasible for persons with mild cognitive impairments and early AD; none of the studies provided significant evidence for improving or maintaining cognitive functions or for transfer of training to everyday skills and tasks (Mueller, 2016). Based on the evidence that practice effects in single domains do not transfer to everyday tasks, some scientists have argued that the "belief that cognitive training and brain games can forestall or prevent dementia is based upon little more than hope and hype," and that there is no mechanism to explain the modulation of the disease process through computerized cognitive training (Ratner & Atkinson, 2015, p. 2613). Instead, they argue that in order to continue to be able to perform complex everyday tasks that require multiple cognitive domains, such as cooking, driving, and using email, people should continue to engage in these tasks over practicing brain games.

The ACTIVE study that randomly assigned 2,802 cognitively intact adults to one of three domain-specific cognitive training programs (memory, reasoning, or speed of processing) or a control group found no significant difference in the incidence of dementia for intervention or control groups after five years of measurement (Ball et al., 2002; Unverzagt et al., 2012). Still a multi-billion-dollar industry continues to market products to vulnerable individuals (Owen et al., 2010). Neuroscientists from the Stanford Center on Longevity and the Berlin Max Planck Institute for Human Development published a document endorsed by 76 leading neuroscientists from around the world stating,

> The strong consensus of this group is that the scientific literature does not support claims that the use of software-based "brain games" [e.g., Luminosity, Cogmed, and BrainHQ] alters neural functioning in ways that improve general cognitive performance in everyday life, or prevent cognitive slowing and brain disease.
>
> *(Hambrick, 2014)*

Ratner and Atkinson (2015) caution that the dangers of believing in the health benefits of brain games are that people will waste time playing games when they could be doing activities with more specific benefits, and that people with dementia could blame themselves for not having played brain games.

Internal Memory Strategies

A meta-analysis revealed that older adults without cognitive impairments could learn internal strategies; despite evidence for generalization to standardized test performance, little evidence was provided for generalization to daily activities (Gross et al., 2012). The most common strategies, usually trained in a group setting, included visual imagery, and face-name and name-learning strategies, with more than one strategy targeted. Gross and colleagues emphasized that clinicians should not overlook the self-generated and idiosyncratic strategies used by persons with memory impairments, whose unique strengths and weaknesses must be considered. Signal detection analysis revealed that typical older adults with better attention, verbal, and episodic memory were more likely to learn target mnemonic strategies and retain them one year later than those with poorer initial test scores (Fairchild, Friedman, Rosen, & Yesavage, 2013). Fairchild and colleagues (2013) also recommended the use of booster sessions to promote maintenance of initial treatment gains. Thus, for persons with dementia, internal strategies are rarely used and should be used only for clients who show evidence of ability to use these strategies during dynamic assessment. Even in the early stages, persons with dementia might not have the awareness, learning ability, or motivation to use internal memory techniques.

External Memory and Communication Strategies

External cues and aids are used to effect changes in functional behaviors or to support memory for facts. External strategies may be more effective for persons with dementia than internal, as they aim to compensate for the impairment while reducing the demands on a person's effortful memory processing (Camp et al., 2000). External aids can be used for goals that pertain to basic wants and needs, safety, orientation, social needs, functional behaviors, and engagement in meaningful activities, among others. To be person-centered, the ICF (WHO, 2001), life participation (Kagan et al., 2008), and unmet needs (Kunik et al., 2003) models should be enmeshed in the design and delivery of external aids.

External aids can be used for information processing impairments at all levels – encoding, consolidation, and retrieval – and for all aspects of memory (see Chapter 3 for more on memory and language deficits in AD and other dementias). The senses of vision, hearing, smell, and touch are essential for recognition and recall of information. When the senses begin to fail due to disease or the aging process, everyday functioning is compromised, requiring supports or substitutes for the degraded information. External aids can enhance the sensory features of stimuli, making them more salient, and creating a prosthetic environment. Important associations between auditory, visual, or tactile features and past experiences of the person with memory impairment are triggered by enhanced sensory cues (Garrett & Yorkston, 1997). Sensory aids that combine multiple sensory features may have increased salience. Table 6.3 provides a hierarchy of sensory cues to consider in developing effective interventions.

Working memory, or encoding, deficits are prevalent in persons with dementia, manifested in behaviors such as repetitive questions or demands, need for frequent reminders of what to do, where to go, and what they were saying. Persons with dementia may respond negatively when not given enough time to process and comprehend complex auditory information. In the case of repetitive questions, the answer is usually conveyed verbally by the caregiver, and is often recognized and acknowledged by the person with dementia, but the answer is not processed and stored for later retrieval. Hence, the question gets repeated. Sometimes the problem is that the amount of information to be processed or encoded exceeds the person's processing capacity. When caregivers reduce the amount of verbal information presented at a time and use written plus picture cues to support comprehension, the person with dementia can better encode the desired information, which should improve these interactions (e.g., Bourgeois, Dijkstra, Burgio, & Allen-Burge, 2001).

External memory strategies facilitate the encoding and consolidation of new information or circumvent the process by providing access to the desired information without needing it to be stored for later retrieval (Bourgeois, 2014; Parenté & Hermann, 2010; Sohlberg & Turkstra, 2011). Rehabilitation therapists have a long history of training persons with memory impairments due to brain injuries to use written strategies, such as memory notebooks, diaries, note taking, appointment calendars, and planners. If important information that is presented verbally is written down immediately, the odds of being able to remember that information because one can read it are increased.

Over the degenerative course of AD, word-finding and other retrieval problems worsen and require strategies that provide alternate routes to the information (March, Wales, & Pattison, 2003). In persons with primary progressive aphasia, this is even more apparent (Reilly, 2016). Deficits in retrieval from long-term memory storage commonly manifest in conversations, where reciprocity of information giving and receiving is expected for a satisfying interaction. Interactions become jeopardized by lack of informative content exchange. External memory aids in print and electronic formats have been developed to access semantic storage via alternate pathways, allowing people to continue to participate in reciprocal conversations. Additionally, a wide variety of external memory strategies can be designed for other functional behaviors and issues by taking advantage of cues in the environment to trigger retrieval from long-term memory storage. Some external memory strategies use specific auditory, visual, or other sensory cues to enhance recognition and recall of important information, whereas others provide a variety of cues to stimulate multiple memory systems (Bourgeois, 2014; Parenté & Hermann, 2010; Sohlberg & Turkstra, 2011). Examples of external aids for a variety of goals will be described in detail below.

TABLE 6.3 A Hierarchy of Sensory Cues

Auditory		
Speech:	Sentences	Open-ended questions, general directions, statements
		Either-or questions, commands, specific directions
		Close technique, one-step directions
		(Books on tape; radio talk shows, conversation)
	Phrases:	Multiword phrase (command, statement)
	Words:	Single word (command, statement)
Environment:		Unfamiliar sounds and noises
		Familiar sounds: doorbells, telephone, sirens, and animal sounds
		Unfamiliar voices: strangers
		Familiar voices: family and friends
Visual		
Gestures:		Formal sign language system
		Pantomime
		Single gesture
Graphic:		Written text: Books and newspapers (multiparagraph, storyline)
		Written text: Multiple sentences (single paragraph)
		Written text: Single sentence
		Written text: Phrase
		Written text: Single word
		Complex picture (photographs, and multiple objects and persons)
		Simpler picture (photographs, single subject, and environmental signs and symbols)
Picture:		Photograph
		Color drawing: realistic or abstract art
		Black and white; line drawing
Colors		Color coding; environmental (wallpaper, carpeting, etc.)
		Color icons: red = stop, and green = go
Physical and Tactile		
Physical		Shadowing
		Physical guidance and prompting (minimal)
		Physical guidance and prompting (maximal)
		Full assistance
Textural		Texture coding; environmental (wallpaper, carpeting, etc.)
		Texture icons; sandpaper = rough, and silk = smooth
Objects		Actual three-dimensional objects, and abstract two-dimensional objects
Olfactory		
Familiar smells		Comfort foods (bread, cookies, and baby powder)
		Familiar smells (wet animal, flowers, new car, fresh-mowed grass, etc.)
Environmental		Familiar places (bakery, gas station, etc.)
		Dangerous smells (fire, smoke, gas, etc.)

Each type of external aid can serve as a compensatory strategy for a variety of problems, e.g., a written cue card can serve as a sensory aid (i.e., visual stimulus), a trigger of long-term memories, and/or an encoding strategy (i.e., rereading the card) (Bourgeois, 2014; Sohlberg & Turkstra, 2011). One person might use Post-It notes because writing the information down helps him to process the information, but he does not tend to need to look at the note later, while another person uses Post-It notes to aid in retrieval of information. Likewise, one person might leave a voicemail message for herself to help her to encode the information, and she may or may not listen to the message later, while another person uses voicemail as a retrieval strategy. The types of external aids used by persons with dementia, particularly, in the early stages, can look a lot like those used by the average busy person – smartphone, wall calendar, pill reminders. As the dementia progresses, strategies need to be modified to continue to match the person's profile of deficits and strengths.

While some people instinctively develop a system that meets their individual needs, there are many others who require some training to design and implement an efficient and effective memory strategy system. For example, elders with memory impairments may need structured training to use a simple calendar reliably. Evidence shows that people with memory impairments can use technology to compensate for their impairments, but more research is needed on persons with degenerative diseases (Jamieson, Cullen, McGee-Lennon, Brewster, & Evans, 2014). Anecdotal reports of overly complex and cumbersome routines (e.g., multiple bell timers to remember several steps in a task or overly detailed computer calendars) that become the focus of one's daily life to the detriment of other activities suggest the need for memory strategy classes or counseling sessions for the general public as well as those with diagnosed memory impairments. Table 6.4 lists the examples of external memory strategies.

External Aids for Conversation and Communication of Basic Wants and Needs. A systematic review of methods to enhance verbal communication in persons with AD documented the benefits of memory wallets and memory aids (i.e., memory books, memory wallets, communication cards) on the conversations of persons with dementia (Egan et al., 2010; Hopper et al., 2013). These communication aids were initially designed by Bourgeois (1990, 1992a, 1992b) in the exploration of the use of written and picture cues to assist in the retrieval of personal information necessary to maintain conversations between persons with AD and their caregivers. Memory wallets and books were designed to improve conversational interactions between persons with

TABLE 6.4 Examples of External Memory Aid Strategies for Various Types of Memory

Strategies to Enhance Sensory Memory

Enlarged print, bright colors, high contrast, highlighting, and color coding
Personal objects
Nametags, pillboxes, Post-It notes, and cards
Hearing aids and assistive listening devices

Strategies to Enhance Memory Encoding and/or Retrieval

Timers, alarms
Signs, labels, cue cards, and calendars
Shopping lists, string on finger
Memory book pages, cue cards, and memo boards
Daily planners, electronic planners
Electronic voice organizers and voice message devices
Training: repetition, practice, and routine use
Computers, cell phones, and multifunctional watches
Putting objects in a special place (e.g., hanging keys by door; glasses on nightstand)

moderate dementia and their caregivers (Bourgeois, 1990). Figure 6.1 presents a variety of memory wallets and memory books used to stimulate conversation and memory.

Books usually have 8- × 11-inch pages, and wallets are often made of pages that are approximately 3- × 5-inch pages. The number of pages should reflect the person's cognitive abilities and functional goals. Persons with more severe impairments usually require fewer pages (i.e., 5–10, rather than 20–30). Memory books/wallets contain simple declarative sentences and a relevant photograph or illustration (one per page). The information to be included in a memory aid is solicited from the person with dementia and his or her family or caregivers; important biographical information (e.g., date and location of birth, parents, siblings, spouse, and educational milestones), daily activity information (e.g., meal times and details, bathing and grooming, and leisure activities), and other relevant personal information (e.g., answers to repeated questions) are among the facts included in the memory aid (see Chapter 5 for related assessment tools aimed at designing memory and communication aids). When personal photographs are not available, a variety of clip art, magazine pictures, and line drawings can be used to illustrate the written statements. Bourgeois (2013) has published a manual detailing the possible types and formats of memory aids; instructions for making the memory aids wearable and portable are also included.

In a series of single-subject experimental design studies, Bourgeois (1990, 1992b) provided evidence for the effects of memory wallets in conversations. In baseline conversations without a memory wallet, persons with moderate dementia provided limited and repetitive or unintelligible information about their family, their life, and their day. Access to the memory wallet during the treatment condition enabled them to read aloud each sentence and then elaborate about the topic, increasing the number of factual statements significantly and decreasing repetitiveness and ambiguity. Systematic replications of this approach reveal that memory wallets were effective with persons with greater cognitive and sensory deficits as long as the visual stimulus characteristics of the memory aid matched the persons' deficits and strengths (Bourgeois, 1992b).

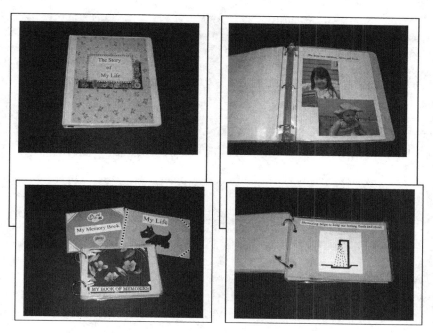

FIGURE 6.1 Memory Wallets and Memory Books

The usefulness of memory wallets/books in conversations was also demonstrated with other types of partners and settings, such as peers (Bourgeois, 1993) or nursing assistants (Bourgeois et al., 2001; Burgio et al., 2001; Dijkstra, Bourgeois, Burgio, & Allen, 2002) in the nursing home, and volunteers at an adult daycare program (Bourgeois & Mason, 1992). Studies of memory wallets/books have also found increased turn-taking and topic maintenance (Bourgeois, 1993; Bourgeois & Mason, 1996; Hoerster, Hickey, & Bourgeois, 2001; Spilkin & Bethlehem, 2003). These findings revealed that reading is relatively preserved into the middle, and sometimes later, stages of dementia. There is increasing evidence that the written modality may be relatively spared in dementia and that orthographic information can access semantic information that is not accessible by other auditory or verbal input modalities (Bourgeois, 2001). Additionally, use of memory wallets resulted in reduced partner prompting and conversational dominance (Hoerster et al., 2001). Social validation findings also reveal a positive impact on communication in these studies (Bourgeois, 1992b; Bourgeois & Mason, 1996; Hoerster et al., 2001). Findings have been replicated with persons with severe dementia (Andrews-Salvia, Roy, & Cameron, 2003; McPherson et al., 2001).

Other types of external cues have also been used with persons with dementia to improve their communication. External aids for conversation might be designed on smartphones (Maier, Özkil, Bang, & Hysse Forchhammer, 2015), tablets, or computers, or on digital photo frames (with or without voice messages). People with moderate AD were able to use communication boards, but required training on how to use them; voice output systems were distracting to persons with AD, thereby impeding their conversational abilities (Fried-Oken, Rowland, Daniels, & Oken, 2012). The use of dolls and stuffed animals has become popular in the past two decades. Although some question the ethical issues around this intervention, older adults have reported benefits in a qualitative study (Alander, Prescott, & James, 2015), and treatment studies have found improvements in engagement and communication (Mitchell, McCormack, & McCance, 2016). Other tangible stimuli, such as "look inside" purses and multisensory boxes can also result in improved engagement in conversation (Griffiths, Dening, Beer, & Tischler, 2016). Smells, such as the burning of candles with a pine scent or gingerbread and vanilla scents, may trigger memories of Christmas trees and baking cookies with their mother, and lead to satisfying conversational interactions. A memory aid in the form of an autobiographical timeline was developed together with the person with dementia, using information from family, resulting in improved retrieval of semantic and autobiographical memories during interactions (Lalanne, Gallarda, & Piolino, 2015). Regardless of the type of external aids and cues used to improve communication, communication partners will take on more responsibility for their implementation as the disease progresses (see Chapters 9 and 10 for caregiver training procedures).

External Aids for Orientation and Safety. Visual cues are thought to trigger associated long-term memories that have accumulated over years of sensory experiences. Objects in the environment, photographs, and traffic signs can cue long-term memories for iconic symbols that are recognized with little effort. Attention to the stimulus characteristics of the environment in dementia-specific units of nursing homes, such as physical design, sensory features, and the social environments, has resulted in the creation of supported living environments to increase adaptive behaviors and enhance safety (Mazzei, Gillan, & Cloutier, 2014). Simple visual cues have frequently been the basis of effective interventions to increase orientation and to decrease responsive behaviors for persons with dementia. Signs indicating the name of the nursing home and day and date are often used to facilitate reality orientation.

A variety of auditory and visual cues have been used to prevent exit seeking and promote safe wandering, including: stop signs, grid lines on the floor, door and elevator murals, and door alarms (e.g., Kincaid & Peacock, 2003; Mazzei et al., 2014). Additionally, placing a particular object or materials along the pacing route of an individual can cue him or her to engage in an alternate activity (i.e., a laundry basket with towels to be folded). Visual cues can also be used to promote wayfinding in nursing homes. A vase of bright red flowers cued a person to her assigned table in the dining room (Leseth & Meader, 1995). Personal photographs and large-print nameplates helped nursing home residents to find their own rooms and prevent unwanted access to other resident rooms (Nolan, Mathews, & Harrison, 2001). The simplicity and effectiveness of these kinds of visual cues have led to the adoption of color schemes, street signs, and personalized front doors and mailboxes as a popular marketing strategy for residential facilities (Zeisel, Hyde, & Shi, 1999). Improved visual and other sensory cues in the dining environment have outcomes of improved mealtime behaviors and eating (Chaudhury, Hung, & Badger, 2013). (See Chapter 7 for more on environmental modifications.)

External Aids for Responsive Behaviors. Sensory cues that trigger positive automatic behaviors or memories can reduce anxieties and disruptive behaviors, for example, soothing "white noise" (waterfall and nature sounds) listened to via headphones to recall a previous nature walk provides a calming effect (Burgio, Scilley, Hardin, Hsu, & Yancy, 1996). Other sensory cues, such as tactile, olfactory, and gustatory cues, have also been effective in triggering memory and maintaining functional behaviors (Griffiths et al., 2016). For example, a whistling teakettle may trigger long-held memories for the process of making a cup of tea. Reduced distress and increased meaningful engagement have been found in studies of doll therapy in persons with dementia (Mitchell et al., 2016). Similarly, decreased agitation and improved family visiting were documented when a variety of handmade, therapeutically based sensorimotor recreational items (e.g., an activity apron, an electronic busy box, a look-inside purse, and squeezies) were given to nursing home residents with severe dementia (Buettner, 1999).

Written text cues can be used with more complex everyday behaviors to increase cooperation and maximize independence with care routines, as well as to reduce responsive behaviors such as repetitive questions. When the person with dementia can no longer write down information reliably for him or herself, caregivers can use external aids in the form of memory wallets/books, cue cards, memo boards, and signs to facilitate encoding and retrieval of the desired information (Bourgeois, 2014). Bourgeois (1994) reported decreasing the repetitive questions of a father to his daughter concerning the whereabouts of his wife with a page in his memory book that said, "My wife, Lillian, died of heart disease in 1967." Bourgeois et al. (1997) expanded the purpose of external aids from memory wallets/books for conversation to improve other types of functional behaviors and reduce responsive behaviors. Repetitive requests and questions were reduced by including a page in the memory wallet that answered the question and having the caregivers redirect their spouse to the memory aid by saying, "The answer is in your memory book," or "Read this _____" (handing her a written instruction for an alternate activity). The frequency of repetitive questions was reduced significantly after treatment.

For persons whose pacing route included the kitchen, spouses were trained to write messages and activity suggestions on an erasable memo board magnetically attached to the refrigerator to decrease anxiety (e.g., "I'll be home for dinner") and to increase desired behaviors (e.g., "Please water the plants"). Caregivers reported generalizing the use of reminder cards to a variety of situations; one wife kept index cards in the car on which to write the answer to the constant query, "Where are we going?" Others used cards in church and on a bus trip; another caregiver designed a "fake" letter from the Internal Revenue Service to remind her husband that he had submitted his tax return and that his refund check had been deposited in his bank account (Bourgeois et al., 1997). Figure 6.2 illustrates a variety of graphic cueing systems (e.g., cue cards and memo boards) for encoding and retrieval of information.

Additionally, for persons with dementia living in the community, a variety of external aids are available to increase safety. Information pendants, medic alert devices, and safe-return bracelets

FIGURE 6.2 Graphic Cueing Systems: Reminder Cards and Memo Boards

containing personal information (i.e., name and address) and medical information (i.e., diagnosis and allergies) (Alzheimer's Association, 2016) require little effort on the part of the person with dementia to have access to important personal and safety information. The wide variety of technology available to increase safety in home environments for community-dwelling persons with dementia is beyond the scope of this chapter, but a few examples include alarms and special locks on doors to prevent wandering from the home and stove alarms. (See Chapter 7 for more on environmental modifications.)

External Aids for ADLs and Meaningful Activities. These external strategies can also be useful for family or staff caregivers when memory and communication difficulties lead to responsive behaviors during care routines and decreased engagement in meaningful activities. Nursing aides were trained to use portable, laminated memory and communication cards with their residents with moderate to severe dementia to increase comprehension and cooperation with care activities, such as showering, feeding, and grooming (Bourgeois et al., 2001). Each resident had a collection of personalized cards that addressed responsive behaviors during ADLS that were identified by their nursing aide. Each card had a picture related to the ADL plus a positive statement about engaging in the ADL such as "Showering makes me feel warm and clean," or "Eating helps me stay strong and healthy." Before initiating an ADL, nursing aides presented the appropriate card to the resident, asked them to read it, and then asked them to proceed with the activity.

Nursing aides reported increased compliance and cooperation with care activities and decreased negative reactions when using the cards. Residents in the experimental group (memory books + staff intervention) had more positive verbalizations with staff and peers when memory cards were present (Bourgeois et al., 2001). Use of memory and communication strategies plus caregiver training such as this might also increase independence in ADLs if the person with dementia has a better understanding of what is happening. Simple verbal reminders at regularly scheduled intervals have been effective at reducing incontinence in nursing home residents (prompted voiding technique; Schnelle, 1990). For some persons with dementia, having a written schedule for voiding can encourage them to use the toilet more frequently and more independently. Training caregivers to use these types of written cues is essential to their success. An interactive CD-ROM training program for reminder card use by nursing aides in the nursing home increased nursing aide knowledge of and intention to use the strategy and perceived self-efficacy in intervening with the responsive behaviors of persons with dementia (Irvine, Ary, & Bourgeois, 2003).

(See Chapters 9 and 10 for more on caregiver training.) Figure 6.3 illustrates examples of memory and communication cards used in long-term care settings.

Other external aids in the environment can also improve performance of ADLs and engagement in activities at home or in a nursing home. Labels on drawers or cupboards can facilitate finding needed belongings for ADLs. Organizational strategies can improve the visual salience of objects, for example, silverware trays, desk supply organizers, and closet organizers facilitate recognizing desired objects. Signs with task analyses for ADLs can maximize independence in completing the activity (e.g., "Step 1: get out the toothpaste and toothbrush. Step 2: put toothpaste on toothbrush..."). Posting signs to suggest activities ("Please arrange the flowers" next to an activity area with dried flowers and vases) or a white board with a schedule of the day's activities can increase participation in leisure activities. Providing written plus picture aids with task analyses for activities, such as the instructions for a simple card or board game, can also increase participation in those activities, revealing that the problem was not loss of interest, but rather difficulty with memory retrieval related to the activity (Eisner, 2013). Additionally, visual enhancements can increase a person's attention to the importance of visual cues. For example, enlarging the print on signs or cards, using paper or cards with a light background with dark text (e.g., pale yellow with dark print might work better for older adults' eyes), creating high-contrast distinctions, or using personal objects can improve ability to benefit from visual cues. Nursing home residents with dementia preferred wayfinding signs with bright green, blue, and magenta backgrounds and white lettering (Brush, Camp, Bohach, & Gertsberg, 2015).

Prospective Memory. External memory aids for prospective memory, or remembering to initiate an action in the future, have become commonplace. Faced with a myriad of facts to remember, chores to do, and appointments and activities to attend in their daily life, people use external aids routinely to circumvent the need to encode and store all of that information. External aids for prospective memory can be low technology, such as Post-It notes, grocery lists, activity schedules, and wall calendars, or high technology, such as the apps on smartphones, tablets, and computers that store information and provide prompts to retrieve information using a variety of alarm and messaging features. Audio recorders and voicemail can be used to record information as a reminder to do an activity later. Examples of visual cueing strategies include having a routine place and location for specific objects, such as hanging the car keys by the door, or putting the empty container of a needed item in the car to remember to stop at the store. Written notes are used as external memory aids for important information that needs to be remembered; having a concrete, tangible written note obviates the need to encode and store it internally.

Persons with mild cognitive impairment or early stages of dementia can be aware of their deficits and use external strategies on their own to mask their symptoms (e.g., the retired businessman

FIGURE 6.3 Memory and Communication Cards Used in Long-Term Care Settings

who starts to use a planner again or the retired college professor who keeps a small notebook to record people's names and words he has forgotten recently). Later, they may request memory rehabilitation, when these systems no longer work for them and need to be modified. They will then participate alongside their clinicians in modifying their systems to improve effectiveness, or in developing and evaluating new systems to meet their needs. They might benefit from apps that serve to adapt the smartphone functions to their needs (Maier et al., 2015). Additionally, persons with MCI and early dementia can benefit from attending cognitive stimulation and rehabilitation programs delivered in a group format, such as memory strategy classes (Fritsch et al., 2014).

As the dementia progresses, the person or caregiver may seek out assistance with modifying their strategies or designing new strategies that are more effective for their cognitive abilities and deficits. Camp, Foss, O'Hanlon, and Stevens (1996) demonstrated positive outcomes when training persons with dementia to incorporate calendar use into their daily routine via a spaced retrieval training protocol. Medication adherence is an issue for many people with dementia, and attempts to intervene with dose administration systems have had small effects (Elliott, Goeman, Beanland, & Koch, 2015). A variety of visual and written cueing systems, such as seven-day medication organizers (Park & Kidder, 1996), and pill containers with a visual organizational chart (Park, Morrell, Frieske, & Kincaid, 1992) or timed alarms (Leirer, Morrow, Tanke, & Pariante, 1991) were found to increase adherence by elderly users. As technology evolves at a rapid pace, persons with memory impairments and their caregivers can look forward to useful apps specific to their needs (e.g., Talk Me Home), simplified smartphones, smart wall calendars, and wearable technology that is designed for their needs (Maier et al., 2015).

Considerations for Designing Memory and Communication Aids. Factors to consider before selecting and designing an external aid include: the individual's level of literacy, degree and severity of cognitive impairment, and level of self-awareness of his or her memory problems, preserved cognitive abilities, and motivation to compensate for deficits. A person's ethnic, cultural, linguistic, and educational background should also be considered (Hopper et al., 2013). Additionally, the person's premorbid familiarity with and use of such aids, the amount of training required in the use of the aid, and the costs associated with the aid and with training should be considered. Familiar and simpler aids and assistive technology that are user-friendly and fit well into their established strategies are the more feasible choices for persons with dementia (Arntzen, Holthe, & Jentoft, 2016). They must also address needs that are important to the person and engage the family caregivers, who play an essential role in whether and how assistive technology is used by persons with dementia (Arntzen et al., 2016). When assistive technology is not designed well, it can increase confusion and decrease self-efficacy in persons with dementia, and become annoying and intrusive for caregivers. However, assistive technology when used well can create positive feelings related to being in control and feeling safe.

Additionally, the person's cognitive and sensory deficits and strengths must be considered; physical abilities of mobility and manual dexterity must also be considered when designing handheld aids, such as memory books/wallets or handheld devices (Bourgeois, 2013). If the person is mobile and has the sensory capability, the memory aid should be small and portable, such as a wallet, or some cards on a ring. The aid should be kept with the person by wearing it on a lanyard, necklace, wristband, or belt, if possible. For persons who use wheelchairs or walkers, a bag might be attached to carry the memory book. Preferably, a plastic pocket will be sewn onto the bag so that the memory aid is visible to all and easily accessible.

For visual aids, font and picture size and contrast must match visual abilities (Bourgeois, 2013). For auditory cues, the person's hearing must be considered. For example, the alarms used for persons who are not supposed to get out of a bed or chair alone can only be effective if the person can hear them, and many of the alarms have a high frequency pitch that is difficult for many older adults to hear. For persons with sensory challenges, additional cues or cue enhancement may be required to ensure ability to use external aids. Other sensory modalities may be enlisted as necessary to provide the appropriate information to maintain function (e.g., audio or tactile cues are used more often with persons with low vision).

Memory aids or enhanced stimuli alone, however, may not serve an encoding or retrieval function that produces desired changes in a person's functioning without training or routine and repetitive exposure (Hopper et al., 2013; Zeisel et al., 1999). Visual cues by themselves, even if they are in the direct path of the intended recipient, do not guarantee that they are seen, recognized, and responded to as desired. Even simple environmental aids, such as signs and labels, may need periodic practice in identifying, reading, and discussing them to maintain their salience and intended function. Vague visual or auditory cues may remind the person that *something* needs to be remembered, but not *what* (Woods, 1996). For example, the person must be able to recall the reason for a visual signal such as a "string on the finger" or an alarm as a reminder. Persons with dementia can be taught to attend to and respond to visual or auditory stimuli. For example, persons with dementia can be trained to sit or lie back down when they hear an alarm, or they can be taught to use more salient written reminders than a vague "string on the finger." Caregivers

---

Case 6.1 Use of Memory Book as Disease Progresses

Scenario: Mrs. Jones has early-stage dementia and attends an adult day facility, where she was given a memory wallet consisting of 30 pages of biographical information. The aid was made by a friendly visitor with the assistance of her daughter. At the second visit, when Mrs. Jones came to the page that stated, "I was a high school teacher 30 years before retiring," she paused, turned over the page, and said, "Did you know that I taught just about every grade and subject? My first teaching job was a fifth-grade social studies class." She had written a list of schools, grade levels, and subjects on the back of the page.

Nine months later, when Mrs. Jones was asked to tell the visitor about her life using the memory wallet, she started reading at the first page, continuing until she reached the last page, and then she started over from the beginning and read until the visitor suggested they get a snack. A year later, Mrs. Jones smiled when asked to talk about her life, held the memory wallet, but did not start reading. When the visitor read aloud the first page, she smiled and patted the picture. As the visitor continued reading each page and commenting about the pictures, Mrs. Jones continued smiling and patting the pictures, and on occasion would repeat a word that the visitor had said.

Explanation: The nature of communicative interaction changes as the disease progresses. In the early stage, Mrs. Jones was aware that the visitor had heard that she was a retired schoolteacher, and she planned to elaborate on that idea by making notes for herself about her different jobs during her career. She was capable of an equitable conversation; her pragmatics were intact, and her language and memory skills allowed her to plan for a more satisfying second conversation. Later, Mrs. Jones' pragmatics declined, and the interaction became one-sided. She read her memory wallet repetitively, reflecting her desire to maintain social closeness with the visitor. By the advanced stage, Mrs. Jones had lost her verbal abilities, but not her desire to communicate, which she did by smiling, patting the wallet, and echoing an occasional word. The visitor, at this point, was entirely responsible for carrying on the conversation by reading and elaborating on the wallet content.

may need to point out, identify, and rehearse the cue with the person to make it noticeable and to keep it salient so that it becomes incorporated into daily use. Many of the reports of successful aid use have involved family and nursing aides who ensured that the aids were available and prompted their use at appropriate times (Bourgeois et al., 1997, 2001).

Clinicians must consider that feelings of confidence in using assistive technology relate to success and mastery of the tool without needing a lot of training (Arntzen et al., 2016). Successful memory-enhancing systems require premorbid familiarity and/or multisensory salient features; some new systems will also require training (e.g., spaced retrieval training). For example, when introducing a novel cueing system, such as an enlarged plate switch with a picture of a nurse taped to it as an alternative call button, training the person with dementia "to touch the picture when you need a nurse" would be necessary (Garrett & Yorkston, 1997). Thus, types and design of aids and training needs must be considered in implementation of external aids.

Training Procedures

The nihilistic belief that persons with dementia are unable to acquire new information and skills or to retrieve and use them when needed due to their encoding and/or retrieval deficits has been challenged for the past two decades. Evidence is accruing that persons with mild to moderate dementia can learn new information, or relearn "forgotten" information, using appropriate training strategies, such as spaced retrieval, a memory-training strategy described below (Hopper et al., 2013). Training can ensure that external memory aids are used routinely and retain their recognition, organizational, and memory or communication-supporting value for persons with mild to moderate dementia. Successful cognitive rehabilitation, particularly using spaced retrieval training and external memory aids, has been reported in the literature. Researchers continue to seek out the most effective training procedures and to determine who responds best to memory training interventions. Sohlberg and Turkstra (2011) have suggested the use of training protocols that incorporate a variety of effective instruction techniques (e.g., error control techniques) and variables such as massed versus distributed practice and intensity of practice. Effective instruction techniques include spaced retrieval training (SR), errorless learning, vanishing cues, and specific instruction (Hopper et al., 2013). One of the problems in examining the evidence for specific training procedures with persons with dementia is that several of the procedures overlap, and inadequate descriptions of training methods and procedural fidelity limit our ability to discern how procedures are being used (Hopper et al., 2013).

Errorless Learning

Errorless learning occurs when clinicians use cues and instructional strategies that minimize the chance of the client making errors (Clare & Jones, 2008). The neuropsychological rehabilitation principle of "errorless learning" is based on the interaction of two types of memory: declarative (explicit) and nondeclarative (implicit or procedural) memory (Squire, 1994). (See Chapter 3 for more information on declarative versus nondeclarative memory in persons with dementia.) To learn and retain new information, persons with memory deficits should engage in "errorless" practice with the new information. Declarative memory deficits prevent self-monitoring and self-correcting of responses during training, so inaccurate learning can occur (Fish, Manly, Kopelman, & Morris, 2015). Therefore, errors during training must be inhibited by not allowing a time delay before the response and not prompting with a hierarchy of cues. For example, a clinician teaching a client her name, Angela, allowed the client to hesitate and respond, "I'm not sure; I think it starts with an A; is it Andrew?" The clinician should have interrupted her, provided her with the correct name for her immediate repetition. She did eventually learn the correct name, but four months later at follow-up, she called the clinician "Andrew" (Bourgeois et al., 2003).

In a systematic review, 10 studies that included participants with mild to severe dementia showed that persons with dementia can learn new information with errorless learning techniques (Hopper et al., 2013). Another review criticized much of the errorless learning literature for having low ecological validity, so these researchers examined only studies that taught everyday functional tasks (de Werd, Boelen, Olde Rikkert, & Kessels, 2013). Many of the studies in both reviews compared the effects of error*less* and error*ful* (i.e., trial-and-error) learning. Research has often concluded that errorless learning is more efficient and produces more accurate learning than errorful conditions (e.g., Baddeley & Wilson, 1994; Clare et al., 2000, 2001; Fish et al., 2015), but reviews reveal conflicting reports (Clare & Jones, 2008; Hopper et al., 2013). In a literature review of errorless learning studies in persons with dementia, Li and Liu (2012) suggested that errorless learning might be impacted by the type of information to be learned, with superior results when the information is more specific in nature. The review by de Werd et al. (2013) reported that errorless learning is effective for teaching meaningful tasks, which are often retained at followup. Fish et al. (2015) reported that methodological confounds interfere with the interpretation of the studies with conflicting findings. They suggested that when all other factors are equal, errorless learning has an advantage over errorful learning in people with memory disorders. Errorless learning is often used in conjunction with other methods, such as vanishing cues, spaced retrieval training (Hopper et al., 2013), and multicomponent cognitive rehabilitation (e.g., Amieva et al., 2016). Clare and Jones (2008) reported that a range of methods can be used to achieve errorless learning, such as vanishing cues and SR training, which makes it difficult to compare methods.

Vanishing Cues

Another way to conduct errorless learning is the method of vanishing cues (Glisky, Schacter, & Tulving, 1986). In this technique, which is designed for more complex information or behaviors, the client is provided with enough information to provide the correct response on the initial trial. Over subsequent successful trials, the information is gradually withdrawn and the client is required to respond with fewer cues (de Werd et al., 2013), or after unsuccessful trials, additional cues are added and then faded (Sohlberg, Ehlhardt, & Kennedy, 2005). Many studies use the approach that leads to errorless learning, making it difficult to tease apart the benefit from each type of training procedure. In three vanishing cues studies in a systematic review, persons with mild to moderate dementia were able to achieve their goals with vanishing cues, with better recall accuracy than during errorful learning conditions, but the limited number of studies and conceptual overlap with errorless learning prevent conclusions about efficacy (Hopper et al., 2013). Another review found that vanishing cues was effective to promote errorless learning in teaching everyday procedural or nonprocedural tasks (de Werd et al., 2013). More research is needed to better understand the application and outcomes of these techniques with procedural variations designed to address the individual learning styles of clients with memory impairment.

Cueing Hierarchies

The most common teaching strategy employed by SLPs is the use of cueing hierarchies to elicit desired behaviors (for a review, see Patterson, 2001). Cueing hierarchies are used frequently for teaching individuals with acquired neurological communication impairments to perform certain communication behaviors, such as word finding. Cueing hierarchies (CH) are a systematic and graded sequence of cues that have increasing power. Treatment protocols have been established using CHs to guide the selection and sequencing of cues. Clinicians evaluate an individual's response to each cue type and design a unique training hierarchy based on the relative strength or power of each cue to elicit the desired response. Bollinger and Stout (1976) described this procedure as response-contingent small-step treatment that can be accomplished in an ascending or descending sequence to elicit the desired response with the least powerful cue. In her review of CHs in word retrieval studies, Patterson (2001) found two common ways to implement this technique: traditional CHs using descending and ascending movement, and modified CHs using descending cues only.

Bourgeois and colleagues (2003) directly compared the use of SR and CH to train fact and strategy goals with persons with dementia. The CH used included semantic cues ("Something to look at"), phonemic cues ("ac" first syllable of the target Activity List), visual cues (point to list), and tactile cues (touch and hold list), followed by imitation ("I look at my activity list"). The study found that persons with dementia learned goals using both strategies within a similar time frame, but at the four-month follow-up, more goals learned through SR were remembered.

Spaced Retrieval

Training Procedures. Spaced retrieval (SR), a memory-training procedure, involves the systematic recall of facts and procedures over successively longer intervals and the retention of the information for long time periods (Brush & Camp, 1998; Camp, 2006). Camp (2006) described the four types of learning that are used in SR training, as follows. SR is based on a shaping paradigm applied to memory, using repetition priming and classical conditioning. Repetition priming is thought to be the component of nondeclarative memory that involves the ability to improve performance with repeated practice, which can occur without effort or conscious processing. The "spacing effect" phenomenon results in better learning when practice is distributed over time, rather than mass practiced. This type of unconscious, automatic learning remains relatively preserved in persons with Alzheimer's dementia until the late stages. SR capitalizes on this preserved strength.

SR also frequently incorporates other types of effective instruction practices to ensure successful learning of target information or behaviors: vanishing cues and errorless learning (Hopper et al., 2013). This is often accomplished by capitalizing on relatively preserved reading skills (Bourgeois, 2001, 2013) to promote errorless learning with cue cards that are gradually faded (unless use of the cue card is the target behavior) to help persons to achieve a wide variety of goals. Errorless learning is achieved through the timing of the prompt and response, which is strictly monitored to prevent the person from producing an incorrect response (Wilson, Baddeley, Evans, & Shiel, 1994). If a person does make an error, then corrective feedback is used, so that each trial ends with the correct response. Balota, Duchek, Sergent-Marshall, and Roediger (2006) found that corrective feedback resulted in better performance than not providing this feedback.

In a SR training session, the clinician states the purpose of the session and provides the prompt-response pairing that will be used throughout the duration of the training procedure. Some studies have used uniform lengths of intervals, but most use expanded intervals. Various methods have been reported for expanding the time intervals (see Box 6.4). Often, a correct response results in doubling the time interval before the next prompt. Incorrect responses elicit the modeling and repetition of the correct response, followed by using the last successful interval. With expanding intervals, a correct response results in doubling the time interval before the next prompt (e.g., 0, 15, 30 seconds, 1, 2, 4, 8 minutes). Incorrect responses elicit the modeling and repetition of the correct response, then going back to the last successful interval. An alternative schedule has also shown success: 5, 10, 20, 40, and 60 seconds; then expanded by 30 seconds up to 3 minutes; then by 1 minute up to 6 minutes; and then by 2 minutes, with training sessions up to 30 minutes (Cherry & Simmons-D'Gerolamo, 2004; Hawley & Cherry, 2008).

The expectation of an immediate correct response is important in preventing incorrect responses; any hesitation should elicit the therapist's modeled response and the person's immediate repetition. This can initially feel unnatural to most clinicians, who have been trained in a cueing protocol that allows the person several seconds to produce a response before providing increasingly informative cues to eventually elicit the correct response. The counterintuitive errorless learning procedure, however, results in rapid and durable acquisition of the target response (Bourgeois et al., 2003; Camp, Foss, O'Hanlon, & Stevens, 1996). (See Box 6.4 for the outline of procedures in a SR training session.)

A wide variety of goals have been targeted using SR training, from remembering specific facts (e.g., family members' names and their room number) to using functional strategies (e.g., the use of a memo board or scheduled activities card, or safe swallowing strategies). (See Box 6.5 for examples of goals targeted in SR). Training procedures for a motor behavior may or may not include elicitation of the motor behavior in each trial, depending on the behavior. Sometimes a verbal response is elicited during the training trials if the motor behavior would take too much time, and then each session must be ended with the execution of the trained strategy. For example, in teaching a client to look at a card to remember her room number, the clinician should say at the end of the SR training, "Great, now let's go find your room," and walk with the client to the room; or if the person is learning to look at the activities board to find out what is happening, the session must end with "Great, now let's go see what's happening today" while walking to the

---

Box 6.4 Outline of Spaced Retrieval Training Session (Brush & Camp, 1998)

- In a Spaced Retrieval training session, the clinician begins the training by stating the purposes of the session and provides the prompt-response pair:

  - "Today I am going to help you remember where your room is. Your room number is written on this card (shows card). When you want to remember where your room is, I want you to look at your card."

- The clinician then prompts the person with dementia to produce the target response:

  - "How do you remember where your room is?"
  - If an immediate, correct response is given ("I look at my card."), the clinician replies:
  - "That's correct, and I want you to remember that because I will be asking you again in a few minutes."

- The time interval is doubled, and the clinician repeats the prompt:

  - "How do you remember where your room is?"

- If an immediate correct response is not given, then the clinician cues the client to look at the cue card and models the correct response, then gives the prompt again.
- The time interval goes back to the last successful interval.
- Training continues until the client is able to recall the correct response independently at the beginning of the next session.

activities board. This ensures that the trained verbal response is associated with the actual desired task, correct room finding, or looking at the activities board. Camp (1999) explained that the effectiveness of pairing verbal and motor behaviors is due to the nondeclarative nature of the conditioned association of verbal and motor behaviors.

For certain motor behaviors, the client produces the behavior in addition to the verbal response all through the training. For example, with a client who is learning to lock the wheelchair brakes before standing, the clinician gives the verbal prompt, "What should you do before you stand up?" The client responds verbally, "Lock my wheelchair brakes," while reaching to lock the brakes. The clinician provides hand-over-hand modeling of the behavior if client does not give the immediate, correct response. In this case, it is less important for the client to give the verbal response, as a verbal response is not necessary in functional use of the behavior and the person is doing the motor behavior during training trials. When teaching participants to use a walker, the cue of "show me" was given if the participant only gave a verbal response (Creighton, Davison, van der Ploeg, Camp, & O'Connor, 2015). Table 6.5 provides examples of typical SR prompts and responses. Finally, clinicians must ensure that clients understand the purpose and importance of the strategies or aids that they are being taught to use, and be motivated to use them (Creighton et al., 2015).

Evidence for SR Training. Persons with dementia caused by a variety of diseases have been shown to benefit from SR training, including persons with Alzheimer's dementia (Camp, Foss, Stevens, & O'Hanlon, 1996; Camp & McKitrick, 1992; McKitrick, Camp, & Black, 1992), Parkinson's disease dementia (Hayden & Camp, 1995), Korsakoff's dementia (Camp & Schaller, 1989), vascular and mixed dementia (e.g., Abrahams & Camp, 1993; Bird et al., 1995), and postanoxia dementia (Bird et al., 1995). Hayden and Camp (1995) demonstrated that persons with

TABLE 6.5 Examples of Typical SR Prompts and Responses

Remembering Names and Facts

T: "If you can't think of the name of something, describe it or tell what you do with it. Now what do you do if you cannot think of the name of something?"
C: "I describe it." or "I tell what I do with it."

Compensatory Swallow Technique

T: "After you swallow your food, take a sip of liquid. What do you do after you swallow your food?"
C: "I take a sip of liquid."

Safety

T: "Make sure you feel the back of the chair on your legs before you sit down. What do you do before you sit down?"
C: "I feel the back of the chair on my legs."
T: "When you walk with your walker, please stay inside it like this. How do you walk with your walker?"
C: "I stay inside it like this."

Repetitive Questions

T: "You live at Menorah Park. Where do you live?"
C: "I live at Menorah Park."

Use of External Cues

T: "If you want to know what activities are planned today, you come over here and read this schedule. Where can you look to find out what activities are planned?"
C: "I can go here to read this schedule."

Note
T = Therapist C = Client.

Box 6.5 Examples of Goals Targeted with SR Training with Persons with Dementia

Names of objects or people:

- names of common objects (e.g., Abrahams & Camp, 1993)
- face–name and object–location associations (e.g., Clare et al., 2000, 2001, 2002; Hawley & Cherry, 2008)
- family members' names (Joltin, Camp, & McMahon, 2003)
- pill name recall (Hochhalter, Bakke, Holub, & Overmier, 2004)

Prospective and recent episodic memory:

- to remember to perform a future action (Camp, Foss, Stevens, & O'Hanlon, 1996)
- to remember information about recent events (Small, 2012)

External aid/strategy use or functional behaviors:

- to use a strategy (e.g., "look at the calendar"; Camp, Foss, O'Hanlon, & Stevens, 1996)
- to use external memory aids (Bourgeois et al., 2003)
- to use cue cards for safe swallowing strategies (Benigas & Bourgeois, 2013)
- mealtime and eating behaviors (Lin et al., 2010)
- to use a walker (Creighton et al., 2015)
- to use a beeper to cue to use the toilet (Bird, Alexopoulos, & Adamowicz, 1995)
- to use voicemail (Thivierge, Simard, Jean, & Grandmaison, 2008)

---

dementia associated with PD could learn new motor activities through SR when, under ordinary conditions, they could not.

Systematic reviews have documented the effectiveness of SR training for persons with mild to moderate dementia in 15 and nine studies, respectively (Hopper et al., 2005, 2013). In the 2005 review, 13 studies showed that some or all participants learned the target information or behaviors. The updated systematic review by Hopper et al. (2013) documented further evidence for use of SR training with persons with mild to moderate dementia learning recall of facts or performance of tasks, but evidence was lacking for persons with moderate-severe to severe dementia. Both reviews reported that the strength of evidence is limited due to the small number of studies, heterogeneity of interventions, and low to moderate methodological quality. Most studies report recall accuracy as the outcomes, and not all studies report on generalization and maintenance of the target information or behaviors, but those that do have found recall for up to a few months.

One systematic review looked at 12 studies specifically targeting semantic information (Oren, Willerton, & Small, 2014). Again, SR training was shown to be effective for persons with mild to moderate dementia, and some studies found maintenance despite increasing severity of cognitive deficits over time. A literature review of SR interventions for persons with dementia examined 34 studies, including three RCTs, and found wide variability in the quality of the studies, the methodologies, and the outcome measures (Creighton, van der Ploeg, & O'Connor, 2013). The review concluded that SR training is effective in teaching people with dementia to learn information and behavioral strategies, and encouraged researchers to include more functional and clinically relevant target behaviors and outcomes in their studies. The outcomes measured in SR training studies have often included percent correct or number of trials correct of the target behavior (Hopper et al., 2013). Studies should also train more personally relevant goals and examine the noncognitive benefits of SR training using tools that are validated for persons with dementia (Creighton et al., 2013, 2015), such as QoL or attitude toward the behavior being trained. For example, SR training has been shown to result in increased QoL ratings (Hawley & Cherry, 2008) and improved attitude toward the functional strategy (walker use) (Creighton et al., 2015).

Generalization and maintenance of SR training effects have been included in some studies. In a systematic review, 12 of 15 studies documented strong maintenance of trained behaviors, and six of 15 studies reported generalized training effects to functional daily living tasks (Hopper et al., 2005). In two single-case experimental designs, generalization and maintenance of the target behaviors was found in some participants. Two of three long-term care (LTC) residents learned and generalized the behavior of reading staff members' nametags outside of the training sessions; the third resident fell and had a significant cognitive decline and was not able to complete the study (Hickey & How, 2008). Two of three residents generalized and maintained their individualized target behaviors (e.g., finding room, cane use) with expanding interval SR training (Hickey, Lawrence, & Landry, 2011); anecdotal evidence showed later that one participant maintained the trained information for over 4 years with no additional training.

Booster sessions have been found to improve long-term retention of target behaviors. Participants who had booster sessions at 6, 12, and 18 weeks after training maintained the gains across a 6-month period (Cherry, Hawley, Jackson, & Boudreaux, 2009). The group that did not receive booster sessions had a notable decline, however, with as little as three SR sessions at six months post, they improved performance to the same level as participants in the booster group. In LTC, rehabilitation clinicians can provide the SR training and create a maintenance plan for the nursing assistants to provide boosters. Also, periodic screenings could be used to identify those requiring booster sessions, and they could then be provided with a short-term SR intervention.

Critical Variables. To determine the most efficient training paradigm, clinicians have begun to question which variables are the most critical determinants of efficient learning in individuals with cognitive disorders. Camp and colleagues have described the critical components of the SR technique to be (a) the doubling or halving of time intervals between prompts, (b) the exact wording of the task prompt, (c) the nature of the interval activity (unrelated to the task), and (d) training to a time criterion. The relative effects of some of these specific types of variables on training outcomes have been investigated, for example use of expanding versus uniform intervals. Some studies have found no benefit of expanded over uniform intervals (e.g., Hochhalter et al., 2004; Hochhalter, Overmier, Gasper, Bakke, & Holub, 2005), while others have found a benefit of expanded over uniform intervals (e.g., Balota et al., 2006; Hawley & Cherry, 2008; Hawley, Cherry, Boudreaux, & Jackson, 2007). Likewise, Hickey et al. (2011) found no gains with uniform intervals in a single-case experimental design with three LTC residents with moderate dementia, whereas two of three residents learned the individualized target behaviors with expanding intervals. Hawley et al. (2007) also found that the expanding interval group did better than the uniform interval group with learning face-name associations with photos and then live person transfer, which also resulted in increased self-esteem and quality of life.

Training schedules (fixed versus variable amount of sessions) have been compared, with better effects revealed for the group that received the most sessions compared to the group that received a fixed number (six) of sessions on alternate days over a 2-week period (Cherry & Simmons-D'Gerolamo, 2004). Dosage requirements are not clear from studies so far, but in most studies, training occurs at least two to five times weekly, with sessions lasting 30–90 minutes. Many of the studies are conducted in long-term care or adult day programs, where it might be easier to conduct intensive training. However, this might be prohibitively expensive or impractical outside of a research study; thus, once weekly sessions were provided to community-dwelling participants with mild to moderate dementia (Materne, Luszcz, & Bond, 2014). Acquisition of the individualized target behaviors was positively associated with cognitive levels at the outset of the study, however, retention after training was not related to cognitive decline; the researchers postulated that motivation may have been related to learning and retention. Those who showed 1-week retention after three training sessions were more likely to retain the information or behavior in follow-up. This suggests that if the person is not progressing after four sessions, then some adjustments to the training should be considered, possibly adding booster sessions conducted by caregivers (Hawley & Cherry, 2008) or over the telephone (Bourgeois, Lenius, Turkstra, & Camp, 2007). Positive results were found when delivering SR treatment over the telephone to provide daily training to persons with dementia (Joltin et al., 2003).

Unfortunately, many studies do not describe what happens during the intervals. One study investigated the effects of new versus formerly known information as well as the content of activities or conversation during the intervals (Hopper, Drefs, Bayles, Tomoeda, & Dinu, 2010). Both new and formerly known information was learned with SR training; learning was reduced when the intervals contained information related to the target behavior. Intervals can contain filler tasks, such as logic, word, or numerical puzzles (Bourgeois et al., 2003; Haslam, Hodder, & Yates, 2011; Hopper et al., 2010), playing games or looking at magazines (Materne et al., 2014) or conversations (Camp and Schaller, 1989).

Studies should also further investigate training family caregivers (Clare et al., 2000; Hawley & Cherry, 2008; McKitrick & Camp, 1993; or staff caregivers (Hunter, Ward, & Camp, 2012) to provide the training. Hunter et al. (2012) found that nursing assistants could be trained to deliver SR training effectively. Staff were provided a keychain with a laminated prompt card of the specific prompt-response pair for each resident. This ensured use of the proper prompt-response pair without having to remember the prompt-response or to refer to case notes, and it was easily passed on to the next shift. Four of the five participants learned the target behaviors, including two who were trained on two goals concurrently. In follow-up, staff reported using SR, but there were barriers, such as time pressure, staff turnover, and forgetting to use the technique. To make the technique more feasible for usual care, policy, clinical, and management level endorsements and supports are required. When staff used the technique, they reported an increased sense of achievement in their jobs. Hunter et al. suggested including teaching staff to use SR training in new staff orientation, with refreshers for staff on a periodic basis.

Further research is needed to investigate the impact of variables such as motivation and cognitive level, as well as the types of noncognitive outcomes that are achieved and the critical variables for SR training (Creighton et al., 2013; Materne et al., 2014). Usefulness of the information or behavior might have an impact on learning and retention, but many studies have used nonpersonalized goals, e.g., face- or object-name associations. Face-name associations can be made more relevant by having the person learn names of familiar people, which could facilitate a better sense of belonging (Hawley & Cherry, 2008). Evidence is also needed for how many goals can be trained with SR training at once, with preliminary evidence that two goals can be trained at the same time (Hunter et al., 2012). Despite variability in training methods (e.g., training conditions, interval schedules, duration, type of goals, participants' severity and type of dementia) SR training studies provide consistent evidence for learning of information and behaviors (Creighton et al., 2013). There is not yet evidence for the superiority of one methodology of SR training over another (Hopper et al., 2013).

Finally, the underlying cause of a responsive behavior or failure to use a strategy must be determined to determine whether SR training is the most appropriate training procedure, and if so, to design a proper prompt-response pair. If a behavior is due to anxiety rather than a memory problem or if the repeated prompt in SR training causes anxiety, then this training procedure is not likely to be effective or appropriate. For example, Hunter et al. (2012) report a case of a woman who produced repetitive questions around who would help her find her room after meals. She became more anxious from fear of failing in SR training, and could not be distracted from rehearsing the correct response during the intervals. See Box 6.6 for additional case examples.

Prospective Memory Training

Prospective memory is remembering to act on an intention in the future, such as remembering to take medicine or pay a bill (Fish et al., 2015). This requires not only episodic memory, but it is also reliant on executive functions. Prospective memory training has taken various forms, with overlap with errorless learning, SR training, and external memory aid training (Fish et al., 2015). As the client demonstrates success at remembering to do the task, the time interval for task recall is increased. Originally designed for persons with brain injuries, the training paradigm varies multiple variables to obtain generalization to functional everyday activities (Sohlberg & Mateer, 2001). For example, the type of task can vary from a one-step motor command to a multistep functional task. The time interval between prompts (or time delay) for task execution is systematically

---

Box 6.6 Case Examples of Anxiety-Driven Behaviors that Do Not Respond to SR Training

Both clients lived in a nursing home and were referred by staff for responsive behaviors:

Mr. MacIsaac spent much of his waking hours wandering the facility, and would frequently go to the front reception desk to ask for a glass of water. Using SR, the SLP trained him to go to the nursing station to ask for water. The client was able to identify the nursing station, and he would perform the behavior in training. However, he did not always drink the water when he received it, and he continued to go to the reception desk to ask for water. The receptionist, nursing staff, and clinician further analyzed his behaviors and came to the conclusion that he was able to remember where to get water, but he was seeking attention and positive interaction with the receptionist.

Mrs. Thibodeau moved into the facility after her daughter, who had been her caregiver, died. Mrs. Thibodeau asked repetitive questions around where her daughter was, why she was in the facility, and when she could go home. Staff were unsure of whether to tell her every time that her daughter had died, as they were uneasy about potentially provoking more anxiety. However, the SLP found that she seemed to calm down when engaging in conversation about her daughter's death and her need for care. A memory card was made stating that her daughter died, and another was made stating that her granddaughter and great-granddaughter visit her every week. She was then trained to look at the cards when she wondered why she was in the facility. In the first training session, in response to the prompt, "what should you look at when you wonder why you are here?" the client began to immediately respond, "My daughter died, didn't she. And I can't take care of myself. I'm scared to be alone. I'm not going to be alone, am I?" This made it clear that she required intervention for anxiety and loneliness more than for memory. Rather than continue SR training, the client was left with the memory cards and other behavioral interventions that encouraged meaningful engagement in activities were implemented (see Chapter 7 for information on those interventions).

increased with successful performance. The activity engaged in during the intervals between executed tasks can range from quiet monitoring of the passage of time to conversation with the clinician or completion of other therapy tasks such as worksheets. Finally, the type of prompt used to signal task initiation can vary from the use of an alarm to the independent monitoring of the passage of time by the client. The effectiveness of this training paradigm was evaluated in several studies with brain-injured clients (Fish et al., 2015; Raskin & Sohlberg, 1996; Sohlberg, White, Evans, & Mateer, 1992); prospective memory performance increased on training tasks, with evidence of generalization to real-world tasks for some clients. Research is needed on the effectiveness of this technique for persons with dementia.

Conclusion

A variety of interventions to enhance memory and communication for persons with dementia have been described. The available evidence for pharmacological and nonpharmacological interventions suggests that both types of interventions have some efficacy for certain uses, but the fact that behavioral interventions may be more cost effective and have no side effects should give them priority (Alves et al., 2013; Olazáran et al., 2010). Some studies suggest that additional staffing is not needed to implement behavioral approaches (Volicer, Simard, Heartquist Pupa, Medrek, & Riorden, 2006). Given the constraints on healthcare resources around the world, the most effective and efficient interventions must be implemented in the most cost-effective ways (e.g., possibly through group treatment, utilization of volunteers). As evidence accrues, researchers are calling on health systems to provide better access to cognitive stimulation and cognitive rehabilitation programs for persons with dementia (e.g., Amieva et al., 2016; Hunter et al., 2012; Khan, Corbett, & Ballard, 2014). (See more information in Chapter 4 on considerations across treatment settings and US Medicare reimbursement.)

Cognitive rehabilitation using external memory and communication strategies and effective training procedures, such as SR training, hold promise for achieving person-centered, meaningful goals. Further evidence is needed documenting the efficacy and efficiency of interventions, and the most critical client variables that influence response to procedures. While high-quality RCTs and single-subject experimental designs are needed to answer some of the questions quantitatively, qualitative studies would also improve our understanding of memory and communication and the way that people engage with different interventions. For example, conversation analysis studies would enrich our understanding of communication between persons with dementia and caregivers and other communication partners' support or scaffold interactions with persons with dementia, which could be useful in developing and evaluating communication supports and training programs (Kindell, Keady, Sage, & Wilkinson, 2016). Additionally, studies should use more ecologically valid targets, and should transfer training to usual caregivers (Hunter et al., 2012).

Clinicians who provide person-centered interventions to improve the functional status of clients with dementia would be well advised to conduct person-centered assessments using the "Flip the Rehab Model" approach (described in Chapter 5), and then consider the available evidence and select intervention techniques that fit each client's scenario. The careful collection of data to document the effectiveness of interventions with each individual client is also imperative. Interventions should aim to follow the suggested guiding principles of: maximizing independent functioning for as long as possible; maintaining QoL through supported participation and engagement in desired activities; and achieving these goals through procedures that are personally relevant to the client and are trained within functional contexts. Meaningful goals can be accomplished by capitalizing on the person's strengths, using effective training procedures, and training caregivers and communication partners in meaningful contexts.

References

202 E. M. Hickey and M. S. Bourgeois

Box 6.7 Resources for Implementing Effective Interventions

Resources for Information on Pharmacological Interventions:

- www.fda.gov
- www.nia.nih.gov/alzheimers/publication/alzheimers-disease-medications-fact-sheet
- www.alz.org/research/science/alzheimers_disease_treatments.asp#approved

Resources for Caregivers on Memory and Communication Aids

- Bourgeois, M.S. (2013). *Memory Books and Other Graphic Cueing Systems: Practical Communication and Memory Aids for Adults with Dementia.* Baltimore: Health Professions Press.
- Best Alzheimer's Products: consumer source for memory aids with voice recording features (e.g., talking photo album, talking tiles); http://store.best-alzheimers-products.com/
- *The Memory Handbook*, Alzheimer's Society: information on memory, strategies, and aids for those with mild memory loss; www.alzheimers.org.uk/site/scripts/download_info.php?fileID=2204

Resources for Clinicians on Cognitive-Communicative Deficits and Practices:

- American Speech-Language-Hearing Association:
  - Practice Portal – Dementia: www.asha.org/Practice-Portal/Clinical-Topics/Dementia/
  - *Person-Centered Focus on Function: Dementia*; www.asha.org/uploadedFiles/ICF-Dementia.pdf
- Academy of Neurologic Communication Disorders and Sciences:
  - Evidence Based Clinical Research; https://ancds.memberclicks.net/evidence-based-clinical-research#Dementia
  - *Systematic Review and Practice Recommendations for Use of Spaced-Retrieval Training with Individuals with Dementia*; www.ancds.org/assets/docs/EBP/summary_technical_report_1_spaced-retrieval_training.pdf
- Benigas, J. E., Brush, J. A., & Elliot, G. M. (2016). *Spaced Retrieval Step by Step*. Baltimore: Health Professions Press.

References

Aarsland, D., Laake, K., Larsen, J. P., & Janvin, C. (2002). Donepezil for cognitive impairment in Parkinson's disease: A randomized controlled study. *Journal of Neurology, Neurosurgery and Psychiatry, 72*(6), 708–712.

Abrahams, J. P., & Camp, C. J. (1993). Maintenance and generalization of object naming training in anomia associated with degenerative dementia. *Clinical Gerontologist, 12*(3), 57–72.

Aguirre, E., Woods, R. T., Spector, A., & Orrell, M. (2013). Cognitive stimulation for dementia: A systematic review of the evidence of effectiveness from randomized controlled trials. *Ageing Research Reviews, 12*(1), 253–262. http://dx.doi.org/10.1016/j.arr.2012.07.001.

Alander, H., Prescott, T., & James, I. A. (2015). Older adults' views and experiences of doll therapy in residential care homes. *Dementia, 14*(5), 574–588. doi:10.1177/1471301213503643.

Algase, D. L., Beck, C., Kolanowski, A., Whall, A., Berent, S., Richards, K., & Beattie, E. (1996). Need-driven dementia-compromised behavior: An alternative view of disruptive behavior. *American Journal of Alzheimer's Disease, 11*(6), 10–19. doi:10.1177/153331759601100603.

Alves, J., Magalhães, R., Thomas, R. E., Gonçalves, Ó. F., Petrosyan, A., & Sampaio, A. (2013). Is there evidence for cognitive intervention in Alzheimer disease? A systematic review of efficacy, feasibility, and cost-effectiveness. *Alzheimer Disease & Associated Disorders, 27*, 195–203. doi:10.1097/WAD.0b013e318 27bda55.

Alzheimer's Association. (2016). *Safe return.* Retrieved February 22, 2017, from www.alz.org/national/documents/brochure_masr_enrollment.pdf.

Alzheimer's Disease Education and Referral Center [ADEAR] (2016, August). *Alzheimer's disease medications fact sheet.* NIH Publication No. 16-AG-3431.

American Speech-Language-Hearing Association. (2005). Roles of speech-language pathologists in the identification, diagnosis, and treatment of individuals with cognitive-communication disorders: Position statement (ASHA Supplement No. 25), Rockville, MD: Author.

Amieva, H., Robert, P. H., Grandoulier, A.-S., Meillon, C., De Rotrou, J., Andrieu, S., ... Dartigues, J.-F. (2016). Group and individual cognitive therapies in Alzheimer's disease: The ETNA3 randomized trial. *International Psychogeriatrics, 28*, 707–717. doi:10.1017/S1041610215001830.

Anderson, J., Arens, K., Arens, K., & Coppens, P. (2001). Spaced retrieval vs. memory tape therapy in memory rehabilitation for dementia of the Alzheimer's type. *Clinical Gerontologist, 24*(1–2), 123–139. doi:10.1300/J018v24n01_09.

Andrews-Salvia, M., Roy, N., & Cameron, R. M. (2003). Evaluating the effects of memory books for individuals with severe dementia. *Journal of Medical Speech-Language Pathology, 11*(1), 51–59.

Arkin, S. M. (1996). Volunteers in partnership: An Alzheimer's rehabilitation program delivered by students. *American Journal of Alzheimer's Disease and Other Dementias, 11*(1), 12–22.

Arkin, S. M. (1997). Alzheimer memory training: Quizzes beat repetition, especially with more impaired. *American Journal of Alzheimer's Disease and Other Dementias, 12*(4), 147–158.

Arkin, S. M. (1999). Elder rehab: A student-supervised exercise program for Alzheimer's patients. *The Gerontologist, 39*(6), 729–735.

Arkin, S. M. (2001). Alzheimer rehabilitation by students: Interventions and outcomes. *Neuropsychological Rehabilitation, 11*(3–4), 273–317.

Arkin, S. (2005). *Language-enriched exercise for clients with Alzheimer's disease.* Tucson, AZ: Desert Southwest Fitness.

Arkin, S. (2007). Language-enriched exercise plus socialization slows cognitive decline in Alzheimer's disease. *American Journal of Alzheimer's Disease and Other Dementias, 22*(1), 62–77.

Arkin, S. (2011). Service learning students as treatment providers. *Topics in Geriatric Rehabilitation, 27*(4), 301–311. doi:10.1097/TGR.0b013e31821e5a90.

Arntzen, C. A., Holthe, T., & Jentoft, R. (2016). Tracing the successful incorporation of assistive technology into everyday life for younger people with dementia and family carers. *Dementia, 15*, 646–662. doi:10.1177/1471301214532263.

Assaf, S., Barak, Y., Berger, U., Paleacu, D., Tadger, S., Plonsky, I., & Baruch, Y. (2016). Safety and efficacy of medical cannabis oil for behavioral and psychological symptoms of dementia: An open label, add-on, pilot study. *Journal of Alzheimer's Disease, 51*(1), 15–19. doi:10.3233/JAD-150915.

Astell, A. J., Ellis, M. P., Bernardi, L., et al. (2010). Using a touch screen computer to support relationships between people with dementia and caregivers. *Interact Comput, 22*(4), 267–275.

Baddeley, A. D., & Wilson, B. A. (1994). When implicit learning fails: Amnesia and the problem of error elimination. *Neuropsychologia, 32*(1), 53–68.

Bahar-Fuchs, A., Clare, L., & Woods, B. (2013). Cognitive training and cognitive rehabilitation for mild to moderate Alzheimer's disease and vascular dementia (Review). *Cochrane Database of Systematic Reviews 2013, Issue 6.* Art. No.: CD003260. doi:10.1002/14651858.CD003260.pub2.

Ball, K., Berch, D. B., Helmers, K. F., Jobe, J. B., Leveck, M. D., Marsiske, M., ... Willis, S. L. (2002). Effects of cognitive training interventions with older adults. *Journal of the American Medical Association, 288*, 2271–2281. doi:10.1001/jama.288.18.2271.

Balota, D. A., Duchek, J. M., Sergent-Marshall, S. D., & Roediger, H. L. III. (2006). Does expanded retrieval produce benefits over equal interval spacing? Explorations of spacing effects in healthy aging and early stage Alzheimer's disease. *Psychology & Aging, 21*, 19–31.

Ballard, C., Creese, B., Corbett, A., & Aarsland, D. (2011). Atypical antipsychotics for the treatment of behavioral and psychological symptoms in dementia, with a particular focus on longer term outcomes and mortality. *Expert Opinion on Drug Safety, 10*(1), 35–43. doi:10.1517/14740338.2010.506711.

Bayles, K. A., Kim, E. S., Azuma, T., Chapman, S. B., Cleary, S., Hopper, T., & Zientz, J. (2005). Developing evidence-based practice guidelines for speech-language pathologists serving individuals with Alzheimer's dementia. *American Journal of Medical Speech Language Pathology, 13*(4), xiii–xxv.

Bayles, K. A., Kim, E., Chapman, S. B., Zientz, J., Rackley, A., Mahendra, N., & Hopper, T. (2006). Evidence-based practice recommendations for working with individuals with dementia: Simulated presence therapy. *Journal of Medical Speech-Language Pathology, 14*(3), xiii–xxi.

Benigas, J. E., & Bourgeois, M. (2016). Using spaced retrieval with external aids to improve use of compensatory strategies during eating for persons with dementia. *American Journal of Speech-Language Pathology, 25*, 321–324. doi:10.1044/2015_AJSLP-14-0176.

Bird, M., Alexopoulos, P., & Adamowicz, J. (1995). Success and failure in five case studies: Use of cued recall to ameliorate behaviour problems in senile dementia. *International Journal of Geriatric Psychiatry, 10*(4), 305–311.

Birks, J., McGuinness, B., & Craig, D. (2013). Rivastigmine for vascular cognitive impairment. *Cochrane Database of Systematic Reviews 2013, Issue 5.* Art. No.: CD004744. doi:10.1002/14651858.CD004744.pub3.

Black, S., Román, G. C., Geldmacher, D. S., Salloway, S., Hecker, J., Burns, A., & Donepezil 307 Vascular Dementia Study Group. (2003). Efficacy and tolerability of donepezil in vascular dementia: Positive results of a 24-week, multicenter, international, randomized, placebo-controlled clinical trial. *Stroke, 34*(10), 2323–2330.

Boczko, F. (1994). The breakfast club: A multi-modal language stimulation program for nursing home residents with Alzheimer's disease. *The American Journal of Alzheimer's Disease and Other Dementias, 9*(4), 35–38.

Bollinger, R. L., & Stout, C. E. (1976). Response-contingent small-step treatment: Performance-based communication intervention. *Journal of Speech and Hearing Disorders, 41*(1), 40–51.

Bourgeois, M. S. (1990). Enhancing conversation skills in Alzheimer's disease using a prosthetic memory aid. *Journal of Applied Behavior Analysis, 23*(1), 29–42.

Bourgeois, M. S. (1991). Communication treatment for adults with dementia. *Journal of Speech, Language, and Hearing Research, 34*(4), 831–844.

Bourgeois, M. S. (1992a). *Conversing with memory impaired individuals using memory aids: A memory aid workbook.* Gaylord, MI: Northern Speech Services.

Bourgeois, M. S. (1992b). Evaluating memory wallets in conversations with patients with dementia. *Journal of Speech, Language, and Hearing Research, 35*(6), 1344–1357.

Bourgeois, M. S. (1993). Effects of memory aids on the dyadic conversations of individuals with dementia. *Journal of Applied Behavior Analysis, 26*(1), 77–87.

Bourgeois, M. S. (1994). Teaching caregivers to use memory aids with patients with dementia. *Seminars in Speech and Language, 15*(4), 291–305.

Bourgeois, M. S. (2001). Is reading preserved in dementia? *The ASHA Leader, 6*(9), 5.

Bourgeois, M.S. (2013). *Memory books and other graphic cueing systems: Practical communication and memory aids for adults with dementia.* Baltimore: Health Professions Press.

Bourgeois, M. (2014, March). *A functional approach to assessment in dementia: Some new ideas.* Paper presented at ASHA Healthcare Conference, Las Vegas, NV.

Bourgeois, M. (2015, November). *Innovative treatments for persons with dementia.* Paper presented at ASHA Research Symposium, Denver, CO.

Bourgeois, M. S., Brush, J., Elliot, G., & Kelly, A. (2015). Join the revolution: How Montessori for aging and dementia can change long-term care culture. *Seminars in Speech and Language, 36*, 209–214. http://dx.doi.org/10.1055/s-0035-1554802.

Bourgeois, M. S., Burgio, L. D., Schulz, R., Beach, S., & Palmer, B. (1997). Modifying the repetitive verbalization of community-dwelling patients with AD. *The Gerontologist, 37*(1), 30–39.

Bourgeois, M. S., Camp, C., Rose, M., White, B., Malone, M., Carr, J., & Rovine, M. (2003). A comparison of training strategies to enhance use of external aids by persons with dementia. *Journal of Communication Disorders, 36*(5), 361–378.

Bourgeois, M., Dijkstra, K., Burgio, L., & Allen-Burge, R. (2001). Memory aids as an AAC strategy for nursing home residents with dementia. *Augmentative and Alternative Communication, 17*(3), 196–210.

Bourgeois, M. S., Lenius, K., Turkstra, L., & Camp, C. (2007). The effects of cognitive teletherapy on reported everyday memory behaviours of persons with chronic traumatic brain injury. *Brain Injury, 21,* 1245–1257. http://dx.doi.org/10.1080/02699050701727452.

Bourgeois, M. S., & Mason, L. A. (1996). Memory wallet intervention in an adult day care setting. *Behavioral Interventions, 11*(1), 3–18.

Boyle, M., Mahendra, N., Hopper, T., Bayles, K. A., Azuma, T., Clearly, S., & Kim, E. (2006). Evidence-based practice recommendations for working with individuals with dementia: Montessori-based interventions. *Journal of Medical Speech-Language Pathology, 14*(1), xv–xxv.

Brodaty, H., & Arasaratnam, C. (2012). Meta-analysis of nonpharmacological interventions for neuropsychiatric symptoms of dementia. *The American Journal of Psychiatry, 169,* 946–953.

Brush, J. A., & Camp, C. J. (1998). Using spaced-retrieval training as an intervention during speech-language therapy. *Clinical Gerontologist, 19*(1), 51–64.

Brush, J., Camp, C., Bohach, S., & Gertsberg, N. (2015). Developing signage that supports wayfinding for persons with dementia. *Canadian Nursing Home, 26*(1), 4–11. Retrieved from http://nursinghome magazine.ca/.

Buckley, J. S., & Salpeter, S. R. (2015). A risk-benefit assessment of dementia medication: Systematic review of the evidence. *Drugs Aging, 32,* 453–467. doi:10.1007/s40266-015-0266-9.

Buettner, L. L. (1999). Simple pleasures: A multilevel sensorimotor intervention for nursing home residents with dementia. *American Journal of Alzheimer's Disease and Other Dementias, 14*(1), 41–52.

Burgio, L. D., Allen-Burge, R., Roth, D. L., Bourgeois, M. S., Dijkstra, K., Gerstle, J., & Bankester, L. (2001). Come talk with me: Improving communication between nursing assistants and nursing home residents during care routines. *The Gerontologist, 41*(4), 449–460.

Burgio, L., Scilley, K., Hardin, J. M., Hsu, C., & Yancey, J. (1996). Environmental "white noise": An intervention for verbally agitated nursing home residents. *Journal of Gerontology Series B: Psychological Sciences and Social Sciences, 51*(6), P364–P373.

Camargo, C. H. F., Justus, F. F., & Retzlaff, G. (2015). The effectiveness of reality orientation in the treatment of Alzheimer's disease. *American Journal of Alzheimer's Disease & Other Dementias, 30*(5), 527–532. doi:https://doi.org/10.1177/1533317514568004.

Camp, C. J. (1999). Memory interventions for normal and pathological older adults. In R. Schulz, G. Maddox, & M. P. Lawton (Eds.), *Annual review of gerontology and geriatrics: Focus on interventions research with older adults* (pp. 155–189). New York: Springer.

Camp, C. J. (2006). *Montessori-based activities for persons with dementia* (Vol. 1). Baltimore: Health Professions Press.

Camp, C. J., Bird, M. J., & Cherry, K. E. (2000). Retrieval strategies as a rehabilitation aid for cognitive loss in pathological aging. In R. D. Hill, L. Bäckman, & A. S. Neely (Eds.), *Cognitive rehabilitation in old age* (pp. 224–248). New York: Oxford University Press.

Camp, C. J., Foss, J. W., O'Hanlon, A. M., & Stevens, A. B. (1996). Memory interventions for persons with dementia. *Applied Cognitive Psychology, 10*(3), 193–210.

Camp, C. J., Foss, J. W., Stevens, A. B., & O'Hanlon, A. M. (1996). Improving prospective memory task performance in persons with Alzheimer's disease. In M. A. Brandimonte, G. Einstein, & M. McDaniel (Eds.), *Prospective memory: Theory and applications* (pp. 351–367). Hillsdale, NJ: Lawrence Erlbaum.

Camp, C. J., Judge, K. S., Bye, C. A., Fox, K. M., Bowden, J., Bell, M., Valencic, K., & Mattern, J. M. (1997). An intergenerational program for persons with dementia using Montessori methods. *The Gerontologist, 37,* 688–692. https://doi.org/10.1093/geront/37.5.688.

Camp, C. J., & McKitrick, L. A. (1992). Memory interventions in Alzheimer's-type dementia populations: Methodological and theoretical issues. In R. L. West & J. D. Sinnott (Eds.), *Everyday memory and aging: Current research and methodology* (pp. 155–172). New York: Springer-Verlag.

Camp, C. J., & Schaller, J. R. (1989). Epilogue: Spaced-retrieval memory training in an adult day-care center. *Educational Gerontology, 15*(6), 641–648.

Camp, C. J., & Skrajner, M. J. (2004). Resident-Assisted Montessori Programming (RAMP): Training persons with dementia to serve as group activity leaders. *The Gerontologist, 44*(3), 426–431.

Cao, L., Tan, L., Wang, H. F. et al. (2016) Dietary patterns and risk of dementia: A systematic review and meta-analysis of cohort studies. *Molecular Neurobiology, 53*(9), 6144. doi:10.1007/s12035-015-9516-4.

Chaudhury, H., Hung, L., & Badger, M. (2013). The role of physical environment in supporting person-centered dining in long-term care: A systematic review of the literature. *American J of Alzheimers Dis Other Demen, 28*(5), 491–500. doi:10.1177/1533317513488923.

Cherry, K. E., Hawley, K. S., Jackson, E. M., & Boudreaux, E. O. (2009). Booster sessions enhance the long-term effectiveness of spaced retrieval in older adults with probable Alzheimer's disease. *Behavior Modification, 33*(3), 295–313. doi:10.1177/0145445509333432.

Cherry, K., E., & Simmons-D'Gerolamo, S. S. (2004). Spaced-retrieval with probably Alzheimer's. *Clinical Gerontologist, 27*(1–2), 139–157.

Chiang, K.-J., Chu, H., Chang, H.-J., Chung, M.-H., Chen, C.-H., Chiou, H.-Y., & Chou, K.-R. (2010). The effects of reminiscence therapy on psychological well-being, depression, and loneliness among the institutionalized aged. *Int J Geriatr Psychiatry, 25*, 380–388. doi:10.1002/gps.2350.

Clare, L., & Jones, R. S. P. (2008). Errorless learning in the rehabilitation of memory impairment: A critical review. *Neuropsychology Review, 18*, 1–23. doi:10.1007/s11065-008-9051-4.

Clare, L., Wilson, B. A., Carter, G., Breen, K., Gosses, A., & Hodges, J. R. (2000). Intervening with everyday memory problems in dementia of Alzheimer type: An errorless learning approach. *Journal of Clinical and Experimental Neuropsychology, 22*(1), 132–146. doi:10649552.

Clare, L., Wilson, B. A., Carter, G., Hodges, J. R., & Adams, M. (2001). Long-term maintenance of treatment gains following a cognitive rehabilitation intervention in early dementia of Alzheimer type: A single case study. *Neuropsychological Rehabilitation, 11*(3), 477–494.

Clare, L., Wilson, B. A., Carter, G., Roth, I., & Hodges, J. R. (2002). Relearning face-name associations in early Alzheimer's disease. *Neuropsychology, 16*, 538–547.

Clark, L. W. (1995). Interventions for persons with Alzheimer's disease: Strategies for maintaining and enhancing communicative access. *Topics in Language Disorders, 15*(2), 47–66.

Cohen-Mansfield, J. (2005). Nursing staff members' assessments of pain in cognitively impaired nursing home residents. *Pain Management Nursing, 6*(2), 68–75.

Corbett, A., Burns, A., & Ballard, C. (2014). Don't use antipsychotics routinely to treat agitation and aggression in people with dementia. *BMJ, 349*, g6420. doi:10.1136/bmj.g6420.

Cotelli, M., Manenti, R., & Zanetti, O. (2012). Reminiscence therapy in dementia: A review. *Maturitas, 72*, 203–2015.

Creighton, A. S., Davison, T. E., van der Ploeg, E. S., Camp, C. J., & O'Connor, D. W. (2015). Using spaced retrieval training to teach people with dementia to independently use their walking aids: Two case studies. *Clinical Gerontologist, 38*, 170–178. doi:10.1080/07317115.2014.988899.

Creighton, A. S., van der Ploeg, E. S., & O'Connor, D. W. (2013). A literature review of spaced-retrieval interventions: A direct memory intervention for people with dementia. *International Psychogeriatrics, 25*, 1743–1763. doi:10.1017/S1041610213001233.

Cummings, J. L., Geldmacher, D., Farlow, M., Sabbagh, M., Christensen, D., & Betz, P. (2013). High-dose donepezil (23 mg/day) for the treatment of moderate and severe Alzheimer's disease: Drug profile and clinical guidelines. *CNS Neuroscience and Therapeutics, 19*, 294–301. doi:10.1111/cns.12076.

Declercq, T., Petrovic, M., Azermai, M., Vander Stichele, R., De Sutter, A. I. M., van Driel, M. L., & Christiaens, T. (2013). Withdrawal versus continuation of chronic antipsychotic drugs for behavioural and psychological symptoms in older people with dementia (Review). *Cochrane Database of Systematic Reviews, 3*, 1–80. doi:10.1002/14651858.CD007726.pub2.

Dempsey, L., Murphy, K., Cooney, A., Casey, D., O'Shea, E., Devane, D., … Hunter, A. (2014). Reminiscence in dementia: A concept analysis. *Dementia, 13*(2), 176–192. doi:10.1177/1471301212456277.

de Werd, M. M. E., Boelen, D., Olde Rikkert, M. G. M., & Kessels, R. P. C. (2013). Errorless learning of everyday tasks in people with dementia. *Clinical Interventions in Aging, 8*, 1177–1190. http://dx.doi.org/10.2147/CIA.S46809.

Dijkstra, K., Bourgeois, M., Burgio, L., & Allen, R. (2002). Effects of a communication intervention on the discourse of nursing home residents with dementia and their nursing assistants. *Journal of Medical Speech-Language Pathology, 10*, 143–157.

Egan, M., Bérubé, D., Racine, G., Leonard, C., & Rochon, E. (2010). Methods to enhance verbal communication between individuals with Alzheimer's disease and their formal and informal caregivers:

A systematic review. *International Journal of Alzheimer's Disease, Volume 2010*, Article ID 906818, 12 pages, doi:10.4061/2010/906818.

Ehret, M. J., & Chamberlin, K. W. (2015). Current practices in the treatment of Alzheimer disease: Where is the evidence after phase III trials? *Clinical Therapeutics, 37*, 1604–1616. http://dx.doi.org/10.1016.j.clinthera.2015.05.510.

Eisner, E. (2013). *Engaging and communicating with people who have dementia: Finding and using their strengths.* Baltimore: Health Professions Press.

Elias, S. M. S., Neville, C., & Scott, T. (2015). The effectiveness of group reminiscence therapy for loneliness, anxiety and depression in older adults in long-term care: A systematic review. *Geriatric Nursing, 36*, 372–380. http://dx.doi.org/10.1016/j.gerinurse.2015.05.004.

Elliott, R. A., Goeman, D., Beanland, C., & Koch, S. (2015). Ability of older people with dementia or cognitive impairment to manage medicine regimens: A narrative review. *Current Clinical Pharmacology, 10*, 213–221.

Esposito, Z., Belli, L., Toniolo, S., Sancesario, G., Bianconi, C., & Martorana, A. (2013). Amyloid beta, glutamate, excitotoxicity in Alzheimer's disease: Are we on the right track? Review article. *CNS Neuroscience & Therapeutics, 19*, 549–555. doi:10.1111/cns.12095.

Fairchild, J. K., Friedman, L., Rosen, A. C., & Yesavage, J. A. (2013). Which older adults maintain benefit from cognitive training? Use of signal detection methods to identify long-term treatment gains. *International Psychogeriatrics, 25*, 607–616. doi:10.1017/S1041610212002049.

Farina, N., Llewellyn, D., Isaac, M., & Tabet, N. (2017). Vitamin E for Alzheimer's dementia and mild cognitive impairment. *Cochrane Database of Systematic Reviews 2017, Issue 1*. Art. No.: CD002854. doi:10.1002/14651858.CD002854.pub4.

Farrimond, L. E., Roberts, E., & McShane, R. (2012). Memantine and cholinesterase inhibitor combination therapy for Alzheimer's disease: A systematic review. *BMJ Open, 2*(3), e000917. doi:10.1136/bmjopen-2012-000917.

Feil, N. (1992). Validation therapy. *Geriatric Nursing, 13*(3), 129–133.

Feil, N., & de Klerk-Rubin, V. (1992). *Validation: The Feil method: How to help the disoriented old-old.* Cleveland, OH: Edward Feil.

Ferris, S. H., Schmitt, F. A., Saxton, J. et al. (2011). Analyzing the impact of 23 mg/day donepezil on language dysfunction in moderate to severe Alzheimer's disease. *Alzheimers Res Ther, 3*, 22.

Fish, J. E., Manly, T., Kopelman, M. D., & Morris, R. G. (2015). Errorless learning of prospective memory tasks: An experimental investigation in people with memory disorders. *Neuropsychological Rehabilitation, 25*(2), 159–188. doi:10.1080/09602011.2014.921204.

Folsom, J. C. (1968). Reality orientation for the elderly mental patient. *Journal of Geriatric Psychiatry, 1*(2), 291–307.

Fried-Oken, M., Rowland, C., Daniels, D., & Oken, B. (2012). AAC to support conversation in persons with moderate Alzheimer's disease. *Augmentative and Alternative Communication, 28*(4), 219–231. doi:10.3109/07434618.2012.732610.

Fritsch, T., McClendon, M. J., Wallendal, M. S., Smyth, K. A., Geldmacher, D. S., Hyde, T. F., & Leo, G. J. (2014). Can a memory club help maintain cognitive function? A pilot investigation. *Activities, Adaptation, & Aging, 38*, 29–52. doi:10.1080/01924788.2014.878873.

Garrett, K. L., & Yorkston, K. M. (1997). Assistive communication technology for elders with cognitive and language disabilities. In R. Lubinski & D. J. Higginbotham (Eds.), *Communication technologies for the elderly* (pp. 203–234). San Diego, CA: Singular.

Gill, C., & McCabe, C. (2016, August). Preparation, clinical support, and confidence of speech and language therapists working with people with dementia in Ireland. Paper presented at the 30th World Congress of the International Association of Logopedics and Phoniatrics, Dublin, Ireland.

Glisky, E. L., Schacter, D. L., & Tulving, E. (1986). Learning and retention of computer-related vocabulary in amnesic patients: Method of vanishing cues. *Journal of Clinical and Experimental Neuropsychology, 8*(3), 292–312.

Griffiths, S., Dening, T., Beer, C., & Tischler, V. (2016). Mementos from Boots multisensory boxes: Qualitative evaluation of an intervention for people with dementia: Innovative practice. *Dementia, 0*(0), 1–9. doi:10.1177/1471301216672495.

Gross, A. L., Parisi, J. M., Spira, A. P., Kueider, A. M., Ko, J. Y., Saczynski, J. S., Samus, Q. M., & Rebok, G. W. (2012). Memory training interventions for older adults: A meta-analysis. *Aging & Mental Health, 16*(6), 722–734. http://dx.doi.org/10.1080/13607863.2012.667783.

Hambrick, D. Z. (2014). Brain training doesn't make you smarter. Retrieved January 5, 2017, from www.scientificamerican.com/article/brain-training-doesn-t-make-you-smarter/.

Haslam, C., Hodder, K. I., & Yates, P. J. (2011). Errorless learning and spaced retrieval: How do these methods fare in healthy and clinical populations? *Journal of Clinical and Experimental Neuropsychology, 33*, 432–447. http://dx.doi.org/10.1080/13803395.2010.533155.

Hawley, K. S., & Cherry, K. E. (2008). Memory interventions and quality of life for older adults with dementia. *Activities, Adaptation, and Aging, 32*(2), 89–102. doi:10.1080/01924780802142958.

Hawley, K. S., Cherry, K. E., Boudreaux, E. O., & Jackson, E. M. (2007). A comparison of adjusted spaced retrieval versus a uniform expanded retrieval schedule for learning a name–face association in older adults with probably Alzheimer's disease. *Journal of Clinical and Experimental Neuropsychology, 30*, 639–649.

Hayden, C. M., & Camp, C. J. (1995). Spaced-retrieval: A memory intervention for dementia in Parkinson's disease. *Clinical Gerontologist, 16*(3), 80–82.

Hickey, E. M., & How, S. (2008, May). Spaced-retrieval training for persons with dementia: Maintenance and generalization. Paper presented at the annual Clinical Aphasiology Conference, Jackson, WY.

Hickey, E. M., Lawrence, M., & Landry, A. (2011, June). Comparison of expanded versus equal interval recall training in persons with Dementia. Paper presented at the annual Clinical Aphasiology Conference, Ft. Lauderdale, FL.

Hochhalter, A. K., Bakke, B. L., Holub, R. J., & Overmier, J. B. (2004). Adjusted spaced retrieval training: A demonstration and initial test of why it is effective. *Clinical Gerontologist, 27*(1–2), 159–168.

Hochhalter, A. K., Overmier, J. B., Gasper, S. M., Bakke, B. L., & Holub, R. J. (2005). A comparison of spaced retrieval to other schedules of practice for people with dementia. *Experimental Aging Research, 31*, 101–118.

Hoerster, L., Hickey, E. M., & Bourgeois, M. S. (2001). Effects of memory aids on conversations between nursing home residents with dementia and nursing assistants. *Neuropsychological Rehabilitation, 11*(3–4), 399–427.

Hopper, T. (2003). "They're just going to get worse anyway": Perspectives on rehabilitation for nursing home residents with dementia. *Journal of Communication Disorders, 36*(5), 345–359. doi:10.1016/S0021-9924(03)00050-9.

Hopper, T. (2016). Not cured … but improved. *The ASHA Leader, 21*(6), 44–51. doi:10.1044/leader.FTR1.21062016.44.

Hopper, T., Bourgeois, M., Pimentel, J., Qualls, C. D., Hickey, E., Frymark, T., & Schooling, T. (2013). An evidence-based systematic review on cognitive interventions for individuals with dementia. *American Journal of Speech-Language Pathology, 22*(1), 126–145.

Hopper, T., Cleary, S., Oddson, B., Donnelly, M. J., & Elgar, S. (2007). Service delivery for older Canadians with dementia: A survey of speech–language pathologists. *Canadian Journal of Speech-Language Pathology & Audiology, 31*(3), 114–126.

Hopper, T., Drefs, S. J., Bayles, K. A., Tomoeda, C. K., & Dinu, I. (2010). The effects of modified spaced retrieval training on learning and retention of face–name associations by individuals with dementia. *Neuropsychological Rehabilitation, 20*(1), 81–102.

Hopper, T., Mahendra, N., Kim, E., Azuma, T., Bayles, K. A., Cleary, S. J., & Tomoeda, C. K. (2005). Evidence-based practice recommendations for working with individuals with dementia: Spaced-retrieval training. *American Journal of Medical Speech-Language Pathology, 13*(4), xxvii–xxxiv.

Hunter, C. E. A., Ward, L., & Camp, C. J. (2012). Transitioning spaced retrieval training to care staff in an Australian residential aged care setting for older adults with dementia: A case study approach. *Clinical Gerontologist, 35*(1), 1–14. doi:10.1080/07317115.2011.626513.

Huntley, J. D., Gould, R. L., Liu, K. et al. (2015). Do cognitive interventions improve general cognition in dementia? A meta-analysis and metaregression. *BMJ Open, 5*, e005247. doi:10.1136/bmjopen-2014-005247.

Ikeda, M. (2017). Pharmacotherapy in dementia with Lewy bodies. In K. Kosaka (Ed.), *Dementia with Lewy bodies*. Switzerland: Springer International.

Irvine, A. B., Ary, D. V., & Bourgeois, M. S., & (2003). An interactive multi-media program to train professional caregivers. *Journal of Applied Gerontology, 22*(2), 269–288.

Jamieson, M., Cullen, B., McGee-Lennon, M., Brewster, S., & Evans, J. J. (2014). The efficacy of cognitive prosthetic technology for people with memory impairments: A systematic review and meta-analysis. *Neuropsychological Rehabilitation, 24*(3–4), 419–444. http://dx.doi.org/10.1080/09602011.2013.825632.

Jeffrey, S. (2013). FDA approves Exelon patch for severe Alzheimer's. Medscape, available at www. medscape.com/viewarticle/807062.

Jiang, X., Huang, J., Song, D., Deng, R., Wei, J., & Zhang, Z. (2017). Increased consumption of fruit and vegetables is related to a reduced risk of cognitive impairment and dementia: Meta-analysis. *Frontiers in Aging Neuroscience, 9*, 18. http://doi.org/10.3389/fnagi.2017.00018.

Jokanovic, N., Tan, E. C. K., Dooley, M. J., Kirkpatrick, C. M., & Bell, J. S. (2015). Prevalence and factors associated with polypharmacy in long-term care facilities: A systematic review. *JAMDA, 16*, 535.e1–535. e12 http://dx.doi.org/10.1016/j.jamda.2015.03.003.

Joltin, A., Camp., C. J., & McMahon, C. M. (2003). Spaced-retrieval over the telephone: An intervention for persons with dementia. *Clinical Psychologist, 7*(1), 50–55.

Kagan, A., Simmons-Mackie, N., Rowland, A., Huijbregts, M., Shumway, E., McEwen, S., ... Sharp, S. (2008). Counting what counts: A framework for capturing real-life outcomes of aphasia intervention. *Aphasiology, 22*, 258–280. http://dx.doi.org/10.1080/02687030701282595.

Kallio, E.-L., Öhman, H., Kautiainen, H., Hietanen, M., & Pitkälä, K. (2017). Cognitive training interventions for patients with Alzheimer's disease: A systematic review. *Journal of Alzheimer's Disease, 56*, 1349–1372. doi:10.3233/JAD-160810.

Kavanagh, S., Gaudig, M., Van Baelen, B. et al. (2011). Galantamine and behavior in Alzheimer disease: Analysis of four trials. *Acta Neurol Scand, 124*(5), 302–308.

Khan, Z., Corbett, A., & Ballard, C. (2014). Cognitive stimulation therapy: Training, maintenance, and implementation in clinical trials. *Pragmatic and Observational Research, 5*, 15–19.

Kim, E. S., Clearly, S. J., Hopper, T., Bayles, K. A., Azuma, T., & Rackley, A. (2006). Evidence-based practice recommendations for working with individuals with dementia: Group reminiscence therapy. *Journal of Medical Speech-Language Pathology, 14*(3), xxiii–xxxiv.

Kincaid, C., & Peacock, J. R. (2003). The effect of a wall mural on decreasing four types of door-testing behaviors. *Journal of Applied Gerontology, 22*(1), 76–88.

Kindell, J., Keady, J., Sage, K., & Wilkinson, R. (2016). Everyday conversation in dementia: A review of the literature to inform research and practice. *Int J Lang Comm Disord, 00*(0), 1–15. doi:10.1111/1460-6984.12298.

Kitwood, T. (1997) *Dementia reconsidered: The person comes first.* Buckingham, UK: Open University Press.

Kueider, A., Parisi, J., Gross, A., & Rebok, G. (2012). Computerized cognitive training with older adults: A systematic review. *PLOS ONE, 7*(7), e40588. doi:10.1371/journal.pone.0040588.

Kunik, M., Martinez, M., Snow, A., Beck, C., Cody, M., Rapp, C. et al. (2003). Determinants of behavioral symptoms in dementia patients. *Clinical Gerontologist, 26*(3–4), 83–89.

Lachaine, J., Beauchemin, C., Legault, M., & Bineau, S. (2011). Economic evaluation of the impact of memantine on time to nursing home admission in the treatment of Alzheimer disease. *Can J Psychiatry, 56*(10), 596–604.

Lalanne, J., Gallarda, T., & Piolino, P. (2015). "The Castle of Remembrance": New insights into a cognitive training programme for autobiographical memory in Alzheimer's disease. *Neuropsychological Rehabilitation, 25*(2), 254–282. doi:http://dx.doi.org/10.1080/09602011.2014.949276.

Lam, V., Hackett, M., & Takechi, R. (2016). Antioxidants and dementia risk: Consideration through a cerebrovascular perspective. *Nutrients, 8*, 828; doi:10.3390/nu8120828.

Lampit, A., Hallock, H., & Valenzuela, M. (2014). Computerized training in cognitively healthy older adults: A systematic review and meta-analysis of effect modifiers. *PLOS Medicine, 11*(11), 1–18. doi:10.1371/journal.pmed.1001756.

Laver, K., Dyer, S., Whitehead, C., Clemson, L., & Crotty, M. (2016). Interventions to delay functional decline in people with dementia: A systematic review of systematic reviews. *BMJ Open, 6*, 1–13. doi:10.1136/bmjopen-2015-010767.

Lazar, A., Thompson, H., & Demiris, G. (2014). A systematic review of the use of technology for reminiscence therapy. *Health Education & Behavior, 41*(15), 515–615. doi:10.1177/1090198114537067.

Leirer, V. O., Morrow, D. G., Tanke, E. D., & Pariante, G. M. (1991). Elders' nonadherence: Its assessment and medication reminding by voice mail. *The Gerontologist, 31*(4), 514–520.

Leseth, L., & Meader, L. (1995). Utilizing an AAC system to maximize receptive and expressive communication skills of a person with Alzheimer's disease. *ASHA AAC Special Interest Division Newsletter, 4*, 7–9.

Li, R., & Liu, K. P. (2012). The use of errorless learning strategies for patients with Alzheimer's disease: A literature review. *International Journal of Rehabilitation Research, 35*(4), 292–298.

Li, Y., Hai, S., Zhou, Y., & Dong, B. R. (2015). Cholinesterase inhibitors for rarer dementias associated with neurological conditions. *Cochrane Database of Systematic Reviews 2015, Issue 3*. Art. No.: CD009444. doi:10.1002/14651858.CD009444.pub3.

Lin, L.-C., Huang, Y.-J., Su, S.-G., Watson, R., Tsai, B., & Wu, S.-C. (2010). Using spaced retrieval and Montessori-based activities in improving eating ability for residents with dementia. *International Journal of Geriatric Psychiatry, 25*(10), 953–959.

Livingston, G., Kelly, L., Lewis-Holmes, E., Baio, G., Morris, S., Patel, N., Omar, R., Katona, C., & Cooper, C. (2014). Non-pharmacological interventions for agitation in dementia: Systematic review of randomized controlled trials. *British Journal of Psychiatry, 205*, 436–442

Mahendra, N., & Arkin, S. (2003). Effects of four years of exercise, language, and social interventions on Alzheimer discourse. *Journal of Communication Disorders, 36*(5), 395–422.

Mahendra, N., Hopper, T., Bayles, K., Azuma, T., Cleary, S., & Kim, E. (2006). Evidence-based practice recommendations for working with individuals with dementia: Montessori-based interventions. *Journal of Medical Speech-Language Pathology, 14*(1), xv–xxv.

Mahendra, N., Kim, E., Bayles, K. A., Hopper, T., Cleary, S. J., & Azuma, T. (2006). Evidence-based practice recommendations for working with individuals with dementia: Computer-assisted cognitive interventions (CACIs). *Journal of Medical Speech-Language Pathology, 13*(4), xxxv–xliv.

Maier, A., Özkil, A. G., Bang, M. M., & Hysse Forchhammer, B. (2015). Remember to remember: A feasibility study adapting wearable technology to the needs of people aged 65 and older with Mild Cognitive Impairment (MCI) and Alzheimer's dementia. *Proceedings of International Conference on Engineering Design (ICED 2015), 1*, 331–340. Retrieved February 4, 2017, from http://orbit.dtu.dk/files/107110242/Remember_to_remember.pdf.

March, E., Wales, R., & Pattison, P. (2003). Language use in normal ageing and dementia of the Alzheimer type. *Clinical Psychologist, 7*(1), 44–49.

Materne, C. J., Luszcz, M. A., & Bond, M. J. (2014). Once-weekly spaced retrieval training is effective in supporting everyday memory activities in community dwelling older people with dementia. *Clinical Gerontologist, 37*(5), 475–492. doi:10.1080/07317115.2014.907591.

Mazzei, F., Gillan, R., & Cloutier, D. (2014). Exploring the influence of environment on the spatial behavior of older adults in a purpose-built acute care dementia unit. *Am J Alzheimers Dis Other Demen, 29*(4), 311–319. doi:10.1177/1533317513517033.

McGuinness, B., Craig, D., Bullock, R., Malouf, R., & Passmore, P. (2014). Statins for the treatment of dementia. *Cochrane Database of Systematic Reviews 2014, Issue 7*. Art. No.: CD007514. doi:10.1002/14651858.CD007514.pub3.

McKitrick, L. A., & Camp, C. J. (1993). Relearning the names of things: The spaced-retrieval intervention implemented by a caregiver. *Clinical Gerontologist, 14*(2), 60–62.

McKitrick, L. A., Camp, C. J., & Black, F. W. (1992). Prospective memory intervention in Alzheimer's disease. *The Journal of Gerontology, 47*(5), 337–343.

McPherson, A., Furniss, F. G., Sdogati, C., Cesaroni, F., Tartaglini, B., & Lindesay, J. (2001). Effects of individualized memory aids on the conversation of persons with severe dementia. *Aging & Mental Health, 5*(3), 289–294.

Microsoft Game Studios. (2003). *Rise of nations* [Video game]. Retrieved from www.microsoftstudios.com/.

Mitchell, G., & Agnelli, J. (2015) Person-centred care for people with dementia: Kitwood reconsidered. *Nursing Standard, 30*, 7, 46–50.

Mitchell, G., McCormack, B., & McCance, T. (2016). Therapeutic use of dolls for people living with dementia: A critical review of the literature. *Dementia, 15*(5), 976–1001. doi:10.1177/1471301214548522.

Moyle, W., El Saifi, N., Draper, B., Jones, C. Beattie, E., Shum, D., … O'Dwyer, S. (2017). Pharmacotherapy of persons with dementia in long-term care in Australia: A descriptive audit of central nervous system medications. *Curr Drug Saf, Feb 9.* doi:10.2174/1574886312666170209113203. [Epub ahead of print] Retrieved on February 22, 2017.

Mueller, K. (2016). A review of computer-based cognitive training for individuals with mild cognitive impairment and Alzheimer's disease. *Perspectives of the ASHA Special Interest Groups, SIG 2, 1*(1), 47–60.

Neal, M., & Barton Wright, P. (2003). Validation therapy for dementia. *Cochrane Database of Systematic Reviews 2003, Issue 3.* Art. No.: CD001394. doi:10.1002/14651858.CD001394.

Nintendo. (2007). *Big Brain Academy: Wii Degree* [Video game]. Redmond, WA: Author.

Nolan, B. A. D., Mathews, R. M., & Harrison, M. (2001). Using external memory aids to increase room finding by older adults with dementia. *American Journal of Alzheimer's Disease and Other Dementias, 16*(4), 251–254.

Olazarán, J., Reisberg, B., Clare, L., Cruz, I., Peña-Casanova, J., del Ser, T., … & Muñiz, R. (2010). Non-pharmacological therapies in Alzheimer's disease: A systematic review of efficacy. *Dementia and Geriatric Cognitive Disorders, 30*(2), 161–178.

Oren, S., Willerton, C., & Small, J. (2014). Effects of spaced retrieval training on semantic memory in Alzheimer's disease: A systematic review. *JSLHR, 57,* 247–270. doi:10.1044/1092-4388(2013/12-0352).

Orrell, M., Aguirre, E., Spector, A., Hoare, Z., Woods, R. T., Streater, A., … & Russell, I. (2014). Maintenance cognitive stimulation therapy for dementia: Single-blind, multicentre, pragmatic randomised controlled trial. *The British Journal of Psychiatry, 204*(6), 454–461. doi:10.1192/bjp.bp. 113.137414.

Owen, A. M., Hampshire, A., Grahn, J. A., Stenton, R., Dajani, S., Burns, A. S., … Ballard, C. G. (2010). Putting brain training to the test. *Nature, 465,* 775–778. doi:10.1038/nature09042.

Parenté, R., & Herrmann, D. (2010). *Retraining cognition: Techniques & applications* (3rd ed.). Austin, TX: Pro-Ed.

Park, D. C., & Kidder, D. P. (1996). Prospective memory and medication adherence. In M. A. Brandimonte, G. Einstein, & M. McDaniel (Eds.), *Prospective memory: Theory and applications* (pp. 369–390). Hillsdale, NJ: Lawrence Erlbaum.

Park, D. C., Morrell, R. W., Frieske, D., & Kincaid, D. (1992). Medication adherence behaviors in older adults: Effects of external cognitive supports. *Psychology and Aging, 7*(2), 252–256.

Parsons, C. (2016). Withdrawal of antidementia drugs in older people: Who, when and how? *Drugs & Aging.* doi:10.1007/s40266-016-0384-z.

Patterson, J. P. (2001). The effectiveness of cueing hierarchies as a treatment for word retrieval impairment. *Perspectives on Neurophysiology and Neurogenic Speech and Language Disorders, 11*(2), 11–18.

Pimentel, J. (2009). Contextual thematic group treatment for individuals with dementia. *Perspectives in Neurogenic Communication Disorders,* 135–141.

Posit Science. (2013). *Brain Fitness Program* [Computer program]. San Francisco, CA: Author.

Purves, B. A., Phinney, A., Hulko, W., Puurveen, G., & Astell, A. J. (2014). Developing CIRCA-BC and exploring the role of the computer as a third participant in conversation. *American Journal of Alzheimer's Disease & Other Dementias, 30*(1), 101–107. doi:10.1177/1533317514539031.

Raskin, S. A., & Sohlberg, M. M. (1996). The efficacy of prospective memory training in two adults with brain injury. *The Journal of Head Trauma Rehabilitation, 11*(3), 32–51.

Ratner, E., & Atkinson, D. (2015). Why cognitive training and brain games will not prevent or forestall dementia. *JAGS, 63*(12), 2612–2614.

Reeve, E., Bell, J. S., & Hilmer, S. N. (2015). Barriers to optimizing prescribing and deprescribing in older adults with dementia: A narrative review. *Curr Clin Pharmacol, 10*(3), 168–177.

Reilly, J. (2016). How to constrain and maintain a lexicon for the treatment of progressive semantic naming deficits: Principles of item selection for formal semantic therapy. *Neuropsychological Rehabilitation, 26*(1), 126–156. doi:10.1080/09602011.2014.1003947.

Reisberg, B., Doody, R., Stöffler, A., Schmitt, F., Ferris, S., & Möbius, H. (2003). Memantine in moderate-to-severe Alzheimer's disease. *New England Journal of Medicine, 348*(14), 1333–1341.

Reus, V., Fochtmann, L. J., Eyler, A. E., Hilty, D. M., Horvitz-Lennon, M., Jibson, M. D., … & Yager, J. (2016). The American Psychiatric Association practice guideline on the use of antipsychotics to treat agitation or psychosis in patients with dementia. *Am J Psychiatry, 173*(5), 543–546.

Rogalski, Y., & Quintana, M. (2013). Activity engagement in cognitive aging: A review of the evidence. *Perspectives on Neurophysiology and Neurogenic Speech and Language Disorders, 23*(1).

Santo Pietro, M. J., & Boczko, F. (1997). The Breakfast Club and related programs. In B. Shadden & M. A. Toner (Eds.), *Aging and communication* (pp. 341–359). Austin, TX: Pro-Ed.

Santo Pietro, M. J., & Boczko, F. (1998). The Breakfast Club: Results of a study examining the effectiveness of a multi-modality group communication treatment. *American Journal of Alzheimer's Disease and Other Dementias, 13*(3), 146–158.

Saxton, J., McGonigle, K. L., Swihart, A. A., & Boller, F. (1993). *Severe impairment battery.* Bury St. Edmunds, UK: Thames Valley.

Schneider, L. S., Dagerman, K. S., Higgins, J. P., & McShane, R. (2011). Lack of evidence for the efficacy of memantine in mild Alzheimer disease. *Arch Neurol, 68*(8), 991–998.

Schnelle, J. F. (1990). Treatment of urinary incontinence in nursing homepatients by prompted voiding. *Journal of the American Geriatrics Society, 38*(3), 356–360.

Small, J. A. (2012). A new frontier in spaced retrieval memory training for persons with Alzheimer's disease. *Neuropsychological Rehabilitation, 22*(3), 329–361. doi:10.1080/09602011.2011.640468.

Smith, G., House, P., Yaffe, K., Ruff, R., Kennison, R., Mahncke, H., & Zelinski, E. (2009). A cognitive training program based on principles of brain plasticity: Results from the Improvement in Memory with Plasticity-Based Adaptive Cognitive Training (IMPACT) study. *Journal of the American Geriatrics Society, 57*(4), 594–603.

Sohlberg, M. M., Ehlhardt, L., & Kennedy, M. (2005). Instructional techniques in cognitive rehabilitation: A preliminary report. *Seminars in Speech & Language, 26*, 268–279. doi:10.1055/s-2005-922105.

Sohlberg, M. M., & Mateer, C. A. (2001). *Cognitive rehabilitation: An integrative neuropsychological approach.* New York: Guilford Press.

Sohlberg, M. M., & Turkstra, L. (2011). *Optimizing cognitive rehabilitation: Effective instructional methods.* New York: Guilford Press.

Sohlberg, M. M., White, O., Evans, E., & Mateer, C. (1992). An investigation into the effects of prospective memory training. *Brain Injury, 6*(2), 139–154.

Spector, A., Davies, S., Woods, B., & Orrell, M. (2000). Reality orientation for dementia: A systematic review of the evidence of effectiveness from randomized controlled trials. *The Gerontologist, 40*, 206–212. https://doi.org/10.1093/geront/40.2.206.

Spector, A., Gardner, C., & Orrell, M. (2011). The impact of cognitive stimulation therapy groups on people with dementia: Views from participants, their carers, and group facilitators. *Aging & Mental Health, 15*(8), 945–949. http://dx.doi.org/10.1080/13607863.2011.586622.

Spilkin, M., & Bethlehem, D. (2003). A conversation analysis approach to facilitating communication with memory books. *Advances in Speech Language Pathology, 5*, 105–118.

Squire, L. R. (1994). Declarative and nondeclarative memory: Multiple brain system supporting learning and memory. In D. L. Schacter & E. Tulving (Eds.), *Memory systems 1994* (pp. 203–232). Cambridge, MA: MIT Press.

Sun, M.-K., Nelson, T. J., & Alkon, D. (2015). Towards universal therapeutics for memory disorders. *Trends in Pharmacological Sciences, 36*(6), 384–394. http://dx.doi.org/10.1016/j.tips.2015.04.004.

Tampi, R. R. & Tampi, D. J. (2014). Efficacy and tolerability of benzodiazepines for the treatment of behavioral and psychological symptoms of dementia: A systematic review of randomized controlled trials. *American Journal of Alzheimer's Disease & Other Dementias, 29*(7), 565–574.

Tan, C. C., Yu, J. T., Wang, H. F., Tan, M. S., Meng, X. F., Wang, C. et al. (2014). Efficacy and safety of donepezil, galantamine, rivastigmine, and memantine for the treatment of Alzheimer's disease: A systematic review and meta-analysis. *Journal of Alzheimer's Disease, 41*(2), 615–631.

Tan, M.-S., Yu, J.-T., Tan, C.-C., Wang, H.-F., Meng, X.-F., Wang, C., … & Tan, L. (2015). Efficacy and adverse effects of ginkgo biloba for cognitive impairment and dementia: A systematic review and meta-analysis. *Journal of Alzheimer's Disease, 43*, 589–603. doi:10.3233/JAD-140837.

Thivierge, S., Simard, M., Jean, L., & Grandmaison, E. (2008). Errorless learning and spaced retrieval techniques to relearn instrumental activities of dialing living in mild Alzheimer's disease: A case report study. *Neuropsychiatric Disease and Treatment, 4*, 987–999. http://dx.doi.org/10.3109/02703181.2013.796037.

Tija, J., Briesacher, B. A., Peterson, D., Liu, Q., Andrade, S. E., & Mitchell, S. L. (2014). Use of medications of questionable benefit in advanced dementia. *JAMA Intern Med, 174*(11), 1763–1771. doi:10.1001/jamainternmed.2014.4103.

Tsoi, K. K. F., Hirai, H. W., Chan, J. Y. C., & Kwok, T. C. Y. (2016). Time to treatment initiation in people with Alzheimer disease: A meta-analysis of randomized controlled trials. *JAMDA, 17,* 24–30. http://dx.doi.org/10.1016/j.jamda.2015.08.007.

Unverzagt, F., Guey, L., Jones, R. et al. (2012). ACTIVE cognitive training and rates of incident dementia. *J Int Neuropsychol Soc, 18,* 669–677.

Volicer, L., Simard, J., Heartquist Pupa, J., Medrek, R., & Riorden, M. E. (2006). Effects of continuous activity programming on behavioral symptoms of dementia. *Journal of the American Medical Directors Association, 7,* 426–431. https://doi.org/10.1016/j.jamda.2006.02.003.

Wilson, B. A., Baddeley, A., Evans, J., & Shiel, A. (1994). Errorless learning in the rehabilitation of memory impaired people. *Neuropsychological Rehabilitation, 4*(3), 307–326.

Wong, C. W. (2016) Pharmacotherapy for dementia: A practical approach to the use of cholinesterase inhibitors and memantine. *Drugs & Aging, 33*(7), 451–460. doi:10.1007/s40266-016-0372-3.

Woods, B., Aguirre, E., Spector, A. E., & Orrell, M. (2012). Cognitive stimulation to improve cognitive functioning in people with dementia. *Cochrane Database of Systematic Reviews, Issue 2.* Art. No.: CD005562. doi:10.1002/14651858.CD005562.pub2.

Woods, R. T. (1996). Psychological "therapies" in dementia. In R. T. Woods (Ed.), *Handbook of the clinical psychology of ageing* (pp. 575–600). New York: John Wiley.

Woods, R. T., Orrell, M., Bruce, E., Edwards, R. T., Hoare, Z., Hounsome, B., … Russell, I. (2016) REMCARE: Pragmatic multi-centre randomised trial of reminiscence groups for people with dementia and their family carers: Effectiveness and economic analysis. *PLoS ONE, 11*(4), e0152843. doi:10.1371/journal.pone.0152843.

World Health Organization. (2001). *International classification of functioning, disability and health (ICF).* Geneva, Switzerland: Author.

Yang, M., Xu, D. D., Zhang, Y., Liu, X., Hoeven, R., & Cho, W. C. S. (2014). A systematic review on natural medicines for the prevention and treatment of Alzheimer's disease with meta-analyses of intervention effect of ginkgo. *The American Journal of Chinese Medicine, 42*(3), 505–521. doi:10.1142/S019 2415X14500335.

Yesavage, J. A. et al. (2008). Acetylcholinesterase inhibitor in combination with cognitive training in older adults. *Journals of Gerontology: Psychological Sciences, 63B,* P288–P294.

Zeng, L., Zou, Y., Kong, L., Wang, N., Wang, Q., … & Liang, W. (2015). Can Chinese herbal medicine ajunctive therapy improve outcomes of senile vascular dementia? Systematic review with meta-analysis of clinical trials. *Phytotherapy Research, 29,* 1843–1857. doi:10.1002/ptr.5481.

Zeisel, J., Hyde, J., & Shi, L. (1999). Environmental design as a treatment for Alzheimer's disease. In L. Volicer & L. Bloom-Charette (Eds.), *Enhancing the quality of life in advanced dementia* (pp. 206–222). Philadelphia: Taylor & Francis.

Zientz, J., Rackley, A., Chapman, S. B., Hopper, T., Mahendra, N., & Cleary, S. (2007a). Evidence-based practice recommendations: Caregiver-administered active cognitive stimulation for individuals with Alzheimer's disease. *Journal of Medical Speech-Language Pathology, 15*(3), xxvii–xxxiv.

Zientz, J., Rackley, A., Chapman, S. B., Hopper, T., Mahendra, N., Kim, E. S., & Cleary, S. (2007b). Evidence-based practice recommendations for dementia: Educating caregivers on Alzheimer's disease and training communication strategies. *Journal of Medical Speech-Language Pathology, 15*(1), iii–xiv.

7

INTERPROFESSIONAL INTERVENTIONS FOR PARTICIPATION AND QUALITY OF LIFE

Ellen M. Hickey, Michelle S. Bourgeois, and Jennifer Brush

Models of care and interventions for persons with dementia have evolved over the past few decades, with an explosion of interest in holistic and nonpharmacological approaches to intervention for the behavioral and psychological symptoms of dementia (BPSDs), or responsive behaviors. The developments in social models of health and person-centered care have influenced research and policy development, prompting culture change in long-term care (LTC), as described in Chapters 1 and 4. Approaches to care for persons with dementia reflect the increased emphasis on person-centered care and aim to maximize functioning and quality of life (QoL), with attention to both the physical and social environments where care is provided. Person-centered care promotes choice, dignity, respect, self-determination, and purposeful living for persons with dementia (Kitwood, 1997; Kitwood & Bredin, 1992), which is reflected in the evolution in policy and philosophy of caring for persons with dementia.

The cognitive-communicative interventions that were discussed in Chapter 6 come primarily from the perspectives of speech–language pathology and (neuro)psychology, with an emphasis on capitalizing on the preserved skills and personal interests of each client. This chapter explores additional nonpharmacological interventions from a broader range of interprofessional perspectives, still focusing on preserved skills, personal interests, and contextual training, while also emphasizing environmental adaptations to improve participation and QoL. Both design of care settings and programming are important in caring for persons with dementia (Forrest & Cohen, 2004). Some models of care and specific interventions will be described in this chapter to illustrate the possibilities; however, this chapter is a starting point, not an exhaustive list of all possible interventions.

While further research is needed, evidence is available for clinicians to build the case for holistic behavioral and environmental interventions for persons with dementia to increase independence, life participation, and QoL. Some of the newest intervention approaches do not yet have a significant base of evidence, but they utilize person-centered care and evidence regarding effective supports for participation and QoL for persons with dementia. For example, a recent innovation in dementia care is the Montessori for Ageing and Dementia model, which emphasizes a team approach to provide a prepared physical and social environment for maximum functioning and QoL of persons with dementia (Bourgeois, Brush, Elliot, & Kelly, 2015). In addition to the need for more research, there is a need for more and better implementation of nonpharmacological interventions that improve QoL and reduce BPSDs.

The Interprofessional Team

Collaborative care should be delivered by an interprofessional team, including a speech-language pathologist (SLP), with the client and family at the center of the team to maximize treatment outcomes. A comprehensive, person-centered assessment should be conducted by the interprofessional team to develop an evidence-based plan of care with functional, personalized goals. Good communication among team members is imperative to avoid unnecessary redundancies in care or gaps in care so that the team can maximize functional outcomes. Team agreement on care plans and interprofessional education on strategies allows for more strategies that can be applied during the sessions and can be more easily integrated into the person's daily routine, maximizing outcomes despite ongoing trends toward shorter lengths of stay in medical and rehabilitation settings (Chatfield, Christos, & McGregor, 2012).

The interprofessional team composition will depend on the care setting. In most in-patient medical settings, the team will minimally include a physician, nursing staff, social worker, family members, and caregiver; rehabilitation professionals and spiritual care staff are other likely team members (Chatfield et al., 2012). In most settings, physicians are responsible for overseeing the person's care, relying on information from the whole team. In medical settings and LTC, nurses and nursing assistants (or support workers) are often responsible for delivering most aspects of daily care, from supervising or assisting the person with activities of daily living to giving medications; they often have essential information and tips for other team members on caring for the client. Social workers are often the case managers who deal with the legal and financial aspects of the client's care. Some social workers will also provide counseling services for clients and their family members. Spiritual care staff attend to the person's spiritual wellbeing and can assist the person in attending religious ceremonies or receiving sacraments, and they might also offer counseling services, depending on the setting and how much time they spend there.

In LTC, the leisure activities staff, dining, and housekeeping staff are also integral members of the team, and are likely to have very useful information for the medical and rehabilitation team members. While performing their duties, housekeeping staff often interact with or observe the residents, so they are in tune with the person's daily routines for waking, eating, spending time in the room versus common areas, attending activities, and toileting; they can provide the team with essential information about changes in routines and patterns. For example, housekeeping staff might notice patterns such as a person's cough or mood varying with position or with time of day, or patterns of reactions to other residents or specific staff members. When seeing a client in home healthcare, there might be fewer team members. Home care can make interprofessional collaboration more challenging due to the lack of in-person contact among team members; however, the opportunity to deliver intervention in the person's own context offers many benefits.

Rehabilitation professionals on the team across types of settings might include physical therapists, occupational therapists, recreation therapists, music therapists, and SLPs. Physical therapists work with clients on their overall strength and mobility, and possibly positioning. Occupational therapists work with clients on activities of daily living (ADLs) from a broad perspective that includes positioning needs, physical abilities, and cognitive abilities; they are usually involved in procuring assistive technology and equipment (e.g., walkers, wheelchairs, special beds). Recreation therapists and leisure activities staff may develop strategies and tools for the client to participate in favorite pastimes and engage them in one-on-one or group activities. Music therapists may deliver interventions that aim to improve some functional skill related to communication or memory, to engage the person in meaningful activity, or to provide pleasant experiences that enhance QoL. SLPs focus on intervening with the cognitive and communicative aspects of the person's functioning to decrease responsive behaviors and to maximize activities, participation, and meaningful engagement. Each rehabilitation discipline has contributed various sensory-, environmental-, and activity-focused techniques to enhance positive behaviors and to reduce responsive behaviors in persons with dementia.

Barriers to Participation and Quality of Life

Much of the research on this topic has been conducted in LTC, therefore, the focus here is on LTC settings, but some parallels could be made to other settings. When older adults with AD are overburdened cognitively, they exhibit responsive behaviors as a way of expressing unmet needs, such as: restlessness, wandering, shadowing, sundowning, or combativeness (Mowrey, Parikh, Bharwani, & Bharwani, 2012), or physical or verbal agitation and aggression (Zeisel et al., 2003). Both internal and external stressors can lead to boredom, disengagement, or dissatisfaction with the surrounding environment, triggering responsive behaviors, or BPSDs (Mowrey et al., 2012). Evidence for the impact of the social and physical environment of LTC settings on functional behaviors, wellbeing, and BPSDs will be discussed first, as these features can be targets for interventions to improve participation and QoL of LTC residents. Garcia and colleagues (Garcia, Espinoza, Lichtenstein, & Hazukda, 2012) conducted focus groups of family members and staff who felt that the social environment was more important than the physical characteristics of the environment, except for noise, which had the biggest impact on behavior and QoL of residents. Specialized physical design features were not sufficient for promoting wellbeing among residents; qualities of the social environment were thought to be more critical than the physical features. Factors that influence the social environment include the characteristics of the residents themselves, visitors or volunteers, and the staff.

Social Environment in LTC. The social environments of nursing homes are influenced by the social climate and contact with other residents (Schenk, Meyer, Behr, Khulmey, & Holzhausen, 2013) and the institutional rules that prevent people with disabilities from being integrated into the social interaction and activities of the nursing home (Lubinski, 1995). Traditionally, the social and physical environments of nursing homes were not conducive to social interaction, often leading to social isolation and loneliness, particularly for those with cognitive or communicative impairments (e.g., Jacelon, 1995; Kaakinen, 1995; Motteran, Trifiletti, & Pedrazza, 2016; Schenk et al., 2013). Residents report implicit rules regarding the type and amount of talk that is acceptable in nursing homes, including beliefs that they should not bother the staff unnecessarily with conversation, talk too much, talk about loneliness, talk to those who are senile or difficult to communicate with, have private conversations in front of others, or complain (Kaakinen, 1995). Residents often perceive that they have few conversational partners and limited topics of choice to share with others (Jacelon, 1995), and spend approximately 85% of their time without any social interaction (Voelkl, Winkelhake, Jeffries, & Yoshioka, 2003).

Residents' physical and cognitive impairments are positively correlated with decreased engagement and increased conflict and distress in nursing home residents (e.g., Bradshaw, Playford, & Riazi, 2012; Mjørud, Engedal, Røsvik, & Kirkevold, 2017; Mor et al., 1995; Schroll, Jónsson, Mor, Berg, & Sherwood, 1997). When residents with disabilities attempt social integration, their efforts are often met with rejection because of this conflict and distress, propagating the social isolation. Only one-third of residents are comfortable talking with other residents (Schroll et al., 1997). Many alert residents do not want to reside with cognitively impaired residents (Lévesque, Cossette, & Potvin, 1993). Additionally, low staff to resident ratio and the presence of rigid organizational rules/regulations was related to increased disruptive behavior and decreased resident QoL (Garcia et al., 2012).

Lubinski (1995) described nursing home environments as "communication impaired environments" due to limited opportunities for meaningful communication; unfortunately, this remains true in too many LTC facilities despite some efforts to provide person-centered care. Caregiver-resident relationships are co-constructed, however, and many staff do participate in relationship-oriented communication in addition to their necessary task-oriented communication (Westerhof, van Vuuren, Brummans, & Custers, 2016). Staff who prompt residents to participate and interact may increase their QoL (Clare, Whitaker, Woods, & Quinn, 2013). Implementation of recommended changes in person-centered care with a focus on active engagement and QoL would result in these positive interactions in more care facilities. (Staff caregiver education and training interventions are discussed in Chapter 10.)

Physical Environment in LTC. The physical environment can also impact communication, functioning, and wellbeing of persons with dementia. Features of the physical environment can discourage social interaction due to a lack of private areas, poor lighting, temperature and noise, and furniture arrangements that are not conducive to interactions (Garre-Olmo et al., 2012). High temperature levels and many hours spent in the bedroom with low lighting are not conducive for wellbeing, and high noise levels are associated with less social interaction in persons with severe dementia (Garre-Olmo et al., 2012). Communication participation can be restricted by poor or absent environmental cues, visual clutter, inadequate lighting, and noisy conditions (Brush, Calkins, Bruce, & Sanford, 2012). The fear of getting lost may lead to decreased exploration and social engagement (Davis, Byers, Nay, & Koch, 2009). Additionally, the beauty shop may be the only area of a nursing home that encourages social interaction on personal topics (Sigman, 1985).

The quality of public and private spaces clearly impacts residents positively or negatively depending on the characteristics of the spaces (e.g., Clare et al., 2013; Motteran et al., 2016; van Hoof et al., 2016). Examples of physical attributes of the environment that contribute to confusion and disorientation include monotony and repetitive elements of architectural composition that lack reference points (Marquardt, Schmieg, & Marquardt, 2009), such as long white hallways with many equally spaced doors (Passini Pigot, Rainville, & Tétreault, 2000). Elevators, floor patterns, dark lines, and dark surfaces can cause anxiety and disorientation (Passini et al., 2000). Inadequate lighting in public areas (Netten, 1989) and poor signage (Rule, Milke, & Dobbs, 1992) are also detrimental to persons with dementia.

Both physical and social environment interventions are necessary to maximize independence, and to promote participation, engagement, and QoL of persons with dementia. Physical interventions target types of spaces available and specific design features. Other interventions emphasize modifications to the social environment and activities programming, using individual and group activities or intervention approaches, such as programs designed to maintain identity and personal interests, to be creative, and to engage in social participation, as discussed in the following sections.

Evolution of Culture Change Policies and Models of LTC

Even though over 50 years have passed since Lindsley (1964) proposed the use of prosthetic environments (i.e., supportive physical and social environments to overcome the sensory and social barriers faced by persons with dementia), progress in implementation of supportive environments has been slow and most of the changes have occurred in the last 10–20 years, as the culture change of person-centered care (PCC) has grown. PCC promotes choice, dignity, respect, self-determination, and purposeful living for persons with dementia (Kitwood, 1997; Kitwood & Bredin, 1992). The PCC culture change movement of the past two decades (Weiner & Ronch, 2003) has prompted the development of a variety of LTC models (e.g., the Eden Alternative, Green House/Small House, Wellspring, and Pioneer Network) to transform LTC from task-oriented to person-centered and to create less "institutional" and more "homelike" environments (Robinson & Gallagher, 2008). The aims of these models are to maintain a sense of wellbeing by: reducing confusion, agitation, and depression; improving social interaction and engagement; prompting maintenance of daily living activities; and triggering memory to maintain communication, social function, and mobility (Bourgeois et al., 2015; Kitwood & Bredin, 1992).

Dementia-specific environmental designs, such as special care units in the nursing home or "memory care" facilities, were developed to decrease the complexity of the environment, use sensory stimuli and cues to increase orientation and awareness, and create a low-stimulation and comfortable environment (Gitlin, Liebman, & Winter, 2003). Innovative LTC models also focus on the social environment, such as the relationship-centered approach of Evercare (Kane, Keckhafer, Flood, Bershadsky, & Siadaty, 2003). Aging in Place (Szanton et al., 2011) is a model that enables persons with dementia to stay home longer by providing services in the community instead of LTC. The QoL of LTC residents was evaluated in an extensive study of 350 assisted living and nursing homes: the Collaborative Studies of Long-Term Care (Zimmerman, Sloane, Heck, Maslow, & Schulz, 2005a). Better QoL was found in persons with dementia when facilities had specialized workers who received more training to encourage more participation in activities (Zimmerman et al., 2005b). Other notable factors included staff involvement in care planning, staff that provided choices and supported resident decision-making, positive resident-staff communication, and the use of fewer antipsychotic and sedative medications.

With the burgeoning PCC movement in many countries, the late 1990s into the 2000s saw a LTC culture change that put resident choice before institutional efficiency. For example, in the United States since 2000, the Centers for Medicare and Medicaid Services (CMS) revised regulations to better reflect this shift in priorities, mandating that facilities provide environments that promote autonomy, preferences, and choice, and the assistance necessary for people to fulfill those choices. See Box 7.1 for examples of how CMS changed the guidance for over 20 of their key regulatory segments, called Tags (483.15(b), Tag F242).

The ABLE Model. As described in Bourgeois et al. (2015), the ABLE model (Roberts, Morley, Walters, Malta, & Doyle, 2015) is a new person-centered approach to dementia care, incorporating elements from a social ecological model (Galik, 2010) and the Montessori method

---

Box 7.1 Examples from CMS (2000) Regulations (Tags in Parentheses)

The Resident has the Right to:

- Choose activities and schedules (F242).
- Interact with members of the interdisciplinary team, friends, and family both inside and outside the care community (F172 and F242).
- Make choices about aspects of his or her life in the care community that are important to him or her (F242).
- Participate in care planning F280).
- Refuse treatment (F155).
- Both quality of care (F309) and QoL (F240) that recognizes each individual and enhances dignity.
- Achieve the highest practicable level of wellbeing (F309).
- The same rights as any resident of the United States (F151).

(Montessori, 1964), which is inherently person-centered. The four core areas of the model are: A) abilities and capabilities of the resident, B) background of the resident, L) leadership, cultural change, and education, and E) physical environment changes (Roberts et al., 2015). The ABLE care model was trialed on one unit of the Wattle facility in Rural Northwest Healthcare in Australia. Sixteen residents lived on the unit: 10 had severe cognitive impairment; 12 received antipsychotic medications; 11 received sedatives. Implementation consisted of key features: stakeholder engagement; staff education and training on Montessori activities and ongoing support from a dementia consultant for 18 months; and home-like interior and exterior environment modifications. Stakeholder engagement involved implementation planning meetings with residents, families, staff, nurse unit manager, a dementia consultant, a cognitive rehabilitation therapist, and a project manager. Eighteen staff received two days of dementia care training, two days of Montessori activity training, and ongoing support from a dementia consultant for 18 months. Colorful, home-like interior spaces were designed with interactive wall spaces for specific uses (e.g., music, reading, physical activities, social interaction, domestic activities), personalized doors, and use of signage and name badges. (See Box 7.2 for aspects of the ABLE model and Figure 7.1 for a photo of a flower arranging activity station.) An exterior space was designed with many features of a rural home environment (e.g., chicken coop, raised garden beds, BBQ).

Changes in "person-centeredness of care" as a function of the training were documented. The Tool for Understanding Residents' Needs as Individual Persons (TURNIP; Edvardsson, Fetherstonhaugh, & Nay, 2011) was used to survey staff and families before training and 12–14 months after implementation. Results showed improved staff knowledge and attitudes about dementia, the person-centeredness of the care organization, and the content of the care provided. There was a marked reduction in medication usage with 100% elimination of antipsychotic usage and sedative usage decreased from 67% to 2% (Roberts et al., 2015). Additionally, resident responsive behaviors due to unmet needs were reduced markedly. Staff testimonials highlight the positive changes that result from this program (see www.youtube.com/watch?v=dYN7I87bXeY).

Box 7.2 The ABLE Model (Roberts et al., 2015)

Core ABLE areas:

A = abilities and capabilities of the resident
B = background of the resident
L = leadership, cultural change, and education
E = physical environment changes

Key Features of Implementation:

1. Stakeholder engagement
2. Education and training in dementia care and Montessori principles for activity programming
3. Ongoing support from a dementia consultant for 18 months
4. Environmental modifications using Montessori principles to create a home-like atmosphere

(See www.youtube.com/watch?v=1LCRrcxlrXE)

FIGURE 7.1   Flower Arranging Activity Station in a Facility using the ABLE Model

Source: Roberts et al., 2015. Used with permission from Anne Kelly.

Montessori for Ageing and Dementia

Maria Montessori developed the Montessori approach to educating children, with an emphasis on self-paced learning and developmentally appropriate activities, and this idea has been applied to intervening with persons with dementia (Camp, 1999; Camp et al., 1997). Montessori for Ageing and Dementia resulted from the collaboration of researchers from Australia, Canada, and the US who were implementing similar programs in their countries. This approach extends PCC and emphasizes a team approach to provide a prepared physical environment for persons with dementia. The Montessori approach encourages care providers to view persons with dementia as still having preserved competencies that can be capitalized upon to promote a satisfying life (Bourgeois et al., 2015). Elliot's *DementiAbility* program (Ducak, Denton, & Elliot, 2016; Elliot, 2011) incorporates Montessori principles and focuses on the person's abilities, needs, interests, and strengths. Worthwhile and meaningful roles are created during routines and activities that are conducted within a supportive environment. The creation of a prepared and supportive physical environment was based in part on evidence for the benefits of using visual cues with persons with dementia (e.g., Bourgeois, 2013). This program relies on staff training and a team approach, as well as organizational changes that require a commitment by nursing home leaders to implement changes to care 24 hours a day (Bourgeois et al., 2015). Elliot also encourages facilities to record and evaluate outcomes of incorporating the *DementiAbility* program. Improvements have been shown in one facility on quality indicators such as medication usage, number of falls, infection rates (Grandview Lodge, 2013), and data are being collected in other facilities.

While people sometimes associate the Montessori approach simply with activities, Montessori for Ageing and Dementia encompasses all aspects of care for persons with dementia. The Association Montessori Internationale (AMI; http://ami-global.org) formed an Advisory Committee to develop training standards, materials, and a certification program for Montessori for Aging and Dementia (Elliot, Kelly, Brush, & Bourgeois, 2015). See Box 7.3 for the Montessori for Ageing and Dementia Charter. The overall aim of the program is to provide opportunities for adults with dementia to be enabled, engaged, and enriched in a prepared environment. This can be achieved by gaining the commitment of LTC leaders to facilitate major changes in operations, providing on-site education on the program for all staff, and conducting follow-up visits to ensure implementation fidelity.

> ## Box 7.3 Montessori for Ageing and Dementia Charter (AMI, 2015)
>
> All older adults and persons with dementia have the right to a caring community that is aligned with the individual's needs, interests, abilities, skills, and strengths for optimal social, emotional, physical, and cognitive support. This environment is carefully prepared to meet and nurture the needs of each person, providing opportunity for success, choice, enhanced independence, and self-initiated activity. Lives are enriched through the engagement in roles, routines, and activities, fostering a sense of belonging and wellbeing.
>
> (Available at http://brushdevelopment.com/wp-content/uploads/2015/09/AMIMAGAD Brochure-6_2015.pdf)

The Montessori for Ageing and Dementia approach instructs staff to assess each person upon joining the community to learn their individual strengths, interests, and needs. They invite residents to engage in individualized activities and provide a role for the person to contribute meaningfully to the community (e.g., arranging flowers for dining tables, passing out hand towels, or saying a blessing before meals). Personalized memory cues are developed for ease of navigation in personal and private spaces within the environment. This approach has a team focus and staff training. All staff members including dietary, housekeeping, and recreation staff receive didactic training, as well as individualized feedback and mentoring. These interventions can also be implemented in the home setting after educating families and home care staff about the philosophy and process.

Evidence for Person-Centered Care Approaches

While regulations (e.g., CMS regulatory segments in the United States) provide a framework for excellence in PCC, they have not been fully realized across the spectrum of LTC settings. A review of 24 studies of person-centered interventions found some beneficial effects for residents' psychological wellbeing, decreased behavioral symptoms, and psychotropic medication use in LTC residents with dementia (Li & Porock, 2014). PCC and/or person-centered environments were examined in a randomized controlled trial (RCT) in 38 homes with 601 persons with dementia (Chenoweth et al., 2014). Quality of care interactions and resident emotional responses to care showed improvements, but there were no additive benefits for QoL or agitation. Variability in the level of detail in program or intervention descriptions (e.g., staff training and degree of program implementation) limits the strength of the current evidence for PCC approaches, and rigorous measurement of PCC is needed (Bourgeois et al., 2015). Program implementation depends on the institutional management environment, such as the degree to which the management supports and helps the staff to carry out PCC (Li & Porock, 2014). Measures of sleep, mood, responsive behaviors, and ADL functioning should be included in outcome measures of wellbeing, in addition to the typical measures of psychological functioning. More rigorous research is needed to guide development of future PCC approaches.

Physical Environment Interventions

As noted in the discussion of the ABLE and Montessori for Ageing and Dementia models, a prepared and supportive environment is important for wellbeing and functioning of persons with dementia (Bourgeois et al., 2015). Nursing home leaders, clinicians, and families can capitalize on the environment to promote maximum safety, functioning, and QoL for persons with dementia (Day, Carreon, & Stump, 2000; Gitlin et al., 2003; Marquardt, Bueter, & Motzek, 2014; Soril et al., 2014). The goals of adaptations to the physical environment include: to decrease responsive behaviors; to increase wellbeing; to provide safety and reduce exiting behaviors; to improve privacy and dignity issues; to increase activities, participation, and engagement. Effective environmental interventions accomplish these goals by following these principles: (1) decrease environmental complexity by relaxing the rules and the expectations for residents and by minimizing distractions for residents; (2) increase orientation and awareness using sensory stimuli and cues; (3) create a comfortable environment with low to medium stimulation (Gitlin et al., 2003). The priority of the strategies should be to provide predictability, familiarity, and structure while also meeting the needs of the staff. Some of these environmental changes have also been found to benefit staff and relationships between staff and residents (Lee, Chaudury, & Hung, 2016). Staff reported that smaller-scale environments create a more homelike feel and promote social interaction between staff and residents, improving QoL for residents and work experiences for staff (Lee et al., 2016).

While there are limitations in the number and methodologies of studies, evidence from systematic reviews shows that environmental interventions are beneficial to persons with dementia (e.g., Marquardt et al., 2014). Soril et al. (2014) examined the effectiveness of built environment interventions in treating BPSDs among residents in LTC settings in a literature review from 1995 to 2013, finding a broad range of interventions. There was not convincing evidence for one type of intervention over others, and no studies reported worsening of responsive behaviors following a built environment intervention. Many older facilities are not ideal buildings, but positive changes can be made using effective design elements involving furniture arrangements, lighting, and décor. Some new facilities are being built based on the evidence for effective environmental features, usually resulting in a more homelike rather than institutional feel of the setting (Bourgeois et al., 2015). For example, use of plants, animals, artwork, adequate lighting, furniture arrangements, and interior finishes have a significant influence on persons with dementia and their wellbeing (e.g., Brawley, 2002; Brush et al., 2012; Calkins, 2001, 2005; Danes, 2002; Day et al., 2000; Forrest & Cohen, 2004; Gitlin et al., 2003; Noreika, Kujoth, & Torgrude, 2002; Teresi, Holmes, & Ory, 2000; Zeisel et al., 2003).

Building Design and Structure

Several structural characteristics appear to impact persons with dementia. A noninstitutional design, especially in dining rooms, creates a more homelike feel. Facilities with a residential character and common spaces that varied in ambiance and provided activities or music were associated with reduced social withdrawal and depression (Anderiessen, Scherder, Gossens, & Sonneveld, 2014; Gotestam & Melin, 1987; Zeisel et al., 2003). Smaller units create a more conducive environment for functional behaviors and for wayfinding (Marquardt et al., 2009). The size and structure of doorways, and the size, shape, and pattern of hallways/connective spaces can affect freedom of movement and functioning. Doors between rooms can be removed or added depending on the need for the space; e.g., removing a door may facilitate room finding, such as finding the bathroom. Circular designs with rest areas can be used to allow the residents to walk without being obstructed or reaching a dead end (Forrest & Cohen, 2004).

A common link between major activity centers of the facility (e.g., craft rooms, hair salon, courtyard, and offices) that is open to both interior and exterior spaces allows the residents to see what is going on in the next space, and to either observe or join in activities of interest (Danes, 2002). On the other hand, many facilities have long hallways with a nursing station located somewhere on the hall with residents often lined up facing into the hallway, rather than facing each other. A negative impact from long hallways on residents' behavior was found in two studies: residents displayed higher restlessness and anxiety (Elmståhl, Annerstedt, & Åhlund, 1997), and more violence (Isaksson, Astrom, Sandman, & Karlsson, 2009). Even with a long hallway, modifications can be made, such as arranging furniture so that residents may sit and face each other, which may encourage interaction.

The availability and location of common versus private spaces with freedom of movement between them is important (Danes, 2002). Informal, common areas were just as important as, if not more important than, the formal areas for structured activities; residents tended to congregate and socialize in a more natural way, such as sitting on couches or at kitchen tables to talk within the informal common areas (Danes, 2002). Residents also need private and personalized spaces (Anderiesen et al., 2014; Morgan & Stewart, 1998; Sigman, 1985; Zeisel et al., 2003). Buildings can either be designed with private bedrooms or with other private rooms that residents may use, particularly with visitors. The lack of private spaces in care facilities restricts residents' opportunities for meaningful conversation with family and other visitors. Many family-focused activities require an element of "family only" participation that require privacy so that families can maintain connections, particularly as the person is less able to participate in outings (Anderiesen et al., 2014).

Privacy and personalized spaces are related to behavioral health outcomes, such as reduced anxiety, aggression, and psychotic problems, and improved sleep (Morgan & Stewart, 1998; Zeisel et al., 2003). Additionally, choice and control over one's social and physical environment was associated with positive adjustment, and sustained health and wellbeing (Kane & Kane, 1987), and confirms personal identity and meaning of spaces. Furniture, the arrangement of rooms, personal possessions, and familiar routines within the care setting can reinforce one's personal identity and enhance QoL (Calkins & Cassella, 2007; Rubinstein & de Medeiros, 2005).

Visual Strategies and Cues

Visual Barriers. Visual strategies and cues can be implemented to improve functional behaviors and engagement, and to decrease wandering and exit-seeking behaviors. The illusion of barriers

---

Box 7.4 Environmental Design

A multilevel care facility was designed with the changing levels of needs of persons with dementia in mind. On the dementia unit, there was a kitchen and a living room with a fireplace. There was also an enclosed courtyard that the residents could freely access, with only one door from the dementia unit. The SLP observed that the residents seemed at home in this setting and would invite her to sit in their kitchen or by their fireplace to talk. They would also congregate together, sitting at the family-style kitchen table. Once they needed a higher level of skilled care, the residents were moved to a skilled nursing unit. Here, the residents could congregate in a lounge area. This time, the lounge area was across from the nurses' station, enclosed in glass, so that the nurses could keep an eye on the residents at all times. The lounge was designed with several different interest areas, including a variety of sensorimotor activities and tactile stimuli that residents with severe cognitive deficits could enjoy. The SLP observed that there seemed to be more interaction among residents and fewer incidents of agitated behaviors or repetitive questions directed at the nurses, as the residents were not lined up facing the nurses' station, and they had interesting activities to pursue.

can be created to improve safety and decrease wandering (Padilla, 2011). Consideration should be given to the design of entrances and exits to buildings or floors (Day et al., 2000; Gitlin et al., 2003; Zeisel et al., 2003). Covers can be placed on panic bars and doorknobs to decrease exit behaviors. Creative visual stimuli can be used to disguise exits to reduce exit attempts, such as camouflaging exit doors or elevators with cloth barriers or wall murals, and placing grid patterns or mirrors in front of doors. Some residents with milder cognitive impairments may still detect the door by people coming and going (Kincaid & Peacock, 2003; Mazzei, Gillian, & Cloutier, 2014). Additionally, well-camouflaged exits and silent electronic door locks rather than alarms can result in fewer residents with depression (Zeisel et al., 2003), and less instances of agitation (Kincaid & Peacock, 2003). Wall murals can also contribute to a less institutionalized feeling of the facility (Kincaid & Peacock, 2003). See Box 7.5 for a description of a door mural used to increase safety, with photo shown in Figure 7.2. Additionally, color contrasts and patterns can be used to create the illusion of barriers, such as dark patterns against light, which are perceived as three-dimensional and create the illusion of steps or holes in the floor (Passini et al., 2000).

Object Arrangement. Objects and furniture can provide interest areas and stimuli to engage the resident and to decrease wandering behavior and agitation. The objects in the environment should be age, gender, and culturally appropriate (Mahendra, 2001). Objects should also facilitate the residents' mood and recall of fond memories, and provide a sense of security. As discussed in Chapter 6, external aids support the ability to recall memories and focus the communication context (e.g., toys and memory wallets). Memory boxes, rotating displays of artwork, and themed interest areas are possible interventions that can make visits with family or friends more enjoyable, and decrease wandering and agitation (Cohen-Mansfield & Werner, 1998; Forrest & Cohen, 2004; Guwaldi, 2013). Memory boxes can also help staff to get to know the residents on a more personal level and to connect with them (Guwaldi, 2013). Some facilities use rotating displays of artwork in the hallways to give the residents and their visitors something to talk about, perhaps making visits more enjoyable.

Cohen-Mansfield and Werner (1998) found that walking paths with multisensory activity centers resulted in decreased exit seeking, better mood, and better engagement with family members. Similarly, Forrest and Cohen (2004) described a building that was designed to control agitation. The facility also had home-like themed living areas and smaller activity centers that were

---

Box 7.5 Use of Door Murals to Increase Safety

Nursing home residents with dementia were frequently exhibiting door testing on locked, alarmed doors that went into the facilities management areas of the building (e.g., laundry, facilities maintenance). Some residents would figure out the code to the doors, and others would "sneak" in behind a staff member, posing a safety concern for residents and a challenge to staff members. The SLP suggested a door mural across the doors, specifically with an ocean scene because many of the residents of the facility lived close to the ocean. The idea was that the residents would enjoy looking at the ocean scene, but would not want to enter. The under-the-ocean scene was not quite what the SLP had in mind, but it worked! At first, some residents appeared to examine the mural to figure out what it was. Others simply stopped paying attention to the doors altogether. Within a few days, the door-testing behaviors had nearly disappeared and this extremely low rate of door opening attempts has remained for several years. The administrator was so pleased at this cost-effective, successful intervention that she had the painter create a mural on another door, also with success.

FIGURE 7.2   Door Mural to Decrease Resident Entry Attempts to Facilities Management Area

designed to encourage the residents to linger and become engaged in an activity (e.g., music, reading, games, or congregating with other residents). The results of such design features resulted in a greater community sense and more interaction and engagement (Hikichi et al., 2015).

Signs can also be used to increase orientation and wayfinding, as well as participation in activities (see Figure 7.3). Signs should be large and easy to understand, but in addition, residents need to be trained to use the signs, as signs alone may not impact residents' orientation (Day et al., 2000). Brush, Camp, Bohach, and Gertsberg (2015) found that only signs that were designed

FIGURE 7.3   Sign in Resident's Room to Remind Her to Look at Her Activity Calendar and Attend Activities

---

Box 7.6 Examples of Interventions to Support Wayfinding and Orientation

- Signage designed using input from individuals with dementia regarding colors and choice of icons improved wayfinding ability (Brush et al., 2015)
- Memory boxes outside resident rooms (Gulwadi, 2013)
- Memorable reference points (landmarks)
- Consistent association of activities with certain locations (Zgola, 1990)
- Signage that illustrates the contents or activities in a room (Van Hoof, Kort, Duijnstee, Rutten, & Hensen, 2010)

---

based on resident preferences for font size and color were effective for increasing wayfinding and independence; lime green, royal blue, and raspberry colors were preferred sign colors by persons with dementia.

Sensory-Enhancing Adaptations

Sensory overstimulation and understimulation can both contribute to confusion and agitation, and even hallucinations, in persons with dementia, so caregivers need to strike a careful balance in the level of stimulation (Day et al., 2000; Gitlin et al., 2003; Marquardt et al., 2014). Recommendations include removing unnecessary clutter, eliminating overstimulating televisions, alarms, and overhead paging, and providing tactile stimulation in surfaces and wall hangings (Day et al., 2000). Zeisel et al. (2003) found that one of the most significant factors in behavioral correlates of health is understandable and controlled sensory stimuli. Residents who can comprehend sensory stimuli have less verbal aggression and agitation, and fewer psychotic problems (Burgio, Scilley, Hardin, Hsu, & Yancey, 1996; Cohen-Mansfield & Werner, 1997; Zeisel et al., 2003). Thus, clinicians should attend to all types of sensory deficits and stimuli of residents.

Vision. Nursing home residents are more likely to have visual impairments than older adults living in the community (West et al., 2003), which reduce the eyes' ability to receive light, to adapt to changes in light, to tolerate glare, and to discriminate color (Noell–Waggoner, 2002). Aging often results in altered color perception due to the lens yellowing, slower adaption times between different light levels, and the requirement for more light than a younger person (Bouma, Weale, & McCreadie, 2006). Older adults with dementia often have visual perception deficits (Hwang, 2014), with reduced depth perception and the loss of contrast sensitivity (Shikder, Mourshed, & Price, 2012). Visual impairments are a predictor of increased falls, greater dependency on others for activities of daily living, and difficulty identifying and understanding objects in the environment (Skelton et al., 2013).

Clinicians should be aware of the visual deficits and abilities of residents and how the types of stimuli in the environment may affect functional abilities. Visual characteristics that should be considered in design features include quality and quantity of light, colors and color contrasts, and size of stimuli (Brush, Meehan, & Calkins, 2002; Noell–Waggoner, 2002; Teresi et al., 2000). Consideration should be given to the contrast between different elements in a room; lack of contrast can act as a barrier to functional behaviors. For example, a white toilet on a white floor can be difficult for a person with dementia to perceive. These features should be considered not just for building design, but also for other stimuli such as types of signs and décor (Brush et al., 2002, 2015).

Older adults need more light exposure, with less glare from light sources or reflective surfaces, and flicker-free lighting, uniformity in ambient lighting, and a balance of daylight and artificial light (Brush et al., 2002). Standards for the quantity and quality of light needed should be used, with uniformity in ambient lighting, and a balance of daylight and artificial light without glare (Noell-Waggoner, 2002). Sheers should be used to reduce glare while letting light in, rather than room-darkening blinds. Older adults require three to five times more light than younger adults. Light should be oriented toward the visual task of interest and not into the person's eyes, and she suggested that for the best color rendition, lamps with a high rating on a color-rendering index (scale of 100) should be used.

When planning for task lighting, planners should ensure that task lights (e.g., a desk lamp) are in reach and easy to use (Noell-Waggoner, 2002). Rather than having lamps with small switches that are hard to find underneath the lampshade, the facility should use lamps that turn on and off by touching the base. Finally, Teresi et al. (2000) suggested the use of yellow rather than blue fluorescent or incandescent lighting to reduce glare. Strategies should be used to minimize glare to increase resident comfort, minimize falls, and maximize attention span include, e.g., some flooring materials absorb glare, and light-colored fabrics and paints softly reflect the light. Additional strategies are use of light fixtures that shield the light source and reduce glare; transitional spaces (e.g., entry lobby) between indoors and outdoors to allow persons to adjust to different levels of brightness (which can take up to 10 minutes); and maximizing daylight from windows through light-shelves, which reflect light on to the ceiling thereby reducing glare (Brawley, 2006; Brawley & Taylor, 2001; Figueiro, 2008; Noell-Waggoner, 2004).

Because of the lower levels of light that are received into an older person's eyes, color may not be discriminated properly. High-contrast color usage can be used to compensate for this, such as black on white backgrounds or blue on yellow backgrounds (Teresi et al., 2000). Teresi et al. advised against the use of blue and green together, as these colors will not be discriminated from each other properly. The use of colors with medium tone is good because those that are darker than medium are seen as gray or black (e.g., navy or burgundy). To maximally plan colors, clinicians can obtain a gray scale from an art supply store to ensure the most useful contrasts, or one is available in the Environment and Communication Assessment Toolkit (Brush et al., 2012). Wall colors that are a medium tone with a light color on ceilings (Noell-Waggoner, 2002), or in a neutral color with contrasting colors to highlight thresholds, and extra light and contrasting colors to underline the presence of obstacles (Teresi et al., 2000) are best for older persons with dementia.

Bright Light Therapy. In a systematic review of 33 environmental interventions, bright light therapy appeared to regulate mood and sleep–wake cycles in some individuals (Padilla, 2011). Some researchers suggest that nursing home residents need opportunities to be exposed to bright natural light (Martin et al., 2006), either by going outdoors or sitting in a heated atrium (Torrington & Tregenza, 2007). Morning bright-light exposure is more effective in reducing depression than evening-light exposure (Joseph, 2006; Wallace-Guy et al., 2002). Supplementing natural daylight with bright artificial lighting has similar health benefits for regulating circadian rhythms (Joseph, 2006). When a constant level of light intensity was maintained to control for the effects of natural daylight changes across the afternoon, there were improvements in behavior (La Garce, 2004). In contrast, a dawn–dusk light therapy had no effects on behavior, cognition, depression, or sleep (Fontana et al., 2003). Increasing overall levels of illumination has been found to reduce the number of night time awakenings and excessive daytime sleeping while controlling for glare and temperature (Joseph, 2006; Martin et al., 2006; Shochat, Martin, Marler, & Ancoli-Israel, 2000; Torrington & Tregenza, 2007). More research on this approach is needed.

Acoustics and Auditory Stimuli. The acoustic atmosphere of most facilities is not conducive to residents' functional abilities. For example, Sloane, Mitchell, Calkins, and Zimmerman

(2000) measured sound pressure levels of 60–70 decibels in dining rooms and at nursing stations; this is the level of loud conversation. Noise levels in care settings have been found to exceed recommendations by the Environmental Protection Agency of 40–50 decibels (Bharathan et al., 2007). Teresi et al. (2000) reported that there is a relationship between noise and negative functional outcomes. Noise may create negative impacts on wellbeing (Garcia et al., 2012) and amount of social interaction (Garre-Olmo et al., 2012).

Given that most residents have hearing disabilities, environmental planners should consider the auditory stimulation and acoustics of each space, and efforts should be made to create a good acoustic environment or to improve the acoustic properties of the space. Auditory interventions can be used to reduce agitation and to increase functional behaviors. A physical space that dampens acoustic stimuli, such as with curtains in the dining room and carpet in high traffic areas (Alessi & Schnelle, 2000; McClaugherty & Burnette, 2001), will improve the acoustic properties, but many residential facilities avoid the use of carpets because they are harder to keep clean. Acoustical ceiling tiles also dampen acoustic stimuli (Brawley, 2006; Brawley & Taylor, 2001; Joseph & Ulrich, 2007; Mahmood, Chaudury, & Gaumont, 2009). On the other hand, hard, nonporous surfaces cause sound to bounce from one surface to another, creating a difficult acoustical environment for older adults (Alessi & Schnelle, 2000; Brawley & Taylor, 2001). Low-noise equipment is helpful, or isolating noisy equipment (e.g., ice machine) into separate rooms (Brawley, 2006; McClaugherty & Burnette, 2001), and using maintenance equipment should be scheduled to minimize disruption (Brawley, 2006).

Burgio et al. (1996) reported the positive effects of environmental "white noise" (e.g., water sounds) audiotapes on verbal agitation in nursing home residents with severe dementia. In the Gitlin et al. (2003) review, eight studies involved some form of auditory stimulation (e.g., soothing music, natural sounds, or white noise), and three studies evaluated music in combination with other sensory-based strategies. (Music-based interventions will be discussed later, under combination strategies.) Gitlin et al. found that 10 out of 11 studies reported improvements after auditory interventions. There were many methodological inconsistencies, however, that made it difficult for Gitlin et al. to make specific recommendations based on the findings. For example, the amount and type of exposure to auditory stimulation differed across studies, outcome measures differed, and different interventions did not always result in different results. Gitlin et al., however, did note that it appears that some form of soothing auditory sounds reduces agitation.

Another aspect of auditory intervention that is often overlooked or not attended to adequately is that of hearing aid usage by residents with dementia. Hearing aids are often underutilized in nursing homes with one barrier being excessive background noise (Pryce & Gooberman-Hill, 2012). Palmer, Adams, Bourgeois, Durrant, and Rossi (1999) studied the impact of hearing aid usage on responsive behaviors in eight persons with Alzheimer's disease residing at home. Family caregivers completed pre- and post-treatment outcome measures. Participants wore their hearing aids for 4–13 hours per day. After hearing aid treatment, one to four responsive behaviors were significantly reduced for all participants. Based on a hearing handicap instrument, nearly all caregivers indicated that hearing handicap had been significantly reduced. Palmer et al. also noted that those with the lowest cognitive function received the least benefit from wearing hearing aids. The care plan for residents with hearing impairment should include that nursing staff ensure that hearing aid batteries are working and the hearing aids are worn consistently.

Outdoor Environments and Therapeutic Gardens

Persons with dementia, particularly those who live in care facilities, often do not get adequate exposure to the outdoors. Increasing free access to the outside, including to therapeutic gardens, may increase the QoL of persons with dementia (Brawley, 2002; Day et al., 2000). Studies have reported the benefits of horticultural therapy and garden settings in the reduction of pain and falls, improvement in attention, lessening of stress, and lowering of "as needed" medications and antipsychotics, which are important factors in improving the QoL and possibly reducing costs in long-term care (Detweiler et al., 2012). Exposure to therapeutic gardens can also reduce agitation, even if looking out of a large window at the garden (Edwards, McDonnell, & Merl, 2012). Therapeutic gardens with safe, secure outside spaces may offer many other benefits as well, including encouraging walking and other forms of exercise, providing opportunities for socialization and sensory stimulation, as well as providing other fun and meaningful activities (Brawley, 2002; Edwards et al., 2012). Access to therapeutic gardens reduced elopement attempts and improved sleep (Stewart, 1995). Therapeutic gardening for people with young-onset dementia resulted in a renewed sense of purpose and increased wellbeing, despite cognitive decline (Duggan, Blackman, Martyr, & Van Schaik, 2008; Hewitt, Watts, Hussey, Power, & Williams, 2013). A number of factors should be considered in planning for therapeutic garden designs, including: making the space highly visible to residents, through a large window, atrium, or outdoors (Brawley, 2002; Detweiler et al., 2012; Edwards et al., 2012); selecting appropriate plants (Detweiler et al., 2012); creating interesting walking paths, ensuring smooth paving surfaces that curtail glare and walking surfaces that are slip resistant, creating clearly distinguishable borders of the pathway, using uniform texture and color on the pathway, and providing spaces for privacy as well as activities (Edwards et al., 2012). Outdoor spaces can include open spaces for exercise, nooks for solitude or visits with family (Brawley, 2002; Whear et al., 2014), and porches for doing activities, resting, or eating. If residents have access to outdoors, they may also engage in other purposeful, physical activities, such as raking, or hanging clothes on a line. These activities may be enjoyable and stimulating for residents who were accustomed to completing them previously. Having the opportunity to engage with natural sensory stimuli, such as plants, flowers, trees, and wildlife, can enhance the QoL of persons with dementia (Brawley, 2002; Edwards et al., 2012). For those who are not able to go outdoors but enjoyed gardening, an activity can be done with real or artificial flowers to engage the person with that interest (see Figure 7.4).

FIGURE 7.4   Gardening Activity

Social Environment Interventions: Individual and Group Activities

Clinicians and families should ensure that persons with dementia are able to maintain participation in the meaningful and satisfying activities of one's daily life through individualized care plans. It is the enjoyment and gratification from particular activities that contribute to our uniqueness as individuals. Unfortunately, many activities based on premorbid hobbies and interests are complex and require the skills that are deteriorating due to dementia. A classic example of decreased participation is when the avid poker player's friends ask his wife to plan alternate activities for the usual poker day so they can avoid confronting him with the fact that he can no longer play competitively. Another example is when the devoted letter writer deflects questions about her much shorter and simpler letters with comments like "I'm so busy lately, I can hardly keep up with my writing." Another example of symptomatic behaviors is the lay reader who begins to decline invitations to participate in the church service with the excuse, "I need to get my glasses checked." This change in participation often occurs too slowly to be noticed by others and is rarely attributed to memory impairment. However, the avoidance of familiar activities and social withdrawal do, in fact, signal the individual's emerging awareness that cognitive skills are not as sharp as they once were. A complete list of familiar and pleasurable hobbies and activities, past and current levels of participation in those activities, and a rank ordering of the most important activities to maintain for future enjoyment should be obtained. With this information, the interdisciplinary team can focus on designing supportive strategies for the most important activities.

Social and Participation Barriers

As the language and cognitive skills of persons with dementia deteriorate with advancing disease, their social partners develop increasingly negative impressions of their ability to maintain social competence and independence (Lubinski, 1995). This is particularly problematic in the nursing home environment, where caregivers' lowered expectations of the residents contribute to activity limitations and the condition of premature "learned helplessness." It is also a problem in home and community settings, when caregivers and families assume the duties and responsibilities of the person with dementia (e.g., managing finances) and relieve them of others (e.g., driving). Social withdrawal, depression, and decreasing participation in favorite activities are signs of the need for intervention. Researchers have begun to document the types of preserved language and cognitive abilities that can help adults with dementia maintain a socially interactive life. QoL among adults with dementia depends in part on the frequency and quality of verbal interactions they have with their caregivers (Bourgeois, Dijkstra, & Hickey, 2005).

Thus, clinicians should also attend to social groups, particularly in day care or LTC facilities. Professionals can identify the organization and composition of social groups, as well as the interactions within these groups (Gitlin et al., 2003). Some examples of strategies for increasing socialization include the simulated presence of family members via audio or video recordings (e.g., Woods & Ashley, 1995) or via personal message cards (Evans, Cheston, & Harris, 2015), structured group activity programs (e.g., Camp & Skrajner, 2004), animal-assisted interventions (e.g., Bernabei et al., 2013), and intergenerational programs (e.g., Galbraith, Larkin, Moorhouse, & Oomen, 2015). Clinicians should examine the evidence for interventions, or the theory and principles behind interventions when there is no scientific evidence available for an intervention (i.e., the intervention is based only on expert opinion). The interventions recommended here apply learning principles to dementia intervention and target everyday functional behaviors, rather than abstract underlying cognitive skills (Holland, 2003); as noted in Chapter 6, abstract cognitive training is not supported by evidence for generalization to improvements in functional behaviors.

Maintaining Self-Identity Through Social Roles and Adapted Work

Successful communicative interaction allows adults with dementia to remain part of social networks and to maintain their roles in these networks. Certain roles, such as a teacher, advice giver, or nurturer, are some of the common ways that people interacted with each other throughout their lifetime; these familiar interactions tend to follow script-like sequences. Camp and Skrajner (2004) demonstrated that adults with early-stage dementia were able to function as group leaders for a small-group activity of memory bingo. They were able to learn procedures involved in leading a group and were able to engage in this role effectively. Similarly, Camp et al. (1997) reported on the preserved teaching role behaviors demonstrated by residents with severe dementia when asked to interact with toddlers using Montessori materials.

Fulfilling a helping or teaching role may have additional psychological benefits, such as higher self-esteem and wellbeing (Liang, Krause, & Bennett, 2001). Dijkstra, Bourgeois, Youmans, and Hancock (2006) examined the effects of two different information-providing roles, an advice-giving role and a teacher role, to assess whether preserved knowledge in community-dwelling adults with moderate dementia could be activated, resulting in qualitatively different conversational content as a function of assigned roles. Study 1 examined differences in language production for a social conversation versus an advice-giving role. Participants were asked, in counterbalanced sessions with the experimenter, to converse about or to provide advice about three topics (marriage, children, and church). Study 2 assessed the extent to which adults with dementia were able to assume a teacher role and to demonstrate preserved knowledge of action sequences and instructive language during a cooking task. In both studies, participants were expected to fulfill these roles by drawing from previous experiences in the remote past as a parent, sibling, or friend, when they gave advice or taught others how to make a recipe. The results confirmed that adults with moderate dementia were able to fulfill role-specific tasks notwithstanding deficits in short-term memory, working memory, and episodic memory, as long as these tasks took place in an appropriate social and communicative context and as long as the role to be fulfilled was adequately triggered. These findings suggest that preserved discourse and role-related abilities in adults with dementia may allow these individuals to engage in interactions involving active, established social roles. Successfully assuming specific roles may also contribute to a better QoL and more rewarding social interactions with peers and caregivers.

In another study of community-dwelling persons with early to moderate dementia, Maddox and Burns (1999) described the development and evaluation of the Adapted Work Program (AWP), a sheltered workshop for male veterans attending a day care program. This work program was based on conceptual models from occupational therapy (i.e., the Allen cognitive disabilities framework; Allen, 1988) and from nursing (i.e., the progressively lowered stress threshold; Hall & Buckwalter, 1987). The AWP provides structured work activities at different performance levels to enhance self-esteem and meaningful roles. The types of work tasks included collating and stapling print materials, labeling envelopes, inspecting and sorting surgical towels, folding blankets, and portioning and wrapping food for the cafeteria. To allow for continued success, demonstrations, visual cues, and other strategies and adaptations were provided for the more moderately impaired participants. Results of a pilot study of 12 individuals who attended the four-hour-per-day program three days a week for a full year revealed positive effects on participants' mood, as measured by the Geriatric Depression Scale (Yesavage et al., 1983), and some improvement on a self-esteem measure (Rosenberg, 1965); control subjects showed declining scores on the same measures. Furthermore, participants and caregivers reported feelings of success in task performance, and of satisfaction with the work role and the maintenance of social relationships.

Maintaining Participation in Social Groups

Question–Asking Reading. Activity programming for LTC residents and adult day clients may include a "current events" group or newspaper reading by a staff member. However, for persons with dementia, this type of activity often leads to disruptive behaviors or passivity due to the length and/or complexity of stories read, or the lack of familiar context for the stories. For persons with dementia who have strengths in reading skills, Question-Asking Reading (QAR) is an alternative intervention that can promote participation in newsgroup activities through the use of written cues (Stevens, Camp, King, Bailey, & Hsu, 1998; Stevens, King, & Camp, 1993). QAR utilizes external prompts to encourage active participation and to facilitate increased comprehension of the text that is read. The suggested routine for the group activity follows: Orientation involves talking about the day's activity as well as general orientation information, such as the day, date, and surroundings, then introduction to the passage; written cue cards for questions are distributed, designed to prompt discussion about the story to be read; a two-paragraph text is distributed and read, with one group member reading the first paragraph, and group members taking turns asking questions using their cue cards to think of questions about the text; then the next paragraph is read and questions are asked.

Results of a QAR study revealed that participants interacted more with each other and with staff, and exhibited better text comprehension and better retention of the information, as compared to typical reading groups. It is important to note that the role of the leader is significant in engaging the participants in the QAR procedure initially, but with repeated exposure to the QAR procedures, participants require fewer prompts to read in turn, ask and answer questions, and offer novel insights on the topic. This type of activity could be modified to meet the cognitive needs and abilities of the group members, for example, modifying the passage length and complexity, and/or the specificity of the cue cards. The idea is to have the group members actively engaged in a reading and discussion activity, rather than passively listening to a staff member or volunteer read to them. See Case 7.1 for an illustration of such activities.

Poetry–Writing Groups. Other reading-related interventions, such as book clubs and poetry-writing groups, have been developed to enhance communication and reminiscence and to prevent the negative predicament of excess social disability (Ryan, Meredith, MacLean, & Orange, 1995). Poetry-writing groups evolved from reminiscence sessions where a group leader would stimulate conversation on a specific topic (e.g., spring, the beach, and school days), write down the memories and feelings of participants, and then read aloud the phrases as poetry (Hagens, 1995; Koch, 1977;

Box 7.7 Suggested Routine for Question-Asking Reading

- Orientation
- Distribute question cue cards (e.g., "Ask about a word that is hard to say," "Ask about the main idea," "Ask about what happens next," "Ask about a specific detail in the story," and "Ask if anyone knows additional information on this topic.")
- Distribute two-paragraph text
- Group reading of paragraph 1
- Question asking
- Group reading of paragraph 2
- Question asking

(Source: Stevens et al., 1993)

Case 7.1 Illustration of Maintaining Participation

An SLP began working in a LTC facility in the fall of 2001. Each day she would walk past the activity room, often hearing an activity assistant reading the newspaper to a group of residents. There were many stories in the newspaper that the SLP felt were inappropriate to read to the residents because they might be negatively impacted by hearing such bad news every day, while possibly not fully understanding what was happening in the world (e.g., stories about anthrax in mailings, terror threats, and the war in Afghanistan). She was concerned about the impact of these stories on the residents' wellbeing. The SLP worked with the activities assistant to teach her to use the Question-Asking Reading technique to engage the residents in reading stories of interest from their past that would encourage them to use their intact remote memories and interests in discussions about the readings.

Schuster, 1998). In Hagens' (1995) "reminisce and write" group, participants wrote down words into a poetry format. Then researchers solicited objects related to the poem from family members to construct a remembering box with photographs and other personally relevant objects from the person's past life that elicited memories and conversation when shared with staff and family. The remembering box, a framed copy of their poem, and a large photograph of the resident were displayed in the resident's room; the authors conducted staff in-services and encouraged staff to use the materials with residents over a 14-month period. Staff reported using the boxes and poems as communication tools, to learn the histories of the residents, and to redirect residents during periods of agitation or sadness.

A review of the literature found that family and nursing home staff reported improved self-esteem of residents and improved relationships with staff and family after reading the writings of the group (Hagens, Beaman, & Ryan, 2003). More recently, Petrescu, MacFarlane, and Ranzijn (2014) conducted a one-on-one short structured interview with the four participants of a series of poetry writing workshops and found they all reported benefiting from the workshops, but their experiences differed greatly. Themes included competence and self-efficacy, personal growth, wanting to contribute, and poetry writing as a way of coping with the progression of the condition.

Timeslips™. *Timeslips™* (George & Hauser, 2014) is a story-telling activity that prompts improvisational stories with surreal picture cards (e.g., an elephant sitting next to a girl on a park bench). Open-ended questions are used by facilitators to initiate storytelling while the participants' responses are written down by a scribe and turned into a story that is read back to the group periodically. These whimsical stories entertain participants while also containing details from the participants' lives. Research on *TimeSlips™* has identified specific benefits for residents (increased creativity, improved QoL, positively altered behavior, and involvement in meaningful activity), for staff members (learning new practices, developing a deeper understanding of residents, involvement in meaningful activity, and thinking creatively around programmatic challenges), and for the nursing home community (nurturing relationships and improved atmosphere) (George & Hauser, 2014).

Maintaining Lifelong Interests Through Modified Activities

Strength-Based Programming Eisner (2001, 2013) developed an approach for the selection of interest-appropriate materials and activities that is based on the personal strengths and interests of the individual. This intervention approach was developed using the theory of multiple intelligences (Gardner, 1983, 1993), which is the idea that all persons have individual strengths and weaknesses, and that their areas of strength can be identified in the types of activities and the career path that they have chosen. In addition, persons with dementia continue to demonstrate areas of relative strength, often reflecting premorbid interests, which should be identified and capitalized on in designing activities for them. Both editions of Eisner's manuals provide "can-do" activities that capitalize on each of the multiple intelligences to increase engagement and QoL of persons with dementia, and can be modified as cognitive deficits worsen (Bourgeois, 2001). Examples of activities that can be conducted across each domain of multiple intelligences are displayed in Table 7.1. See Case 7.2 for an

TABLE 7.1 Strength–Based Programming Based on Theory of Multiple Intelligences

Intelligence Types	Examples of Activities
Verbal-linguistic	Communication cards, memory wallets, and word games
Logical-mathematical	Card and board games, jigsaw puzzles, and organizational tasks
Visual-spatial	Crafts and picture games
Tactile-kinesthetic	Dance, exercise, ball games, and dolls and plush toys
Auditory-musical	Music, sound games, and toys with sound effects
Interpersonal	Discussions, drama, storytelling, group games, and dolls and toys
Intrapersonal	Writing journals, collages of personal items, and solitare
Naturalistic	Picnics, nature walks, gardening, animals, nature shows and videos, and science games and activities

Source: For strength-based programming, Eisner (2001, 2013); and for theory of multiple intelligences, Gardner (1993).

Case 7.2 Illustration of Modifying an Activity – Scrabble

Level 1. In the game of Scrabble, participants select seven random tiles with letters of the alphabet and attempt to formulate words with the letters for the maximum possible points using a game board. Words are placed on the game board in a crossword puzzle format, to intersect with existing words on the board. The game continues until participants' tiles no longer form words to add to the board. The winner has accumulated the most points from the added values of his or her individual word plays. This game requires good vocabulary, spelling, attention, prediction, and working memory skills.

Level 2. To simplify the rules of the game, Scrabble could be played without the game board, eliminating the crossword puzzle aspect of the game. Players can select randomly seven letter tiles and attempt to formulate a word with the letters. On each player's turn, he or she can place the word in the middle of the table for all to see; scores can be accumulated by adding the values of each letter tile for each word played. If no word can be formulated, players can use a turn to trade in tiles.

Level 3. Scrabble letter tiles can be used for a word- and/or letter-matching game. Word cards can be prepared in advance on topics of interest (e.g., school days: pencil, paper, teacher, math, science, spelling, etc.), and players uncover tiles from the pile in the middle of the table to match the letters on their card. As a group activity, players can take turns picking a tile and matching it to their card; as a solitary activity, a person can match tiles to letters on the word card for as long as this activity is engaging.

(Based on Bourgeois, 2001; Eisner, 2001, 2013)

example of how a favorite activity can be modified with cognitive deterioration. Also see Figures 7.5 and 7.6 for examples of strength-based activities: a photo of a reading or conversation book with tactile stimulation for those who have verbal and tactile-kinesthetic interests, and a photo of a basket of yarn that could be used to make something, to talk about the different colors and textures, or simply to feel and manipulate.

Handbag Intervention. There is no limit to the types of personalized activities that have been developed and modified to satisfy the need for meaningful and interesting ways to engage persons with dementia. Buse and Twigg (2014) explored the role of handbags in the everyday lives of women with dementia. Their study revealed the significance of handbags in supporting the women's identities. The bags and the objects inside served as "biographical" and "memory"

FIGURE 7.5 Conversation Book about Pets with Tactile Stimulation

FIGURE 7.6 Basket of Yarn for Reminiscence or Tactile Stimulation

FIGURE 7.7 Joke Book for a Modified Joke Telling Activity

objects. Also noteworthy, the handbags were used to create personal or private spaces for the women. Creative arts activities may also provide an avenue for maintaining interests and identity, but these will be discussed separately later.

Montessori–Based Activities. As noted previously, the Montessori for Ageing and Dementia approach is a holistic model that goes beyond activity programming to the overall way that care is delivered. However, some clinicians and caregivers might use Montessori-based activities without having the DementiAbility (Elliot; www.dementiability.com) training or the whole program implemented in their facilities. These activities provide learners with cognitive stimulation and opportunities to interact successfully and meaningfully with their environment. They contain explicit cues about how to complete the activity. They also focus on recognition, rather than recall, making them ideal activities for persons with dementia to promote maintenance of previous skills and strengths. Camp and colleagues developed successful interventions that use Montessori principles for persons with dementia in adult day programs (Judge, Camp, & Orsulic-Jeras, 2000) and LTC settings (Camp et al., 1997; Orsulic-Jeras, Judge, & Camp, 2000; Vance, Camp, Kabacoff, & Greenwalt, 1996), and evaluated them with well-designed, controlled, and quasi-experimental studies. Participants have included persons with dementia interacting with each other (e.g., Camp & Skrajner, 2004), with preschool children (e.g., Camp et al., 1997), with staff (e.g., Schneider, Diggs, Orsulic, & Camp, 1999), or with family members (Schneider & Camp, 2002).

In two manuals of Montessori activities for persons with dementia, a series of activities that involve the active manipulation of concrete materials in purposeful, personally relevant ways are described with instructions (Camp, 2001; Joltin, Camp, Noble, & Antenucci, 2012). Montessori activities provide learning tasks in sensory, motor, and abstract domains that encourage independence, confidence, and contributions to society. Each activity is started at a simple level and gradually increases in complexity while providing structured repetition, immediate feedback, and a high probability of success to promote unconscious learning. This type of learning is based on priming, motor learning, and implicit memory, which are relatively spared in AD and related dementias (Camp, 1999). Some examples of the types of activities are tool use and scooping for fine and gross motor skills; sound, scent, color, and shape identification and sorting for sensory skills; and counting and conceptual sorting for abstract cognitive skills. See Table 7.2 for further examples of activities.

When older adults with dementia were asked to show preschool children how to complete Montessori tasks, they were able to do so easily and without prompting (Camp et al., 1997). Participants appeared to have a positive self-perception and increased sense of self-worth, reduced behavior problems, and more functional behaviors when serving in this teacher role (Camp et al.). Furthermore, Montessori activities resulted in significantly more constructive engagement, less passive engagement, and more pleasure (Orsulic-Jeras et al., 2000). Training persons with early-stage dementia to be leaders of a small-group Montessori-based activity for persons with more advanced dementia resulted in effective leader skills and increased engagement, satisfaction, and

TABLE 7.2 Examples of Montessori Programming Activities

Type of Activities	Examples
Motor	Scooping, polishing objects, cylinder blocks, dressing frames
Sensory	Sound cylinders, scent identification, tactile sorting, color and shape matching
Abstract	Number rods and counting, sandpaper letters, sorting tasks (e.g., emotions, or plant versus animal), geography activities

Source: Camp (1999) and Camp et al. (1997).

pleasure in comparison to standard activity programming by activities staff (Camp & Skrajner, 2004; Skrajner et al., 2014). Schneider and Camp (2002) reported positive benefits of training family visitors to use Montessori activities; residents had significantly more active and less passive engagement with visitors, and the visitors reported that they felt significantly less burden in their visits and that they saw positive changes in their loved ones.

Pleasant Events. Pleasant Events interventions were first applied to older adults with depression (Zeiss & Lewinsohn, 1986), and then to home-dwelling persons with dementia and their caregivers, based on the premise that engaging in desired pleasant activities would reduce feelings of depression. Using the Pleasant Events Schedule–AD (Teri & Logsdon, 1991) to identify a comprehensive list of desirable activities, Teri, Logsdon, Uomoto, and McCurry (1997) first trained caregivers to increase the frequency of these specific Pleasant Events in the daily routine of the person with dementia. They then trained caregivers to use problem-solving strategies, using a Behavior Therapy–Problem-Solving intervention, to overcome the barriers preventing the implementation of increased pleasant events. Results revealed that Pleasant Events–Problem-Solving interventions are correlated with lower levels of reported depression in persons with dementia.

Nursing assistants (NAs) were trained to perform individualized activities with residents of a dementia special care unit (Lichtenberg, Kemp-Havican, MacNeill, & Johnson, 2005). The activities were identified on each resident's Pleasant Events Schedule–AD (Teri & Logsdon, 1991) or were suggested by the NAs. A mixed design was used to examine the effects of this intervention on residents' wellbeing. For residents in the experimental group, the program involved an explanation of the relationship between daily activities and one's feelings, relaxation exercises, mood ratings (on a scale of 1–10) before and after the activities, and a 15–20-minute individual activity. Examples of activities included engaging with correspondence (e.g., cards and letters), reminiscing, socializing, pampering, bird watching, reading, walking, and fixing things. See Case 7.3 for an example of the need for Pleasant Events for residents with dementia. Results for the experimental group revealed a significant improvement in the Behave – AD (Reisberg et al., 1987), as well as fewer troublesome and dangerous behaviors after treatment and higher mood ratings

---

Case 7.3 Illustration of Pleasant Activities

A woman moved into a nursing home after her husband died and her children realized how much their father had been compensating for her memory deficits. She appeared quite depressed, which exacerbated her cognitive deficits. The staff discovered that a former church friend of hers was living in the facility, and put them in the same room. The women were often found together, wandering the facility looking for something to do. Sometimes one woman would begin to cry and ask when she could go home, and the other would then either try to console her or also become upset. The facility administrator found the women trying to leave the building one day, so he asked them to help out with a task. He gave one woman a ball of yarn, and handed the other woman the end of the yarn and asked her to unroll the ball and make a new one. When the SLP saw the women sitting near the front door, engaged in this activity, she asked what they were doing. One woman answered, "Somebody asked us to make a new ball of yarn out of a perfectly good ball of yarn. They must think we're 'cuckoo' or something!" The SLP then walked the women to the activities room and asked them to assist with folding placemats that had been laundered. The women were much more pleased with this activity, and as the staff began giving them more pleasant and meaningful activities to do, the women had fewer crying episodes and escape attempts.

immediately after the activities; in contrast, the control group displayed more troublesome behaviors after the study. Thus, Pleasant Events interventions can reduce responsive behaviors and increase opportunities for positive engagement in home-dwelling or LTC residents with dementia. This intervention is supported by randomized controlled trials.

Simple Pleasures. Simple Pleasures is a therapeutic recreation activity that is designed to reduce isolation, inactivity, and agitation (Buettner, 1997, 1999; Kolanowski, Buettner, Costa, & Litaker, 2001). The idea behind Simple Pleasures is to provide age- and stage-appropriate recreational items for nursing home residents and to teach staff, families, and volunteers how to make and to use the items to interact with the residents. Simple Pleasures items consist of a variety of handmade, therapeutically based sensorimotor recreational items (e.g., an activity apron, an electronic busy box, a look-inside purse, and squeezies). The types of Simple Pleasures designed by the investigators reflected the Need-Driven Dementia Compromised Behavior Model (Algase et al., 1996; Kunik et al., 2003) discussed in earlier chapters. See Table 7.3 for examples of Simple Pleasures, and Case 7.4 for an example of a client for whom a toolbox was used to increase engagement and decrease responsive behaviors. See Figure 7.8 for an example of a crocheted

TABLE 7.3 Simple Pleasures

Type of Activity/Stimulation	Examples
Sensori-motor activities	Squeezies (balloons filled with bird seed); stuffed fish, butterfly; patchwork sewing cards; "wave machines" (e.g., starry nights or ocean wave – plastic bottle filled with mineral oil, glitter, star-shaped sequins, or seashells)
Reminiscence, language, cognitive	Look-inside purses, briefcases, and tackle boxes; home decorator kits (e.g., book of wallpaper, carpet, fabric, and paint swatches); message magnets: words and phrases on magnet strips; picture dominoes and bingo; dolls
Tactile manipulation; sensorimotor	Table ball game (roll tennis ball into wooden box with holes); latchbox (wooden board with various latches, hinges, and locks to manipulate); activity aprons
Heat	Hand muff; hot water bottle cover; lap blanket
Ambulatory	Wanderer's cart (made with PVC pipe)

Source: Buettner (1999).

Case 7.4 Case Illustration of a Memory Box for Engagement

Mr. Pearson, who worked as a mechanic for over 70 years, entered a LTC facility. Mr. Pearson was not able to discuss details of his work, nor did he initiate interactions with other residents. He often wandered around the facility looking for something to do, frequently manipulating objects and looking for things to "fix." An activities assistant made a memory box constructed from a toolbox, labeled with the name of the auto body shop where the man worked for all those years. Inside, she put toy cars, pictures of cars and car parts, tools, and other memorabilia that would allow the resident to reminisce about his time as a mechanic. The staff were instructed to place the toolbox near the resident whenever he began wandering and looking for something to do. Mr. Pearson's troublesome behaviors decreased, and the staff enjoyed interactions with the resident related to his favorite topic.

FIGURE 7.8   Crocheted Handmuff with "Twiddlers" for Tactile-Kinesthetic Engagement

handmuff with "twiddlers" sewn on for those who enjoy tactile-kinesthetic engagement, and Figure 7.9 for a doll wearing clothes with "twiddlers" sewn on for those who enjoy interacting with a doll or manipulating the objects for tactile-kinesthetic stimulation.

In a study using a crossover design, Buettner (1999) found decreased agitation, increased engagement and interaction, and increased frequency of and satisfaction with family visits when Simple Pleasures were given to nursing home residents with dementia. Additionally, Simple

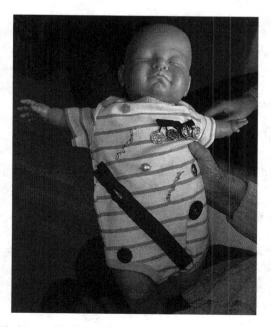

FIGURE 7.9   Doll with Clothing with "Twiddlers" Attached

Pleasures interventions can be very economical, as Buettner recommended that volunteers (e.g., church auxiliaries or guilds) make them. In Buettner's project, 450 volunteers were trained to make the items. In a small treatment study, Kolanowski et al. (2001) selected Simple Pleasures to enrich the physical and social environment, and matched the activities to each person's style of interest and premorbid personality traits (e.g., extraversion and openness). Results revealed that mean time on task was significantly higher during the treatment than control condition, but there was no significant difference in degree of participation between conditions. Additionally, there was increased positive affect during the treatment condition, but no difference in level of negative affect, mood, or dementia behaviors across treatment or control. However, during the treatment condition, the participants had more days when no dementia behaviors were exhibited, as compared to during the control condition.

Maintaining Connections and Interactions

Simulated Presence. Family or staff caregivers often use radio, television, and/or movies to try to occupy or entertain persons with dementia. Sometimes a person may enjoy listening to a favorite radio program, or watching a favorite movie or the same televised football game repeatedly. Eventually, however, people with dementia often lose interest, even for familiar movie classics or favorite sporting events. This is often due to under- or overstimulation with this type of activity, leading to passivity or agitation for some persons, particularly as cognitive deficits become more severe. Radio or video programs may have too much complex dialogue, and too little or too much action; there may be too much visual and/or auditory stimulation, making it difficult to understand what is happening.

Interventionists have, therefore, sought an alternative to radio, movies, and television. One such alternative is homemade audiotapes or videotapes made specifically for the individual with dementia; for example, family members may tape themselves talking to their relative, which provides a "simulated presence" (Woods & Ashley, 1995). In this intervention, a family member fills out a memory inventory form about topics that typically elicit positive emotions in the resident during visits, and then makes a personalized, interactive audiotape that contains references to preserved memories with two to three themes, repeated in different ways (e.g., important life events, loved ones, hobbies, and interests). Family members are encouraged to use phrases of affection. The tape is edited and silent pauses are added, so the resident has the opportunity to respond to the tape. This provides some form of social contact, while capitalizing on preserved long-term memories to engage the individual in reminiscing and to elicit positive emotions.

Woods and Ashley (1995) reported decreased social isolation and agitation in the residents who participated, and recommended "simulated presence" for nursing home residents who respond well to family and other familiar people. In a series of four studies, researchers have documented that SimPres audiotapes made by family members or nursing home staff reduced agitation at a rate 14% greater than usual care and 46% greater than the placebo condition, and reduced withdrawn behavior 25% more often than with usual care and double the rate of the placebo conditions (Camberg, Woods, & McIntyre, 1999). Alternatively, videotapes could be made by family members, and may also include stories, songs, or activities. A family video could be a useful tool for staff to use to comfort or redirect a confused or agitated resident. Overall, studies to support Simulated Presence Therapy show modest benefits.

Additionally, many residents do not have family connections who are able to provide the recordings. Therefore, an alternative intervention, Personal Message Cards, was developed to be more accessible. The Personal Message cards utilise commercially available talking greetings card with a short recorded audio message, and personalized with photographs if desired. Each time the card is opened, the recipient hears the message and the card can also be personalised with photographs. Evans et al. (2015) evaluated the impact of message cards, but had a poor response rate for the feedback (10/24 participants); nine of the 10 respondents reported that the goals of using the cards were met. They found that even people with severe dementia were able to benefit from the Personal Message Cards.

Video Respite™. Commercial video recordings are available for persons with dementia who do not have family to make personalized videotapes (Lund, Hill, Caserta, & Wright, 1995), or who desire more variety in videotapes. Video Respite™ videos are highly interactive and engage the person with dementia in a variety of therapeutic activities (e.g., reminiscence, music, and exercise). Individuals are encouraged to follow along and participate with the activities and conversations on the videos. Lund et al. (1995) demonstrated that Video Respite™ engages persons with dementia (e.g., smiling, laughing, and commenting) for longer periods of time than other video presentations (e.g., classic movies and television shows). Other findings included a reduction in responsive behaviors, such as complaining, withdrawing, wandering, and asking repetitive questions; reduced depression; and increased self-esteem and self-awareness. This intervention can be very useful for family members caring for a person with dementia at home, so that the caregiver can prepare dinner or take a shower without worrying about entertaining the person with dementia; staff caregivers can use Video Respite™ as an individual or group activity.

Maintaining Spirituality and Religious Practices

While research studies on interventions to maintain spirituality are limited, there is a small and growing number of papers. There are anecdotal reports on persons with dementia who can continue to participate in singing hymns or reciting prayers long after one would expect the person to be able to do so (e.g., in advanced stages of dementia, when the person has become predominantly nonverbal) (e.g., Roff & Parker, 2003; Stuckey, Post, Ollerton, FallCreek, & Whitehouse, 2002). There are also some correlational studies that investigate the impact of religious identity and/or religious attendance on cognitive function in older adults (e.g., Van Ness & Kasl, 2003). The literature that is available, as well as clinical common sense, suggests that holistic care plans for persons with dementia include meeting their spiritual and religious needs in addition to their physical, cognitive, and social and emotional needs (e.g., Bell & Troxel, 2001; Powers & Watson, 2011; Roff & Parker, 2003; Stuckey et al., 2002). The consensus is that spiritual and religious practices are meaningful activities that can offer a person a way to remain engaged; to connect with family, friends, and caregivers; and to stimulate mental activity. Because clinicians may not be familiar with or comfortable with a person's spiritual or religious practices, they should collaborate with family caregivers as well as the faith community to promote participation in spiritual and religious practices for as long as possible (Roff & Parker, 2003).

Spiritual activities should be a multisensory experience (e.g., music, aroma, touch, verbal) (Stuckey et al., 2002). Religious practices can stimulate cognitive activity because they use many domains of intelligence (e.g., verbal, musical, and emotional) and because religious services require both perception and production activities (e.g., listening to sermons, reciting prayers, and singing songs) (Van Ness & Kasl, 2003). Because people with dementia have preserved long-term memories, these strengths can be used in planning spiritual activities. For people who learned religious prayers and songs in childhood, these became overlearned and rote through ongoing practice and rehearsal. Singing hymns and reciting prayers are often more automatic verbal behaviors than engaging in more spontaneous topics of conversation (Roff & Parker, 2003). These long-remembered rituals and prayers may provide comfort and reassurance to persons with dementia. Marston (2001) developed recommendations for development and use of a prayer list that could be used with persons in the early stages of dementia and modified for those in later stages: (a) exploring the meaning of prayer and how prayer is most effective; (b) reviewing how a prayer list would work; and (c) developing and using the prayer list.

Inclusion of spiritual needs in the care plan also dignifies the person with dementia by recognizing the need to feel connected, loved, and hopeful, and to feel valued as a person and not just a patient or resident (Bell & Troxel, 2001). Furthermore, even persons with advanced dementia may have spiritual needs that must be attended to at the end of life, a time when spiritual experiences may be the most profound for an individual. Persons with dementia and their caregivers reported that they used religious or spiritual explanations to cope and to come to peace with the dementing illness. They also reported being able to use their spirituality or religion to find "gifts amid loss" (Stuckey et al., 2002, p. 204), and that it allowed them to live in the moment and to appreciate the blessings they did have. Furthermore, attention to relationships as spiritual connections assisted the persons with dementia and their caregivers in coping.

To promote continued participation in the faith community, Roff and Parker (2003) described a model of a spiritual team, called a Care Team. The Care Team model trains volunteers on ways to provide service for persons with dementia and their caregivers, and to promote their spiritual growth and practice. Where such a service is not available, clinicians should work collaboratively with faith leaders and members of the faith community to meet the needs of persons with dementia. Professional chaplains can educate staff about how to provide spiritual support and how to accommodate diversity (Powers & Watson, 2011), and SLPs can train members of the faith team how to support communication and engagement in spiritual activities; for example, SLPs can train the faith team to use compensatory strategies, such as those described in Chapter 6. Another suggestion is to incorporate spiritual or religious content into Montessori activities. For example, a Montessori activity could be sorting names of Bible characters into those from the Old or New Testament, or to arrange the verses of a hymn or prayer into the proper order.

Although many experts have advocated the inclusion of spirituality in the care plan, there is a lack of evidence to support any particular intervention recommendation. Evidence is also needed from a variety of religious and ethnic traditions, and clinicians need to be sensitive to the diversity of needs across their clients from various backgrounds (Stuckey et al., 2002). Future research should also investigate the impact of the clinician's own beliefs about spiritual and religious practices on the clinical outcomes (Marston, 2001).

Creative Arts Interventions

Creative arts interventions may encompass music, dance, and/or visual arts, or any combination of these approaches. The arts have long been considered to have positive effects on individuals and communities, and to be an integral part of health. A distinction must be made between art therapy and arts and health activities, with the former being conducted by a qualified clinical therapist and the latter being delivered by artists, educators, nurses, and museum staff (Young, Camic, & Tischler, 2016). Literature from both types of services will be discussed, but the emphasis is on how SLPs and other rehabilitation professionals and caregivers can incorporate activities that connect with past hobbies and interests in the creative arts to engage individuals with dementia, to provide cognitive stimulation, and to promote communication. Sometimes SLPs can work collaboratively with art, dance, or music therapists, but this is not always possible. If not, SLPs may incorporate some forms of creative arts activities within their scope in working with persons with dementia.

A review of 17 studies on community-based arts programs for persons with dementia revealed cognitive benefits of arts programs (Young et al., 2016). The three studies on literary arts programs included oral reading and storytelling groups (e.g., TimeSlips, which was discussed earlier in the chapter). These programs facilitate communication and discussion among participants, and may improve cognitive processes of attention and memory. The seven studies on performing arts included caregiver singing, group singing, background and live music, participatory dance and dance performance. Listening to live music had benefits for those in the early stage of dementia, with better wellbeing, communication, social contact, and participation. The most robust finding was for singing groups and programs, which resulted in better sustained attention across severity levels; persons with mild dementia also showed improvements in episodic and working memory, executive function, and general cognition. There was only one study that involved dance; students from the National Ballet School elicited reminiscence from the participants with dementia and then created and performed seasonal dances based on the stories told. Cognitive benefits were found even though the participants were not actively engaged in dancing; some discussed the memories of their young adulthood that were provoked by watching the dance. The seven studies on visual art programs included art-making, art-education, and art-viewing and also resulted in better sustained attention and provided intellectual engagement with more opportunities for social communication in those with mild-moderate severity. Encouraging persons with dementia to make art has significant benefits on episodic memory in early and moderate dementia and verbalization during interventions, and may result in increased engagement in activities and spontaneous communication. Results are promising, and more research with better methodologic rigor is needed to further examine the cognitive benefits as well as behavioral and QoL outcomes.

Persons with dementia should have the opportunity to be actively involved in creating art forms, not just listening or watching, particularly if this was an important part of their life in the past. Clinicians should apply understanding of spared cognitive processes (e.g., procedural memory) and strength-based intervention principles in engaging persons with dementia in the arts. For example, persons with dementia have been found to have intact remote procedural memory for making music, such as preserved piano-playing ability (Crystal, Grober, & Masur, 1989) and preserved rhythmic abilities in individuals in the later stages who have lost other functional skills (Clair, Bernstein, & Johnson, 1995). Pairing a preferred musical stimulus and related questions resulted in increased verbal communication and increased nonverbal engagement (Mahendra, 2001).

Given the available evidence, music therapy shows promise for managing the responsive behaviors of persons with dementia and for increasing their QoL. Clair and Ebberts (1997) found that caregivers reported more satisfaction in their visits after the onset of a music therapy program during visits with persons with dementia. This is similar to the effect of the Montessori activities described above. Chavin (2002) suggested the following options for setting up music programs for persons with dementia in LTC: (a) develop a music therapy program with a board-certified music therapist; (b) develop a specialized music program with a music therapist; (c) develop a one-on-one or small-group music program within the activity programming; or (d) bring in professional musicians to perform on a regular basis. Chavin (2002) also suggested that we keep in mind that music may change a person's mood for the better or for the worse, and that it may affect a person positively or negatively; in addition, remember that not everyone enjoys music, and some people are particularly selective in the music that is enjoyable. Finally, clinicians should evaluate the successfulness of music programs by considering a variety of issues, such as the size of the group, the response of each individual, and the appropriateness of the music selections and activities. Music therapy is supported by quasi- and non-experimental studies.

The arts are an important aspect of cultures and permeate many aspects of daily life. Music, dance, and visual arts activities should be consistent with participants' preferences in the arts, which is often related to their cultural background, age, gender, religion, ethnicity, or culture, but one should not assume what a person's preferences are based solely on knowledge of those demographic characteristics. Persons with dementia may have difficulty verbally communicating with caregivers about their preferences related to the arts. An SLP could train the caregivers to use supported communication to facilitate an interaction around preferences (and other needs), and encourage the caregivers to pay attention to the nonverbal signals that a person might exhibit regarding preferences and engagement with the arts programs.

Pet Therapy Animal-Assisted Interventions

Some behavioral and/or environmental interventions include the presence of live, stuffed, or robotic animals. Researchers have suggested that animals may stimulate remote memories and/or promote engagement in persons with dementia, possibly by providing a shared, tangible context for communication (e.g., Hopper, Bayles, and Tomoeda, 1998; Mahendra, 2001; Shibata, 2012). Dogs are often used for pet therapy, and may live at the facility, may assist in occupational or physical therapy goals (i.e., animal-assisted therapy), or may come in as a visitor for the residents with volunteers. Bernabei et al. (2013) conducted a review of 18 studies on animal-assisted interventions for people with dementia. They found positive impacts, such as decreased agitation, and improved social interaction with improved communication. Few studies assessed mood or cognitive functions; they showed better coping ability but no impact on cognitive functions. A few studies of various types of animal-assisted interventions will be discussed.

Hopper and colleagues (1998) used toys, including a stuffed dog, in the environment of four LTC residents with dementia during a conversational task and assessed communication scores. Results revealed increased information units when conversing in the presence of the toys; however, for three out of four participants, total words and frequency of verbal initiations did not change significantly in the presence or absence of toys. Results also revealed that there was no effect of how realistic the toys were. Other researchers have demonstrated that stuffed animals increased alertness, smiling, and nodding and decreased agitation (Bailey, Gilbert, & Herweyer, 1992) and that they increased life satisfaction, psychosocial function, social competence, and personal neatness and decreased depression (Francis & Baly, 1986).

Some residential facilities are including live animals as part of the environment, often cats, birds, or dogs, as the underlying philosophy is changing to make residential facilities more homelike (Thomas, 1994). While most studies and programs involve cats and dogs, a quasi-experimental study with 71 participants with dementia and 71 staff members examined the effects of an aquarium in three LTC units (Edwards, Beck, & Lim, 2014). After the aquarium was introduced, improvements were seen in terms of residents' decreases in uncooperative, irrational, or inappropriate behaviors, and better sleep. Additionally, staff reported greater satisfaction. Researchers concluded that aquariums are potentially useful interventions for dementia units.

A review of 19 studies of dog-assisted therapy conducted by Cipriani et al. (2013) found that 12 of the studies reported statistically significant outcomes related to QoL. An RCT of therapy with human–only therapist versus human plus dog was conducted with 55 people with mild-moderate dementia in three Australian LTC facilities (Travers, Perkins, Rand, Bartlett, & Morton, 2013). Participants with lower pre-treatment depression had more improvement in their depression scores when in the animal-assisted therapy condition than the human-only condition. Participants in the dog-assisted condition displayed better QoL in one facility. These promising results suggest that further rigorous research should be conducted to determine the benefits of animal-assisted therapy.

Additionally, dogs are now being trained as service animals for persons with dementia, known as "Dementia dogs," in Israel and Scotland (Coren, 2014; www.dementiadog.org). Dementia dogs are on a leash and are trained to walk ahead of the owner and lead the person with dementia home when given the command, "Home," or when a beeping signal is delivered by a family member through a GPS device. The Dementia dogs are also trained to stay with their person and alert others for help if the person with dementia is not able to walk home or if the person falls, and to track the scent of the person if they are separated. The dogs are also trained to help around the house, reminding the owner to feed the dogs and themselves, to take medicine, to use the toilet, and other basic needs. This innovation has not seen controlled studies yet, but anecdotal evidence suggests that Dementia dogs have a promising future. In a related type of project, smartphones are being mounted on a dog's back and they are trained to deliver the phone to their owner when an alarm is emitted; research evidence is limited to a case study of a healthy woman, but the aim is to train the dogs with persons with dementia (Oshima, Harada, Yasuda, Machishima, & Nakayama, 2014).

Bernabei et al. (2013) also noted the potential for robotic animal interventions. Research suggests that robotic animals (PARO) may also be used as therapeutic agents to improve QoL, with similar responses as with a live animal or baby, including stroking, holding, and talking to the robotic animal (Shibata, 2012). Preliminary evidence for use of PARO suggests that a robotic animal also has similar effects as a live animal, and may reduce depression and agitation, and improve communication. Animal visitation was investigated across three types of visits between 18 women with dementia in long-term care and a 17-year-old boy visited the persons with dementia in three conditions: alone, with a live dog, and with the SONY robotic "pet" (AIBO) (Kramer, Friedmann, & Bernstein, 2009). The residents responded positively to all three types of visits, but the visits with the live animal or robot prompted more interaction than without an animal. Interestingly, the AIBO produced the best results with increased resident-initiated conversation and longer eye gaze than with the live animal, which holds promise for the future of animal therapy.

Overall, more evidence is needed, but there is enough evidence to say that some persons with dementia can benefit from animal-assisted interventions, ranging from animal companions or visitors to therapy assistants to service dogs. Clinicians should determine whether pets were an important part of a person's life and provide such treatments in cases where animals and pets may be soothing. Even for those who were not pet owners, animals may improve QoL and increase opportunities for interaction. The positive findings of stuffed animals are encouraging, given concerns about animal allergies or any other hygienic concerns that may arise in care facilities. Clinicians may introduce such interventions and make careful observations to provide evidence for each of their clients. See Case 7.5 for examples of responses to animal-assisted interventions.

Intergenerational Programming

Intergenerational programming can be used in adult day programs, assisted living, nursing homes, or older adults' own homes. Earlier intergenerational programs were prompted by federal policies and academic initiatives (Aday, Rice, & Evans, 1991; Aday, Sims, & Evans, 1991; Baecher-Browii, 1997; Chamberlain, Fetterman, & Maher, 1994), and then grew with the increased emphasis on service learning, which incorporates community service into education, in colleges and universities throughout the United States (Campus Compact, 1994). Intergenerational programs can be an important antidote to the growing divide and decreasing interactions across generations (George, Whitehouse, & Whitehouse, 2011). These programs have been utilized across disciplines, including social work (Gesino & Siegel, 1995; Wilson & Simson, 1991), occupational therapy (Greene, 1998), psychology (Fretz, 1979), sociology and anthropology (McGowan, 1994; McGowan &

Case 7.5 Examples of Responses to Animal-Assisted Intervention by Three Women with Alzheimer's Dementia

All three women had severe cognitive-linguistic deficits with the majority of spoken language production unintelligible.

Reactions to a live dog:

- Display positive affect and begin to talk intelligibly immediately, e.g.:

  - "Aren't you just the cutest little thing. You're the cutest puppy, aren't you?" (repeated)
  - "I bet they're hungry. They want a cookie." After giving treats, the dog began to beg for more, and she replied, "You're a greedy one. You want more cookies."

- Stroke the dog's head or back.

Reactions to a mechanical cat that makes "meow" sounds, purrs, and moves its head and front paws:

- Hug and stroke the cat.
- Speak to the cat in complete and intelligible sentences.
- One woman was engaged meaningfully with the cat for 20 minutes without cues.

Blankenship, 1994), gerontology (Yamashita, Kinney, & Lokon, 2011), and speech-language pathology (Arkin, 1996).

Intergenerational programs and service learning have common requirements of reciprocity of benefits for both the recipient and provider of services (Greene, 1998). Benefits for both groups of participants may include a sense of being part of a larger society, improved self-esteem, and increased awareness of progress in one's own life (Aday, Sim, & Evans, 1991; Chamberlain et al., 1994). Additional benefits for older adults may include receiving needed services, and for the students, decreasing ageism, gaining practical experience, and increasing interest in gerontology careers. Intergenerational programs appear to be a valuable mechanism to decrease social isolation and to improve societal integration of youth and older adults. Qualitative reports of college students' journals (McGowan & Blankenship, 1994) and reaction worksheets (Gesino & Siegel, 1995) showed that the students modified their self-identity and decreased ageism as a result of their experiences with older adults.

A small study with experimental control was conducted in which older adults with dementia who were in the intervention group volunteered in hour-long structured sessions in a kindergarten class and an older elementary class in alternating weeks for five months (George & Singer, 2011). Results revealed that the older adults in the intervention group experienced less stress, which the researchers noted as an important finding given that stress might be a risk factor for dementia, and this increasingly common intervention could potentially modify that risk factor. This study took place at the Intergenerational School, a charter school in Cleveland, OH, which aims to bring the generations together for creative exchange; the school may ultimately provide a useful way to nurture social and civic responsibility and to address needed social challenges (George et al., 2011).

There is a growing body of literature providing evidence for the impacts of intergenerational programs. A scoping review of 27 articles reported that the most common types of intergenerational programs involved music, visual and performing arts, and narrative and storytelling programs; other programs incorporated Montessori, education, mentorship, and recreation activities (Galbraith et al., 2015). There were three themes across the studies: program design, outcomes for the youth, and outcomes for the persons with dementia. When there are mutually beneficial or meaningful activities, intergenerational programs can provide benefits to students as well as to the persons with dementia. Outcomes for youth were categorized into perceptions of aging and dementia, behavior, mood and enjoyment, and skill development and character building. Outcomes for the persons with dementia were categorized into sense of self (purpose); mood, with largely positive impacts on affect; behavior, with improvements in many studies in positive and on-task behaviors and a decrease in agitation; and social engagement and engagement in activity. The researchers concluded that, despite methodological flaws in the study and too small a number of studies to compare across interventions, intergenerational programs are supported by evidence. They noted that education and training of facilitators and youth participants is necessary prior to the intergenerational interactions.

Finally, some of the programs described in previous sections have included an intergenerational component, for example the roles study by Dijkstra et al. (2006), the Montessori program conducted between preschool children and residents with dementia (Camp et al., 1997), and the Volunteers in Partnership program (Arkin, 1996; Mahendra & Arkin, 2003). Other activity-based interventions could also be easily carried out within an intergenerational context (e.g., strength-based programming, Pleasant Events, and art therapy programs).

Conclusion

Evidence is available now to support the implementation of interprofessional interventions that modify the physical and/or social environments of persons with dementia. While progress has been made in developing innovations in person-centered care, the future of dementia care needs to see stronger research studies and better implementation of evidence-based environmental modifications and behavioral interventions. Interventions should capitalize on preserved abilities and personal strengths and interests to promote maximum functioning and QoL in persons with dementia. Further, many of the behavioral interventions, and some of the physical environment interventions, are low-cost interventions, particularly when compared to the amount of money that is spent on medications that have little evidence for improving BPSDs or QoL. Given limited resources across most countries and settings, clinicians are urged to join the culture change movement to implement these low-cost, person-centered interventions to improve participation and QoL of persons with dementia in whatever setting they may be residing or receiving services. Lastly, SLPs sometimes have to educate other members of the care team about our role and appropriate referrals. See Box 7.8 for an example of how to gain support for SLP services. Also see Box 7.9 for a list of resources that could be used by clinicians or suggested to families for implementing nonpharmacological interventions.

Box 7.8 Illustration of Gaining Support for Services

An SLP started a new job in a nursing home. She was eager to implement the strategies she had learned about in her training. The SLP whom she replaced, however, worked only with residents with dysphagia or dysarthria. After a few weeks, the SLP's caseload had decreased and she had time to screen other residents. One resident of interest to the SLP was Mrs. Franklin, who sat in the hallway and spit at, kicked, punched, and called names to people walking by. The SLP spoke to the nursing staff about Mrs. Franklin's responsive behaviors and her lack of positive interactions with others, and requested a referral for intervention. The social worker and nursing staff stated, "Why would you see her? What could you possibly do with her?" The SLP did a chart review, and found that this was actually a change of condition – Mrs. Franklin previously did not initiate any interaction and was very lethargic most of the time. Based on the ability to document this change in condition, and Mrs. Franklin's increased potential to participate in treatment given her increased alertness, the SLP was able to obtain the referral. The SLP learned that Mr. Franklin lived in the independent apartments next to the facility. When he visited, Mrs. Franklin was quiet and content, but they rarely talked. Mr. Franklin was skeptical but more than happy to have someone attempt to help his wife to communicate. The SLP went to his apartment and worked with Mr. Franklin to select pictures of Mrs. Franklin's life and family, and to make a memory wallet. This couple had a tremendously interesting life together! Mrs. Franklin was very pleased to read the memory wallet and converse about the topics. She told stories of living in Europe; recalled her daughter, who had died at the age of 18; and was proud to discuss her accomplishments as a teacher. Her husband sat and watched, with tears rolling down his face, as he discovered that his wife had not forgotten all these important details of their life – she just needed assistance to recall them and to converse about them. Furthermore, the staff began to surround Mrs. Franklin, rather than avoid her, because they wanted to know more about the amazing things this woman had done in her life. The responsive behaviors quickly disappeared because Mrs. Franklin now had a way to initiate positive interaction with many conversation partners. The memory wallet also kept her mind stimulated when she was alone. The SLP soon had such a big caseload (including many residents with cognitive-communication disorders) that she had a waiting list and the rehab company had to send in an extra SLP to help her catch up with all the referrals!

Box 7.9 Resources

Resources for Activities and Engagement

101 Activities, Alzheimer's Association: www.alz.org/living_with_alzheimers_101_activities.asp

Activities to do with Your Parent Who Has Alzheimer's Dementia, Judity A. Levy: Ms. Levy is an Occupational Therapist with personal and professional experience with persons with Alzheimer's dementia; published by CreateSpace Independent Publishing Platform

Alzheimer's Store: products designed for persons with Alzheimer's such as puzzles, therapy dolls, one-button radio, simple music player, painting activities, games, and activity boards; www.alzstore.com/alzheimers-dementia-activities-s/1673.htm

Best Alzheimer's Products: products for entertainment (e.g., simple music player, flipper remote control, one-button radio, DVDs, Video Respite series, CDs), nurturing and comfort activities (e.g., dolls and stuffed animals), reading and photographic collections, coloring books, and other activities; http://store.best-alzheimers-products.com/

Can Do Activities for Adults with Alzheimer's Disease: Strength-based Communication and Programming, Eileen Eisner: published by Pro-Ed Inc.

Creating Moments of Joy (5th ed.), Jolene Brackey: published by Purdue University Press

Dementiability: information, workshops, videos, publications, and other resources on Montessori methods for dementia; www.dementiability.com/

Engaging and Communicating With People Who Have Dementia: Finding and Using Their Strengths, Eileen Eisner: published by Health Professions Press

Keeping Busy: The Dementia Activities Specialist: games, books, and activities for persons with dementia and professionals delivering group programs; http://keepingbusy.com/puzzles-for-dementia/

MindStart: products designed by an occupational therapist for persons with dementia for leisure and stimulation including puzzles, games, coloring books, word games, books, and lacing cards; www.mind-start.com/Alzheimers-and-dementia-products-from-MindStart.html

Montessori-Based Activities for Persons with Dementia, Volumes 1 & 2, Cameron J. Camp: published by Health Professions Press

My House of Memories app, National Museums Liverpool and Innovate Dementia: interactive collection of images, music, and information on objects from life in England from 1920 to 1980 to facilitate reminiscence and exploration of areas of interest; www.liverpoolmuseums.org.uk/learning/projects/house-of-memories/my-house-of-memories-app.aspx

Taking Part: Activities for People with Dementia, Alzheimer's Society; https://shop.alzheimers.org.uk/books/taking-part-activities-for-people-with-dementia?search=Taking%20part&description=true

Adult Literacy Resources

New Readers Press: publisher of books for English learners, including a series of easy-to-read books for pleasure reading; www.newreaderspress.com/pleasure-reading

News for You: available from New Readers Press, subscribers have access to easy-to-read news articles; text audio can be played in full or sentence by sentence; www.newreaderspress.com/news-for-you-online

News in Levels: post news stories from around the world written in three levels with the option to listen to the audio recording of the text; simplified text and audio recording of *Robinson Crusoe* is also available; www.newsinlevels.com/

Shadowbox Press: publisher of a collection of books for persons with dementia; www.shadowboxpress.com/products/conversation-cards-two-deck-set

Two-Lap Book series, Health Professions Press; www.healthpropress.com/product/two-lap-book-series/

Emma Rose Sparrow, author, available through Amazon CreateSpace Independent Publishing Platform: series of books designed for persons with Alzheimer's disease; www.amazon.com/Emma-Rose-Sparrow/e/B00N09DY10

Appendix 7.1: Speech Therapy Involvement with the Sunset Club

Ellen Hickey, Ph.D., CCC-SLP

October 12, 2001

Goals of speech therapy involvement: increase verbal participation and interaction among residents, and increase use of recognition cues for memory deficits.

Use strength–based programming: idea of multiple intelligence theory...

- Determine each person's strengths, and build on those strengths (e.g., Mrs. Jones = verbal; Mrs. Smith = motor).
- Provide necessary support in areas of weakness...

  > For example, Mrs. Smith: strengths in motor skills and weakness in verbal skills; when doing verbal activities, provide written cues for her participation, and link verbalizations to motor behaviors; and provide much positive reinforcement and opportunities for her to feel proud during motor activities.

Increasing verbal participation: whether a strength or weakness, most residents with dementia will have word-finding deficits to some extent ... need to emphasize strengths and not highlight weaknesses in this area...

- Ask open-ended questions that do not have right or wrong answers, but have many possible answers ("What do you think about...?").
- Encourage interaction for the sake of personal connection rather than to obtain right or wrong answers.
- Avoid yes–no questions if you are trying to get the residents discussing – if yes or no will answer the question, that is all you are likely to get, especially from those with weakness in verbal skills.
- Provide written cues, such as...

  - For example, if doing a naming activity, use cards that have the name printed on the picture, change the task from naming to oral reading, and then ask the resident to elaborate on it.
  - For example, if discussing current events:
    - use a poster board, dry-erase board, or easel to write names of people, places, and events.
    - give index cards to each resident with written cues related to the topic, such as "I am registered Democrat. I voted for Jimmy Carter."
    - read a brief story related to current events, give residents with lower verbal ability index cards with a question to pose to the group that is related to the story, and allow residents with greater verbal ability to answer the questions (provide them written cues as needed, such as on the dry-erase board, etc.).

- Use pictures, drawing, gestures, and pointing to supplement verbal input and output to enhance communication. Have scrap paper available near each resident to write cues or draw, or cue them to use other communication modalities to get their message across.

- Use memory books and communication cards in small-group conversation (2–3 residents) – allow residents to look at each other's books.
- Use themes to tie activities together – music, discussion, motor games, and so on.

References

Aday, R. H., Rice, C., & Evans, E. (1991a). Intergenerational Partners Project: A model linking elementary students with senior center volunteers. *The Gerontologist, 31*(2), 263–266.

Aday, R. H., Sims, C. R., & Evans, E. (1991b). Youth's attitudes toward the elderly: The impact of intergenerational partners. *Journal of Applied Gerontology, 10*(3), 372–384.

Algase, D. L., Beck, C., Kolanowski, A., Whall, A., Berent, S., Richards, K., & Beattie, E. (1996). Need-driven dementia-compromised behavior: An alternative view of disruptive behavior. *American Journal of Alzheimer's Disease and Other Dementias, 11*(6), 10–19.

Allen, C. K. (1988). Occupational therapy: Functional assessment of the severity of mental disorders. *Hospital and Community Psychiatry, 39*(2), 140–142.

Alessi, C. A., & Schnelle, J. F. (2000). Approach to sleep disorders in the nursing home setting: Review article. *Sleep Medicine Reviews, 4*, 45–56. https://doi.org/10.1053/smrv.1999.0066.

Anderiesen, H., Scherder, C., Gossens, R., & Sonneveld, M. (2014). A systematic review – physical activity in dementia: The influence of the nursing home environment. *Applied Ergonomics, 45*, 1678–1686.

Arkin, S. M. (1996). Volunteers in partnership: An Alzheimer's rehabilitation program delivered by students. *American Journal of Alzheimer's Disease and Other Dementias, 11*(1), 12–22.

Baecher-Browii, D. (1997). Why a geriatric center? *Journal of Gerontological Social Work, 28*(1–2), 163–170.

Bailey, J., Gilbert, E., & Herweyer, S. (1992). To find a soul. *Nursing, 22*(7), 63–64.

Bell, V., & Troxel, D. (2001). Spirituality and the person with dementia: A view from the field. *Alzheimer's Care Today, 2*(2), 31–45.

Bernabei, V., De Ronchi, D., La Ferla, T., Moretti, F., Tonelli, L., Ferrari, … & Atti, A. R. (2013). Animal-assisted interventions for elderly patients affected by dementia or psychiatric disorders: A review. *Journal of Psychiatric Research, 47*(6), 762–773.

Bharathan, T., Glodan, D., Ramesh, A., Vardhini, B., Baccash, E., Kiselev, P., & Goldenberg, G. (2007). What do patterns of noise in a teaching hospital and nursing home suggest? *Noise & Health, 9*(35), 31–34.

Bouma, H., Weale, R. A., & McCreadie. C. (2006). Technological environments for visual independence in later years. *Gerontechnology, 5*(4), 187–194.

Bourgeois, M. S. (2001). Matching activity modifications to the progression of functional changes. In E. Eisner (Ed.), *Can do activities for adults with Alzheimer's disease* (pp. 101–107). Austin, TX: Pro-Ed.

Bourgeois, M. S. (2013). *Memory and communication aids for people with dementia*. Baltimore: Health Professions Press.

Bourgeois, M. S., Brush, J., Elliot, G., & Kelly, A. (2015). Join the revolution: How Montessori for aging and dementia can change long-term care culture. *Seminars in Speech and Language, 36*, 209–214. http://dx.doi.org/10.1055/s-0035-1554802.

Bourgeois, M., Dijkstra, K., & Hickey, E. (2005). Impact of communicative interaction on measuring quality of life in dementia. *Journal of Medical Speech Language Pathology, 13*, 37–50.

Bradshaw, S. A., Playford, E. D., & Riazi, A. (2012). Living well in care homes: A systematic review of qualitative studies. *Age and Ageing, 41*, 429–440. doi:10.1093/ageing/afs069.

Brawley, E. C. (2002). Therapeutic gardens for individuals with Alzheimer's disease. *Alzheimer's Care Today, 3*(1), 7–11.

Brawley, E. C. (2006). *Design innovations for aging and Alzheimer's: Creating caring environments*. Hoboken, NJ: John Wiley & Sons.

Brawley, E. C., & Taylor, M. (2001). Strategies for upgrading senior care environments: Designing for vision. *Nursing Homes, 50*(6), 28–30.

Brush, J., Calkins, M., Bruce, C., & Sanford, J. (2012). *Environment and communication assessment toolkit for dementia care*. Baltimore: Health Professions Press.

Brush, J., Camp, C., Bohach, S., & Gertsberg, N. (2015). Creating supportive wayfinding for persons with dementia. *Canadian Nursing Home, 26*(1), 4–11.

Brush, J. A., Meehan, R. A., & Calkins, M. P. (2002). Using the environment to improve intake for people with dementia. *Alzheimer's Care Quarterly, 3*, 330–338.

Buettner, L. L. (1997). *Simple Pleasures: A multi-level sensory motor intervention for nursing home residents with dementia*. Binghamton, NY: Binghamton University Press.

Buettner, L. (1999). Simple Pleasures: A multilevel sensorimotor intervention for nursing home residents with dementia. *American Journal of Alzheimer's Disease and Other Dementias, 14*(1), 41–52.

Burgio, L., Scilley, K., Hardin, J. M., Hsu, C., & Yancey, J. (1996). Environmental "white noise": An intervention for verbally agitated nursing home residents. *The Journals of Gerontology Series B: Psychological Sciences and Social Sciences, 51*(6), P364–P373.

Buse, C., & Twigg, J. (2014). Women with dementia and their handbags: Negotiating identity, privacy and "home" through material culture. *J Aging Studies, 30*(1), 14–22.

Calkins, M. P. (2001). The physical and social environment of the person with Alzheimer's disease. *Aging & Mental Health, 5*(Suppl. 1), 74–78. http://dx.doi.org/10.1080/713650003.

Calkins, M. P. (2005). Environments for late-stage dementia. *Alzheimer's Care Today, 6*(1), 71–75.

Calkins, M., & Cassella, C. (2007). Exploring the cost and value of private versus shared bedrooms in nursing homes. *Gerontologist, 47*, 169–183. https://doi.org/10.1093/geront/47.2.169.

Camberg, L., Woods, P., & McIntyre, K. (1999). SimPres: A personalized approach to enhance well-being in persons with Alzheimer's disease. In L. Volicer & L. Bloom-Charette (Eds.), *Enhancing the quality of life in advanced dementia* (pp. 126–139). Philadelphia: Brunner/Mazel.

Camp, C. J. (1999). *Montessori-based activities for persons with dementia* (Vol. 1). Beachwood, OH: Menorah Park Center for the Aging.

Camp, C. J. (2001). From efficacy to effectiveness to diffusion: Making the transitions in dementia intervention research. *Neuropsychological Rehabilitation, 11*, 495–517. doi:10.1080/09602010042000079.

Camp, C. J., Judge, K. S., Bye, C. A., Fox, K. M., Bowden, J., Bell, M., … & Mattern, J. M. (1997). An intergenerational program for persons with dementia using Montessori methods. *The Gerontologist, 37*(5), 688–692.

Camp, C. J., & Skrajner, M. J. (2004). Resident-assisted Montessori programming (RAMP): Training persons with dementia to serve as group activity leaders. *The Gerontologist, 44*(3), 426–431.

Campus Compact. (1994). *Annual report*. Providence, RI: Brown University.

Chamberlain, V. M., Fetterman, E., & Maher, M. (1994). Innovation in elder and child care: An intergenerational experience. *Educational Gerontology, 20*(2), 193–204.

Chatfield, L., Christos, S., & McGregor, M. (2012). Interdisciplinary therapy assessments for the older adults. *Perspectives of the ASHA Special Interest Groups, 17*, 11–16. doi:10.1044/gero17.1.11.

Chavin, M. (2002). Music as communication. *Alzheimer's Care Today, 3*(2), 145–156.

Chenoweth, L., Forbes, I., Fleming, R., et al. (2014). PerCEN: A cluster randomized controlled trial of personcentered residential care and environment for people with dementia. *Int Psychogeriatr, 26*(7), 1147–1160.

Cipriani, J., Cooper, M., DiGiovanni, N. M., Litchkofski, A., Nichols, A. L., & Ramsey, A. (2013). Dog-assisted therapy for residents of long-term care facilities: An evidence-based review with implications for occupational therapy. *Physical & Occupational Therapy in Geriatrics, 31*(3), 214–240.

Clair, A. A., Bernstein, B., & Johnson, G. (1995). Rhythm playing characteristics in persons with severe dementia including those with probable Alzheimer's type. *Journal of Music Therapy, 32*(5), 113–131.

Clair, A. A., & Ebberts, A. G. (1997). The effects of music therapy on interactions between family caregivers and their care receivers with late stage dementia. *Journal of Music Therapy, 34*, 148–164. https://doi.org/10.1093/jmt/34.3.148.

Clare, L., Whitaker, R., Woods, R. T., & Quinn, C. (2013). AwareCare: A pilot randomized controlled trial of an awareness-based staff training intervention to improve quality of life for residents with severe dementia in long-term care settings. *International Psychogeriatrics, 25*(1), 128–139. doi:https://doi.org/10.1017/S1041610212001226.

Cohen-Mansfield, J., & Werner, P. (1997). Management of verbally disruptive behaviors in nursing home residents. *The Journals of Gerontology Series A: Biological Sciences and Medical Sciences, 52*(6), M369–M377.

Cohen-Mansfield, J., & Werner, P. (1998). The effects of an enhanced environment on nursing home residents who pace. *The Gerontologist, 38*(2), 199–208.

Coren, S. (2014, January 21). Assistance dogs for Alzheimer's and dementia patients. *Psychology Today*. Retrieved on April 17, 2017 from www.psychologytoday.com/blog/canine-corner/201401/assistance-dogs-alzheimers-and-dementia-patients.

Crystal, H. A., Grober, E., & Masur, D. (1989). Preservation of musical memory in Alzheimer's disease. *Journal of Neurology, Neurosurgery, and Psychiatry, 52*(12), 1415–1416.

Danes, S. (2002). Creating an environment for community. *Alzheimer's Care Today, 3*(1), 61–66.

Davis, S., Byers, S., Nay, R., & Koch, S. (2009). Guiding design of dementia friendly environments in residential care settings: Considering the living experience. *Dementia, 8*, 185–203. doi:10.1177/147130120 9103250.

Day, K., Carreon, D., & Stump, C. (2000). The therapeutic design of environments for people with dementia: A review of the empirical research. *The Gerontologist, 40*(4), 397–416.

Detweiler, M., Sharma, T., Detweiler, J., Murphy, P., Lane, S., Carman, J., Chudhary, A., Halling, M., & Kim, K. (2012). What is the evidence to support the use of therapeutic gardens for the elderly? *Psychiatry Investig, 9*(2), 100–110.

Dijkstra, K., Bourgeois, M., Youmans, G., & Hancock, A. (2006). Implications of an advice-giving and teacher role on language produce in adults with dementia. *The Gerontologist, 46*(3), 357–366.

Ducak, K., Denton, M., & Elliot, G. (2016). Implementing Montessori methods for dementia in Ontario long-term care homes: Recreation staff and multidisciplinary consultants' perceptions of policy and practice issues. *Dementia* (Advanced Online publication). doi:10.1177/1471301215625342.

Duggan, S., Blackman, T. Martyr, A. & Van Schaik, P. (2008). The impact of early dementia on outdoor life. *Dementia, 7*(2), 191–204.

Edvardsson, D., Fetherstonhaugh, D., & Nay, R. (2011). The tool for understanding residents' needs as individual persons (TURNIP): Construction and initial testing. *J Clin Nurs, 20*(19–20), 2890–2896.

Edwards, C. A., McDonnell, C., & Merl, H. (2012). An evaluation of a therapeutic garden's influence on the quality of life of aged care residents with dementia. *Dementia, 12*(4), 494–510.

Edwards, N. E., Beck, A. M., & Lim, E. (2014). Influence of aquarium on resident behavior and staff satisfaction in dementia units. *Western Journal of Nursing Research, 36*(10), 1309–1322.

Elmståhl, S., Annerstedt, L., & Åhlund, O. (1997). How should a group living unit for demented elderly be designed to decrease psychiatric symptoms? *Alzheimer Disease and Associated Disorders, 11*, 47–52.

Eisner, E. (2001). *Can do activities for adults with Alzheimer's disease: Strength-based communication and programming.* Austin, TX: Pro-Ed.

Eisner, E. (2013). *Engaging and communicating with people who have dementia: Finding and using their strengths.* Baltimore: Health Professions Press.

Elliot, G. (2011). *Montessori Methods for Dementia™: Focusing on the person and the prepared environment.* Oakville, Ontario, Canada: Dementiability Enterprises.

Elliot, G., Kelly, A., Brush, J., & Bourgeois, M. (2015). Dr. Montessori meets DementiAbility. Presented at The General Meeting of the Association Montessori International (AMI), Amsterdam, Holland.

Evans, N., Cheston, R., & Harris, N. (2015). Personal message cards: An evaluation of an alternative method of delivering simulated presence therapy. *Dementia, 15*(6), 1703–1715. doi:10.1177/1471301215574363.

Figueiro, M. G. (2008). A proposed 24 hour lighting scheme for older adults. *Lighting Research & Technology, 40*, 153–160. doi:10.1177/1477153507087299.

Fontana, G. P., Kraüchi, K., Cajochen, C., Someren, E., Amrhein, I., Pache, M., … Wirz-Justice, A. (2003). Dawn–dusk simulation light therapy of disturbed circadian rest-activity cycles in demented elderly. *Experimental Gerontology, 38*(1–2), 207–216.

Forrest, M. M., & Cohen, J. (2004). Marrying design/organization and programming to create a home and community for Alzheimer's residents. *Alzheimer's Care Today, 5*(1), 9–12.

Francis, G., & Baly, A. (1986). Plush animals: Do they make a difference? *Geriatric Nursing, 74*(3), 140–143.

Fretz, B. R. (1979). College students as paraprofessionals with children and the aged. *American Journal of Community Psychology, 7*(3), 357–360.

Galbraith, B., Larkin, H., Moorhouse, A., & Oomen, T. (2015). Intergenerational programs for persons with dementia: A scoping review. *Journal of Gerontological Social Work, 5*(4), 357–378. doi:10.1080/01634372. 2015.1008166.

Galik, E. (2010). Function-focused care for LTC residents with moderate-to-severe dementia: A social ecological approach. *ANN Longterm Care, 18*(6), 27–32.

Garcia, C. H., Espinoza, S. E., Lichtenstein, M., & Hazuda, H. P. (2012). Health literacy associations between Hispanic elderly patients and their caregivers. *Journal of Health Communication, 18*(Suppl. 1), 256–272. doi:10.1044/gero17.1.11.

Gardner, H. (1983). *Frames of mind: The theory of multiple intelligences.* New York: Basic.

Gardner, H. (1993). *Multiple intelligences: The theory in practice.* New York: Basic.

Garre-Olmo, J., Planas-Pujol, X., Lopez-Pousa, S., Weiner, M. F., Turon-Estrada, A., Juvinyà, D., ... Vilalta-Franch, J. (2012). Cross-cultural adaptation and psychometric validation of a Spanish version of the Quality of Life in Late-Stage Dementia Scale. *Qual Life Res, 19*(3), 445–453.

George, D., & Hauser, D. (2014). "I'm a storyteller!" Exploring the benefits of TimeSlips Creating Expression program at a nursing home. *Am J Alz Dis & Oth Dementias, 29*(8), 678–684.

George, D. G., & Singer, M. E. (2011). Intergenerational volunteering and quality of life for persons with mild to moderate dementia: Results from a 5-month intervention study in the United States. *The American Journal of Geriatric Psychiatry, 19*(4), 392–396.

George, D., Whitehouse, C., & Whitehouse, P. (2011). A model of intergenerativity: How the intergenerational school is bringing the generations together to foster collective wisdom and community health. *Journal of Intergenerational Relationships, 9*(4), 389–404. http://dx.doi.org/10.1080/15350770.2011.619922.

Gesino, J. P., & Siegel, E. (1995). Training gerontological social workers for nursing home practice. *Gerontology & Geriatrics Education, 15*(4), 69–82.

Gitlin, L. N., Liebman, J., & Winter, L. (2003). Are environmental interventions effective in the management of Alzheimer's disease and related disorders? *Alzheimer's Care Today, 4*(2), 85–107.

Gotestam, K. G., & Melin, L. (1987). Improving well-being for patients with senile dementia by minor changes in the ward environment. In L. Levi (Ed.), *Society, stress, and disease* (pp. 295–297). Oxford, UK: Oxford University Press.

Grandview Lodge (2013). *Grandview Lodge annual report 2013.* Ontario, Canada. Available at www.haldimandcounty.on.ca/residents.aspx?id=268. Accessed May 29, 2015.

Greene, D. (1998). Reciprocity in two conditions of service learning. *Educational Gerontology, 24*(5), 411–424.

Guwaldi, G. (2013). Establishing continuity of self-memory boxes in dementia facilities for older adults: Their use and usefulness. *Journal of Housing for the Elderly, 27*(1/2), 105–119. doi:10.1080/02763893.210 2.754817.

Hagens, C. (1995). Reminisce and write: A creative writing program for the nursing home. *Long Term Care Journal, 5*(2), 9–10.

Hagens, C., Beaman, A., & Ryan, E. B. (2003). Reminiscing, poetry writing, and remembering boxes: Personhood-centered communication with cognitively impaired older adults. *Activities, Adaptation, & Aging, 27*(3–4), 97–112.

Hall, G. R., & Buckwalter, K. C. (1987). Progressively lowered stress threshold: A conceptual model for care of adults with Alzheimer's disease. *Archives of Psychiatric Nursing, 1*(6), 399–406.

Hewitt, P., Watts, C., Hussey, J., Power, K., & Williams, T. (2013). Does a structured gardening programme improve well-being in young-onset dementia? A preliminary study. *Br J Occupational Therapy, 76*(8), 355–361.

Hikichi, H., Kondo, N., Kondo, K., Aida, J., Takeda, T., & Kawachi, I. (2015). Effect of a community intervention programme promoting social interactions on functional disability prevention for older adults: Propensity score matching and instrumental variable analyses. *J. Epidemiol. Comm. Health, 69*(9), 905–910. doi:10.1136/jech-2014-2015345.

Holland, A. L. (2003). Improving communication skills in individuals with dementia. *Journal of Communication Disorders, 36*(5), 325–326.

Hopper, T., Bayles, K. A., & Tomoeda, C. K. (1998). Using toys to stimulate communication function in individuals with Alzheimer's disease. *Journal of Medical Speech-Language Pathology, 6*(2), 73–80.

Hwang, Y. (2014). Influence of building materials with directional textures on the visual perceptions of elderly with Alzheimer's disease. *Intern. J. Geron, 8*(3), 147–151.

Isaksson, U., Åström, S., Sandman, P.-O., & Karlsson, S. (2009). Factors associated with prevalence of violent behaviour among residents living in nursing homes. *Journal of Clinical Nursing, 18*, 972–980. doi:10.1111/j.1365-2702.2008.02440.x.

Jacelon, C. S. (1995). The effect of living in a nursing home on socialization in elderly people. *Journal of Advanced Nursing, 22*(3), 539–546.

Joltin, A., Camp, C., Noble, B. H., & Antenucci, V. M. (2012). *A different visit: Activities for caregivers and their loved ones with memory impairments*. Beachwood, OH: Menorah Park Center for Senior Living.

Joseph, A. (2006). *The impact of light on outcomes in healthcare settings*. Issue Paper No. 2. Concord, CA: The Center for Health Design.

Joseph, A., & Ulrich, R. (2007). *Sound control for improved outcomes in healthcare settings*. Issue Paper No. 4. Concord, CA: The Center for Health Design.

Judge, K. S., Camp, C. J., & Orsulic-Jeras, S. (2000). Use of Montessori-based activities for clients with dementia in adult day care: Effects on engagement. *American Journal of Alzheimer's Disease and Other Dementias, 15*(1), 42–46.

Kaakinen, J. (1995). Talking among elderly nursing home residents. *Topics in Language Disorders, 15*(2), 36–46.

Kane, R. A., & Kane, R. L. (1987). *Long-term care: Principles, programs, and policies*. New York: Springer.

Kane, R. L., Keckhafer, G., Flood, S., Bershadsky, B., & Siadaty, M. S. (2003). The effect of Evercare on hospital use. *Journal of the American Geriatrics Society, 51*, 1427–1434. http://onlinelibrary.wiley.com/doi/10.1046/j.1532-5415.2003.51461.x/full.

Kane, R. A., Lum, T. Y., Cutler, L. J., Degenholtz, H. B., & Yu, T. C. (2007). Resident outcomes in small-house nursing homes: A longitudinal evaluation of the initial green house program. *J Am Geriatr Soc, 55*, 832–839.

Kincaid, C., & Peacock, J. R. (2003). The effect of a wall mural on decreasing four types of door-testing behaviors. *Journal of Applied Gerontology, 22*(1), 76–88.

Kitwood, T. (1997). *Dementia reconsidered: The person comes first*. Milton Keynes, UK: Open University Press.

Kitwood, T., & Bredin, K. (1992). Towards a theory of dementia care: Personhood and well-being. *Ageing Soc, 12*, 269–287.

Koch, K. (1977). *I never told anybody: Teaching poetry writing in a nursing home*. New York: Random House.

Kolanowski, A. M., Buettner, L., Costa, P. T., & Litaker, M. (2001). Capturing interests: Therapeutic recreation activities for persons with dementia. *Therapeutic Recreation Journal, 35*(3), 220–235.

Kramer, S. C., Friedmann, E., & Bernstein, P. L. (2009). Comparison of the effect of human interaction, animal-assisted therapy, and AIBO-assisted therapy on long-term care residents with dementia. *Anthrozoös, 22*(1), 43–57.

Kunik, M. E., Martinez, M., Snow, A. L., Beck, C. K., Cody, M., Rapp, C. G., … & Hamilton, J. D. (2003). Determinants of behavioral symptoms in dementia patients. *Clinical Gerontologist, 26*(3–4), 83–89.

Lee, S. Y., Chaudhury, H., & Hung, L. (2016). Exploring staff perceptions on the role of physical environment in dementia care setting. *Dementia, 15*(4), 743–755.

Lévesque, S., Cossette, S., & Potvin, L. (1993). Why alert residents are more or less willing to cohabit with cognitively impaired peers: An exploratory model. *The Gerontologist, 33*(4), 514–522.

Li, J., & Porock, D. (2014). Resident outcomes of person-centered care in long-term care: A narrative review of interventional research. *International Journal of Nursing Studies, 51*, 1395–1415.

Liang, J., Krause, N. M., & Bennett, J. M. (2001). Social exchange and well-being: Is giving better than receiving? *Psychology and Aging, 16*(3), 511–523.

Lichtenberg, P. A., Kemp-Havican, J., MacNeill, S. E., & Johnson, A. S. (2005). Pilot study of behavioral treatment in dementia care units. *The Gerontologist, 45*(3), 406–410.

Lindsley, O. R. (1964). Geriatric behavioral prosthetics. In R. Kastenbaum (Ed.), *New thoughts on old age* (pp. 41–60). New York: Springer.

Lubinski, R. (1995). State-of-the-art perspectives on communication in nursing homes. *Topics in Language Disorders, 15*(2), 1–19.

Lund, D. A., Hill, R. D., Caserta, M. S., & Wright, S. D. (1995). Video Respite™: An innovative resource for family, professional caregivers, and persons with dementia. *The Gerontologist, 35*(5), 683–687.

Maddox, M. K., & Burns, T. (1999). Adapted Work Program: A sheltered workshop for patients with dementia. In L. Volicer & L. Bloom-Charette (Eds.), *Enhancing the quality of life in advanced dementia* (pp. 56–77). Philadelphia: Brunner/Mazel.

Mahendra, N. (2001). Direct interventions for improving the performance of individuals with Alzheimer's disease. *Seminars in Speech and Language, 22*(4), 291–303.

Mahendra, N., & Arkin, S. (2003). Effects of four years of exercise, language, and social interventions on Alzheimer disease. *Journal of Communication Disorders, 36*(5), 395–422.

Mahmood, A., Chaudhury, H., & Gaumont, A. (2009). Environmental issues related to medication errors in long-term care: Lessons from the literature. *Health Environments Research & Design Journal, 2*(2), 42–59.

Marquardt, G., Bueter, K., & Motzek, T. (2014). Impact of the design of the built environment on people with dementia: An evidence-based review. *Health Environments Research & Design Journal, 8*(1), 127–157. doi:10.1177/193758671400800111.

Marquardt, G., Schmieg, P., & Marquardt, G. (2009). Dementia-friendly architecture: Environments that facilitate wayfinding in nursing homes. *American Journal of Alzheimer's Disease and Other Dementias, 24*, 333–340. doi:0.1177/1533317509334959.

Marston, D. C. (2001). Prayer as a meaningful activity in nursing homes. *Clinical Gerontologist, 23*(1–2), 173–178.

Martin, J. L., Webber, A. P., Alam, T., Harker, J. O., Josephson, K. R., & Alessi, C. A. (2006). Daytime sleeping, sleep disturbance, and circadian rhythms in the nursing home. *Am J Geriatr Psychiatry, 14*(2), 121–129. doi:10.1097/01.JGP.0000192483.35555.a3.

Mazzei, F., Gillan, R., & Cloutier, D. (2014). Exploring the influence of environment on the spatial behavior of older adults in a purpose-built acute care dementia unit. *Am J Alzheimers and Other Dementias, 29*(4), 311–319.

McClaugherty, L., & Burnette, K. D. (2001, January). Are nursing facilities too noisy? *Provider, 27*(1), 39–41.

McGowan, T. G. (1994). Mentoring-reminiscence: A conceptual and empirical analysis. *The International Journal of Aging and Human Development, 39*(4), 321–336.

McGowan, T. G., & Blankenship, S. (1994). Intergenerational experience and ontological change. *Educational Gerontology, 20*(6), 589–604.

Mjørud, M., Engedal, K., Røsvik, J., & Kirkevold, M. (2017). Living with dementia in a nursing home, as described by persons with dementia: A phenomenological hermeneutic study. *BMC Health Services Research, 17*(93), 1–9. doi:10.1186/s12913-017-2053-2.

Montessori, M. (1964). *The Montessori method*. New York: Schocken Books.

Mor, V., Branco, K., Fleishman, J., Hawes, C., Phillips, C., Morris, J., & Fries, B. (1995). The structure of social engagement among nursing home residents. *The Journals of Gerontology Series B: Psychological Sciences and Social Sciences, 50*(1), P1–P8.

Morgan, D. G., & Stewart, N. J. (1998). Multiple occupancy versus private rooms on dementia care units. *Environment and Behavior, 30*(4), 487–504.

Motteran, A., Trifiletti, E., & Pedrazza, M. (2016). Well-being and lack of well-being among nursing home residents. *Ageing International, 41*, 150–166. doi:10.1007/s12126-016-9240-z.

Mowrey, C., Parikh, P., Bharwang, G., & Bharwnaj, M. (2012). Application of behavior-based ergonomics therapies to improve quality of life and reduce medication usage for Alzheimer's/dementia residents. *American Journal of Alzheimer's Disease & Other Dementias, 28*(1), 35–41.

Netten, A. (1989). The effect of design of residential homes in creating dependency among confused elderly residents: A study of elderly demented residents and their ability to find their way around homes for the elderly. *International Journal of Geriatric Psychiatry, 4*(3), 143–153.

Noell-Waggoner, E. (2002). Light: An essential intervention for Alzheimer's disease. *Alzheimer's Care Today, 3*(4), 343–352.

Noell-Waggoner, E. (2004). Lighting solutions for contemporary problems of older adults. *Journal of Psychosocial Nursing and Mental Health Services, 42*(7), 14–20. doi:10.3928/02793695-20040301-01.

Noreika, J., Kujoth, J., & Torgrude, S. (2002). Using a post occupancy evaluation to guide bathroom design in a dementia specific, assisted-living facility. *Alzheimer's Care Today, 3*(1), 32–37.

Orsulic-Jeras, S., Judge, K. S., & Camp, C. J. (2000). Montessori-based activities for long-term care residents with advanced dementia: Effects on engagement and affect. *The Gerontologist, 40*(1), 107–111.

Oshima, C., Harada, C., Yasuda, K., Machishima, K., & Nakayama, K. (2014). The effectiveness of assistance dogs mounting ICT devices: A case study of a healthy woman and her dog. In S. Yamamoto (Eds.), *Human interface and the management of information. Information and knowledge in applications and services. Lecture notes in computer science, vol. 8522*. Springer, Cham.

Padilla, R. (2011). Effectiveness of environment-based interventions for people with Alzheimer's disease and related dementias. *American Journal of Occupational Therapy, 65*(5), 514–530.

Palmer, C. V., Adams, S. W., Bourgeois, M., Durrant, J., & Rossi, M. (1999). Reduction in caregiver-identified responsive behaviors in patients with Alzheimer disease post-hearing-aid fitting. *Journal of Speech, Language, and Hearing Research, 42*(2), 312–328.

Passini, R., Pigot, H., Rainville, C., & Tétreault, M.-H. (2000). Wayfinding in a nursing home for advanced dementia of the Alzheimer's type. *Environment and Behavior, 32*, 684–710.

Petrescu, I., MacFarlane, K., & Ranzijn, R. (2014). Psychological effects of poetry workshops with people with early stage dementia: An exploratory study. *Dementia, 13*(2), 207–215.

Powers, B. A., & Watson, N. M. (2011). Spiritual nurturance and support for nursing home residents with dementia. *Dementia, 10*(1), 59–80.

Pryce, H., & Gooberman-Hill, R. (2012). "There's a hell of a noise": Living with a hearing loss in residential care. *Age & Ageing, 41*(1), 40–46. doi:https://doi.org/10.1093/ageing/afr112.

Reisberg, B., Borenstein, J., Salob, S. P., Ferris, S. H., Franssen, E., & Georgotas, A. (1987). Behavioral symptoms in Alzheimer's disease: Phenomenology and treatment. *The Journal of Clinical Psychiatry, 48*(Suppl. 5), 9–15.

Roberts, G., Morley, C., Walters, W., Malta, S., & Doyle, C. (2015). Caring for people with dementia in residential aged care: Successes with a composite person-centered care model featuring Montessori-based activities. *Geriatr Nurs, 36*(2), 106–110.

Robinson, G. E., & Gallagher, A. (2008). Culture change impacts quality of life for nursing home residents. *Topics in Clinical Nutr., 23*(2), 120–130.

Roff, L. L., & Parker, M. W. (2003). Spirituality and Alzheimer's disease care. *Alzheimer's Care Today, 4*(4), 267–270.

Rosenberg, M. (1965). *Society and the adolescent self-image.* Princeton, NJ: University Press.

Rubinstein, R. L., & de Medeiros, K. (2005). Home, self, and identity. In G. Rowles & H. Chaudhury (Eds.), *Home and identity in late life* (pp. 47–62). New York: Springer.

Rule, B. G., Milke, D. L., & Dobbs, A. R. (1992). Design of institutions: Cognitive functioning and social interactions of the aged resident. *Journal of Applied Gerontology, 11*, 475–488.

Ryan, E. B., Meredith, S. D., MacLean, M. J., & Orange, J. B. (1995). Changing the way we talk with older adults: Promoting health using the Communication Enhancement Model. *The International Journal of Aging and Human Development, 41*(2), 87–105.

Schenk, L., Meyer, R., Behr, A., Kuhlmey, A., & Holzhausen, M. (2013). Quality of life in nursing homes: Results of a qualitative resident survey. *Quality of Life Research, 22*, 2929–2938. doi:10.1007/s11136-013-0400-2.

Schneider, N. M., & Camp, C. J. (2002). Use of Montessori-based activities by visitors of nursing home residents with dementia. *Clinical Gerontologist, 26*(1–2), 71–84.

Schneider, N. M., Diggs, S., Orsulic, S., & Camp, C. J. (1999). Nursing assistants teaching Montessori activities. *Journal of Nurse Assistants, 6*, 13–15.

Schroll, M., Jónsson, P. V., Mor, V., Berg, K., & Sherwood, S. (1997). An international study of social engagement among nursing home residents. *Age and Ageing, 26*(Suppl. 2), 55–59.

Schuster, E. (1998). A community bound by words: Reflections on a nursing home writing group. *Journal of Aging Studies, 12*(2), 137–147.

Shibata, T. (2012). Therapeutic seal robot as biofeedback medical device: Qualitative and quantitative evaluations of robot therapy in dementia care. *Proceedings of the IEEE, 100*(8), 2527–2538. doi:10.1109/JPROC.2012.2200559.

Shikder, S., Mourshed, M., & Price, A. (2012). Therapeutic lighting design for the elderly: A review. *Perspectives in Public Health, 132*, 282–291. doi:10.1177/1757913911422288.

Shochat, T., Martin, J., Marler, M., & Ancoli-Israel, S. (2000). Illumination levels in nursing home patients: Effects on sleep and activity rhythms. *Journal of Sleep Research, 9*, 373–379. doi:10.1046/j.1365-2869.2000.00221.x.

Sigman, S. J. (1985). Conversational behavior in two health care institutions for the elderly. *Institutional Journal of Aging and Human Development, 21*(2), 137–154.

Skelton, D. A., Howe, T. E., Ballinger, C., Neil, F., Palmer, S., & Gray, L. (2013). Environmental and behavioural interventions for reducing physical activity limitation in community-dwelling visually impaired older people. *Cochrane Database of Systematic Reviews 2013, Issue 6.* Art. No.: CD009233. doi:10.1002/14651858.CD009233.pub2.

Skrajner, M. J., Haberman, J. L., Camp, C. J., Tusick, M., Frentiu, C., & Gorzelle, G. (2014). Effects of using nursing home residents to serve as group activity leaders: Lessons learned from the RAP project. *Dementia, 13*(2), 274–285.

Sloane, P. D., Mitchell, C. M., Calkins, M., & Zimmerman, S. I. (2000). Light and noise levels in Alzheimer's disease special care units. *Research and Practice in Alzheimer's Disease, 4,* 241–249.

Soril, L. J. J. J., Leggett, L. E., Lorenzetti, D. L., Silvius, J., Robertson, D., Mansell, L. et al. (2014). Effective use of the built environment to manage behavioral and psychological symptoms of dementia: A systematic review. *PLoS ONE, 9*(12), e115425. doi:10.1371/journal.pone.0115425.

Stevens, A. B., Camp, C. J., King, C. A., Bailey, E. H., & Hsu, C. (1998). Effects of a staff implemented therapeutic group activity for adult day care clients. *Aging & Mental Health, 2*(4), 333–342.

Stevens, A. B., King, C. A., & Camp, C. J. (1993). Improving prose memory and social interaction using question asking reading with adult day care clients. *Educational Gerontology, 19*(7), 651–662.

Stewart, J. T. (1995). Management of behavior problems in the demented patient. *American Family Physician, 52*(8), 2311–2320.

Stuckey, J. C., Post, S. G., Ollerton, S., FallCreek, S. J., & Whitehouse, P. J. (2002). Alzheimer's disease, religion, and the ethics of respect for spirituality: A community dialogue. *Alzheimer's Care Today, 3*(3), 199–207.

Szanton, S. L., Thorpe, R. J., Boyd, C., et al. (2011). Community aging in place, advancing better living for elders: A bio-behavioral-environmental intervention to improve function and health-related quality of life in disabled older adults. *J Am Geriatr Soc, 59*(12), 2314–2320.

Teresi, J. A., Holmes, D., & Ory, M. G. (2000). The therapeutic design of environments for people with dementia: Further reflections and recent findings from the National Institute on Aging Collaborative Studies of Dementia Special Care Units. *The Gerontologist, 40*(4), 417–421.

Teri, L., & Logsdon, R. G. (1991). Identifying pleasant events for Alzheimer's disease patients: The Pleasant Events Schedule–AD. *The Gerontologist, 31*(1), 124–127.

Teri, L., Logsdon, R. G., Uomoto, J., & McCurry, S. M. (1997). Behavioral treatment of depression in dementia patients: A controlled clinical trial. *Journal of Gerontology Series B: Psychological Sciences and Social Sciences, 52*(4), P159–P166.

Thomas, W. H. (1994). *The Eden alternative: Nature, hope, and nursing homes.* Columbia, MO: University of Missouri.

Torrington, J. M., & Tregenza, P. R. (2007). Lighting for people with dementia. *Lighting Research and Technology, 39,* 81–97. doi:10.1177/1365782806074484.

Travers, C., Perkins, J., Rand, J., Bartlett, H., & Morton, J. (2013). An evaluation of dog-assisted therapy for residents of aged care facilities with dementia. *Antrozoös: A multidisciplinary journal of the interactions of people and animals, 26*(2), 213–225.

Vance, D. Camp, C., Kabacoff, M., & Greenwalt, L. (1996). Montessori methods: Innovative interventions for adults with Alzheimer's disease. *Montessori Life, 8,* 10–12.

Van Hoof, J., Kort, H. S. M., Duijnstee, M. S. H., Rutten, P. G. S., & Hensen, J. L. M. (2010). The indoor environment and the integrated design of homes for older people. *Building and Environment, 45*(5), 1244–1261.

van Hoof, J., Verbeek, H., Janssen, B. M., Eijkelenboom, A., Molony, S. L., Felix, E., Nieboer, K. A., Zwerts-Verhelst, E. L. M., Sijstermans, J. J. W. M., & Wouters, E. J. M. (2016). A three perspective study of the sense of home of nursing home residents: The views of residents, care professionals, and relatives. *BMC Geriatrics, 16*(169), 1–15. doi:10.1186/s12877-016-0344-9.

Van Ness, P. H., & Kasl, S. V. (2003). Religion and cognitive dysfunction in an elderly cohort. *Journal of Gerontology Series B: Psychological Sciences and Social Sciences, 58*(1), S21–S29.

Voelkl, J. E., Winkelhake, K., Jeffries, J., & Yoshioka, N. (2003). Examination of a nursing home environment: Are residents engaged in recreation activities? *Therapeutic Recreation Journal, 37,* 300–314.

Wallace-Guy, G. M., Kripke, D. F., Jean-Louis, G., Langer, R. D., Elliott, J. A., & Tuunainen, A. (2002). Evening light exposure: Implications for sleep and depression. *Journal of the American Geriatrics Society, 50,* 738–739. doi:10.1046/j.1532-5415.2002.50171.x.

Weiner, A. S., & Ronch, J. L. (2003). *Culture change in long-term care.* New York: Routledge.

West, S. K., Friedman, D., Muñoz, B., Roche, K. B., Park, W., Deremeik, J., ... & German, P. (2003). A randomized trial of visual impairment interventions for nursing home residents: Study design, baseline characteristics and visual loss. *Ophthalmic Epidemiology, 10*(3), 193–209.

Westerhof, G. J., van Vuuren, M., Brummans, B. H. J. M., & Custers, A. F. J. (2014). A Buberian approach to the co-construction of relationships between professional caregivers and residents in nursing homes. *Gerontologist, 54*, 354–362. https://doi.org/10.1093/geront/gnt064.

Whear, R., Coon, J. T., Bethel, A., Abbott, R., Stein, K., & Garside, R. (2014). What is the impact of using outdoor spaces such as gardens on the physical and mental well-being of those with dementia? A systematic review of quantitative and qualitative evidence. *Journal of the American Medical Directors Association, 15*, 697–705. http://dx.doi.org/10.1016/j.jamda.2014.05.013.

Wilson, L. B., & Simson, S. (1991). The role of social work in intergenerational programming. *Journal of Gerontological Social Work, 16*(1–2), 87–96.

Woods, P., & Ashley, J. (1995). Simulated presence therapy: Using selected memories to manage responsive behaviors in Alzheimer's disease patients. *Geriatric Nursing, 16*(1), 9–14.

Yamashita, T., Kinney, J. M., & Lokon, E. J. (2011). The impact of a gerontology course and a service-learning program on college students' attitudes toward people with dementia. *Journal of Applied Gerontology, 32*(2), 139–163.

Yesavage, J. A., Brink, T. L., Rose, T. L., Lum, O., Huang, V., Adey, M., & Leirer, V. O. (1983). Development and validation of a geriatric depression screening scale: A preliminary report. *Journal of Psychiatric Research, 17*(1), 37–49.

Young, R., Camic, P. M., & Tischler, V. (2016). The impact of community-based arts and health interventions on cognition in people with dementia: A systematic literature review. *Aging & Mental Health, 20*(4), 337–351. doi:10.1080/13607863.2015.1011080.

Zeisel, J., Silverstein, N. M., Hyde, J., Levkoff, S., Lawton, M. P., & Holmes, W. (2003). Environmental correlates to behavioral health outcomes in Alzheimer's special care units. *The Gerontologist, 43*(5), 697–711.

Zeiss, A. M., & Lewinsohn, P. M. (1986). Adapting behavioral treatment for depression to meet the needs of the elderly. *Clinical Psychologist, 39*(4), 98–100.

Zgola, J. (1990). Alzheimer's disease and the home: Issues in environmental design. *American Journal of Alzheimer's Disease & Other Dementias, 5*(3), 15–22.

Zimmerman, S., Sloane, P. D., Heck, E., Maslow, K., & Schulz, R. (2005a). Introduction: Dementia care and quality of life in assisted living and nursing homes. *Gerontologist, 45*(Spec No. 1), 5–7.

Zimmerman, S, Sloane P. D., Williams, C. S., et al. (2005b). Dementia care and quality of life in assisted living and nursing homes. *Gerontologist, 45*(Spec No. 1), 133–146.

8

EATING AND SWALLOWING

Description, Assessment, and Intervention

Ellen M. Hickey, Stuart Cleary, Pamela Coulter, and Michelle S. Bourgeois

People with dementia may experience a wide variety of difficulties during meals, including meal-time challenges (i.e., social/behavioral challenges), eating difficulties, and swallowing disorders (Aselage, 2010; Watson & Green, 2006). Mealtime, eating, and swallowing problems are of concern in the care of persons with dementia because of their prevalence and potential adverse effects on health and quality of life (Alagiakrishnan, Bhanjib, & Kurianc, 2013; Clavé & Shaker, 2015; Giebel, Sutcliffe, & Challis, 2015). Mealtime, eating, and swallowing abilities are integrally related, and are influenced by multiple factors that need to be considered in assessment and treatment. As dementia progresses and problems become more severe, decisions must be made that balance the potential health risks and impacts on quality of life, respecting the wishes of the person with dementia and family. A person-centered, interprofessional team approach with clients and their families at the center of the team is imperative to ensure best practice and optimal outcomes.

This chapter describes the characteristics of mealtime, eating, and swallowing difficulties, and the factors that influence persons with dementia during mealtimes, and the consequences of these challenges. The chapter also guides clinicians in person-centered assessment and treatment approaches to increase safety, maximize nutrition and hydration, and enhance the overall meal-time experience for persons with dementia. Ultimately, clinicians aim to maintain quality of life over the course of dementia progression. Finally, the chapter discusses end-of-life care, as pertains to feeding and swallowing.

Characteristics

First, important distinctions will be made around terminology (based on Aselage, 2010; Watson & Green, 2006). *Mealtime behaviors* pertain to the social aspects of participating in meals (e.g., communication around wants and needs, and the social behaviors and cultural rituals around meals) and *eating*, which is the process of delivering food and drink to the mouth. *Swallowing* is the process of transferring food and drink from the mouth to the stomach. Though our focus in this chapter is eating and swallowing, we will also address mealtime behaviors, as people with dementia may have difficulties across all three areas, and they can sometimes be hard to tease apart.

When a person with dementia has difficulty with eating and/or swallowing, a variety of risks and potential consequences arise, extending from health issues to quality of life impacts related to the social and cultural aspects of eating (Aselage & Amella, 2010; Brush, Meehan, & Calkins, 2002; Calkins & Brush, 2003; Liu et al., 2016). Rituals around sharing meals are often a part of one's cultural identity, memories, and quality of life (Bloomfield & Pegram, 2012; Brush et al., 2002; Kofod & Birkemose, 2004; Wallin, Carlander, Sandman, Ternestedt, & Håkanson, 2014). The social behaviors of mealtimes may be impacted by environmental factors or cognitive-communicative deficits, with impacts becoming more significant over the disease progression. In the early to middle stages of dementia, eating ability (and most basic ADLs) is usually relatively intact, but there is a decline in the later stages of dementia (Arrighi, Gélinas, McLaughlin, Buchanan, & Gauthier, 2013; Aselage & Amella, 2010; Giebel et al., 2014, 2015; Kai et al., 2015). As the later stages ensue, problems with chewing and swallowing also become more common.

Hospitalized persons with dementia and dysphagia are at increased risk for aspiration pneumonia, malnutrition, sepsis, mechanical ventilation, anorexia, and mortality, and have longer hospital stays with higher care costs, as compared to those with dementia without dysphagia (Paranji, Paranji, Wright, & Chandra, 2017). Among nursing home residents, those with dementia are at a higher risk for weight loss, inadequate nutrition, and eating disability, with increased risk for those with comorbidities, advanced dementia, and for those on multiple medications (Bell, Tamura, Masaki, & Amella, 2013; Slaughter, Eliasziw, Morgan, & Drummond, 2011; Slaughter & Hayduk, 2012). Factors impacting eating and swallowing will be described, including cognitive, behavioral, sensory, physiological, and environmental factors, as described in the next section.

Mealtime Behaviors and Eating

Cognitive and Behavioral Factors. Mealtime behaviors and eating challenges are often related to cognitive deficits. Eating is one of the last functional behaviors to be lost in the course of AD, and there is a predictable course of deterioration of these skills. For example, in the early stages of dementia, persons who live in the community may have trouble with grocery shopping and meal preparation (e.g., initiation, planning, memory of recipes, safe preparation) or forget to eat (Arrighi et al., 2013; Brush et al., 2002; Douglas & Lawrence, 2015; Sato et al., 2014). Nursing home residents with dementia may have difficulty finding the dining room, remembering when meals are served, making food choices, and maintaining socially appropriate conversations and manners (Genoe et al., 2012; Kai et al., 2015). Attention deficits and perceptual difficulties increase with disease progression, making it difficult for the person to stay seated through the entire meal, resist distractions, and manipulate utensils and condiment packets (Brush et al., 2002). They may also overstuff their mouths and begin eating nonfood items (particularly persons with bv-FTD).

As cognitive deficits in orientation, attention, perception, and executive functioning become more severe, mealtime and eating behaviors become more challenging, manifesting as difficulties with: maintaining awareness, attention, and interest during meals, recognizing and locating food, initiating and sequencing self-feeding, using utensils, responding to smells, following simple verbal commands, and communicating preferences and needs (Aselage & Amella, 2010; Lee & Song, 2015; Rogus-Pulia, Malandraki, Johnson, & Robbins, 2015; Wu & Lin, 2015). Behavioral and psychiatric symptoms, such as lack of recognition of environment or tablemates, delusions, and hallucinations, also complicate mealtime behaviors and eating (Amella, 2004; Arrighi et al., 2013; Aselage & Amella, 2011; Lee & Song, 2015; Njegovan, Man-Son-Hing, Mitchell, & Molnar, 2001; Stockdell & Amella, 2008).

Responsive behaviors that can impact mealtimes are wandering, pacing, and physical aggression (Liu et al., 2016). In the later stages, as cognitive deficits become more severe and responsive behaviors are more common, a person with dementia may throw, spit out, or push away food, refusing to eat (Lee & Song, 2015; Liu et al., 2016; Wu & Lin, 2015). The person may use fingers to eat, resist feeding assistance (turning away head, not opening the mouth, not swallowing, pushing away), spit or throw food, and exhibit disruptive vocalizations (Aselage & Amella, 2010, 2011; Gilmore-Bykovskyi, 2015). Despite some predictability in progression, individual variation is expected in terms of which abilities are lost, and the order and rate of loss (Arrighi et al., 2013).

Sensory Factors. Sensory factors can impact both mealtime behaviors and eating, putting one at risk for limited eating and drinking (Behrman, Chouliaras, & Ebmeier, 2014; Briller, Proffitt, Perez, & Calkins, 2001). There are several age-related physical changes in vision that contribute to eating problems, including decreases in pupil size and reaction time, reduced contrast and color saturation and discrimination, loss of peripheral vision, and difficulties with depth perception and spatial orientation (Behrman et al., 2014; Brush et al., 2002; Lee & Song, 2015; Rizzo, Anderson, Dawson, & Nawrot, 2000). Visual stimuli include the amount of distraction (e.g., people coming and going), lighting (quantity and quality), and visual contrasts between table and dishes and between dishes and food (Douglas & Lawrence, 2015; Koss & Gilmore, 1998). Visual hallucinations may also impact mealtime behaviors and eating, particularly for persons with DLB (Behrman et al., 2014). These problems might make it difficult for a person with dementia to be able to perceive the items on a tray, and they often get frustrated or overwhelmed trying, and may give up.

Hearing loss and difficulty hearing in noisy environments (with and without hearing aids) interfere with the social interactions possible in dining situations; for some, wearing hearing aids creates discomfort due to the amplification of environmental sounds, as well as sounds of their own chewing (Baucom, 1996; Behrman et al., 2014; Roberts & Durnbaugh, 2002). The amount and types of auditory stimuli include the background noise from machines and cooking (e.g., ice machine, and dishes and silverware clanging) and people talking, as well as the ability of the client to attend to conversations or verbal instructions at his or her table (Calkins & Brush, 2003). Sensory changes in smell and taste that impact identification and recognition of foods may be related to age, medications, Alzheimer's disease, Parkinson's disease dementia (PDD), and fronto-temporal lobar degeneration (Behrman et al., 2014; Omar, Mahoney, Buckley, & Warren, 2013; Sakai, Ikeda, Kazui, Shigenobu, & Nishikawa, 2016; Williams & Weatherhead, 2013). Decreased sensitivity and recognition of sweet tastes may actually contribute to persons with AD desiring sweet foods (Sakai et al., 2016). These problems might contribute to the decreased appetite often seen in persons with dementia.

Physiological Factors. Appetite is a significant physiological factor in adequate nutritional intake in persons with dementia, who may experience either decreased or increased appetite, related to appetite regulation (Kai et al., 2015; Sato et al., 2014; Simmons & Schnelle, 2003) or mood disturbance (e.g., depression, indifference, and apathy) (Liu et al., 2016; Simmons & Schnelle, 2003). Neuroimaging studies have revealed that problems with appetite might be due to cortical lesions in the left anterior cingulate cortex, which is known to cause reduced appetite, apathy, and decreased goal-directed behaviors, and extrinsic motivations for eating (Hu et al., 2002; Ismail et al., 2008). Other findings implicate the orbitofrontal cortex, which processes gustatory, olfactory, and visual information and is activated in processing unpleasant flavors and odors and the feelings of being satiated (Ismail et al., 2008). In persons with behavioral variant-frontotemporal dementia (bv-FTD), increased caloric intake related to increased appetite is associated with atrophy in the cingulate cortices, thalamus, and cerebellum. In semantic-variant primary progressive aphasia, these three areas plus the orbitofrontal cortex and nucleus accumbens show atrophy (Ahmed et al., 2016).

Other causes of decreased eating include: medication side effects (e.g., antidepressants), other health problems (e.g., overactive thyroid, liver problems, and kidney failure), and infections (e.g., bladder infections) (Gillick & Mitchell, 2002). Physical stressors, such as fatigue, pain, chronic illnesses, constipation, lack of dentures or poorly fitting dentures, and medications that decrease the appetite or reduce saliva, will also interfere with eating and may lead to inadequate intake (Keller, Chambers, Niezgoda, & Duizer, 2012; Roberts & Durnbaugh, 2002). Generalized weakness, grip strength, sitting balance, and mobility can also contribute to eating difficulties (Liu et al., 2016).

Factors in the Physical and Social Environment. According to the International Classification of Functioning, Disability and Health (ICF; WHO, 2001), environmental factors include the physical, social, and attitudinal aspects of everyday life situations. A variety of these factors may put older persons at risk of reduced quantity and/or quality of eating and drinking, or increased dependency on assistance (Lee & Song, 2015; Slaughter et al., 2011; Slaughter & Hayduk, 2012). For those living in the community, the environment may not be conducive to adequate food and liquid intake, possibly due to isolation (social or geographic), limited income (Genoe et al., 2012; Rehm, Peñalvo, Afshin, & Mozaffarian, 2016), or other issues. Research in the US has shown that even those older adults without dementia are prone to consuming a poor or intermediate diet quality, as defined by the American Heart Association (Rehm et al., 2016).

As they enter residential care, mealtimes are just one area in which persons with dementia experience loss of control, possibly impacting their mealtime participation. Those with dementia are particularly at risk for malnutrition and dehydration, especially in institutional settings. Nursing home residents with dementia who ate in their rooms, rather than in a dining room with other residents, had more difficulty with self-feeding (Lee & Song, 2015). Across 45 assisted living and nursing home facilities, 54% of the observed residents had low food intake and 51% of them had low fluid intake (Reed, Zimmerman, Sloane, Williams, & Boustani, 2005); greater food and fluid intake was related to staff monitoring of residents, having meals in a public dining area, and the presence of non-institutional features, such as tablecloths and not eating from trays.

For those who eat in common areas, the external stressors of loud noises or music, crowding of people and mobility aids, an institutionalized environment, bland food on institutional trays, poor lighting, and behavior of tablemates impact dining in institutional settings (Brush et al., 2002; Douglas & Lawrence, 2015; Roberts & Durnbaugh, 2002). A variety of mealtime and eating issues related to caregiver behaviors have been reported, including inaccurate documentation of oral food and fluid consumption and nutritional supplementation, failure to identify residents in need of intervention, overestimation of need for feeding assistance by residents, and lack of routine assessment of residents' food preferences, which may change with AD (Gilmore-Bykovskyi, 2015; Hanson, Ersek, Lin, & Carey, 2013; Kai et al., 2015; Pioneer Network, 2011; Simmons & Schnelle, 2003).

Lack of staffing in the dining room may result in inadequate supervision of eating or inadequate feeding assistance for residents who need it (e.g., no verbal prompts, limited social engagement, food bites are too large, and residents are fed too quickly) (Amella, 1999; Aselage & Amella, 2011; Liu et al., 2016; Pioneer Network, 2011; Simmons & Schnelle, 2003, 2006; Ullrich & Crichton, 2015). The quality of interactions with caregivers can improve or contribute to mealtime difficulties such as responsive behaviors, agitation, and intake (Aselage & Amella, 2010, 2011). Nursing assistants might use a task-oriented approach to mealtime with residents, which leads to a depersonalized, "assembly-line" style of care, causing stress to both staff and residents, reducing mealtime pleasure, and increasing the frequency of resistance, agitation, and other responsive behaviors (Aselage & Amella, 2011; Gilmore-Bykovskyi, 2015; Liu, Galik, Boltz, Nahm & Resnick, 2015; Roberts & Durnbaugh, 2002). Some of these caregiver behaviors may stem from the organizational culture of a facility and priorities of care, such as an emphasis on participation and independence versus intake and length of time to feed.

Responsive behaviors in persons with severe dementia are often a means of communication (e.g., biting a straw when a cup is being withdrawn to indicate the wish to have another drink) rather than resistance. When nursing staff members are not properly trained, the presence of responsive behaviors can make it difficult to effectively provide feeding assistance (Douglas & Lawrence, 2015). Caregiver behaviors that may elicit responsive behaviors are feeding too quickly, controlling behavior and language (e.g., "Eat your beans," in a commanding tone), and task-centered behaviors (e.g., ignoring the person's conversation to focus on feeding, or outpacing feeding with ability to enjoy and swallow food) (Aselage & Amella, 2011; Gilmore-Bykovskyi, 2015). Caregivers must investigate possible triggers of responsive behaviors, problem solve, and evaluate the outcome (e.g., adjusting room temperature for increased comfort, or modifying their own feeding behaviors). Inaccurate interpretation of resistive or agitated behavior as lack of coop-eration or a desire to stop eating can result in a meal being ended prematurely, thus reducing nutritional intake (Amella & Batchelor-Aselage, 2014; Aselage & Amella, 2011).

Cultural and Religious Factors of Residents and Caregivers. Dining practices and food choices differ between cultures and can impact behavior and intake during meals (Liu et al., 2016). Habits, such as saying grace prior to a meal or waiting for all tablemates to receive their food before eating, could be misinterpreted as a person with dementia delaying initiation of eating. Religious beliefs can influence what foods are acceptable by dictating fasting during certain periods or abstinence from certain foods, and cultural practices influence the preference for certain foods, particularly "comfort foods" when feeling unwell. These cultural and religious practices may have been easy to deal with at one time when some communities were quite homogenous, but with increasing diversity, differences may present challenges to dining services of long-term care facili-ties, necessitating creative solutions.

Caregivers' own religious or health beliefs may also influence how they feed people, or how they interpret responsive behaviors. For example, staff of Christian nursing homes in Germany were more likely to interpret resistance to feeding assistance (e.g., closing mouth during feeding) as a will to die than staff in secular nursing homes (Kuehlmeyer et al., 2015). Those in secular homes might interpret these behaviors as a sign of discomfort, or a wish to stop eating (Kuehlmeyer et al., 2015). Caregivers must be mindful of how their own beliefs and interpretations of behavior impact interactions and contribute to feeding difficulties (Amella & Batchelor-Aselage, 2014; Kuehlmeyer et al., 2015). Facilities that have a religious affiliation might have policies around end-of-life care that impact decision-making (e.g., Catholic facilities that will not allow removal of alternative feeding methods).

Food Quality and Presentation. The presentation and quality of food and drink affects how much we enjoy our meal. Nursing home residents with advanced dementia with eating and swal-lowing difficulties may have limited choices in foods that they enjoy eating (Hanson et al., 2013). For residents who have difficulty recognizing foods, being served pureed foods with no recogniz-able form compounds the issue (Keller et al., 2012). Older persons on therapeutic diets (e.g., reduced salt, sugar, fat) and dysphagia diets (e.g., pureed, minced) are at increased risk of weight loss because of the unappetizing changes to the taste of food, decreased nutrient density, and limited choices (Keller et al., 2012; Pioneer Network, 2011). Compared to regular textured foods, pureed diets may provide approximately 400 fewer calories a day (Keller et al., 2012). The Pioneer Network Food and Dining Clinical Task Force recommends liberalizing the diets of nursing home residents, using therapeutic diets only when essential, based on poor tolerance, the goals of care, and the prevalence of weight loss for those on therapeutic diets.

Swallowing

Swallowing involves getting food from the mouth to the pharynx and into the esophagus so that it can be passed to the stomach. Swallowing disorders, or dysphagia, may be classified as oral, pharyngeal, or esophageal, based on where in the system challenges are encountered. If not properly diagnosed and managed, these deficits often lead to serious medical conditions, such as dehydration, malnutrition, laryngospasm, bronchospasm, aspiration pneumonia, or asphyxia (Clavé & Shaker, 2015; Liu, Cheon, & Thomas, 2014). Speech-language pathologists most often work with people with oral and pharyngeal swallowing deficits, and occasionally those with esophageal deficits. Prevalence, signs and symptoms, and consequences of dysphagia will be described.

Prevalence of Dysphagia. Prevalence of dysphagia differs across persons with different types of dementia, based on the pathophysiology, which might also cause a neuromuscular disorder. In studies that did not identify the dementia type, prevalence of dysphagia was reported as 6–13% in persons with mild dementia (Park et al., 2013; Sato et al., 2014), 83% in persons with moderate-severe dementia (Park et al., 2013), and 80% in advanced dementia (Hanson et al., 2013). In persons with AD, 32% and 29–44% have been reported in the mild and moderate-severe stages, respectively (Alagiakrishnan et al., 2013). Persons with AD most commonly have oral stage deficits, usually related to cognitive deficits, such as not attending to food in the mouth or not remembering to chew and swallow. Additionally, symptoms such as slow oral transit time result from an underlying impairment in sensation in persons with AD.

Dysphagia prevalence in persons with other types of dementia was reported to be 47% for vascular dementia, 25% for FTD, and 57% for frontotemporal lobar degeneration (Alagiakrishnan et al., 2013), and 32% for dementia with Lewy bodies (DLB) and PDD, with 92% of these cases confirmed with videofluoroscopic swallow study (Londos et al., 2013). Regardless of diagnosis, dysphagia is a common problem in nursing home residents with dementia (Park et al., 2013). In addition to swallowing problems related to cognitive deficits, some diseases that cause dementia also cause neuromuscular deficits resulting in dysphagia, possibly with an earlier onset, for example: Parkinson disease (Volonté, Porta, & Comi, 2002), progressive supranuclear palsy and multi-system atrophy (Walshe, 2014), and Huntington disease (Kagel & Leopold, 1992). Pharyngeal stage deficits may be seen in persons with dementia with Lewy bodies and PDD due to Parkinsonism (Londos et al., 2013; Walshe, 2014). Persons with vascular dementia may exhibit both oral and pharyngeal dysphagia (Alagiakrishnan et al., 2013; Walshe, 2014). The prevalence of dysphagia is higher among persons with AD than FTD (Alagiakrishnan et al., 2013), but compared to AD, persons with FTD may show more indiscriminate eating behaviors (e.g., eating nonfood items), and persons with semantic dementia frequently change food preferences (Alagiakrishnan et al., 2013).

Symptoms of Dysphagia. Symptoms of oral and pharyngeal dysfunction include: trouble with chewing; anterior loss of food and liquids; pocketing of food in the buccal cavities; difficulty initiating swallowing; a slow swallow; nasal regurgitation; drooling and difficulty managing secretions; wet voice quality; aspiration; choking and coughing episodes; food sticking in the pharynx and/or larynx; and weight loss (Park et al., 2013; Sato et al., 2014). In addition to the impact of cognitive deficits on swallowing, oral stage problems might also be caused by neuromuscular weakness and incoordination, reduced range of motion, and oral apraxia that prevent adequate lip and tongue control. Other oral stage problems include: reduced lip seal, oral clearance, bolus formation, and transfer of bolus to the pharynx. Persons with dementia may have difficulty with bolus manipulation (Aselage & Amella, 2011), although biting, chewing, and swallowing may be less impaired relative to feeding abilities (Lee & Song, 2015; Wu & Lin, 2015).

In the pharyngeal stage, delayed pharyngeal swallow, multiple swallows per bolus, decreased hyolaryngeal elevation, pharyngeal residue, laryngeal penetration, and aspiration may be present (Affoo, Foley, Rosenbek, Shoemaker, & Martin, 2013; Alagiakrishnan et al., 2013; Sato et al., 2014; Walshe, 2014). Pharyngeal stage symptoms may include delayed pharyngeal swallow, spillage of the bolus into the pharynx before initiation of the swallow, pharyngeal residue in the pyriform sinuses and valleculae, laryngeal penetration, and aspiration (Alagiakrishnan et al., 2013;

Londos et al., 2013; Walshe, 2014). Other deficits revealed by objective assessment included esophageal dysmotility, decreased salivation, and as the disease progresses, reduced ability to clear laryngeal penetration, and silent aspiration (Cersosimo & Benarroch, 2012; Kalf, de Swart, Bloem, & Munneke, 2012).

Outcomes of Eating and Swallowing Challenges

Malnutrition, Dehydration, and Weight Loss. Malnutrition is a widespread problem in older people around the world (Allen, Methven, & Gosney, 2014). As dementia progresses, problems with decreased appetite, reduced recognition of thirst, and forgetting to eat and drink often lead to malnutrition and dehydration, and their associated complications such as weight loss and death (Aselage & Amella, 2010; Liu et al., 2014; Hanson, Ersek, Lin, & Carey, 2013; Jensen, Compher, Sullivan, & Mudlin, 2013; Roberts & Durnbaugh, 2002). Caregivers must consistently monitor food and fluid intake, as well as signs of malnutrition, dehydration, or aspiration (Foley, Affoo, & Martin, 2015), both in home and residential settings. Low body mass index and malnutrition are significant problems in long-term care, with malnutrition affecting 30–85% of nursing home residents (Landi et al., 1999; Saletti, Lindgren, Johansson, & Cederholm, 2000; Simmons & Reuben, 2000), and cognitive decline can be accelerated by undernutrition (Brooke & Ojo, 2015; Hooper et al., 2016). Weight loss is a significant problem in persons with dementia (Ball et al., 2015).

Consumption of less than 75% of the served meal is considered to be a clinically significant eating problem according to the *Minimum Data Set* (MDS). Simmons and Schnelle (2003) reported that the majority of nursing home residents have low oral food and fluid intake, according to the MDS criterion, and that those with cognitive deficits are at particularly high risk for malnutrition. Others have argued that behavioral disturbances (e.g., irritability, agitation, and disinhibition), rather than severity of cognitive deficits, are related to altered food selection that may contribute to malnutrition (Greenwood et al., 2005). Beyond poor appetite regulation, persons with AD tend to display a preference for carbohydrates, especially sweets, rather than proteins. See Box 8.1 for signs of poor nutrition and hydration.

Box 8.1 Malnutrition and Dehydration Warning Signs

Signs of malnutrition and dehydration:

- Weight loss, skin changes, skin breakdown (e.g., pressure sores), infections, dizziness, fatigue, irritability, increased confusion, increased falls, and mortality

Additional signs:

- Malnutrition: incontinence, weakness, brittle hair, hair loss, and increased susceptibility to infections
- Dehydration: dry mouth/tongue and cracked lips, sunken eyes, low urine output, dark-colored urine, constipation, lethargy, and dizziness, low blood pressure, muscle cramps, "skin pinch" on back of hand that maintains shape

(Sources: Jensen et al., 2013; Kofod & Birkemose, 2004; Roberts & Durnbaugh, 2002)

Quality of Life. A reduction in quality of life for persons with dementia (PWD) can result from long-standing mealtime difficulties (Liu et al., 2014; Pioneer Network, 2011). Transitioning to modified texture diets can mean eating merely for the sake of nutrition, rather than enjoyment, and can result in feelings of sadness, frustration, depression, and upset (Ullrich & Crichton, 2015). The presence of eating and swallowing problems may result in social consequences as well (Calkins & Brush, 2003; Wallin et al., 2014). Thus, providing nutrition and enjoyable mealtimes are common concerns in caring for elders, particularly for those with dementia (Gillick & Mitchell, 2002; Njegovan et al., 2001; Watson & Green, 2006). Caregivers should use mealtime as an opportunity to make residents feel like a part of the community and to recognize them as dignified adults (Bowlby Sifton, 2002; Hellen, 2002).

For family members caring for a loved one with dementia at home, challenges with food intake and weight loss can cause anxiety, guilt, and stress, and significantly increase caregiver burden, especially if not expected (Ball et al., 2015). Family members reported difficulties that were related to cognition (forgetfulness, confusion, disorientation), physical decline (dysphagia, decrease in appetite, visuospatial deficits, recognition of food), responsive emotions (frustration, anger, isolation, fear), independent functional skills (self-feeding and utensil use), and responsive behaviors (aggression, hoarding food). Caregivers perceived that they had received inadequate education from professionals involved in their family member's care, and independently sought this knowledge from dietitians, the internet, and support groups, or some drew on their own professional nursing knowledge.

Assessment

The goals of assessment can be delineated across the ICF: impairment, activities and participation, contextual factors, and quality of life (WHO, 2001). As noted previously, care is best delivered by a collaborative, person-centered, interprofessional team. Team composition depends on the setting (e.g., home, nursing home, hospital) and the type of mealtime problem being addressed, but most often, speech-language pathologists (SLPs) work collaboratively with nursing staff, dietitians/nutritionists, occupational therapists (OTs), and physicians to manage eating and swallowing challenges. Other team members may include physical therapists (PTs), recreation therapists and activities staff, psychologists, and social workers.

Clinicians need to understand the purpose and goals of assessment to determine the appropriate procedures to be used (which is also described in Chapter 5 on assessment of cognitive-communicative abilities). Goals of assessment vary from screening to differential diagnosis to assessment for treatment planning and measuring outcomes. Screenings are used to determine whether there is a potential problem that warrants a skilled assessment; they are usually conducted by a nurse, OT, or SLP. Generally, the goal of differential diagnosis is to diagnose the nature and severity of the impairment and identify the resulting safety risks and health consequences of the impairment. If this information is not already available, then assessment for treatment planning will incorporate these goals as well.

When the purpose of assessment is to design a plan of care (POC), procedures must also allow the clinician to: determine the client's and caregiver's goals; identify unmet needs, and the impacts on participation in mealtime and quality of life; and identify internal and external factors that contribute to eating and swallowing challenges, as well as strengths that can be used to compensate for challenges. Strengths should be viewed broadly, and might be found in the client, in the caregiver, or in other aspects of the environment. Assessment for treatment planning should be holistic and allow authentic choice making by the client and family; see Chapter 5 for discussion of tools that support communication for choice-making.

In assessment for treatment planning, the clinician must assess potential to benefit from skilled SLP services, to be able to determine whether the POC will be restorative-based or maintenance-based, and to document reasonable expectations for progress (see Chapter 4 for more on these issues). Ideally, the assessment process is collaborative and should include an interprofessional team including nurses, caregivers, physicians, professional dietitians/nutritionists, OTs, physiotherapists, and others (Walshe, 2014). A psychologist or social worker may be an integral part of the team when there are contentious decisions around balancing risk/safety and the desires of the client and family.

Screening

Nursing and other staff members need to be aware of the observable signs of dysphagia, to be able to screen for swallowing problems and make appropriate referrals to the SLP. One behavior that nursing staff can monitor in screenings is rinsing ability, which is independently predictive of dysphagia in persons with AD (Sato et al., 2014). A tool that has been developed for self-report of swallowing problems, the EAT-10 (Belafksy et al., 2008), is currently being tested for validity for use with persons with dementia (available at www.nestlenutrition-institute.org/Education/practical-tools/Documents/EAT-10_Swallowing_Assessment_Tool.pdf).

A screening tool that was developed for use in nursing homes is The Meal Assistance Screening Tool (MAST; Steele, 1996). This was designed for nursing staff to identify the types and severity of mealtime difficulties experienced by nursing home residents, in eight categories: mealtime pre-requisites (e.g., alert or drowsy), seating and positioning problems, dentition and oral hygiene, type of diet provided, type of assistance provided, intake, challenging behaviors (e.g., yelling and hoarding), and eating problems (e.g., dysphagia). Using the MAST to assess 349 nursing home residents, 87% of them had problems, including dysphagia (68%), poor oral intake (46%), positioning problems (35%), and responsive behaviors (40%) (Steele, Greenwood, Ens, Robertson, & Seidman-Carlson (1997). Better oral intake was seen for residents with severe cognitive impairment than those with mild to moderate cognitive impairment due to the fact that many of the residents with severe impairments received partial or total feeding assistance.

Chart Review and Case History

The chart review and case history are important for determining important background factors, such as medical diagnosis and history of dysphagia. The SLP must review notes from the interprofessional team, particularly physicians and/or nurses, for evidence of a history of dysphagia, signs or symptoms of dysphagia, including decreased food and liquid intake, weight loss, fever, chest congestion, and/or pneumonia. Orders for current diet and liquid intake must also be noted, not just for dysphagia recommendations but also for allergies and medical restrictions (e.g., low-salt diet or diabetic diet). Other aspects of health status or care to note include gastrointestinal disorder, medications, the presence of a feeding tube, and the need for suctioning (McCullough et al., 2000). Notes from nurses, or the nutritionist or OT might also indicate observations of coughing or choking while eating or drinking, assistance with feeding, and food preferences. Results of chest X-rays (e.g., right lower lobe lung infiltrate), swallowing studies (e.g., videofluoroscopy), and lab results (e.g., evidence of dehydration or malnutrition) are also important to note.

With respect to the context of eating, the clinician should obtain information regarding where, when, what, how often, how much, and with whom a person is accustomed to eating (Calkins & Brush, 2003). Other considerations include whether the client enjoyed doing other activities (e.g., TV, radio, or newspaper) while eating, and whether the client is a slow or fast eater. Any changes to that familiar context of eating may contribute to eating and/or swallowing problems. The SLP should also conduct an interview with the client if possible, and with caregivers, asking questions related to the above information. The SLP must determine the client's perception and awareness of any eating or swallowing problems. If the client is unfamiliar to the SLP, the interview is also an opportunity to gather information regarding cognitive-communicative status. The clinician can also verify or add to these findings with observation of habitual mealtime behaviors, including social aspects, and eating or feeding.

Positioning

The client's typical positioning during meals is an important consideration. The SLP should note the body posture and head posture of the client, as well as his or her ability to modify positioning given instructions or spontaneously. The ideal position for eating and swallowing, for most persons, is sitting upright in a chair with knees and hips at 90-degree angles, with the head positioned straight over the spine. Compensatory positioning strategies can be examined as needed, such as flexing the head with a "chin tuck." Often in the late stage of dementia, the head will be chronically flexed or hyperextended, and the focus of the assessment will be on determining the use of adaptive feeding equipment for that position (Hellen, 2002). Postural supports and alternative seating should also be considered in conjunction with PTs and OTs.

Structural-Functional Examination of the Swallowing Mechanism

The structural-functional examination is conducted so that the clinician can identify signs of neuromuscular problems that could cause oral/pharyngeal dysphagia. This assessment might be more limited than when used with clients without cognitive deficits, as clients in the moderate to later stages of dementia may have difficulty understanding the procedures and following instructions (Alagiakrishnan et al., 2013; see Yorkston, Beukelman, Strand, & Hakel, 2010; or see Duffy, 2013). If the client has difficulty following instructions for volitional movements, then one strategy for observing movements is to engage the client in an imitation "game" such that the person imitates various oral-motor behaviors, such as lip pursing, jaw opening, and so on.

The clinician should start with observation, looking for evidence of the client's saliva production and saliva management (e.g., drooling, excessive saliva in the mouth, or dry mouth, which could be medication related). Drooling may indicate the client is likely to have anterior loss of food or liquids. Observations should be made of the face, lips, tongue, uvula, and jaw muscles for the health of tissues, and for symmetry, strength, range of motion, and coordination. Facial/lip droop, asymmetrical tongue or weakness with limited movement or coordination might be related to difficulty with bolus manipulation and oral clearance; the clinician might observe pocketing of food in the cheek or food residue on the tongue or palate, even hours after a meal is over. Jaw weakness may lead to decreased chewing, or spasticity in the jaw muscles could cause pain during chewing. Asymmetrical uvula or difficulty building oral pressure ("puff up your cheeks") might be a sign of weakness in the velum that could lead to nasal regurgitation.

The clinician should also observe respiratory patterning (e.g., respiratory rate, and abdominal versus thoracic breathing). Sensory assessment may be limited by the client's cognitive abilities, but the SLP may note any positive or negative behaviors related to various types of tastes, temperatures, and textures, as well as gently touching the outside of the cheek or touching the tongue with a tongue blade, spoon, or lemon swab. Sensory problems can also lead to difficulty with oral clearance (i.e., pocketing of food in the cheek). If possible, the structural-functional exam should include assessment of the strength and quality of the volitional cough and swallow. If the person is unable to respond to commands, the clinician should note reflexive coughs and swallows, observing laryngeal elevation and voice quality after a cough or swallow. Assessment of the gag reflex is usually not indicated, given poor reliability and lack of a meaningful association with dysphagia (McCullough et al., 2000), as well as the likelihood of confusing or upsetting the client.

Finally, the client's speech and voice production during the exam can also give signs of the integrity of the structures involved in swallowing. The clinician should note presence or absence of dysarthria, and intelligibility of speech (McCullough et al., 2000). The clinician should also note the client's voice quality (e.g., dysphonia, breathy, harsh, or wet and gurgly). Judgments of dysphonia and wet voice quality may also be reliably obtained from sustained phonation. Presence of wet voice quality may indicate dysphagia.

Clinical ("Bedside") Evaluation of Eating and Swallowing Behaviors

Several assessment tools have been developed for use with persons with dementia, and/or for use in the nursing home setting; a few will be described here. In general, the tools designed for eating assessment examine the ability of the person to get the food and drink from dish to mouth, and the tools designed for swallowing assessment examine the ability of the person to manage the food and liquid within the oral cavity and to swallow the bolus safely. Regardless of the tool used, the clinician should collect data on a number of factors that may influence the client's ability to eat, including the context of feeding, as described above.

Eating and swallowing behaviors should be assessed under habitual conditions as well as ideal conditions to determine current problems and potential for improvement. The clinician should note the effect of auditory and visual sensory variables and environmental factors on the ability of the client to eat, as described under sensory and environmental factors above. The Environment and Communication Assessment Toolkit (ECAT; Brush, Calkins, Bruce, & Sanford, 2011) can be used to evaluate the impact of features of personal (e.g., the person's room) and public spaces (e.g., the dining room), identifying low-cost, person-centered environmental modifications, such as lighting changes and ambient noise reduction, to improve the individual's functioning (Bruce, Brush, Sanford, & Calkins, 2013).

Mealtime Behaviors and Eating Assessment. All involved caregivers (e.g., nurses, OTs, SLPs, dietitians) can observe mealtime behaviors, such as social behaviors with others during meals. OTs generally conduct the evaluation of whether a client needs assistance for eating or should be fed by caregivers. This involves assessing range of motion, strength, and endurance of the upper extremities; grasp and release ability; and visual-motor integration abilities that impact use of utensils (Hellen, 2002). The clinician should note the client's attention to items placed in front of him or her (e.g., is there visual scanning difficulty from a field cut or neglect?) and ability to identify food and liquid items and utensils appropriately (e.g., is there an agnosia or other perceptual problem?). In addition, the clinician should evaluate the client's ability to initiate eating and to manipulate the utensils to feed oneself (Lee & Song, 2015) (e.g., is there an executive function problem or an apraxia?). If caregivers feed the person, the clinician should assess the client's response to feeding. In any case, the clinician should also note any feeding aversive behaviors (as described above; Stockdell & Amella, 2008).

While several assessment tools have been developed to determine the need for feeding assistance for nursing home residents, most have not undergone adequate psychometric testing (Aselage, 2010), with the exception of the Edinburgh Feeding Evaluation in Dementia Scale (EdFED; Stockdell & Amella, 2008) which was developed to identify eating difficulties and level of feeding assistance needed by persons with late-stage dementia. The questionnaire consists of 11 items, with subjective judgments made on the frequency of 10 observable behaviors and the present level of assistance required during meals. For example, items include behaviors such as: refuses to eat, turns head away, spits out food, leaves mouth open, as well as items to indicate the amount of supervision or assistance the person needs. The questionnaire takes five or more minutes to complete, whether by observation by a member of the care team (e.g., nurse), or caregiver report. The EdFED has undergone much psychometric assessment, with good results for: internal consistency (Watson, 1996), reliability (Watson, McDonald, & McReady, 2001), construct validity (Watson, Green, & Legg, 2001), convergent and discriminant validity (Watson, 1997; Watson, Green, & Legg, 2001). The Chinese version of the EdFED has been validated (Liu, Watson, & Lou, 2013), and preliminary psychometric testing completed on an Italian translation (Bagnasco et al., 2015). Advantages of using the EdFED include its ease of use, time efficiency, sensitivity to change over time, and demonstrated reliability and validity. This tool can also be used in the community and in caregiver interviews.

Swallowing Assessment. As part of the clinical swallowing evaluation, a variety of swallowing behaviors should be assessed. The swallowing assessment should only be initiated after a structural-functional exam and provision of oral hygiene care, if required. The dysphagia evaluation often begins with just a sip of water so that if there are significant concerns about swallowing safety and aspiration, the person will not have ingested any food or liquid that is more likely to cause infection. From there, the clinician administers a variety of foods and liquids with varying textures and consistencies, in both controlled trials and habitual self-feeding trials.

With respect to chewing, the clinician should note the type of chewing pattern (e.g., a rotary pattern or a suck–swallow pattern) and adequacy of chewing different textures of foods. With respect to manipulation and movement of the bolus, the clinician should note the effect of textures on the person's ability to form a cohesive bolus versus the food falling apart into various parts of the mouth, and the ability to hold food in the mouth. As cognitive deficits and/or motor deficits begin to interfere with the oral stage, some clients will need altered food textures and food restrictions (e.g., soft foods only, and no combinations of liquids and solids, such as in soups) to ensure safety of forming and manipulating a bolus. These modifications will be discussed further under the treatment section of this chapter.

In the pharyngeal stage, the clinician should note the speed and adequacy of laryngeal excursion. The swallowing process happens very quickly, although initiation of the swallow may be slower in individuals with dementia. By placing four fingers on the front of the client's neck, in the laryngeal and base of tongue areas, the clinician should be able to palpate immediate movement of the laryngeal structures up and forward. Clinicians should note signs of delayed or inadequate laryngeal excursion, coughing, throat cleaning and/or wet voice quality immediately or shortly after swallowing, or complaints of food feeling "stuck in the throat." McCullough et al. (2000) found that clinicians could reliably judge trial swallows of thin and thick liquids and puree consistencies for the following measures: prolonged total swallow duration, presence of oral stasis after the swallow, and overall swallowing function.

Another aspect of the swallowing assessment is the impact on quality of life. This is an essential aspect when it comes to making decisions regarding interventions, sometimes making decision-making contentious between the client, family, and healthcare team. There is an assessment tool to address this area, called the SWAL-QOL (McHorney et al., 2000a, 2000b, 2002, 2006). This is a 44-item self-report tool that examines both the perceived impairment and how a swallowing disorder impacts a person's daily life, feelings, and activities. The tool is sensitive to severity of dysphagia, and has documented reliability and validity, although it has not been tested with persons with cognitive impairments. A related tool, the SWAL-CARE (McHorney et al., 2002) is a 15-item tool that asks the client/family to give feedback on satisfaction with care. These tools are meant to be used to document treatment effectiveness. Given the nature of the self-report task and the reliance on memory and awareness of deficits, this tool may be difficult for people with moderate dementia, but it might be useful for people in the early stages of dementia who have neuromuscular disorders that accompany dementia early in the disease process.

Instrumental Swallowing Assessments

In acute or outpatient settings, if there are any suspicions of pharyngeal swallowing difficulty, clients are referred for instrumental swallowing assessment (e.g., a modified barium swallow or videofluoroscopy swallow study, or fiberendoscopic evaluation of swallowing [FEES]) with a physician's order. Given the possible low reliability of clinical bedside evaluation measures (McCullough et al., 2000) and the lack of ability to detect silent aspiration or to fully evaluate the efficacy of compensatory strategies to prevent aspiration (e.g., Leder, Sasaki, & Burrell, 1998; Logemann, 2003), some have suggested that instrumental swallow assessment is necessary in all cases. Compensatory strategies are patient specific and can be tested for efficacy during an instrumental swallow assessment, such as the effect of certain intense tastes, bolus temperatures, or carbonation triggering the pharyngeal phase of the swallow faster, or the use of a chin tuck position to prevent aspiration (Rösler et al., 2015).

When working with persons with dementia in the nursing home setting, however, there is controversy regarding the referral for instrumental assessment of swallowing, based on a number of factors. These factors range from logistical and financial concerns (e.g., transportation) to the complications of removing a person with dementia from the habitual setting for assessment, which is often confusing and might not give a good indication of habitual swallowing abilities. In combination with cognitive and behavioral deficits that interfere with ability to follow instructions and fully participate in the assessment, these problems may limit the practicality (Walshe, 2014). Instrumental assessment in an unfamiliar environment should only be pursued when the information yielded from a clinical assessment is inadequate to obtain the information needed for the goals of the assessment (Pioneer Network, 2011).

Alternatively, conducting FEES in the natural environment is a better approach for those clients who would be able to cooperate with the procedure (Leder et al., 1998). Advantages of FEES include: It detects silent aspiration at bedside, using minimally invasive procedures without contrast material or radiation, allowing this assessment to be administered as often as necessary. However, FEES is invasive and might prompt responsive behaviors too, regardless of setting. Decisions for use must still be weighed with the necessity for and utility of the information to be gained. The SLP must work with the interprofessional team to consider risks versus benefits of various procedures, as well as risks of swallowing symptoms and whether the information to be gained will make a difference in choices to be made regarding dysphagia management (e.g., will the client and/or family choose oral feeding or drinking regardless of the results of instrumental assessment?).

Treatment of Eating and Swallowing

The goals of eating and swallowing interventions can also be delineated across the domains of the ICF. They vary from those focused on improving the ability to eat or to swallow safely (e.g., to use a safe swallow strategy to prevent aspiration) or to use strategies to improve nutrition and hydration (e.g., to follow written cue cards to increase intake of food and liquids), to those focused on the participation, engagement, quality of life aspects (e.g., to increase pleasure in the dining experience). The goals must be determined in collaboration with the client and family, and any applicable team members, considering all assessment information, potential to benefit from treatment, and the desires of the client and family. At times, this requires a balance between increasing safety and accepting risk in order to best accommodate the desires of the client and family and to preserve independence and dignity. Each client and family will have their own level of risk tolerance, and decisions will have to take this into account. Regardless, eating and swallowing goals are not simply to ensure adequate intake, but to enhance overall physical, mental, and emotional well-being, considering each individual's unique circumstances.

There are a variety of approaches that can be used to improve eating and swallowing in persons with dementia. As noted above, many challenges are related to environmental factors (physical, social, and attitudinal), as well as cognitive, sensory, and physiological changes that make it difficult for persons with dementia to engage in safe intake of the proper quantity and quality of food and liquids, let alone to maintain independence, dignity, and quality of life. Clinicians use the client's and family's goals and information gained from the assessment to design a POC that is person-centered, as well as reasonable and necessary, choosing the most effective and/or efficient interventions to use for the given circumstances. If mealtime behaviors are an issue, then caregivers should use the Need-Driven Dementia-Compromised Behavior model (e.g., Algase et al., 1996; Kunik et al., 2003) to first reduce stressors on the client. Once responsive behaviors are reduced, then the clinician may address other deficits and intervene to promote nutrition (Roberts & Durnbaugh, 2002). The interventions to be discussed below are grouped into several overarching categories that encompass modifiable factors that influence eating and swallowing: environmental factors, food selection, cognitive and memory strategies and training, and caregiver interventions.

Modifying the Environment

When older adults move into assisted living or long-term care, they often have to adjust to changes in the context of eating. This adjustment is to be expected, as facilities cannot possibly accommodate every individual's eating preferences. However, some accommodation for the needs and preferences of individuals must be made to ensure person-centered care. Satisfaction with mealtime is affected by the food quality, quantity, and social context. The healthcare team may assist individuals with dementia in meeting nutrition and quality of life goals at mealtimes by reducing or eliminating environmental factors that interfere with eating (Lee & Song, 2015). Suggestions for enhancing aspects of the dining experience will be described, including the dining context, sensory stimuli, and music. Additional resources are provided in Box 8.5 at the end of this chapter.

Dining Context and Social Routines. Experts often recommend introducing a more home-like or more naturalistic setting to improve the overall dining experience for persons with dementia living in residential care (e.g., Aselage & Amella, 2010; Brush et al., 2002, 2011; Calkins & Brush, 2003; Douglas & Lawrence, 2015; Hellen, 2002). Improvements in oral food and fluid intake have been found with improvements to the dining environment, social stimulation, and staff attention (Douglas & Lawrence, 2015; Lee & Song, 2015). For persons who have lived alone for many years, a move to a residential facility, where expectations include eating in a group setting, may be stressful. For others who may have been lonely after a spouse died or friends moved away, this move to a group setting may be a welcome change. As noted previously, the person's eating history should include whether meals were eaten alone or with others, and this information should be considered in determining the most functional context for eating (Pioneer Network, 2011). Engaging in familiar routines surrounding meals is also important. For those who have always prayed before meals, the rushed context of many residential dining rooms may be prohibitive; offering a prayer or moment of silence before meals may reduce this problem (Hellen, 2002).

The optimal context to increase function and wellbeing is a low-stimulus environment with small groups and compatible tablemates (Hellen, 2002). A fine dining approach, either restaurant or buffet style, is recommended in the earlier stages of dementia to improve opportunities for more favored foods, increased opportunities for interaction, and more intake (Aselage & Amella, 2010; Pioneer Network, 2011; Roberts & Durnbaugh, 2002). The dining room milieu should be quiet and small with limited activity, and have small tables with armchairs designed not to tip; additionally, there should be adequate staff with proper training to assist residents to eat in a timely manner so that they do not have to wait. Family style dining as an environmental enhancement may also have beneficial effects for individuals with dementia (Altus, Engelman, & Mathews, 2002; Aselage & Amella, 2010; Douglas & Lawrence, 2015; Liu et al., 2015). Presenting food with serving bowls and empty plates compared to prepared food trays has a positive effect (Altus et al., 2002). Similarly, home-style dining where personal choice and independence were supported, resulted in improved food intake, nutritional status, and quality of life in long-term care residents (Ruigrok & Sheridan, 2006). A behavioral communication intervention designed to address the physiological and social interaction needs of residents with dementia resulted in decreased wandering, increased sitting, greater food consumption, and stable weight in three residents with dementia (Beattie, Algase, & Song, 2004).

At home, it may be helpful for family members to remain at the table until their family member with dementia has finished eating and to converse during the meal (Aselage & Amella, 2010). Others leaving the table may be a cue to stop eating, or the person may not wish to remain at the table alone once the enjoyable social interaction has ceased. For persons with dementia who dislike being monitored during meals or snacks at which the caregiver is not eating, having a cup of tea or water while the person finishes eating may make the caregiver's presence more natural. Additionally, for some it is considered poor manners to eat or drink in front of others who are not; the caregiver having a drink of water may make the situation feel more comfortable and enjoyable for the person with dementia.

Adaptations and Assistance During Meals. There are various levels and forms of mealtime adaptations and assistance. Eating independence can be improved with use of adaptive seating (e.g., for those with poor sitting balance), adaptive utensils, place set up, and cutting up food (Liu et al., 2016). Appropriate verbal prompts and praise provided by caregivers can increase food intake (Altus et al., 2002; Aselage & Amella, 2011; Liu et al., 2016). When cueing and other modifications (i.e., finger foods) no longer work for individuals with more advanced dementia, careful hand feeding should be offered, particularly if an individual is losing weight (AGS, 2014; Gillick & Mitchell, 2002; Hanson et al., 2013). In such cases, nurse supervisors, OTs, and/or SLPs need to provide training and supervision to ensure that the staff consistently use appropriate person-centered, safe feeding techniques that emphasize both safety and dignity (see Box 8.2). Caregivers must be mindful that the risk of aspiration is higher for persons who are dependent on others for feeding (Correia, Morillo, Filho, & Mansur, 2010). When being fed, a person has reduced control over coordinating swallow timing with presentation of food. Caregivers must also be careful not to misinterpret a person not opening the mouth as a signal to stop eating entirely; it could also communicate misunderstanding of what is expected, the need to finish the previous spoonful, or the need to clear the mouth with a liquid wash (Correia et al., 2010).

Caregivers must also monitor oral hygiene, and may need to give assistance in this area, particularly as dementia progresses. Individuals in the moderate to later stages of dementia often have poor oral health. The importance of oral hygiene in the care of people with dementia cannot be over-emphasized, as regular mouth care is critical in preventing bacterial overgrowth and

Box 8.2 Appropriate Communication and Assistance for Person-Centered Feeding

Communication:

- Verbal: Greet the person upon arrival, use a positive tone of voice, use simple sentences, show empathy, express approval ("I've enjoyed having lunch with you.") and interest ("I hear chocolate cake is your favorite. Is that right?"), maintain orientation; avoid talking too much, as this may be distracting
- Nonverbal: Make eye contact, use positive facial expression, touch and speak gently, "back-channel" responses ("hmm"), nod in affirmation
- Carefully observe the person's behaviors and adjust social interaction to ensure that they are facilitating, not hindering, eating

Assistance:

- Use adaptive equipment as needed (e.g., rubber spoons, plate guard, built-up cutlery handles, nosey cups)
- Encourage the person to help (e.g., if the person has picked up an item required by the staff, say courteously, "Oh, would you pass that to me please? ... Thank you.")
- Cut meat, remove nonfood items from the tray, open cartons, offer fluids throughout the meal, wipe crumbs and dribble from the mouth
- Provide choice, monitor comfort
- Allow the person to swallow one spoonful at a time, not only to ensure safety, but also the pleasures of eating
- Do not: force feed, mix pureed foods, outpace the person's ability to swallow the food, misinterpret a person not opening the mouth as a signal to stop eating entirely

(Based on Gilmore-Bykovskyi, 2015; Kayser-Jones & Schell, 1997; Roberts & Durnbaugh, 2002; Rogus-Pulia et al., 2015; Simmons, Osterweil, & Schnelle, 2001)

---

subsequent development of pneumonia due to aspiration of secretions (Pioneer Network, 2011; Rogus-Pulia et al., 2015). Excellent oral care is a requirement for persons with dementia and dysphagia, particularly for those who are appropriate for a Frazier free water protocol to improve hydration.

Sensory Stimuli. Several simple environmental modifications for increasing dining success include limiting extraneous stimulation (e.g., removing nonfood items from table before serving food), increasing the lighting (e.g., add lights to the corners and perimeter of the dining room), decreasing glare (e.g., use of window sheers and tablecloths), decreasing shadows, fixing flickering lights, using solid colors or only simple patterns on surfaces and textiles, and increasing the visual contrast of the food and place setting (e.g., dark tablecloth and light dishes) (Aselage & Amella, 2010; Behrman et al., 2014; Brush et al., 2002; Calkins & Brush, 2003; Douglas & Lawrence, 2015; Hellen, 2002; Kingston, 2017; Lee & Song, 2015; Liu et al., 2016; Roberts & Durnbaugh, 2002; Whear et al., 2014).

Older adults require three times as much light as younger ones (Koss & Gilmore, 1998). Enhanced lighting and enhanced visual contrasts in table settings can be used to increase food intake and to reduce negative behaviors (Brush et al., 2002; Koss & Gilmore, 1998). When these visual modifications were made in place settings, researchers observed increased frequency and quality of conversations with staff, and increased ability to find and use a napkin and to follow simple directions, and reduced distractibility, anxiety, and assistance needed (Brush et al., 2002). The use of colored rather than clear drinking glasses, to increase visibility, resulted in patients consuming 50% more water (Kingston, 2017).

Other modifications to the visual and auditory stimuli in the environment include decreasing TVs and radios playing, the number of people coming and going, and staff shouting and talking to each other; this may be facilitated by holding meals in smaller rooms (Behrman et al., 2014; Calkins & Brush, 2003). To absorb as much of the background noise as possible, the dining room should contain furniture and drapes made of fabric, such as fabric-covered acoustic panels that drape down from the ceiling and on the walls (Behrman et al., 2014; Calkins & Brush, 2003).

Another strategy to decrease environmental noise is to put up wall partitions with high-rated acoustic material to block out noise from the kitchen, ice machine, and tray service areas. Unfortunately, many residential facilities limit the use of fabrics and textiles for ease of cleaning and enhanced sanitation, but the resulting hard surfaces also serve to increase acoustic energy. The smell of foods cooking or coffee brewing can help to orient persons with to mealtime, stimulate appetite, and improve food intake (Behrman et al., 2014; Cleary, Van Soest, Milke, & Misiaszek, 2008). Finally, caregivers should ensure that residents' hearing aids and glasses are in place for meals, unless the noise of the environment and of their own chewing is distressing with hearing aids (Behrman et al., 2014; Hellen, 2002; Roberts & Durnbaugh, 2002).

Music. A music intervention during dinner may result in increased food intake and decreased depression, irritability, and restlessness in residents with dementia. Different types of music may produce different effects on residents – some may become calmer, while others may spend more time eating. When listening to "soothing" or "calming" music at mealtimes, residents with dementia had decreased mealtime agitation (Douglas & Lawrence, 2015; Hicks-Moore, 2005; Ho et al. 2011), and at a calmer pace (Douglas & Lawrence, 2015). Nursing home residents ate 20% more calories with familiar background music playing during lunchtimes (Thomas & Smith, 2009).

Despite these positive results, a systematic review of mealtime interventions concluded a weak level of evidence overall in studies examining the influence of soothing mealtime music on agitation (Liu et al., 2014). Anecdotally, there are residents who dislike music during meals either because the choice in music is not to their taste, or it interferes with their ability to hear tablemates. Another systematic review found seven studies where music was introduced during meals suggested a benefit in decreasing physical aggression, irritability, verbal and physical agitation, and non-aggressive physical behaviors; these effects may persist up to two weeks after discontinuing the playing of mealtime music (Whear et al., 2014). Music types that may elicit these benefits include relaxing music in particular (e.g., nature sounds, instrumental, and classical), pop, and music from the 1920s/30s.

Overall, music appears to hold promise as an intervention to enhance mealtimes and to improve nutritional intake among some individuals with dementia in long-term care settings. Confidence in knowledge about expected outcomes, dosage, and type of music that are most beneficial would improve with more robust research methodology. As always, person-centered care dictates that staff find out about preferences for individual clients.

Case 8.1 Illustration of Modifying the Physical and Social Environment

Brenda was a pleasant, middle-aged woman who lived in a skilled nursing facility and had advanced frontotemporal dementia. She herself had worked as a nurse previously. When awake, Brenda was very alert to her surroundings, thoroughly enjoyed "people-watching" and listening to others converse, but was no longer able to express herself verbally. Brenda typically ate her pureed meals in the dining room with staff assistance with feeding and cueing to swallow her food and clear her mouth. She often did not finish her meals, consuming less than 40% of her food at times, and was losing weight.

One contributing factor was that there were many distractions in the dining room, including multiple conversations between staff and residents or other staff, sound from a television that was often left on and behind Brenda, and many people present and walking around. Another factor was that to finish 100% of her meal, Brenda often required 40–60 minutes of one-on-one staff time as she chewed slowly, was often distracted, held food in her mouth, and often required repeated cues to swallow. Her food often needed to be reheated. Staff generally felt they could not spend this much time with Brenda due to other demands on their time in providing care to other residents.

The nursing clinical leader arranged to have Brenda fed in her room with a staff member who was dedicated to feeding her at that time. Brenda enjoyed looking at the staff member, listening to her music, or having the staff member "chat" with her or sing to her. With the reduced sensory input, Brenda was better able to attend to eating and the staff member's cues, while still having the pleasure of socializing. Occasionally another staff member would come in and Brenda would perk up even more and begin to chew more quickly and swallow with less cueing as she watched them and listened to them chatting. The staff made sure to include Brenda during these conversations with eye contact, smiles, and by referencing her (e.g., "You like this sunny weather too, don't you Brenda?"). With this dedicated assistance and optimal sensory and social environment, Brenda began to finish more of her meals and gain weight.

Food Selection, Modifications, and Intake

Food Selection. Prior to beginning any intervention to improve nutritional status, caregivers should be aware of appropriate goals for food and fluid intake for persons with dementia, which is determined by the dietitian/clinical nutritionist. Successful mealtimes require a personalized approach, with knowledge of individual food preferences; when food intake is poor at meals, the person may be encouraged to eat by providing choices or by providing the person's "comfort food" (Hellen, 2002). For those who are concerned about saving some of their food for later, caregivers may offer food that is wrapped and does not spoil. For those who are overwhelmed by the perception of too much food, serving one food or course at a time may also improve food intake by simplifying the meal and making the amount of food appear less overwhelming (Ball et al., 2015; Gillick & Mitchell, 2002; Hellen, 2002). Provision of finger foods has been found to increase intake and decrease weight loss (Abdelhamid et al., 2016). Along with high-calorie supplements, assisted feeding, appetite stimulants, and modified foods are all evidence-based options to promote weight gain for people with dementia and feeding problems, either used individually or in combination (Jackson, Currie, Graham, & Robb, 2011). Nutritional supplements are more likely to be consumed when served in a glass than via a straw in the container (Allen et al., 2014).

Case 8.2 Illustration of Mealtime Modifications at Home

Marian had been caring at home for her husband Gerry who was clinically diagnosed with AD several years previously. With her own worsening health problems, Marian had been finding it increasingly difficult to care for Gerry alone while on the waitlist for a nursing home bed, especially as his physically and verbally aggressive behaviors had been steadily increasing. Marian struggled with Gerry not finishing meals (he became distracted and seemed to lose interest in the food, stating he was full), yet consumed excessive quantities of sugary drinks between meals. The latter was additionally problematic as Gerry was incontinent. She worried about him getting enough to eat, drinking the right amount of fluids, the amount of sugar he was consuming in pop and juice, the work of preparing meals that went uneaten, and food being wasted.

A resourceful woman, Marian started preparing meals like pasta or sandwiches. When not finished, they could easily be put in the fridge and presented as a newly prepared and tasty meal when Gerry again expressed hunger. Sandwiches were also useful in that Gerry could eat them while wandering around their home. She also placed their dining table in a corner of their condominium so that the chairs faced the corner, thus reducing distraction. She removed the cans of pop and bottles of juice they had always kept in their fridge, so that there was only ever one or two bottles of juice and water. These changes reduced this source of confrontation and care burden.

Dysphagia Diets. As dementia progresses, dietary modifications are common. Altered food textures and fluid consistencies may be recommended for persons with oropharyngeal dysphagia, with the goals of improving swallowing safety and efficiency (Garcia, Chambers, & Molander, 2005). Modified food textures such as soft, chopped, minced, or puree may be recommended for persons with reduced tongue, masticatory, or pharyngeal muscle strength to decrease effort, choking on solid pieces of food, and the risk of oral and pharyngeal residue after swallowing (Keller et al., 2012; Steele et al., 2015). Thickened fluids are often recommended to slow transit time and decrease the risk of penetration and aspiration, but they also increase the risk of post–swallow pharyngeal residue, with the risk increasing as the thickness is increased (Steele et al., 2015).

Due to problems with staff accurately thickening liquids, some facilities may choose to only provide one option of thickened liquid (i.e., honey/moderately thick pre-thickened drinks) to reduce errors (i.e., nectar for honey). This choice, however, comes with its own risks. Residents who would most appropriately drink nectar thick beverages, if only offered honey thick, may have increased pharyngeal residue, decreased fluid intake, and derive less enjoyment from beverages (Steele et al., 2015). Additionally, thickened liquids may increase the risk of dehydration (Garcia et al., 2005). As fluid thickness is increased, more intake is required to meet hydration requirements. As dehydration exacerbates cognitive impairment, and has other negative effects on functioning, it is important that SLPs carefully determine the need for thickened liquids and recommend them sparingly. Some research evidence exists for allowing small sips of water in a carefully controlled protocol (see Cleary, Yanke, Masuta & Wilson, 2016) and only after oral hygiene has been provided.

When foods are mechanically altered, particularly when pureed, the nutrient density of fat, protein, and calories is decreased, food may become unrecognizable due to changes in shape and color, and it may be considered unpalatable due to changes in flavor, all increasing the risk of malnutrition and weight loss. When considering the recommendation of dysphagia diets, clinicians should give serious thought to the risk of decreased intake, pleasure with eating, and quality of life

(Keller et al., 2012; Pioneer Network, 2011; Ullrich & Crichton, 2015). Thus, to enhance nutritional status, hydration, and quality of life, and decrease the risk of weight loss in older persons living in nursing homes, the use of therapeutic, mechanically altered, and dysphagia diets should be avoided unless absolutely necessary (Pioneer Network, 2011). Clients (according to capacity) and families/substitute decision-makers must be engaged in decisions around dysphagia diets; how this is done can influence how acceptable the recommended diet is. When these diets are justified and acceptable to the PWD and their family, they should be monitored and discontinued if use is no longer required (e.g., after overcoming pneumonia, swallowing function returns to baseline, or effective compensatory strategies are implemented), the goals of care change (e.g., comfort care), or there are negative consequences like weight loss (Pioneer Network, 2011). See Box 8.3 for "Dos and Don'ts" of engaging the client and family in decision-making around dysphagia diets.

With a person on a modified texture diet or someone who does not consume adequate amounts of food, ensuring adequate nutrition requires a focus on the energy content of foods offered, not just the volume. Diets should include foods that are high in energy and naturally rich in nutrients or enriched (Keller et al., 2012; Spindler, 2002). Providing sensory stimulation through food odors and flavor enhancement improves appetite, tolerance, and intake (Douglas & Lawrence, 2015; Keller et al., 2012; Yen, 1996), and providing foods that look and smell appealing in adequate portions also improves appetite (Keller et al., 2012; Roberts & Durnbaugh, 2002). Additionally, nutritional supplements may improve food intake, body weight, and body mass index in PWD (Liu et al., 2014). See Box 8.4 for strategies to increase the appeal and nutritional value of mechanically altered foods.

Terminology, operational definitions, and food classifications differ between facilities, healthcare disciplines, companies, and regions (Cichero et al., 2016). This can make transitions between levels of care or facilities difficult, unless there is adequate communication about what food and

---

Box 8.3 Involving Clients and Families in Decision-Making for Modified Foods and Liquids

DO:

- Educate the client and family about the nature of modified textures and consistencies, the benefits and risks of such an intervention.
- Use supported communication and choice-making tools to engage the client maximally (to their capacity) (see Chapters 5 and 6 for more on such communication tools).
- Be actively involved in developing an acceptable management plan.
- Offer what the person can have: "Would you like some ice cream or vanilla pudding?"
- Convey concern for wellbeing (e.g., "I know your mum enjoys coffee, but because when she drinks liquids that aren't thickened they go into her airway, we're worried about coffee being unsafe for her.")

DON'T:

- Approach the client and family with a set of recommendations for approval without informing and involving them.
- Avoid punitive and limiting language such as, "you can't have a cookie."

(Ullrich & Crichton, 2015)

Box 8.4 Strategies to Increase the Appeal and Nutritional Value of Mechanically Altered Foods

Adding appeal
- Increase sensory stimulation with food odors, a variety of flavors and temperatures.
- Present foods in their pre-modified form using food molds (e.g., minced chicken in the form of a chicken breast, or pureed carrots in the shape of a carrot).
- Offer pureed foods that are naturally this consistency (e.g., mashed potatoes, yogurt, mousse).
- Offer foods that are finely chopped and soft, which may be as well tolerated in terms of chewing and swallowing, and the flavor may not be as degraded as it is when pureed.
- Keep food items separate on a plate.
- Provide foods that look and smell appealing, and in adequate portions.
- Enhance flavor with salt, herbs, sweet sauces, honey, or sugar.

Enhancing nutrient value
- Include high energy foods (e.g., butter, oil, nuts, sauces/gravy, ice cream, and cheese).
- Include naturally nutrient-rich foods (e.g., fruits, vegetables, and oils).
- Include nutrient-enriched foods (e.g., cereals that are vitamin fortified).
- Add skim milk powder, egg albumen, carbohydrate-based thickeners, and rice-based enriched cereal.

(Based on: Ball et al., 2015; Behrman et al., 2014; Douglas & Lawrence, 2015; Keller et al., 2012; Roberts & Durnbaugh, 2002; Rogus-Pulia et al., 2015; Spindler, 2002; Williams & Weatherhead, 2013; Yen, 1996)

---

liquid recommendations the person is being transferred with. This has resulted in development of standardized protocols in some countries (e.g., USA, Canada, New Zealand). In November 2015, the International Dysphagia Diet Standardization Initiative (IDDSI) presented the IDDSI Framework (Cichero et al., 2016). The initiative was an international and multidisciplinary collaboration to standardize preparation, operational definitions, and terminology for modified textures and consistencies. The standard has been recognized by ASHA, endorsed by the New Zealand Speech-language Therapists' Association, and adopted by the Canadian Dysphagia Industry Group with full implementation planned for 2019 (http://iddsi.org/).

Cognitive Approaches

Compensatory Strategies. Given that most of the eating challenges in persons with early stages of AD are due to cognitive deficits, cognitive strategies can be devised to improve eating and swallowing behaviors, and the overall dining experience. In the early stage of dementia, the person may still be living relatively independently at home, with some assistance provided with shopping and meal preparation. Several creative approaches can be used, including written and graphic cues, to help maintain this level of independence. For example, shopping lists can be organized according to the organization of one's grocery store by making columns in accordance with the aisles of the grocery store. See Table 8.1 for an example. Additionally, strategies to identify food that is out of date and to organize refrigerators and cupboards can be developed through the use of written cues and labels.

Calendars can be made to list the meals that will be eaten each day, and crossed off to help the person remember whether or not he or she has eaten. Cooking can also be maintained through the use of written cues and timers, or simplified with the use of a microwave. When the person is unable to prepare hot meals, "Meals on Wheels" may be arranged to serve one hot meal per day. This sometimes has the added benefit of a small amount of socialization with the person delivering the meal.

In the middle stages, cognitive, psychiatric, and behavioral disturbances may affect eating and swallowing. For example, some residents refuse to go to the dining hall due to fears of being poisoned or of not being able to pay for their meals. Hellen (2002) recommended several creative strategies for dealing with responsive behaviors. For example, a take-out box can be used if there is concern about being poisoned; or a letter can be provided stating that the person has paid his or her "dues," which includes meals; or a "paid in full" meal ticket can be provided (see Table 8.2 for an example). As cognitive deficits increase, mealtime may become more confusing and simplification is needed, such as using multisensory cues to foster recall of mealtime memories, and using a task analysis to simplify the components of eating and to sequence eating activities consistently, offering one item at a time and using one-step directions (Calkins & Brush, 2003; Gillick & Mitchell, 2002; Hellen, 2002).

As discussed in Chapter 5, SLPs can develop use of external strategies to improve functional behaviors. For example, written reminder cards can be made for safe swallowing during meals, or for the multiple instructions in a swallowing evaluation. For persons with more severe cognitive deficits, cards can be made for each step in the eating and swallowing process: Open your mouth, chew, and swallow. Reminder cards may also be used to facilitate use of specific swallowing

TABLE 8.1 Example of Grocery Shopping List, Organized by Store Aisles

Aisle 1: Produce	Aisle 2: Bread, crackers	Aisle 3: Cereals
Aisle 4: Cleaning products	Aisle 5: Healthcare products	Aisle 6: Soda, chips, snack foods
Aisle 7: Frozen vegetables, dinners	Aisle 8: Frozen desserts	Aisle 9: Dairy and eggs (milk, cheese, yogurt)

TABLE 8.2 Example of Meal Ticket

```
┌────────────────────────────────────────────────┐
│                                                  │
│            Islandview Village                    │
│                                                  │
│                 MEAL TICKET                      │
│                                                  │
│        Name: _____     │
│                                                  │
│                 paid in full                     │
│                                                  │
└────────────────────────────────────────────────┘
```

strategies, such as chin tuck positioning, or alternating liquids and solids. These strategies may help to maintain independence over a longer period of time, or to minimize the amount of cueing and assistance needed. See Table 8.3 for examples of reminder cards.

Spaced Retrieval Training + Written Cues. When the person with dementia has oral-pharyngeal dysphagia, the person may benefit from the use of spaced retrieval training and written cue cards to recall safe swallowing strategies, as illustrated below. Brush and Camp (1998) described the successful training of an 86-year-old resident of a long-term care facility to use a compensatory strategy for his dysphagia, which was trained with the spaced retrieval training procedure. After a thorough swallowing assessment (bedside and radiographic) revealed that the resident needed to alternate bites of food with sips of liquid to clear the food from the valleculae, the clinician began training with a visual cue card ("After you swallow your food, take a sip of liquid"). Using the spaced retrieval technique, the clinician prompted, "What do you do after you swallow your food?" The resident responded, "I take a sip of liquid," and the clinician prompted him to take a sip. During training, the visual prompt was changed to read, "Chew-swallow-sip," and then removed when the resident was remembering to take a sip 83% of the time. At the 8-week follow-up session, the resident completed the compensatory technique 95% of the time, requiring only one reminder per meal to use the safe swallowing technique. Also note the strategies in Appendix 8.1 for a variety of cognitive-related eating and swallowing challenges.

More recently, Benigas and Bourgeois (2016) used spaced retrieval training with written and graphic cues, to teach five nursing home residents with dementia compensatory swallowing behaviors. The investigators used the results of a comprehensive eating and swallowing evaluation, which included videofluoroscopic findings, and they observed the PWD eating a typical meal in order to select compensatory strategies for each individual (e.g., chin tuck, small bites, double swallow, swallow and cough). These strategies were printed on cue cards and taught using the spaced retrieval paradigm. All five participants learned to use compensatory strategies to eat safely, and four were able to have their diets upgraded with use of the visual cue. In addition, social validation ratings showed that judges who were naïve to the treatment conditions scored participants' performance of compensatory behaviors as significantly improved from baseline observations.

Montessori-based Activities + Spaced Retrieval Training. Other investigators have found a positive effect of Montessori-based activities and spaced retrieval training to reduce feeding difficulties and increase independence with self-feeding (Liu et al., 2015). Wu, Lin, Wu, Lin, & Liu (2013) implemented a treatment program combining spaced retrieval training and Montessori-based activities with 63 persons with dementia in three nursing homes in Taiwan. Twenty-five persons at one nursing home received a standardized protocol for 24 sessions over 8 weeks, and 38 persons in two nursing homes had an individualized program for 10–35 sessions. A control group of 27 persons at a fourth nursing home received care as usual. At the end of the program, compared to the pre-test, those in both intervention groups demonstrated improved Chinese-EdFED scores, increased intake, and some weight gain at the 6-month follow-up. Positive differences

TABLE 8.3 Written Cues for Eating and Swallowing Challenges

1. Food labels for items in refrigerator

   | **Chicken, May 22, 2017** |

   | **Green beans, May 22, 2017** |

2. Food labels for cupboards

   | **Canned soups and vegetables** |

   | **Pasta, rice, cereals** |

   | **Herbs, spices, flours** |

3. Meal menu

   ## Isleview Manor
   May 22, 2017
   ### Today's menu:
   Green beans
   Mashed potatoes
   Chicken
   Brownie
   Coffee or tea

4. Eating sequence

   Open mouth

   Chew

   Swallow

5. Safe eating/swallowing

   1. Sit up straight
   2. Take a small sip
   3. Chin down
   4. Swallow

   Take a bite
   Chew and chew
   Swallow
   Take a sip
   Start over

6. Swallowing evaluation

   1. Take a sip
   2. Keep it on my tongue
   3. Wait
   4. Swallow

7. Oral hygiene

   1. Get denture box
   2. Remove dentures
   3. Put dentures in box
   4. Fill box with water
   5. Put denture tablet in water
   6. Close denture box
   7. Get cup
   8. Put water in cup
   9. Rinse mouth with water

compared to pre-test data were measured at 1-, 3-, and 6-month follow-ups. Interestingly, the physical exercise part of the Montessori-based intervention appeared to improve grip strength, upper extremity strength, and sitting balance (Liu et al., 2016). These initial findings of this type of intervention are suggestive of the utility of spaced retrieval training and Montessori-based interventions to improve eating independence, intake, and weight gain. Further research is needed that improves on the methodological limitations (e.g., lack of randomization or multiple baseline measurements) and provides additional evidence.

Providing Support for Caregivers

Caregivers are responsible for monitoring and providing cueing or assistance for safe eating and swallowing, adapting interventions along with the progression of cognitive deficits. Unfortunately, staff training is often not sufficient for use of the most effective and efficient procedures. Staff may find residents' responsive or aversive behaviors pose a significant barrier to providing feeding assistance, and mealtime thus becomes one of the most challenging parts of providing care (Aselage & Amella, 2010; Douglas & Lawrence, 2015; Simmons & Schnelle, 2003). Thus, researchers have developed training programs designed to help staff to understand eating and swallowing problems in persons with dementia, and the best ways to assist their residents. Effective caregiver training programs can result in residents spending more time eating, and having less difficulty with eating (Liu et al., 2014). In addition to the environmental and cognitive strategies already suggested in the above sections, optimal ways for staff to cue or to feed residents will be discussed.

Staff training should emphasize a person-centered, rather than a task-oriented, approach for mealtime with residents (Gilmore-Bykovskyi, 2015; Hellen, 2002; Roberts & Durnbaugh, 2002), so as to reduce the stress of both staff and residents and the risk of triggering agitation or resistance. The care team must ensure that all suitable procedures and strategies have been attempted before beginning the more invasive feeding by staff; and staff must provide such care in ways that will protect the persons' autonomy and dignity (Pioneer Network, 2011; Simmons & Schnelle, 2003). This also requires having enough staff available to follow through with a person-centered approach (Hellen, 2002). Refer back to Box 8.2 for descriptions of appropriate communication and assistance for person-centered feeding behaviors.

In general, staff should be taught about how self-feeding and swallowing abilities change with dementia and the underlying factors that contribute to these challenges (e.g., apraxia). Understanding how their own behaviors, beliefs, attitudes, and use of a person-centered approach may change resident behaviors and outcomes may also prove beneficial. Techniques to provide appropriate hands-on assistance (e.g., bridging, chaining, and hand over hand), as well as communication strategies that will enhance cueing (e.g., the use of a calm, slow style, and short sentences) should also be taught (Hellen, 2002). Staff should be taught about offering reinforcement and encouragement for self-feeding efforts, and to sit in front of the person when providing cueing or assistance. One-on-one assistance during eating through the use of verbal prompts and reinforcement has been shown to be effective in improving eating performance of individuals with dementia (Liu et al., 2015).

In a three-week pre-post caregiver training study with 26 residents with midstage AD and 52 staff, Roberts and Durnbaugh (2002) found that staff were able to identify appropriate interventions significantly more often in post-training than in pre-training. Whereas overall food consumption did not differ, food selection included more nutritious and less non–nutritious foods. Simmons and Schnelle (2003) investigated the effects of a 2-day trial of feeding assistance on residents' oral food and fluid intake during meals, with a significant increase in their mealtime intake in response to the intervention. More cognitive and physical impairment was associated with a higher increase in oral intake in response to the intervention.

Scheduling group education sessions with caregiving staff is one challenge of such feeding skills training interventions in nursing homes. Batchelor-Murphy, Amella, Zapka, Mueller, and Beck (2015) performed a feasibility study exploring the use of a 30-minute online training presentation that staff could complete when most convenient, paired with direct coaching on feeding skills as a group. Control group caregivers only completed pre-post questionnaires and were observed by researchers. Both groups of staff increased the number of target feeding skill behaviors, possibly reflecting the influence of the pre-intervention questionnaire as it included questions on specific behaviors that were subsequently taught in the training program. Batchelor-Murphy and colleagues (2015) found that intervention group staff increased the amount of time spent feeding residents, whereas the control group staff decreased time spent feeding residents. Food intake in the training group doubled, whereas in the control group, intake decreased by more than half. This type of training program is promising to improve food intake in residents with dementia living in a skilled nursing facility, and requires more research (Batchelor-Murphy et al., 2015).

Manning et al. (2012) reported a significant increase in oral intake of older adults in a hospital-based setting when patients were fed by volunteers. Volunteer feeding assistants spent more than twice the amount of time feeding patients than nurses were able to spend. Similar positive outcomes have been reported by others (see Dory, 2004; Lipner, Bosler & Giles, 1990). Staff caregivers could be assigned to feed more complex residents, whereas volunteers could provide cueing and assistance to those who need less skilled care. Because many hospitals and nursing homes have volunteers, the use of volunteers in feeding individuals with dementia could be a valuable method to improve care during mealtimes with little increase in operating cost to the facility or time burden to the staff (Douglas & Lawrence, 2015).

Support groups may provide a source of emotional support and useful information about preparing modified dishes and managing responsive behaviors associated with meals. Support groups may be general to dysphagia *or* dementia topics (see Box 8.5 for resources at the end of this chapter). One example of a support group specific to the needs of male spouses is the Men's Cooking Group in Toronto, Ontario. Hosted by the Alzheimer Society Toronto and in partnership with a local church, the Men's Group was developed for men caring for their wives with dementia who are learning to cook for the first time. Participants learn about grocery budgeting, cooking, and are able to connect with others with similar experiences (http://alz.to/blog/whats-dinner-tonight/).

Amella and Batchelor-Aselage's (2014) developed the C3P Model for evaluating and intervening with mealtime challenges. This model was developed to assist formal and informal caregivers to assess, implement change, and evaluate outcomes of changes by asking what is working well and what is not during mealtimes. Amella and Batchelor-Aselage's C3P Model demonstrates its utility

---

Case 8.3 Illustration of a Caregiver Intervention

Cleary (2006) reported a case study in which a variety of strategies were utilized to increase independence and safety in eating/swallowing for a man with PDD. The staff members were trained to implement the following strategies: seat him at a consistent place and follow a predictable routine in the dining room, place a Plexiglas barrier around his eating area to prevent him from eating extraneous items (e.g., sugar packets), and provide one food item at a time. This client reportedly was very distractible at meals, ate independently only 20% of the time, had severe weight loss due to poor intake, and experienced two choking episodes before intervention. After the intervention, he reportedly ate independently 70% of the time and gained nine pounds in the first 45 days of intervention.

in its systematic and practical approach to analyzing how the *person* with dementia, the *place* (i.e., the environment), and other *people* (i.e., caregivers) can be modified to make mealtimes more positive. The program has a train–the–trainer element, to enable caregivers and volunteers to train others at their home facilities.

Eating Issues in End-Stage Dementia

Eating is one of the last functional behaviors to be lost in the course of dementia (Mitchell, 2015). In the late stages, persons with dementia are fed by staff. This period can last from a few months to several years, but when the person consistently spits out food, pushes away the spoon, and gags on or refuses to drink liquids, it becomes necessary to decide on either a palliative care approach or tube feeding (Mitchell, 2015). Weight loss is a predictor of death in advanced dementia (Hanson et al., 2013). Decisions about feeding at this stage are complicated and contentious. The SLP has an important role in providing families and other caregivers with information as they make decisions about how to proceed.

Pneumonia. In general, poor nutrition is a contributor to risk for infection, and dysphagia is a risk factor for both poor nutrition and pneumonia. Foley et al. (2015) conducted a systematic that revealed that people with dementia are more likely to have pneumonia than older adults without dementia, and they are more likely to die of pneumonia. While dysphagia is not the only cause of pneumonia, it is one of the causes in persons with dementia, and risk is associated with aspiration, particularly in those with feeding tubes and reflux. Pneumonia is more likely the more severe the cognitive deficits, and cognitive deficits worsen after a bout of pneumonia. They also noted that pharyngeal dysphagia may be worsened by the side effects of some medications (e.g., some neuroleptics).

Palliative Care. The goal of palliative care is the best quality of life for patients and their families by providing care that is life affirming, does not hasten or postpone death, provides relief from pain, addresses psychological and spiritual needs, and supports both patients and families (Pollens, 2004). Palliative, or comfort, care involves offering food and drink only to the extent the person continues to accept and enjoy them. The goal of hand feeding at this stage is to provide food to the extent that it is comfortable for the patient, rather than to ensure a prescribed caloric intake

---

Case 8.4 Illustration of a Multicomponent Intervention

In the long-term care unit of a multi-level care facility, where there were only occasional SLP services, the residents with severe dementia were lined up in the hall and being fed by nursing assistants, who were squeezing pureed food into their mouths with a large syringe. Staff were talking amongst themselves, and the residents were either passively taking the food or showing agitation. The SLP received a referral for an evaluation, and requested real dishes and silverware for the assessment, which staff thought was pointless. They were quite surprised when the resident was able to eat her whole tray without signs of unsafe swallowing!

The SLP used the following strategies: remove distracting items, offer one item at a time, talk to the resident in a calm voice, give one-step directions, and use written reminder cards for each step (open your mouth, chew, and swallow). The SLP then offered in-service training and demonstrations for nursing staff. The staff were apprehensive initially, but soon learned that the strategies did not increase their workload and that, in fact, some residents became much easier to feed and less agitated. Administrators and families were delighted!

(Mitchell, 2015). In some facilities, "comfort trays" are used at the end of life to offer hydration, consisting of items such as water, Jell-O, and ice cream.

Tube Feeding. Tube feeding is a second care option for individuals with advanced dementia who can no longer take food or fluids by mouth. Tube feeding requires either the insertion of a tube via the nasal passages, through the esophagus and into the stomach (nasogastric), or the insertion of a percutaneous endoscopic gastrostomy (PEG) tube from the mouth, through the esophagus, into the stomach, and through an incision in the stomach wall and skin. This latter procedure is performed by giving the person a mild sedative and a local anesthetic to numb the skin, and is well tolerated by most (Gillick & Mitchell, 2002). Evidence suggests that tube feeding does not lengthen survival or improve quality of life in persons with end-stage dementia, nor does earlier insertion have a different outcome (Foley et al., 2015; Goldberg & Altman, 2014; Nourhashémi et al., 2012; Teno et al., 2012).

The American Geriatrics Society Ethics Committee and Clinical Practice and Models of Care Committee developed a position statement on the use of feeding tubes in advanced dementia. They concluded that observational research evidence indicates that the benefits of tube feeding do not outweigh the substantial associated treatment burdens (AGS, 2014). The committees noted that there is preponderance of evidence to demonstrate that feeding tubes do not prevent aspiration pneumonia, prolong survival or promote wound healing in persons with late-stage dementia (e.g., Alagiakrishnan et al., 2013; Dharmarajan & Unnikrishnan, 2004), and may result in adverse outcomes related to complications (e.g., infection, increased risk of pressure ulcers, pneumonia) with feeding tube placement.

The decision to place a feeding tube or to offer a palliative approach to care through hand feeding is a difficult one for caregivers. There are ethical concerns, family beliefs and values, family burdens and other issues to be considered (Fernandez-Viadero, Jimenez-Sanz, Verduga, & Crespo, 2015). Caregivers are often understandably concerned when their loved ones with advanced dementia stop eating. They may be reassured with information that patients at the end-of-life experience little to no hunger or thirst, and the potential discomfort of a dry mouth can be alleviated with mouth swabs or ice chips (Gillick & Mitchell, 2002; McCann, Hall, & Groth-Juncker, 1994). When the discussion and or recommendation to not insert a PEG is brought up with caregivers, it may be wrongly interpreted as a recommendation that will mean "no food" or "no care" for their loved one (Goldberg & Altman, 2014). It should be emphasized to caregivers that hand feeding instead of tube feeding does not imply that medical care has been stopped, but rather that care is focused on palliation (Mitchell, 2015). Caregivers have a better experience in making the decision about tube feeding when using a decision aid (Hanson et al., 2011).

The SLP's Role in End-of-Life Care. Irwin (2006) described the role of the SLP in making end-of-life decisions, particularly with regard to the feeding of patients with advanced dementia. Although SLPs often participate in the development and implementation of nutrition care plans in long-term care facilities (White, 2005), some studies have shown that they may not have adequate knowledge about the operation and consequences of tube feeding or safe oral intake to be a strong advocate for the patient's preferences (Davis & Conti, 2003). Few SLPs are reported to be members of the palliative or hospice care team in spite of the fact that patients with advanced dementia may experience dysphagia and require recommendations and precautions for food and liquid consistencies, and oral intake facilitation techniques. In some cases, however, SLPs have contributed significantly to management decisions reducing tube placements (Monteleoni & Clark, 2004). Both ASHA and Speech-Language and Audiology Canada (SAC) have produced materials to help guide SLPs working in these contexts (ASHA, n.d.; SAC, 2016). Eggenberger and Nelms (2004) suggested that SLPs who want to enhance the ability of family members to make informed nutritional and end-of-life decisions for their loved one should integrate the current best practice evidence and their clinical expertise when providing feeding recommendations. Clinicians, therefore, have developed tools to aid families and medical professionals in the decision-making process (Eggenberger & Nelms, 2004; Mitchell, Tetroe, & O'Connor, 2001). More information about quality of life, end-of-life decision-making, and advance directives can be found in Chapter 11.

Box 8.5 Resources for Clinicians, Clients, Families

For Clinicians: Optimizing Mealtimes and Dining Practices in Skilled Nursing Facilities:

- Pioneer Network Resource Library – Dining: resources to facilitate implementation of the recommendations of the Pioneer Network Food and Dining Clinical Standards Task Force (2011) and to enhance dining for residents of skilled nursing facilities; www.pioneernetwork.net/resource-library
- International Dysphagia Diet Standardisation Initiative: information for professionals on the IDDSI; http://iddsi.org/about-us/

For Clients, Families, and Caregivers:

- Dysphagia Diet: consumer source for thickeners, adaptive utensils, pureed food, pre-thickened drinks, recipes, and dysphagia cookbooks; www.dysphagia-diet.com/default.aspx
- National Foundation of Swallowing Disorders: review of dysphagia cookbooks; http://swallowingdisorderfoundation.com/which-dysphagia-cookbook-is-right-for-you/
- Dysphagia Solutions: products, recipes, advice, and instructional videos for consumers and family members; www.dysphagiasupplies.com/
- Gourmet Puree: puree recipe books available for purchase; http://essentialpuree.com/
- DysDine – Dysphagia Dining: maintained by graduate students in speech-language pathology, this site offers recipes, discussion boards, resources, and restaurant reviews; www.dysdine.com/

For Clients and Families: Support Groups and Online Forums:

- Agevillage.com Forums: hosts French language message boards on a variety of topics on aging; http://forums.agevillage.com/
- ALZConnected, Alzheimer's Association: hosts a message board for caregivers with a variety of topics; has a Spanish forum; www.alzconnected.org/default.aspx
- Alzheimer's Association – Caregiver Support Groups: consumers and caregivers can search for support groups in their state; www.alz.org/care/alzheimers-dementia-support-groups.asp
- AsantCafé, Alzheimer Society of Alberta and Northwest Territories: an online discussion forum for persons with dementia and caregivers; www.asantcafe.ca/
- Alzheimer Society Canada: provincial Alzheimer Societies host or connect people with local support groups; www.alzheimer.ca/en/provincial-office-directory
- National Foundation of Swallowing Disorders: maintains a list of swallowing support groups in the US, hosts themed online community forums, and provides resources for SLPs interested in starting a support group; the support groups listed are not specific to those with dementia; http://swallowingdisorderfoundation.com/swallowing-support-groups/

Appendix 8.1 Strategies for Mealtime, Eating, and Swallowing Challenges in Persons with Dementia

Challenges and Strategies

Shopping, Storing Food, and Preparing Meals
- Use organized lists
- Write labels and dates on foods in refrigerator
- Write category labels in pantry and cupboards
- Timers
- Simplified written recipes
- Microwave
- Help prepare foods: Put on sauces and dressing, butter bread, and cut food
- "Meals on Wheels"

Loss of Interest in Eating, or Poor Appetite
- Emphasize meal routines
- Assist with meal preparation to get multisensory stimulation
- Provide a limited number of immediate choices (show menu or food pictures)
- Provide frequent small meals and snacks
- Provide small portions, individually
- Provide foods that look like real food, and use real dishes and silverware
- Look for natural social opportunities to offer food and drink, such as offering an ice cream if going to the garden in the summer, a warm mug of broth on a cold afternoon by the fire, or a drink of water while doing an activity together

Overeating
- Provide distractions and alternative activities
- Limit access, and provide low-calorie snacks
- Use checklist of meals – check off after each meal eaten

Safety: Impulsive eating & food preparation
- Supervise eating rate
- Remind person to take small bites and sips
- Use written reminder card for small bites and sips
- Cut into bite size, and serve at a safe temperature

Memory Deficits: Forgets to eat or forgets how to eat
- Use a schedule card and alarms
- Use reminder cards: For example, "Eating keeps me strong and healthy"
- Use reminder cards with steps: multiple steps per card, or one step per card (e.g., "Open mouth," "Chew," and "Swallow")
- Imitation
- Verbal and gestural cues
- Written cues: "I am eating green beans"
- Physical assistance – get them started (e.g., place spoon or sandwich in hand)

Attention Deficits: Discontinues eating, distracted
- Remind to continue eating (e.g., invitingly say, "have some more soup," with a hand gesture indicating the soup)
- Reduce distracting background noise (e.g., turn off TV)
- Position so that they have their backs toward thoroughfares

Perceptual Deficits: Smell and taste; vision; tactile
- Throw out spoiled food – use labels
- Enhance foods – use salt substitutes, sugar substitutes, and sweet versus sour
- Use a mixture of temperatures and textures (if not orally defensive)
- Enhance presentation: color contrast among placemat, bowl, and food
- Remove tray and all nonfood items
- Provide items that look like real food
- Provide one or two items at a time
- Maximize lighting
- Offer carbonated beverages which may provide additional stimulation and oral sensation of the liquid

Executive Functions (Initiation, Planning, Sequencing)
- Verbal cue to start eating
- Place the spoon in the person's hand
- Scoop some food onto the spoon, rest it on the plate on the side of dominant hand, and verbally cue them (Invitingly: "Have some meatloaf."), and/or guide their hand to the spoon
- Spaced retrieval training
- Written cues on a card

Agitation and Pacing
- Need extra calories
- Reduce distractions (e.g., eat at the table, not in front of the TV)
- Eat one-on-one (then join in family meal)
- Eat one item at a time
- "Cocktail party" approach – eat "by the way" with finger foods
- Use a calm, slow approach in providing assistance
- Allow the person to eat alone as necessary
- Engage in conversation or an activity to prevent agitation while waiting for food (e.g., look at photography book; feed baby doll a bottle)
- Evaluate if person is uncomfortable, in pain, or is attempting to communicate something
- Have a cup of tea or water and engage the person and/or tablemates in conversation if appropriate to create a more natural and socially enjoyable experience

Eating Resistance Behaviors
- Gently touch spoon to lower lip to cue mouth opening
- Evaluate the situation – comfort (check for repositioning need or pain levels), temperature of food and room (check if the food needs to be reheated or if the person needs a sweater or the thermostat adjusted), still trying to swallow (observe external indications of laryngeal elevation)
- If refusing food, offer a drink, and vice versa
- Alternate between foods (meat, vegetables, potatoes, dessert)
- Give the person and break and engage him or her

Mechanics of Eating
- Accept and accommodate messiness: Use plastic tablecloths, napkins, and shirt protectors; offer a warm damp face towel at the end of the meal to clean hands and face
- Use plateguard and weighted utensils
- Use bowls and "scoopable" foods that require a spoon only
- Use finger foods
- Cut up the person's food before serving

Supplements and Enhancers
- Add protein (e.g., soy) powders to milk
- Provide shakes as snacks
- Add fiber using wheat germ
- Load on sauces, gravy, butter, shredded cheese, and so on to increase calories
- Put sweet supplements on foods (chocolate syrup and jellies)
- Use salts (or salt substitutes) and spices

Dehydration
(Note: Dehydration exacerbates cognitive deficits!)
- Note if person is not accurately perceiving thirst
- Frequently offer drinks, particularly when the temperature is hot, humid, or very dry
- Provide easily accessible drinks (e.g., individual servings such as juice boxes)
- Avoid asking yes–no questions (i.e., "Do you want a drink?")

Swallowing Disorders (i.e., dysphagia): Choking hazards
- Avoid hot dogs, popcorn, crackers, and "mixed" textures
- For persons with oral residue, for some taking a drink may help to clear the mouth, for others it poses a risk of aspiration
- Crush pills (consult pharmacist first)

Swallowing Disorders (i.e., dysphagia): Need modified diet and/or liquids
- Regular: bacon, chicken, broccoli, salad
- Soft: toast, hamburger, cooked vegetables
- Ground: banana, baked fish, scrambled eggs
- Puree: applesauce, cream of wheat, grits, yogurt, pudding, thin mashed potato, ice cream (if no thin liquid restriction)
- Slightly thick
- Nectar/mildly thick
- Honey/moderately thick
- Pudding/extremely thick

Swallowing Disorders (i.e., dysphagia): Stops chewing prematurely; needs cues to swallow; "squirreling" in cheeks
- Verbally cue (e.g., "chew your food")
- Gently stroke the person's cheek
- Use a verbal or tactile cue (e.g., "swallow", gently stroke the person's throat if they are comfortable with this)
- Cue the person to clear the food from their cheeks (e.g., "finish the food in your mouth")
- Gently stroke the person's cheek upward from the jaw line to push the food up out of the cheek

Warning signs – Contact your doctor for a referral to a speech-language pathologist if you notice ANY of the following:
- Holding food in mouth, requires cues to swallow
- Food left in mouth (collected in cheek or on tongue)
- Throat clearing during and after meals
- Coughing during and after meals
- Wet or gurgly voice
- Weight loss
- Fever
- Pneumonia

End Stage: Severely Limited Eating
(Note: Changes should not be sudden)
Changes to expect:
- Swallowing problems, not chewing food, refusing to eat, not recognizing food, and eating non-edibles

Limited intake:
- Provide comfort tray: selection of fluids, Jell-O, ice cream, and the like

Oral Hygiene Problems
Signs:
- Food avoidance (toast, meat, etc.), mouth ulcers, thrush medications, and sensitive gums

Dentures
- Provide assistance in cleaning (visual support and verbal cues)
- Obtain adjustment by dentist if weight changes

Oral cleaning:
- Use written reminder cards for tooth brushing
- Use glycerin swabs
- Ensure that mouth is clear of all food before and after each meal and snack

Source: Adapted from Melton and Bourgeois (2004).

References

Abdelhamid, A., Bunn, D., Copley, M., Cowap, V., Dickinson, A., Gray, L., … Hooper, L. (2016). Effectiveness of interventions to directly support food and drink intake in people with dementia: Systematic review and meta-analysis. *BMN Geriatrics, 16*(26), 1–18. doi:10.1186/s12877-016-0196-3.

Affoo, R. H., Foley, N., Rosenbek, J., Shoemaker, J. K., & Martin, R. E. (2013). Swallowing dysfunction and autonomic nervous system dysfunction in Alzheimer's disease: A scoping review of the evidence. *Journal of the American Geriatrics Society, 61*, 2203–2213. doi:10.1111/jgs.12553.

Ahmed, R. M., Irish, M., Henning, E., Dermody, N., Bartley, L., Kiernan, M. C., … Hodges, J. R. (2016). Assessment of eating behavior disturbance and neural networks in frontotemporal dementia. *Journal of the American Medical Association, 73*, 282–290. doi:10.1001/jamaneurol.2015.4478.

Alagiakrishnan, K., Bhanjib, R. A., & Kurianc, M. (2013). Evaluation and management of oropharyngeal dysphagia in different types of dementia: A systematic review. *Archives of Gerontology and Geriatrics, 56*, 1–9. http://dx.doi.org/10.1016/j.archger.2012.04.011.

Algase, D. L., Beck, C., Kolanowski, A., Whall, A., Berent, S., Richards, K., & Beattie, E. (1996). Need-driven dementia-compromised behavior: An alternative view of disruptive behavior. *American Journal of Alzheimer's Disease, 11*, 10–19. doi:abs/10.1177/153331759601100603.

Allen, V. J., Methven, L., & Gosney, M. (2014). Impact of serving method on the consumption of nutritional supplement drinks: Randomized trial in older adults with cognitive impairment. *Journal of Advanced Nursing, 70*(6), 1323–1334. doi:10.1111/jan.12293.

Altus, D., Engelman, K., & Mathews, M. (2002). Using family-style meals to increase participation and communication in persons with dementia. *Journal of Gerontological Nursing, 28*(9), 47–53. doi:10.3928/0098-9134-20020901-09.

Amella, E. J. (1999). Factors influencing the proportion of food consumed by nursing home residents with dementia. *Journal of the American Medical Society, 47*, 879–885. doi:10.1111/j.1532-5415.1999.tb03849.x.

Amella, E. (2004). Feeding and hydration issues for older adults with dementia. *Nursing Clinics of North America, 39*(3), 607–623.

Amella, E. J., & Batchelor-Aselage, M. B. (2014). Facilitating ADLs by caregivers of persons with dementia: The C3P model. *Occupational Therapy in Health Care, 28*, 51–62. doi:10.3109/07380577.2013.867388.

American Geriatrics Society [AGS] Ethics Committee and Clinical Practice and Models of Care Committee (2014). American Geriatrics Society feeding tubes in advanced dementia position statement. *J Am Geriatr Soc, 62*(8), 1590–1593. doi:10.1111/jgs.12924.

American Speech-Language-Hearing Association (ASHA). (n.d.). *Dementia: End-of-life issues.* Retrieved February 20, 2017 from www.asha.org/PRPSpecificTopic.aspx? folderid=8589935289&section=Treatm ent#End-of-Life_Issues.

Arrighi, H. M., Gélinas, I., McLaughlin, T. P., Buchanan, J., & Gauthier, S. (2013). Longitudinal changes in functional disability in Alzheimer's disease patients. *International Psychogeriatrics, 25*, 929–937. doi:10.1017/S1041610212002360.

Aselage, M. B. (2010). Measuring mealtime difficulties: Eating, feeding and meal behaviours in older adults with dementia. *Journal of Clinical Nursing, 19*, 621–631. doi:10.1111/j.1365-2702.2009.03129.x.

Aselage, M. B., & Amella, E. J. (2010). An evolutionary analysis of mealtime difficulties in older adults with dementia. *Journal of Clinical Nursing, 19*, 33–41. doi:10.1111/j.1365-2702.2009.0269.x.

Aselage, M. B., & Amella, E. J. (2011). State of the science: Alleviating mealtime difficulties in nursing home residents with dementia. *Nursing Outlook, 59*, 210–214. doi:10.1016/j.outlook.2011.05.009.

Bagnasco, A., Watson, R., Zanini, M., Rosa, F., Rocco, G., & Sasso, L. (2015). Preliminary testing using Mokken scaling of an Italian translation of the Edinburgh Feeding Evaluation in Dementia (EdFED-I) scale. *Applied Nursing Research, 28*, 391–396. http://dx.doi.org/10.1016/j.apnr.2015.02.003.

Ball, L., Jansen, S., Desbrow, B., Morgan, K., Moyle, W., & Hughes, R. (2015). Experiences and nutrition support strategies in dementia care: Lessons from family carers. *Nutrition & Dietetics, 72*, 22–29. doi:10.1111/1747-0080.12107.

Batchelor-Murphy, M., Amella, E. J., Zapka, J., Mueller, M., & Beck, C. (2015). Feasibility of a web-based dementia feeding skills training program for nursing home staff. *Geriatric Nursing, 36*, 212–218. http://dx.doi.org/10.1016/j.gerinurse.2015.02.003.

Baucom, A. (1996). *Hospitality design for the graying generation: Meeting the needs of a growing market.* New York: John Wiley.

Beattie, E., Algase, D., & Song, J. (2004). Keeping wandering nursing home residents at the table: Improving food intake using a behavioral communication intervention. *Aging & Mental Health, 8*, 109–116. doi:10.1080/13607860410001649617.

Behrman, S., Chouliaras, L., & Ebmeier, K. P. (2014). Considering the senses in the diagnosis and management of dementia. *Maturitas, 77*, 305–310. http://dx.doi.org/10.1016/j.maturitas.2014.01.003.

Belafsky, P. C., Mouadeb, D. A., Rees, C. J., Pryor, J. C., Postma, G. N., Allen, J., & Leonard, R. J. (2008). Validity and reliability of the eating assessment tool (EAT-10). *Annals of Otology Rhinology & Laryngology, 117*(12), 919–924.

Bell, C. L., Tamura, B. K., Masaki, K. H., & Amella, E. J. (2013). Prevalence and measures of nutritional compromise among nursing home patients: Weight loss, low body mass index, malnutrition, and feeding dependency, a systematic review of the literature. *Journal of the American Directors Association, 14*, 94–100. http://dx.doi.org/10.1016/j.jamda.2012.10.012.

Benigas, J., & Bourgeois, M. S. (2016). Using spaced retrieval with external aids to improve use of compensatory strategies during eating for persons with dementia. *American Journal of Speech Language Pathology, 25*(3), 321–324.

Bloomfield, J., & Pegram, A. (2012). Improving nutrition and hydration in hospital: The nurse's responsibility. *Nursing Standard, 26*, 52–56. http://dx.doi.org/10.7748/ns2012.04.26.34.52.c9065.

Bowlby Sifton, C. (2002). Eating and nutrition: Nurturing, food, and community life. *Alzheimer's Care Quarterly, 3*(4), iv–v. Retrieved from http://journals.lww.com/actjournalonline.

Briller, S., Proffitt, M., Perez, K., & Calkins, M. (2001). *Creating successful dementia care settings: Vol. 1. Understanding the environment through aging senses.* Baltimore: Health Professions.

Brooke, J., & Ojo, O. (2015). Oral and enteral nutrition in dementia: An overview. *British Journal of Nursing, 24*(12), 624–628.

Bruce, C., Brush, J. A., Sanford, J. A., & Calkins, M. P. (2013). Development and evaluation of the Environment and Communication Assessment Toolkit with speech-language pathologists. *Seminars in Speech & Language, 34*(1), 42–51. doi:10.1055/s-0033-1337394.

Brush, J., Calkins, M., Bruce, C., & Sanford, J. (2011). *Environment and Communication Assessment Toolkit for dementia care (ECAT).* Baltimore: Health Professions Press.

Brush, J. A., & Camp, C. J. (1998). Spaced retrieval during dysphagia therapy: A case study. *Clinical Gerontologist, 19*, 96–99. Retrieved from www.tandfonline.com/loi/wcli20.

Brush, J. A., Meehan, R. A., & Calkins, M. P. (2002). Using the environment to improve intake for people with dementia. *Alzheimer's Care Quarterly, 3*, 330–338. Retrieved from www.alzfdn.org/Publications/afa-care-quarterly/.

Calkins, M. P., & Brush, J. A. (2003). Designing for dining: The secret of happier mealtimes. *Alzheimer's Care Quarterly, 4*(1), 73–76. Retrieved from www.alzfdn.org/Publications/afa-care-quarterly/.

Cersosimo, M. G., & Benarroch, E. E. (2012). Pathological correlates of gastrointestinal dysfunction in Parkinson's disease. *Neurobiology of Disease, 46*, 559–564. doi:10.1016/j.nbd.2011.10.014.

Cichero, J. A. Y., Lam, P., Steele, C. M., Hanson, B., Chen, J., Dantas, R. O., … Stanschus, S. (2016). Development of international terminology and definitions for texture-modified foods and thickened fluids used in dysphagia management: The IDDSI framework. *Dysphagia.* doi:10.1007/s00455-016-9758-y.

Clavé, P., & Shaker, R. (2015). Dysphagia: Current reality and scope of the problem. *Nature Reviews Gastroenterology & Hepatology, 12*, 259–270. doi:10.1038/nrgastro.2015.49.

Cleary, S. (2006). Shifting paradigms: Treating swallowing and eating problems in dementia. *Communiqué, 20*(2), 4–7.

Cleary, S., Van Soest, D., Milke, D., & Misiaszek, J. (2008). Using the smell of baking bread to facilitate eating in residents with dementia. *Canadian Nursing Home, 19*, 6–13.

Cleary, S., Yanke, J., Masuta, B., & Wilson, K. (2016). Free water protocols. *Canadian Nursing Home, 27*(3), 8.

Correia, S. D. M., Morillo, L. S., Filho, W. J., & Mansur, L. L. (2010). Swallowing in moderate and severe phases of Alzheimer's disease. *Arq Neuropsiquiatr, 68*(6), 855–861.

Davis, L. A., & Conti, G. J. (2003). Speech-language pathologists' roles and knowledge levels related to non-oral feeding. *Journal of Medical Speech-Language Pathology, 13*(1), 15–30. Retrieved from www.pluralpublishing.com/journals_JMSLP.htm.

Dharmarajan, T., & Unnikrishnan, D. (2004). Tube feeding in the elderly. The technique, complications, and outcome. *Postgraduate Medicine, 115*, 51–54. http://dx.doi.org/10.3810/pgm.2004.02.1443.

Dory, M. (2004). Enhancing the dining experience in long-term care: Dining With Dignity program. *Journal of Nutrition for the Elderly, 23*(3), 99–109. http://dx.doi.org/10. 1300/J052v23n03_07.

Douglas, J. W., & Lawrence, J. C. (2015). Environmental considerations for improving nutritional status in older adults with dementia: A narrative review. *Journal of the Academy of Nutrition and Dietetics, 115*, 1815–1831. http://dx.doi.org/10.1016/j.jand.2015.06.376.

Duffy, J. (2013). *Motor speech disorders: Substrates, differential diagnosis, and management* (3rd ed.). Toronto: Mosby.

Eggenberger, S., & Nelms, T. (2004). Artificial hydration and nutrition in advanced Alzheimer's disease: Facilitating family decision-making. *Journal of Clinical Nursing, 13*, 661–667. doi:10.1111/j.1365-2702.2004.00967.x.

Fernandez-Viadero, C., Jimenez-Sanz, M., Verduga, R., & Crespo, D. (2015). Some questions about dementia and tube feedings. *J Am Geriatr Soc, 63*(7), 1490. doi:10.1111/jgs.13551.

Foley, N. C., Affoo, R. H., & Martin, R. E. (2015). A systematic review and meta-analysis examining pneumonia-associated mortality in dementia. *Dementia and Geriatric Cognitive Disorders, 39*, 52–67. doi:10.1159/000367783.

Garcia, J. M., Chambers, E., & Molander, M. (2005). Thickened liquids: Practice patterns of speech-language pathologists. *American Journal of Speech Language Pathology, 14*(1), 4–13.

Genoe, M. R., Keller, H. H., Martin, L. S., Dupuis, S. L., Reimer, H., Cassolato, C., & Edward, G. (2012). Adjusting to mealtime change within the context of dementia. *Canadian Journal on Aging, 31*, 173–194. doi:10.1017/S0714980812000098.

Giebel, C. M., Sutcliffe, C., & Challis, D. (2015). Activities of daily living and quality of life across different stages of dementia: A UK study. *Aging & Mental Health, 19*, 63–71. http://dx.doi.org/10.1080/13607863.2014.915920.

Giebel, C. M., Sutcliffe, C., Stolt, M., Karlsson, S., Renom-Guiteras, A., Soto, M., … Challis, D. (2014). Deterioration of basic activities of daily living and their impact on quality of life across different cognitive stages of dementia: A European study. *International Psychogeriatrics, 26*, 1283–1293. doi:10.1017/S104 1610214000775.

Gillick, M. R., & Mitchell, S. L. (2002). Facing eating difficulties in end-stage dementia. *Alzheimer's Care Quarterly, 3*(3), 227–232. Retrieved from www.alzfdn.org/Publications/afa-care-quarterly/.

Gilmore-Bykovskyi, A. L. (2015). Caregiver person-centeredness and behavioral symptoms during mealtime interactions: Development and feasibility of a coding scheme. *Geriatric Nursing, 26*, S10–S15. http://dx. doi.org/10.1016/j.gerinurse.2015.02.018.

Goldberg, L. S., & Altman, K. W. (2014). The role of gastrostomy tube placement in advanced dementia with dysphagia: A critical review. *Clinical Interventions in Aging, 9*, 1733–1739. http://doi.org/10.2147/CIA.S53153.

Greenwood, C. E., Tam, C., Chan, M., Young, K. W. H., Binns, M. A., & van Reekum, R. (2005). Behavioral disturbances, not cognitive deterioration, are associated with altered food selection in seniors with Alzheimer's disease. *Journal of Gerontology: Medical Sciences, 60A*, 499–505. https://doi.org/10.1093/gerona/60.4.499.

Hanson, L. C., Carey, T. S., Caprio, A. J. et al. (2011). Improving decision-making for feeding options in advanced dementia: A randomized, controlled trial. *JAGS, 59*(11), 2009–2016.

Hanson, L. C., Ersek, M., Lin, F. C., & Carey, T. S. (2013). Outcomes of feeding problems in advanced dementia in a nursing home population. *Journal of the American Geriatrics Society, 61*, 1692–1697. doi:10.1111/jgs.12448.

Hellen, C. R. (2002). Doing lunch: A proposal for a functional well-being assessment. *Alzheimer's Care Quarterly, 3*(4), 302–315.

Hicks-Moore, S. (2005). Relaxing music at mealtime in nursing homes: Effects on agitated patients with dementia. *Journal of Gerontological Nursing, 31*(12), 26–32. doi:10.3928/0098-9134-20051201-07.

Ho, S.-Y., Lai, H.-L., Jeng, S.-Y., Tang, C.-W., Sung, H.-C., & Chen, P.-W. (2011). The effects of researcher-composed music at mealtime on agitation in nursing home residents with dementia. *Archives Psychiatric Nursing, 25*(6), 49–55.

Hooper, L., Bunn, D. K., Downing, A., Jimoh, F. O., Groves, J., … & Shepstone, L. (2016). Which frail older people are dehydrated? The UK DRIE study. *J Gerontol A Biol Sci Med Sci, 71*(10), 1341–1347. doi:10.1093/gerona/glv205.

Hu, X., Okamura, N., Arai, H., Higuchi, M., Maruyama, M., Itoh, M., … Sasaki, H. (2002). Neuro-anatomical correlates of low body weight in Alzheimer's disease: A PET study. *Progress in Neuropsycho_pharmacology and Biological Psychiatry, 26*, 1285–1289. http://dx.doi.org/10.1016/S0278-5846(02)00291-9.

Irwin, W. (2006). Feeding patients with advanced dementia: The role of the speech-language pathologist in making end-of-life decisions. *Journal of Medical Speech-Language Pathology, 14*, xi–xiii.

Ismail, Z., Hermann, N., Rothenburg, L. S., Cotter, A., Leibovitch, F. S., Rafi-Tari, S., … Lanctôt, K. L. (2008). A functional neuroimaging study of appetite loss in Alzheimer's disease. *Journal of the Neurological Sciences, 271*, 97–103. http://dx.doi.org.ezproxy. library.dal.ca/10.1016/j.jns.2008.03.023.

Jackson, J., Currie, K., Graham, C., & Robb, Y. (2011). The effectiveness of interventions to reduce under-nutrition and promote eating in older adults with dementia: A systematic review. *JBI Library of Systematic Reviews, 9* (37), 1509–1550. doi:10.11124/jbisrir-2011-119.

Jensen, G. L., Compher, C., Sullivan, D. H., & Mullin, G. E. (2013). Recognizing malnutrition in adults: Definitions and characteristics, screening, assessment, and team approach. *JPEN: Journal of Parenteral and Enteral Nutrition, 37*(6), 802–807. doi:10.1177/0148607113492338.

Kagel, M. C., & Leopold, N. A. (1992). Dysphagia in Huntington's disease: A 16 year retrospective. *Dysphagia, 7*, 106. doi:10.1007/BF02493441.

Kai, K., Hashimoto, M., Amano, K., Tanaka, H., Fukuhara, R., & Ikeda, M. (2015). Relationship between eating disturbance and dementia severity in patients with Alzheimer's disease. *PLoS ONE, 10*(8), 1–10. doi:10.1371/journal.pone.0133666.

Kalf, J. G., de Swart, B. J. M., Bloem, B. R., & Munneke, M. (2012). Prevalence of oropharyngeal dysphagia in Parkinson's disease: A meta-analysis. *Parkinsonism and Related Disorders, 18*, 311–315. doi:10.1016/j.parkreldis.2011.11.006.

Kayser-Jones, J., & Schell, E. (1997). The effect of staffing on the quality of care at mealtime. *Nursing Outlook, 45*(2), 64–72.

Keller, H., Chambers, L., Niezgoda, H., & Duizer, L. (2012). Issues associated with the use of modified texture foods. *The Journal of Nutrition, Health & Aging, 16*, 195–200. doi:10.1007/s12603-011-0160-z.

Kingston, T. (2017). Promoting fluid intake for patients with dementia or visual impairments. *British Journal of Nursing, 26*, 98–99. doi:10.12968/bjon.2017.26.2.98.

Kofod, J., & Birkemose, A. (2004). Meals in nursing homes. *Scandinavian Journal of Caring Sciences, 18*, 128–134. doi:10.1111/j.1471-6712.2004.00276.x.

Koss, E., & Gilmore, C. G. (1998). Environmental interventions and functional abilities of AD patients. In B. Vellas, J. Filten, & G. Frisoni (Eds.), *Research and practice in Alzheimer's disease* (pp. 185–191). New York: Serdi/Springer.

Kuehlmeyer, K., Schuler, A. F., Kolb, C., Pflegewirt, D., Borasio, G. D., & Jox, R. J. (2015). Evaluating nonverbal behavior of individuals with dementia during feeding: A survey of the nursing staff in residential care homes for elderly adults. *Journal of the American Geriatrics Society, 63*, 2544–2549. doi:10.1111/jgs.13822.

Kunik, M., Martinez, M., Snow, A., Beck, C., Cody, M., Rapp, C. et al. (2003). Determinants of behavioral symptoms in dementia patients. *Clinical Gerontologist, 26*(3–4), 83–89.

Landi, F., Zuccala, G., Gambassi, G., Incalzi, R. A., Manigrasso, L., Pagano, F., … Bernabei, R. (1999). Body mass index and mortality among old people living in the community. *American Journal of the Geriatrics Society, 47*, 1072–1076. doi:10.1111/j.1532-5415.1999.tb05229.x.

Leder, S. B., Sasaki, C. T., & Burrell, M. I. (1998). Fiberoptic endoscopic evaluation of dysphagia to identify silent aspiration. *Dysphagia, 13*, 19–21. doi:10.1007/PL00009544.

Lee, K. M., & Song, J.-A. (2015). Factors influencing the degree of eating ability among people with dementia. *Journal of Clinical Nursing, 24*, 1707–1717. doi:10.1111/jocn.12777.

Lipner, H., Bosler, J., & Giles, G. (1990). Volunteer participation in feeding residents: Training and supervision in a long-term care facility. *Dysphagia, 5*(2), 89–95. doi:10.1007/BF02412650.

Liu, W., Cheon, J., & Thomas, S. A. (2014). Interventions on mealtime difficulties in older adults with dementia: A systematic review. *International Journal of Nursing Studies, 51*, 14–27. http://dx.doi.org/10.1016/j.ijnurstu.2012.12.021.

Liu, W., Galik, E., Boltz, M., Nahm, E.-S., Lerner, N., & Resnick, B. (2016). Factors associated with eating performance for long-term care residents with moderate-to-severe cognitive impairment. *Journal of Advanced Nursing, 72*, 348–360. doi:10.1111/jan.12846.

Liu, W., Galik, E., Boltz, M., Nahm, E.-S., & Resnick, B. (2015). Optimizing eating performance for older adults with dementia living in long-term care: A systematic review. *Worldviews on Evidence-Based Nursing, 12*, 228–235. doi:10.1111/wvn.12100.

Liu, W., Watson, R., & Lou, F. (2013). The Edinburgh Feeding Evaluation in Dementia scale (EdFED): Cross-cultural validation of the simplified Chinese version in mainland China. *Journal of Clinical Nursing, 23*, 45–53. doi:10.1111/j.1365-2702.2012.04250.x.

Logemann, J. (2003). Dysphagia and dementia: The challenge of dual diagnosis. *The ASHA Leader, 8*, 1–5. doi:10.1044/leader.FTR4.08032003.1.

Londos, E., Hanxsson, O., Hirsch, I. A., Janneskog, A., Bülow, M., & Palmqvist, S. (2013). Dysphagia in Lewy body dementia: A clinical observational study of swallowing function by videofluoroscopic examination. *BMC Neurology, 13*(140), 1–5. www.biomedcentral.com/1471-2377/13/140.

Manning, F., Harris, K., Duncan, R., Walton, K., Bracks, J., Larby, L., … Batterham, M. (2012). Additional feeding assistance improves the energy and protein intakes of hospitalized elderly patients. A health services evaluation. *Appetite, 59*, 471–477. http://dx.doi.org/10.1016/j.appet.2012.06.011.

McCann, R., Hall, W., & Groth-Juncker, A. (1994). Comfort care for terminally ill patients: The appropriate use of nutrition and hydration. *JAMA, 274*, 1236–1246.

McCullough, G. H., Wertz, R. T., Rosenbek, J. C., Mills, R. H., Ross, K. B., & Ashford, J. R. (2000). Inter- and intrajudge reliability of a clinical examination of swallowing in adults. *Dysphagia, 15*, 58–67. doi:10.1007/s004550010002.

McHorney, C. A., Bricker, D. E., Robbins, J., Kramer, A. E., Rosenbek, J. C., & Chignell, K. A. (2000a). The SWAL-QOL Outcomes tool for oropharyngeal dysphagia in adults: II. Item reduction and preliminary scaling. *Dysphagia, 15*, 122–133.

McHorney, C. A., Bricker, D. E., Robbins, J., Kramer, A. E., Rosenbek, J. C., Chignell, K. A., Logemann, J. A., & Clarke, C. (2000b). The SWAL-QOL Outcomes tool for oropharyngeal dysphagia in adults: I. Conceptual foundation and item development. *Dysphagia, 15*, 115–121.

McHorney, C. A., Martin-Harris, B., Robbins, J., & Rosenbek, J. (2006). Clinical validity of the SWAL-QOL and SWAL-CARE outcomes tools with respect to bolus flow measures. *Dysphagia, 21*(3), 141–148. doi:10.1007/s00455-005-0026-9.

McHorney, C. A., Robbins, J., Lomax, K., Rosenbek, J. C., Chignell, K. A., Kramer, A. E., & Bricker, D. E. (2002). The SWAL-QOL and SWAL-CARE Outcomes tool for oropharyngeal dysphagia in adults: III. Documentation of reliability and validity. *Dysphagia, 17*, 97–114.

Melton, A., & Bourgeois, M. (2004, February). *Feeding and swallowing issues in dementia.* Invited presentation at the Pilot Club's Annual Alzheimer Update, Tallahassee, FL.

Mitchell, S. L (2015). Advanced dementia. *New England Journal of Medicine, 372*, 2533–2540. doi:10.1056/NEJMcp1412652.

Mitchell, S., Tetroe, J., & O'Connor, A. (2001). A decision aid for long-term tube-feeding in cognitively impaired older persons. *Journal of the American Geriatrics Society, 49*, 313–316. doi:10.1046/j.1532-5415.2001.4930313.x.

Monteleoni, C., & Clark, E. (2004). Using rapid-cycle quality improvement methodology to reduce feeding tubes in patients with advanced dementia: Before and after study. *British Medical Journal, 329*, 491–494. https://doi.org/10.1136/bmj.329.7464.491.

Njegovan, V., Man-Son-Hing, M., Mitchell, S., & Molnar, F. (2001). The hierarchy of functional loss associative with cognitive decline in older persons. *Journal of Gerontology A: Biological Science & Medical Science, 56*, M638–M643. https://doi.org/10. 1093/gerona/56.10.M638.

Nourhashémi, F., Gillette, S., Cantet, C., Stilmunkes, A., Saffon, N., Rougé-Bugat, M. E., … Rolland, Y. (2012). End-of-life care for persons with advanced Alzheimer disease: Design and baseline data from the ALFINE study. *The Journal of Nutrition, Health & Aging, 16*, 457–461. doi:10.1007/s12603-011-0333-9.

Omar, R., Mahoney, C. J., Buckley, A. H., & Warren, J. D. (2013). Flavour identification in fronto_temporal lobar degeneration. *Journal of Neurology, Neurosurgery, & Psychiatry, 84*, 88–93. doi:10.1136/jnnp-2012-303853.

Paranji, S., Paranji, N., Wright, S., & Chandra, S. (2017). A nationwide study of the impact of dysphagia on hospital outcomes among patients with dementia. *American Journal of Alzheimer's Disease & Other Dementias, 32*, 5–11. doi:10.1177/1533317516673464.

Park, Y.-H., Han, H.-R., Oh, B.-M., Lee, J., Park, J., Yu, S. J., & Chang, H. K. (2013). Prevalence and associated factors of dysphagia in nursing home residents. *Geriatric Nursing, 34*, 212–217. http://dx.doi.org/10.1016/j.gerinurse.2013.02.014.

Pioneer Network, Food and Dining Clinical Standards Task Force. (2011). *New dining practice standards.* Retrieved from www.pioneernetwork.net/resource-library/.

Pollens, R. (2004). Role of the speech-language pathologist in palliative hospice care. *Journal of Palliative Medicine, 7*, 694–702. doi:10.1089/jpm.2004.7.694.

Reed, P., Zimmerman, S., Sloane, P., Williams, C., & Boustani, M. (2005). Characteristics associated with low food and fluid intake in long-term care residents with dementia. *The Gerontologist, 45*, 74–80. https://doi.org/10.1093/geront/45.suppl_1.74.

Rehm, C. D., Peñalvo, J. L., Afshin, A., & Mozaffarian, D. (2016). Dietary intake among US adults, 1999–2012. *Journal of the American Medical Association, 316*, 2542–2553. doi:10.1001/jama.2016.7491.

Rizzo, M., Anderson, S. W., Dawson, J., & Nawrot, M. (2000). Vision and cognition in Alzheimer's disease. *Neuropsychologia, 38*, 1157–1169. http://dx.doi.org/10.1016/S0028-3932(00)00023-3.

Roberts, S., & Durnbaugh, T. (2002). Enhancing nutrition and eating skills in long term care. *Alzheimer's Care Quarterly, 3*(4), 316–329. Retrieved from www.alzfdn.org/Publications/afa-care-quarterly/.

Rogus-Pulia, N., Malandraki, G. A., Johnson, S., & Robbins, J. (2015). Understanding dysphagia in dementia: The present and the future. *Current Physical Medicine and Rehabilitation Reports, 3*, 86–97. doi:10.1007/s40141-015-0078-1.

Rösler, A., Pfeil, S., Lessmannc, H., Höder, J., Befahr, A., & von Renteln-Kruse, W. (2015). Dysphagia in dementia: Influence of dementia severity and food texture on the prevalence of aspiration and latency to swallow in hospitalized geriatric patients. *Journal of the American Medical Directors Association, 16*, 697–701. http://dx.doi.org/10.1016/j.jamda.2015.03.020.

Ruigrok, J., & Sheridan, L. (2006). Life enrichment programme: Enhanced dining experience, a pilot project. *International Journal of Health Care Quality Assurance Incorporating Leadership in Health Services, 19*, 420–429. http://dx.doi.org/10.1108/09526860610680067.

Sakai, M., Ikeda, M., Kazui, H., Shigenobu, K., & Nishikawa, T. (2016). Decline of gustatory sensitivity with the progression of Alzheimer's disease. *International Psychogeriatrics, 28*, 511–517. doi:10.1017/S1041610215001337.

Saletti, A., Lindgren, E. Y., Johansson, L., & Cederholm, T. (2000). Nutritional status according to Mini Nutritional Assessment in an institutionalised elderly population in Sweden. *Gerontology, 46*, 139–145. doi:10.1159/000022149.

Sato, E., Hirano, H., Watanabe, Y., Edahiro, A., Sato, K., Yamane, G., & Katakura, A. (2014). Detecting signs of dysphagia in patients with Alzheimer's disease with oral feeding in daily life. *Geriatrics & Gerontology International, 14*, 549–555. doi:10.1111/ggi.12131.

Simmons, S., Osterweil, D., & Schnelle, J. (2001). Improving food intake in nursing home residents with feeding assistance: A staff analysis. *Journal of Gerontology, 56A*, M790–M794. https://doi.org/10.1093/gerona/56.12.M790.

Simmons, S. F., & Reuben, D. (2000). Nutritional intake monitoring for nursing home residents: A comparison of staff documentation, direct observation, and photography methods. *Journal of the American Geriatrics Society, 48*, 209–213. doi:10.1111/j.1532-5415.2000.tb03914.x.

Simmons, S. F., & Schnelle, J. F. (2003). Implementation of nutritional interventions in long-term care. *Alzheimer's Care Quarterly, 4*(4), 286–296.

Simmons, S. F., & Schnelle, J. F. (2006). Feeding assistance needs of long-stay nursing home residents and staff time to provide care. *Journal of the American Geriatrics Society, 54*, 919–924. doi:10.1111/j.1532-5415.2006.00812.x.

Slaughter, S. E., Eliasziw, M., Morgan, D., & Drummond, N. (2011). Incidence and predictors of eating disability among nursing home residents with middle-stage dementia. *Clinical Nutrition, 30*, 172–177. doi:10.1016/j.clnu.2010.09.001.

Slaughter, S. E., & Hayduk, L. A. (2012). Contributions of environment, comorbidity, and stage of dementia to the onset of walking and eating disability in long-term care residents. *Journal of the American Geriatrics Society, 60*, 1624–1631. doi:10.1111/j.1532-5415.2012.04116.x.

Speech-Language and Audiology Canada (SAC). (2016). *The role of speech-language pathologists, audiologists and communication health assistants in end-of-life care*. Retrieved from www.sac-oac.ca/sites/default/files/resources/end-of-life_position-statement_en.pdf.

Spindler, A. A. (2002). Nutritional considerations for persons with Alzheimer's disease. *Alzheimer's Care Quarterly, 3*(4), 289–301.

Steele, C. (1996). *Meal assistance screening tool*. Ontario: Steele.

Steele, C. M., Alsanei, W. A., Ayanikalath, S., Barbon, C. E., Chen, J., Cichero, J. A., ... Wang, H. (2015). The influence of food texture and liquid consistency modification on swallowing physiology and function: A systematic review. *Dysphagia, 30*, 2–26. doi:10.1007/s00455-014-9578-x.

Steele, C., Greenwood, C., Ens, I., Robertson, C., & Seidman-Carlson, R. (1997). Mealtime difficulties in a home for the aged: Not just dysphagia. *Dysphagia, 12*, 45–50. doi:10.1007/PL00009517.

Stockdell, R., & Amella, E. J. (2008). The Edinburgh Feeding Evaluation in Dementia Scale: Determining how much help people with dementia need at mealtime. *American Journal of Nursing, 108*(8), 46–54. doi:10.1097/01.NAJ.0000327831.51782.8e.

Teno, J. M., Gozalo, P. L., Mitchell, S. L., Kuo, S., Rhodes, R. L., Bynum, J. P. W., & Mor, V. (2012). Does feeding tube insertion and its timing improve survival? *J Am Geriatr Soc, 60*, 1918–1921.

Thomas, D. W., & Smith, M. (2009). The effect of music on caloric consumption among nursing home residents with dementia of the Alzheimer's type. *Activities, Adaptation, & Aging, 33*(1), 1–16. http://dx.doi.org/10.1080/01924780902718566.

Ullrich, S., & Crichton, J. (2015). Older people with dysphagia: Transitioning to texture-modified food. *British Journal of Nursing, 24*, 686–692.

Volonté, M. A., Porta, M., & Comi, G. (2002). Clinical assessment of dysphagia in early phases of Parkinson's disease. *Neurological Sciences, 23*, S121–S122. doi:10.1007/s100720200099.

Wallin, V., Carlander, I., Sandman, P.-O., Ternestedt, B.-M., & Håkanson, C. (2014). Maintaining ordinariness around food: Partners' experiences of everyday life with a dying person. *Journal of Clinical Nursing, 23*, 2748–2756. doi:10.1111/jocn.12518.

Walshe, M. (2014). Oropharyngeal dysphagia in neurodegenerative disease. *Journal of Gastroenterology and Hepatology Research, 3*, 1265–1271. doi:10.6051/j.issn.2224-3992.2014.03.408-2.

Watson, R. (1996). The Mokken scaling procedure (MSP) applied to the measurement of feeding difficulty in elderly people with dementia. *International Journal of Nursing Studies, 33*, 385–393. http://dx.doi.org/10.1016/0020-7489(95)00058-5.

Watson, R. (1997). Construct validity of a scale to measure feeding difficulty in elderly patients with dementia. *Clinical Effectiveness in Nursing, 1*, 114–115. http://dx.doi.org/10.1016/S1361-9004(06)80014-2.

Watson, R., & Green, S. M. (2006). Feeding and dementia: A systematic literature review. *Journal of Advanced Nursing, 54*(1), 86–93.

Watson, R., Green, S. M., & Legg, L. (2001). The Edinburgh Feeding Evaluation in Dementia Scale #2 (EdFED #2): Convergent and discriminant validity. *Clinical Effectiveness in Nursing, 5*(1), 44–46.

Watson, R., MacDonald, J., & McReady, T. (2001). The Edinburgh Feeding Evaluation in Dementia Scale #2 (EdFED #2): Inter- and intra-rater reliability. *Clinical Effectiveness in Nursing, 5*(1), 184–186.

Whear, R., Abbott, R., Thompson-Coon, J., Bethel, A., Rogers, M., Hemsley, A., ... Stein, K. (2014). Effectiveness of mealtime interventions on behavior symptoms of people with dementia living in care homes: A systematic review. *Journal of the American Medical Directors Association, 15*, 185–193. http://dx.doi.org/10.1016/j.jamda.2013.10.015.

White, H. (2005). Nutrition in advanced Alzheimer's disease. *North Carolina Medical Journal, 66*, 307–312.

Williams, K., & Weatherhead, I. (2013, May). Improving nutrition and care for people with dementia. *British Journal of Community Nursing, 18*(Suppl 5), S20–S25. doi:10.12968/bjcn.2013.18.Sup5.S20.

World Health Organization. (2001). *International classification of functioning, disability, and health.* Geneva: Author.

Wu, H.-S., & Lin, L.-C. (2015). Comparing cognition, mealtime performance, and nutritional status in people with dementia with or without ideational apraxia. *Biological Research for Nursing, 17*, 199–206. doi:10.1177/1099800414536773.

Wu, H. S., Lin, L. C., Wu, S. C., in, K. N., & Liu, H. C. (2013). The effectiveness of spaced retrieval combined with Montessori-based activities in improving the eating ability of residents with dementia. *Journal of Advanced Nursing, 70*, 1891–1901. doi:10.111/jan.12352.

Yen, P. (1996). When food doesn't taste good anymore. *Geriatric Nursing, 17*, 44–45. doi:10.1016/S0197-4572(96)80014-0.

Yorkston, K. M., Beukelman, D. R., Strand, E. A., & Hakel, M. (2010). *Management of motor speech disorders in children and adults* (3rd ed.). Austin, TX: Pro-Ed.

9

FAMILY CAREGIVER ISSUES AND TRAINING

Michelle S. Bourgeois

The purpose of this chapter is to highlight the important role of caregivers in the treatment continuum for persons with dementia, as well as the role of the speech-language pathologist (SLP) and interprofessional team in advising and supporting caregivers throughout this process. A caregiver is a relative or friend who provides help with personal needs and household chores to another person without payment (National Alliance for Caregiving and the American Association of Retired Persons [NAC/AARP], 2015). In past years, the SLP's work with caregivers was to provide assistance *indirectly* to persons with dementia through their caregivers, primarily in the form of education about the diagnosis and future planning (Clark, 1997). In the past two decades, much more attention has been directed toward designing and evaluating direct interventions for persons with dementia, but the importance of including caregivers in the intervention process has not diminished. Most of the research reveals the need for a menu of training approaches for caregivers based on their unique demographic characteristics and a variety of socioeconomic factors (e.g., educational level, cultural background), as well as their support needs and relationship to the care recipient. The role of the SLP and interprofessional team is to provide education, support, training, and counseling to caregivers of persons with dementia from diagnosis through the end of life.

An understanding of the specific needs and characteristics of each caregiver allows the healthcare professional to successfully match the appropriate support and training approach to each unique caregiver. A summary of what is known about caregivers, including considerations for what different caregivers might bring to the situation, their needs and expectations, their emotional and physical health risks, and the types of barriers that prevent them from benefiting from services offered will be described. The team must gauge the range of potential emotional and psychosocial barriers to acceptance and implementation of caregiving recommendations. Lastly, the types of interventions available to caregivers will be delineated, including a range of approaches from generic educational and supportive models, to communication-specific training programs.

Researchers' conceptualization of the process of caregiving has evolved since the publication of Pearlin's stress process model of caregiving (Pearlin, Mullan, Semple, & Skaff, 1990). In this model, the many types of problems experienced by the caregiver (e.g., objective problems with the care recipient and their own subjective responses to these problems) are **stressors** that contribute to negative and positive caregiver (and care recipient) **outcomes** (e.g., poor health and depression, institutionalization) and secondary stressors of family conflict and work, employment, and financial strains. The resources that modify or regulate the relationship between the stressors and the outcomes are the **moderators** (Aneshensel, Pearlin, Mullan, Zarit, & Whitlatch, 1995). The entire caregiving process operates within the social, economic, and cultural context of the individual caregiver and his or her unique **background and contextual** variables. Without moderating factors, these stressors can lead to negative caregiving outcomes (e.g., caregiver depression, anxiety, anger, poor health, mortality, and institutionalization of the person with dementia). However, the factors that tend to moderate the stressors and lead to more positive caregiving outcomes include having: access to social support (i.e., instrumental and emotional), access to interventions designed to address caregiving challenges, and effective coping strategies that provide a sense of mastery and self-esteem.

Interventions have revealed that when caregivers can identify positive aspects of caregiving they report significantly lower levels of depression, burden, and subjective health (e.g., Cohen, Colantonio, & Vernich, 2002). Folkman's revised stress process model (Folkman, 2008) highlights the importance of coping responses as mediators of stress (see Figure 9.1). When coping responses are adaptive (e.g., problem-focused coping that leads to a favorable resolution), the caregiving outcome likely leads to positive emotions. In contrast, when coping responses are maladaptive (e.g., avoidance coping that leads to unfavorable or no resolution), caregivers experience additional distress. Therefore, recent caregiver interventions are incorporating meaning-based coping strategies into other successful intervention approaches, such as problem-solving skills (Judge, Yarry, & Orsulic-Jeras, 2014).

The individual characteristics and situations of each caregiver create an almost infinite array of response possibilities. A multitude of factors impact the caregiving equation, including age, gender, education, race and ethnicity, socioeconomic status and financial resources, the composition of family networks, the health and coping skills of the caregiver, the quality of the caregiver–care recipient relationship, and their physical proximity. The many factors to consider when working with the caregivers of persons with dementia are described in the following section.

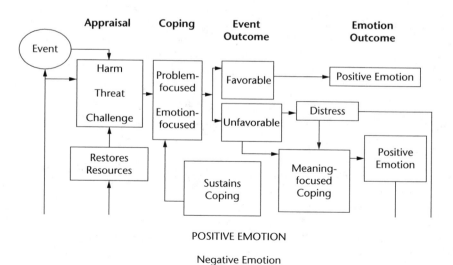

FIGURE 9.1   Folkman's Revised Stress Process Model

Source: Folkman, S. (2008). The case for positive emotions in the stress process. *Anxiety, Stress, and Coping, 21*(1), 3–14. Reprinted with permission from Taylor and Francis Ltd.

Caregiver Characteristics

The most important support for persons with dementia may well be their caregivers. A survey by the National Alliance for Caregiving and the American Association of Retired Persons (NAC/AARP, 2015) estimated that there are 39.8 million caregivers in the United States, providing 18.1 billion hours of unpaid care. Two-thirds of caregivers are non-Hispanic White families, 10% are African-American, and 20% are Hispanic. Most caregivers (66%) live with the care recipient in the community and 23% of caregivers are "sandwich generation" caregivers who care not only for an aging parent with dementia, but also for children under age 18 (Alzheimer's Association, 2016). Two-thirds of caregivers are women and married; one-third are daughters who spend more time caregiving than male caregivers; and more wives give care than husbands. Overall, caregiving women experience higher levels of burden, depression, and impaired health than men; this is thought to be because women spend a greater amount of time caregiving, do a greater number of caregiving tasks, and care for persons with a greater number of behavioral problems (Alzheimer's Association, 2016).

The number of dementia caregivers continues to increase as the baby boomers age, life expectancy increases, and medical technology advances (Schulz & Martire, 2004). The shift in healthcare focus from acute to chronic diseases is resulting in more persons requiring caregiving for longer durations and for more types of tasks. Two decades ago, 10% of the elderly population (2.97 million persons) required help with activities of daily living (ADLs), such as dressing and bathing, and 23.2% of the elderly population (6.26 million) required help with instrumental activities of daily living (IADLs), such as shopping and finances (Van Nostrand, Furner, & Suzman, 1993). In 2015, caregivers provided an average of 24.4 hours/week of care, 60% of which was help with ADLs (NAC/AARP, 2015). These numbers are predicted to increase in the coming years when the Baby Boomers have attained 65 years of age (Centers for Disease Control and Prevention, 2013).

Family caregivers often have difficulty pinpointing the exact time when caregiving began because the types of care provided are the typical tasks one family member would do for the other, whether or not they had a chronic illness or disability (e.g., cooking meals and doing the laundry; Schulz & Quittner, 1998). When care exceeds the boundaries of what is normal (e.g., help with bathing and toileting), family caregivers may admit that their helping role has changed. Family and friends provide 75% of care, and the remaining 25% of care is purchased (Schulz & Martire, 2004). National surveys of family caregivers reveal the majority of caregivers of a person with dementia are middle-aged, married females who work at least part-time (NAC/AARP, 2015). These caregivers provide care primarily to a parent, grandparent, friend, aunt or uncle, or spouse, and many of them have children in the home. Most caregivers live with the disabled person, providing an average of five years of care at an estimated rate of approximately 40.5 hours per week (NAC/AARP, 2015). The types of tasks included in caregiving range from IADLs (e.g., transportation, grocery shopping, housework, medication administration, managing finances) to ADLs (e.g., dressing, bathing, feeding, and toileting).

Caregiving for any individual with a disability is burdensome, but the range, frequency, and severity of cognitive deficits and responsive behaviors displayed by persons with dementia can produce stresses that are physically demanding and unremitting (Ory, Yee, Tennstedt, & Schulz, 2000). As a loved one's function declines, and the duration, amount, and intensity of caregiving increase, caregiver perceptions of their own burden and depression become increasingly negative (Epstein-Lubow et al., 2012). Most caregivers report lower incomes and lower self-reported health, and as a result, most are at risk for psychological distress and burden, psychiatric and physical illness, and economic stressors (Alzheimer's Association, 2016).

Factors Related to the Caregiving Experience

Many factors influence the perceptions associated with caregiving, including the relationship of the care provider to the care recipient (i.e., spouse, son or daughter, other relative, or friend), the nature of the relationship (e.g., loving or adversarial), the role of the caregiver (e.g., primary versus secondary), age, gender, education, financial resources, proximity to the care recipient, and ethnicity. In-depth analyses of all of these caregiving variables are beyond the scope of this chapter, but are available in other resources (e.g., Burgio, Gaugler, & Hilgeman, 2016; Miller et al., 2013; NAC/AARP, 2015). A summary of some of the factors critical to the health professional's understanding of caregivers' circumstances is provided below.

Type of Relationship to Care Recipient: Spouses. The relationship of the caregiver to the care recipient is known to influence the caregiving experience (Brodaty et al., 2014; Kim et al., 2016; Reed et al., 2014; Yee & Schulz, 2000). Spousal caregivers are thought to provide the most extensive and comprehensive care because of the nature of the marital relationship (NAC/AARP, 2015). Rose-Rego, Strauss, and Smyth (1998) found gender differences in psychological, social, and physical wellbeing in their caregiving sample. Caregiving wives reported more negative feelings, including depression, about caregiving than did husbands. This difference may have been related to differences in women's attentiveness to their emotions, their willingness to report negative symptoms, their use of emotion-focused coping strategies, and the nature of the caregiving tasks. Similarly, Kim et al., (2016) found that wives providing personal care were more depressed than wives providing assistance with instrumental care, but there were no differences in caregiving husbands' depression related to type of caregiving tasks. They reported a continuing need for research on strategies to reduce the distress of caregiving wives providing personal care. In a French study comparing caregivers' responses to the Neuropsychiatric Inventory (NPI) to describe their care recipients' behaviors and the Zarit Burden Interview, Dauphinot and colleagues (2015) found that while disease stage and etiology were not significantly related, the specific behaviors that were related included apathy, agitation, aberrant motor behavior, appetite disorders, and irritability. In contrast, an Italian study reported more caregiver burden in AD caregivers than VaD caregivers (D'Onofrio et al., 2014). In Japan, caregiver burden was found to be associated with cognitive stage of AD and types of caregiving tasks required (Kamiya, Sakurai, Ogama, Maki, & Toba, 2014). In spite of significant need for assistance, it has been reported that wives often have difficulty accepting help from others, which was thought to be related to needing assistance in recognizing problems, accepting direction from others, and recognizing help needs (Brown and Alligood, 2004). In contrast, caregiving husbands expressed feelings of isolation and invisibility in their care work, reported a combined management and nurturing caregiving style, and persevered due to feelings of commitment, responsibility, and devotion to their wife (Brown & Alligood, 2004; Russell, 2001). The impact of caregiving on spouses is influenced by the nature of their marital relationship. When spouses report low marital cohesion and satisfaction, they also report more depression (Rankin, Haut, & Keefover, 2001). Their perceptions of the level of marital affection and marital satisfaction are inversely related to their grief responses to the dementia diagnosis (Lindgren, Connelly, & Gaspar, 1999). Disagreement about the effects of caregiving on the caregiver can cause relationship strain between spouses, even when there is little disagreement about the care recipient's needs (Lyons, Zarit, Sayer, & Whitlatch, 2002). Spouses feel more burdened and depressed about their caregiving responsibilities than adult children caregivers, particularly when their spouse has physical impairments and behavior problems (Pinquart & Sörensen, 2003). Responsive behaviors, especially emotional lability, were associated with negative wellbeing in wives and younger (<65 years old) husbands (Croog, Sudilovsky, Burleson, & Baume, 2001). Relationship satisfaction with the care recipient has been found to predict frustration and embarrassment and impact of caregiving on caregivers' lives (Springate & Tremont, 2014). Finally, communication impairments due to dementia also contribute to the experience of caregiving burden; there is a continuing need for caregiver training of effective communication strategies to decrease burden and improve communication satisfaction (Watson, Aizawa, Savundranayagam, & Orange, 2013).

Type of Relationship to Care Recipient: Adult Children and Their Siblings. Much research has focused on understanding adult children caregivers and the effects of a multitude of variables such as family composition, gender, geographical proximity, and marital status on the extent of care being given to their elderly parents (Fulton, 2005; Moon, Rote, & Beatty, 2016; Pinquart & Sörensen, 2011; Stoller, Forster, & Duniho, 1992). For example, adult children are more likely to be involved in the caregiving process when the parent is widowed and has functional or cognitive impairment, and if they live nearby (Crawford, Bond, & Balshaw, 1994; Stoller et al., 1992). In fact, even prior to caregiving, adult children who are in good health and have positive family norms for caregiving have increased expectations for primary involvement in caregiving when the time arrives; a large network of sisters, however, decreases the expectation for primary responsibility for parental care (Franks, Pierce, & Dwyer, 2003). Recent reviews add that Baby Boomer caregivers whose parent is in non-nursing home residential care report a low level of providing help with daily activities, better physical health, better emotional wellbeing, and a higher level of informal help than caregivers of parents living in the community who had more secondary and financial stressors (Moon et al., 2016). This suggests that residential care of the parent may be beneficial for caregivers' physical and emotional health.

Daughters, with or without siblings, are more likely to provide caregiving assistance than sons (Dwyer & Coward, 1991). They also tend to give a wider range of care, such as assistance with ADLs and IADLs (Dwyer, Henretta, Coward, & Barton, 1992; Horowitz, 1985). Daughters' involvement in caregiving is greatest when they are not married (Connidis, Rosenthal, & McMullin, 1996) and when parents are more impaired (Crawford et al., 1994). Widowed mothers prefer the help of daughters to the help of sons if both are nearby (Crawford et al., 1994), especially if more assistance is needed (Stoller et al., 1992). Widowed mothers even seem to grow closer to their daughters (Lopata, 1987) and more distant from their sons (Atchely, 1988). Daughters report stronger feelings of attachment, and think their parent(s) to be in greater need of help than sons, which may explain their greater caregiving involvement (Cicirelli, 1983). Gender role attitudes reflecting higher expectations from daughters compared to sons might be another explanation for their greater involvement in caregiving (Finley, 1989). However, not all studies report differences in feelings of attachment toward parents between daughters and sons (Crawford et al., 1994). Adult daughters report doing more personal care and household chores (Dwyer & Coward, 1991) than sons who help with other chores, such as money management, home repairs, and transportation (Collins & Jones, 1997). This gendered division of labor does not hold for spousal caregivers, who provide more similar types and amounts of care to their spouses than do adult children (Tennstedt, Crawford, & McKinlay, 1993).

The adult child caregiving role is substantially different from the spousal caregiving role; adult children have to acknowledge that they no longer are in a position to receive help and support from, but now must provide assistance and emotional support to, their parents. It can be difficult for children to make this change (Connidis et al., 1996) and maintain feelings of intimacy, interconnectedness, and reciprocity (Kaye & Applegate, 1990). The change in caregiving role has an impact on interpersonal relationships in caregiving dyads; for adult children, the level of affection is a decisive factor in giving care, whereas for spouses, feelings of obligation are important (Connidis et al., 1996).

The impact of siblings on the caregiving equation is also important. For example, the amount and intensity of care provided by siblings to elderly parents are influenced by both their availability and proximity, as well as by their behavior (Fulton, 2005). When a sibling starts to provide assistance to a parent, the odds of another sibling initiating assistance increase. However, when a sibling stops providing assistance, the other sibling is more likely to discontinue assistance (Dwyer et al., 1992). Adult children caregivers without siblings perform a role that is similar to the spousal caregiver role because caregiving responsibilities cannot be shared with a close family member (Lustbader & Hooyman, 1994). Adult children without siblings appear to have greater role responsibilities, but also have a more positive reaction to caregiving and a smaller extent of feelings of abandonment than adult children caregivers with siblings (Barnes, Given, & Given, 1992). The availability of siblings to share caregiving responsibilities increases the potential for conflict. Daughters as primary caregivers seem to experience more conflict with sisters than brothers, with sisters feeling guilty about not doing more (Brody, Hoffman, Kleban, & Schoonover, 1989). Adult children with siblings expect their siblings to share the caregiver burden and feel abandoned if they do not receive this help and support. Regardless of the presence of helping siblings, however, caregivers reported a negative impact of their assistance on their health over time. In addition, they reported receiving less affective support and experiencing increased feelings of abandonment over time (Barnes et al., 1992). For daughters, support from their husband or friends was more important and prevalent than that from a sibling due to the potential for sibling conflict (Brody, Litvin, Hoffman, & Kleban, 1992).

The Caregiving Role: Primary Versus Secondary Caregivers. In addition to the caregiver's relationship to the care recipient, his or her role as either the primary or secondary caregiver impacts the nature and outcomes of the care provided. Caregiving responsibilities are usually assumed by one person, the primary caregiver; however, secondary caregivers have been reported to provide supplementary assistance with a wide variety of tasks (Pruchno, Peters, & Burant, 1995; Tennstedt, McKinlay, & Sullivan, 1989). As a result of different expectations on either side, there are potential disagreements and divergent perceptions about caregiving. Family conflicts arise between primary and secondary caregivers regarding issues of parental illness and the level of assistance required from the family (Semple, 1992). Often, the advice provided from other family members is experienced as stressful (MaloneBeach & Zarit, 1995).

Bourgeois, Beach, Schulz, and Burgio (1996) found that primary and secondary caregivers exhibited 64% disagreement on perceptions of primary caregiver coping efficacy, 51% disagreement on primary caregiver strain, and 46% disagreement on perception of responsive behavior, with greater agreement on measures of more objective behaviors. This degree of disagreement between caregivers may account for dissatisfaction in perceptions of support and contribute to higher levels of stress. Instead of reducing burden and stress, disagreement or other upsetting elements of the relationship between primary and secondary caregivers could be stronger than positive effects of support (Pagel, Erdly, & Becker, 1987). Disagreement contributes to feelings of strain and burden among caregivers, thereby increasing the likelihood of placement in a nursing home.

Disagreement about responsive behavior can also result in divergent reactions to them by the caregiver, resulting in an increase in responsive behavior. Insight into differences in coping behavior among primary and secondary caregivers can help to explain differences in disagreements. According to content analyses of interviews with caregivers (Gottlieb & Gignac, 1996), adult children tend to use wishful thinking as a coping strategy more often than spouses. However, this does not relate closely to actual responsive behaviors of their parent, nor does it adequately reflect their caregiving strain. A second difference in coping strategies is that adult female children caregivers seem more optimistic, whereas spouses use humor more to deal with the caregiving burden. Third, adult children seek (outside) help to a greater extent than spouses.

For coping strategies to be effective for both primary and secondary caregivers and care recipients, primary caregivers have to be aware of their coping strategies and coordinate them with those of the secondary caregivers. Primary and secondary caregivers should also decide on a division of caregiving tasks that are complementary. For instance, during a family meeting, the primary and secondary caregivers could set up a realistic and specific schedule for caregiving, encouraging participation without trying to equate types of help (Zarit & Edwards, 1999).

A cross-sectional study of 90 primary and 90 secondary caregivers of dependent elderly people in Portugal reported that while secondary caregivers reduced the burden of primary caregivers and delayed institutionalization of the care recipient, neither group was efficient at managing caregiving-related stress (Barbosa, Figueiredo, Sousa, & Demain, 2011). Similarly, Lou and colleagues found that 70% of primary Chinese caregivers had secondary caregivers, but primary caregivers had a higher likelihood of psychological distress when the care recipient expressed a negative mood (Lou, Kwan, Chong, & Chi, 2013). This suggests that both primary and secondary caregivers need services that provide emotional support.

Race, Ethnicity, and Culture. In our diverse society, differences in race, ethnicity, and culture cannot be overlooked when providing services to caregivers. Sensitivity to the different needs and responses to caregiving challenges of caregivers from diverse backgrounds will enhance positive outcomes. In the United States, the four federally designated ethnic minority categories are American Indian/Alaska Native, Asian/Pacific Islander, Black, and Hispanic (Yeo, 1996). Within these classifications, differences in national origin, culture, and language further diversify the groups. For example, Young and Gu (1995) reported their Asian sample to include native Hawaiian, Japanese, Vietnamese, Cambodian, Chinese, and Filipino elders. Factors such as degree of acculturation and ethnic identity, education, income, and religious affiliation, among others, influence the degree to which caregivers access available resources and supports for their family member with dementia. Pinquart and Sörensen (2005) have developed a model representing the many factors influencing ethnic differences in stressors, resources, and outcomes related to caregiving (Table 9.1).

Healthcare professionals must provide appropriate and culturally sensitive services to diverse populations. This can be particularly challenging when (a) a person does not speak the language of the healthcare team, (b) the symptoms of dementia (e.g., confusion and memory loss) are viewed as normal aging processes in other cultures, (c) cultural traditions of family responsibility and gender roles preclude the acceptance of outside help, and (d) there are cultural differences in the perception of institutionalization and/or health-related and end-of-life decision-making

TABLE 9.1 Factors Influencing Ethnic Differences in Caregiving Variables

---

Race and Ethnicity Influences
Caregiver Factors
Resources and Cultural Norm (positive appraisal, faith, problem-focused coping, pre-caregiving health, informal social support, use of formal services
Other Background Variables (age, gender, family position, co-residence, employment, education, income)

Caregiver Outcomes
Burden and Gain due to:
Care Receiver Health and Functioning (objective care needs; ADL limitations, cognitive status, problem behaviors)
Amount of Care Provided (hours per day, number of tasks); Positive caregiving experiences
Psychological and Physical Health Outcomes (depression, illness)

Source: Adapted from Pinquart and Sörensen, 2005.

(Yeo, 1996). Cultural differences occur in multiple domains, including psychosocial health, life satisfaction, caregiving appraisals, spirituality, coping, self-efficacy, physical functioning, social support, filial responsibility, familyism, views toward elders, use of formal services and health care (Nápoles, Chadiha, Eversly, & Monreno-John, 2010).

Resources to educate professionals about racial, cultural, and ethnic differences needed are listed in Table 9.2 (Botsford, Clarke, & Gibb, 2011; Edgerly, Montes, Yau, Stokes, & Redd, 2003; Santo Pietro & Ostuni, 2003). There has been some effort to translate diagnostic tests, educational materials about dementia, and caregiver resources into different languages (e.g., Alzheimer Association Website; Fuh, Wanh, Liu, & Wang, 1999), but this is an area in need of further development. Nápoles and colleagues (2010) reviewed the caregiving literature for ethnic and cultural tailoring and found only 11 studies that reported cultural tailoring. Eight of these studies were from the Resources for Enhancing Alzheimer's Caregiver Health (REACH) initiative, a group of NIA-funded projects that evaluated caregiver training studies designed for a sampling of ethnic groups (56% Caucasian, 24% Black, and 19% Hispanic) (Wisniewski et al., 2003).

A meta-analysis of 116 empirical studies examining racial and ethnic differences in caregiving found that non-White participants are 30% more likely: to be caregivers; to be adult children, friends, or other family members; to have a lower socioeconomic status; to have worse physical health; to spend more than 13 hours per week in caregiving activities; and to receive more informal support (McCann et al., 2000; Pinquart & Sörensen, 2005). Additionally, these responsibilities increase with age for married persons. Minority elders tend to report: lower levels of stress, burden, and depression; to hold stronger beliefs about filial support; and to be more likely to use faith, prayer, and religion as coping strategies (Connell & Gibson, 1997; Koenig et al., 1992). More specifically, African American caregivers' higher religiosity than Whites contributed to more positive feelings about caregiving, lower anxiety, and lower feelings of bother by the care

TABLE 9.2 Sources Describing Caregivers of Different Ethnicities in the US

Ethnicity	References
American Indian/Alaska Native	Carter (2015), Jervis and Manson (2002)
Asian/Pacific Islander	
• Chinese	Braun and Browne (1998); Teng (1996)
• Japanese	Tempo and Saito (1996)
• Filipino	McBride and Parreno (1996)
• Korean	Youn, Knight, Jeong, and Benton (1999)
• Vietnamese	Yeo, Uyen Tran, Hikoyeda, and Hinton (2001) Yee, Nguyen, and Ha (2003)
• Hmong	Gerdner, Tripp-Reimer, and Yang (2005)
African American	Barnes, Mendes de Leon, Bienias, and Evans (2004) Dilworth-Anderson, Goodwin, and Williams (2004) Lewis and Ausberry (1996)
Hispanic	
• Spanish	Mungas (1996); Taussig and Ponton (1996)
• Mexican	Briones, Ramirez, Guerrero, and Ledger (2002) Chiriboga, Black, Aranda, and Markides (2002) Gallagher-Thompson, Talamantes, Ramirez, and Valverde (1996), Llanque and Enriquez (2012)
• Cuban and Puerto Rican	Henderson (1996)

recipient's behavior (Roff et al., 2004). In fact, feelings of respect for an older family member often lead to "normalization" of responsive behaviors and delayed dementia evaluation (Cloutterbuck & Mahoney, 2003).

Similarly, Native American populations whose cultural value of idealizing elders for their wisdom and high moral values may explain the cognitive decline in dementia as either part of normal aging or a transition to the next world, and may choose to depend solely on the family for caregiving (Jervis & Manson, 2002). Native families face a multitude of challenges related to poverty and living in rural areas or on reservations, where there are not many formal services or long-term care facilities. These factors and the lack of understanding of dementia may lead to severe caregiver stress, elder neglect, and elder abuse (Paveza et al., 1992; Whitehouse, Lerner, & Hedera, 1993).

There have been conflicting findings regarding prevalence of depression in Latino caregivers. Latino caregivers are mostly women in their 40s, and are unpaid caregivers for parents or parents-in-law in the caregiver's home; they tend to report high levels of depression, low availability of informal support, and underutilization of formal services (Ayalon & Huyck, 2001; Llanque & Enriquez, 2012). In some studies, Latino caregivers displayed the highest level of depression, as compared to Japanese, African Americans, and Whites (Adams, Aranda, Kemp, & Takagi, 2002; Pinquart & Sörensen, 2005). In another study, however, adult children Latino caregivers reported less depression, lower levels of role captivity, and higher self-acceptance than White caregivers; feelings of role captivity were stronger predictors of negative versus positive caregiving outcomes than ethnicity (Morano & Sanders, 2005). Highly acculturated Mexican American caregivers reported greater depression than noncaregivers (Hahn, Kim & Chiriboga, 2011), suggesting that a better understanding of acculturation differences among Hispanic/Latino caregivers would lead to better tailoring of interventions.

In general, less is known about the caregiving and coping strategies of Asian groups (e.g., Chinese, Japanese, Korean, and Filipino), especially the Vietnamese and Hmong (Thompson, Gallagher-Thompson, & Haley, 2003). Multi-ethnic Asian informal caregivers in Singapore reported higher burden when the care recipient had dementia, communication difficulties, and more care needs (e.g., feeding and bathing) (Vaingankar et al., 2016). However, there are some innovative intervention programs targeting the specific needs and challenges of ethnic minority caregivers, such as the Los Angeles' El Portal Latino Alzheimer's project, San Francisco's Japanese Kimochi, Inc., and the John XXIII Multiservice Chinese Outreach Center (Edgerly et al., 2003).

The Alzheimer's Association (https://alz.org/) and the Administration on Aging (https://aoa.acl.gov/) have programs and materials for many ethnic cultures, including an Asian Pacific Islanders Toolkit for dementia caregivers. The Caregiving Alliance has similar resources (www.caregiver.org/asian-pacific-islander-dementia-care-network).

Research into the barriers to accessing culturally appropriate services for ethnic minority elders underscores the economic, geographic, cultural, and linguistic differences that are important factors in the social and healthcare delivery systems, as well as perceptions of and stigma associated with cognitive impairment (Nápoles et al., 2010). More attention needs to be paid to cultural tailoring to overcome barriers related to familyism, language, literacy, protecting elders, and logistical barriers. This information will extend the literature on caregiving minority families, their extended social networks, and help-seeking processes in an effort to improve the quality of care and management of dementia in all healthcare settings.

Box 9.1 Other Factors That Impact Caregiving: Special Categories of Caregivers

- Caregivers who are taking care of their homosexual partner face challenges related to prejudice and insensitivity in their interactions with health services, and the lack of interventions and support services that meet their needs (Moore, 2002).
- The caregivers of people with younger-onset dementia are usually younger themselves, still working, and have children at home. They are often unprepared for the demands of caregiving and, as a result, experience increased burden and feel more isolated (Arai, Matsumoto, Ikeda, & Arai, 2007).
- Persons with Down's syndrome have a high risk of developing Alzheimer's disease in middle age, resulting in additional challenges of diagnosing and managing the symptoms (Margallo-Lana et al., 2007; Stanton & Coetzee, 2003). Additional information about this condition can be found at www.emedicinehealth.com/alzheimers_disease_in__down_syndrome/article_em.htm.
- In cases of a second marriage later in life when one partner develops dementia, specific issues regarding the person with dementia's capacity to marry and feelings of obligation on the part of the caregiving spouse can cause conflict in the relationship and with the adult children of both partners (Peisah & Bridger, 2008).

Risks and Benefits of Caregiving

Caregivers of all types may have different expectations and stresses related to caregiving responsibilities. This may lead to different caregiving outcomes, including physical health and mental health outcomes of the caregiver, and the risk of institutionalization of the care recipient (Argimon, Limon, Vila, & Cabezas, 2005). Measures of physical health outcomes include: self-rated global health, frequency and types of medical conditions, health-related behaviors, medications, and hospitalizations, and physiological changes (e.g., immune functioning, hypertension, and cardiac health; Bookwala, Yee, & Schulz, 2000). In studies comparing the physical health outcomes of caregivers and noncaregivers, caregivers reported lower overall global health, more physical health problems, less physical activity and sleep, and increased medication use (Brodaty et al., 2014). Caregivers have poorer immune functioning, higher cardiovascular risk factors, and increased blood pressure (Mausbach, 2014) than noncaregiving controls. Mental health, or psychiatric, outcomes include self-report measures of wellbeing, depression, anxiety, and psychiatric drug use. Dementia caregivers report increased depression and anxiety in comparison to age- and gender-based controls (Epstein-Lubow et al., 2012). Overall, caregiver physical and mental health, as well as other risk factors (e.g., gender, financial status, and personality variables), predict negative caregiving outcomes (Ory et al., 2000). For example, increased depression and anxiety and limited social support are related to negative physical health (Li, Seltzer, & Greenberg, 1997). Poor physical health is related to increased caregiver-reported depression (Harwood, Barker, Ownby, & Duara, 2000).

One of the strongest and recurring findings in this literature is the relationship between care recipient factors and the mental and physical health outcomes of caregivers. A person's responsive behaviors are especially predictive of negative caregiver physical and mental health (Hooker et al., 2002; O'Rourke & Tuokko, 2000). When there is increased dependency in ADLs in addition to responsive behaviors (e.g., disinhibition and limited awareness), there are reports of increased caregiver depression (Alzheimer's Association, 2016). Informal support from family and friends was found to diminish when the person with dementia shows increased responsive behaviors and functional limitations, resulting in more caregiver-reported depression and burden (Clyburn, Stones, Hadjistavropoulos, & Tuokko, 2000). Overall, caregiver stress is related to the severity of dementia, the type and amount of responsive behaviors exhibited, the amount of support the caregiver receives, and the fact that these factors change over time as the disease progresses; a well-functioning support system and a high quality of social services to the caregiving dyad have a positive impact on burden and strain (Alzheimer's Association, 2016).

When the caregiver is no longer healthy, mentally or physically, and the caregiver's quality of life diminishes, the person with dementia is at increased risk of institutionalization (Gaugler, Yu, Krichbaum, & Wyman, 2009). Other factors that increase risk of institutionalization include inadequate caregiver coping strategies, caregiver stress, insufficient support for the caregiver, and disagreement among caregivers. As well, having a caregiver with any of the following characteristics increase risk of institutionalization: an adult child as a primary caregiver, a relatively young caregiver (e.g., a grandchild), an employed child caregiver, or a caregiver with lower morale (Montgomery & Kosloski, 1994). Client characteristics that are risk factors for institutionalization include: advanced age, poor health, lower functional status, problems with ADLs, cognitive impairment, and living alone without access to a support group of family or friends.

In general, adult children caregivers with financial resources, who provide substantial care to old parents who are highly dependent on them, are at the greatest risk of institutionalizing their parent (Gaugler et al., 2009). Although nursing home placement might seem like a good solution to reduce caregiver stress for the caregiver, research has shown that this stress generally does not decrease after institutionalization (Moon et al., 2016). Caregivers are not always ready for this step when professionals advise them to put their relative in a nursing home (Zarit & Knight, 1996). In contrast, attention to the caregiver's health risks in the form of increased support (e.g., assistance for ADLs, overnight help, and fewer caregiving hours) was found to improve caregiver mental functioning (Markowitz, Gutterman, Sadik, & Papadopoulos, 2003) and decrease the risk of care recipient institutionalization (Gaugler et al., 2000). This portends well for the potential possible impact of intervention on caregiving outcomes.

McKinlay, Crawford, and Tennstedt (1995) found that caregiving is not always perceived as stressful. In fact, NAC/AARP survey caregivers reported the feeling that best described their caregiving experience was happiness (48.9%) and love (17.3%); feelings of burden, obligation, sadness, and anger ranged from 2.5% to 15.2%. There is a growing literature on the positive aspects of caregiving that suggests that some caregivers find satisfaction and rewards in providing care and that this results in reduced reports of caregiver stress and in other improved caregiver outcomes (Cohen et al., 2002; Miller & Lawton, 1997; Roff et al., 2004). In a study of 978 spouse and child caregivers, Raschick and Ingersoll-Dayton (2004) found that female caregivers experience more caregiving "costs" than do male caregivers, and that adult children caregivers experience more rewards than do spousal caregivers. The care recipient's helpfulness, however, was found to have a greater impact on spousal than adult children caregivers.

Barriers to Obtaining Assistance with Caregiving

Professionals (e.g., social workers and case managers) often express frustration with caregivers who appear reluctant to implement suggested caregiving strategies and recommendations for formal services. In addition to the psychosocial variables that define the caregiver (e.g., relationship, gender, and ethnicity), additional psychological factors have been identified that impact such caregiving situations and outcomes. There appear to be unspoken barriers that prevent the adoption of particular strategies that exist without the overt awareness of the caregiver. Albert (1990) suggested that caregivers might be reluctant to acknowledge the extent of the disruption on the household of the care recipient's illness until they become so stressed that minor problems precipitate catastrophic reactions. Rubinstein (1990) explained that there might be psychological and symbolic meanings of the term *home* that contribute to the commitment to care for the person with dementia at home. For example, issues of control, security, family history, independence, comfort, and protection are all related to the idea that keeping a sick person at home means that the person is not fully "sick." Some caregiving families figure out their own management strategies, such as using routines for caregiving tasks and redefining parent–child roles (Albert, 1990), that are effective for a while; other families struggle in a mode of constant crisis management and delay the search for and acceptance of outside help. Yet recent surveys are finding that persons with dementia have more hospital stays, skilled nursing facility stays, and home healthcare visits than other older people (Alzheimer's Association, 2016) suggesting that Baby Boomer caregivers are seeking out assistance for caregiving challenges (Moon et al., 2016).

Other issues that pose often insurmountable barriers to obtaining adequate help include the social stigma and feelings of failure associated with seeking help, the lack of knowledge of the existence of services, the overwhelming array of choices available once identified, the fears of the cost of the services, the possibility of the person's refusal to cooperate with services, and lack of transportation. Once the caregiver has been convinced to try a service, new problems arise, including dissatisfaction with the services provided and conflict between caregivers and service providers involving differences in beliefs about the focus and intensity of caregiving tasks (Corcoran, 1993; Weinberger et al., 1993; Zarit, 1990). It may seem obvious that there is a need to understand the lifestyle, values, and goals of the caregiver, as well as his or her caregiving style, in order to provide effective services (Corcoran, 1994), but unless one uses the appropriate assessment tools to determine these caregiving characteristics, they might be overlooked. For example, Corcoran (1994) discovered that most men prefer a task–oriented approach to caregiving, whereas most women prefer a parental model emphasizing the physical and emotional health of the care recipient.

Tools such as *Personhood in Dementia Questionnaire* (Hunter et al., 2013), *Ways of Coping Questionnaire* (Lazarus & Folkman, 1984), *Communicating With Others: What's My Style or Hidden Feelings That Influence Communication* (Ostuni & Santo Pietro, 1991) should be helpful in identifying the important factors to be addressed in order to engender a positive, trusting relationship with the caregiver and to increase the possibility of positive caregiving outcomes. Toth-Cohen and colleagues (2001) outlined the four key factors to consider when working with caregivers of persons with dementia in their homes to be (a) understanding the personal meaning of home for the family, (b) viewing the caregiver as a "lay practitioner," (c) identifying the caregiver's beliefs and values, and (d) recognizing the demand characteristics of the services provided.

Finally, the most important variable in caregiving interventions may well be time. It is necessary to recognize that it may take more time than anticipated or desired for the caregiver to understand the extent of his or her caregiving challenges, to identify and accept the resources available, and to make the necessary changes in thinking and management styles to create a positive caregiving outcome. Bourgeois and colleagues (Bourgeois, Schulz, Burgio, & Beach, 2002) kept track of how long it took for caregivers to attempt or adopt a suggestion from a professional. In some cases, even with repeated suggestions over time, it took 6–12 months before the caregiver was able to overcome his or her personal barriers to the suggested strategy. Variability in time reflects the complexity of caregiving issues and the continuum of caregivers and caregiving styles. Professionals should not become disheartened when caregivers need time to change. Instead, professionals should understand that people require different amounts of time to be able to accept recommendations that may be in conflict with or differ from their own personal beliefs, family history, and coping styles. We need to trust that most caregivers will eventually be ready to try something new, and when that time comes, we need to be ready to support them in their efforts.

Interventions for Family Caregivers

The past decades have seen a proliferation of interventions developed to improve the psychosocial-emotional responses and dementia management skills of family caregivers (Burgio et al., 2016; Gitlin & Hodgson, 2015). With few exceptions, the interventions have been applied to a variety of caregivers, including spouses, adult children, siblings, friends, and paid caregivers. Burgio et al. (2016) conducted a systematic review of 40 previous systematic reviews and meta-analyses. They described a variety of types of caregiving interventions, including: psychoeducational (offering information, resources, and services), supportive (support groups focused on sharing ideas and solutions to problems), respite (providing in-home or site-specific time away from caregiving), psychotherapy (individual and family counseling), and multicomponent (providing a combination of education, support, respite, and therapy). In spite of this wealth of research, Burgio and colleagues (2016) caution that this literature still lacks high-quality evidence due to few randomized controlled trials (RCTs), sampling differences among studies, variability in study designs, heterogeneity of outcome measures, and questionable statistical power of some trials, resulting in moderately positive intervention efficacy.

Psychoeducational interventions address a variety of treatment purposes, including: to enhance the caregiver's knowledge (Brennan, Moore, & Smyth, 1991; Brodaty, Roberts, & Peters, 1994), to increase cognitive skills in problem solving (Labrecque, Peak, & Toseland, 1992), to reduce dysfunctional thoughts (Gallagher-Thompson & Steffen, 1994), to improve coping (Gallagher-Thompson & DeVries, 1994), to increase behavior management skills (Bourgeois et al., 2002), to improve caregivers' perceptions of their loved one's quality of life (Fletcher & Eckberg, 2014), to improve understanding of communication challenges in dementia (Purves & Phinney, 2012), and to modify positive and negative affect (Teri & Uomoto, 1991; Toseland, Rossiter, Peak, & Smith, 1990). Burgio et al. (2016) found that psychoeducational interventions produced strong evidence in reducing psychological morbidity, and short-term benefits on caregiver burden, depression, and wellbeing (e.g., Thompson et al., 2007). Psychoeducational + skills-building interventions showed additional reductions in depression and improvement in quality of life (Elvish, Lever, Johnstone, Cawley, & Keady, 2013). An individualized, home-based intervention program for managing problem behaviors in Taiwan was found to better reduce physically aggressive behavior than the control condition of receiving written instructions and telephone support (Huang et al., 2013). Support group interventions were judged to be modestly effective at reducing caregivers' distress; however, when a problem-solving component was added to the support group positive effects were seen (Cooke et al., 2001). In addition, a greater reduction in caregiver distress was measured when education was delivered individually than in groups (Selwood et al., 2007). In spite of the progress documented in improving caregivers' skills and reducing stress and burden through intervention, caregivers still report that they're "flying by the seat of our pants" and want more advanced courses or continuing support (Samia, Hepburn, & Nichols, 2012).

Respite interventions are designed to provide relief from caregiving in the form of respite care or adult day care. In these treatments, time away from caregiving responsibilities is intended to result in positive changes in mood, quality of life, and feelings about caregiving, but this does not always happen (Theis, Moss, & Pearson, 1994; Zarit, Greene, Ferraro, Townsend, & Stephens, 1996). Changes in physical health and sleep improvements have been the result of two studies of short-term institutional respite (Caradoc-Davies & Harvey, 1995; Larkin & Hopcroft, 1993). Caregivers, however, do not take advantage of this intervention as often as it is available. Lawton,

Brody, and Saperstein (1989) found that only 58% of caregivers in their study utilized the services. The effects of respite interventions are few and conflicting; some studies report having some effects on burden, depression, and wellbeing (e.g., Sörenson, Pinquart, & Duberstein, 2002), but others report no consistent or enduring effects (Cooper, Balamurali, Selwood, & Livingston, 2007), or no effects (Maayan, Soares-Weiser, & Lee, 2014).

Psychotherapy, and cognitive-behavioral therapy in particular, has shown consistent, positive effects on caregiver outcomes (Sörenson et al., 2002), possibly due to the intensity and time factors associated with individual-delivered intervention. Inconsistencies across studies in effects on caregiver and care-recipient outcomes were reported. For example, group-delivered interventions may yield more caregiver benefits (Thompson et al., 2007), but care-recipient institutionalization may not be influenced by the intervention (Vernooij-Dassen, Draskovic, McCleery, & Downs, 2011). A 4-hour Mindfulness intervention measured increased wellbeing (acceptance, presence, peace, and hope), and decreased reactivity and caregiver burden (Hoppes, Bryce, Hellman, & Finlay, 2012). Many other promising interventions are addressing caregiver challenges in creative ways such as volunteering (Guerra, Demain, Figueiredo, & De Sousa, 2012), increasing physical activity (Loi et al., 2014), and attending a reminiscence group with the person with dementia (Melunsky et al., 2015).

Multiple Component Interventions. While many intervention models have a single or primary focus of the treatment provided, the multiplicity of caregiver needs, however, has resulted in interventions consisting of multiple components. For example, early multicomponent interventions provided a combination of educational sessions, care planning, support groups, or a "buddy" (Ingersoll-Dayton, Chapman, & Neal, 1990); education and respite (Mohide et al., 1990; Oktay & Volland, 1990); or information, counseling, problem-solving, and a support group (Demers & Lavoie, 1996). Counseling on multiple topics, such as problem-solving, time management, and stress reduction (Toseland & Smith, 1990), and individual and family counseling designed to increase knowledge and affective responses to caregiving (Mittelman et al., 1995; Mittelman, Ferris, Shulman, Steinberg, & Levin, 1996) have improved caregiving outcomes for a wider range of caregivers. The addition of cognitive and behavioral skills training to intervention models has also contributed to positive caregiving outcomes (Gallagher-Thompson & DeVries, 1994; Gallagher-Thompson & Steffen, 1994).

While the majority of these studies are older, they are still relevant, as recent reviews have found that multicomponent interventions demonstrated the most consistent findings of efficacy for both caregiver and care-recipient outcomes (Burgio et al., 2016; Gitlin & Hodgson, 2015). Multiple meta-analyses confirmed effects ranging from small but significant on measures of depression (Parker, Mills, & Abbey, 2008), to moderate benefits for a variety of caregiver outcomes, and delayed institutionalization of the care recipient (Brodaty & Arasaratnam, 2012; Olazarán et al., 2010). These positive results were also seen with internet-delivered interventions for dementia caregivers (e.g., Boots et al., 2014).

A major concern with these multipronged approaches is that it is difficult to know which specific component of the intervention contributed most to the caregiving outcome. In these times of fiscal constraint, it is important to provide the best services possible at the least cost. For example, Hinchliffe, Hyman, Blizard, and Livingston (1995) provided drug therapy, behavioral, coping, and cognitive skills training, respite, *and* education to caregivers; it is unknown which aspects of the intervention were helpful, and all components may not be needed. Therefore, it is important to try to match the most effective intervention components to the particular needs of specific caregivers and to avoid providing unnecessary or ineffective service components. Too many choices may overwhelm caregivers or lead to nonuse of services. Yet, a meta-analysis of 30 psychosocial interventions for caregivers (Brodaty, Green, & Koschera, 2003) documented significant benefits in caregiver psychological distress and caregiver knowledge, particularly when the care recipients were involved in the intervention (i.e., when caregivers learned how to modify their family members' behaviors), the programs were more intensive, and the programs were tailored to caregivers' needs. Some of the interventions even delayed nursing home admission (Eloniemi-Sulkava, Sivenius, & Sulkava, 1999; Mittelman et al., 1996; Riordan & Bennett, 1998).

Efforts are now under way to compare treatment components within multicomponent interventions for their relative effectiveness. For example, Bourgeois and colleagues (2002) compared the effects of two well-defined and well-monitored skills training intervention approaches, care recipient change or self-change, with a control condition in which caregivers received a quasi-treatment (group class, home visits, and care recipient behavior tracking). Their multicomponent intervention was designed specifically to extend the generalizability of the most promising caregiver-focused skills training packages (Lovett & Gallagher, 1988), and care recipient-focused skills training approaches (Pinkston, Linsk, & Young, 1988; Zarit, Anthony, & Boutselis, 1987). Spousal caregivers in both intervention groups demonstrated significant improvements in a variety of caregiver outcome measures, such as depression, perceived health, caregiver strain, and self-efficacy, as a result of successfully implementing care recipient change or self-change programs. Caregivers who were taught to implement care recipient-focused behavior change programs in this study were highly effective in decreasing responsive behaviors, demonstrating maintenance of treatment gains over time. Caregivers who were taught to change their own behavior in response to caregiving challenges demonstrated significantly higher self-ratings of mood at the post-intervention and follow-up assessments. The effects of the interventions were most evident for the outcomes that directly reflected the skills directly targeted by the training (i.e., teaching behavior management skills reduced responsive behavior; teaching mood-elevating procedures improved mood ratings), and less so for those outcomes that were hypothesized to be related to the skills but not directly trained (e.g., anger and perceived health). These findings suggest that future interventions should assess the individual caregiver's specific training needs and tailor intervention to address directly those issues to maximize the desired outcomes. Differences in acceptability (i.e., implementation) of treatment plans between the two treatment groups suggested that caregivers might have different opinions about the behaviors they wanted to change, as well as perceived difficulty of implementing behavior change programs involving other individuals. Future interventions should be designed to offer a menu of behavior change strategies with therapist guidance in the selection process based on a caregiver needs assessment.

The analysis of different treatment components or treatment packages through a variety of outcome measures is also important for understanding the relationship between treatment components and outcomes. For example, Steffen (2000) compared a home-delivered videotaped Coping With Frustration class plus telephone follow-up with traditional face-to-face Coping With Frustration classes and a waiting list group and found that both treatment groups reported significant improvements in depression, hostility, and confidence in their ability to handle caregiving challenges, whereas the control group did not. Similar results were seen by Eisdorfer et al. (2003) and Mahoney, Tarlow, and Jones (2003) in their telephone-based cognitive-behavioral interventions; caregivers reduced their stress and depression and increased life satisfaction compared to minimal education and support groups. Glueckauf, Bourgeois, Massey, Pomidor, and Stine (2004) compared internet-delivered and telephone-delivered Positive Caregiving classes to dementia family caregivers and found substantial increases in self-efficacy perceptions, and reduced caregiver burden post training for both treatment groups. These studies have all been conducted with caregivers living in metropolitan and urban areas.

Glueckauf, Ketterson, Loomis, and Dages (2004) and Glueckauf et al. (2005) designed a telephone-delivered modification of the Positive Caregiving classes specifically for a rural population; the Alzheimer's Rural Care Healthline (ARCH) program was designed to compare the effects of the telephone-based caregiving classes with a minimal education and support control condition on caregivers' depression, perceived self-efficacy, and burden. In a follow-up study Glueckauf and colleagues (2012) compared telephone-based and face-to-face Cognitive Behavior Therapy (CBT) interventions with African American dementia caregivers with depression and found that both telephone-based and face-to-face CBT produced improvements in depression, subjective burden, and assistance support in these caregivers. Replication with a larger sample size ($N = 106$) is currently in progress.

In 1995, the National Institute on Aging and the National Institute on Nursing Research funded six intervention research programs designed to evaluate the effectiveness of different multicomponent interventions for family caregivers of persons with AD (Schulz et al., 2003). Each intervention model aimed to change specific caregiving stressors, and the caregivers' appraisal of and response to the stressors, and to address the specific needs of culturally diverse racial and ethnic majority and minority populations. This unique NIH initiative required adherence to the randomized controlled clinical trial requirements of (a) random assignment to treatment and control conditions, (b) common outcome measures, and (c) identical measurement intervals. The interventions were (a) Individual Information and Support strategies, (b) Group support and Family Systems Therapy, (c) Psychoeducation and Skill-based training approaches, (d) Home-based environmental interventions, and (e) Enhanced technology support systems. Analyses of the combined data from these studies revealed that caregivers in intervention conditions reported reduced burden and reduced depression compared to those in control conditions. Specifically, women and individuals with high school or less education reported lower burden, whereas caregivers who were Hispanic, had less than a high school education, and were nonspouses reported lower depression than similar caregivers in the control conditions (Schultz et al., 2003).

Schulz and colleagues (2003) pointed out that although these intervention studies have provided more insight into which strategies are useful for enhancing outcomes for different caregivers, the effects of these interventions on burden, depression, and other indicators of psychological wellbeing remain small to moderate. They hypothesized that the reason for these disappointing effects may be that caregivers cannot be categorized into single syndromal groups that are the target of a specific intervention. Caregivers may instead have problems of varying intensities in multiple areas and may need different intervention components tailored to address those specific issues. The attempt to find a "one-size-fits-all" intervention remains unsuccessful and most likely unrealistic.

This important finding led to the funding of a second phase of intervention studies, called Resources for Enhancing Alzheimer's Caregiver Health (REACH) II. The purpose of these studies was to evaluate an intervention composed of multiple treatment components (safety, self-care, social support, emotional wellbeing, and responsive behaviors) that were specifically tailored to the individual caregiver. A risk appraisal instrument determined the intensity of each treatment component a caregiver required. Those treatments were delivered using the most effective combination of active techniques, such as role-playing and interactive practice, in-home visits, and telephone-based support found in the REACH studies. Hispanic, Caucasian, and Black caregivers demonstrated significantly greater improvement in quality of life indicators (depression, burden, self-care, and social support) at six months post-treatment compared to control group caregivers. However, there were no significant effects on institutionalization of the care-recipient as a result of treatment at six months (Belle et al., 2006). A longer follow-up period might have revealed differences between groups and interventions for ethnically diverse dementia caregivers. As shown in Schulz and Martire's (2004) model (Figure 9.2), the many different types of intervention are thought to address different stressors and health processes; research is ongoing to better match interventions with desired outcomes.

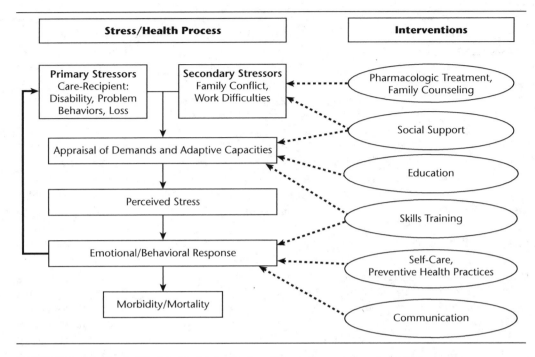

FIGURE 9.2 The Stress/Health Model Applied to Caregiving and Associated Interventions

Source: Reprinted with permission: Schulz and Martire (2004).

Communication-Focused Dementia Caregiver Interventions

Family caregivers of a person with dementia report that attempting to communicate with their loved one can be stressful (Clark & Witte, 1995). This is probably due to not understanding the communication problems associated with dementia, nor having the skills needed to prevent or repair communication breakdowns. As a result, caregivers may develop misconceptions about changes in communication, unrealistic expectations of communicative interactions, and negative communication patterns with their family member with dementia (Ripich, Ziol, & Lee, 1998). Investigations of the relationship between communication problems and caregiving burdens reveal that specific semantic and pragmatic breakdowns in language processing by persons with dementia result in responsive behaviors that are stressful to caregivers (Savundranagam, Hummert, & Montgomery, 2005). For example, word-finding difficulties interfere with topic maintenance in a conversation (Ripich, 1994), and misunderstood conversations lead to caregiver frustration (Orange, 1995). Therefore, it follows that caregivers need assistance to understand the progressive decline in communication skills over the course of dementia, the impact on responsive behaviors, and strategies to ease the stress and burden of impaired communication.

There are many publications for caregivers concerning the changes in communication behaviors related to dementia. Those written by SLPs describe the communication impairments and preserved abilities across mild, moderate, and severe stages of the disease (e.g., Rau, 1993; Santo Pietro & Ostuni, 2003). Other, more general guidebooks also contain chapters on communication challenges and recommended strategies for improving communication (e.g., Mace & Rabins, 2017; Tappen, 1997).

Research on the many common sense recommendations for caregivers about how best to communicate with persons with dementia has been forthcoming in the literature with mixed results. For example, Hendryx-Bedalov (1999) noted that persons with AD appeared to have more difficulty responding to abstract rather than concrete language during mealtime conversations; however, when caregivers were taught to use more concrete questions, the responses of the person with AD were not much different from when they were asked abstract questions. Similarly, Tappen and colleagues (Tappen, Williams-Burgess, Edelstein, Touhy, & Fishman, 1997) taught caregivers three conversation-enhancing strategies (i.e., closed-ended questions, respecting personhood, and topic maintenance) and documented their increased use of these strategies with relatively little differential effect on the persons with dementia who responded positively to all strategies. Caregivers report dissatisfaction with some recommended strategies that they have tried without much success, such as using a slow rate of speech and short utterances (Orange, 1995).

Small and Gutman (2002) reviewed the literature to identify all the recommended communication strategies for caregivers (see Table 9.3 for a list of the 10 most frequently recommended strategies). Caregivers were then asked to rate the frequency of use and effectiveness of each of these strategies. Similar to other reports in the literature, short simple speech and asking one question or giving one instruction at a time were judged effective techniques (Kemper, Anagnopoulos, Lyons, & Heberlein, 1994; Small, Gutman, Makela, & Hillhouse, 2003; Small, Kemper, & Lyons, 1997). In contrast to Small et al. (1997), these caregivers reported dissatisfaction with paraphrased speech, and they did not use the following strategies very often: slowed speech, eliminating distractions, approaching from the front, and maintaining eye contact. As Small and Gutman pointed out, there is still a great need for research on the efficacy of these recommended strategies in real-life situations. Although many of the above-reviewed caregiving interventions addressed communication-related issues in a general way, family caregivers need specific training, such as identifying communication problems and applying communication strategies, to improve communicative interactions. Several studies have begun to address these issues directly; for example, caregivers have been taught to use memory aids to enhance conversations (Bourgeois, 1992) and to reduce repetitive requests (Bourgeois et al., 1997). In other research, caregivers were taught to improve repair strategies (Orange & Colton-Hudson, 1998). In addition to improving communication, these studies have also found reduced caregiver-reported stress. Haberstroh and colleagues (2011) evaluated the TANDEM program for teaching informal caregivers to use communication-maintaining strategies and found significant improvement in the use of strategies over time and caregiver mood during training sessions, but no effects on caregiver burden.

TABLE 9.3 Rank Order of the Most Frequently Recommended Communication Strategies

1. Use short, simple sentences.
2. Speak slowly.
3. Ask one question or give one instruction at a time.
4. Approach slowly and from the front; establish and maintain eye contact.
5. Eliminate distractions (e.g., TV and radio).
6. Avoid interrupting the person; allow plenty of time for responding.
7. Use yes–no rather than open-ended questions.
8. Encourage circumlocution during word-finding problems.
9. Repeat messages with the same wording.
10. Paraphrase repeated messages.

Source: Small and Gutman (2002).

To address formal caregivers' training needs, Bourgeois and colleagues developed a program to teach nursing assistants (NAs) to use memory wallets with residents with dementia during ADLs (Burgio et al., 2001). Didactic sessions covered information about dementia-related behaviors, the relationship between responsive behaviors and communication deficits, the use of written cues to support communication, and an approach strategy for interactions. NAs were observed during care interactions with residents and provided feedback on their use of the strategies, including Announce (Hello, Mrs. Smith, I'm Mary), specific one-step instructions (Please read this: "Showering makes me feel fresh and clean"; Let's go take a shower), and Praise (Thank you for helping me with your nightgown). Results showed that trained NAs talked more, used positive statements more frequently, and tended to increase the number of specific instructions given to residents, without increasing the total time giving care to residents. These effects maintained for 2 months. In a similar study, Wilson, Rochon, Mihailidis, and Leonard (2012) taught NAs to use task-focused verbal and nonverbal communication strategies while assisting residents with moderate to severe dementia in handwashing. Trained NAs were observed to use one direction at a time, close-ended questions, paraphrased repetition, encouraging comments, and stated the resident's name to facilitate task completion. More information about training professional caregivers can be found in Chapter 10.

In their systematic review of 13 studies designed to enhance verbal communication between individuals with Alzheimer's disease and their formal and informal caregivers, Egan, Bérubé, Racine, Leonard, and Rochon (2010) cautioned that methodological concerns (e.g., small sample sizes, nonrandom group assignment) limited the strength of the evidence for the interventions. Nevertheless, they found the use of memory aids showed the clearest effectiveness for improving participants' discourse, with promising results for the Breakfast Club intervention (Santo Pietro & Boczko, 1998).

Teaching Caregivers to Use Memory Aids. As mentioned in Chapter 6, family caregivers have been taught to use memory wallets and memory books to improve conversations with the person with dementia (Bourgeois, 1994). When the perceptions of the caregivers in that study did not match the objective data (i.e., spouses were not impressed with the improvement in conversation about familiar historical content when other behavior problems persisted), Bourgeois and colleagues (1997) explored the benefits of teaching caregivers to use targeted written text to modify caregiver-identified repetitive verbal behaviors that were reported to be disruptive and to prevent satisfying communicative interactions. For example, if the caregiver was distressed that the person with AD repeatedly asked about a deceased relative, then a page was made for the memory book that stated the facts (e.g., "My husband, Jim, was laid to rest in St. Mary's Cemetery on March 14, 2002"). In each case, a written statement and cue format were developed to address the unique concern of the person, ranging from a reminder card that read, "We are going to the grocery store," to an erasable memo board on the refrigerator that read, "Today is Monday. Jane will be home at 3 o'clock." Results revealed that, in addition to caregivers reporting reductions in the frequency of repeated verbalizations with the use of these written tools, they also expressed satisfaction with their own ability to modify a previously frustrating problem.

It must be noted that the caregivers in this study were part of a larger study (Bourgeois et al., 2002) and were asked to keep track of the frequency of the most stressful responsive behaviors of their spouse with AD over the course of the study. In some cases, the data sheets revealed that the problems identified as very stressful were in fact very rare in occurrence. Only those that persisted over time that were addressed with a written memory aid strategy. It was suggested that the recording of data itself might be an effective intervention for helping the caregiver to be more objective about the frequency of particularly challenging behaviors.

As Bourgeois et al. (2002) reported, however, control group caregivers who did not receive training in memory aids may have become more objective about the responsive behaviors of their spouse with AD because of data recording, but the frequency of the challenging behaviors was not changed as a result of data recording alone. Recording the frequency of responsive behaviors is, however, an important precursor to the development of an effective intervention. Appendix 9.1 includes examples of data-recording sheets recommended for caregivers and instructions for their use.

Several other tools for working with caregivers have also been included at the end of this chapter. Appendix 9.2 contains caregiver instructions for making memory aids. Appendix 9.3 has caregiver instructions for having satisfying conversations with the care recipient using a memory aid. Appendix 9.4 contains caregiver instructions for developing and using written cues (in the form of reminder cards).

A popular SLP-developed program, the FOCUSED Program (Ripich, 1994), was adapted from a communication skills training program developed for nursing assistants (Ripich, Wykle, & Niles, 1995; Ripich, Ziol, Durand, & Fritsch, 1999) to address the needs of family caregivers. Based on an interactive discourse model of conversational exchanges, this seven-step program, called the FOCUSED program, teaches caregivers specific conversation skills (**f**ace-to-face, **o**rientation, **c**ontinuity, **u**nsticking, **s**tructure, **e**xchange, and **d**irect). See Table 9.4 for a description of each strategy. This training program is designed to be used in six two-hour modules and includes a trainer's manual, a caregiver's guide, pre- and post-assessments, reminder cards on which are printed the FOCUSED principles, and an instructional videotape (*Alzheimer's Disease Communication Guide: The FOCUSED Program for Caregivers*; Ripich & Wykle, 1996).

Ripich et al. (1998) evaluated this program with 19 caregivers (15 women and four men) and a waitlist control group of 18 caregivers (15 women and three men). The treatment group attended four 2-hour sessions. Both groups completed an assessment battery, consisting of measures of wellbeing (positive and negative affect), depression, health, stress and burden (general and communication hassles), and knowledge of AD and communication, in each of four phases: pre-training, immediately, and 6 and 12 months post training. Treatment caregivers demonstrated

TABLE 9.4 FOCUSED Communication Strategies

Face-to-face	Face the person with AD. Call his or her name. Touch the person. Gain and maintain eye contact.
Orientation	Orient the person to the topic by repeating key words several times. Repeat and rephrase sentences. Use nouns and specific names.
Continuity	Continue the same topic of conversation for as long as possible. Restate the topic throughout the conversation. Indicate that you are introducing a new topic.
Unsticking	Help the person become "unstuck" by suggesting the intended word. Repeat the sentence using the correct word. Ask, "Do you mean …?"
Structure	Structure your questions so that the person can recognize and repeat a response. Provide two simple choices at a time. Use yes–no questions.
Exchange	Keep up the normal exchange of ideas in everyday conversation. Keep the conversation going with comments like "Oh, how nice," or "That's great." Do not ask "test" questions.
Direct	Keep sentences short, simple, and direct. Put the subject of the sentence first. Use and repeat nouns rather than pronouns. Use hand signals, pictures, and facial expressions.

Source: Ripich and Wykle (1996).

significant decreases in communication hassles and increases in knowledge about AD and communication in post-training, which maintained at 6 and 12 months, compared to control caregivers, who did not show these effects. No changes were reported in any of the other measures of affect, depression, health, or general caregiving hassles. This study provides support for the effectiveness of a communication-focused skills training program to produce changes in communicative interactions between caregivers and their family member with dementia. Byrne and Orange (2005) pointed out, however, that this program was "not based on a theoretical framework that justifies its program elements" (p. 196), and as Small and Gutman (2002) found, not all of the recommended strategies have been reported to be effective. Therefore, SLPs must be sure to monitor the effects of any treatment program that recommends the FOCUSED strategies.

As mentioned in earlier chapters, many responsive behaviors exhibited by persons with dementia appear related to communication and cognitive impairments that can be modified successfully with communication- or memory-enhancing interventions designed by SLPs. Therefore, the role of the SLP in working with caregivers is multidimensional. SLPs can teach caregivers about the cognitive and communicative deficits and strengths of the person with dementia as the disease progresses. They can convey specific strategies and techniques for supporting and maintaining satisfying conversations and for modifying related responsive behaviors. It is important to note that SLPs can be reimbursed for training caregivers; in Chapter 4, examples of caregiver treatment goals are provided. In addition, SLPs can recognize the other psychosocial and emotional needs of caregivers and make recommendations for other services, including educational materials, websites, support groups, and other relevant community resources. Table 9.5 provides a list of the educational topics that are beneficial to caregivers; Table 9.6 is a list of websites and internet resources for caregivers. Finally, SLPs can provide counseling services to caregivers struggling emotionally with caregiving challenges. As discussed in Chapter 11, the functional approaches suggested in this book for treating the person with dementia and their caregivers are designed to help maintain a quality of life in the face of the many difficulties related to a degenerative disease such as dementia and to assist with end-of-life communication.

TABLE 9.5 Examples of Caregiver Education Topics

Dementia: Definition, stages, expected course, and treatment
Understanding Alzheimer's disease and related dementias
Characteristics of Alzheimer's disease and related dementias
Communication skills
Behavior management
Activities of daily living (ADLs); bathing, dressing, toileting, and feeding
Medical care: Diagnostic evaluation, treatment, and drug studies
Nursing and home healthcare services
Respite and day care services
Residential care and nursing home options
Support groups
Counseling services
Transportation services
Local agency services
Legal issues and services
Financial issues and services

TABLE 9.6 Websites and Internet Resources for Family Caregivers

Administration on Aging: www.aoa.gov
Source for long-term care ombudsmen: www.aoa.gov/prof/aoaprog/elder_rights/
LTCombudsman/ltc_ombudsman.asp
Alzheimer Disease Education and Referral Center (ADEAR): www.alzheimers.org
Alzheimer's Association: www.alz.org
Alzheimer's Foundation of America: www.alzfdn.org
American Geriatrics Society: www.americangeriatrics.org
Area Agency on Aging: www.n4a.org
Source for eldercare local community services: www.n4a.org/locator
Family Caregiver Alliance: www.caregiver.org
Mayo Clinic: www.mayoclinic.com/health/alzheimers–caregivers
Medline Plus: www.nlm.nih.gov/medlineplus/alzheimerscaregivers.html
National Family Caregiver Support program: www.fullcirclecare.org
Online Caregiver magazine: www.caregiver.com
Source of CD-ROM training materials: www.orcahealth.com
Source of large–print and adaptive household and leisure materials: www.eldercorner.com
Source of Video Respite tapes and other Alzheimer's–related materials: www.healthpropress.com

Case 9.1 Illustration of a Caregiver Intervention

The conference room at the Capital Area Regional Hospital was fast becoming crowded for the monthly meeting of "Caregivers: Education and Support." Mr. and Mrs. Wong; Juanita Hernandez and her sister, Maria; the Johnson family (siblings Jamar, Jerrell, and Jenisha); Mrs. Bernadette Sterling; Burton Hughes; and several other newcomers were chatting quietly. The social worker, Mary Washington, was checking with the guest speaker, Dr. Henry, about the projector and his handouts for tonight's presentation. Within minutes everyone found a seat, and Ms. Washington made some welcoming remarks and introduced the speaker and his topic, "Recent Advances in Dementia Medications." As Dr. Henry began his lecture, Ms. Washington surveyed the assembled group and reflected on their progress in the past months.

Mr. and Mrs. Wong, middle-aged professionals and second-generation Taiwanese, were caring for Mr. Wong's father with dementia. Several months ago, Mrs. Wong had called in distress; her husband expected her to quit her job to care for his father, who was exhibiting uncharacteristic behaviors (e.g., putting clothing in shopping bags, buying cigarettes at the corner grocery, and asking strangers for directions to the bus station). They had sent him to Taiwan to visit his siblings during the summer, but upon his return he denied that he had seen anyone he knew or that he had had anything to eat for the entire three weeks. Ms. Washington advised Mrs. Wong to make an appointment with their family physician. Subsequent to Mr. Wong Sr.'s dementia diagnosis, Mr. and Mrs. Wong began attending this group, and over the past few months they had implemented several suggestions: They hired a personal assistant to spend the daytime hours with Mr. Wong, fixing his meals, playing chess with him, and taking him to the Asian Social Club for their afternoon men's group. Mr. Wong Jr. made an appointment with an attorney to discuss financial and medical decision-making.

Juanita Hernandez and her sister, Maria, both single mothers with several young children, were sharing responsibility for their mother with dementia. Their mother, Ana Luz, had cared for an extended family of more than 25 foster children over the years, but had been unable to complete any of her routine household activities for many months. She spent hours sitting in a chair on the porch, watching the passersby; she forgot to bathe or change her clothing. On the day when Maria arrived home to hear her young son screaming in his crib, apparently unattended for hours, Juanita and her sister arranged for a medical evaluation. It has been a very difficult six months for these sisters, trying to enlist the help of other siblings to share in the care of their mother as well as multiple small children. But Ms. Washington remembers vividly the family meeting she facilitated at Ana Luz's home; several other sisters and two brothers had an emotional time learning that their mother with dementia required such close supervision and assistance. But they were quick to volunteer for a variety of activities at specific times, as Ms. Washington noted these on an erasable monthly calendar; each sister agreed to spend one day a week at their mother's house watching the babies and preparing meals. One brother offered to do the yard work and take out the garbage weekly; the other planned to take Ana Luz to church on Sundays. It has not always gone as smoothly as everyone had hoped, but they have recently started having a family potluck dinner at Ana Luz's after church on Sunday, and that is helping everyone plan for the coming week.

It was rewarding to see the Johnson family all in attendance tonight. Siblings Lamar, Jerrell, and Shaniqua have their own families and many personal challenges, but they have been able to help their beloved uncle Oscar to get diagnosed and moved to an assisted living facility. Last month, they mentioned the facility staff were concerned that Oscar was not attending his usual activity programs and was missing meals; the Johnsons are hoping to get some ideas tonight about how to get their uncle to take his medications correctly.

Mrs. Bernadette Sterling and Burton Hughes are both in their 70s. They met last year at the hospital's adult day care facility, where their spouses spent the daytime hours. Mr. Sterling died a few months ago, but Mrs. Sterling still attends these meetings. Mr. Hughes has come to the meeting tonight for ideas about how to handle his wife's fears about the new day care staff member who has a foreign accent. Mrs. Sterling is remembering when Ms. Washington first suggested adult day care for her husband; she had just dismissed that idea because her husband's illness had made him quick to say anything that came to mind and she was afraid he would say something racist in public. She regrets the many months she waited until she was so worn out from caregiving that day care was her only hope. But she was determined to avoid placing her husband in a nursing home; her fears were put to rest when she watched the staff anticipate potentially difficult situations and carefully redirect him to a positive activity. Mr. Hughes' wife will be fine once he alerts the staff to watch for signs that she is becoming fearful.

As the presentation winds down and Dr. Henry is answering questions from the audience, Ms. Washington notices that a couple of last meeting's newcomers are not present tonight. Seth McCory, a busy young attorney, had asked her at the end of the meeting for other sources of information about dementia; she gave him a list of reputable websites and a bibliography of books and pamphlets to get him started learning about his mother's diagnosis. Mary Smith, the freelance photographer, whose only relative was an aunt in another state who was calling her daily with troubling questions, needed the toll-free helpline number for advice when these unexpected calls occurred. As different as each of these caregivers are, there are different solutions for their needs. Ms. Washington is relieved that her hospital and her community have the wealth of resources needed to meet the needs of everyone who is dealing with the challenges of dementia.

Appendix 9.1: Example Data-Recording Sheets and Instructions for Caregivers

Day	Count Problem: Cannot Find Room	Count Problem: Asks What Time It Is
Monday		
Tuesday		
Wednesday		
Thursday		
Friday		
Saturday		
Sunday		

1. Ask the caregiver to identify and describe the responsive behaviors.
2. Determine which are the most stressful behaviors, and write them on the data sheet.
3. Discuss a time for recording behaviors (use the same time every day, such as after breakfast or dinner, or before bed).
4. Practice recording with verbal role-play.
5. One week later, review the data sheet. Discuss frequencies. Decide on the problem to remediate.

Appendix 9.2: Making Memory Aids: Family Caregiver Instructions

1. Complete a "Memory Aid Information Form" (see Appendices 5.3 and 5.4).
2. Make a written list of all possible sentences to include in the memory aid.
3. Choose an appropriate number of written sentences or reproducible pages to include in the memory aid for your family member.
4. Find family pictures that clearly illustrate each of the sentences. Magazine pictures and other souvenirs or familiar items, such as maps, concert programs, ticket stubs, invitations, and greeting cards, can also be included to illustrate the pages.
5. Choose the size of memory aid that you feel is most appropriate for your family member. Memory wallets are recommended for persons who live at home and still go on outings outside of the home; memory books are better for persons who are housebound or in nursing homes, and who may have trouble turning small pages. Wearable memory wallets are also valuable in the nursing home or assisted living setting.
6. Assemble the supplies needed to make the memory aid. Remember the scissors, the glue, and a black ink pen.
7. Print sentences in black ink and large letters, or use your computer to type the words on the pages.
8. Trim and paste pictures onto relevant pages.
9. Slip book pages into clear plastic page protectors or laminated wallet pages. Using a hole-punch, make holes for each wallet page.
10. Put all book pages into a three-ring notebook, and wallet pages into a wallet with 1" rings.
11. Read the "Guidelines for Having a Satisfying Conversation" (Appendix 9.3).
12. Share the memory aid with its new owner.

Source: © Michelle S. Bourgeois, Ph.D.

Appendix 9.3: Guidelines for Having a Satisfying Conversation

1. ***Ask*** them to have a conversation with you.
    "Mary, I'd really like to talk with you today. Would you mind if I sat down beside you?"
2. ***Guide*** the conversation onto specific topics and ***redirect*** the conversation back to the topic when the person begins to ramble.
    "Mary, let's talk about your family now – please tell me all about them."
3. ***Reassure*** them and ***help out*** when they get stuck or can't find the word they want to use.
    "That's OK, Bob; what else can you tell me about your life?"
4. ***Smile*** and ***act interested*** in whatever they're talking about, even if you're not quite sure what they are trying to say.
5. ***THANK*** them for talking with you.

What to *Avoid* During Conversations

DO NOT quiz the person or ask lots of specific questions.
"Now who is this person? I know you know: Who is it?"
DO NOT correct or ***contradict*** something that was stated as a fact even if you know it's wrong.
"No, that's not John. That's Jason, remember, your grandson Jason?"

Source: © Michelle S. Bourgeois, Ph.D.

Appendix 9.4 Reminder Cards: Using Written Cues in the Home and Nursing Home

When a question is repeated a few seconds after you have just answered it, a **reminder card** may help to keep the information in mind. Follow these easy steps for successful remembering:

1. State the answer to the question or concern.
2. Write the answer on an index card or notepad.
3. Read the card aloud with the person, and give it to him or her.
4. When the question is repeated, *do not* say the answer. *Instead*, say, "Read the card."
5. Do this each time the question is repeated.

Examples

Q: When am I going to the store?
A: **I am going to the store after lunch.** (Write this on the card.)
Q: Where are we going?
A: **We are going to church.** (Write this on the card.)
Q: Where is my paycheck?
A: **My money is safe in the bank.** (Write this on the card.)

Helpful Hints

Print a clear message.
Use large print. Use a few, simple, positive words.
Make the message personal.
Use personal pronouns (*I, my, we*) in the message.

Read the message aloud.

If there are reading errors, change the message.

Source: © Michelle S. Bourgeois, Ph.D.

References

Adams, B., Aranda, M., Kemp, R., & Takagi, K. (2002). Ethnic and gender differences in distress among Anglo-American, African-American, Japanese-American and Mexican-American spousal caregivers of persons with dementia. *Journal of Clinical Geropsychology, 8*(4), 279–301.

Albert, S. M. (1990). The dependent elderly, home health care, and strategies of household adaptation. In J. F. Gubrium & A. Sankar (Eds.), *The home care experience* (pp. 19–36). Newbury Park, CA: Sage.

Alzheimer's Association (2014). *Alzheimer's disease facts and figures. Special report: Women and Alzheimer's disease.* Retrieved December 22, 2015, from www.alz.org/downloads/Facts_ Figures_2014.pdf.

Alzheimer's Association (2016). Alzheimer's disease facts and figures. *Alzheimer's & Dementia,12*(4), 1–84.

Aneshensel, C., Pearlin, L., Mullan, J., Zarit, S., & Whitlatch, C. (1995). *Profiles in caregiving: The unexpected career.* New York: Academic Press.

Arai, A., Matsumoto, T., Ikeda, M., & Arai, Y. (2007). Do family caregivers perceive more difficulty when they look after patients with early onset dementia compared to those with late onset dementia. *Int J Geriatr Psychiatry, 22*, 1255–1261.

Argimon, J., Limon, E., Vila, J., & Cabezas, C. (2005). Health-related quality-of-life of caregivers as a predictor of nursing-home placement of patients with dementia. *Alzheimer Disease and Associated Disorders, 19*(1), 41–44.

Atchely, R. C. (1988). *The social forces in later life.* Belmont, CA: Wadsworth.

Ayalon, L., & Huyck, M. (2001). Latino caregivers of relatives with Alzheimer's disease. *Clinical Gerontologist, 24*(3/4), 93–106.

Barbosa, A., Figueiredo, S., Sousa, L., & Demain, S. (2011). Coping with the caregiving role: Differences between primary and secondary caregivers of dependent elderly people. *Aging and Mental Health, 15*(4), 490–499.

Barnes, C., Given, B., & Given, C. (1992). Caregivers of elderly relatives: Spouses and adult children. *Health & Social Work, 17*, 282–289.

Barnes, L., Mendes de Leon, C., Bienias, J., & Evans, D. (2004). A longitudinal study of Black-White differences in social resources. *Journal of Gerontology: Social Sciences, 59B*, S146–S153.

Belle, S., Burgio, L., Burns, R. Coon, D., Czaja, S. J., Gallagher-Thompson, D., et al. (2006). Enhancing the quality of life of dementia caregivers from different ethnic or racial groups: A randomized, controlled trial. *Annals of Internal Medicine, 145*, 727–738.

Bookwala, J., Yee, J., & Schulz, R. (2000). Caregiving and detrimental mental and physical health outcomes. In G. Williamson, P. Parmelee, & D. Shaffer (Eds.), *Physical illness and depression in older adults: A handbook of theory, research, and practice* (pp. 93–131). New York: Plenum.

Boots, L. M., de Vugt, M. E., van Knippenberg, R. J., Kempen, G. I., & Verhey, F. R. (2014). A systematic review of internet-based supportive interventions for caregivers of patients with dementia. *International Journal of Geriatric Psychiatry, 29*, 331–344.

Botsford, J., Clark, C. L., & Gibb, C. E. (2011). Research and dementia, caring and ethnicity: A review of the literature. *Journal of Research in Nursing, 16*(5), 437–449.

Bourgeois, M. (1992). Evaluating memory wallets in conversations with patients with dementia. *Journal of Speech and Hearing Research, 35*, 1344–1357.

Bourgeois, M. (1994). Teaching caregivers to use memory aids with patients with dementia. In Caregiving in Alzheimer's disease II: Caregiving interventions. *Seminars in Speech and Language, 15*(4), 291–305.

Bourgeois, M., Beach, S., Schulz, R., & Burgio, L. (1996). When primary and secondary caregivers disagree: Predictors and psychosocial consequences. *Psychology and Aging, 11*, 527–537.

Bourgeois, M., Burgio, L., Schulz, R., Beach, S., & Palmer, B. (1997). Modifying repetitive verbalization of community dwelling patients with AD. *The Gerontologist, 37*, 30–39.

Bourgeois, M., Schulz, R., Burgio, L., & Beach, S. (2002). Skills training for spouses of patients with Alzheimer's disease: Outcomes of an intervention study. *Journal of Clinical Geropsychology, 8*, 53–73.

Braun, K., & Browne, C. V. (1998). Perceptions of dementia, caregiving, and help seeking among Asian and Pacific Islander Americans. *Health Social Work, 23*(4), 262–274.

Brennan, P., Moore, S., & Smyth, K. (1991). ComputerLink: Electronic support for the home caregiver. *Advances in Nursing Science, 13*(4), 14–27.

Briones, D., Ramirez, A., Guerrero, M., & Ledger, E. (2002). Determining cultural and psychosocial factors in Alzheimer disease among Hispanic populations. *Alzheimer Disease and Associated Disorders, 16*, S86–S88.

Brodaty, H., & Arasaratnam, C. (2012). Meta-analysis of nonpharmacological interventions for neuropsychiatric symptoms of dementia. *The American Journal of Psychiatry, 169*, 946–953.

Brodaty, H., Green, A., & Koschera, A. (2003). Meta-analysis of psychosocial interventions for caregivers of people with dementia. *Journal of the American Geriatrics Society, 51*, 657–664.

Brodaty, H., Roberts, K., & Peters, K. (1994). Quasi-experimental evaluation of an educational model for dementia caregivers. *International Journal of Geriatric Psychiatry, 9*, 195–204.

Brodaty, H., Woodward, M., Boundry, K., Ames, D., Balshaw, R., & PRIME Study Group. (2014). Prevalence and predictors of burden in caregivers of people with dementia. *The American Journal of Geriatric Psychiatry, 22*, 756–765.

Brody, E. M., Hoffman, C., Kleban, M. H., & Schoonover, C. B. (1989). Caregiving daughters and their local siblings: Perceptions, strains, and interactions. *The Gerontologist, 29*, 529–538.

Brody, E., Litvin, S., Hoffman, C., & Kleban, M. (1992). Differential effects of daughters' marital status on their parent care experiences. *The Gerontologist, 32*, 58–67.

Brown, J., & Alligood, M. (2004). Realizing wrongness: Stories of older wife caregivers. *Journal of Applied Gerontology, 23*(2), 104–119.

Burgio, L., Allen-Burge, R., Roth, D., Bourgeois, M., Dijkstra, K., Gerstle, J., et al. (2001). Come talk with me: Improving communication between nursing assistants and nursing home residents during care routines. *The Gerontologist, 41*, 449–460.

Burgio, L. D., Gaugler, J. E., & Hilgeman, M. M. (Eds.) (2016). *The spectrum of family caregiving for adults and elders with chronic illness.* New York: Oxford University Press.

Byrne, K., & Orange, J. B. (2005). Conceptualizing communication enhancement in dementia for family caregivers using the SHO-ICF framework. *Advances in Speech-Language Pathology, 7*(4), 187–202.

Caradoc-Davies, T., & Harvey, J. (1995). Do social relief admissions have any effect on patients or their caregivers? *Disability and Rehabilitation, 17*(5), 247–251.

Carter, P. (2015). State of caregiving for people with dementia in Indian country. Retrieved December 2016, from https://ruralhealth.und.edu/presentations/pdf/101915-caregiving-for-dementia-in-indian-country.pdf.

Centers for Disease Control and Prevention (2013). *The state of aging and health in America 2013.* Centers for Disease Control and Prevention, US Dept. of Health and Human Services.

Chiriboga, D., Black, S., Aranda, M., & Markides, K. (2002). Stress and depressive symptoms among Mexican American elders. *Journal of Gerontology: Psychological Sciences, 57B*, P559–P568.

Cicirelli, V. G. (1983). Adult children's attachment and helping behaviour to elderly parents: A path model. *Journal of Marriage and the Family, 45*, 815–824.

Clark, L. (1997). Communication intervention for family caregivers and professional health care providers. In B. Shadden & M. A. Toner (Eds.), *Aging and communication* (pp. 251–274). Austin, TX: Pro-Ed.

Clark, L., & Witte, K. (1995). Nature and efficacy of communication management in Alzheimer's disease. In R. Lubinski (Ed.), *Dementia and communication* (pp. 238–256). San Diego, CA: Singular.

Cloutterbuck, J., & Mahoney, D. (2003). African American dementia caregivers: The duality of respect. *Dementia, 2*(2), 221–243.

Clyburn, L., Stones, M., Hadjistavropoulos, T., & Tuokko, H. (2000). Predicting caregiver burden and depression in Alzheimer's disease. *Journal of Gerontology: Social Sciences, 55B*, S2–S13.

Cohen, C., Colantonio, A., & Vernich, L. (2002). Positive aspects of caregiving: Rounding out the caregiver experience. *International Journal of Geriatric Psychiatry, 17*, 184–188.

Collins, C., & Jones, R. (1997). Emotional distress and morbidity in dementia carers: A matched comparison of husbands and wives. *International Journal of Geriatric Psychiatry, 12*, 1168–1173.

Connell, C., & Gibson, G. (1997). Racial, ethnic and cultural differences in dementia caregiving: Review and analysis. *The Gerontologist, 37*, 355–364.

Connidis, I. A., Rosenthal, C. J., & McMullin, J. A. (1996). The impact of family composition on providing help to older parents. *Research on Aging, 18*(4), 402–429.

Cooke, D. D., McNally, L., Mulligan, K. T., Harrison, M. J., & Newman, S. P. (2001). Psychosocial interventions for caregivers of people with dementia: A systematic review. *Aging & Mental Health, 5,* 120–135.

Cooper, C., Balamurali, T. B., Selwood, A., & Livingston, G. (2007). A systematic review of intervention studies about anxiety in caregivers of people with dementia. *International Journal of Geriatric Psychiatry, 22,* 181–188.

Corcoran, M. (1993). Collaboration: An ethical approach to effective therapeutic relationships. *Topics in Geriatric Rehabilitation, 9,* 21–29.

Corcoran, M. (1994, November). *Individuals caring for a spouse with Alzheimer's disease: A descriptive study of caregiving styles.* Paper presented at the Gerontological Society of America Convention, New Orleans, LA.

Crawford, L., Bond, J., & Balshaw, R. (1994). Factors affecting sons' and daughters' caregiving to older parents. *Canadian Journal on Aging, 13*(4), 454–469.

Croog, S., Sudilovsky, A., Burleson, J., & Baume, R. (2001). Vulnerability of husband and wife caregivers of Alzheimer disease patients to caregiving stressors. *Alzheimer Disease and Associated Disorders, 15*(4), 201–210.

Dauphinot, V., Felphin-Combe, F., Mouchoux, C., Dorey, A., Bathsavanis, A., Makaroff, Z., Rouch, I., & Krolak-Salmon, P. (2015). Risk factors of caregiver burden among patients with Alzheimer's disease or related disorders: A cross-sectional study. *Journal of Alzheimers Disease, 44,* 907–916.

Demers, A., & Lavoie, J. (1996). Effect of support groups on family caregivers to the frail elderly. *Canadian Journal on Aging, 15*(1), 129–144.

Dilworth-Anderson, P., Goodwin, P., & Williams, S. (2004). Can culture help explain the physical health effects of caregiving over time among African American caregivers? *Journal of Gerontology: Social Sciences, 59B,* S138–S145.

D'Onofrio, G., Sancaroo, D., Addante, F., Ciccone, F., Cascavilla, L., Paris, F., Picoco, M., Nuzzaci, C., Elia, A., Greco, A., Chiarini, R., Panza, F., & Pilotto, A. (2014). Caregiver burden characterization in patients with Alzheimer's disease or vascular dementia. *International Journal of Geriatric Psychiatry, 30.*

Dwyer, J. W., & Coward, R. T. (1991). A multivariate comparison of the involvement of adult sons versus daughters in the care of impaired parents. *Journal of Gerontology, 46,* S259–S269.

Dwyer, J. W., Henretta, J. C., Coward, R. T., & Barton, A. J. (1992). Changes in helping behaviors of adult children as caregivers. *Research on Aging, 14*(3), 351–375.

Edgerly, E., Montes, L., Yau, E., Stokes, S., & Redd, D. (2003). Ethnic minority caregivers. In D. Coon, D. Gallagher-Thompson, & L. Thompson (Eds.), *Innovative interventions to reduce dementia caregiver stress* (pp. 223–242). New York: Springer.

Egan, M., Bérubé, D., Racine, G., Leonard, C., & Rochon, E. (2010). Methods to enhance verbal communication between individuals with Alzheimer's disease and their formal and informal caregivers: A systematic review. *International Journal of Alzheimer's Disease.* Retrieved from www.ncbi.nlm.nih.gov/pubmedhealth/PMH0030378/.

Eisdorfer, C., Czaja, S., Loewenstein, D., Rubert, M., Arguelles, S., Mitrani, V., et al. (2003). The effect of a family therapy and technology-based intervention on caregiver depression. *Gerontologist, 43,* 521–531.

Eloniemi-Sulkava, U., Sivenius, J. S., & Sulkava, R. (1999). Support program for demented patients and their carers: The role of dementia family care coordinator is crucial. In K. Iqbal, D. Swaab, B. Winblad, & H. M. Wisniewski (Eds.), *Alzheimer's disease and related disorders* (pp. 795–802). West Sussex, UK: John Wiley.

Elvish, R., Lever, S., Johnstone, J., Cawley, R., & Keady, J. (2013). Psychological interventions for carers of people with dementia: A systematic review of quantitative and qualitative evidence. *Counseling and Psychotherapy Research, 13,* 106–125.

Epstein-Lubow, G., Gaudiano, B., Darling, E., Hinckley, M., Tremont, G., Kohn, R., et al. (2012). Differences in depression severity in family caregivers of hospitalized individuals with dementia and family caregivers of outpatients with dementia. *American Journal of Geriatric Psychiatry, 20,* 815–819.

Finley, N. J. (1989). Theories of family labor as applied to gender differences in caregiving for elderly parents. *Journal of Marriage and the Family, 51,* 79–86.

Fletcher, T., & Eckberg, J. (2014). The effects of creative reminiscing on individuals with dementia and their caregivers: A pilot study. *Physical & Occupational Therapy in Geriatrics, 32*(1), 68–84.

Folkman, S. (2008). The case for positive emotions in the stress process. *Anxiety Stress Coping, 21*(1), 3–14.

Franks, M., Pierce, L., & Dwyer, J. (2003). Expected parent-care involvement of adult children. *Journal of Applied Gerontology, 22*(1), 104–117.

Fuh, J., Wanh, S., Liu, H., & Wang, H. (1999). The caregiving burden scale among Chinese caregivers of Alzheimer patients. *Dementia and Geriatric Cognitive Disorders, 10*(3), 186–191.

Fulton, B. R. (2005). Adult child caregivers of persons with Alzheimer's disease: Social exchange, generativity, and the family. *Dissertation Abstracts International, 66*(2-B), 1219.

Gallagher-Thompson, D., & DeVries, H. (1994). Coping with frustration classes: Development and preliminary outcomes with women who care for relatives with dementia. *The Gerontologist, 34*(4), 548–552.

Gallagher-Thompson, D., & Steffen, A. (1994). Comparative effects of cognitive-behavioral and brief psychodynamic psychotherapies for depressed family caregivers. *Journal of Consulting and Clinical Psychology, 62*(3), 543–549.

Gallagher-Thompson, D., Talamantes, M., Ramirez, R., & Valverde, I. (1996). Service delivery issues and recommendations for working with Mexican American family caregivers. In G. Yeo & D. Gallagher-Thompson (Eds.), *Ethnicity and the dementias* (pp. 137–152). Washington, DC: Taylor & Francis.

Gaugler, J., Edwards, A., Femia, E., Zarit, S., Stephens, M., Townsend, A., et al. (2000). Predictors of institutionalization of cognitively impaired elders: Family help and the timing of placement. *Journal of Gerontology: Psychological Sciences, 55B*, P247–P255.

Gaugler, J. E., Yu, F., Krichbaum, K., & Wyman, J. F. (2009). Predictors of nursing home admission for persons with dementia. *Medical Care, 47*(2), 191–198.

Gerdner, L., Tripp-Reimer, T., & Yang, D. (2005). Perception and care of elders with dementia in the Hmong American community. *Alzheimer's & Dementia, 1*(Suppl. 1), S54–S55.

Gitlin, L., & Hodgson, N. (2015). Caregivers as therapeutic agents in dementia care: The evidence-base for interventions supporting their role. In J. E. Gaugler, & R. L. Kane (Eds.), *Family caregiving in the new normal* (pp. 305–356). London, UK: Academic Press.

Glueckauf, R. L., Bourgeois, M., Massey, A., Pomidor, A., & Stine, C. (2004, June). *Alzheimer's Rural Care Healthline: Supporting rural caregivers across Florida* (Grant No. 2004103). Tampa, FL: Johnny Byrd, Sr. Alzheimer's Center and Research Institute.

Glueckauf, R., Davis, W., Willis, F., Sharma, D., Gustafson, D. J., Hayes, J., Stutzman, M., et al. (2012). Telephone-based, cognitive-behavioral therapy for African American dementia caregivers with depression: Initial findings. *Rehabilitation Psychology, 57*(2), 124–139.

Glueckauf, R., Ketterson, T., Loomis, J., & Dages, P. (2004). Online support and education for dementia caregivers: Overview, utilization, and initial program evaluation. *Telemedicine Journal and e-Health, 10*, 223–232.

Glueckauf, R. L., Stine, C., Bourgeois, M., Pomidor, A., Rom, P., Young, M. E., et al. (2005). Alzheimer's Rural Care Healthline: Linking rural caregivers to cognitive-behavioral intervention for depression. *Rehabilitation Psychology, 50*, 346–354.

Gottlieb, B., & Gignac, M. (1996). Content and domain specificity of coping among family caregivers of persons with dementia. *Journal of Aging Studies, 10*(2), 137–155.

Guerra, S., Demain, S., Figueiredo, D., & De Sousa, L. (2012). Being a Volunteer: Motivations, fears and benefits of volunteering in an intervention program for people with dementia and their families. *Activities, Adaptation & Aging, 36*(1), 55–78.

Haberstroh, J., Neumeyer, K., Krause, K., Franzmann, J., & Pantel, J. (2011). TANDEM: Communication training for informal caregivers of people with dementia. *Aging & Mental Health, 15*(3), 405–413.

Hahn, E., Kim, G., & Chiriboga, D. (2011). Acculturation and depressive symptoms among Mexican American elders new to the caregiving role: Results from the Hispanic-EPESE. *Journal of Aging and Health, 23*(3), 417–432.

Harwood, D., Barker, W., Ownby, R., & Duara, R. (2000). Caregiver self-rated health in Alzheimer's disease. *Clinical Gerontologist, 21*(4), 19–33.

Henderson, J. N. (1996). Cultural dynamics of dementia in a Cuban and Puerto Rican population in the United States. In G. Yeo & D. Gallagher-Thompson (Eds.), *Ethnicity and the dementias* (pp. 153–166). Washington, DC: Taylor & Francis.

Hendryx-Bedalov, P. (1999). Effects of caregiver communication on the outcomes of requests in spouses with dementia of the Alzheimer's type. *International Journal of Aging and Human Development, 49,* 127–148.

Hinchliffe, A., Hyman, I., Blizard, B., & Livingston, G. (1995). Behavioural complications of dementia: Can they be treated? *International Journal of Geriatric Psychiatry, 10,* 839–847.

Hooker, K., Bowman, S., Coehlo, D., Lim, S., Kaye, J., Guariglia, R., et al. (2002). Behavioral change in persons with dementia: Relationships with mental and physical health of caregivers. *Journal of Gerontology: Psychological Sciences, 57B,* P453–P460.

Hoppes, S., Bryce, H., Hellman, C., & Finlay, E. (2012). The effects of brief Mindfulness training on caregivers' well-being. *Activities, Adaptation & Aging, 36,* 147–166.

Horowitz, A. (1985). Sons and daughters as caregivers to older parents: Differences in role performance and consequences. *The Gerontologist, 25,* 5–10.

Huang, H.-L., Kuo, L.-M., Chen, Y.-S., Liang, J., Huang, H.-L., Chiu, Y.-C., Chen, S.-T., Sun, Y., Hsu, W.-C., & Shyu, Y.-L. (2013). A home-based training program improves caregivers' skills and dementia patients' aggressive behaviors: a randomized controlled trial. *American Journal of Geriatric Psychiatry, 21*(11), 1060–1070.

Hunter, P. V., Hadjistavropoulos, T., Smythe, W. E., Malloy, D. C., Kaasalainen, S., & Williams, J. (2013). The Personhood in Dementia Questionnaire (PDQ): Establishing an association between beliefs about personhood and health providers' approaches to person-centred care. *Journal of Aging Studies, 27,* 276–287.

Ingersoll-Dayton, B., Chapman, N., & Neal, M. (1990). A program for caregivers in the workplace. *The Gerontologist, 30*(1), 126–130.

Jervis, L., & Manson, S. (2002). American Indians/Alaska Natives and dementia. *Alzheimer Disease and Associated Disorders, 16,* S89–S95.

Judge, K. S., Yarry, S. J., & Orselic-Jeras, S. (2014). Acceptability and feasibility results of a strength-based skills training program for dementia caregiving dyads. *The Gerontologist, 50*(3), 408–417.

Kamiya, M., Sakurai, T., Ogama, N., Maki, Y., & Toba, K. (2014). Factors associated with increased caregivers' burden in several cognitive stages of Alzheimer's disease. *Geriatric Gerontology International, 14*(Suppl. 2), 45–55.

Kaye, L., & Applegate, J. (1990). Men as elder caregivers: A response to changing families. *American Journal of Orthopsychiatry, 60*(1), 86–95.

Kemper, S., Anagnopoulos, C., Lyons, K., & Heberlein, W. (1994). Speech accommodations to dementia. *Journal of Gerontology, 49,* P223–P229.

Kim, M., Dunkle, R., Lehnng, A., Shen, H.-W., Feld, S., & Perone, A. (2016). Caregiver stressors and depressive symptoms among older husbands and wives in the United States. *Journal of Women & Aging.* doi:10.1080/08952841.2016.1223962.

Koenig, H., Cohen, H., Blazer, D., Pieper, C., Meador, K., Shelp, F., et al. (1992). Religious coping and depression among elderly, hospitalized medically ill men. *American Journal of Psychiatry, 149*(12), 1693–1700.

Labrecque, M., Peak, T., & Toseland, R. (1992). Long-term effectiveness of a group program for caregivers of frail elderly veterans. *American Journal of Orthopsychiatry, 62*(4), 575–588.

Larkin, J., & Hopcroft, B. (1993). In-hospital respite as a moderator of caregiver stress. *Health & Social Work, 18*(2), 133–138.

Lawton, M., Brody, E., & Saperstein, A. (1989). A controlled study of respite service for caregivers of Alzheimer's patients. *The Gerontologist, 29*(1), 8–16.

Lazarus, R. S. & Folkman, S. (1984). *Stress, appraisal and coping.* New York: Springer.

Lewis, I., & Ausberry, M. (1996). African American families: Management of demented elders. In G. Yeo & D. Gallagher-Thompson (Eds.), *Ethnicity and the dementias* (pp. 167–174). Washington, DC: Taylor & Francis.

Li, L., Seltzer, M., & Greenberg, J. (1997). Social support and depressive symptoms: Differential patterns in wife and daughter caregivers. *Journal of Gerontology: Social Sciences, 52B,* S200–S211.

Lindgren, C., Connelly, C., & Gaspar, H. (1999). Grief in spouse and children caregivers of dementia patients. *Western Journal of Nursing Research, 21*(4), 521–537.

Llanque, S. M., & Enriquez, M. (2012). Interventions for Hispanic caregivers of patients with dementia: A review of the literature. *American Journal of Alzheimers Disease and Other Dementias, 27*(1), 23–32.

Loi, S., Dow, B., Ames, D., Moore, K., Hill, K., Russell, M., & Lautenschlager, N. (2014). Physical activity in caregivers: What are the psychological benefits? *Archives of Gerontology and Geriatrics, 59*, 204–210.

Lopata, H. (Ed.). (1987). *Widows: Vol. 2. North America.* Durham, NC: Duke University Press.

Lou, V., Kwan, C., Chong, M., & Chi, I. (2013). Associations between secondary caregivers' supportive behaviors and psychological distress of primary spousal caregivers of cognitively intact and impaired elders. *The Gerontologist, 53*, 1–11.

Lovett, S., & Gallagher, D. (1988). Psychoeducational interventions for family caregivers: Preliminary efficacy data. *Behavior Therapy, 19*, 321–330.

Lustbader, W., & Hooyman, N. R. (1994). *Taking care of aging family members: A practical guide* (rev. ed.). New York: Free Press.

Lyons, K., Zarit, S., Sayer, A., & Whitlatch, C. (2002). Caregiving as a dyadic process: Perspectives from caregiver and receiver. *Journal of Gerontology: Psychological Sciences, 57B*, P195–P204.

Maayan, N., Soares-Weiser, K., & Lee, H. (2014). Respite care for people with dementia and their carers. *Cochrane Database of Systematic Reviews 2014, Issue 1.* Art. No.: CD004396. doi:10.1002/14651858. CD004396.pub3.

Mace, N. L., & Rabins, P. V. (2017). *The 36-hour day: A family guide to caring for persons with Alzheimer's disease, related dementing illnesses, and memory loss in later life* (6th ed.). Baltimore: Johns Hopkins University Press.

Mahoney, D., Tarlow, B., & Jones, R. (2003). Effects of an automated telephone support system on caregiver burden and anxiety: Findings from the REACH for TLC intervention study. *Gerontologist, 43*, 556–567.

MaloneBeach, E., & Zarit, S. (1995). Dimensions of social support and social conflict as predictors of caregiver depression. *International Psychogeriatrics, 7*, 25–38.

Margallo-Lana, M., Moore, P., Kay, D., et al. (2007). Fifteen-year follow-up of 92 hospitalized adults with Down's syndrome: Incidence of cognitive decline, its relationship to age and neuropathology. *Journal of Intellectual Disability Research, 51*, 463–477.

Markowitz, J., Gutterman, E., Sadik, K., & Papadopoulos, G. (2003). Health-related quality of life for caregivers of patients with Alzheimer disease. *Alzheimer Disease and Associated Disorders, 17*, 209–214.

Mausbach, B. T. (2014). Caregiving. *American Journal of Geriatric Psychiatry, 22*, 743–745.

McBride, M., & Parreno, H. (1996). Filipino American families and caregiving. In G. Yeo & D. Gallagher-Thompson (Eds.), *Ethnicity and the dementias* (pp. 123–135). Washington, DC: Taylor & Francis.

McCann, J., Herbert, L., Beckett, L., Morris, M., Scherr, P., & Evans, D. (2000). Comparison of informal caregiving by black and white older adults in a community population. *Journal of the American Geriatrics Society, 48*(12), 1612–1617.

McKinlay, J., Crawford, S., & Tennstedt, S. (1995). The everyday impacts of providing informal care to dependent elders and their consequences for the care recipients. *Journal of Aging and Health, 7*, 497–528.

Melunsky, N., Crellin, N., Dudzinski, E., Orrell, M., Wenborn, J., Poland, F., Woods, B., & Charlesworth, G. (2015). The experience of family carers attending a joint reminiscence group with people with dementia: A thematic analysis. *Dementia, 14*(6), 842–859.

Miller, B., & Lawton, M. (1997). Positive aspects of caregiving. Introduction: Finding balance in caregiver research. *The Gerontologist, 37*, 216–217.

Miller, L., Mioshi, E., Savage, S., Lah, S., Hodges, J., & Piquet, O. (2013). Identifying cognitive and demographic variables that contribute to carer burden in dementia. *Dementia & Geriatric Cognitive Disorders, 36*, 43–49.

Mittelman, M., Ferris, S., Shulman, E., Steinberg, G., Ambinder, A., Mackell, J., et al. (1995). A comprehensive support program: Effect on depression in spouse-caregivers of AD patients. *The Gerontologist, 35*(6), 792–802.

Mittelman, M., Ferris, S., Shulman, E., Steinberg, G., & Levin, B. (1996). A family intervention to delay nursing home placement of patients with Alzheimer disease. *Journal of the American Medical Association, 276*(21), 1725–1731.

Mohide, E., Pringle, D., Streiner, D., Gilbert, J., Muir, G., & Tew, M. (1990). A randomized trial of family caregiver support in the home management of dementia. *Journal of the American Geriatrics Society, 38*, 446–454.

Montgomery, R. J. V., & Kosloski, K. (1994). A longitudinal analysis of nursing home placement for dependent elders cared for by spouses vs. adult children. *Journal of Gerontology: Social Sciences, 49*(2), S62–S74.

Moon, H., Rote, S., & Beaty, J. (2016). Caregiver setting and Baby Boomer caregiver stress process: Findings from the National Study of Caregiving (NSOC). *Geriatric Nursing,* 1–6.

Moore, W. (2002). Lesbian and gay elders: Connecting care providers through a telephone support group. *Journal of Gay and Lesbian Social Services, 14,* 23–41.

Morano, C., & Sanders, S. (2005). Exploring differences in depression, role captivity, and self-acceptance in Hispanic and non-Hispanic adult children caregivers. *Journal of Ethnic & Cultural Diversity in Social Work, 14*(1/2), 27–46.

Mungas, D. (1996). The process of development of valid and reliable neuropsychological assessment measures for English- and Spanish-speaking elderly persons. In G. Yeo & D. Gallagher-Thompson (Eds.), *Ethnicity and the dementias* (pp. 33–46). Washington, DC: Taylor & Francis.

Nápoles, A. M., Chadiha, L., Eversley, R., & Moreno-John, G. (2010). Developing culturally sensitive dementia caregiver interventions: Are we there yet? *American Journal of Alzheimer's Disease & Other Dementia, 25*(5), 389–406.

National Alliance for Caregiving and the American Association of Retired Persons (NAC/AARP). (2015). *Family caregiving in the US: Findings from a national survey: Final report.* Bethesda, MD: National Alliance for Caregiving. Retrieved November 6, 2015, from http://assets.aarp.org/rgcenter/il/caregiving_09_fr.pdf.

Oktay, J., & Volland, P. (1990). Posthospital support program for the frail elderly and their caregivers: A quasi-experimental evaluation. *American Journal of Public Health, 80*(1), 39–46.

Olazarán, J., Reisberg, B., Clare, L., Cruz, I., Pena-Casanova, J., Del Ser, T., et al. (2010). Nonpharmacological therapies in Alzheimer's disease: A systematic review of efficacy. *Dementia & Geriatric Cognitive Disorders, 30,* 161–178.

Orange, J. B. (1995). Perspectives of family members regarding communication changes. In R. Lubinski (Ed.), *Dementia and communication* (pp. 168–186). San Diego, CA: Singular.

Orange, J. B., & Colton-Hudson, A. (1998). Enhancing communicating in dementia of the Alzheimer's type: Caregiver education and training. *Topics in Geriatric Rehabilitation, 14,* 56–75.

O'Rourke, N., & Tuokko, H. (2000). The psychological and physical costs of caregiving: The Canadian study of health and aging. *Journal of Applied Gerontology, 19*(4), 389–404.

Ory, M., Yee, J., Tennstedt, S., & Schulz, R. (2000). The extent and impact of dementia care: Unique challenges experienced by family caregivers. In R. Schulz (Ed.), *Handbook on dementia caregiving: Evidence-based interventions for family caregivers* (pp. 1–32). New York: Springer.

Ostuni, E., & Santo Pietro, M. J. (1991). *Getting through: Communicating when someone you care for has Alzheimer's disease.* Vero Beach, FL: Speech Bin.

Pagel, M., Erdly, W., & Becker, J. (1987). Social networks: We get by with (and in spite of) a little help from our friends. *Journal of Personality and Social Psychology, 53,* 793–804.

Parker, D., Mills, S., & Abbey, J. (2008). Effectiveness of interventions that assist caregivers to support people with dementia living in the community: A systematic review. *International Journal of Evidence-based Healthcare, 6,* 137–172.

Paveza, G., Cohen, D., Eisendorfer, C., Freels, S., Semla, T., Ashford, J. W., et al. (1992). Severe family violence and Alzheimer's disease: Prevalence and risk factors. *Gerontologist, 32,* 493–497.

Pearlin, L., Mullan, J., Semple, S., & Skaff, M. (1990). Caregiving and the stress process: An overview of concepts and their measures. *The Gerontologist, 30*(5), 583–594.

Peisah, C., & Bridger, M. ((2008). Abuse by marriage: The exploitation of mentally ill older people. *International Journal of Geriatric Psychiatry, 23,* 883–888.

Pinkston, E. M., Linsk, N. L., & Young, R. N. (1988). Home-based behavioral family treatment of the impaired elderly. *Behavior Therapy, 19*(3), 331–344.

Pinquart, M., & Sörensen, S. (2003). Associations of stressors and uplifts of caregiving with caregiver burden and depressive mood: A meta-analysis. *Journal of Gerontology: Psychological Sciences, 58B,* P112–P128.

Pinquart, M., & Sörensen, S. (2005). Ethnic differences in stressors, resources, and psychological outcomes of family caregiving: A meta-analysis. *The Gerontologist, 45,* 90–106.

Pinquart, M., & Sörensen, S. (2011). Spouses, adult children, and children-in-law as caregivers of older adults: A meta-analytic comparison. *Psychology and Aging, 26*(1), 1–14.

Pruchno, R., Peters, N., & Burant, C. (1995). Mental health of coresident family caregivers: Examination of a two-factor model. *Journal of Gerontology: Psychological Sciences, 50B*, P247–P256.

Purves, B., & Phinney, A. (2012). Family voices: A family systems approach to understanding communication in dementia. *Canadian J Speech-Language Pathology and Audiology, 36*(4), 284–300.

Rankin, E., Haut, M., & Keefover, R. (2001). Current marital functioning as a mediating factor in depression among spouse caregivers in dementia. *Clinical Gerontologist, 23*(3/4), 27–44.

Raschick, M., & Ingersoll-Dayton, B. (2004). The costs and rewards of caregiving among aging spouses and adult children. *Family Relations, 53*(3), 317–325.

Rau, M. T. (1993). *Coping with communication challenges in Alzheimer's disease.* San Diego, CA: Singular.

Reed, C., Belger, M., Dell'Agnello, G., et al. (2014). Caregiver burden in Alzheimer's disease: Differential association in adult-child and spousal caregivers in the GERAS observational study. *Dementia Geriatric Cognitive Disorders Extra, 4*(1), 51–64.

Riordan, J., & Bennett, A. (1998). An evaluation of an augmented domiciliary service to older people with dementia and their carers. *Aging & Mental Health, 2*, 137–143.

Ripich, D. (1994). Functional communication with AD patients: A caregiver training program. *Alzheimer Disease and Associated Disorders, 8*, 95–109.

Ripich, D., & Wykle, M. (1996). *Alzheimer's disease communication guide: The FOCUSED program for caregivers.* San Antonio, TX: Psychological Corporation.

Ripich, D., Wykle, M., & Niles, S. (1995). Alzheimer's disease caregivers: The FOCUSED program: A communication skills training program helps nursing assistants to give better care to patients with disease. *Geriatric Nursing, 16*, 15–19.

Ripich, D. N., Ziol, E., Durand, E. J., & Fritsch, T. (1999). Training Alzheimer's disease caregivers for successful communication. *Clinical Gerontologist, 21*(1), 37–57.

Ripich, D., Ziol, E., & Lee, M. (1998). Longitudinal effects of communication training on caregivers of persons with Alzheimer's disease. *Clinical Gerontologist, 19*, 37–55.

Roff, L., Burgio, L., Gitlin, L., Nichols, L., Chaplin, W., & Hardin, J. M. (2004). Positive aspects of Alzheimer's caregiving: The role of race. *Journal of Gerontology: Psychological Sciences, 59B*, P185–P190.

Rose-Rego, S. K., Strauss, M. E., & Smyth, K. A. (1998). Differences in the perceived well-being of wives and husbands caring for persons with Alzheimer's disease. *The Gerontologist, 38*, 224–230.

Rubinstein, R. L. (1990). Culture and disorder in the home care experience: The home as the sickroom. In J. F. Gubrium & A. Sankar (Eds.), *The home care experience* (pp. 37–58). Newbury Park, CA: Sage.

Russell, R. (2001). In sickness and in health: A qualitative study of elderly men who care for wives with dementia. *Journal of Aging Studies, 15*, 351–367.

Samia, L., Hepburn, K., & Nichols, L. (2012). "Flying by the seat of our pants": What dementia family caregivers want in an advanced caregiver training program. *Research in Nursing & Health, 35*, 598–609.

Santo Pietro, M. J., & Boczko, F. (1998). The Breakfast Club: Results of a study examining the effectiveness of a multi-modality group communication treatment. *American Journal of Alzheimer's Disease, 13*, 146–158.

Santo Pietro, M., & Ostuni, E. (2003). *Successful communication with persons with Alzheimer's disease: An inservice manual* (2nd ed.). St. Louis, MO: Elsevier Science.

Savundranagam, M. Y., Hummert, M., & Montgomery, R. (2005). Investigating the effects of communication problems on caregiver burden. *Journal of Gerontology: Social Sciences, 60B*, S48–S55.

Schulz, R., Burgio, L., Burns, R., Eisdorfer, C., Gallagher-Thompson, D., Gitlin, L., et al. (2003). Resources for enhancing Alzheimer's caregiver health (REACH): Overview, site-specific outcomes, and future directions. *Gerontologist, 43*, 514–520.

Schulz, R., & Martire, L. (2004). Family caregiving of persons with dementia: Prevalence, health effects, and support strategies. *American Journal of Geriatric Psychiatry, 12*, 240–249.

Schulz, R., & Quittner, A. (1998). Caregiving through the life span: An overview and future directions. *Health Psychology, 17*, 107–111.

Selwood, A., Johnston, K., Katona, C., Lyketsos, C., & Livingston, G. (2007). Systematic review of the effect of psychological interventions on family caregivers of people with dementia. *Journal of Affective Disorders, 101*, 75–89.

Semple, S. (1992). Conflict in Alzheimer's caregiving families: Its dimensions and consequences. *The Gerontologist, 32*, 648–655.

Small, J. A., & Gutman, G. (2002). Recommended and reported use of communication strategies in Alzheimer caregiving. *Alzheimer Disease and Associated Disorders, 16,* 270–278.

Small, J. A., Gutman, G., Makela, S., & Hillhouse, B. (2003). Effectiveness of communication strategies used by caregivers of persons with Alzheimer's disease during activities of daily living. *Journal of Speech, Language and Hearing Research, 46,* 353–367.

Small, J. A., Kemper, S., & Lyons, K. (1997). Sentence comprehension in Alzheimer's disease: Effects of grammatical complexity, speech rate, and repetition. *Psychology and Aging, 12,* 3–11.

Sörensen, S., Pinquart, M., & Duberstein, P. (2002). How effective are interventions with caregivers? An updated meta-analysis. *The Gerontologist, 42*(3), 356–372.

Springate, B., & Tremont, G. (2014). Dimensions of caregiver burden in dementia: Impact of demographic, mood, and care recipient variables. *American Journal of Geriatric Psychiatry, 22*(3), 294–300.

Stanton, L. R. & Coetzee, R. H. (2003). Down's syndrome and dementia. *Advances in Psychiatric Treatment, 10*(1), 50–58.

Steffen, A. M. (2000). Anger management for dementia caregivers: A preliminary study using video and telephone interventions. *Behavior Therapy, 31,* 281–299.

Stoller, E. P., Forster, L. E., & Duniho, T. S. (1992). Systems of parent care within sibling networks. *Research on Aging, 14*(1), 28–49.

Tappen, R. (1997). *Interventions for Alzheimer's disease: A caregiver's complete reference.* Baltimore: Health Professions.

Tappen, R., Williams-Burgess, C., Edelstein, J., Touhy, T., & Fishman, S. (1997). Communicating with individuals with Alzheimer's disease: Examination of recommended strategies. *Archives of Psychiatric Nursing, 21,* 249–256.

Taussig, I. M., & Ponton, M. (1996). Issues in neuropsychological assessment for Hispanic older adults: Cultural and linguistic factors. In G. Yeo & D. Gallagher-Thompson (Eds.), *Ethnicity and the dementias* (pp. 33–46). Washington, DC: Taylor & Francis.

Tempo, P., & Saito, A. (1996). Techniques of working with Japanese American families. In G. Yeo & D. Gallagher-Thompson (Eds.), *Ethnicity and the dementias* (pp. 109–122). Washington, DC: Taylor & Francis.

Teng, E. (1996). Cross-cultural testing and the cognitive abilities screening instrument. In G. Yeo & D. Gallagher-Thompson (Eds.), *Ethnicity and the dementias* (pp. 77–85). Washington, DC: Taylor & Francis.

Tennstedt, S., Crawford, S., & McKinlay, J. (1993). Determining the pattern of community care: Is coresidence more important than caregiver relationship? *Journal of Gerontology, 48,* S74–S83.

Tennstedt, S. L., McKinlay, J. B., & Sullivan, L. M. (1989). Informal care for frail elders: The role of secondary caregivers. *The Gerontologist, 29,* 677–683.

Teri, L., & Uomoto, J. M. (1991). Reducing excess disability in dementia patients: Training caregivers to manage patient depression. *Clinical Gerontologist, 10,* 49–63.

Theis, S., Moss, J., & Pearson, M. (1994). Respite for caregivers: An evaluation study. *Journal of Community Health Nursing, 77*(1), 31–44.

Thompson, C. A., Spilsbury, K., Hall, J., Birks, Y., Barnes, C., & Adamson, J. (2007). Systematic review of information and support interventions for caregivers of people with dementia. *BMC Geriatrics, 7,* 18.

Thompson, L., Gallagher-Thompson, D., & Haley, W. (2003). Future directions in dementia caregiving intervention research and practice. In D. Coon, D. Gallagher-Thompson, & L. Thompson (Eds.), *Innovative interventions to reduce dementia caregiver stress* (pp. 299–311). New York: Springer.

Toseland, R. W., Rossiter, C. M., Peak, T., & Smith, G. C. (1990). Comparative effectiveness of individual and group interventions to support family caregivers. *Social Work, 35,* 209–217.

Toseland, R. W., & Smith, G. C. (1990). Effectiveness of individual counseling by professional and peer helpers for family caregivers of the elderly. *Psychology and Aging, 5,* 256–263.

Toth-Cohen, S., Gitlin, L., Corcoran, M., Eckhardt, S., Johns, P., & Lipsitt, R. (2001). Providing services to family caregivers at home: Challenges and recommendations for health and human service professions. *Alzheimer's Care Quarterly, 2,* 23–32.

Vaingankar, J., Chong, S., Abdin, E., Picco, L., Jeyagurunathan, A., Zhang, Y., Sambasivam, R., Chua, B., Ng, L., Prince, M., & Subramaniam, M. (2016). Care participation and burden among informal caregivers of older adults with care needs and association with dementia. *International Psychogeriatrics, 28*(2), 221–231.

Van Nostrand, J., Furner, S., & Suzman, R. (Eds.). (1993). *Health data on older Americans, United States: 1992* (Ser. 3). Hyattsville, MD: National Center for Health Statistics.

Vernooij-Dassen, M., Draskovic, I., McCleery, J., & Downs, M. (2011). Cognitive reframing for carers of people with dementia. *The Cochrane Database of Systematic Reviews, Nov. 9*(11), CD005318.

Watson, B., Aizawa, L., Savundranayagam, M., & Orange, J. B. (2013). Links among communication, dementia, and caregiver burden. *Canadian J Speech-Language Pathology and Audiology, 36*(4), 276–283.

Weinberger, M., Gold, D., Divine, G., Cowper, P., Hodgson, L., Schreiner, P., et al. (1993). Social service interventions for caregivers of patients with dementia: Impact on health care utilization and expenditures. *Journal of the American Geriatrics Society, 41*, 153–156.

Whitehouse, P., Lerner, A., & Hedera, P. (1993). Dementia. In K. Heilman (Ed.), *Clinical neuropsychology* (pp. 603–645). New York: Oxford University Press.

Wilson, R., Rochon, E., Mihailidis, A., & Leonard, C. (2012). Examining success of communication strategies used by formal caregivers assisting individuals with Alzheimer's disease during an activity of daily living. *Journal of Speech, Language, and Hearing Research, 55*, 328–341.

Wisniewski, S. R., Belle, S. H., Marcus, S. M., Burgio, L. D., Coon, D. W., Ory, M. G., ... Schulz, R. (2003). The Resources for Enhancing Alzheimer's Caregiver Health (REACH): Project design and baseline characteristics. *Psychology and Aging, 18*(3), 375–384. http://doi.org/10.1037/0882-7974.18.3.375.

Yee, B., Nguyen, H., & Ha, M. (2003). Chronic disease health beliefs and life style practices among Vietnamese adults: Influence of gender and age. *Women & Therapy, 26*(1/2), 111–125.

Yee, J., & Schulz, R. (2000). Gender differences in psychiatric morbidity among family caregivers: A review and analysis. *The Gerontologist, 40*, 147–164.

Yeo, G. (1996). Background. In G. Yeo & D. Gallagher-Thompson (Eds.), *Ethnicity and the dementias* (pp. 3–7). Washington, DC: Taylor & Francis.

Yeo, G., Uyen Tran, J., Hikoyeda, N., & Hinton, L. (2001). Conceptions of dementia among Vietnamese American caregivers. *Journal of Gerontological Social Work, 36*, 131–152.

Youn, G., Knight, B., Jeong, H., & Benton, D. (1999). Differences in familism values and caregiving outcomes among Korean, Korean American, and White American dementia caregivers. *Psychology and Aging, 14*(3), 355–364.

Young, J., & Gu, N. (1995). *Demographic and socioeconomic characteristics of elderly Asian and Pacific Island Americans.* Seattle, WA: National Asian Pacific Center on Aging.

Zarit, S. H. (1990). Interventions with frail elders and their families: Are they effective and why? In M. P. Stevens, J. H. Crowther, S. E. Hobfoil, & D. L. Tennenbaum (Eds.), *Stress and coping in later life* (pp. 147–158). Washington, DC: Hemisphere.

Zarit, S. H., Anthony, C., & Boutselis, M. (1987). Interventions with caregivers of dementia patients: Comparison of two approaches. *Psychology and Aging, 2*(3), 225–232.

Zarit, S. H., & Edwards, A. (1999). Family caregiving: Research and clinical interventions. In R. Woods (Ed.), *Psychological problems of ageing.* London: John Wiley.

Zarit, S. H., Greene, R., Ferraro, E., Townsend, A., & Stephens, M. (1996, November). Adult day care and the relief of caregiver strain: Results of the adult day care collaborative study. Symposium presented at the annual meetings of the Gerontological Society of America, Washington, DC.

Zarit, S. H., & Knight, B. G. (Eds.). (1996). *A guide to psychotherapy and aging: Effective clinical interventions in a life-stage context.* Washington, DC: APA.

10

PROFESSIONAL AND PARAPROFESSIONAL CAREGIVER TRAINING AND SUPERVISION

Natalie F. Douglas, Michelle S. Bourgeois, and Ellen M. Hickey

Estimates suggest that, by the year 2050, there will be approximately 131.5 million people with a dementia diagnosis in the world (Alzheimer's Disease International, 2016). When the family can no longer manage the person with dementia at home, or when there is no family to provide care, residential care is the logical option. There are over 1.4 million Americans living in skilled nursing facilities (SNFs) (Harris-Kojetin, Sengupta, Park-Lee, & Valverde, 2013). Of that number, 68% of residents have some form of cognitive impairment including mild cognitive impairment, moderate-severe cognitive impairment, and/or other dementia related disorders (Alzheimer's Association, 2012). In this setting, care is provided largely from staff in the nursing department, as well as the activities department. The staff hired to provide care to the frail elderly range from nurses in managerial positions who have advanced degrees to certified nursing assistants (CNAs) in paraprofessional positions who often have a high school education. CNAs hold approximately 65% of all positions in long-term care (Trinkoff, Storr, Lerner, Yang, & Han, 2016). The job of a CNA is demanding under the best of circumstances, and the challenges of providing quality care to persons with dementia are many. Accordingly, efforts are under way to develop effective staff training programs and desirable work environments in times of high staff turnover and few staff incentives.

In 1987, the federal government mandated that nursing homes provide a therapeutic, rather than custodial, model of care (Omnibus Budget Reconciliation Act [OBRA] of 1987, 1991). Since then, the nursing home industry has struggled to meet the expectations of lawmakers and families. CNAs are required to receive 75 hours of basic training upon employment and to take 12 hours per year of continuing education (CMS, 2012). Yet a report on CNA training, published by the Office of the Inspector General ([OIG], 2002), emphasized that staff training has not kept pace with the needs of the nursing home industry. Research efforts have resulted in a better understanding of the personnel who make caregiving their profession, as well as the challenges they face on the job and the types of supports (e.g., training) that help them to provide quality care. Still, CNAs report needing more training, especially in the management of responsive behaviors, in information about depression and aggression, and in communicating more effectively with residents with dementia (Trinkoff et al., 2016). The OIG (2002) report identified additional training needs related to teamwork, coping with death and dying, time management, and new technologies. Researchers have found that inadequate training and inadequate staffing were the two main reasons for the perception that nursing homes in the United States are not providing quality care (Trinkoff et al., 2016). One must acknowledge the variables that often undermine the desired therapeutic model of care, including the costs of providing these services and the limited resources at every level from federal, to state, to the individual. Nevertheless, progress is being made toward the goal of quality therapeutic care for those in need.

Staff Characteristics

Certified nursing assistants provide most resident care in long-term care facilities (Squillace et al., 2009). Since CNAs are not licensed, there are not any federal regulations concerning CNA workload. Some states have regulations, but not all. For example, in Michigan, a CNA ratio of 8 : 1 is required in the morning, 12 : 1 in the afternoon, and 15 : 1 at night (NH Regulations Plus, 2011). On the other hand, the state of Alabama does not have any required CNA to resident ratios. This large variability in workload can provide serious quality of care problems (Schnelle, Schroyer, Saraf, & Simmons, 2016). Inadequate staffing patterns, among other employment challenges, result in high turnover. Some national estimates of CNA turnover range from 15% to 80% annually (Schnelle et al., 2016). Another study reports that 66% of CNAs turn over annually in long-term care settings in the United States (Trinkoff et al., 2013). In a nationwide study of skilled nursing facilities and long-term care communities, CNA turnover was associated with more pressure ulcers, pain, and urinary tract infections among residents even when controlling for staffing, skill mix, number of beds, and profit-status (Trinkoff et al., 2013). Thus, high staff turnover is one of the long-term care industry's biggest challenges, giving rise to issues related to the continuity of care and the expense of constant staff training and retraining.

The reasons for high turnover are many and are often related to job satisfaction. Job characteristics that influence satisfaction include workload, pay and benefits, perceived autonomy, job pride, and professional interactions, among others (Chou, Boldy, & Lee, 2002). Workload and staffing patterns are major contributors to job dissatisfaction (Squires et al., 2015). Indeed, Squires and colleagues concluded in their systematic review of the CNA job satisfaction literature that individual factors that contributed to CNA job satisfaction included empowerment and autonomy. Organizational factors that contributed to CNA job satisfaction included facility resources and workload.

The CNA's job is particularly difficult both physically and emotionally. Many residents require assistance with personal care tasks that involve lifting and transferring. A variety of behaviors that are exhibited by persons with dementia, such as verbal abuse, physical agitation, and wandering,

---

Box 10.1 Key Facts to Know about CNAs

1. They are usually overworked.
2. They are usually underpaid.
3. They sustain remarkable stress levels.
4. They shoulder most of resident responsibility without power or authority.
5. They feel pressure to meet unreasonable workload expectations, and as such, they sometimes feel the need to "cut corners."
6. Resident outcomes are better if they are empowered (participate in decision-making about policy and care).
7. They value personal growth opportunities.
8. A resident-centered environment promotes job-related wellbeing.

can be difficult to manage on a daily basis. The frequent incidence of resident death can cause emotional strain, and decreased quality of life for the CNA (Liang, Hsieh, Lin, & Chen, 2014). Data also indicate an increase in stress for CNAs when it is necessitated that the CNA call family members who may or may not care deeply for the resident. The mental health of CNAs was noted to improve if these paraprofessionals perceived themselves to feel empowered to complete their job responsibilities (Liang et al., 2014). Speech-language pathologists may contribute to a CNA's feeling of empowerment by training them in specific areas that directly impact a resident's well-being, including communication, cognition, and swallowing. This ultimately leads to the CNA understanding the resident better, impacting all levels of care.

Staff Training Needs

The evolution of staff training in dementia care has been described as paralleling the increase in knowledge about dementia from simple descriptions of the disease process itself and application to the "medical" model, to behavioral approaches designed to teach specific caregiving strategies, to person-centered models that teach staff to view the world through the eyes of their clients (Ortigara & Rapp, 2004). Person-centered approaches have expanded over the last decade, and are now the focus of most long-term care facilities. Speech-language pathologists (SLPs) can use person-centered approaches while teaching skills to professional and paraprofessional staff so that they can better provide for the communication, cognitive, and swallowing needs of long-term care residents. SLPs are uniquely positioned to maximize potential in these areas with an orientation in staff training programs toward quality of life, independence, and purposeful living.

Cognitive, communication, and swallowing needs impact an individual's physical and psychosocial health, regardless of where on the severity spectrum they fall. For example, people with cognitive impairments may disengage from activities and experience social isolation, boredom, and restlessness. This lack of engagement may precipitate negative neuropsychological behaviors such as aggression, wandering, or refusal of medical care. In some cases, these negative neuropsychological behaviors lead to the administration of inappropriate antipsychotic medications due to lack of staff training in nonpharmacological interventions or perceived lack of staff time and resources to implement the interventions (Daly, Bay, Levy, & Carnahan, 2015).

The Role of SLPs in Staff Training

SLPs are highly qualified to train caregivers in dementia care, given that they are trained with at least a master's degree with specific training in the processes that underlie communication, such as language, speech, attention, memory and executive functions. SLPs are additionally specialized in balancing the safety and pleasure of eating. Their skills are invaluable to people with dementia and those who care for them. SLPs are poised to tackle these needs through evidence-based training of other therapists, nursing professionals and paraprofessionals, and even administrators/leaders in long-term care. When professional and paraprofessional caregivers are trained by SLPs, the result is improved communication, cognition, and swallowing outcomes for people with dementia (Hopper et al., 2013). Thus, SLPs add significant value to long-term care settings (American Speech-Language-Hearing Association [ASHA], 2016). For example, potential value added by SLPs includes residents' ability to: maintain independence in meals and other ADLs, maintain and expand social networks, communicate wants, needs, and desires in the most optimal ways possible, and engage in meaningful everyday activities and conversations.

Furthermore, SLPs have an ethical responsibility to train professional caregivers in long-term care settings as part of the highest quality plan of care for residents with dysphagia and cognitive-communication disorders due to dementia (ASHA, 2016). ASHA developed an evidence-based compendium to guide SLP practice patterns. Preferred practice patterns for SLPs working with people with dementia are outlined here: www.asha.org/Practice-Portal/Clinical-Topics/Dementia/. Roles and responsibilities concerning professional caregiver training are outlined in Table 10.1.

Although SLPs have an ethical, valuable, and critical role in educating professional caregivers in SNFs, there are identified barriers to providing this training (Douglas et al., 2014). SLPs often report a lack of buy-in and carryover of training by professional caregivers. Furthermore, even when there is buy-in with individual caregivers, the institutional culture and climate may interfere with change (Douglas & Hickey, 2015). Therefore, it is helpful to widen the lens and examine theoretical aspects of human behavior change prior to implementing specific skill training.

Adult Learning Principles

Behavioral interventions require human behavior change. SLPs can benefit from a strong base of support for encouraging behavior change by examining literature from adult learning theory. Knowles (1980) identified principles of adult learning, and later expanded upon them (Knowles, Holton, & Swanson, 2005). Table 10.2 highlights six adult learning principles adapted from Knowles et al. (2005).

TABLE 10.1 Roles and Responsibilities of SLPs Working with Individuals with Dementia and Professional Caregivers

Educating other professionals, third-party payers, and legislators on the needs of persons with dementia and the role of SLPs in diagnosing and managing cognitive communication and swallowing disorders associated with dementia

Educating caregivers about possible communication difficulties and providing strategies to facilitate effective communication

Providing indirect intervention through the individual's caregivers and environmental modification

Consulting and collaborating with other professionals, family members, caregivers, and others to facilitate program development and to provide supervision, evaluation, and/or expert testimony, as appropriate

Serving as an integral member of an interdisciplinary team working with individuals with dementia and their families/caregivers

Source: ASHA, n.d. (www.asha.org/PRPSpecificTopic.aspx?folderid=8589935289&section=Roles_and_Responsibilities)

TABLE 10.2 Adult Learning Principles

Learning Principle	Learner Thought
1. The need to know	Why do I need to know this?
2. The learner's self-concept	I am responsible for my own decisions.
3. The role of the learners' experiences	I have experiences I value, and you should respect them.
4. Readiness to learn	I learn because my circumstances are changing.
5. Orientation to learning	Learning will help me deal with the situation in which I find myself.
6. Motivation	I learn because I want to.

Source: Adapted from Knowles et al. (2005), as stated in Taylor and Hamdy (2013, p. e1563).

Adult learners need to perceive a valid rationale for why they are being trained in a specific area. For example, if an SLP is training a CNA in a specific communication strategy, part of that training should explicitly state the value of the training for not only the resident with dementia, but also for the CNA. Providing examples of how our suggested cognitive supports and interventions can help a person with dementia, as well as improve the overall environment for other residents and make the CNA's job easier are all possible "need to knows" that are valuable for a CNA during training (see Box 10.2 for specific examples of CNA "need to knows.")

Although SLPs may complete training with professional caregivers frequently, incorporating adult learning principles may be key to more effective training, and ultimately, better care for residents with dementia. If a paraprofessional caregiver perceives a readiness to change based upon a current situation in which they find themselves, learning may be enhanced. A popular psychologist states, "How is that working for you?" Likewise, if a professional caregiver is struggling daily to help a person with dementia to take a shower, an SLP can provide on-site training in this moment to support quality care. A professional or paraprofessional caregiver may be oriented to learn in this situation due to the perceived need for support.

As adults, learners recognize that they are responsible for their own decisions (learning principle 2). A similar concept to this principle is self-efficacy (Bandura, 1997). Adults are more apt to complete tasks in which they perceive themselves to be successful, and in situations where they believe they have a locus of control for decision-making (Bandura, 1988). If it is possible to train a professional caregiver according to a set of choices as opposed to one prescribed action, that training will be more in line with principles of adult learning. Rather than giving a caregiver one prescribed solution for a problem, one could teach the caregiver several possible solutions to a problem. For example, if a resident in a long-term care community is demonstrating responsive behaviors that are disruptive to others, it may be helpful to suggest multiple strategies or activities to redirect the resident instead of just one generic activity. A volunteer may be available to take the resident for a walk. Similarly, there may be three or four person-centered activities that are available to support redirection of the resident. Multiple choices can empower CNAs to customize their residents' care based upon the situation.

Previous experiences of learners should be acknowledged and incorporated into training programs. Most paraprofessional and professional caregivers have experiences with persons with dementia prior to participating in caregiver training by an SLP, as well as other life experiences that are relevant. These experiences shape the learning process, so part of SLP caregiver training should include at least one explicit statement that honors the value of the paraprofessional and professional caregivers' life experiences. Perhaps the caregiver has a loved one with dementia that they are caring for at home right now. Maybe the professional or paraprofessional caregiver is only a few credits away from achieving the next level of education, but experienced an intense family situation where he or she had to quit school. Perhaps the caregiver has worked at the facility for 20 years and feels that some of the long-term residents are like family. The incorporation and value of these life experiences into the training program supports adult learning.

Box 10.2 Examples of CNA "Need to Knows"

Decreased instances of the resident with dementia pressing the call button unnecessarily
Decreased instances of the resident communicating through shouting out
Decreased instances of exit-seeking behaviors
Increased instances of the resident with dementia actively engaging in meaningful activities
Increased instances of the resident doing ADLs with cueing rather than physical assistance

---

Box 10.3 Example of the Role of the Learner's Experiences

While the SLP is conducting training in use of cognitive supports for persons with dementia, an activities assistant states that her grandmother had dementia and she and her mom took care of her at their home. She states that she became an activities assistant because she felt that she was "a natural" at finding ways to communicate with her grandmother and to engage her in meaningful activities. Rather than trying to minimize the activity assistant's desire to tell her story, the SLP asks her for more details and expands on the successes to drive home some key points.

The most difficult adult learning principle to incorporate into a training program is the sixth: motivation. Adults learn best when they are motivated, intrinsically or extrinsically, to learn. Extrinsic motivations may include money, recognition, or the need for continuing education to maintain licensure. Intrinsic motivations may include a desire to be a lifelong learner, a deep passion for the subject matter, a special fondness for caring for persons with dementia, or a drive for continued quality improvement in the workplace. Michie and colleagues (Michie, Atkins, & West, 2014; Michie, van Stralen, & West, 2011) have expanded upon these adult learning principles to further illustrate best practices in behavioral interventions, as follows in the sections below.

Behavior Change Wheel

Michie and colleagues (2011, 2013, 2014) have successfully studied key aspects in promoting behavior change. Figure 10.1 shows the behavior change wheel, a visual depiction of the many theoretical aspects that should be considered in behavioral interventions.

In the most inner part of the circle, three key features related to behavior change are stated: (1) capability, (2) motivation, and (3) opportunity (Michie et al., 2011). If a person is asked to change a certain behavior, he or she must be both physically and psychologically *capable* to make the change. Aligned with adult learning principles, the person should also be *motivated* to change their behavior. In this model, reflective motivation is motivation by more external factors, such as the professional or paraprofessional caregiver recognizing that they will be evaluated by a superior on their performance. Automatic motivation consists of more internal factors such as emotional responses or an internal disposition. Finally, the person must have *opportunities* to demonstrate the changed behavior; situations should be physically and/or socially constructed to prompt the newly trained behavior. In training professional or paraprofessional caregivers to use cognitive supports, the caregiver should: (1) feel both physically and psychologically capable to implement the cognitive support (such as an external memory aid); (2) be motivated in some way to implement the cognitive support; and (3) have ample opportunities to implement the cognitive support. See Box 10.4 for examples.

Consistent with behavior change theories, if behavior is to change, the trainer should intervene simultaneously, consistently, and at many levels. For example, professional or paraprofessional caregivers should be trained often, in many contexts, and the item to be trained should have support from the overall healthcare organization (Harvey & Kitson, 2016). The behavior to be changed should be precisely identified and a full understanding of the behavior should be achieved by both the trainer and the trainee. A specific behavior change technique should then be introduced. Behavior change techniques are exemplified in the darkest, middle portion of the circle in Figure 10.1 and include: education, persuasion, incentivization, coercion, training, restriction,

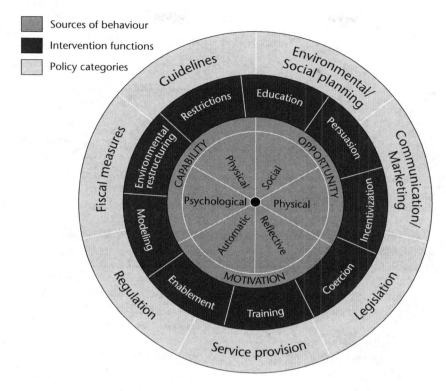

FIGURE 10.1 The Behavior Change Wheel

Source: © 2011 Michie et al. licensee BioMed Central Ltd. Creative Commons Attribution License (http://creativecommons.org/licenses/by/2.0).

Box 10.4 How Does Behavior Change?

1. Capability
    e.g., the CNA knows how to design an effective memory card for repetitive questions
2. Motivation
    e.g., the CNA feels good knowing that she helped to improve the quality of life of the resident, as well as the overall atmosphere due to fewer responsive behaviors
3. Opportunity
    e.g., a box of index cards, pictures, and a marker are kept at the nursing station to quickly make memory cards as the need arises

---

environmental restructuring, modeling and enablement. Table 10.3 outlines the definitions of each behavioral change intervention, along with an example of a potential application to SLP training of professional or paraprofessional caregivers.

The final and outer most circles in the behavior change wheel exemplify policy categories that impact behavior change. Human behavior change is complex, and it is necessary to recognize the influence of policies on professional caregivers' behaviors. For example, communication and marketing campaigns within a skilled nursing facility can support behavior change ("We support individual choice in dementia care!"). Clinical guidelines support behavior change, although they

TABLE 10.3 Behavioral Change Interventions and Professional or Paraprofessional Caregiver Training Applications

Intervention	Definition	Application to Professional or Paraprofessional Caregiver Training
Education	Increasing knowledge or understanding	Provide basic information about communication in dementia
Persuasion	Using communication to induce positive or negative feelings or stimulate action	Use imagery to motivate increases in implementing external memory aids and other cognitive supports
Incentivization	Creating expectation of award	Use prize drawings for professional caregivers who are "caught" implementing positive communication strategies with residents with dementia
Coercion	Creating expectation of punishment or cost	Write-up professional caregivers who are not implementing positive communication strategies for residents with dementia
Training	Imparting skills	Provide advanced training to "champions" of residents with dementia
Restriction	Using rules to reduce the opportunity to engage in the target behavior	Regulatory efforts to significantly penalize facilities who use physical restraints or prescribe unnecessary antipsychotic medications to residents with dementia
Environmental restructuring	Changing the physical or social context	Providing electronic reminders within professional caregivers' charting systems to use positive ways to engage residents with dementia
Modeling	Providing an example for people to aspire to or imitate	Video vignettes or real-life models of appropriate strategy implementation in action
Enablement	Increasing means/reducing barriers to increase capability or opportunity	On-site behavioral support; engagement and cognitive support materials are easily physically accessible in multiple environments

Source: Michie et al., 2011, p. 7.

are sometimes difficult to implement in the real world. With respect to the national mandate to reduce inappropriate use of anti-psychotic medications to residents with dementia, the rate has decreased significantly in the past five years largely in part due to nonpharmacological interventions (CMS, 2016). SLPs are well-suited to train professional caregivers in such nonpharmacological interventions such as engagement in meaningful and purposeful activities.

Fiscal, regulation, legislation, and service provision policies can also impact behavior change. For example, productivity requirements often hinder best practices for SLPs training professional or paraprofessional caregivers in long-term care settings. As the need for continued quality dementia care increases, it will be imperative to consider alternatives to how SLPs deliver and bill for services. One alternative may be to align the payment of SLPs more closely with the salary of that of a social worker or director of recreation. For example, social workers, directors of nursing, directors of recreation, and directors of administration are paid a set salary per year. These professionals have measures for productivity within their job descriptions that determine whether they are meeting job requirements. Physical and occupational therapists' and SLPs' productivity and value, on the other hand, are determined by the number of minutes they spend providing skilled services with residents (Douglas, 2016). Since professional or paraprofessional caregiver training requires intervening at multiple levels (CNAs, licensed practical nurses [LPNs], registered nurses [RNs], other therapists, physicians) and frequently (small 5-minute bursts throughout teachable moments in the day), this is much more amenable to a salary structure, as opposed to a "see Mr. Smith for 45 minutes today" structure for optimal productivity (see Box 10.5).

Value- versus volume-based care as outlined by the Affordable Care Act (Blumenthal, Abrams, & Nuzum, 2015) furthermore implores SLPs to train professional caregivers using evidence-based adult learning models. Living communities where people with dementia reside would be wise to adopt service-oriented policies that support optimal communication from professional caregivers as implemented by SLPs. Environmental or social planning also impacts behavior change. Professional caregivers may be more apt to embrace communication strategies, individual choice, purposeful activities, and engagement if the physical environment supports such practices. Home-like environments that are less institutionalized and medicalized are the way of the future in dementia care, and SLPs training professional caregivers may have higher quality outcomes in these progressive environments (Bourgeois, Brush, Elliot, & Kelly, 2015).

Training Programs

Examples of Effective Training Programs

Since the first edition of this book, there has been an explosion of training programs for both professional and family caregivers of people with dementia. While these programs have varying degrees of scientific evidence, it is hopeful that this issue is receiving much more attention by both scientific and healthcare communities. Part of the mission of the Rosalynn Carter Institute for Caregiving is to curate research about caregiving supports and interventions (www.rosalynncarter.org). Based out of a service unit of Georgia Southwestern University, this institute exists to support both family and professional caregivers through the provision of resources including locating support groups and jargon-free publications such as "Dealing with Dementia." Under the research section of caregiver training for people with dementia, there are over 30 evidence-based caregiver training programs available, addressing cognitive restructuring, self-care, communication training, skills training, and education. Other notable published professional caregiver programs are reviewed below.

In 1996, Bourgeois and Burgio were funded by the National Institute on Aging to evaluate a CNA training program ("Increasing Effective Communication in Nursing Homes," R01 AG 13008–04) designed to increase and improve the communicative interactions between residents with dementia and CNAs. The program included a didactic in-service (with a manual and handouts);

Box 10.5 Case Example

Mr. Smith has moderate dementia and requires viewing external memory aids to shower. When he is looking at the memory aid, he can shower almost independently; however, he requires assistance of at least two people if he does not view the aid. As per best and evidence-based practices, the SLP will provide better quality care if she coaches the professional caregiver to train Mr. Smith to use the aid in the moment, in the actual context, while Mr. Smith is showering, as opposed to seeing Mr. Smith by himself for 45 minutes. Incorporating principles of adult learning as the SLP trains the professional caregiver will support quality care for residents with dementia, and alternative service delivery models should be considered.

on-the-job, individualized skills training; personalized resident memory books; and a formal staff management system to evaluate the effects of training CNAs to use communication skills and memory books with their residents with dementia (Bourgeois, Dijkstra, Burgio, & Allen, 1998). In the pilot study (Allen-Burge, Burgio, Bourgeois, Sims, & Nunnikhoven, 2001), each of 12 CNAs received two 1-hour didactic in-services, followed by 2 weeks of individualized on-the-job training. A 12-page personalized memory booklet consisting of biographical, orientation, and daily schedule information was constructed for each resident. By the end of the second week of on-the-job training, eight of the 12 CNAs had achieved a performance score of 80% accuracy in using the trained skills, including increased use of instructions and positive statements. Residents were observed to be in possession of their memory books during 70% of the observations post intervention and to demonstrate increased rates of speaking compared to baseline observations. In addition, visitors and other residents were observed to be talking more frequently with residents with memory books after treatment implementation. This effect was particularly striking for the rate of positive statements made by any person in the environment post intervention, including the resident. Some of these effects were shown to maintain at the one-month follow-up assessment.

The subsequent study increased the on-the-job training period to 4 weeks, and specific minor details of the formal staff management system were tailored to the needs of individual nursing homes in the two study locations (Burgio et al., 2001). Trained CNAs talked more, used positive statements more frequently, and provided more specific instructions to residents during care activities, without increasing the total amount of caregiving time. These positive changes in CNA behavior were still evident 2 months after the research staff had left the facilities. The staff management system included training of the LPNs and RNs who observed CNAs during care activities and provided immediate verbal performance feedback. In addition, CNAs monitored their own skill performance by completing a self-monitoring form at the end of their shift. These forms were entered in a weekly lottery, with the winner choosing from a variety of incentives (e.g., the opportunity to leave work earlier than scheduled, extra pay, and goodie bags). Other incentives included public recognition of job performance criterion attainment by posting their names on an Honor Roll. An in-depth analysis of the components of the communication skills training program (Bourgeois, Dijkstra, Burgio, & Allen, 2004) revealed that CNAs significantly increased their use of effective skills and instructions, and decreased their use of ineffective instructions.

During baseline observations, CNAs displayed low rates of all skills and instructions, except for *announcing care* and *addressing resident by name*, which were used 70–80% of the time (Bourgeois et al., 2004). Treatment group CNAs needed an average of 8.35 sessions of one-to-one training with feedback ($SD = 2.86$; range $= 3–15$) to achieve job performance criteria. The Communication Skills Checklist was the tool used during care activity observations by research staff and trained LPNs to document skill performance and to share with CNAs for feedback purposes. During post-training observations, CNAs showed significant improvements over baseline for the effective skills (*address resident by name*, *introduce self by name*, *announce every activity*, and *wait 5 seconds*), for effective instructions (*short and clear instructions*, positive feedback, and talk about resident's life), and ineffective instructions (*multistep instructions* and *unhelpful questions*). At the 3-month follow-up observation, these behaviors maintained or exceeded post-training rates. Personalized memory books were present during 84.3% of training sessions, but were used during only 26.5% of follow-up sessions (Bourgeois et al., 2004). Despite this, the overall quality of communicative interactions during care interactions improved. Before training, CNAs' communication style was task focused and neutral; after training, CNAs were more positive and engaged in social and personalized conversations with the residents during care.

Hobday, Savik, Smith, and Gaugler (2010) evaluated an internet-based multimedia education program aimed at training CNAs. The program, titled CARES® (connect with the resident; assess behavior; respond appropriately; evaluate what works; share with the team) is designed to support direct care workers in providing dementia care. Through internet modules incorporating role-play and problem-based learning techniques, CNAs increased both their knowledge, skills, and perceptions of competence related to dementia care. Participants also reported decreased stress in their daily interactions with people with dementia. The internet-based program also supported the continued feasibility of internet-based training options.

A very well-studied program includes the STAR-C, formulated by Teri and colleagues (2012). It is a family caregiver training program that is systematic and standardized, yet it could be flexible to the local context, including CNAs. In this program, community consultants are trained in tailored problem-solving strategies, and then these consultants in turn train the direct care worker or family member. After caregivers were trained in this program, people with dementia were noted to increase pleasant events, communication skills, and problem-solving abilities. It is noteworthy that individual case consultation proved important to achieving these positive outcomes.

Technology such as videos and the internet can be key components in professional and para-professional training programs. Irvine, Ary, and Bourgeois (2003) randomly assigned CNAs to treatment conditions, comparing a videotaped lecture-based training program to an interactive multimedia computer training program on CD-ROM. The CNAs rated videotaped vignettes of caregiving situations before and after training. CNAs who received the interactive computer training demonstrated significantly more correct responses at post-test than did the videotape training participants; they were also more likely to report intention to use the correct strategies and to have increased self-efficacy to use the correct strategies.

Maslow, Fazio, Ortigara, Kuhn, and Zeisel (2013) used videos to review materials and incorporated leadership meetings within their person-centered care dementia training programs. Specific action plans included the formulation of short- and long-term goals, along with a brainstorming session to anticipate challenges and behaviors. Individual coaching and small groups further enforced the material of this training. The authors recommend low or no cost awards to incentivize the training process (gift certificates, monthly celebrations), and they also suggest the evaluation and revision of the training as needed. Adult learning principles are also highlighted in this review, as the authors connect emotional learning of the direct caregiver with improved outcomes for people with dementia.

Passalacqua and Harwood (2012) tested a series of workshops, called VIPS, which were designed to train valuing people, individualized care, personal perspectives, and an opportune social environment. The VIPS program was designed to support positive communication in long-term care settings. An underlying philosophy of the program was a strength-based and failure-free environment. The training took place for 1-hour sessions over the course of 4 weeks and included information about normal aging, Alzheimer's disease, communication strategies, managing behavior, personal care, ways to promote quality of life and participation and activities, a focus on caregiving and family, and finally, ethics. A combination of vignettes, PowerPoint presentations, role-play, and guided visualization was incorporated to convey the material. Testing of the workshops showed that participants demonstrated decreased personalization of negative comments from residents, increased empathy for residents, and increased hope for residents. The program was judged to be highly feasible to incorporate into other skilled nursing facility settings as well.

Another example of successful implementation of an evidence-based intervention into a community setting is a detailed skill management program delivered by occupational therapists (OTs) that was supported by randomized controlled trials in the past (Gitlin, Winter, & Corcoran, 2003). This intervention, called Skills 2 Care, was later translated into a home health agency private practice (Gitlin, Jacobs, & Earland, 2010). Delivered in a person's home by an OT, the program was additionally integrated into OTs' current therapy workflow to allow the program to be reimbursed by Medicare part B. The intervention itself consists of custom-tailored interventions for home safety (including decluttering the environment), reducing responsive behaviors through problem-solving strategies, and enhancing overall communication (Gitlin et al., 2010).

Results of Gitlin and colleagues' work (Gitlin et al., 2010) indicated continued positive outcomes even though the intervention was delivered by typical OTs in a community setting. Most clinicians were satisfied with the treatment and intended to use the treatment even after the end of the study. In terms of organizational buy-in, for example, the researchers found that having a dedicated community setting-based coordinator and early adopters of the intervention to be helpful in the successful translation of the program. In this study, agreement of participation and OTs who volunteered served as markers for such buy-in. Fidelity monitoring in the form of treatment protocol review and caregiver surveys in terms of treatment delivery, treatment receipt, and treatment enactment also contributed to the successful translation of this program. Finally, the successful translation of this program into a community setting was also attributed to coaching in terms of three individual phone calls with each trained therapist and 5 monthly group phone calls to discuss difficult cases and to reinforce core components of the treatment (Gitlin et al., 2010).

Finally, a training program that has become more classic in the literature describes a communication strategy training program for CNAs when communicating with people with dementia. The FOCUSED program trains CNAs to keep communication face to face, to orient people with dementia to the topic, to provide continuity with topic, to "unstick" communication breakdowns, to structure questions to be yes/no or have two-optioned choices, to maintain a pleasant, typical exchange, and to keep sentences short and direct (Ripich, Wykle, & Niles, 1995). Outcomes reported included more favorable attitudes toward people with dementia with possible quality of life increases for residents with dementia. More recently, researchers at the University of Queensland have outlined strategies to support communication and memory when interacting with people with dementia (Conway & Chenery, 2016). They have shown that the implementation of MESSAGE (maximize attention, expression and body language, keep it simple, support their conversation, assist with visual aids, get their message, and encourage and engage in communication) and RECAPS (reminders, environment, consistent routines, attention, practice, simple steps) communication strategies have resulted in improved knowledge and self-efficacy for direct care workers in healthcare settings. Video examples and vignettes of these strategies in action can be found freely accessible here www.youtube.com/watch?v=LC8pv2XX5lg and www.youtube.com/watch?v=pupgSd-3sx0.

Characteristics of Effective Training Programs

Although specificities of training programs may vary, the literature base provides general strategies that should be employed to support the best chances for effective training. These are surmised from the literature reviewed above and stated in Table 10.4.

TABLE 10.4 Characteristics of Effective Training Programs

1. Use multiple modalities (video, print, live demonstration).
2. Tailor training to specific needs of individuals.
3. Complete training in short, in the moment, bursts as opposed to longer didactic sessions.
4. Adopt a coaching, collaborative philosophy.
5. Recognize the contributions and value of the trainees.
6. Assess outcomes of the training and revise as necessary.

The Challenge of Supervision and Sustainability

Sustainability, or the problem of the trained skill continuing after the training is completed, is not a problem unique to professional caregiver training in dementia care. Most behavioral treatments are at risk for both "drift" away from the target being trained and complete extinction of the trained behavior. For example, if an SLP trains a CNA to use a memory or communication aid before completing a daily activity with the resident with dementia, such as dressing, will the CNA continue using the memory aid 2 hours after the training? Two weeks after the training? Two years after the training?

The literature base in implementation science can inform the sustainability of our professional caregiving practices. Sustainability refers to the duration, maintenance, or continued delivery of an evidence-based healthcare intervention. Factors that support sustainability include continued coaching, measurement of the fidelity of the target behavior, and a framework of continuous evaluation and problem solving (National Implementation Research Network, n.d.). As such, changes in policies and procedures may be required to sustain desired behaviors. It is necessary to have target behaviors dependent upon the organizational infrastructure and not necessarily the person delivering the behavior (especially considering the high turnover rate of CNAs). Research needs are great in the sustainability of healthcare interventions; however, preliminary research reports that training, managerial practices, financial practices, and organizational contextual factors can help achieve sustainability (Proctor et al., 2015).

For example, recent attention has been given to the factors outside of the clinician that impact healthcare service delivery. Data indicate that negative organizational cultures and climates lead to decreased patient safety, employee burnout, and increased employee turnover. On the other hand, positive organizational cultures and climates are associated with increased patient safety, improved employee satisfaction, and longer sustainability of innovative treatment to benefit clients (see Douglas & Hickey, 2015 for a review). There is a call for further study of organizational-level interventions to support best clinical service delivery.

Although challenging, SLPs are tenacious enough to take on the necessary work to lead organizational systems to support practices that facilitate quality of life, purposeful living, and optimal communication for people with dementia. Evidence-based professional caregiver training is the starting point toward equitable services for all residents with dementia in skilled nursing facilities and long-term care communities. This evidence needs to be put into practice, and further evidence needs to be gathered, particularly for the durability of the training effects.

Conclusion

This chapter outlined characteristics of professionals and paraprofessionals who may work with adults with dementia in skilled nursing or similar settings. Staff in nursing and activities departments face many challenges in their demanding jobs. Effective staff training programs and innovations to create desirable work environments are needed. Speech-language pathologists play a critical role in training staff to optimize outcomes for people with dementia. This chapter emphasized training programs that use evidence-based strategies and adult learning principles to support behavior change. Forward-thinking clinical practice will embrace such principles that may eventually influence models of service provision for the SLP working with individuals with dementia in skilled nursing and long-term care communities. Future clinical practice for the SLP in skilled nursing and long-term care communities will also include the intentional dismantling of silos. Interprofessional practice may impact the perceived power differential between SLPs and other professionals and paraprofessionals, supporting our ultimate goal of person–centered, relevant, and meaningful outcomes for people with dementia.

References

Allen-Burge, R., Burgio, L. D., Bourgeois, M. S., Sims, R., & Nunnikhoven, J. (2001). Increasing communication among nursing home residents. *Journal of Clinical Geropsychology, 7*, 213–230. doi:10.1023/A:1011343212424.

Alzheimer's Association. (2012). 2012 Alzheimer's disease facts and figures. *Alzheimer's and Dementia, 8*, 131–168. http://dx.doi.org/10.1016/j.jalz.2012.02.001.

Alzheimer's Disease International. (2016). *Dementia statistics.* Retrieved October 29, 2016, from www.alz.co.uk/research/statistics.

American Speech-Language-Hearing Association. (n.d.). *Practice portal: Dementia.* Retrieved October 24, 2016, from www.asha.org/Practice-Portal/Clinical-Topics/Dementia/.

American Speech-Language-Hearing Association. (2016, March 1). *Code of ethics.* Available from www.asha.org/Code-of-Ethics/.

Bandura, A. (1997). *Self-efficacy: The exercise of control.* New York: Freeman.

Bandura, A. (1988). Organizational application of social cognitive theory. *Australian Journal of Management, 13*, 275–302. doi:10.1177/031289628801300210.

Blumenthal, D., Abrams, M., & Nuzum, R. (2015). The Affordable Care Act at 5 years. *The New England Journal of Medicine, 372*, 2451–2458. doi:10.1056/NEJMhpr1503614.

Bourgeois, M. S., Brush, J., Elliot, G., & Kelly, A. (2015). Join the revolution: How Montessori for aging and dementia care can change long-term care culture. *Seminars in Speech and Language, 36*, 209–214. doi:10.1055/s-0035-1554802.

Bourgeois, M., Dijkstra, K., Burgio, L., & Allen, R. (1998). *Increasing effective communication in nursing homes: In-service workshop training manual, videotapes, and documentation forms.* Tallahassee, FL: Department of Communication Disorders, Florida State University.

Bourgeois, M. S., Dijkstra, K., Burgio, L. D., & Allen, R. S. (2004). Communication skills training for nursing aides of residents with dementia: The impact of measuring performance. *Clinical Gerontologist, 27*, 119–138. http://dx.doi.org/10.1300/J018v27n01_10.

Burgio, L. D., Allen-Burge, R., Roth, D. L., Bourgeois, M. S., Dijkstra, K., Gerstle, J., … Bankester, L. (2001). Come talk with me: Improving communication between nursing assistants and nursing home residents during care routines. *The Gerontologist, 41*, 449–460. doi:10.1093/geront/41.4.449.

Chou, S., Boldy, D., & Lee, A. (2002). Measuring job satisfaction in residential aged care. *International Journal for Quality in Health Care, 14*, 49–54.

Centers for Medicare and Medicaid Services (CMS). (2012). Code of Federal Regulations. Title 42 – Public health, Part 483: Requirements for states and long term care facilities. Retrieved June 15, 2017, from www.ecfr.gov/cgi-bin/text-idx?c=ecfr&tpl=/ecfrbrowse/Title42/42cfr483_main_02.tpl.

Centers for Medicare and Medicaid Services (CMS). (2016). *CMS launches partnership to improve dementia care in nursing homes.* Updated August 5, 2016. Retrieved October 24, 2016 from www.nhqualitycampaign.org/dementiaCare.aspx.

Conway, E. R., & Chenery, H. J. (2016). Evaluating the MESSAGE communication strategies in dementia training for use with community-based aged care staff working with people with dementia: A controlled pretest-post-test study. *Journal of Clinical Nursing, 25*, 1145–1155. doi:10.1111/jocn.13134.

Daly, J. M., Bay, C. P., Levy, B. T., & Carnahan, R. M. (2015). Caring for people with dementia and challenging behaviors in nursing homes: A needs assessment geriatric nursing. *Geriatric Nursing, 36*, 182–191. http://dx.doi.org/10.1016/j.gerinurse.2015.01.001.

Douglas, N. F. (2016). Organizational context associated with time spent evaluating language and cognitive-communicative impairments in skilled nursing facilities: Survey results within an implementation science framework. *Journal of Communication Disorders, 60*, 1–13. http://dx.doi.org/10.1016/j.jcomdis.2015.11.002.

Douglas, N. F., & Hickey, E. (2015). Creating positive environments in skilled nursing facilities to support best practice implementation: An overview and practical suggestions. *Seminars in Speech & Language, 36*, 167–178. http://dx.doi.org/10.1055/s-0035-1551838.

Douglas, N. F., Hinckley, J. J., Haley, W. E., Andel, R., Chisolm, T. H., & Eddins, A. C. (2014). Perceptions of speech-language pathologists linked to evidence-based practice use in skilled nursing facilities. *American Journal of Speech-Language Pathology, 23*, 612–624. doi:10.1044/2014_AJSLP-13-0139.

Gitlin, L. N., Jacobs, M., & Earland, T. V. (2010). Translation of a dementia caregiver intervention for delivery in homecare as a reimbursable Medicare service: Outcomes and lessons learned. *The Gerontologist, 50*, 847–854. doi:10.1093/geront/gnq057.

Gitlin, L. N., Winter, L., & Corcoran, M. (2003). Effects of the home environmental skill-building program on the caregiver–care recipient dyad: 6-month outcomes from the Philadelphia REACH Initiative. *The Gerontologist, 43*, 532–546. doi:10.1093/geront/43.4.532.

Harris-Kojetin, L., Sengupta, M., Park-Lee, E., & Valverde, R. (2013). Long-term care services in the United States: 2013 overview. *Vital and Health Statistics, 3*(37). Retrieved June 16, 2017, from Centers for Disease Control and Prevention website: www.cdc.gov/nchs/data/nsltcp/long_term_care_services_2013. pdf.

Harvey, G., & Kitson, A. (2016). PARIHS revisited: From heuristic to integrated framework for the successful implementation of knowledge into practice. *Implementation Science, 11*(33), 1–13. doi:10.1186/s13012-016-0398-2.

Hobday, J. V., Savik, K., Smith, S., & Gaugler, J. E. (2010). Feasibility of internet training for care staff of residents with dementia: The CARES® program. *Journal of Gerontological Nursing, 36*(4), 13–21. doi:10. 3928/00989134-20100302-01.

Hopper, T., Bourgeois, M., Pimentel, J., Qualls, C. D., Hickey, E., Frymark, T., & Schooling, T. (2013). An evidence-based systematic review on cognitive interventions for individuals with dementia. *American Journal of Speech-Language Pathology, 22*, 126–145. doi:10.1044/1058-0360.

Irvine, A. B., Ary, D. V., & Bourgeois, M. S. (2003). An interactive multi-media program to train professional caregivers. *Journal of Applied Gerontology, 22*, 269–288. doi:10.1177/0733464803022002006.

Knowles, M. S. (1980). *The modern practice of adult education: From pedagogy to andragogy* (rev. ed.). New York: Cambridge – the Adult Education Company.

Knowles, M. S., Holton, E. F., & Swanson, R. A. (2005). *The adult learner: The definitive classic in adult education and human resource development* (6th ed.). Boston: Elsevier.

Liang, Y.-W., Hsieh, Y., Lin, Y.-H., & Chen, W.-Y. (2014). The impact of job stressors on health-related quality of life of nursing assistants in long-term care settings. *Geriatric Nursing, 35*, 114–119. http://dx.doi. org/10.1016/j.gerinurse.2013.11.001.

Maslow, K., Fazio, S., Ortigara, A., Kuhn, D., & Zeisel, J. (2013). From concept to practice: Training in person-centered care for people with dementia. *Generations – Journal of the American Society on Aging, 37*(3), 100–107. Retrieved June 16, 2017, from www.asaging.org/generations-journal-american-society-aging.

Michie, S., Atkins, L., & West, R. (2014). *The behavior change wheel: A guide to designing interventions.* Surrey, UK: Silverback Publishing.

Michie, S., Richardson, M., Johnston, M. Abraham, C., Francis, J., Hardeman, W., … Wood, C. E. (2013). The behavior change technique taxonomy (v1) of 93 hierarchical clustered techniques: Building an international consensus for the reporting of behavior change interventions. *Annals of Behavioral Medicine, 46*, 81–95. doi:10.1007/s12160-013-9486-6.

Michie, S., van Stralen, M. M., & West, R. (2011). The behavior change wheel: A new method for characterizing and designing behavior change interventions. *Implementation Science, 6*(42), 1–11. doi:10.1186/1748-5908-6-42.

National Implementation Research Network (NIRN). (n.d.). *About NIRN.* Retrieved October 27, 2016, from http://nirn.fpg.unc.edu/about-nirn.

NH Regulations Plus. (2011). *Nursing services-staffing ratios.* Retrieved October 27, 2016, from www.hpm. umn.edu/nhregsplus/NH%20Regs%20by%20Topic/Topic%20Nursing%20Services%20-%20 Staffing%20Ratios.html.

Office of the Inspector General (OIG). (2002). *Nurse aide training report.* Retrieved October 27, 2016, from http://oig.hhs.gov/oci/reports/oci-05-01-00030.pdf.

Omnibus Budget Reconciliation Act (OBRA) of 1987. (1991, October). *The Federal Register, 56*(48), 865–921.

Ortigara, A., & Rapp, C. G. (2004). Caregiver education for excellence in dementia care. *Alzheimer's Care Quarterly, 5*, 179–180. Retrieved October 27, 2016, from http://journals.lww.com/actjournalonline/pages/default.aspx.

Passalacqua, S. A., & Harwood, J. (2012). VIPS communication skills training to paraprofessional dementia caregivers: An intervention to increase person-centered dementia care. *Clinical Gerontologist, 35*, 425–445. http://dx.doi.org/10.1080/07317115.2012.702655.

Proctor, E., Luke, D., Calhoun, A., McMillen, C., Brownson, R., McCrary, S., & Padek, M. (2015). Sustainability of evidence-based healthcare: Research agenda, methodological advances, and infrastructure support. *Implementation Science, 10*(88), 1–13 doi:10.1186/s13012-015-0274-5.

Ripich, D. N., Wykle, M., & Niles, S. (1995). Alzheimer's disease caregivers: The FOCUSED program: A communication skills training program helps nursing assistants to give better care to patients with Alzheimer's disease. *Geriatric Nursing, 16*, 15–19. http://dx.doi.org/10.1016/S0197-4572(05)80073-4.

Schnelle, J. F., Schroyer, L. D., Saraf, A. A., & Simmons, S. F. (2016). Determining nurse aide staffing requirements to provide care based on resident workload: A discrete event simulation model. *The Journal of Post-Acute and Long-Term Care Medicine, 17*, 970–977. http://dx.doi.org/10.1016/j.jamda.2016.08.006.

Squillace, M. R., Remsburg, R. E., Harris-Kojetin, L. D., Bercovitz, A., Rosenoff, E., & Han, B. (2009). The national nursing assistant survey: Improving the evidence base for policy initiatives to strengthen the certified nursing assistant workforce. *Gerontologist, 49*, 185–197. doi:10.1093/geront/gnp024.

Squires, J. E., Hoben, M., Linklater, S., Carlteon, H. L., Graham, N., & Estabrooks, C. A. (2015). Job satisfaction among care aides in residential long-term care: A systematic review of contributing factors, both individual and organizational. *Nursing Research and Practice, Article ID 157924*, 1–24, doi:http://dx.doi.org/10.1155/2015/157924.

Taylor, D. C. M., & Hamdy, H. (2013). Adult learning theories: Implications for learning and teaching in medical education: AMEE guide no. 83. *Medical Teacher, 35*, e1561–e1572. doi:10.3109/0142159X.2013.828153.

Teri, L., McKenzie, G., Logsdon, R. G., McCurry, S. M., Bollin, S., Mead, J., & Menne, H. (2012). Translation of two evidence-based programs for training families to improve care of persons with dementia. *The Gerontologist*, 1–8. doi:10.1093/geront/gnr132.

Trinkoff, A. M., Han, K., Storr, C. L., Lerner, N., Johantgen, M., & Gartrell, K. (2013). Turnover, staffing, skill mix, and resident outcomes in a national sample of US nursing homes. *The Journal of Nursing Administration, 43*, 630–636. doi:10.1097/NNA. 0000000000000004.

Trinkoff, A. M., Storr, C. L., Lerner, N. B., Yang, B. K., & Han, K. (2016). CNA training requirements and resident care outcomes in nursing homes. *The Gerontologist*, 1–8. doi:10.1093/geront/gnw049.

11

QUALITY OF LIFE AND END OF LIFE ISSUES

Ellen M. Hickey and Michelle S. Bourgeois

The ultimate objective in providing person-centered care to persons with dementia is to enhance or maintain their desired quality of life (QoL) in the face of medical conditions that limit communicative, cognitive, and social functioning. The degree to which QoL is impacted in persons with dementia and their caregivers has been the focus of much research in the past few decades. Quality of life is a subjective notion that is difficult to quantify but essential to consider. As governments and organizations around the world have moved toward outcomes-based management, patient-/client-reported outcomes and satisfaction, and accountability, the need for useful QoL assessment tools has intensified. While there is agreement that QoL impacts persons with dementia and their caregivers, there is no conclusive way to measure the impacts. Research has shown that self-report and proxy report (staff or family report of the person's QoL) differ. This chapter provides suggestions for QoL measurement, and then discusses issues around pain management, advance care planning, and end of life issues. Suggestions for improving QoL of persons with dementia are in Chapters 6 through 8.

Quality of Life in Persons with Dementia

Defining Quality of Life

One challenge in measuring QoL in research and clinical settings is the considerable difficulty in defining the construct of QoL, which has such different meanings to different individuals and groups. These definitions can then be used to create meaningful, person-centered assessment tools that reflect the important domains of QoL. Researchers around the globe have been struggling with the conceptualization of QoL for older people over the past few decades, recognizing that it may be different for older than for younger adults. Below is a summary of some of the research on QoL conceptualization, and research findings for older adults, those living in institutions, and those with dementia.

Domains of QoL. Researchers have faced difficulties in the development of assessment tools due to inconsistency in definitions and in determining specific domains to include, and challenges in developing reliable procedures for the measurement of subjective experiences (Dempster & Donnelly, 2000; Volicer & Bloom-Charette, 1999). Though definitions have been debated, many have not strayed far from the notion of "the good life" (George & Bearon, 1980). Some conceptualizations of QoL involve perceptions of life satisfaction in general, or broad dimensions of physical and mental wellbeing or satisfaction. Life satisfaction is conceptualized by some as satisfaction with life progression, current situations, prospects, and general senses of happiness and wellbeing (George & Bearon, 1980).

Social and cultural factors impact perceptions of health and QoL (Saxena, O'Connell, and Underwood, 2002), including which domains are important in different countries and cultures (Kane, 2003). Studies of QoL of older adults living in long-term care (LTC) across many countries have shown similar results, albeit mostly amongst Caucasian participants in economically developed countries (e.g., Clare, Rowlands, Bruce, Surr, & Downs, 2008; Godin, Keefe, Kelloway, & Hirdes, 2015; Mjørud, Engedal, Røsvik, & Kirkevold, 2017; Motteran, Trifiletti, & Pedrazza, 2016; Schenk, Meyer, Behr, Kuhlmey, & Hozhausen, 2013; van Hoof et al., 2016). Gender, race, ethnicity, and religion should be considered when assessing QoL, and when making decisions about providing care (Cunningham, Burton, Hawes-Dawson, Kington, & Hays, 1999; Saxena et al., 2002). Also, the types of health conditions that are prevalent tend to vary to some extent across racial, ethnic, and socioeconomic groups (e.g., the prevalence of diabetes, hypertension, and heart disease; Smith & Kington, 1997).

Lawton (1991) proposed one of the first comprehensive conceptualizations of QoL for older persons, with four domains: objective environment (physical attributes), perceived QoL (subjective life satisfaction), psychological wellbeing (emotional state), and behavioral competence (physical health, functional competence, cognition, time use, and social behavior). This model was then applied to persons with dementia (Lawton, 1994). Other conceptualizations include specific dimensions of QoL, involving overlapping factors, such as: global impression of QoL, emotional and behavioral functioning and wellbeing, feelings and mood, intellectual and cognitive functioning, social functioning and wellbeing, the existence of a support network, the ability to pursue and enjoy interests and recreation, energy and vitality, physical wellbeing, functional wellbeing, response to surroundings, as well as environmental, occupational, and financial factors (Howard & Rockwood, 1995; Kane, 2003; Rabins, Kasper, Kleinman, Black, & Patrick, 1999; Silberfeld, Rueda, Krahn, & Naglie, 2002; Volicer & Bloom-Charette, 1999). A sense of identity and self-worth is important for QoL at any age, including in older adults and for those living in LTC (e.g., Hellberg, Augustsson, & Hellstrom Muhli, 2011; Mjørud et al., 2017). Torrison and colleagues (2016) conducted a factor analysis that revealed three factors important in QoL: physical, social, and psychological wellbeing.

Health-Related Quality of Life (HRQoL). HRQoL measurement often includes measures of physical and/or mental functions, including ADL measures. Functional status, an indication of how independently an individual can complete activities of daily living (ADLs), has often been equated with HRQoL. A systematic review of 100 articles on HRQoL over a 10-year period revealed that there is little consistency in the conceptualization of HRQoL, and the variations in terminology across models make it difficult to compare across studies (Bakas et al., 2012). HRQoL is usually viewed as a dynamic, subjective, and multidimensional construct that most commonly includes physical, social, psychological, and spiritual factors. Bakas et al. (2012) found that most of the reviewed studies came up with their own conceptualization of HRQoL, but there were three models that were used repeatedly in the literature. They recommended that researchers consistently use one model to allow for more comparability across studies; they suggested the Ferrans, Zerwic, Wilbur, and Larson (2005) model, because it added important individual and environmental characteristics. They also reported that the *International Classification of Functioning, Disability, & Health* (World Health Organization, 2001) might be most useful in guiding interventions because of its mapping framework for how health conditions impact people.

The WHO Quality of Life (WHOQOL) Group (1993, 1995) defined *quality of life* as "an individual's perception of their position in life, in the context of the culture and value systems in which they live and in relation to their goals, expectations, standards, and concerns." In the development of the WHOQOL-100, the WHOQOL Group (1998) found six domains of health-related quality of life that are important across the countries studied: physical health, psychological health, level of independence, social health, environmental health, and spirituality, religiousness, and personal beliefs. The Group then developed a supplementary module, the WHOQOL SRPB (spirituality, religiousness, personal beliefs). Through focus groups and pilot testing held internationally, they found eight facets that were of importance across cultural groups that had good psychometric properties: spiritual connection, meaning and purpose in life, awe, wholeness and integration, spiritual strength, inner peace, hope and optimism, and faith. Additional facets were important around work, but did not have adequate psychometric properties in testing: kindness to others, code to live by, acceptance of others, forgiveness, death and dying, miscellaneous (e.g., control over one's life, detachment and attachment), and freedom to practice beliefs and rituals. The most recent model, the PROMIS conceptual model (PROMIS Network, 2011), based on the WHO definition of health, incorporates a comprehensive array of aspects of physical, mental, and social health (see Figure 11.1). The PROMIS conceptual framework (2011) appears to cover all the important QoL domains specific to dementia, as described in following sections.

QoL in Institutionalized Older Adults. Researchers have been examining the dimensions of QoL for institutionalized older adults for decades. Recent research studies across many countries have replicated earlier studies, revealing consistent important dimensions of QoL, for example: choice, control and autonomy, recognition of competence, privacy, peace and quiet, feeling at home, safety and security, social contacts, meaningful activities, and interactions with staff (e.g., Clare et al., 2008; Godin et al., 2015; Mjørud et al., 2017; Motteran et al., 2016; Schenk et al.,

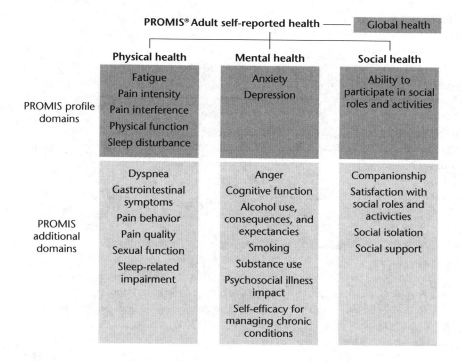

FIGURE 11.1 PROMIS Conceptual Framework (www.nihpromis.org/measures/domain framework)

2013; van Hoof et al., 2016). Other themes that are important to QoL and satisfaction in LTCs include spirituality (e.g., Motteran et al., 2016), identity (e.g., Hellberg et al., 2011; Mjørud et al., 2017), dignity, and food and mealtime enjoyment (e.g., Burack, Weiner, Reinhardt, & Annunziato, 2012; Godin et al., 2015; van Hoof et al., 2016). The impact of the quality of public and private spaces also appears in many studies (e.g., Clare et al., 2013; Motteran et al., 2016; van Hoof et al., 2016).

The dimension of social contact, which arises across studies, was particularly prominent in the interviews collected by Schenk and colleagues (2013) using the documentary method with persons who could verbally respond to a semi-structured narrative interview. The dimension of social contact had four sub-dimensions: social climate, contact with other residents, contact with nursing and care staff, and contact with one's family. *Social climate* had to do with the overall atmosphere of the home, with importance placed on friendly and harmonious relationships. *Contact with other residents* showed variability across participants in terms of expectations of the social relations in the LTC (e.g., people to do things for, people to share enjoyment with, having someone to trust); this sub-dimension showed improvement in the life situation for those who were lonely prior to moving into the home and made friends there, but not for those who did not make friends. *Contact with one's family* was important to social wellbeing. *Contact with nursing and care staff* revealed that the participants appreciate staff who show empathy and engagement with the residents.

Similar findings around social contact are found repeatedly. Shared spaces can both facilitate and impede social contact with other residents and visitors (Motteran et al., 2016). An important aspect of social contact for LTC residents is the quality of interactions with professional caregivers, particularly given that some studies find that participants are either not interested in interactions with other residents or they are not able to interact with them due to communication or cognitive challenges (e.g., Bradshaw, Playford, & Riazi, 2012; Cahill & Diaz-Ponce, 2011; Mjørud et al., 2017). Staff capability to support three basic needs of autonomy, relatedness, and competence is essential (Custers, Kuin, Riksen-Walraven, & Westserhof, 2011). Nursing home residents need to feel acknowledged as a human being and to have love and be loved (Lundin, Berg, & Muhli, 2013). Staff who prompt residents to participate and interact may increase their QoL (Clare et al., 2013). Staff engaging in relational aspects of their job in addition to physical care duties was important in several studies, and respect for privacy is essential (e.g., Bradshaw et al., 2012; Custers et al., 2011; Mjørud et al., 2017; Ryan, Byrne, Spykerman, & Orange, 2005). Furthermore, caregiver-resident relationships are co-constructed, and staff do participate in relationship-oriented communication in addition to their necessary task-oriented communication (Westerhof, van Vuuren, Brummans, & Custers, 2016; also see Chapter 10).

Another particularly relevant dimension is having meaningful and enjoyable activities, which could involve feeling useful and engaged or experiencing positive emotions during activities (e.g., Godin et al., 2015; Schenk et al., 2013). Nursing home residents often feel a sense of loss, and having meaningful activities might counteract some of that loss (Mjørud et al., 2017). Although most of these studies were conducted with LTC residents who are cognitively intact or only mildly impaired, these themes are particularly relevant to speech-language pathologists (SLPs), as well as other members of the interprofessional team who provide intervention in LTC. SLPs can provide interventions that facilitate meaningful engagement in activities and interactions; see Chapters 6 and 7 for more details on interventions. The results of these studies also provide evidence that can provide direction down the broader path of culture change occurring in many LTCs around the world. See Box 11.1 for important factors in QoL of LTC residents.

QoL in Persons with Dementia. Studies on persons with dementia have investigated the factors that are most important for their QoL. In focus groups, persons with dementia reported that they valued reminiscing about the past and "making the best of it" "one day at a time"

Box 11.1 Important Factors in Quality of Life of Persons Living in LTCs

- Choice, control and autonomy, recognition of competence
- Identity, spirituality, dignity
- Privacy, peace and quiet
- Feeling at home, safety and security
- Social contacts and interactions with staff
- Meaningful activities and mealtime enjoyment

(Thorgrimsen et al., 2003). A systematic review of review papers on the needs and subjective experiences of persons with dementia revealed two key themes: coming to terms with the disease and maintaining normality (von Kutzleben, Schmid, Halek, Holle, & Bartholomeyczik, 2012). A significant factor in decreased family contact upon admission to a LTC was the presence of dementia (Port et al., 2001). A qualitative, interview-based study of Australian LTC residents with dementia revealed that positive QoL was related to relationships with family and others, a need for control over their lives, and a need to feel like they were contributing to their community (Moyle, Fetherstonhaugh, Greben, Beattie, & AusQoL Group, 2015). Given the importance of social engagement, it is important to note that those with depression or cognitive deficits are commonly found to have poor social engagement (Achterberg et al., 2003). Several studies have found that lower QoL was associated with depression, cognitive impairment, and impaired ADLs (Barrios, Verdelho, Narciso, Goncalves-Pereira, Logsdon, & de Mendonca, 2013; Bosboom, Alfonso, Eaton, & Almeida, 2012; Conde-Sala, Garre-Olmo, Turro-Garriga, Lopez-Pousa, & Vilalta-Franch, 2009; Logsdon, Gibbons, McCurry, & Teri, 1999, 2002). A more recent study found only a weak association with cognition and functional abilities (Lacey, Bobula, Rudell, Alvir, & Leibman, 2015). Other studies found no association between cognition and QoL, but a consistent association with depressed mood (Chua et al., 2016; Giebel, Sutcliffe, & Challis, 2015; Naglie et al., 2011; Woods et al., 2014).

Woods et al. (2014) also found other factors that were important in QoL, including: irritability and self-concept of the person with dementia; quality of the relationship between care recipient and care provider; and male gender. Self-reports of QoL in people with dementia have also been found to be related to the person's comorbidities (Buckley et al., 2012) and performance of individual ADLs (Giebel et al., 2015). No simple relationship exists between cognition or activity limitations and QoL in people with dementia, but depression is a consistent factor associated with QoL, according to two reviews (Banerjee et al., 2009; Beerens, Zwakhalen, Verbeek, Ruwaard, & Hamers, 2013). Much remains to be understood about the longitudinal effects of dementia on QoL (Beerens et al., 2013), and there is a need for high-quality longitudinal studies (Beerens et al., 2014).

Quality of Life Measurement Challenges

In the past few decades, significant efforts have been made to develop quality of life measures and patient-/client-reported outcomes for people with dementia. There are more than 10 dementia-specific instruments available, with some variability in the different domains measured and the ways that data are collected, and some used frequently internationally while others are used more specifically in certain countries. This section will discuss the challenges in mode of administration and proxy versus self-report that researchers face in creating reliable and valid QoL measures for persons with dementia. Different types of respondents (e.g., client, staff, family) have different conceptualizations of QoL and varying perspectives on the QoL of persons with dementia, but all perspectives can be useful depending on the purpose of collecting the data (Godin et al., 2015).

Mode of Administration. An important consideration in QOL assessment in older adults with dementia is mode of administration (e.g., independent self-report questionnaires versus an interview-based approach or proxy report). Some have suggested that, for persons with dementia, QoL instruments must be completed in an interview with an examiner (Novella et al., 2001). Alternatively, visual analogue scales can be used to simplify assessment procedures for individuals who have cognitive and communicative disorders (e.g., Scherder & Bouma, 2000). LTC residents with dementia were able to reliably respond to visual analogue scales about QoL (Bourgeois, Dijktra, & Hickey, 2005a, 2005b; Hickey & Bourgeois, 2000). Rand and Caeils (2015) suggested that participatory action research to determine survey questions and modes of administration and use of visual aids to support communication can be used with persons with dementia to self-report their QoL.

Persons with mild to moderate cognitive impairment can provide consistent responses to questions about their preferences, their choices, and their involvement in decisions regarding their daily lives when appropriate cognitive-communicative supports are used (Bourgeois, Camp, Antenucci, & Fox, 2016; Feinberg & Whitlatch, 2001). Persons with dementia have also reported QoL using innovative supports such as taking photos that reflect what matters in their QoL and discussing the photos (van Hoof et al., 2016). As dementia progresses, assumptions are sometimes made that with increasing memory loss, people have compromised insight into their condition, which could potentially make their responses to QoL measures unreliable. Researchers have come to varying conclusions about whether awareness of the disease and insight into deficits influences self-report of QoL scores (Banerjee et al., 2009; Giebel et al., 2015; Hurt et al., 2010; Lacey et al., 2015; Selai, Vaughan, Harvey, & Logsdon, 2001; Sousa, Santos, Arcoverde, & Simões, 2013; Thorgrimsen et al., 2003; Woods et al., 2014).

Proxy Reports. Proxy reports can be obtained from family members, friends, or professional caregivers who know the client well, as additional information, or in place of self-report for those no longer able to provide self-report (Beerens et al., 2014; Godin et al., 2015; Kane et al., 2005; Robertson et al., 2017). Proxy reports or observations are better options than exclusion of people with severe deficits from outcomes measurement, but they are usually more negative than self-reports (Arons, Krabbe, Schölzel-Dorenbos, van der Wilt, & Olde Rikkert, 2013; Bruvik Ulstein, Ranhoff, & Engedal, 2012; Buckley et al., 2012). A systematic review of 17 studies showed that staff and family member proxy reports were not significantly different for global scores of QoL of LTC residents with dementia, but there were differences between self-report and proxy report, with proxy reports being related to both physical and mental health indicators (Robertson et al., 2017). Individual studies have found differences between staff and family member criteria for conceptualizations of QoL (e.g., Godin et al., 2015), and Robertson and colleagues (2017) suggest that the environment of a care home may impact the findings, with more burnt out staff and more stressful environments resulting in lower QoL ratings.

Some studies have sought to understand whether family member characteristics influence proxy reports, as findings are not consistent across family member proxies. For example, Arons et al. (2013) found that family member proxy reports of QoL were significantly related to proxy characteristics, such as age and financial situation. Bruvik et al. (2012) found smaller differences when the care recipient and caregiver lived together, but larger differences if more neuropsychiatric behaviors were reported. Sousa et al. (2013) found that noncognitive factors, such as depressive symptoms and awareness, accounted for more of the difference in self- versus proxy reports than cognitive impairment.

Other studies of family member proxies have examined whether cognition, function, behaviors, or depression influence QoL ratings. Family member proxy reports have been associated with neuropsychiatric symptoms of dementia (Buckley et al., 2012; Giebel et al., 2015; Robertson et al., 2017). There are inconsistent results of the association between depression and family member proxy reports of QoL. Depression and functioning were consistent predictors of proxy reports of QoL, but measures of cognition and caregiver depression and burden were not (Naglie et al., 2011). Chua et al. (2016) found that depression was more associated with self-report of HRQoL than proxy reports. Additionally, proxies may overestimate the cognitive abilities of persons with dementia and underestimate their emotional wellbeing (Bourgeois et al., 2005a; Hickey & Bourgeois, 2000).

Whether staff or family proxies, the type of proxy informant and the relationship to the care recipient can impact results. Kane et al. (2005) found that family proxy reports were statistically significantly correlated with LTC residents' reports of QoL on the domains of comfort, functional competence, privacy, dignity, meaningful activity, security, and autonomy, but not enjoyment or relationships; meanwhile, staff proxy reports were statistically significantly correlated with resident reports on all domains except dignity and relationships. The type of domains addressed can also impact the results of proxy measures. Cheng and Chan (2006) found that family members provide more valid responses on items related to less observable items (e.g., usual activities, and anxiety and depression), whereas clinicians provide more valid responses on more observable items (e.g., mobility and self-care). A systematic review found that family members' rated QoL lower when more restraints were used, the person had lived in the home for longer, and when the family contributed more to fees (Robertson et al., 2017).

The lack of concordance between resident and proxy ratings in LTC settings may be related to the amount and quality of their verbal and social interactions. Communication difficulties impede social interaction and constrain participation in self-reported QoL measurements (Brod, Stewart, Sands, & Walton, 1999). When residents do not express themselves clearly, caregivers often misinterpret what they are trying to communicate. Another finding that lends to the idea of ratings being influenced by how well the proxy knows the person is better agreement when the primary nurse completed the proxy measure (Gräske, Fischer, Kuhlmey, & Wolf-Ostermann, 2012). One suggestion to remedy this problem, which needs further evaluation, is to train proxies to find out about their care recipients' perceived QoL through structured conversations prior to completing QoL measures.

Bourgeois et al. (2005a) administered the DQoL by self-report and proxy report with LTC residents with dementia and their care staff (nursing assistants/continuing care assistants) before and after a 10-minute conversation about QoL topics. This conversation was supported by written cue cards (augmented verbal procedure) to elicit accurate responses from individuals. Resident and staff ratings demonstrated significantly greater agreement on QoL indicators in the post-conversation ratings than pre-conversation ratings. Anecdotal observations of the nurse aides' comments during interactions revealed surprise and sometimes disbelief at persons' responses, suggesting that proxy informants often assume they know what residents like and dislike, and can be surprised when residents' responses contradict their assumptions. That proxy assumptions might differ significantly from persons' opinions has serious potential consequences for important QoL decision-making; errors could be made by proxies that impact a person's QoL. One must consider the type of tool being used, or the type of proxy available, and choose the tool and proxy accordingly, or use more than one type of proxy to obtain a broader perspective on the individual's QoL.

Quality of Life Assessment Tools

Quality of life measures are either generic instruments that can be used with people with any health condition, or disease specific. Researchers have been developing tools specific to persons with dementia that elicit reliable responses, given the importance of self-report of QoL whenever possible. When self-report becomes too challenging, either proxy report or observational scales are used. A review of dementia-specific QoL measures revealed 15 measures that have been reported in the literature (Perales, Cosco, Stephan, Haro, & Brayne, 2013); see Box 11.2 for examples of measures. Of these, most have been developed in the USA, but five have been validated in other countries; and none have had psychometric properties assessed on population-based samples. The self-report tools are tested on people with mild to moderate dementia, while proxy reports and observational tools are more likely to be tested on people with moderate to severe dementia. While the tests share some common domains, the conceptualizations of domains are not consistent, so anyone seeking to use these tools will need to examine the conceptualization of a tool before deciding to determine if the tool meets their measurement needs. Domains most commonly include: mood, social interaction, enjoyment of activities or sense of aesthetics, and self-esteem or self-concept; other possible domains are cognition, activities, health, living conditions, and feelings of usefulness (Perales et al., 2013). Due to ongoing issues with psychometrics or comprehensiveness of available tools, Bowling and colleagues (2015) have called for development of a broader, more rigorous tool to measure QoL in people with dementia.

Dementia–Specific Self-Report Measures. Researchers have recommended the use of self-rated depression and QoL in Alzheimer's dementia treatment trials (e.g., Naglie et al., 2011). A few of the existing tools will be described here. The first self-report measures of dementia-specific QoL were purportedly developed using Lawton's model of QoL, including the Dementia Quality of Life Scale (DQoL; Brod, 1998; Brod et al., 1999) and the Quality of Life–Alzheimer's Disease Scale (QoL-AD; Logsdon et al., 1999). However, a systematic review found that Lawton's model was not fully tapped in the DQoL and QoL-AD, and other tools were not based on any model at all, or were based only on HR-QoL and had little social relevance (Bowling et al., 2015). These remain the most commonly used tools.

The DQoL (Brod, 1998; Brod et al., 1999) was based on results of three caregiver focus groups that identified domains that are important to persons with dementia. The DQoL has 29 items and takes approximately 10 minutes to administer. The result is an overall score and five subscale scores: self-esteem, positive affect, negative affect, feelings of belonging, and sense of aesthetics. The DQoL has acceptable reliability and validity for persons with mild to moderate cognitive deficits (MMSE > 11). Thorgrimsen and colleagues (2003) found that participants with MMSE scores below 10 had difficulty completing the DQoL, even though they passed the screening tool

---

Box 11.1 Important Factors in Quality of Life of Persons Living in LTC

- Choice, control and autonomy, recognition of competence
- Identity, spirituality, dignity
- Privacy, peace and quiet
- Feeling at home, safety and security
- Social contacts and interactions with staff
- Meaningful activities and mealtime enjoyment

provided with the instrument. The DQoL has been tested in the USA, China, Japan, Spain, the United Kingdom, and the Netherlands (Perales et al., 2013).

The QoL-AD (Logsdon et al., 1999) was based on a literature review of quality of life in dementia, and contains 13 items: physical health, energy, mood, living situation, memory, family, marriage, friends, chores, fun, money, self, and life as a whole. The developers for this scale reported acceptable reliability and validity for both self-report and proxy report. Reliability and validity were further investigated by Thorgrimsen and colleagues (2003) by comparing the QoL-AD to other measures, as well as gathering perspectives of persons with dementia and care-givers (family and staff) in focus groups. Results revealed that the QoL-AD has good validity and reliability, even for persons with severe cognitive deficits. Promising results were found for use of this tool in acute care, but more research is needed (Torrison et al., 2016). Also, participants had an easier time completing the QoL-AD than the DQoL, and the QoL-AD demonstrated sensit-ivity to change (Selwood, Thorgrimsen, & Orrell, 2005; Thorgrimsen et al., 2003). Given its ease of administration over a wide range of dementia severity and its strong psychometric properties, the QoL-AD has been used in clinical research internationally (Whitehouse, Patterson, & Sami, 2003). The DQoL was thought to be preferable for research purposes due to better discriminant capacity, while the QoL-AD was preferable for consultations in geriatric care because it is quicker and easier to administer. A comparison of the French language versions of the DQoL and the QoL-AD revealed that both tests had adequate psychometric properties (Wolak-Thierry, Novella, Barbe, Morrone, Mahmoudi, & Jolly, 2015). The QoL-AD has been tested in the USA, China (Cantonese and Mandarin), Taiwan, Spain, Japan, Brazil, Korea, France (and French Switzerland), Mexico, and the UK (Perales et al., 2013).

The DEMQOL (Smith et al., 2005, 2007) is a self-report measure with 28 items that fall into four domains: health and wellbeing, cognitive functioning, social relationships, and daily activities. There is also a global QoL item, but it does not count toward the overall score. The DEMQOL can be administered to people with mild to moderate dementia with good validity and reliability; this tool is not appropriate for people with severe dementia. Chua et al. (2016) found that the DEMQOL is an accurate measure of individual HRQoL, but that subscale scores should not be used. The DEMQOL and DEMQOL-proxy (described below) were used in an investigation to develop a tool to measure quality-adjusted life-years (QALYs) for people with dementia (Mulhern et al., 2013). QALYs are commonly used to measure the benefits and cost-effectiveness of inter-ventions, including improvements in QoL as well as other areas being treated (e.g., memory or engagement). The DEMQOL tools cannot be used as is for this purpose because they do not incorporate preference information. Mulhern et al. (2013) suggested that the DEMQOL tools be used alongside a generic QoL measure, such as the European Quality of Life-5 Dimensions (EQ-5D; Brooks, Rabin, & de Charro, 2003) to determine the benefits of interventions, but they do not recommend the use of generic QoL instruments alone. The DEMQOL has been tested in the UK and Spain (Perales et al., 2013).

Generic Self-Report Measures. The Neuro-QoL measure (Cella et al., 2011; Gershon et al., 2012) has the potential to be an appropriate choice for assessing QoL in persons with dementia. To date, the Neuro-QoL has been validated with many neurological populations, including some who may present with cognitive deficits or a dementia syndrome, including: stroke, traumatic brain injury, Parkinson's disease, Huntington's disease, multiple sclerosis, and ALS. This tool reli-ably assesses several domains of QoL, including physical, mental, and social wellbeing (www.neuroqol.com). The Neuro-QoL was designed to be a self-report measure, but it can also be administered by proxy report. It comes in two forms: Short Forms, which are 5–10 fixed items for one domain, and Computer Adaptive Tests, which have 4–12 items that are dynamically administered.

Single-domain assessments have been used in some situations to represent overall QoL. Sousa et al. (2013) warned that discrete measures of cognition or level of function are not good indicators of QoL, as important factors that influence QoL will be missed. Other single-domain assessments may give a better window into QoL. Given the relationship of depression and QoL, clinicians may use depression measures as a single-domain predictor of QoL. The Geriatric Depression Scale (GDS; Yesavage et al., 1983) is frequently used in LTCs. Isella, Villa, and Appollonio (2005) examined the utility of short forms to screen and quantify depression in persons with mild to moderate dementia; results supported the use of the GDS-4 for screenings and the GDS-15 for evaluation of severity. People with dementia who have an MMSE score greater than 14 could complete the GDS-15, and more research is needed for those with MMSE scores of 10–14 (Conradsson et al., 2013). Alternatively, clinicians could use a tool that was designed to measure depression in people with dementia, such as the Cornell Scale for Depression in Dementia (CSDD; Alexopoulus, Abrams, Young, & Shamoian, 1988), which has 19 items that address mood-related signs, behavioral disturbance, physical signs, cyclic functions, and ideational disturbance. The CSDD was found to be a valid tool in participants at a memory disorders clinic (Knapskog, Barca, Engedal, & The Cornell Study Group, 2011).

Communication-Related Self-Report Measures. Communication disorders are a reality of dementia, so it is important to assess how communication difficulties may affect the resident's quality of life. The Quality of Communication Life Scale (QCL; Paul-Brown, Frattali, Holland, Thompson, & Caperton, 2004) addresses the role of communication in QoL. The QCL measures the personal and environmental factors that impact meaningful life participation, and includes one item on the person's overall quality of life (Paul-Brown et al., 2004). The QCL was originally designed to be completed independently by persons with aphasias, dysarthrias, and other neurological communication disorders; people with dementia were not included in the test development. Bourgeois et al. (2005b) found that persons with dementia were able to reliably complete the instrument when the examiner sat with the residents, read the instructions, gave sufficient time for residents to respond, and gave appropriate prompts for the resident to respond, as needed.

As described in Chapter 5 on assessment for treatment planning, another potentially effective procedure for eliciting valid and reliable opinions directly from persons with dementia is a labeled picture card category-sorting procedure based on Montessori methods (Camp, 2006; Camp & Skrajner, 2004; van der Ploeg, Eppingstall, Camp, & Runci, 2013). Using written and picture cues in an enhanced visual/sorting procedure, caregivers can elicit opinions about QoL indicators from persons with dementia. Additionally, when staff caregivers have conversations with persons with dementia using such a task, the residents will verbalize more and with less confusion, which will improve the nursing staff's ability to validly complete proxy reports of QoL. VoiceMy-Choice™ (VMC; Bourgeois et al., 2016) and Talking Mats® (www.talkingmats.com; Murphy, Gray, van Achterberg, Wyke, & Cox, 2010) are two visually formatted decision-making tools that are available.

Dementia-Specific Proxy-Report Measures. The DQoL and QoL-AD can also be used as proxy measures, and it may be useful to collect both self-report and proxy report using one of these tools to compare perspectives of the person with dementia and the caregiver. Other scales were developed specifically as proxy measures, for example, the Alzheimer Disease Related Quality of Life Scale (ADRQL; Rabins et al., 1999) and the DEMQOL-Proxy (Smith et al., 2005, 2007). The ADRQL results in a global QoL score by summing five domain scores: social interaction, awareness of self, enjoyment of activities, feelings and mood, and response to surroundings. The DEMQOL-proxy has 31 items plus an overall QoL item (Smith et al., 2005, 2007). The proxy version contains items that fall in the same four domains as the self-report

DEMQOL. This tool can be used with caregivers of people with mild to severe dementia with excellent reliability; however, the subscale scores are less reliable and should not be used (Chua et al., 2016).

Given the frequent associations between QoL and neuropsychiatric behaviors in persons with dementia (e.g., Benhabib, Lanctôt, Eryavec, Li, & Herrmann, 2013; Hurt et al., 2008), another tool that could be used as an indication of QoL is the Neuropsychiatric Inventory (Cummings et al., 1994; Cummings, 1997; www.npitest.net). This tool was found to be reliable and valid and has 12 domains related to neuropsychiatric behaviors, including: delusions, hallucinations, agitation/aggression, dysphoria, anxiety, euphoria, apathy, disinhibition, irritability/lability, aberrant motor activity, night-time behavioral disturbances, and appetite and eating abnormalities. The NPI can be used with multiple types of dementia, and does not focus only on Alzheimer's disease. If a caregiver indicates that one of the domains is present, then the full set of items for that domain is administered, indicating both frequency of the behavior and caregiver distress related to the behavior. Of note, the NPI is available in over 40 different languages and several dialects of some languages (e.g., English, Spanish, French, Cantonese); a complete listing can be found on the test website (http://npitest.net/npi/translations.html). There are five versions of the NPI, 10- and 12-item versions (NPI-10; Cummings et al., 1994; NPI-12, Cummings, 1997), a LTC version (NPI-NH; Wood et al., 2000), a brief questionnaire (NPI-Q; Kaufer et al., 2000), and a clinician version, which allows the clinician to have input into the ratings (NPI-C; de Medeiros et al., 2010). This measure was sensitive to change in a pharmacological treatment study (Benhabib et al., 2013).

Dementia-Specific Observational Measures. Observational measures have the potential to document change in patients' positive affect and/or experiences and may be useful outcome measures for interventions. However, Kane (2003) warned that this approach is difficult to implement due to staffing considerations and the possible rarity of some behaviors being observed. Observers require training to provide valid and reliable ratings, and the likelihood of observing the target behaviors during a brief observation period may be quite low. Furthermore, Kane noted that observation of QOL should not be limited to weekday working hours, as a resident's QoL is shaped by events that happen throughout the day. Observations of affect and other indicators of QoL can be useful with persons with severe cognitive deficits.

One observational rating tool has been available under several different names. It was first published as the Philadelphia Geriatric Center Affect Rating Scale (Lawton, Van Haitsma, & Klapper, 1996a, 1996b), then the Apparent Affect Rating Scale (AARS; Lawton, Van Haitsma, Perkinson, & Ruckdeschel, 1999), and currently the Observed Emotion Rating Scale (Lawton, Van Haitsma, & Klapper, 1996b). This scale is available at www.abramsoncenter.org/media/1199/observed-emotion-rating-scale.pdf, and is used to assess persons with moderate to severe dementia. The tool has five domains: pleasure, anger, anxiety/fear, sadness, and general alertness. A trained clinician, who knows the person well, observes the person's facial expressions for 10 minutes to make the ratings of the extent or duration of each domain. Lawton and colleagues found that persons with dementia express less positive affect than other LTC residents.

The Quality of Life in Dementia scale (QUALID; Weiner et al., 2000; Weiner & Hynan, 2015) was developed specifically to measure QoL of persons in late-stage dementia living in LTC facilities. Trained observers observe residents over a 1-week period and then rate 11 observable behaviors (e.g., smiles, is irritable, enjoys eating). The QUALID was shown to have good internal consistency, excellent test-retest and interrater reliability, and adequate construct validity. The QUALID was reliable in documenting QoL in people with dementia in their last week of life (Hendriks, Smalbrugge, Hertogh, & van der Steen, 2014). The QUALID is valid for single points in time for persons with moderate to severe dementia; it may not be sensitive to change over time or useful as an outcome measure, however, as it did not change longitudinally during a pharmacological treatment study, even though other measures of behavioral and psychiatric symptoms showed improvements (Benhabib et al., 2013). The QUALID has undergone cross-cultural adaptation and psychometric validation to create a Spanish version, which correlated with the QOL-Visual Analogue Scale, Pain-Visual Analogue Scale, and NPI-NH (Garre-Olmo et al., 2010). The QUALID has also been tested in Sweden.

In summary, QoL is a complex construct with varying conceptualizations and opinions about the most relevant domains. There are now quite a few tools available to assess QoL in persons with dementia, and QoL should be measured in intervention trials for people with dementia, whether pharmacological or behavioral. Perales et al. (2013) provided a useful review of HRQoL scales for dementia and have made many suggestions regarding choice of a scale that reflect the issues addressed above. For example, one should consider where a test was developed and validated and in what languages, for which severity levels, and which types of data collection methods. Other important considerations are the purpose of the assessment, the conceptualization of the domains and items included, as well as psychometric properties and scoring.

Assessing and Managing Pain

Pain is an important component of health-related quality of life. There is evidence that 50–80% of persons with dementia in LTC experience pain related to musculoskeletal, gastrointestinal, and cardiac conditions (Corbett et al., 2012). Other causes of pain include fecal impaction, urinary retention, unrecognized fracture, and surgical abdomen (Volicer & Hurley, 2015). People with dementia are less likely to receive treatment for pain than people without cognitive impairments (Hoffman, van den Bussche, Wiese, Glaeske, & Kaduszkiewicz, 2014). The assessment and treatment of pain is thought to be inadequate because of the lack of understanding of the impact of dementia neuropathology on pain perception and processing in dementia, the limitations of current assessment procedures, the lack of evidence for effective treatment, and the need for more education and training of healthcare professionals (Achterberg et al., 2013). Nurses sometimes think they use evidence-based pain management principles more than they do with older adults in acute care (Coker et al., 2010); examples of strategies that were suggested to eliminate the barriers to pain management include offering pain relief regularly, using pain assessment tools with patients with cognitive impairment, making nonpharmacological treatments available, and helping patients and families to manage side effects.

Assessment of the presence and severity of pain is one of the main responsibilities of nurses, so that they may assist physicians with pain management. An important role for the SLP in the medical setting is to consult with nursing about appropriate communication supports for patients to be able to report their level of pain reliably, or to interpret the nonverbal communicative attempts of patients with cognitive-communicative impairments. Typically, pain assessment is done verbally, by self-report. Nurses ask patients if they have pain, and if they respond affirmatively, they are asked to rate the severity. There are many versions of pain-rating scales; often, clinicians require the person to rate pain on a scale from 0–10, with the instructions that 0 means *no pain at all* and 10 means *the worst pain possible*. Tools such as the Verbal Descriptor Scale (Feldt, Ryden, & Miles, 1998) require the person to endorse one of seven brief pain severity descriptions (from *no pain* to *pain as bad as it could be*). Self-report measures can be used reliably with persons in the earlier stages of dementia, including the Visual Analog Scale (VAS) (Scherder & Bouma, 2000), the Numerical Rating Scale (Herr & Mobily, 1993), and the Faces Pain Scale (FPS; Bieri, Reeve, Champion, Addicoat, & Ziegler, 1990) (Corbett et al., 2012). In a study comparing the reliability of these three scales with 129 persons with severe dementia (MMSE < 11), 61% of them could understand at least one of the scales; interestingly, they found that participants had difficulty with the FPS (Pautex et al., 2006). Scherder and Bouma (2000) compared the Colored Analogue Scale (CAS; McGrath et al., 1996), the Facial Affective Scale (FAS; McGrath et al., 1996), and the FPS; all could be used by persons with mild dementia, but only the CAS was used reliably by persons with moderate to severe dementia.

Fisher et al. (2002) developed and examined an explicit procedure for obtaining self-report pain data from LTC residents with varying levels of cognitive ability. They documented consistent and reliable self-report pain assessments with residents who had a mean MMSE of 15 ($SD=7$). Residents were provided with adequate time and assistance (e.g., verbal prompts) to respond in yes–no and Likert scale response formats using a 17-item modified version of the Geriatric Pain Measure – Modified (GPM-M; Ferrell, Stein, & Beck, 2000; Simmons, Ferrell, & Schnelle, 2002), which was referred to as *GPM-M2*. Evidence for psychometric properties was good, including validity, internal consistency, and stability.

A systematic review of tools to identify pain in persons with dementia revealed many different validated tools used worldwide (Husebo, Achterberg, & Flo, 2016), including the Checklist of Nonverbal Pain Indicators (CNPA; Feldt, 2000), Elderly Pain Caring Assessment 2 (EPCA-2; Morello, Jean, Alix, Sellin-Peres, & Fermanian, 2007), Mobilization-Observation-Behavior-Intensity-Dementia (MOBID; Husebo, Ostelo, & Strand, 2014), Observational Pain Behavior Assessment Instrument (OPBAI; Teske, Daut, & Cleeland, 1983), Pain Assessment for the Dementing Elderly (PADE; Villanueva, Smith, Erickson, Lee, & Singer, 2003), Pain Assessment in Advanced Dementia (PAINAD; Warden, Hurley & Volicer, 2003), and Pain Assessment in Noncommunicative Elderly persons (PAINE, Cohen-Mansfield, 2006), but few of these were implemented regularly, nor were they used to test responsiveness to treatment.

In the presence of communication difficulties, people with dementia may not be able to explain their pain adequately (Ballard, Creese, Corbett, & Aarsland, 2011; Monroe, Parish, & Mion, 2015). Instead, they are known to express pain in nonverbal ways, such as crying out or yelling, restlessness, rocking, rubbing a body part, grimacing, and other aggressive or resistive/defensive behaviors (Ballard et al., 2011; Husebo, Strand, Moe-Nilssen, Husebo, & Ljunggren, 2009). In one study, pain was positively correlated with aggression and agitation but negatively associated with wandering, suggesting that effective pain management might increase mobility as well as decrease aggressive and agitated behaviors (Ahn & Horgas, 2013). Changes in interpersonal interactions, activity patterns or routines, and mental status should be documented as well (AGS Panel on Persistent Pain in Older Persons, 2002).

Even when pain is detected in persons with dementia it might not be treated effectively (Frampton, 2003). Persons with disruptive behaviors may be given antipsychotic medications rather than analgesics (Ballard et al., 2011). Forty-five percent of residents with painful conditions reported in their charts did not receive any pain medications (Plooij, van der Spek, & Scherder, 2012). Patients with dementia who had hip surgery received fewer analgesics than did cognitively intact patients who had the same surgery (Monroe, Misra, & Habermann, 2014; Morrison & Siu, 2000). Systematic pain assessment has been shown to result in both improved pain management (as determined by increased usage of as needed analgesics) and decreased nursing staff distress and burnout (Fuchs-Lacelle, Hadjistavropoulos, & Lix, 2008).

Given the challenges of obtaining reliable self-report data with persons with dementia, observational tools are sometimes used to determine if there are nonverbal signs of pain. For example, the Checklist of Nonverbal Pain Indicators (CNPI; Feldt, 2000) is an observational tool nurses can use to indicate the presence of a variety of verbal and nonverbal behaviors to communicate pain. The PAINAD is another observational tool used in clinical practice (Warden, Hurley, & Volicer, 2003). The PAINAD was developed out of the need for a valid, quick, and reliable way to document observed behaviors indicative of pain, but also to evaluate the increasing numbers of nonpharmacological interventions for pain management such as listening to preferred music (Park, 2010) and others. The instrument includes five categories of behavior (breathing, negative vocalizations, facial expression, body language, and consolability) rated on a scale of 0–2, with a range of 0–10 points. The authors of this instrument reported marginal internal consistency with the original measure (Warden et al., 2003), but follow-up studies have shown good internal consistency and very good inter-rater reliability (Dewaters et al., 2008; Schuler et al., 2007). The PAINAD has been translated into 11 languages. And a free online video demonstration of the PAINAD and three other pain scales is available at http://journals.lww.com/ajnonline/Pages/videogallery.aspx?videoId=16&autoPlay=true. Additional methods of pain assessment in persons with dementia are emerging, for example, computerized assessment of facial expressions (Hadjistavropoulos et al., 2014).

Attention to the problems of assessing and treating pain in persons with cognitive and communicative impairments has been a focus of nursing educators, with good results. After training, similar amounts of analgesic medications were administered during hip fracture recuperation to both cognitively impaired and intact residents who reported similar pain intensity ratings (Feldt & Finch, 2002); nurses in LTC were cautioned, however, that residents with cognitive impairment may not anticipate the need for pain medication and may not request "prn" (as-needed) pain medications. Nursing staff may need to schedule routine medication administration in anticipation of expected periods of pain fluctuation. Reid and colleagues (Reid, O'Neil, Dancy, Berry, & Stowell, 2015) provided a two-hour educational workshop on pain management and found significant improvements in consistency of pain assessment and documentation at three and eight months after training.

Given the documentation of significant difficulty in adequately assessing and managing pain in persons with cognitive deficits, a role for the SLP in working with persons with dementia is to facilitate communication in the process of pain assessment and management. SLPs could provide valuable assistance in this process by interpreting nonverbal expressions of pain for nursing staff when residents are exhibiting responsive behaviors such as agitation. SLPs may act as one of the raters of nonverbal communication, or may assist in adapting existing tools so that persons with cognitive impairments can use them. For example, Lasker (2006), working with nursing staff at a local hospital, revised a visual pain scale to graphically depict facial features associated with different severities of pain (Figure 11.2). Finally, SLPs must keep in mind that "everyone can communicate, everyone does communicate" (Beukelman, Mirenda, & Ball, 2012), and that it is our job to assist other caregivers to figure out what and how people with dementia, who are labeled as "noncommunicative," are communicating.

PAIN SCALE

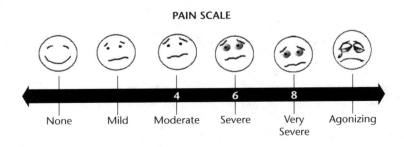

FIGURE 11.2 Visual Pain Scale

Source: Lasker (2006).

End of Life Issues

Given population aging and the increasing prevalence of dementia, the issue of end of life decision-making for persons with dementia is becoming ever more pressing. The goal for all people with dementia should be to maximize quality of life until the end of life. However, as noted above, many people fail to receive interventions that allow them to remain comfortable, and some receive interventions that prolong life without quality of life, even though families report that the goal of care should be comfort (Mitchell et al., 2009). Many organizations and governments are working to develop innovative solutions to reduce the numbers of burdensome transfers for older adults at the end of life. In a nationwide study in the United States, these transfers were found to be costly and avoidable, and often related to indicators of poorer quality end of life care, such as feeding tube insertion, intensive care stays, late hospice referral, and stage IV decubitus ulcers (Gozalo et al., 2011). Increasingly, people are discussing the right to die with dignity, but individual values and wishes around dying are widely variable, and most legislation around assisted dying excludes persons with dementia (Menzel & Steinbock, 2013).

Advance Care Directives

In an ideal world, everyone would prepare an advance care directive document (or "living will") specifying treatment preferences for a variety of medical conditions and end of life care and identifying a healthcare proxy, or substitute decision-maker. These statements should indicate both wishes and preferences for treatments to receive, and directives of which treatments should be refused (Brooke & Kirk, 2016). This could make such decisions less difficult for family and staff caregivers, although controversies remain and advance care directives should be used as a tool to have a conversation rather than a set of rigid commands. Many countries or states have passed legislation that guides the legal process of making these wishes known (Gozalo et al., 2011). Physicians are encouraged to have discussions with their patients while they are still able to make those decisions, and people are urged to have these conversations with their family members, yet, most do not (Garand, Dew, Lingler, & DeKosky, 2011; Kim, Ersek, Bradway, & Hickman, 2015).

In Rao and colleagues' analysis of 7,946 respondents of the 2010 HealthStyles Survey, only 26.3% had an advance directive (Rao, Anderson, Lin, & Laux, 2014). The most reported reason for not having one was lack of awareness of advance directives. A review of 33 studies by van der Steen et al. (2014) revealed active avoidance of advance care plan conversations by people with dementia and their families due to not being ready and willing to be involved in these discussions or passive avoidance due to trust placed in healthcare providers to deliver appropriate care, as well as fear and lack of understanding of the disease trajectory. Additionally, a review by de Vleminck et al. (2014) revealed that physicians avoided initiating the advance care plan process with their patients with dementia because they were uncertain about the person's understanding of the disease and prognosis, or they lacked familiarity with the terminal phases of dementia. Other barriers include questions around when to initiate conversations around advance care planning and who should initiate these discussions, and which documentation to complete (Dickinson et al., 2013; Robinson et al., 2013).

Advance care directives need to be initiated and executed while the person still has decision-making capacity (Kim et al., 2015; Mitchell et al., 2009). Conversations about end of life care can be uncomfortable, particularly when family members disagree, but this is even more problematic when an urgent medical situation arises and substitute decision-makers have not been informed of wishes. Upon hospital admission, patients or their substitute decision-makers are asked to sign a document consenting to treatment. If they have not completed an advance directive form or do not have a copy with them, they are asked to complete one during the admissions process, if competent to do so. Unfortunately, most people with dementia are not competent to complete an advance directive and may not be able to express their own treatment wishes, leaving family members and staff to make difficult choices that are often contentious (Kim et al., 2015).

Whether or not someone has an advance directive, the physician or nurse practitioner could initiate a discussion about care wishes using the Physician Orders for Life-Sustaining Treatments (POLST) paradigm (Bomba, Kemp, & Black, 2012), preferably before a transfer to hospital in an acute situation. The POLST provides a framework for conducting goals-of-care discussions between healthcare providers, patients, and their surrogates (Kim et al., 2015). The decisions made from these discussions are translated directly to medical orders, and can be used across healthcare settings to provide better continuous care. The POLST should be complementary to an advance directive, if the person has one, and should be part of an ongoing conversation between healthcare providers and surrogates as the person's condition changes (Kim et al., 2015). Kim and colleagues' (2015) literature review identified challenges in using the POLST, such as the lack of discussions between physicians, patients, and surrogates about end of life care goals, and the need for training to understand the care options and to communicate with surrogates and patients about the care options. Additionally, states sometimes impose barriers to following the POLST orders, for example, in some states one cannot forego artificial nutrition and hydration unless this is stated in an advance directive. When POLST is used, the outcome is less use of unwanted life-sustaining treatments.

Brooke and Kirk (2016) concluded from their literature review that health professionals need training and education regarding dementia prognosis, advance care planning, and advanced communication skills. The SLP is the ideal interprofessional team member to provide training in communication skills to other team members, as well as to support persons with dementia to be able to communicate about medical treatments and end of life care decisions. This can be done across care settings in which SLPs work with people with dementia (acute care, home care, LTCs). See Box 11.3 for websites to gain more information about advance directives and for resources for the public and/or healthcare providers to have advance directive conversations. Menzel and Steinbock (2013) provide an intriguing, albeit controversial, argument for the right of persons with dementia to have access to physician-assisted dying. They provide six case studies of persons with dementia and the factors that should be weighed in decisions to follow or not follow their end of life care wishes, highlighting the complexity of decisions and the importance of including the person with dementia as much as possible in the process. That might be accomplished more fully with SLP support for communication.

Determining Capacity

Determination of competence and capacity for decision-making is complicated and often stressful for families to initiate. Competence is a legal state that refers to a person's mental soundness to make decisions for specific situations, rather than globally. Only a judge can determine incompetence, otherwise, adults are presumed to be competent. Capacity is a clinical judgment that refers to degree of ability to make an informed decision, and may vary depending on the situation (e.g., decisions about everyday activities and foods versus medical treatments), as well as depending on cognitive fluctuations (Trachsel, Hermann, & Biller-Andorno, 2015). Because decisional capacity is situation specific, the evaluation team needs to understand not only the extent of the decisions required and the potential ramifications of each decision, but also how to communicate the choices effectively to the person with impaired cognition. SLPs could be asked to provide support in capacity evaluations when people have difficulty understanding the questions or lack awareness of

Box 11.3 Resources for Advance Care Planning

- *Five Wishes*, Aging with Dignity: advance directive for medical, personal, emotional, and spiritual needs; www.agingwithdignity.org
- National POLST Paradigm; resources for the public and healthcare professionals around end of life care, and advance care planning; http://polst.org
- *The Conversation Project* encourages people to talk to their significant others and healthcare providers about their end of life wishes; provides a general Your Conversation Starter Kit in eight languages, as well as one specifically for people with dementia and their families, and *How to Talk to Your Doctor* available in four languages; http://the conversationproject.org; http://theconversationproject.org/wp-content/uploads/2017/02/ConversationProject-StarterKit-Alzheimers-English.pdf
- *PREPARE for Your Care* is an interactive website that guides an individual or family through medical decision-making; available in English and Spanish; www.prepareforyourcare.org
- *Go Wish* game, sort cards stating wishes into levels of importance (e.g., to have a doctor who knows me as a whole person); available as a card game for purchase or a free online game; also includes other resources and supports; www.gowish.org from the Coda Alliance; http://codaalliance.org
- *Caring Conversations* workbook, Center for Practical Bioethics – resources for advance directives and durable power of attorney; https://practicalbioethics.org/resources/caring-conversations
- National Hospice and Palliative Care Organization; advance directives for all 50 states and Washington, DC; Spanish option on website; as well as a toll-free number for information and counseling; www.caringinfo.org
- *Advanced Directives – Planning Ahead*, Dr. Neil Wenger, University of California, Los Angeles (UCLA) Health; www.uclahealth.org/neil-wenger
- *End-of-Life Decisions*, Alzheimer's Association; information for consumers and families; www.alz.org/national/documents/brochure_endoflifedecisions.pdf
- *Dementia and End-of-Life Care*, Alzheimer Society of Canada; www.alzheimer.ca/~/media/Files/national/End-of-life-care/EoL_Part_I_e
- Speak Up Campaign – Advance Care Planning Canada; a source of information for consumers, families, and professionals; includes province-specific information for Canadians; includes a video about *5 steps of Advance Care Planning* (Think, Learn, Decide, Talk, Record); www.advancecareplanning.ca
- Dying With Dignity Canada – provides resources and personal support for creating advance directives in Canada; www.dyingwithdignity.ca/download_your_advance_care_planning_kit
- *End of Life Law & Policy in Canada*; provides legal information about advance directives, palliative care, and assisted dying, including national and provincial information; http://eol.law.dal.ca/?page_id=231
- Advance Care Planning Australia – has information about competence and capacity, FAQs, and information about training workshops for the public and health professionals; information on advance care planning is available in 11 languages; http://advancecareplanning.org.au/

their own cognitive challenges. The SLP can serve an important role on the team in determining the extent of comprehension, making suggestions for appropriate assessment tools, and offering support strategies (i.e., visual and written cues).

Allen et al. (2003) developed some objective measures of capacity in their study of correlates of advance care planning in LTCs. Based on a sample of 78 LTC residents with a mean Mini-Mental Status Exam (MMSE; Folstein, Folstein, & McHugh, 1975) score of 14 ($SD = 6.5$), they found that these residents could state a treatment preference but did not understand the treatment situation or the consequences of the treatment choice. Residents who verbally interacted with others were more likely to understand and appreciate treatment choices; in addition, cognitive supports and prompts (Allen & Shuster, 2002) and different response options, such as yes–no versus scaled responses (Fisher et al., 2002) appear to increase the likelihood of participation in treatment planning discussions. Moye, Karel, Azar, and Gurrera (2004) also found that adults with mild dementia could participate in medical decision-making at acceptable legal standards, but the focus of the process should be on having the person describe the reasons for specific medical choices and the implications of those choices on future outcomes, and not to require comprehension of the meaning of specific diagnostic and treatment procedures.

The Role of the SLP in End of Life Decision-Making

As the person's medical condition is predicted to deteriorate, and the need for medical intervention becomes apparent, engaging the person in discussion about advance directives and end of life wishes will be an important and meaningful topic in treatment sessions. The role of the SLP is to ensure communication access about their needs by providing communication health services and resources to support autonomy and improve quality of life. The specific role of the SLP will be determined by each person with dementia and/or family through a process of person-centered care (ASHA, 2017). SLPs must view the person with dementia and family holistically, considering their physical, emotional, psychological, and spiritual needs (ASHA, 2017; www.asha.org; Speech-Language and Audiology Canada, 2016; www.sac-oac.ca/). What the SLP may think is best for the person clinically may not always be accepted as best for the person's quality of life. Decisions that families make will be influenced by their cultural background and spiritual beliefs, and their acceptance of disability, which the SLP must respect (ASHA, n.d.). The clinician must show cultural humility and demonstrate cultural sensitivity when sharing potential treatment recommendations and outcomes (ASHA, 2017). The document *2004–2005 Ethics, Rights, and Responsibilities Standards of the Joint Commission on Accreditation of Healthcare Organizations* addresses this issue in Standard RI.2.80 (see Box 11.4 for link).

The development of alternative communication strategies (e.g., visual and environmental supports) at the end of life will have a facilitative or palliative function, instead of a rehabilitative one. To understand the person's needs, the SLP will need to ask the person to share his or her needs, desires, and preferences for communication interactions, partners, settings, and topics. Appropriate supports enable people with dementia to understand and to express their opinions and preferences reliably, even in the later stages of illness (Bourgeois et al., 2016; see Chapter 5 for more information).

Chang (2015) evaluated the effects of visual aids and written medical vignettes on decision-making for end of life care of 20 persons with mild and moderate dementia. Participants were asked to demonstrate *Understanding, Making a Choice, Reasoning, and Appreciation* of two medical vignettes (Drug Treatment for Dementia, and Feeding Tube Placement for Dysphagia) under two counterbalanced conditions: verbal only or verbal plus visual aids. The visual aids consisted of pictures and text illustrating the two medical vignettes. Transcripts of the experimental sessions were analyzed for quality of the verbal statements made to demonstrate decisional capacity. Results showed that participants demonstrated significantly better overall decisional capacity in *Understanding*, *Reasoning*, and *Appreciation* when supported by visual aids during the decision-making process. Participants in both conditions were able to *Express a Choice*, but only the participants using visual aids were able to explain their rationale for their decision based on the information provided. Participants in the verbal-only condition often stated they would choose whatever option their doctor recommended. The development of these communication support tools and the research documenting their effectiveness should empower SLPs and other healthcare professionals to advocate for the person with dementia to make their own decisions about important quality of life concerns (e.g., use of feeding tubes, nutritional and hydration strategies) (Regan, Tapley, & Jolley, 2014).

Speech–language pathologists must also understand the patterns of functional decline at the end of life, as well as the process of dying. In an examination of the trajectories of functional decline over the last year of life in 747 individuals with a terminal condition, the abilities to eat and transfer were relatively preserved until death was imminent, even for patients with advanced dementia who were completely dependent for other ADLs (Chen, Chan, Kiely, Morris, & Mitchell, 2007). See the resources in Box 11.4 for more suggested resources on hospice and end of life care. The End of Life Resources link from the American Speech-Language-Hearing Association has additional links to websites and articles related to end of life care.

Counseling Opportunities at the End of Life

Holland points out that we need to look for "counseling opportunities" in our therapeutic interactions and to be aware that people may have troubling thoughts that they wish to discuss with someone who is not family (Holland & Nelson, 2013). For example, there may be someone who needs an apology for a wrongdoing in the past; or the location of the will, the key to the safe

---

Box 11.4 Recommended Resources on Hospice and End of Life Care

Websites
- National Hospice and Palliative Care Organization: educational resources for professionals and consumer and family resources for end of life care; www.nhpco.org
- *Position Statement – The Role of Speech-Language Pathologists, Audiologists and Communication Health Assistants in End-of-Life Care*, Speech-Language and Audiology Canada: www.sac-oac.ca/sites/default/files/resources/end-of-life_position-statement_en.pdf
- *End of Life Resources and References*, American Speech-Language-Hearing Association: www.asha.org/SLP/End-of-Life-Resources/

Books
- Gawande, A. (2014). *Being mortal: Medicine and what matters in the end.* New York: Henry Holt & Company, LLC.
- Goldberg, S. (2009). *Lessons for the living: Stories of forgiveness, gratitude, and courage at the end of life.* Boston: Trumpeter Books.
- Kalanithi, P. (2016). *When breath becomes air.* New York: Random House.
- Nuland, S. (1993). *How we die.* New York: Vintage Books.
- Sacks, O. (2015). *Gratitude.* New York: Alfred A. Knopf.

deposit box, or computer passwords may need to be communicated. Holland advises SLPs to develop meaningful therapy activities that would enable the person to express these important details – the SLP could transcribe letters that the person dictates, such as an apology letter, or a letter expressing gratitude for the kind words or loving care provided by a caregiver. The making of a Memory Book, or a book of special recipes or a compendium of advice for the future for the grandchildren could be a meaningful activity to initiate with the person, and then involve the family to complete it. A conversation about the person's accomplishments in life could lead to writing a draft of their obituary; a discussion of the person's favorite prayers and hymns could result in the script of their own funeral service. Family members of persons who have left specific written instructions for their funeral service and who have received gratitude or apology letters after their passing have expressed feeling especially grateful to the clinician who thought to have these conversations with their loved one (Bourgeois, personal communication).

Conclusion

Around the world, there have been changes in legislation and policies that increasingly require the use of patient/client satisfaction and outcomes by hospitals and other healthcare facilities. There have been significant research efforts to understand the quality of life of persons with dementia, whether they are living at home or in care facilities. Common themes in this literature include issues around privacy, self-determination and autonomy, social contact, and the impact of the environment on QoL. Additionally, research studies around the world show that people with mild to moderate dementia can indicate their own QoL and preferences, but this becomes more difficult to obtain when cognitive deficits are severe. Proxy informants can provide their perspectives on QoL, but clinicians and researchers must keep in mind that they are answering from their own perspectives, which will differ from the perspective of the person with dementia. Regardless of the care setting, pain management is an important part of maintaining or enhancing QoL, but this is an area that is lacking for too many people with dementia. Speech-language pathologists have an important role to play in facilitating communication around QoL, pain, and end of life decisions with persons with dementia. Use of supported communication techniques and augmentative communication tools can help people with dementia to participate in their care and day to day life decisions.

For clients like Mary Doe, with no written end of life instructions in their files, it is important to facilitate the communication and documentation of these decisions. Though it can be difficult to help clients with moderate dementia make these decisions for themselves, they are decisions that they deserve to make. The clinician must describe the choices and provide visual aids. The clinician or activity leader must also provide pros and cons of the options given (as shown in the example above). Visuals may be used for the description of pros and cons if necessary to facilitate client understanding.

Case 11.1 Case Example of Visual Supports to Aid Conversation About End of Life Issues

Mary Doe's family members report that they want to respect her wishes in the matter of cremation vs. burial, but they are not sure what she would want. They want to discuss it with her, but they want to be sure that she understands both options. The following is an example that may be beneficial for Mary Doe and her family (or others in a similar situation): Case example provided by Haller (2015), used with permission.

Cremation vs. Burial

Cremation	Burial

What is cremation?  Cremation is the reduction of a deceased body to ashes by burning. (Definition provided by Merriam–Webster Dictionary)	*What is a burial?*  Burial is the act or ceremony of burying a dead person in a grave. (Definition provided by Merriam–Webster Dictionary)
Pros • Less expensive than burial. • Remains/urns are portable. • Remains are able to be split up amongst family members, or stored in a preferred location.	*Pros* • More widely acceptable by society. • Family members may be comforted by a place to visit (plot/tombstone). • May want to be a part of a family burial ground.
Cons • Cremations are not available everywhere, and family may have to search for a facility that performs cremations. • If ashes are lost or destroyed, they cannot be replaced. • If family members disagree with cremation, it may cause tension.	*Cons* • Family must purchase coffin, plot, and tombstone. • Other related costs/fees make burial more expensive. • Cemeteries typically restrict visiting hours, types of monuments, etc.

Which option is your preference?

Cremation	*Burial*
 I would like to be cremated.	 *I would like to be buried.*

References

Achterberg, W., Pieper, M., Dalen-Kok, A., de Waal, M., Husebo, B., Lautenbacher, S., Kunz, M., Scherder, E., & Corbett, A. (2013). Pain management in patients with dementia. *Clin Interv Aging, 8*, 1471–1482.

Achterberg, W., Pot, A., Kerkstra, A., Ooms, M., Muller, M., & Ribbe, M. (2003). The effect of depression on social engagement in newly admitted Dutch nursing home residents. *The Gerontologist, 43*(2), 213–218.

AGS Panel on Persistent Pain in Older Persons (2002). The management of persistent pain in older persons. *J Am Geriatr Soc, 50*(Suppl 6), S205–S224.

Ahn, H., & Horgas, A. (2013). The relationship between pain and disruptive behaviors in LTC residents with dementia. *BMC Geriatr, 13*, 14.

Alexopoulus, G. S., Abrams, R. S., Young, R. C., & Shamoian, C. A. (1988). Cornell scale for depression in dementia. *Biological Psychiatry, 23*(3), 271–284.

Allen, R. S., DeLaine, S. R., Chaplin, W. F., Marson, D. C., Bourgeois, M. S., Dijkstra, K., & Burgio, L. D. (2003). Advance care planning in LTCs: Correlates of capacity and possession of advance directives. *The Gerontologist, 43*(3), 309–317.

Allen, R. S., & Shuster, J. L. (2002). The role of proxies in treatment decisions: Evaluating functional capacity to consent to end-of-life treatments within a family context. *Behavioral Sciences and the Law, 20*, 235–252.

American Speech-Language-Hearing Association (ASHA). (n.d.). *Dementia: End-of-life issues.* Retrieved February 20, 2017, from www.asha.org/PRPSpecificTopic.aspx? folderid=8589935289&section=Treatment#End-of-Life_Issues.

American Speech-Language-Hearing Association (ASHA). (2017). *Practice portal on SLP roles in dementia care.* Retrieved January 10, 2017, from www.asha.org/PRPSpecificTopic.aspx?folderid=8589935289&section=Roles_and_Responsibilities.

Arons, A., Krabbe, P., Schölzel-Dorenbos, C., van der Wilt, G. J., & Olde Rikkert, M. (2013). Quality of life in dementia: A study on proxy bias. *BMC Medical Research Methodology, 13*(110). doi:10.1186/1471-2288-13-110.

Bakas, T., McLennon, S. M., Carpenter, J. S., Buelow, J. M., Otte, J. L., Hanna, K. M., … Welch, J. L. (2012). Systematic review of health-related quality of life models. *Health and Quality of Life Outcomes, 10*(134). doi:10.1186/1477-7525-10-134.

Ballard, C., Creese, B., Corbett, A., & Aarsland, D. (2011). Atypical antipsychotics for the treatment of behavioral and psychological symptoms in dementia, with a particular focus on longer term outcomes and mortality. *Expert Opin Drug Saf, 10*(1), 35–43.

Banerjee, S., Samsi, K., Petrie, C. D., Alvir, J., Treglia, M., Schwam, E. M., & del Valle, M. (2009). What do we know about quality of life in dementia? A review of the emerging evidence on the predictive and explanatory value of disease specific measures of health related quality of life in people with dementia. *International Journal of Geriatric Psychiatry, 24*, 15–24.

Barrios, H., Verdelho, A., Narciso, S., Goncalves-Pereira, M., Logsdon, R., & de Mendonca, A. (2013). Quality of life in patients with cognitive impairment: Validation of the Quality of Life-Alzheimer's Disease scale in Portugal. *International Psychogeriatrics, 25*, 1085–1096.

Beerens, H. C., Sutcliffe, C., Renom-Guiteras, A., Soto, M. E., Suhonen, R., Zabalegui, A., … Hamers, J. P. H. (2014). Quality of life and quality of care for people with dementia receiving long term institutional care or professional home care: The European RightTimePlaceCare Study. *Journal of American Medical Directors Association, 15*(1), 54–61. http://dx.doi.org/10.1016/j.jamda.2013.09.010.

Beerens, H. C., Zwakhalen, S. M. G., Verbeek, H., Ruwaard, D., & Hamers, J. P. H. (2013). Factors associated with quality of life of people with dementia in long-term care facilities: A systematic review. *International Journal of Nursing Studies, 50*(9), 1259–1270.

Benhabib, H., Lanctôt, K. L., Eryavec, G. M., Li, A., & Herrmann, N. (2013). Responsiveness of the QUALID to improved neuropsychiatric symptoms in patients with Alzheimer's disease. *Canadian Geriatrics Journal, 16*(4). Retrieved January 28, 2017, from www.cgjonline.ca/index.php/cgj/article/view/78/155.

Beukelman, D., Mirenda, P., & Ball, L. (2012). *Augmentative and alternative communication: Supporting children and adults with complex communication needs* (4th ed.). Baltimore: Paul H. Brookes Publishing Co.

Bieri, D., Reeve, R. A., Champion, G. D., Addicoat, L., & Ziegler, J. B. (1990). Faces Pain Scale for the self-assessment of the severity of pain experienced by children: Development, initial validation, and preliminary investigation for ratio scale properties. *Pain, 41*, 139–150.

Bomba, P. A., Kemp, M., & Black, J. S. (2012). POLST: An improvement over traditional advance directives. *Cleveland Clinic Journal of Medicine, 79*(7), 457–464. doi:10.3949/ccjm.79a.11098.

Bosboom, P. R., Alfonso, H., Eaton, J., & Almeida, O. P. (2012). Quality of life in Alzheimer's disease: Different factors associated with complementary ratings by patients and family carers. *International Psychogeriatrics, 24*, 708–721.

Bourgeois, M., Camp, C., Antenucci, V., & Fox, K. (2016). VoiceMyChoice™: Facilitating understanding of preferences of residents with dementia. *Advances in Aging Research, 5*, 131–141.

Bourgeois, M., Dijkstra, K., & Hickey, E. (2005a). Impact of communicative interaction on measuring quality of life in dementia. *Journal of Medical Speech Language Pathology, 13*, 37–50.

Bourgeois, M., Dijkstra, K., & Hickey, E. (2005b, November). Assessing quality of life in persons with dementia. Paper presented at the American Speech Language Hearing Association convention, San Diego, CA.

Bowling, A., Rowe, G., Adams, S., Sands, P., Samsi, K., Crane, M., Joly, L., & Manthorpe, J. (2015). Quality of life in dementia: A systematically conducted narrative review of dementia-specific measurement scales. *Aging & Mental Health, 19*(1), 13–31.

Bradshaw, S. A., Playford, E. D., & Riazi, A. (2012). Living well in care homes: A systematic review of qualitative studies. *Age & Ageing, 41*, 429–440. doi:10.1093/ageing/afs069.

Brod, M. (1998). *Dementia quality of life instrument.* San Francisco, CA: Quintiles.

Brod, M., Steward, A. L., Sands, L., & Walton, P. (1999). Conceptualization and measurement of quality of life in dementia: The dementia quality of life instrument (DQoL). *The Gerontologist, 39*, 25–35.

Brooke, J., & Kirk, M. (2016). Advance care planning for people living with dementia. *British Journal of Community Nursing, 19*(10), 490–495.

Brooks, R., Rabin, R., & de Charro, F. (2003). *The measurement and valuation of health status using EQ-5D: A European perspective.* The Netherlands: Kluwer Academic Publishers.

Bruvik, F. K., Ulstein, I. D., Ranhoff, A. H., & Engedal, K. (2012). The quality of life of people with dementia and their family carers. *Dementia Geriatric Cognitive Disorders, 34*, 7–14. doi:10.1159/00003 41584.

Buckley, T., Fauth, E. B., Morrison, A., Tschanz, J., Rabins, P. V., Piercy, K. W., Norton, M., & Lyketsos, C. G. (2012). Predictors of quality of life ratings for persons with dementia simultaneously reported by patients and their caregivers: The Cache County (Utah) study. *International Psychogeriatrics, 24*(7), 1094–1102. doi:10.1017/S1041610212000063.

Burack, O. R., Weiner, A. S., Reinhardt, J. P., & Annunziato, R. A. (2012). What matters most to LTC elders: Quality of life in the LTC. *Journal of American Medical Directors Association, 13*(1), 48–53. http://dx.doi.org/10.1016/j.jamda.2010.08.002.

Cahill, S., & Diaz-Ponce, A. M. (2011). "I hate having nobody here. I'd like to know where they all are": Can qualitative research detect differences in quality of life among LTC residents with different levels of cognitive impairment? *Aging Mental Health, 15*(5), 562–572.

Camp, C. (2006). Montessori-based Dementia Programming™ in long-term care: A case study of disseminating an intervention for persons with dementia. In R. C. Intrieri & L. Hyer (Eds.), *Clinical applied gerontological interventions in long-term care* (pp. 295–314). New York: Springer.

Camp, C. & Skrajner, M. (2004). Resident-assisted Montessori programming (RAMPTM): Training persons with dementia to serve as group activity leaders. *The Gerontologist, 44*, 426–431.

Cella, D., Nowinski, C., Peterman, A., Victorson, D., Miller, D., Lai, J.-S., & Moy, C. (2011). The Neurology Quality of Life measurement initiative. *Archives of Physical Medicine and Rehabilitation, 92*(10 Suppl), S28–S36. doi:10.1016/j.apmr.2011.01.025.

Chang, W. (2015). *Effects of visual stimuli on decision-making capacity of people with dementia for end-of-life care.* Unpublished dissertation. Columbus, OH: The Ohio State University.

Chen, J., Chan, D., Kiely, D., Morris, J., & Mitchell, S. (2007). Terminal trajectories of functional decline in the long-term care setting. *Journal of Gerontology, 62A*(5), 531–536.

Cheng, S., & Chan, A. (2006). Relationship with others and life satisfaction in later life: Do gender and widowhood make a difference? *Journal of Gerontology, 61B*, P46–P53.

Chua, K.-C., Brown, A., Little, R., Matthews, D., Morton, L., Loftus, V., … Banerjee, S. (2016). Quality-of-life assessment in dementia: The use of DEMQOL and DEMQOL-Proxy total scores. *Quality of Life Research, 25*, 3107–3118. doi:10.1007/s11136-016-1343-1.

Clare, L., Rowlands, J., Bruce, E., Surr, C., & Downs, M. (2008). The experience of living with dementia in residential care: An interpretative phenomenological analysis. *The Gerontologist, 48*(6), 711–720.

Clare, L., Whitaker, R., Woods, R. T., Quinn, C., Jelley, H., Hoare, Z., … Wilson, B. A. (2013). Aware-Care: A pilot randomized controlled trial of an awareness-based staff training intervention to improve quality of life for residents with severe dementia in long-term care settings. *International Psychogeriatrics, 25*(1), 128–139. doi:10.1017/S1041610212001226.

Cohen-Mansfield, J. (2006). Pain assessment in noncommunicative elderly persons – PAINE. *Clin J Pain, 22*, 569–575.

Coker, E., Papaioannou, A., Kaasalainen, S., Dolovich, L., Turpie, I., & Taniguchi, A. (2010). Nurses' perceived barriers to optimal pain management in older adults on acute medical units. *Appl. Nurs. Res, 23*, 139–146.

Conde-Sala, J. L., Garre-Olmo, J., Turro-Garriga, O., Lopez-Pousa, S., & Vilalta-Franch, J. (2009). Factors related to perceived quality of life in patients with Alzheimer's disease: The patient's perception compared with that of caregivers. *Int J Geriatr Psychiatry, 24*, 585–594.

Conradsson, M., Rosendahl, E., Littbrand, H., Gustafson, Y., Olofsson, B., & Lövheim, H. (2013). Usefulness of the Geriatric Depression Scale 15-item version among very old people with and without cognitive impairment. *Aging Ment Health, 17*(5), 638–645. doi:10.1080/13607863.2012.758231.

Corbett, A., Husebo, B., Malcangio, M., Staniland, A., Cohen-Mansfield, J., Aarsland, D., & Ballard, C. (2012). Assessment and treatment of pain in people with dementia. *Nat Rev Neurol., 8*(5), 264–274. doi:10.1038/nrneurol.2012.53.

Cummings, J. L. (1997). The Neuropsychiatric Inventory: Assessing psychopathology in dementia patients. *Neurology, 48*, S10–S16.

Cummings, J., Mega, M., Gray, K., Rosenberg-Thompson, S., Carusi, D. A., & Gornbein, J. (1994). The Neuropsychiatric Inventory: Comprehensive assessment of psychopathology in dementia. *Neurology, 44*, 2308–2314.

Cunningham, W. E., Burton, T. M., Hawes-Dawson, J., Kington, R. S., & Hays, R. D. (1999). Use of relevancy ratings by target respondents to develop health-related quality of life measures: An example with African-American elderly. *Quality of Life Research, 8*, 749–768.

Custers, A., Kuin, Y., Riksen-Walraven, M., & Westerhof, G. J. (2011). Need support and wellbeing during morning care activities: An observational study on resident-staff interaction in LTCs. *Ageing & Society, 31*, 1425–1442.

de Medeiros, K., Robert, P., Gauthier, S., Stella, F., Politis, A. … Lyketsos, C. (2010). The Neuropsychiatric Inventory-Clinician Rating Scale (NPI-C): Reliability and validity of a revised assessment of neuropsychiatric symptoms in dementia. *International Psychogeriatrics, 22*(6), 984–994.

de Vleminck, A., Pardon, K., Beernaert, K., Deschepper, R., Houttekier, D., Van Audenhove, C., … Stichele, R. V. (2014). Barriers to advanced care planning in cancer, heart failure and dementia patients: A focus group study on General Practitioners' views and experiences. *PLOS ONE, 9*(1): e84905. doi:10.1371/journal.pone.0084905.

Dempster, M., & Donnelly, M. (2000). How well do elderly people complete individualized quality of life measures: An exploratory study. *Quality of Life Research, 9*, 369–375.

Dewaters, T., Faut-Callahan, M., McCann, J. J., Paice, J. A., Fogg, L., Hollinger-Smith, L., … Stanaitis, H. (2008). Comparison of self-reported pain and the PAINAD scale in hospitalized cognitively impaired and intact older adults after hip-fracture surgery. *Orthopedic Nursing, 27*(1), 21–28. doi:10.1097/01.NOR.0000310607.62624.74.

Dickinson, D., Bamford, C., Exley, C., Emmett, C., Hughes, J., & Robinson, L. (2013). Planning for tomorrow whilst living for today: The views of people with dementia and their families on advance care planning. *Int Psychogeriatr, 25*(12), 2011–2021. doi:10.1017/S1041610213001531.

Feinberg, L., & Whitlatch, C. (2001). Are persons with cognitive impairment able to state consistent choices? *The Gerontologist, 41*(3), 374–382.

Feldt, K. S. (2000). The checklist of nonverbal pain indicators (CNPI). *Pain Manag Nurs, 1*, 13–21.

Feldt, K., & Finch, M. (2002). Older adults with hip fractures: Treatment of pain following hospitalization. *Journal of Gerontological Nursing, 28*(8), 27–35.

Feldt, K. S., Ryden, M. B., & Miles, S. (1998). Treatment of pain in cognitively impaired compared with cognitively intact older patients with hip fractures. *Journal of the American Geriatrics Society, 46*, 1079–1085.

Ferrans, C. E., Zerwic, J. J., Wilbur, J. E., & Larson, J. L. (2005). Conceptual model of health-related quality of life. *J Nurs Scholarsh, 37*(4), 336–342.

Ferrell, B. A., Stein, W. M., & Beck, J. C. (2000). The Geriatric Pain Measure: Validity, reliability and factor analysis. *J Am Geriatr Soc, 48*(12), 1669–1673.

Fisher, S. E., Burgio, L. D., Thorn, B. E., & Allen-Burge, R., Gerstle, J., Roth, D. L., & Allen, S. J. (2002). Pain assessment and management in cognitively impaired LTC residents: Association of certified nursing assistant pain report, Minimum Data Set pain report, and analgesic medication use. *JAGS, 50*(1), 152–156.

Folstein, M. F., Folstein, S. E., & McHugh, P. R. (1975). "Mini-mental state": A practical method for grading the cognitive state of patients for the clinician. *Journal of Psychiatric Research, 12*(3), 189–198.

Frampton, M. (2003). Experience assessment and management of pain in people with dementia. *Age Ageing, 32*(3), 248–251.

Fuchs-Lacelle, S., Hadjistavropoulos, T., & Lix, L. (2008). Pain assessment as intervention: A study of older adults with severe dementia. *Clinical Journal of Pain, 24*(8), 697–707. doi:10.1097/AJP.0b013e31817 2625a.

Garand, L., Dew, M. A., Lingler, J. H., & DeKosky, S. T. (2011). Incidence and predictors of advance care planning among persons with cognitive impairment. *The American Journal of Geriatric Psychiatry, 19*(8), 712–720. doi:10.1097/JGP.0b013e3181faebef.

Garre-Olmo, J., Planas-Pujol, X., Lopez-Pousa, S., Weiner, M. F., Turon-Estrada, A., Juvinyà, D., ... Vilalta-Franch, J. (2010). Cross-cultural adaptation and psychometric validation of a Spanish version of the Quality of Life in Late-Stage Dementia Scale. *Qual Life Res, 19*(3), 445–453.

George, L. K., & Bearon, L. B. (1980). *Quality of life in older persons: Meaning and measurement.* New York: Human Sciences.

Gershon, R. C., Lai, J. S., Bode, R., Choi, S., Moy, C., Bleck, T., Miller, D., Peterman, A., & Cella, D. (2012). Neuro-QOL: Quality of life item banks for adults with neurological disorders: Item development and calibrations based upon clinical and general population testing. *Qual Life Res, 21*(3), 475–486.

Giebel, C. M., Sutcliffe, C., & Challis, D. (2015). Activities of daily living and quality of life across different stages of dementia: A UK study. *Aging & Mental Health, 19*(1), 63–71. doi:10.1080/13607863.2014. 915920.

Godin, J., Keefe, J., Kelloway, E. K., & Hirdes, J. P. (2015). LTC resident quality of life: testing for measurement equivalence across resident, family, and staff perspectives. *Qual Life Res, 24*, 2365–2374. doi:10. 1007/s11136-015-0989-4.

Gozalo, P., Teno, J. M., Mitchell, S. L., Skinner, J., Bynum, J., Tyler, D., & Mor, V. (2011). End-of-life transitions among LTC residents with cognitive issues. *New England Journal of Medicine, 365*(13), 1212–1221. doi:10.1056/NEJMsa1100347.

Gräske, J., Fischer, T., Kuhlmey, A., & Wolf-Ostermann, K. (2012). Quality of life in dementia care: Differences in quality of life measurements performed by residents with dementia and by nursing staff. *Aging & Mental Health, 16*(7), 819–827. http://dx.doi.org/10.1080/13607863.2012.667782.

Hadjistavropoulos, T., Herr, K., Prkachin, K. M., Craig, K. D., Gibson, S. J. ... Smith, J. H. (2014). Pain assessment in elderly adults with dementia. *The Lancet Neurology, 13*(12), 1216–1227.

Haller, B. (2015). *Examples of visual supports to aid conversation about end of life issues.* Unpublished project. Tampa, FL: University of South Florida.

Hellberg, I., Augustsson, V., & Hellstrom Muhli, U. (2011). Seniors' experiences of living in special housing accommodation. *International Journal of Qualitative Studies on Health and Wellbeing, 6*(1), 5894.

Hendriks, S. A., Smalbrugge, M., Hertogh, C. M., & van der Steen, J. T. (2014). Dying with dementia: Symptoms, treatment, and quality of life in the last week of life. *J Pain Symptom Manage., 47*(4), 710–720. doi:10.1016/j.jpainsymman.2013.05.015.

Herr, K. A., & Mobily, P. R. (1993). Comparison of selected pain assessment tools for use with the elderly. *Appl Nurs Res, 6*(1), 39–46.

Hickey, E., & Bourgeois, M. (2000). Health-related quality of life (HR-QOL) in LTC residents with dementia: Stability and relationships among measures. *Aphasiology, 14*, 669–679.

Hoffman, F., van den Bussche, H., Wiese, B., Glaeske, G., & Kaduszkiewicz, H. (2014). Diagnoses indicating pain and analgesic drug prescription in patients with dementia: A comparison to age- and sex-matched controls. *BMC Geriatr, 14*(20).

Holland, A. L., & Nelson, R. L. (2013). *Counseling in communication disorders: A wellness perspective* (2nd ed.). San Diego, CA: Plural Press.

Howard, K., & Rockwood, K. (1995). Quality of life in Alzheimer's disease. *Dementia, 6*, 113–116.

Hurt, C. S., Banerjee, S., Tunnard, C., Whitehead, D. L., Tsolaki, M., Mecocci, P., … Lovestone, S. (2010). Insight, cognition and quality of life in Alzheimer's disease. *J Neurol Neurosurg Psychiatry, 81*(3), 331–336. doi:10.1136/jnnp. 2009.184598.

Hurt, C., Bhattacharyya, S., Burns, A., Camus, V., Liperoti, R., Marriott, A., … Byrne, E. J. (2008). Patient and caregiver perspectives of quality of life in dementia. An investigation of the relationship to behavioural and psychological symptoms in dementia. *Dement Geriatr Cogn, 26*(2), 138–146. doi:10.1159/000149584.

Husebo, B. S., Achterberg, W., & Flo, E. (2016). Identifying and managing pain in people with Alzheimer's disease and other types of dementia: A systematic review. *CNS Drugs, 30*, 481–497.

Husebo, B. S., Ostelo, R., & Strand, L. I. (2014). The MOBID-2 pain scale: Reliability and responsiveness to pain in patients with dementia. *Eur J Pain, 18*(10), 1419–1430.

Husebo, B., Strand, L., Moe-Nilssen, R., Husebo, S., & Ljunggren, A (2009). Pain behaviour and pain intensity in older persons with severe dementia: Reliability of the MOBID Pain Scale by video uptake. *Scand J Caring Sci, 23*(1), 180–189.

Isella, V., Villa, M., & Appollonio, I. (2005). Screening and quantification of depression in mild-to-moderate dementia through the GDS short forms. *Clinical Gerontologist, 24*(3/4), 115–125.

Kane, R. (2003). Definition, measurement, and correlates of quality of life in LTCs: Toward a reasonable practice, research, and policy agenda. *The Gerontologist, 43*, 28–36.

Kane, R., Kane, R., Bershadsky, B., Degenholtz, H., Kling, K., Totten, A., et al. (2005). Proxy sources for information on LTC residents' quality of life. *Journal of Gerontology, 60B*(6), S318–S325.

Kaufer, D. I., Cummings, J. L., Ketchel, P., Smith, V., MacMillan, A., Shelley, T., … DeKosky, S. (2000). Validation of the NPI-Q, a brief clinical form of the neuropsychiatric inventory. *The Journal of Neuropsychiatry and Clinical Neurosciences, 12*(2), 233–239.

Kim, H., Ersek, M., Bradway, C., & Hickman, S. E. (2015). Physician orders for life-sustaining treatment for LTC residents with dementia. *Journal of the American Association of Nurse Practitioners, 27*, 606–614. doi:10.1002/2327-6924.12258.

Knapskog, A. B., Barca, M. L., Engedal, K., & The Cornell Study Group. (2011). A comparison of the validity of the Cornell scale and the MADRS in detecting depression among memory clinic patients. *Dementia and Geriatric Cognitive Disorders, 32*(4), 287–294.

Lacey, L., Bobula, J., Rudell, K., Alvir, J., & Leibman, C. (2015). Quality of life and utility measurement in a large clinical trial sample of patients with mild to moderate Alzheimer's disease: Determinants and level of changes observed. *Value Health, 18*, 638–645.

Lasker, J. (2006). *Pain scale.* Unpublished document. Tallahassee, FL: Florida State University.

Lawton, M. P. (1991). A multidimensional view of quality of life in frail elders. In J. E. Birren, J. E. Lubben, J. C. Rowe, & D. E. Deutchman (Eds.), *The concept and measurement of quality of life in the frail elderly* (pp. 3–27). San Diego, CA: Academic Press.

Lawton, M. P. (1994). Quality of life in Alzheimer disease. *Alzheimer Disease and Associated Disorders, 8*(Suppl. 3), 138–150.

Lawton, M. P., Van Haitsma, K., & Klapper, J. (1996a). Observed affect in LTC residents with Alzheimer's disease. *Journal of Gerontology, 51B*(6), 309–316.

Lawton, M. P., Van Haitsma, K., & Klapper, J. (1996b). *Observed Emotion Rating Scale.* Retrieved January 30, 2017, from www.abramsoncenter.org/PRI.

Lawton, M. P., Van Haitsma, K., Perkinson, M., & Ruckdeschel, K. (1999). Observed affect and quality of life in dementia: Further affirmations and problems. *J Ment Health Aging, 5*(1), 69–81.

Logsdon, R. G., Gibbons, L. E., McCurry, S. M., & Teri, L. (1999). Quality of life in Alzheimer's disease: Patient and caregiver reports. *Journal of Mental Health and Aging, 5*, 21–32.

Logsdon, R. G., Gibbons, L. E., McCurry, S. M., & Teri, L. (2002). Assessing quality of life in older adults with cognitive impairment. *Psychosom Med., 64*, 510–519.

Lundin, A., Berg, L.-E., & Muhli, U. H. (2013). Feeling existentially touched: A phenomenological notion of the wellbeing of elderly living in special housing accommodation from the perspective of care professionals. *International Journal of Qualitative Studies on Health and Wellbeing, 8*, 20587.

McGrath, P. A., Seifert, C. E., Speechley, K. N., Booth, J. C., Stitt, L., & Gibson, M. C. (1996). A new analogue scale for assessing children's pain: An initial validation study. *Pain, 64*, 435–443.

Menzel, P. T., & Steinbock, B. (2013). Advance directives, dementia, and physician-assisted death. *The Journal of Law, Medicine, & Ethics, 41*(2), 484–500. doi:10.1111/jlme.12057.

Mitchell, S. L., Teno, J. M., Kiely, D. K., Shaffer, M. L., Jones, R. N., Prigerson, H. G., ... Hamel, M. B. (2009). The clinical course of advanced dementia. *New England Journal of Medicine, 361*(16), 1529–1538. doi:10.1056/NEJMoa0902234.

Mjørud, M., Engedal, K., Røsvik, J., & Kirkevold, M. (2017). Living with dementia in a LTC, as described by persons with dementia: A phenomenological hermeneutic study. *BMC Health Services Research, 17*, 93. doi:10.1186/s12913-017-2053-2.

Monroe, T. B., Misra, S. K., Habermann, R. C., Dietrich, M. S., Cowan, R. L., & Simmons, S. F. (2014). Pain reports and pain medication treatment in LTC residents with and without dementia. *Geriatr Gerontol Int., 14*, 541–548. doi:10.1111/ggi.12130.

Monroe, T. B., Parish, A., & Mion, L. C. (2015). Decision factors nurses use to assess pain in LTC residents with dementia. *Archives of Psychiatric Nursing, 29*, 316–320.

Morello, R., Jean, A., Alix, M., Sellin-Peres, D., & Fermanian, J. A. (2007). A scale to measure pain in non-verbally communicating older patients: The EPCA-2 Study of its psychometric properties. *Pain, 133*, 87–98.

Morrison, R., & Siu, A. (2000). A comparison of pain and its treatment in advanced dementia and cognitively intact patients with hip fracture. *J Pain Symptom Manage, 19*(4), 240–248.

Motteran, A., Trifiletti, E., & Pedrazza, M. (2016). Wellbeing and lack of wellbeing among LTC residents. *Ageing Int, 41*, 150–166. doi:10.1007/s12126-016-9240-z.

Moye, J., Karel, M., Azar, A. R., & Gurrera, R. J., (2004). Capacity to consent to treatment: Empirical comparison of three instruments in older adults with and without dementia. *The Gerontologist, 44*, 166–175.

Moyle, W., Fetherstonhaugh, D., Greben, M., Beattie, E., & AusQoL Group. (2015). Influencers on quality of life as reported by people living with dementia in long-term care: A descriptive exploratory approach. *BMC Geriatr, 15*(1), 50. doi:10.1186/s12877-015-0050-z.

Mulhern, B., Rowen, D., Brazier, J., et al. (2013). Development of DEMQOL-U and DEMQOL-PROXY-U: Generation of preference-based indices from DEMQOL and DEMQOL-PROXY for use in economic evaluation. *Health Technology Assessment, 17*(5). Southampton, UK: NIHR Journals Library. Retrieved January 17, 2017, from www.ncbi.nlm.nih.gov/books/NBK260320/.

Murphy, J., Gray, C., van Achterberg, T., Wyke, S., & Cox, S. (2010). The effectiveness of the Talking Mats framework in helping people with dementia to express their views on wellbeing. *Dementia, 9*(4), 454–472. doi:10.1177/1471301210381776.

Naglie, G., Hogan, D. B., Krahn, M., Black, S. E., Beattie, B. L., Patterson, C., ... Tomlinson, G. (2011). Predictors of family caregiver ratings of patient quality of life in Alzheimer disease: Cross-sectional results from the Canadian Alzheimer's disease quality of life study. *Am J Geriatr Psychiatry, 19*(10), 891–901.

Novella, J. L., Ankri, J., Morrone, I., Guillemin, F., Jolly, D., Jochum, C., ... Blanchard, F. (2001). Evaluation of the quality of life in dementia with a generic quality of life questionnaire: The Duke health profile. *Dementia and Geriatric Cognitive Disorders, 12*(2), 158–166.

Park, H. (2010). Effect of music on pain for home-dwelling persons with dementia. *Pain Management Nursing, 11*(3), 141–147.

Paul-Brown, D., Frattali, C., Holland, A., Thompson, C., & Caperton, C. (2004). *Quality of communication life scale.* Rockville, MD: ASHA.

Pautex, S., Michon, A., Guedira, M., Emond, H., Le Lous, P. ... Gold, G. (2006). Pain in severe dementia: Self-assessment or observational scales? *J Am Geriatr Soc, 54*(7), 1040–1045.

Perales, J., Cosco, T. D., Stephan, B. C. M., Haro, J. M., & Brayne, C. (2013). Health-related quality-of-life instruments for Alzheimer's disease and mixed dementia. *International Psychogeriatrics, 25*(5), 691–706. doi:10.1017/S1041610212002293.

Plooij, B., van der Spek, K., & Scherder, E. J. (2012). Pain medication and global cognitive functioning in dementia patients with painful conditions. *Drugs Aging, 29*(5), 377–384.

Port, C., Gruber-Baldini, A., Burton, L., Baumgarten, M., Hebel, J. R. … Magaziner, J. (2001). Resident contact with family and friends following nursing home admission. *Gerontologist, 41*(5), 589–596.

PROMIS Network (2011). Retrieved January 7, 2017, from www.nihpromis.com/science/Presentations 2011.aspx?AspxAutoDetectCookieSupport=1.

Rabins, P. V., Kasper, J. D., Kleinman, L., Black, B. S., & Patrick, D. L. (1999). Concepts and methods in the development of the ADRQL: An instrument for assessing health-related quality of life in persons with Alzheimer's disease. *Journal of Mental Health and Aging, 5*, 33–48.

Rand, S. & Caeils, J. (2015). *Using proxies to assess quality of life: A review of the issues and challenges.* Discussion paper 2899. Canterbury, UK: Quality & Outcomes of Person-Centered Care Policy Research Unit. Retrieved January 7, 2017, from www.pssru.ac.uk/archive/pdf/4980.pdf.

Rao, J., Anderson, L., Lin, F., & Laux, J. (2014). Completion of advance directives among U.S. consumers. *Am. J. Pre. Medicine, 46*(1), 65–70.

Regan, A., Tapley, M., & Jolley, D. (2014). Improving end of life care for people with dementia. *Nursing Standard, 28*(48), 37–43. doi:10.7748/ns.28.48.37.e8760.

Reid, M., O'Neil, K., Dancy, J., Berry, C., & Stowell, S. (2015). Pain management in long-term care communities: A quality improvement initiative. *AM Longterm Care, 23*(2), 29–35.

Robertson, S., Cooper, C., Hoe, J., Hamilton, O., Stringer, A., & Livingston, G. (2017). Proxy rated quality of life of care home residents with dementia: A systematic review. *International Psychogeriatrics,* 1–13. doi:https://doi.org/10.1017/S1041610216002167.

Robinson, L., Dickinson, C., Bamford, C., Clark, A., Hughes, J., & Exley, C. (2013). A qualitative study: Professionals' experiences of advance care planning in dementia and palliative care, "a good idea in theory but…" *Palliat Med, 27*(5), 401–408. doi:10.1177/0269216312465651.

Ryan, E. B., Byrne, K., Spykerman, H., & Orange, J. B. (2005). Evidencing Kitwood's personhood strategies: Conversation as care in dementia. In Davis, B. H. (Ed.), *Alzheimer talk, text and context: Enhancing communication.* New York: Palgrave Macmillan.

Saxena, S., O'Connell, K., & Underwood, L. (2002). A commentary: Cross-cultural quality-of-life assessment at the end of life. *The Gerontologist, 42*(Special Issue III), 81–85.

Schenk, L., Meyer, R., Behr, A., Kuhlmey, A., & Hozhausen, M. (2013). Quality of life in LTCs: Results of a qualitative resident survey. *Qual Life Res, 22*, 2929–2938. doi:10.1007/s11136-013-0400-2.

Scherder, E., & Bouma, A. (2000). Visual analogue scales for pain assessment in Alzheimer's disease. *Gerontology, 46*(1), 47–53.

Schuler, M., Becker, S., Kaspar, R., Nikolaus, T., Kruse, A., & Basler, H. D. (2007). Psychometric properties of the German "Pain Assessment in Advanced Dementia Scalae" (PAINAD-G) in LTC residents. *Journal of the American Medical Director Association, 8*(6), 388–395.

Selai, C., Vaughan, A., Harvey, R. J., & Logsdon, R. (2001). Using the QoL-AD in the UK. *International Journal of Geriatric Psychiatry, 16*, 537–538.

Selwood, A., Thorgrimsen, L., & Orrell, M. (2005). Quality of life in dementia: A one-year follow-up study. *International Journal of Geriatric Psychiatry, 20*, 232–237.

Silberfeld, M., Rueda, S., Krahn, M., & Naglie, G. (2002). Content validity for dementia of three generic preference based health related quality of life instruments. *Quality of Life Research, 11*, 71–79.

Simmons, S. F., Ferrell, B. A., & Schnelle, J. F. (2002). Effects of a controlled exercise trial on pain in LTC residents. *Clin J Pain, 18*(6), 380–385.

Smith, J. P., & Kington, R. S. (1997). Race, socioeconomic status, and health in late life. In L. G. Martin & B. J. Soldo (Eds.), *Racial and ethnic differences in the health of older Americans.* Washington, DC: National Academy Press.

Smith, S. C., Lamping, D. L., Banerjee, S., Harwood, R., Foley, B., Smith, P., … Knapp, M. (2005). Measurement of health-related quality of life for people with dementia: Development of a new instrument (DEMQOL) and an evaluation of current methodology. *Health Technol Assess, 9*(10), 1–93, iii–iv.

Smith, S. C., Lamping, D. L., Banerjee, S., Harwood, R. H., Foley, B., Smith, P., … Knapp, M. (2007). Development of a new measure of health-related quality of life for people with dementia: DEMQOL. *Psychol Med, 37*(5), 737–746.

Sousa, M. F. B., Santos, R. L., Arcoverde, C., & Simões, P. (2013). Quality of life in dementia: The role of non-cognitive factors in the ratings of people with dementia and family caregivers. *International Psychogeriatrics, 25*, 1097–1105. doi:https://doi.org/10.1017/S1041610213000410.

Speech-Language and Audiology Canada (March, 2016). Position statement on end-of-life care. Retrieved January 5, 2017, from www.sac-oac.ca/.

Teske, K., Daut, R. L., & Cleeland, C. S. (1983). Relationships between nurses' observations and patients' self-reports of pain. *Pain, 16*, 289–297.

Thorgrimsen, L., Selwood, A., Spector, A., Royan, L., de Madariaga Lopez, M., Woods, R., & Orrell, M. (2003). Whose quality of life is it anyway? The validity and reliability of the Quality of Life–Alzheimer's Disease (QoL-AD) scale. *Alzheimer Disease and Associated Disorders, 17*, 201–208.

Torisson, G., Stavenow, L., Minthon, L., & Londos, E. (2016). Reliability, validity and clinical correlates of the Quality of Life in Alzheimer's disease (QoL-AD) scale in medical inpatients. *Health and Quality of Life Outcomes, 14*(90). doi:10.1186/s12955-016-0493-8.

Traschel, M., Hermann, H., & Biller-Andorno, N. (2015). Cognitive fluctuations as a challenge for the assessment of decision-making capacity in patients with dementia. *American Journal of Alzheimer's Disease & Other Dementias, 30*(4), 360–363. doi:10.1177/1533317514539377.

van der Ploeg, E. S., Eppingstall, B., Camp, C. J., & Runci, S. (2013). A randomized crossover trial to study the effect of personalized, one-to-one interaction using Montessori-based activities on agitation, affect, and engagement in LTC residents with dementia. *International Psychogeriatrics, 25*(4), 565–575.

van der Steen, J. T., van Soest-Poortvliet, M. C., Hallie-Heierman, M., Onwuteaka-Philipsen, B. D., Deliens, L., de Boer, M. E., ... de Vet, H. C. (2014). Factors associated with initiation of advance care planning in dementia: A systematic review. *J Alzheimer's Dis, 40*(3), 743–757. doi:10.3233/JAD-131967.

van Hoof, J., Verbeek, H., Janssen, B. M., Eijkelenboom, A., Molony, S. L., Felix, E., ... Wouters, E. J. M. (2016). A three perspective study of the sense of home of LTC residents: The views of residents, care professionals, and relatives. *BMC Geriatrics, 16*, 169. doi:10.1186/s12877-016-0344-9.

Villanueva, M. R., Smith, T. L., Erickson, J. S., Lee, A. C., & Singer, C. M. (2003). Pain assessment for the dementing elderly (PADE): Reliability and validity of a new measure. *J Am Med Dir Assoc, 4*, 1–8.

Volicer, L., & Bloom-Charette, L. (Eds.). (1999). *Enhancing the quality of life in advanced dementia*. Philadelphia: Brunner/Mazel.

Volicer, L., & Hurley, A. (2015). *Assessment scales for advanced dementia*. Baltimore: Health Professions Press.

von Kutzleben, M., Schmid, W., Halek, M., Holle, B., & Bartholomeyczik, S. (2012). Community-dwelling persons with dementia: What do they need? What do they demand? What do they do? A systematic review on the subjective experiences of persons with dementia. *Aging & Mental Health, 16*(3), 378–390. http://dx.doi.org/10/1080/13607863.2011.614594.

Warden, V., Hurley, A. C., & Volicer, L. (2003). Development and psychometric evaluation of the Pain Assessment in Advanced Dementia (PAINAD) scale. *J Am Med Dir Assoc, 4*, 9–15.

Weiner, M., & Hynan, L. (2015). Quality of life in late-stage dementia. In L. Volicer and A. Hurley (Eds.), *Assessment scales for advanced dementia* (pp. 53–64). Baltimore: Health Professions Press.

Weiner, M. F., Martin-Cook, K., Svetlik, D. A., Saine, K., Foster B., & Fontaine, C. S. (2000). The quality of life in late-stage dementia (QUALID) scale. *J Am Med Dir Assoc, 1*, 114–116.

Westerhof, G. J., van Vuuren, M., Brummans, B. H. J., & Custers, A. F. J. (2016). A Buberian approach to the co-construction of relationships between professional caregivers and residents in LTCs. *The Gerontologist, 54*(3), 354–362. doi:10.1093/geront/gnt064.

Whitehouse, P. J., Patterson, M. B., & Sami, S. A. (2003). Quality of life in dementia: Ten years later. *Alzheimer Disease and Associated Disorders, 17*, 199–200.

Wolak-Thierry, A., Novella, J.-L., Barbe, C., Morrone, I., Mahmoudi, R., & Jolly, D. (2015). Comparison of QoL-AD and DQoL in elderly with Alzheimer's disease. *Aging & Mental Health, 19*(3), 274–278.

Wood, S., Cummings, J. L., Hsu, M. A., et al. (2000). The use of the neuropsychiatric inventory in LTC residents. Characterization and measurement. *Am J Geriatr Psychiatry, 8*(1), 75–83.

Woods, R. T., Nelis, S. M., Martyr, A., Roberts, J., Whitaker, C. J., Markova, I., ... Clare, L. (2014). What contributes to a good quality of life in early dementia? Awareness and the QoL-AD: A cross-sectional study. *Health Qual Life Outcomes, 12*, 94.

World Health Organization. (2001). *International classification of functioning, disability, and health*. Retrieved February 21, 2006, from www3.who.int/icf/icftemplate.cfm.

World Health Organization Quality of Life Group (WHOQOL Group). (1993). Study protocol for the World Health Organization project to develop a Quality of Life assessment instrument (the WHOQOL). *Quality of Life Research, 2*, 153–159.

World Health Organization Quality of Life Group (WHOQOL Group). (1995). The World Health Organization Quality of Life assessment (WHOQOL): Position paper from the World Health Organization. *Social Science and Medicine, 41*, 1403–1409.

World Health Organization Quality of Life Group (WHOQOL Group). (1998). The World Health Organization Quality of Life assessment (WHOQOL): Development and general psychometric properties. *Social Science and Medicine, 46*, 1569–1585.

Yesavage, J. A., Brink, T. L., Rose, T. L., Lum, O., Huang, V., Adey, M., et al. (1983). Development and validation of a geriatric depression screening scale: A preliminary report. *Journal of Psychiatric Research, 17*, 37–49.

AUTHOR INDEX

Page numbers in *italics* denote tables, those in **bold** denote figures.

SUBJECT INDEX

Page numbers in *italics* denote tables.